The Harlem Renaissance

Negrotarians among the Niggerati at the Lafayette Theatre, from a caricature by Miguel Covarrubias. (Courtesy *Vogue*. Copyright © 1936 [renewed 1964] by The Condé Nast Publications Inc.)

The Harlem Renaissance

A HISTORICAL DICTIONARY FOR THE ERA

Edited by
Bruce Kellner

Ref.
700
H284

Greenwood Press
Westport, Connecticut • London, England

Library of Congress Cataloging in Publication Data

Main entry under title:

The Harlem Renaissance.

  Bibliography: p.
  Includes index.
  1. Afro-American arts—New York (N.Y.)—Dictionaries.
2. Harlem Renaissance—Dictionaries. I. Kellner, Bruce.
NX511.N4H37   1984   700′.899607307471   83-22687
ISBN 0-313-23232-6 (lib. bdg.)

Library of Congress Catalog Card Number: 83-22687
ISBN: 0-313-23232-6

First published in 1984

Greenwood Press
A division of Congressional Information Service, Inc.
88 Post Road West
Westport, Connecticut 06881

Printed in the United States of America

10 9 8 7 6 5 4 3 2 1

Copyright acknowledgments

Grateful acknowledgment is made for permission to use selections, from Carl Van Vechten's *Nigger
Heaven*, written by Langston Hughes. Reprinted by permission of Harold Ober Associates Incorporated. Copyright 1926. For permission to include selections from Carl Van Vechten's typed
inventory for the James Weldon Johnson Memorial Collection of Negro Arts and Letters, prepared
1941–64 to accompany various gifts to the collection, grateful acknowledgment is made to Donald
Gallup, Literary Trustee to the Estate of Carl Van Vechten, and to the Collection of American
Literature, the Beinecke Rare Book and Manuscript Library, Yale University. This material cannot
be reprinted without the express written consent of the Van Vechten Estate.

Born an' bred in Harlem,
Harlem to duh bone,
Ah say, born an' bred in Harlem,
Harlem to duh bone...
—Langston Hughes, 1926

Contents

Illustrations

Acknowledgments

My essential debt is to seven industrious contributing essayists who prepared about one-third of the entries, many of which cover most of the major figures of the Harlem Renaissance. Four of them cheerfully accepted assignments in addition to those in their initial agreements, and the other three also cheerfully signed on when the project was well under way and began to swell. I am grateful to them, too, for the pleasurable give-and-take as we met or corresponded, even to pooling resources and writing a few entries in tandem.

In the process of compiling the dictionary, we returned time and again to several sources. They merit special recognition and our joint recommendation to anyone interested in pursuing the subject further. In their order of publication: James Weldon Johnson's* *Black Manhattan,* 1930; Gilbert Osofsky's *Harlem*, 1966; Roi Ottley and William J. Weatherby's *Negro in New York*, 1967; Nathan Irvin Huggins's *Harlem Renaissance*, 1971; Henry T. Sampson's *Blacks in Blackface*, 1980; David Levering Lewis's *When Harlem Was in Vogue*, 1981; and Jervis Anderson's *This Was Harlem*, 1982. This brief list in no way diminishes the significance of the enormous range of sources on which we called.

For two years the staff members of the Helen Ganser Library, at Millersville University where I teach, tracked down an amazing number of obscure publications on the slimmest of leads, and they assisted me in many ways through the library's own excellent holdings, always with good humor and continued interest.

Other libraries deserve acknowledgment too: The James Weldon Johnson Memorial Collection of Negro Arts and Letters, founded by Carl Van Vechten, in the Beinecke Rare Book and Manuscript Library at Yale University; the Schomburg Center for Research in Black Culture at the Harlem Branch of the New York Public Library; Fisk University Library; Columbia University Library; Radcliffe College Library; Lincoln University Library; the National Association

*An asterisk (*) after a name or subject indicates a separate entry in this book.

for the Advancement of Colored People Archive in the Library of Congress; and many other libraries willing to send on interlibrary loan a remarkable range of materials.

The Hatch-Billops Collection is not only a library but a treasure house of taped interviews and oral histories, with typed abstracts, of hundreds of Afro-Americans, many of whom were active during the Harlem Renaissance. I am deeply grateful to Camille Billops and James V. Hatch for the freedom they gave me to make use of this rich lode.

For permission to reprint illustrations and photographs, grateful acknowledgment is made to the following: Collection of American Literature, Beinecke Rare Book and Manuscript Library, Yale University; Condé Nast Publications, Inc.; the Crisis Publishing Company; Alfred A. Knopf,* Inc.; the National Urban League*; Fire!! Press; Regina M. Anderson* Andrews; Richard Bruce Nugent*; Joseph Solomon for the Estate of Carl Van Vechten; Prentiss Taylor*; and Thomas Wirth. Grateful acknowledgment is made to Harold Ober Associates for permission to reprint Langston Hughes's lyric, written for Carl Van Vechten's *Nigger Heaven* and here used as an epigraph. For permission to include heretofore unpublished material from Carl Van Vechten's inventory to the James Weldon Johnson Memorial Collection of Negro Arts and Letters, grateful acknowledgment is made to Donald Gallup, Literary Trustee to the Estate of Carl Van Vechten, and to the Collection of American Literature, the Beinecke Rare Book and Manuscript Library, Yale University.

Donald Angus, Elinor J. (Mrs. Josiah) Marvel, Richard Bruce Nugent, Louise Thompson* Patterson, and Prentiss Taylor were part of the Harlem Renaissance, having lived through it; their infallible memories and vivid recollections have enhanced many of the entries.

For favors of various kinds, I want to thank a number of friends and associates: A'Lelia Bundles, Edward Burns, Sharon Cox, Dan Dietz, Donald Gallup, Eric Garber, Barbara Hunsberger, Kate Kellner, Scot Kriner, Evelyn Lyons, Paul Padgette, Sue Rohrer, Richard Rutledge, David Schoonover, Leo Shelley, Joseph Solomon, Bonnie Szymanski, Tom Wirth, and Frances Zantantas.

Hans Kellner compiled the preliminary bibliography, verified references, and prepared the preliminary index with his customary diligence. Further, in proof-reading much of the material, he kept an eye on my syntax, for which I am beholden.

My thanks also to Greenwood Press for initiating this project and particularly to Cynthia Harris for her patience and good counsel.

To Millersville University, I am grateful for two research grants (1981-1982 and 1982-1983) and for a drastically reduced teaching schedule in the fall of 1983 to facilitate my completing the manuscript.

Finally, I regret that it is too late to thank three people who are surely responsible for my initial interest in the twenties and for my pleasure in the period "when Harlem was in vogue": Nora Holt,* Langston Hughes,* and Carl Van Vechten.*

Introduction

"When Harlem was in vogue," as its best poet Langston Hughes* described the period,[1] the so-called Negro Renaissance blossomed and, with the onslaught of the Depression, wilted. Interest in the subject outside the black community seems to have begun in 1967 when the New York Public Library published *The Negro in New York*, a series of manuscripts prepared by the Federal Writers Project. Until then, the information had gathered a quarter of a century of dust, occasionally disturbed by scholars, in the Schomburg Collection of the Harlem Branch of the library, its publication "deferred and prevented because information contained in it was too startling for conservative taste."[2] That material informed Gilbert Osofsky's *Harlem: The Making of a Ghetto* in 1966, Nathan Irvin Huggins's *Harlem Renaissance* in 1971, more recently David Levering Lewis's *When Harlem Was in Vogue* in 1981, Jervis Anderson's *This Was Harlem* in 1982, and dozens of essays and articles, from all of which anyone considering the period can only gratefully pillage.

"Harlem Renaissance" is actually a misnomer, because the rich surge of black arts and letters during the 1920s was not limited to activity a few blocks north of 125th Street in New York, or even to New York City. "Negro Renaissance" gave way to "Harlem Renaissance" as *colored* gave way to *Negro*, *Negro* to *black*, and more recently *black* to *Afro-American*—sensitivity to names and labels sometimes altering as rapidly as fashions. W.E.B. Du Bois,* generally considered the greatest black activist-intellectual of the century, attacked these epithets in 1928, when a high school student wrote a letter to *The Crisis** to complain that "Negro" was the white race's attempt to make the black race feel inferior. Du Bois replied:

Do not...make the all too common error of mistaking names for things.... If a thing is despised either because of ignorance or because it is despicable, you will not alter matters by changing its name. If men despise Negroes they will not despise them less if Negroes are called "colored" or "Afro-Americans."...Suppose now we could change the name....Would the Negro problem be suddenly and eternally settled?...Your real work...does not lie with names....Your work as a Negro lies in two directions. *First*, to let the world know what there is fine and genuine about the Negro race. And *secondly*, to see that there is nothing about that race which is worth contempt; your contempt, my contempt; or the contempt of the wide, wide world.[3]

Implicit in Du Bois's attitude was the belief he shared with many members of both races that within any group there was what he came to call the "Talented Tenth," 10 percent of its members capable of extraordinary achievement, gifted by the gods and by circumstances, to speak for the rest. If white America could be awakened to that talented tenth in black America, he reasoned, segregation would diminish, conditions would improve, and in time prejudice would disappear.

If, in the bleak landscape of the Depression, Du Bois's belief proved misguided, it was nevertheless optimistic and positive, coming on the threshold of the genial spirit of the "Splendid Drunken Twenties," as white "Negrotarian" Carl Van Vechten* called the decade.[4] The Harlem Renaissance, however, was not born because of the end of the war or the beginning of Prohibition. The 1920s only witnessed a sudden awareness of something that had been long in developing, which after another generation came to its full bouquet during the Black Arts movement of the late 1960s. White America may have first taken notice in 1925, when the *New York Herald Tribune* observed: "We are on the edge, if not already in the midst, of what might not improperly be called a Negro Renaissance.... And it would be one of fate's quaint but by no means impossible revenges if the Negro's real contribution to American life should be in the field of art."[5] Had white America been less parochial, it might have sensed an inevitable change long before, indeed, as early as the turn of the century, when Harlem's color began to change so radically.

At that time black Americans lived at the northern edge of New York City, in an area west of Sixth Avenue around 53rd Street, referred to without any particular derision—but perhaps without affection either—as Black Bohemia. About seventy-five blocks farther north, Harlem was a quiet country town, nearly 300 years old. When an elevated railway came in during the 1890s and expensive apartments began to go up, Harlem became a stronghold of the upper middle class, where wealthy families stabled trotting stock and Oscar Hammerstein erected an opera house. Jews and Negroes were virtually nonexistent there, although some shanty Irish lived down on the northern edge of Central Park in Goatville.

Coincidentally, black newspapers like the New York *Age** and, a few years later, the Chicago *Defender** and even some southern newspapers began to urge Afro-Americans afflicted in the South with low pay and miserable living conditions to take command of their own emancipation. The great migrations began shortly, and in that first decade of the century New York's 300 black families increased to nearly 5,000. They lived in an area of six blocks.

The calendar logistics of what then happened are not always possible to chart, but by 1903 a young realtor, Philip A. Payton, Jr.,* had persuaded some white apartment-house owners to rent at high fees some empty Harlem property to middle-class black tenants, educated professional people eager to escape the slum into which Black Bohemia had begun to decay because of the hordes of ignorant southern indigents. Soon the first block west of Fifth Avenue on 134th Street had become a modest black colony. (More accurately, one would say beige colony, because at that time color lines were drawn within the race itself. There were expressions among Afro-Americans trying to escape the stigma this country had placed on color: ''The Lighter the Whiter,'' for example, and ''White is Right.'') When the colony began to spread, despite attempts by white residents to contain it by forming the Harlem Property Owners' Improvement Association in 1910, a fascinating power struggle ensued. Black capital began to buy up properties on the market. Realtors John E. Nail* and Henry Parker purchased five apartment houses and arranged for St. Philip's Protestant Episcopal Church* to buy thirteen more along 135th Street. Then, in the words of Nail's brother-in-law, James Weldon Johnson,* another of those great figures of the Harlem Renaissance, ''the presence of a single coloured family on a block, regardless of the fact that they might be well-bred people, with sufficient means to buy their new home, was sufficient for precipitate flight. The stampeded whites actually deserted house after house and block after block. Then prices dropped; they dropped lower than the bottom, and such coloured people as were able took advantage of these prices and bought.''[6] Those who weren't able to buy followed too, for when the war came the critical shortage of common labor sent agents for northern industrialists into the South with promises of steady wages, no discrimination, and good schools. According to a Department of Labor report on the subject in 1918, nearly 250,000 black peasants had fled the South—to East St. Louis, Chicago, Washington, New York—skipping ''two generations of social economy and a century and more in civilization,'' a writer during the twenties observed, looking back on the phenomenon.[7]

In this same period—just before and during the war—three powerful figures emerged, each profoundly influential in his own way: W.E.B. Du Bois, James Weldon Johnson, and Marcus Garvey.* On the basis of longevity as well as authority, Du Bois is surely preeminent in an unlikely trio, a sociologist, a Harvard Ph.D., a forceful speaker and writer, and one of the founders of the National Association for the Advancement of Colored People (NAACP),* an organization decrying the accommodation policies of an earlier generation represented by the authority of Booker T. Washington. Du Bois seems to have been an austere man; perhaps no one ever heard him laugh, not in public anyway; but his confrere James Weldon Johnson offered just the ballast necessary to give the movement its force. Johnson's friendly diplomacy and tact made him an ideal envoy between the races, and, unlike Du Bois, he was gregarious. He had been United States consul to Venezuela and then to Nicaragua early in the century, as well as a popular lyricist, writing not only such familiar songs with his brother J. Rosamond Johnson* as ''Under the Bamboo Tree'' but the lyrics for the national anthem of all Afro-Americans, ''Lift Every Voice and Sing.''

Both Du Bois and Johnson were integrationist, strongly opposed to the separatist policies of Marcus Garvey, the third member of the extraordinary trio. Garvey dreamed of a return to Africa for the entire race. Just before the full impact of his brief but undeniable influence, however, in 1917 "the seeds of the Black Renaissance of the Twenties were planted," wrote Arna Bontemps* long afterward. Bontemps was neither the first nor the last black historian to cite 1917 as "definitely...the year."[8]

On 28 July 1917, between 10,000 and 15,000 black American citizens marched down Fifth Avenue. Since the Emancipation Proclamation, nearly 3,000 Negroes had been lynched without trial, and during the preceding several weeks a number of race riots* had occurred around the country, notably in East St. Louis, Illinois. Anticipating by half a century Martin Luther King's great march on Washington, black leaders in Harlem—Du Bois and Johnson among them—organized the first Silent Protest Parade.* It was a striking moment in Harlem's coming of age. Another moment occurred that year when Claude McKay* had two poems celebrating Harlem life accepted by *Seven Arts**; they were the first poems since Paul Laurence Dunbar's dialect pieces during the 1890s to appear under a white imprimatur. Still another reason for marking 1917 as the debut of the Harlem Renaissance occurred three months before the Silent Protest Parade. "The date of the most important single event in the entire history of the Negro in the American Theatre," James Weldon Johnson later wrote, was 5 April 1917, when three plays by white writer Ridgely Torrence, not only about black Americans but portrayed by black Americans, opened on Broadway.[19] They contained no minstrel comedians rattling tambourines and cakewalking, no happy darkies singing on the old plantation, no blackface makeup, but, instead, sympathetic and vulnerable human beings locked in identifiable human situations. America declared war against Germany the following day, however, and interest in theatrical matters—to play such a vital role for Harlem in the years that followed—was temporarily diverted.

Certainly, the impact of the war was felt on black America as well as on white America. Despite the inequities in the country and the black press's continual deriding of Woodrow Wilson's speeches about the rights of a democracy, Harlem was as outraged by the war as the rest of the country. W.E.B. Du Bois's call to set aside differences only echoed avowals from other black leaders, assuring the government in an official report from the NAACP that the nation would find black Americans as loyal as white Americans. Although black Americans had to fight for the right to be loyal, too: the right to be trained and the right to lead troops even of their own race. These pleas only followed continuing ones for the right to vote, the right to be educated, and the right not to be lynched.

Two hundred thousand black soldiers served in France and acquitted themselves well, as history later revealed, even though the U.S. government issued secret directives to the French, smuggled back to America and printed in *The Crisis* of the NAACP, claiming that the black race would create for the white race "a menace of degeneracy were it not that an impassable gulf has been made between them.... Indulgence and familiarity are matters of grievous concern to the Americans.'' The French were advised not to eat with black troops, not to shake hands with them, not even to speak to them ''outside the requirements of military service.''[10] Moreover, the black troops faced not only German ammunition but German propaganda—leaflets inviting them to come over, where they could sit anywhere they liked on the streetcars in Berlin and where they wouldn't get lynched. Propaganda back home consisted of popular songs like ''The Nigger War Bride Blues'' (1917) and ''When the Boys from Dixie Eat the Melon on the Rhine'' (1918). The following year, however, 1,300 black veterans of the 369th Regiment marched up Fifth Avenue to the military tunes of James Reese Europe's* band and with Bill ''Bojangles'' Robinson* as drum major. The French called them ''Hell Fighters,''* the only American unit awarded the Croix de Guerre and the only regiment chosen by the French High Command to lead the march on the Rhine. White America was furious, but black America had been given an identity it refused to relinquish, and W.E.B. Du Bois's editorial in *The Crisis* concluded with a rallying cry:

we are cowards and jackasses if now that the war is over we do not marshal every ounce of our brain and brawn to fight a sterner, longer, more unbending battle against the forces of hell in our own land.

    We *return.*
    We *return from fighting.*
    We *return fighting.*[11]

That was in May. Then came the Red Summer of 1919 with its twenty-five race riots. James Weldon Johnson gave the bloody season its name, and Claude McKay memorialized it in a sonnet in the white magazine the *Liberator*,* ''If We Must Die.''

It is not surprising that in view of these contradictory circumstances—the black heroism that gave the race hope and the flawed democracy that gave the race despair—a man like Marcus Garvey could capture the imaginations of so many Afro-American citizens, particularly those among the ''untalented ninetieth.'' He galvanized his race in a program of self-help and advancement and African nationalism through his Universal Negro Improvement Association (UNIA),* which in 1920 astonished New York with an international convention of parades, speeches, pageants, and a royal investiture to administer a new black nation of more than 25,000 delegates from throughout the world. Garvey founded a shipping line as well, but neither it nor his ''Back to Africa'' movement succeeded. The organization split into separate factions, fed surely by Du Bois's sneering invective against separatism as well as by Garvey's bankruptcy and imprisonment for mail fraud and subsequent deportation. On the other hand, his newspaper *Negro World** gave black Americans a popular outlet, with a strong lineup of staff writers, many of whom went on to more significant work. Further, it printed a great deal of poetry—or what it called poetry—that was mostly inept, including Garvey's own naive doggerel; but this was the first time that black voices had expressed their need, on any large scale at least, to be heard. Fully three years before the *New York Herald Tribune* did so, *Negro World* had begun announcing a "negro renaissance" in its editorials.

The Harlem in which this ferment and activity transpired was very different from that sleepy, turn-of-the-century town. By the 1920s Harlem's six north-south blocks began at 125th Street. Fifth Avenue marked the boundary to the east, where above 131st Street thieves and indigent families were housed in "tenements like crowded dungheaps festering with poverty-stricken and crime-ridden step-children of nature," in Wallace Thurman's* memorable simile.[12] At the height of Harlem's financial success and popularity during the twenties, 2,000 black families were destitute, the average income was about eighteen dollars a week, and many of the 233 people per acre (as opposed to 133 elsewhere in Manhattan) seemed to be surviving on Fifth Avenue. Lenox Avenue was the first block west, Harlem's Bowery, shaky from its subway station and lined with pool halls and dives, with a few restaurants and theaters farther north. But Seventh Avenue was Black Broadway, sleek and spacious, especially from 127th to 134th streets, the Harlem that white thrill seekers came to know when the twenties really began to roar. Here was "the real thing in promenades," according to the *New Yorker*, then a fledgling magazine.[13] Flanked on either side by churches, theaters, business establishments and shops, cabarets and speakeasies, tea rooms and restaurants, Seventh Avenue was thriving and well groomed and active all day, and from five in the afternoon until after midnight it was brilliant and glamorous and exciting as well. Numbers-racket runners, Hindu fakirs, and soapbox orators clung to its corners, with prostitutes, blind musicians, lovers, bolito kings, dancing children, poets, pimps, preachers, and families in between, and at 132nd Street the Tree of Hope,* an aging elm that served as a labor exchange where out-of-work Harlemites had rubbed its bark smooth for good luck. "Harlem takes its ease on one of the widest and most lovely avenues in the city," the *New Yorker* continued, "and although it is but a half-hour from Times Square, it might be a stage set for Egypt in Modern Clothes." Eighth Avenue, Edgecombe and St. Nicholas avenues, and Sugar Hill* to the west—Harlem's border—held some luxury apartments for its middle-class, professional people, business entrepreneurs, social dowagers who presided over Harlem's soirées, and racketeers. Coogan's Bluff, in the northern heights from 145th Street, was also black. The entire area, less than two square miles, held 200,000 Afro-Americans, "more to the square acre," James Weldon Johnson observed, "than in any other place on earth."[14]

In this city within a city lived many literary figures, theater personalities, singers, and musicians, their names later identified inevitably with the Harlem Renaissance, among them Eubie Blake* and Noble Sissle.* Their 1921 musical comedy *Shuffle Along** has been cited often as the true, single impetus for the period: the first black Broadway show of the twenties. It set a pace and style during a period eager for novelties, and after the first week's run business was so heavy that the street on which it was playing had to be designated for one-way traffic. *Shuffle Along* opened with no advance sale and little backing, in a seedy lecture hall in need of renovation; certainly, the cast did not anticipate a long run, and Blake recalled that everyone connected with it was afraid that the love story, in which a black boy kisses a black girl, on stage, in public, would get them all thrown in jail. Instead, its enormous popularity made it a model for most of the shows that followed, many of them with equally invidiously racist titles: *Alabama Bound, Bandana Land, Black Bottom Revue, Black Scandals,* * and of course *Blackbirds,* * of which there were several annual editions with memorable songs like Fats Waller's* "Ain't Misbehavin' " and "Honeysuckle Rose"; *Chocolate Blondes, Chocolate Browns*, and *Chocolate Dandies* *; *Darktown Scandals* and *Darktown Strutters*; *Goin' White*; *Lucky Sambo* *; *North Ain't South* *; and *Raisin' Cane.* *

If the titles smacked of racism, so did some of the songs: as far as popular music was concerned, there had not been much progress since the beginning of the century when a black comedian named Ernest Hogan incensed Afro-Americans with a song called "All Coons Look Alike to Me." The music was essentially imitative of the white tunes downtown (or perhaps it was only Broadway show-tune music rather than racial music). There were exceptions: "Am I Blue?" "Ain't Misbehavin'," "Memories of You," and "Runnin' Wild." More often, however, the songs were simply banal: "I'm a Little Blackbird Looking for a Bluebird," or "There's No Place as Grand as Bandana Land," or "If You've Never Been Vamped by a Brownskin, You've Never Been Vamped at All." At the outset of the twenties, songs truly Negro in origin—spirituals* and blues*—were little known to whites and publicly shunned by blacks. The difference in time between slavery and the Harlem Renaissance was no more than the distance between the Harlem Renaissance and the present, about 60 years, and 300-year-old wounds heal slowly.

Similarly, plays about the lives of ordinary Afro-Americans were unlikely to draw large audiences. "There is a lot of talk about 'art' in this community nowadays," black drama critic Theophilus Lewis* complained. "The best people are all hot for it. But when a craftsman unveils his work and the best people immediately begin chatting about its propriety, instead of discussing the competence of the execution, one is moved to wonder if their esthetic favor is not bogus."[15] When Taylor Gordon* and Paul Robeson* began to give recitals of spirituals in New York, black audiences were less enchanted than white ones; they might sing those "sorrow songs," as W.E.B. Du Bois called them, in the privacy of their homes, but most Afro-Americans wanted to assimilate, not separate, trying to straighten their hair with pomades and bleach their skins with face creams. Lighter was still whiter.

As for the blues, frankly erotic and nothing that respectable, middle-class, cultured "colored people" wanted to disclose, they were usually performed in all-black theaters for all-black audiences or in the dozens of cabarets in Harlem where three-piece bands pounded out rhythms for singers like Bessie Smith.*

Less-celebrated performers are only now beginning to be discovered through new releases of long-forgotten recordings from black record companies like Black Swan Phonograph Corporation* (originally, Harry H. Pace*) that flourished in the twenties. The indestructible Alberta Hunter,* who first sang in Harlem in 1922, was still performing as late as 1984, just to let her audiences at The Cookery in Greenwich Village know what they missed by being born so late. The most popular of these figures was barely recognizable in her old age, an elephantine earth mother croaking out Baptist hymns for Billy Graham; but during the twenties Ethel Waters* was Sweet Mama Stringbean, and she counted among her credentials having been first to sing W. C. Handy's* immortal "St. Louis Blues." Waters went on to become one of America's most distinguished actresses, but she did not appear on Broadway until 1927, and more than another decade elapsed before she had an opportunity to perform in serious drama.

Other black actors were equally repressed by white expectations and black stereotypes. Charles Gilpin,* for example, triumphed in Eugene O'Neill's* *Emperor Jones* in 1920, but few roles were offered to him afterward; Paul Robeson appeared in O'Neill's *All God's Chillun Got Wings* in 1924, but critics and audiences seemed far more interested and sometimes outraged by a black actor appearing with a white actress than in the play or the performances. Not surprisingly, Robeson turned to the recital stage and then drifted into an inconsequential career in English films. After the O'Neill plays, Paul Green's* powerful *In Abraham's Bosom* employed an all-black cast, including the greatly admired Rose McClendon,* and won the Pulitzer Prize in 1926; a year later Du Bose Heyward's* dramatization of his novel *Porgy,* about black life in South Carolina, was an extraordinarily popular success; and in 1930 Marc Connelly's *Green Pastures* overwhelmed white Broadway and ran for two seasons. These plays offered serious roles to serious black actors, despite their paucity and familiar stereotypes among the characters, but they were all by white playwrights. With few exceptions, plays by Afro-Americans only got hearings through little theater groups, performing in the Harlem branches of the New York Public Library and the YMCA, with little attention and no pay. Serious dramatists like Frank Wilson,* who worked full-time as a postman, or Willis Richardson,* a clerk with the U.S. Bureau of Printing and Engraving, found no commercial outlet for their work. The kind of show—largely musical revues—that had a chance on Broadway only extends the partial alphabetical list above: *Rhapsody in Black,* *Strut Miss Lizzie,* *Strut Your Stuff, Struttin' Along, Struttin' Hannah from Savannah, Struttin' Sam from Alabam, Tan Town Topics, Watermelon, We'se Risin'*—all of them invariably imitative, invariably perpetuating racial stereotypes, with pale chorus girls and comedians in blackface makeup.

Beyond all of this musical and theatrical activity, the curiosity of slumming ofays, the hedonism rife during Prohibition, and far beyond the romantic notions of the Universal Negro Improvement Association, an intellectual life continued to develop through the NAACP and the National Urban League.* It attracted less popular attention because serious literature usually attracts less popular attention. A 1924 Civic Club Dinner* served as a prologue to the Harlem Renaissance in literary matters. The dinner was organized by the Urban League at the venerable club, where several influential white editors and publishers, many of whom afterward were eager to publish work by black writers, were among the guests. One editor, Paul Kellog of the *Survey Graphic*,* was so impressed that he devoted an entire issue to the matter: "Harlem: Mecca of the New Negro." To its predominately white subscribers, *Survey Graphic*'s issue the following March served as a significant move toward recognition of the abilities of the "Talented Tenth" that intellectual Afro-Americans were counting on to improve the estimation of the race in the eyes of an ignorant white public.

The movement had no formal organization at that time, and as black poet Robert Hayden later observed, it was more "aesthetic and philosophical than political," its main thrust "integrationist" rather than "separatist," trying to awaken black Americans to their own value in society.[16] Concurrently, *Vanity Fair*,* the leading white magazine for sophisticated readers interested in the arts, introduced black matters to a huge popular public, beginning with a series of articles by the white novelist and music critic Carl Van Vechten, who had been championing Negro arts and letters since the turn of the century. Half a dozen 1925 issues carried such essays: about jazz; about the spirituals; about the blues; about blues singers; a "Prescription for the Negro Theatre" to abandon white imitations; an analysis of the black artist's reluctance to exploit his racial gifts; and introductions to selections of poems by two young writers who clearly exemplify the strongest contradictions in the Harlem Renaissance.

Countee Cullen* wanted desperately to be recognized as a poet, not as a black poet, and he slavishly, sometimes eloquently, imitated John Keats. Langston Hughes,* on the other hand, insisted on being recognized as a black poet, freewheeling his verse through Harlem's seamy pleasures as well as its anguish. They were in their early twenties when Van Vechten introduced their work in 1925, and the following year he was responsible for bringing the Harlem Renaissance more forcibly to the attention of white America with his novel *Nigger Heaven*.* The title alone guaranteed controversy. Two different characters have something to say about the phrase, and in their declarations they express another of the strong contradictions in the period that thousands of new arrivals to Harlem grew to feel during the halcyon days of the Renaissance. In a sleazy cabaret, a girl "rapturously" calls all of Harlem "Nigger Heaven": "I jes nacherly think dis heah is Nigger Heaven!" she exclaims with pleasure, employing the epithet used freely among black Americans, not only as a term of opprobrium but often as a term of endearment.[17] Later in the novel another character reacts very differently to the phrase: "Nigger Heaven! That's what Harlem is. We sit in our places in the gallery of this New York theatre and watch the white world sitting down below in the good seats in the orchestra.... It never seems to occur to them that Nigger Heaven is crowded, that there isn't another seat, that something has to be done."[18] Whatever its limitations as art, *Nigger Heaven* surely popularized the Harlem Renaissance and Harlem itself. The audiences for black shows grew larger and the postmidnight invasions of black cabarets and speakeasies more frequent; many young black writers were suddenly taken up and briefly successful, as white New Yorkers began turning up at literary soirées on Striver's Row* and Rent Parties* on side streets off the avenues.

Not surprisingly, some remarkable nonliterary personalities turned up as well and, with time, have entered Harlem's unique mythology: Pig Foot Mary Dean,* for example, who began her career with a mobile restaurant selling boiled pigs' feet out of a baby carriage and died worth about half a million dollars; Elder Becton,* who preached "a square deal for God" until he got gunned down by gangsters; Father Divine (George Baker*), who succeeded Becton as Harlem's spiritual leader, preaching peace, brotherhood, cleanliness, and abstention from sex in exchange for prayers and sumptuous meals; Gladys Bentley,* a 400-pound entertainer who openly dressed in tailor-made drag and wore a white tuxedo when she married her girl friend in Atlantic City; Caspar Holstein,* who devised the notorious numbers* racket, that system of betting on the daily stock-market reports; Hubert Fauntleroy Julian,* the Black Eagle, who parachuted into Harlem and sold tickets in advance to eager onlookers, and viewing rights to his body to a local undertaker, in case he didn't make it; A'Lelia Walker,* the multimillionaire daughter of the inventor of the hair-straightening process, Sarah Breedlove (Madame C. J.) Walker,* "Queen of the De-Kink," in Osbert Sitwell's apt phrase,[19] who passed her time in her castle above the Hudson River, the Villa LeWaro, with its twenty-four-carat-gold-inlaid piano and black footmen in doublets and hose and white wigs. At the height of the Harlem Renaissance, A'Lelia Walker turned the top floor of her Harlem townhouse into the "Dark Tower,"* where black artists and writers were supposed to rub shoulders and break bread with white visitors. She greeted her guests as they climbed the stairs and charged them fifteen cents apiece to check their hats.

But it is among those writers who mounted the steps to A'Lelia Walker's Dark Tower, whose poems and stories ran in *The Crisis* and *Opportunity*,* whose works—for so long afterward ignored—now turn up with increasing regularity in standard anthologies of American literature, that the Harlem Renaissance gains its lasting value as a cultural phenomenon in our history. First, Jean Toomer*: his brilliant *Cane** is the period's avant-garde. Poets like Georgia Douglas Johnson,* Frank Horne,* and Arna Bontemps, as well as the perennial representatives Langston Hughes and Countee Cullen, now are regularly included in collections of American verse. Zora Neale Hurston* is surely one of the most remarkable renaissance figures, first as an anthropologist responsible for collecting a wealth of valuable folk material throughout the South and later as a gifted novelist, greatly underrated, especially for *Their Eyes Were Watching God*, a book no feminist dare ignore. Walter White,* the powerful gadfly of the NAACP, wrote two novels about the horrors of the South, both angry enough to incinerate themselves, and he also wrote *Rope and Faggot*,* that mad history of lynching and burning in America. James Weldon Johnson contributed an excellent history of Harlem, *Black Manhattan*.* Jessie Fauset,* an editor on *The

Crisis, wrote four interesting novels about black middle-class life. Rudolph Fisher* wrote an engaging detective novel, clearly a forerunner of Chester Himes's *Cotton* books that made such successful movies a few years ago, while Claude McKay* wrote a fine expatriate novel, *Banjo*,* and both of them wrote novels about contemporary high life, Fisher's *Walls of Jericho** and McKay's *Home to Harlem*,* equally good introductions to the period they paint. Both Hughes and Cullen turned their hands to fiction, as well as to more books of verse. Nella Larsen's* two novels reflect her tortured attitudes toward color consciousness, and Wallace Thurman* echoed them from his own ambivalent point of view in *The Blacker the Berry*.* The period was not without its con artists, certainly, as one of Thurman's characters admits with sufficient dispassion in a later novel:

Being a Negro writer these days is a racket and I'm going to make the most of it while it lasts. Sure I cut the fool. But I enjoy it too.... And the only way I can live easily until I have the requisite training is to pass as a writer of potential ability. Voila! I get my tuition paid at Columbia. I rent an apartment and have all the furniture contributed by kind hearted ofays.... I find queer places for whites to go in Harlem...; out of the way primitive churches, sidestreet speakeasies. They fall for it. About twice a year I manage to sell a story. It is acclaimed. I am a genius in the making. Thank God for this Negro literary renaissance. Long may it flourish.[20]

The most uncompromising of the Harlem Renaissance artists, Wallace Thurman is inevitably the writer on whom any such list must conclude. At the height of the period he edited two magazines, *Fire!!** and *Harlem: A Forum of Negro Life*,* in which he collected work from most of the foregoing writers, and several others as well, to thumb their noses at the older generation with poems and stories and essays guaranteed to offend the uptight and staid. When Harlem fell with the stock market crash, and all writers, as Langston Hughes put it, went "rolling down the hill toward the Works Projects Administration,"[21] Thurman created his besotted "Niggerati Manor" in the epitaphic novel *Infants of the Spring*.* He had always been suspicious of the movement anyway, sensing the danger in fads masquerading as art, so the bitter satire was not unexpected: "Whites and blacks clung passionately together as if trying to effect a permanent merger. Liquor, jazz music, and close physical contact had achieved what decades of propaganda had advocated with little success.... Tomorrow all of them will have an emotional hangover.... This...is the Negro Renaissance, and this is about all the whole damn thing is going to amount to."[22]

By 1932, when Thurman's novel was published, Harlem was too hungry to care much about the "New Negro"; certainly, white America didn't. In the New York *Amsterdam News*ature* Kelly Miller* wrote, about the same time, "The bottom layer is always pressed thinnest by the weight superincumbent upon it," noting that with banks failing, religious faith at a low ebb, schools offering no help for employment training, lynching reborn, and only the NAACP still speaking out in protest, Afro-Americans were destined to suffer.[23] Thirty-five years later *The*

Negro in New York disclosed how much. Ten thousand people lived in cellars and basements where the toilet was a tin can in the corner. White families were paying 20 to 25 percent of their wages for housing; blacks were paying 40 to 50 percent when there were any wages to draw on, and if there weren't, they were driven back to the tenements of Lenox and Fifth. The public service companies made clear that they only employed a minimum number of blacks in menial positions and none as "stenographers, clerks, or inspectors."[24] Wage standards disappeared completely; domestic slave markets began to flourish. Venereal disease and pneumonia rates doubled. So did the death rate. One out of ten black infants died, twice the number of white infants. The Harlem General Hospital,* offering medical treatment to 350,000 potential patients, had 273 beds. Black citizens were arrested in droves for racket extortion and prostitution, the best-paying professions, and the Mayor's Commission eventually admitted to discrimination by the police force against Harlem and its residents and to "a studied neglect of its critical problems."[25] Most of this information was suppressed or ignored, following a final explosion on 19 March 1935, when 10,000 black Americans swept through Harlem destroying the property of white merchants. "In the very citadel of America's New Negro," Roi Ottley later wrote, "crowds went crazy like the remnants of a defeated, abandoned, hungry army."[26]

And then, for nearly a generation of further systematic segregation and sporadic rioting and indifference, they waited—until Rosa Parks sat down in the front of a bus in Selma, Alabama, because she was tired. The subsequent dogged and determined efforts of Martin Luther King brought about the Black Arts movement, long overdue; but it was not in the sixties that black became beautiful. That declaration of independence had come in the *Nation* magazine in July 1926, when Langston Hughes wrote:

it is the duty of the younger Negro artist. . .to change through the force of his art that old whispering "I want to be white," hidden in the aspirations of his people, to "Why should I want to be white? I am a Negro—and beautiful!. . . . We younger Negro artists who create now intend to express our individual dark-skinned selves without fear or shame. . . . We know we are beautiful. And ugly too. The tom-tom cries and the tom-tom laughs. . . . We build our temples for tomorrow, strong as we know how, and we stand on top of the mountain, free within ourselves.[27]

The period 1917 to 1935, from Harlem's first silent protest march to its first riot, marks the limits of this Harlem Renaissance dictionary, with perhaps an entry or two on either side as introduction and conclusion. It accounts for significant figures and events and locales—failures as well as successes—in entries varying from about 50 to about 1,500 words. Throughout, "Harlem Renaissance" is used consistently in referring to the period 1917–1935; "black" and "Afro-American" are used more or less interchangeably; and "Negro," when historically accurate or appropriate, is regularly employed without opprobrium.

On occasion, available information determined the amount of space allotted to subjects, although their relative importance to the period was influential. Conversely, many distinguished personalities of whom full-length biographies are readily available have not been given untoward attention at the expense of lesser figures who were also important in the evolution and ferment of the period. Some few earlier people, inactive during the twenties and thirties but strongly influential, are included, while others just beginning their careers at the tail end of the period are not. Politicians and educators and athletes appear in this alphabetical compilation, as well as poets and painters and novelists; so do journalists, racketeers, clergymen, aviators, musicians, junkmen, and postal clerks, if their roles in the Harlem Renaissance were somewhat significant: leading actors require supporting casts in panoramic plays.

The dictionary accounts for the plots and critical receptions of representative novels, films, dramas, and musical entertainments; it covers the newspapers and periodicals of and about Afro-Americans, not only those published in Harlem but those whose influence on Harlem was marked; it includes entries on a few white figures whose involvement with the movement and whose lasting contributions to it were sufficient to warrant attention; it includes entries on subjects as various as churches and cabarets, literary quarterlies and gossip sheets, little theater groups and business organizations; and it includes a few general articles on subjects inextricable from the Harlem Renaissance.

Further, it accounts for a number of figures, publications, and places whose significance seems at first glance far removed from the primary concerns of the Harlem Renaissance. The preoccupation with black arts and letters during the twenties, however, surely stimulated interest in Afro-American matters on a broader scale. The achievements of a black educator in the South may have been facilitated by the popularity of a black singer in the North; it is unlikely that a black person could have run for public office before the Harlem Renaissance; the work of a black poet in a New York magazine may have made possible the publication of work by other black writers in other parts of the country. Such an osmosis may be no more strongly intellectual than it is emotional, but, having occurred, its results demand documentation.

Generally, the dictionary concentrates on its subjects between 1917 and 1935, deliberately truncating earlier and later events, activities, and accomplishments, although accounting for them in summary. Most subjects are identified according to the names by which they were best known and regularly recognized. The surname is followed by the given name or names (unfamiliar or unused given names appear in brackets) or by nicknames or stage names that were used exclusively, when appropriate, or by nicknames that were used occasionally in quotation marks; finally, again when appropriate, full names that differ from familiar ones follow in brackets. Thus: Ellington, [Edward Kennedy] Duke; Armstrong, [Daniel] Louis "Satchmo"; Morton, Jelly Roll [Ferdinand Joseph LaMenthe]; Robinson, Bill "Bojangles" [Luther Robinson]; Taylor, Eva [Irene Gibbons]. In cross-referencing subjects with asterisks when their names appear in various entries, these examples, then, appear as Duke Ellington*; Louis Armstrong*; Jelly Roll Morton*; Bill Robinson* or, because of its wider familiarity, occasionally Bill "Bojangles" Robinson*; and Eva Taylor.* Dates connected with each entry are as complete as extant records have allowed, within the limitations of the compilers' research. "1900," for example, indicates existence or application within a single year, as in the case of a book's publication or of a theatrical opening; "1900–   " indicates that the person is still living or that the organization, place, or publication is still functioning; "1900–?," "?–1900," or "?–?" indicates dates only partially complete. Some cabarets and nightclubs opened and closed so quickly that even a question mark becomes supererogatory. Similarly, subject entries, like "Dance" or "Riots," are undated, although pertinent dates are included in the body of the entry. Writers' works are included if they bear some relevance to the period under consideration. Each entry concludes with its sources, listed chronologically in order of publication. Published sources are offered in abbreviated form, including author or editor, short title, and date, or an abbreviation and date. Following them, sources from manuscripts, scrapbooks, and correspondence are listed; and following them are verbal sources. Each entry closes with the initials of its author or authors. In all quotations from published sources, I have silently corrected obvious typographical errors and errors in spelling and punctuation to avoid riddling pages with [sic].

Several appendixes follow the body of the dictionary. Appendix A provides a chronology of significant events from 1917 to 1935, beginning with the first silent protest march and ending with the first Harlem riot. This short chronology serves as a guide to the period's progress. Appendix B, "A Harlem Renaissance Library," is a chronological listing of books by or about Afro-Americans published during the Harlem Renaissance. Appendix C lists plays and musical entertainments by or about Afro-Americans, and Appendix D is an alphabetical listing of newspapers and other serial publications. Finally, Appendix E is a glossary of Harlem slang—words and phrases in popular use during the twenties and thirties, of which a surprising number have influenced present-day speech and communication.

The bibliography includes full publication information of the sources used in compiling the dictionary as well as others drawn upon for background. Frequently, different editions of the same work have been used by different contributors; therefore, dates of original publication and of reprint are included, if applicable. Works used only in reprint editions include date of initial publication.

An index to a dictionary is not, in the present case, redundant, since many figures and events and locales are referred to regularly and frequently throughout in subject entries other than their own. Through the index, readers may trace ancillary information about subjects of interest to them; furthermore, not every person, place, or thing connected with the Harlem Renaissance warrants a separate subject entry in the dictionary, nor in all cases was sufficient information available to construct one. The index indicates where many of them are discussed.

For the foregoing divisions and decisions, and for the inevitable errors and omissions associated with any work of this scope, I assume responsibility, defending the former and apologizing for the latter.

Bruce Kellner

NOTES

1. Langston Hughes, "When Harlem Was in Vogue," *Town and Country*, July 1940, p. 64.
2. Roi Ottley and William J. Weatherby, eds., *The Negro in New York: An Informal Social History, 1626–1940*, New York: Praeger, 1969, p. 9.
3. W.E.B. Du Bois. "Postscript," *The Crisis*, May 1928, pp. 96–97.
4. Carl Van Vechten, *Fragments from an unwritten autobiography*, New Haven: Yale University Library, 1955, p. 3.
5. Quoted in "Pot-Pourri," *Opportunity*, June 1925, p. 187.
6. James Weldon Johnson, *Black Manhattan* (New York: Knopf, 1930), p. 150.
7. A[lain] L[ocke], "Harlem," *The Survey Graphic Number*, 1 March 1925, p. 630.
8. Arna Bontemps, "The Black Renaissance of the Twenties," *Black World*, November 1970, p. 7.
9. Johnson, *Black Manhattan*, p. 175.
10. "Documents of the War," *The Crisis*, March 1919, pp. 16–17.
11. W.E.B. Du Bois, "Returning Soldiers," *The Crisis*, May 1919, pp. 13–14.
12. Wallace Thurman, *Negro Life in New York's Harlem* (Girard, Kans.: Haldeman-Julius, 1928), p. 8.
13. "The Talk of the Town," *New Yorker*, 9 October 1926, pp. 20–21.
14. Johnson, *Black Manhattan*, p. 147.
15. Theophilus Lewis, "Theatre," *The Messenger*, April 1924, p. 110.
16. Robert Hayden, Preface to *The New Negro*, ed. Alain Locke (New York: Atheneum, 1969), p. ix.
17. Carl Van Vechten, *Nigger Heaven* (New York: Knopf, 1926), p. 15.
18. Van Vechten, *Nigger Heaven*, p. 149.
19. Osbert Sitwell, "New York in the Twenties," *Atlantic Monthly*, February 1962, p. 38.
20. Wallace Thurman, *Infants of the Spring* (New York: Macaulay, 1932), pp. 229–30.
21. Langston Hughes, *The Big Sea* (New York: Knopf, 1940), p. 233.
22. Thurman, *Infants of the Spring*, p. 187.
23. Kelly Miller, "Looking Backward," in *Voices of a Black Nation*, ed. Theodore G. Vincent (San Francisco: Ramparts Press, 1973), p. 58.
24. Ottley and Weatherby, *Negro in New York*, p. 268.
25. Ottley and Weatherby, *Negro in New York*, p. 280.
26. Ottley and Weatherby, *Negro in New York*, p. 275.
27. Langston Hughes, "The Negro Artist and the Racial Mountain," *The Nation*, 23 June 1926, p. 694.

Abbreviations

Three abbreviations appear with regularity in the entries and are used inter-changeably with the full names of the organizations for which they stand:

NAACP   National Association for the Advancement of Colored
               People
UNIA   Universal Negro Improvement Association
TOBA   Theatrical Owners and Bookers Association

In preparing any substantial reference work, editors inevitably transform the published scholarship of others into "standard reference sources." This dictionary calls so often on a number of such works that they have been assigned abbreviations in the spirit of those already widely in use. This liberty applies only to books conforming to alphabetical arrangements of bibliographical, biographical, and historical matters. Full publication information is included in the bibliography. Abbreviations and dates; or authors or editors, short titles, and dates accompany each entry.

AAA   *Afro-American Authors*, ed. William Adams, Boston, 1970.
AAB   *American Authors and Books, 1642–Present*, ed. W. J.
               Burke and W. D. Howe, New York, 1962, 1972.
AAD   *Afro-American Artists: A Bio-Bibliographical Dictionary*,
               ed. Theresa Dickason Cederholm, Boston, 1973.
AAL   *Afro-American Literature*, ed. William Adams, Boston,
               1970.
ASCAP   *ASCAP Biographical Dictionary*, ed. Lynn Farnal Group,
               New York, 1966, 1980.
AWW   *American Women Writers*, ed. Linda Mainiero, New York,
               1979.

BAF	*Blacks in American Films*, by Edward Mapp, Metuchen, N.J., 1974.
BAW	*Black American Writers*, by Geraldine O. Matthews, Boston, 1975.
BAWPP	*Black American Writers Past and Present*, ed. Theresa Gunnels Rush et al., Metuchen, N.J., 1975.
BB	*Blacks in Blackface*, by Henry T. Sampson, Metuchen, N.J., 1980.
BBW	*Blacks in Black and White*, by Henry T. Sampson, Metuchen, N.J., 1977.
BCM	*Blacks in Classical Music*, by Raoul Abdul, New York, 1977.
BDAM	*Biographical Dictionary of Afro-American and African Music and Musicians*, by Eileen Southern, Westport, Conn., 1982.
BEWW	*Biographical Encyclopedia and Who's Who in the American Theatre*, ed. Walter Rigdon, New York, 1966.
BIA	*Blacks in America*, ed. James M. McPherson, Garden City, N.Y., 1971.
Burns Mantle	*The Best Plays of 1919–1920* through *The Best Plays of 1935–1936*, ed. Burns Mantle, New York, 1919–1936.
BWBO	*Black Women in Bands and Orchestras*, by D. Antoinette Handy, 1981.
BWW	*Blues Who's Who*, by Sheldon Harris, New Rochelle, N.Y., 1979.
CA	*Contemporary Authors*, Detroit, 1967–1980.
CB	*Current Biography*, New York, 1940, 1944, 1945, 1951, 1954, 1969, 1980.
CVV	Carl Van Vechten's Typed Inventory, 1941–1964, for the James Weldon Johnson Memorial Collection of Negro Arts and Letters, Beinecke Rare Book and Manuscript Library, Yale University, New Haven, unpublished.
DAB	*Dictionary of American Biography*, ed. American Council of Learned Societies, New York, 1928–1937.
DANB	*Dictionary of American Negro Biography*, ed. Rayford W. Logan and Michael R. Winston, New York, 1982.
DBPA	*Dictionary of Blacks in the Performing Arts*, ed. Edward Mapp, Metuchen, N.J., 1974.
EBA	*Encyclopedia of Black America*, ed. Augustus W. Lowe, New York, 1981.
EJ	*The Encyclopedia of Jazz*, ed. Leonard Feather, New York, 1955, 1960, 1970.
EMT	*Encyclopedia of the Musical Theatre*, ed. Stanley Green, New York, 1976.

ETM	*Encyclopedia of Theatre Music*, ed. Richard Lewine and Alex Simon, New York, 1961.
GD	*Grove's Dictionary of Music and Musicians*; rev. ed. *New Grove Dictionary of Music and Musicians*, New York, 1954, 1955, 1980.
Hatch-Billops	The Hatch-Billops Collection, Inc., Archives of Black American Cultural History, Taped Oral Interviews, New York, unpublished.
JWJ	The James Weldon Johnson Memorial Collection of Negro Arts and Letters, Beinecke Rare Book and Manuscript Library, Yale University, New Haven, scrapbooks and clippings.
MBA	*The Music of Black Americans*, by Eileen Southern, New York, 1971.
NA	*Negro Almanac*, ed. Harry A. Ploski and Warren Marr II, New York, 1976, 1980.
NAW	*Notable American Women, 1607–1950*, ed. Edward T. James et al., Cambridge, Mass., 1971, 1980.
NYT	*New York Times*, 1915–1983.
NYTTR	*New York Times Theatre Reviews*, 1972. All reviews of plays and other theatrical entertainments used as references in the dictionary were drawn from this unpaged compilation. When quoted, the reviews are (parenthetically) identified by date and page in the text of the entries, and NYTTR is listed as the reference source.
PR	*Progress of a Race*, ed. J. L. Nichols and William Crogman, New York, 1920, 1969.
SBAA	*Selected Black American Authors*, by James Page, Boston, 1977.
TCA	*Twentieth Century Authors*, ed. Stanley Kunitz and Howard Haycraft, New York, 1940, 1955.
WWA	*Who's Who in America*, New York, 1930, 1933, 1945, 1950, 1959, 1977, 1979, 1981.
WWB	*Who's Who in Boxing*, ed. Bob Burrill, New Rochelle, N.Y., 1974.
WWBA	*Who's Who Among Black Americans*, Northbrook, Ill., 1976.
WWCA	*Who's Who in Colored America*, New York, 1927, 1933, 1938, 1950.
WWCR	*Who's Who of the Colored Race*, Chicago, 1915.
WWH	*Who's Who in Hollywood, 1900–1976*, ed. David Ragan, New Rochelle, N.Y., 1976.
WWJ	*Who's Who in Jazz*, by John Chilton, Philadelphia, 1972, 1978.
WWT	*Who's Who in the Theatre*, ed. John Parker, New York, 1939, 1952.

WWW — *Who Was Who in America*, New York, 1943, 1947, 1950, 1951, 1963, 1968.

Each entry concludes with the initials of its author:

DA	Desmond Arthur
DD	Dennis B. Downey
MH	Mark Helbling
DI	Diane S. Isaacs
BK	Bruce Kellner
PO	Priscilla Oppenheimer
DS	David Stameshkin
RZ	Robert L. Zangrando

Contributors

DESMOND ARTHUR is a San Francisco music critic whose essays and reviews appear regularly in the *American Record Guide*.

DENNIS B. DOWNEY is Assistant Professor of History at Millersville University of Pennsylvania and author of several essays on American cultural history.

MARK HELBLING is Associate Professor of American Studies at the University of Hawaii and author of many articles on Afro-American arts and letters.

DIANE S. ISAACS, whose research interests lie in the work of black women writers, was Assistant Professor of Afro-American and Women's Studies at the University of Minnesota and is now assistant to the vice president for student affairs at Fordham University, New York.

BRUCE KELLNER is Professor of English at Millersville University of Pennsylvania and author of three books on the life and works of Carl Van Vechten as well as many essays on twentieth-century British and American literature.

PRISCILLA OPPENHEIMER is a free-lance writer and editor in Lancaster, Pennsylvania, and active in women's studies activities.

DAVID STAMESHKIN was Instructor of Black History at Middlebury College, Vermont, and is presently Acting Assistant Dean of Students at Franklin and Marshall College in Lancaster, Pennsylvania.

ROBERT L. ZANGRANDO is Professor of History at the University of Akron, Ohio, and is completing a critical biography of Walter White.

The Silent Protest Parade, 28 July 1917. (Reprinted with Permission of the Crisis Publishing Company.)

W.E.B. Du Bois, 1946, photograph by Carl Van Vechten. (Courtesy of Joseph Solomon for the Estate of Carl Van Vechten, and Kirkwood Community College.)

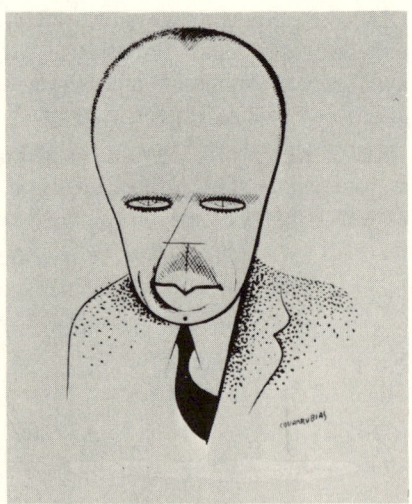

James Weldon Johnson, 1927, caricature by Miguel Covarrubias. (Reprinted by permission of Alfred A. Knopf, Inc., from the dust jacket of James Weldon Johnson, *The Autobiography of an Ex-Coloured Man*, copyright 1927, renewal copyright 1955 Carl Van Vechten.)

Madame C. J. Walker Manufacturing Company was a familiar advertiser in Afro-American magazines and newspapers during the twenties. (From *The Messenger*.)

Shuffle Along, by Eubie Blake, Noble Sissle, Aubrey Lyles, and Irvin C. Miller, 1921. From a postcard. (Collection of the author.)

Josephine Baker in *Revue Nègre*, 1925, anonymous. (Courtesy Donald Angus.)

Frank Wilson and Rose McClendon in *Porgy*, drawing by O'Brian from *Opportunity*, November 1927. (Reprinted with permission of the National Urban League.)

Carl Van Vechten, a Prediction, 1926, caricature by Miguel Covarrubias. (Collection of the author.)

Nora Holt, 1922, photograph by James Hargis Connelly. (Courtesy of The Collection of American Literature, the Beinecke Rare Book and Manuscript Library, Yale University.)

Langston Hughes, Charles S. Johnson, E. Franklin Frazier, Rudolph Fisher, and Hubert Delaney, 1926. (Courtesy of Regina M. Andrews.)

Countee Cullen, 1925, drawing by Winold Reiss. (Reprinted with permission of the National Urban League.)

Zora Neale Hurston, 1934

Walter White, 1932

Claude McKay, 1934

Nella Larsen, 1934

Photographs by Carl Van Vechten. (Courtesy of Joseph Solomon for the Estate of Carl Van Vechten, and The Collection of American Literature, the Beinecke Rare Book and Manuscript Library, Yale University.)

Scottsboro Limited, 1931, lithograph for the play by Langston Hughes, by Prentiss Taylor. (Courtesy of Prentiss Taylor.)

Langston Hughes, 1931, photograph by Baxter Snark. (Courtesy of Prentiss Taylor.)

W. C. Handy, 1932, photograph by Carl Van Vechten. (Courtesy of Joseph Solomon for the Estate of Carl Van Vechten.)

Drawing for Mulattoes from *Ebony and Topaz* by Richard Bruce Nugent, 1927. (Reprinted with permission of the National Urban League. Courtesy of Richard Bruce Nugent.)

Gladys Bentley, 1932, photograph by Carl Van Vechten. (Courtesy of Joseph Solomon for the Estate of Carl Van Vechten, and The Collection of American Literature, the Beinecke Rare Book and Manuscript Library, Yale University.)

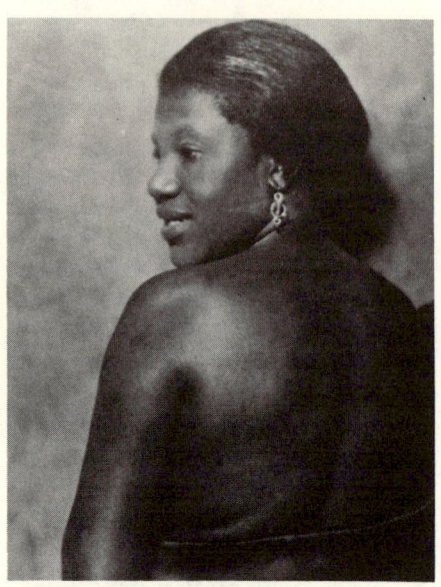

Bessie Smith, 1936, photograph by Carl Van Vechten. (Courtesy of Joseph Solomon for the Estate of Carl Van Vechten.)

Clara Smith, 1925. (Courtesy of The Collection of American Literature, the Beinecke Rare Book and Manuscript Library, Yale University.)

Blues Singer Backstage, from a drawing by E. Simms Campbell, *Opportunity*, October 1929. (Reprinted with permission of the National Urban League.)

Opportunity, September 1928, drawing by D. Edouard Freeman. (Reprinted with permission of the National Urban League.)

Fire!!, November 1926, design by Aaron Douglas. (Courtesy of Tom Wirth and The Fire!! Press.)

Irvin C. Miller Productions, from a 1928 poster. (Collection of the author.)

The Messenger, October 1926, A'Lelia Walker. (Greenwood Press.)

The Harlem Renaissance

A

ABBOTT, ROBERT S[ENGSTACKE] (journalist), 24 November 1870–29 February 1940. The editor of the Chicago *Defender** was born off the coast of Georgia and learned the practical side of his trade as an apprentice printer for the *Savannah News* in his early twenties. Concurrently, he put himself through school at Claflin College in Orangeburg, South Carolina, the Hampton Institute in Hampton, Virginia, and the Kent College of Law in Chicago where he received a degree in 1900. After five years of law practice Abbott founded the Chicago *Defender*, with an initial run of 300 copies, peddling them door-to-door in the beginning. In 1910 he became its editor, urging blacks to go north and later opposing Marcus Garvey's* back-to-Africa movement. By the 1920s Abbott's national weekly had become one of the most influential newspapers in the country, its main circulation being among blue-collar Afro-Americans. He attempted to reach a more sophisticated audience with *Abbott's Monthly*,* a popular but largely unfocused magazine containing poetry, photographs, and a wide variety of topical essays; its three-year run ended in 1933. Abbott was a member of the Illinois Race Relations Commission from 1919. During World War II his paper was credited with having sold $2 million in defense bonds. In 1944 a liberty ship was named in his honor, and he is further memorialized in the continued power of the Chicago *Defender*.
REFERENCE: Roi Ottley, *The Lonely Warrior*, 1955. (BK)

ABBOTT'S MONTHLY (periodical), 1929–1933. For a period of three years beginning in September 1929, Robert Sengstacke Abbott,* editor of the Chicago *Defender*,* published *Abbott's Monthly*, advertising it as "a magazine that's different." With colorful covers, like those of *Cosmopolitan* and *Hearst's International* at the time, featuring popular personalities in glamorized paintings, the issues included articles by writers as diverse as the musical comedy star Salem Tutt Whitney* and the celebrated white lawyer Clarence Darrow. Some

of Langston Hughes's* poems appeared in *Abbott's Monthly*, and an early story by Robert Hayden, one of the most eloquent black voices of the next generation of writers, was included in the June 1931 issue.
REFERENCE: JWJ. (BK)

AFRICANA (musical revue), 1927. Earl Dancer produced this short revue, basing it on a tab show entitled *Miss Calico*. In the leading role of that touring revue Ethel Waters had been accompanied by eight chorus girls, two boys, two comics, and a seven-piece jazz band—the conventional makeup for a travelling company at the time. With additional music and lyrics by Donald Heywood* and a title appropriated from a 1922 tab show, *Africana* opened at the Daly 63rd Street Theatre for seventy-two performances. Ethel Waters repeated "I'm Coming, Virginia," and added several of her familiar songs: "Dinah," "My Special Friend Is Back in Town," and "Shake That Thing." Dancer also included the parody he had written for *Miss Calico* of the popular Broadway play *Lulu Belle*,* "with apologies to Mr. [David] Belasco". *Africana* featured Pickaninny Hill, "the champion cakewalker of the world," the Two Black Dots, a team of low comedians in blackface, and a chorus line clad in banana costumes à la Josephine Baker.* According to the *New York Times*, most of the performers lacked minimum competence.
REFERENCES: Ethel Waters, *His Eye Is on the Sparrow*, 1951; NYTTR, 1972; BB, 1980. (BK)

AFRICANA (operetta), 1934. Donald Heywood* wrote this operetta, included in the *New York Times* list of "gloomy evenings." It featured a mixed cast, a book about civilization versus savagery in Africa in which the son of a Congo king falls in love with a missionary's daughter, and forgettable music. The *Times* reviewer suggested "Whimper of the Jungle" as an alternate title (27 Nov. 1934, p. 26).
REFERENCES: NYTTR, 1972; BB, 1980. (BK)

AFRICAN ORTHODOX CHURCH 1921–c.1935. Marcus Garvey* formed the African Orthodox Church on 28 September 1921 as a means of ending the blacks' subservience to an alien "white" God and Christ. Garvey believed that blacks should worship a black God who made his African sons and daughters in his image. The Reverend George Alexander McGuire,* a prominent black Episcopalian minister in Boston, gave up his pulpit in 1920 to become Chaplain General of Garvey's Universal Negro Improvement Association*; the next year he was ordained a bishop of dignitaries of the Greek Orthodox Church and consecrated as head of the new African Orthodox Church. The ritual of the church followed closely Roman Catholic (Garvey's religion) and Episcopalian doctrines; except for the introduction of a black Madonna, Christ, and God, the new church differed little from other Christian sects. It was, not surprisingly, vilified by black clergymen who accepted a "white" God; however, Africans and some black Caribbeans were highly receptive to the idea of a black deity. McGuire later broke with Garvey, but the church (or at least its ideals) apparently lived on into the 1930s.

REFERENCES: E. David Cronon, *Black Moses*, 1955; John Hendrik Clarke, ed., *Marcus Garvey and the Vision of Africa*, 1974. (DS)

AFRO-AMERICAN (BALTIMORE) (newspaper), 1910– . The Baltimore *Afro-American* began in 1892 as a four-page sheet used to advertise the church and community enterprises of the Reverend William Alexander. John H. Murphy, a fifty-year-old whitewasher, bought the paper from Alexander for $200 in 1910 and merged it with the *Ledger*, a church and community organ published by the Reverend George F. Bragg in the 1890s. Murphy worked full time at publishing the *Afro-American Ledger* (later, *Afro-American*) after 1917, when he stopped accepting other printing business. It was then that the *Afro-American* began to grow from a small weekly of 8,500 circulation to become the largest-selling black paper on the Eastern Seaboard, with a circulation of 38,377 in 1930 and 79,952 in 1937. When Murphy died in 1922 his sons took over operation of the company, which began to print *Afro-American* editions in Washington and Philadelphia in the 1930s. The all-black staff developed a reputation for excellent national and international coverage of news, and Bill Gibson's sports column "Hear Me Talkin' to Ya' " was very popular. The paper's motto was "Independent in all things—neutral in none." The *Afro-American* was the first eastern paper to solidly support a Democratic presidential candidate when it endorsed Al Smith in 1928. Only the *Pittsburgh Courier** had a larger national circulation in the late 1920s and 1930s than the *Afro-American*, with its distinctive green outer sheet.

REFERENCES: Eugene Gordon, "The Negro Press," *The Annals*, 1928; *The Crisis*, Feb. 1938. (DS)

AFRO-AMERICAN FOLKSONGS (book), 1925. In the preface to his book *Afro-American Folksongs: A Study in Racial and National Music*, Henry E. Krehbiel, a noted critic and musicologist, proposed that folk music be subjected to "scientific observation" so that it might be presented as "fit material for artistic treatment." He attempted to analyze the scales, modes, and rhythmic characteristics of African music and to show how these characteristics prevailed in French and Spanish Creole songs and American-English spirituals and folk songs. Krehbiel drew upon published material and second-hand accounts rather than undertaking personal field research, and most of his music examples are presented in academically correct arrangements by Harry Thacker Burleigh* and others. The book for its time was an outstanding scholarly achievement, and it paved the way for further research in the field.

REFERENCES: Henry Edward Krehbiel, *Afro-American Folksongs*, 1914; GD, 1954. (DA)

AGE **(NEW YORK)** (newspaper), 1881–1960. Originally the *Globe*, the New York *Age* was founded in 1881 by several men, including T. Thomas Fortune,* a militant young black journalist. In 1884 Fortune began a successor paper, the *Freeman*, but gave it up in October 1887. It was renamed the New York *Age* by its new editors. In February 1889 Fortune again became editor and served in that capacity until 1907, when the paper ran into deep financial difficulties and its secret financial supporter, Booker T. Washington, apparently decided he wanted Fortune removed. In his place, Fred R. Moore,* a Washington stalwart, ran the paper into the 1930s. Moore turned the *Age* into a mouthpiece of the Tuskegee Machine and of moderate to conservative views on most issues. Furthermore, Moore hired almost his entire staff from family members. This may account for the low rating given the *Age* in the late 1920s by writer Eugene Gordon,* who carefully surveyed the leading black newspapers in the country. Gordon found the *Age* to be a mediocre paper in all respects and ranked it eighth in all-around performance behind papers such as the *Pittsburgh Courier*,* the Chicago *Defender*,* the Baltimore *Afro-American*,* and its New York competitor, the *Amsterdam News*.* The *Age*, which had maintained a near monopoly until the establishment of the *Amsterdam News* and the *New York News* in the early twentieth century, remained a staid paper, according to historian Gilbert Osofsky, until it began to imitate its more successful tabloid competitors in the 1920s.

REFERENCES: Eugene Gordon, "The Negro Press," *The Annals*, 1928; Gilbert Osofsky, *Harlem: The Making of a Ghetto*, 1966; Roi Ottley and William Weatherby, eds., *The Negro in New York*, 1967; Emma Thornbrough, *T. Thomas Fortune*, 1972. (DS)

ALDRIDGE PLAYERS (little theater group), 1926. During the summer of 1926 the Aldridge Players organized to present three one-act plays by Frank Wilson*: "Sugar Cain," "Color Worship," and "Flies." According to Theophilus Lewis,* reviewing them for *The Messenger*,* all were superior to recent offerings by the Krigwa Players,* both dramatically and histrionically. Charles Randolph, Eve Gertrude Nurse, Charlie Taylor, William Jackson, Agnes Marsh, and Wilson himself appeared in the casts. Even though the plays were less successful dramatically than theatrically, Lewis believed "conventional standards of drama" could only be unfairly applied so early in the "development of the Negro little theatre movement," which from its beginnings he had championed in his columns (Aug. 1926, p. 246).

REFERENCE: Theophilus Lewis, "Theatre," *The Messenger*, Aug. 1926. (BK)

ALEXANDER, LEWIS (writer), 4 July 1900–1945. Lewis Alexander was born in Washington, D.C., and attended Howard University and the University of Pennsylvania. From an early age he was involved with various dramatic groups: the Howard Players, the Playwrights' Circle, the Aldridge Players,* and the Ethiopian Art Players,* appearing in New York with the latter. In 1927 he

edited an issue of *Carolina Magazine** featuring the work of young black writers, and he contributed some of his own verse to *Opportunity** and Countee Cullen's* *Caroling Dusk*.* Alexander's conventional quatrains and imitations of Japanese haiku, however, did not reflect the thrust and excitement of the work of other writers of the period, although he wrote on black themes occasionally.
REFERENCE: Langston Hughes and Arna Bontemps, eds., *The Poetry of the Negro*, 1949. (BK)

ALHAMBRA (cabaret), 1926–1932. The Alhambra Theatre* opened its ballroom on Seventh Avenue at 126th Street at a cost of $100,000 in 1926. White customers and black customers usually came on alternate nights. The Depression brought about its demise in 1932.
REFERENCE: David Levering Lewis, *When Harlem Was in Vogue*, 1981. (BK)

ALHAMBRA THEATRE, ?–1932. Located at Seventh Avenue and 126th Street, the Alhambra Theatre customarily offered a three-in-one show: a movie, a musical revue, and a dramatic sketch. The films were usually Hollywood products, although occasionally a black feature was booked in, and the musical section seems to have been largely a series of vaudeville acts. Plays with titles like "Monster Man," "Mighty Lak a Rose," "The Ghost House," and "Carnival Girl" were fleetingly referred to on the theatrical page of the *Inter-State Tattler** as "sketches" or "dramas" or "melodramas," but little information about their content ever appeared. Many of the actors, however, were popular with Alhambra audiences: Amanda Randolph,* Edna Harris, Teddy Blackmon, and Susie Sutton regularly appeared there, invariably praised for their performances.
REFERENCE: *Inter-State Tattler*, 1925–1932. (BK)

ALIX, [LIZA] MAE (entertainer), 31 August 1904–? The "Queen of the Splits," as Mae Alix often billed herself, worked in various nightclubs in Chicago, her hometown, until 1922 as both a singer and dancer. She made some recordings with Louis Armstrong* in 1926 while appearing in a number of New York cabarets, including the Cotton Club,* with Duke Ellington's* orchestra at the Hollywood Club, and at Small's Paradise.* Most of her work was in Chicago through the period, and she seems to have returned there permanently after an appearance in a revue at Connie's Inn* during the 1931–1932 season.
REFERENCE: BWW, 1979. (BK)

ALLEN, CLEVELAND G. (music journalist), March 1887–October 1953. During the 1920s Cleveland Allen was known for his lectures on black folk music and for his regular articles in *Musical America* and professional music journals. He had studied music in his native Greenville, South Carolina, and later at New York University and at the Angelus Academy of Music in New

York. He continued private voice studies thereafter. He was a columnist for the New York *Age** and New York representative for the Chicago *Defender** and *The Freeman* of Indianapolis.
REFERENCE: BDAM, 1982. (PO)

ALL GOD'S CHILLUN GOT WINGS (play), 1924. Eugene O'Neill's* unpopular drama about a mixed marriage between a black intellectual and an inferior white was produced at the Provincetown Playhouse, 15 May 1924, and revived at the Greenwich Village Theatre three months later. The play gained notoriety because a white actress (Mary Blair) was obliged to kiss the hand of a black actor (Paul Robeson*) at the conclusion, kneeling at his feet. Helen McKeller had accepted the lead so long as the actor were white under blackface makeup but quit when Robeson was cast in the part. Furthermore, Mayor Jimmie Walker refused to license the black and white child actors required to appear on stage together in the first scene. At the opening performance, director James Light read the scene in front of the curtain, although at the revival the children appeared together with the permission of the mayor, pending a court ruling. "If the enemies had been less diligent," reported reviewer John Corbin, "there is scant likelihood that it would have attracted attention beyond the small circle of those interested in...the theatre of experiment." Corbin further observed, "Common observation tells us that in many respects, both mental and moral, the average negro is inferior to the average white," and that "ethically and biologically, mixed marriages are undesirable—a crime against the future of our people" (NYT, 18 May 1924, sec. F, p. 1). At the play's revival, there was "sustained apathy and little applause" for this often overwrought melodrama, but Robeson performed with "admirable force" (NYT, 19 Aug. 1924, p. 9).
REFERENCES: *The Crisis*, May 1927; NYTTR, 1972. (BK)

AMBER SATYR (novel), 1932. One of several novels by white writers with black subject matter, Roy Flannagan's *Amber Satyr* is about Luther Harris, a southern mulatto boy who becomes involved with a group of indigent and degenerate white people. When a women begins to lust after him, the neighborhood gossip, strongly influenced by racial prejudice, results in his being lynched. (BK)

AMERICAN NEGRO ACADEMY. See NEGRO ART INSTITUTE.

AMERICAN NEGRO LABOR CONGRESS, 1925. The American Negro Labor Congress, a Communist-controlled organization, met for the first time in Chicago in October 1925. Its stated purpose was to unify all black labor and farmer organizations with sympathetic interracial organizations. The congress hoped eventually to end discrimination against black workers and bring black workers into the mainstream American labor movement. Under the leadership of black Communist Lovett Fort-Whiteman, the congress also planned to form local councils around the country to implement its goals. According to Sterling

Spero and Abram Harris in their 1931 monograph *The Black Worker*, blacks who attended the 1925 congress were immediately disaffected by the fact that the Communists controlled the congress; indeed, they argued that only one more congress was held, and after that the movement folded except for pronouncements by the Moscow-controlled Comintern that the congress be revived as a means of mobilizing black workers under their leadership. The American Negro Labor Congress met virulent opposition from A. Philip Randolph* and other leftists worried about Moscow's control over blacks and American labor; only W.E.B. Du Bois* showed much favor toward it.

REFERENCES: Sterling Denhard Spero and Abram L. Harris, *The Black Worker*, 1931; Theodore Kornweibel, *No Crystal Stair*, 1974. (DS)

AMSTERDAM NEWS (NEW YORK) (newspaper), 1909– . Founded in 1909, the *Amsterdam News* competed effectively with the New York *Age** by concentrating on New York City news and taking strong stances against racism and discrimination. By the late 1920s one critic had rated the *Amsterdam News* well above the *Age* in all categories. Sadie Warren Davis was an effective force as owner of the *Amsterdam News* for many years, and under her leadership the paper was rated as the finest black newspaper in the country by Eugene Gordon* in 1927. Gordon particularly credited the professional staff, including editor-in-chief William Kelly,* his assistant Thelma Berlack,* and sports writer Lionel Dougherty.* In 1935 an attempt to unionize the staff led to a bitter strike when Davis refused to deal with the union. The paper suffered significant economic damage during the strike, and Davis sold out to the business operations of doctors C. B. Powell and P.M.H. Savory in late 1935. Savory was a leading force at the paper until his death in 1965.

REFERENCES: Eugene Gordon, "The Negro Press," *The Annals*, 1928; Roi Ottley and William J. Weatherby, eds., *The Negro in New York*, 1967. (DS)

ANDERSON, [EDMUND LINCOLN] EDDIE (comedian), 18 September 1905–28 February 1977. Long before he became widely known as Jack Benny's "Rochester," Eddie Anderson was active in musical comedy. He won an amateur contest in his native Oakland, California, at the age of thirteen and, after a brief turn as a jockey, became a dancing comedian with touring companies. While still in his teens he appeared as a chorus boy in Mamie Smith's* *Struttin' Along* in 1923, and a year later he appeared as one of the "Three Black Aces" with his brother Cornelius in *Steppin' High*. After a fourteen-week stint dancing at the Plantation Club,* he toured on both the Pantages and Keith circuits in *Steppin' High*. At some early point in this vaudeville work, Jack Benny caught his act and several years later, in preparing his radio show, remembered Eddie Anderson, who became his inseparable, wise-cracking valet Rochester. Anderson acted in several films, notably *The Green Pastures* as an endearing Noah and *Cabin in*

the Sky with Ethel Waters,* but his "Rochester" characterization was sufficiently firm in American mythology to overshadow his other work.
REFERENCE: BB, 1980. (BK)

ANDERSON, GARLAND (playwright), c. 1886–1939. The first Afro-American to have a full-length Broadway production—*Appearances,** in 1925—Garland Anderson left school in Wichita, Kansas, when he was about eleven years old and got a job as a janitor in the Sacramento, California, post office. As a San Francisco bellhop in his thirties, he wrote his play about a black man falsely accused by a white woman of rape called *Don't Judge by Appearances*. After a cross-country tour to raise money, Anderson brought his play with the shortened title *Appearances* to New York for a brief run. It played for a longer period on tour and then went to London, where Anderson became known as the innovator of "Nu-Snack," a malted milk drink. Although he claimed to have written many other plays, in addition to *Extortion* in 1929, he spent his later years as Minister of Constructive Thinking at The Truth Center. He published a book based on his philosophy, *Uncommon Sense* (1937), and lectured widely as well, but few blacks seem to have been interested in his optimistic message.
REFERENCES: Langston Hughes and Milton Meltzer, *Black Magic*, 1971; James V. Hatch, ed., *Black Theatre, U.S.A.*, 1974. (BK)

ANDERSON, HALLIE (dance orchestra conductor), 5 January 1885–9 November 1927. Born in Virginia, Hallie Anderson moved as a child to New York City, where she studied music privately, in the public schools, and at the New York German Conservatory of Music. She formed and led dance orchestras early in the century and gave concerts with the New Amsterdam Musical Association Band. At one time her orchestra, which was integrated by sex and race, numbered one hundred pieces. She promoted an Annual Reception and Ball for many years, beginning in 1905. When large dance orchestras fell out of popular favor, Anderson turned to directing theater bands and in 1919 directed a "Lady Band" at the Lafayette Theatre* in New York.
REFERENCE: BDAM, 1982. (PO)

ANDERSON, MARIAN (singer), 17 February 1902–   . Marian Anderson studied music as a child in her native Philadelphia with the Negro teacher Mary Patterson and in her early teens appeared in recitals in local churches, schools, and YMCA halls and in cantatas and oratorios with Roland Hayes.* Her church, Union Baptist Church, sponsored her vocal studies with Giuseppe Borghetti, and in 1925 she won a vocal competition sponsored by the New York Philharmonic Symphony at Lewisohn Stadium. Recitals in Town Hall in New York and Witherspoon Hall in Philadelphia followed, but she achieved only moderate success.

In 1929, aided by a Julius Rosenwald Fellowship, she went to Europe for further study. Her debut recital in Berlin in 1932 launched her upon a highly

successful European career. Arturo Toscanini, who heard her in recital at Salzburg, described her rich contralto as "a voice that comes once in a hundred years." Under the management of impresario Sol Hurok, she returned to America for triumphant recitals in New York. Despite her great critical and popular acclaim during her first American tours, the Daughters of the American Revolution refused her permission to sing in Constitution Hall in Washington, D.C., because of her color. The White House intervened, and on Easter Sunday 1939 she sang on the steps of the Lincoln Memorial to a crowd of 75,000 people. In her long career, through international tours, recordings, and radio and television appearances, she became one of the best-known and most-loved singers in the world. In 1955 she became the first black singer to appear with the Metropolitan Opera Company, singing the role of Ulrica in Verdi's *Un Ballo in Maschera*. She toured Asia as goodwill ambassador under the auspices of the State Department, served as delegate to the United Nations, and received orders and decorations from the governments of Liberia, France, Finland, Haiti, Japan, the Philippines, and Sweden, as well as degrees and doctorates in music and humane letters. Her autobiography *My Lord, What a Morning!* was published in 1956.
REFERENCES: GD, 1954; WWA, 1959; MBA, 1971. (DA)

ANDERSON [ANDREWS], REGINA M. (librarian, promoter), c. 1900– .
Born in Chicago around the turn of the century, Regina Anderson became assistant to Ernestine Rose at the Harlem Branch of the New York Public Library and organized various amateur groups that performed there. Through her efforts the Negro Experimental Theatre* was founded, and with Gwendolyn Bennett* she was largely responsible for encouraging Charles S. Johnson* to stage the celebrated dinner for young black writers at the Civic Club.* With Ethel Nance* and Louella Tucker, she shared an apartment at 580 Nicholas Avenue on Sugar Hill,* a kind of Harlem Renaissance USO as well as a "probation office and intelligence outpost for the Urban League." Thinly disguised, it was described as the apartment of the heroine in Carl Van Vechten's* *Nigger Heaven.* Regina Anderson wrote plays, including *Climbing Jacob's Ladder*, for the Negro Experimental Theatre, but because of her connection with the library, it was produced under her pseudonym Ursala Trelling. Her picture on the cover of a late 1924 issue of *The Messenger** confirms latter-day reports of her considerable beauty. She later married New York assemblyman William T. Andrews.
REFERENCES: Loften Mitchell, ed., *Voices of the Black Theatre*, 1975; Jervis Anderson, *This Was Harlem*, 1982. (BK)

ANDERSON, SHERWOOD (writer), 13 September 1876–8 March 1941. Born in Camden, Ohio, Sherwood Anderson became a cultural legend after he left his marriage and his paint and roofing business in 1912 to join Floyd Dell, Margaret Anderson, Ben Hecht, and Carl Sandburg as part of the Chicago Renaissance. In 1920 Anderson journeyed south to Mobile, Alabama, and in 1921 he went to Europe. The following year he moved to New Orleans and subsequently to New York. Feeling unable to relate fully to the new movement in the arts, in 1926 he retreated to a farm in Virginia where he made his home for the rest of his life. Although Anderson preferred to be on the intellectual margins of New York, white or black, and his novel *Dark Laughter** (1925) drew heavily upon his several visits to Alabama and Louisiana, he did have contact with certain major figures of the Harlem Renaissance. In 1925 Alain Locke* inquired if he might contribute an article for *The New Negro**; Anderson declined. But the following year, at the request of Jessie Fauset,* Anderson contributed a response to *The Crisis* symposium "The Negro in Art: How Shall He Be Portrayed?"* (May 1926). However, it was Jean Toomer* who provided the most important imaginative contact with the Harlem Renaissance. In 1922 Toomer proposed starting a magazine that would champion black culture and feature black artists and intellectuals. Although Anderson declined to participate, and nothing came of Toomer's idea, the two entered into an intense although short-lived correspondence. Anderson offered encouragement and praise for Toomer's writing and offered to write an introduction as well as to help in the publication of *Cane.** Toomer, in turn, highly praised Anderson's writing, offered constructive advice, and linked his inspiration for *Cane* with Anderson's *Triumph of the Egg* (1921) and *Winesburg, Ohio* (1919).

REFERENCES: Irving Howe, *Sherwood Anderson*, 1951; James Schevill, *Sherwood Anderson*, 1951; Ray Lewis White, ed., *The Achievement of Sherwood Anderson*, 1966; Sherwood Anderson–Jean Toomer Correspondence, 1922, Fisk University. (MH)

ANDLAUER PRODUCTION COMPANY (film company), 1921. In 1921 the Andlauer Production Company was founded to make two films with Jack Johnson,* the prize fighter: *As the World Turns* and *For His Mother's Sake*. The first of them is of some historical interest because of its use of the Kansas City Monarchs and the Detroit Stars, both actual black baseball teams of the period. In the heavy-handed plot, Joe and Tom both love Molly (the latter played by Blanche Thompson). Johnson, playing himself, trains Joe as an athlete. When Joe substitutes for an incapacitated Monarch and wins for the team, the Elks Club gives him a testimonial dinner. Then Tom and Joe slug it out, Molly is accused of theft, Tom is found guilty instead, and Johnson—afforded ample footage to demonstrate his prowess in the boxing ring—gives Molly and Joe a nest egg.

REFERENCE: BBW, 1977. (BK)

ANTHOLOGY OF AMERICAN NEGRO LITERATURE (book), 1929. Similar to Alain Locke's* *New Negro** (1925), V. F. Calverton's *Anthology of American Negro Literature* is both an alert and a testament to the rapid growth in racial art and culture of black Americans in the 1920s. One half of this volume is a broad representation of imaginative literature: fiction, drama, poetry, and the lyrics of labor songs, blues, and spirituals. The second half is a diverse collection of literary, historical, and sociological essays. Although Calverton expanded upon Locke's emphasis that the artist symbolizes and expresses the conscience of his race, he also argued that black art and literature are most fundamentally the reflection of their social and economic context. Nancy Cunard,* who included the introduction in her own anthology *Negro*, said of this earliest full-length collection of black writings, "no better book than this anthology could possibly be recommended" on the subject (p. 82). Calverton, genially identified with the white "Negrotarians" of the period, in Zora Neale Hurston's* coinage, wrote and edited other books as well, many of them Marxist in their sympathies but none of them directly related to black arts and letters. REFERENCES: Nancy Cunard, ed., *Negro*, 1970; William Rose Benét, ed., *The Reader's Encyclopedia*, 1948. (MH)

AN ANTHOLOGY OF VERSE BY AMERICAN NEGROES (book), 1924. Edited by "Southern white men who desire the most cordial relations between the races," *An Anthology of Verse by American Negroes* was readied for publication in 1921 by Newman Ivey White, head of the English department at Trinity College, and Walter Clinton Jackson of the North Carolina College for Women (p. iii). When the book finally appeared in print in 1924, however, the Harlem Renaissance was well under way, and many of the writers represented seemed less than appropriate for the movement, beginning with Phillis Wheatley and George Moses Horton from the late eighteenth and early nineteenth centuries and including several obscure figures before Paul Laurence Dunbar. William Stanley Braithwaite,* Joseph Cotter, Sr.,* and Benjamin Brawley* represented the earlier twentieth-century poets along with James Weldon Johnson*; brief selections by Georgia Douglas Johnson,* Jessie Fauset,* Claude McKay,* and a single poem by Countee Cullen* represented the more recent ones. In between, White and Jackson included selections by a number of black poets otherwise neglected and uncollected, all of modest and conventional accomplishments in both form and content. Walter Everette Hawkins (17 November 1883–?) was a railway mail service clerk whose *Chords and Discords* (1909) was revised and reprinted in Boston in 1920; he wrote other books, according to the biographical notes, including *The Black Soldiers*, about black enlisted men in World War I. Charles B. Johnson (5 October 1880–?) was a Baptist minister in Missouri who had published two volumes of verse, both in 1918: *Songs of My People* and *Mantle of Dunbar*; his work appeared in *The Crisis** in 1923. Edward Smythe Jones (1888–?) walked from his home in Indiana to Harvard in hopes of an education, only to be thrown into a Cambridge jail for vagrancy until he quoted his poems in court, got a job as a janitor, and in 1911 had his verses published in *Sylvan Cabin*. George Reginald Margetson (1877–?) was a station engineer who had published four volumes of his poetry before 1916. Allen J. Mond (1875–?) was a Kansas boiler maker whose *Rhymes, Tales, and Rhymed Tales* appeared in 1906. None of these men produced work of significance; yet the fact of their achievement is itself significant as a foreshadowing of the Harlem

Renaissance. Published by Trinity College in 1924, the *Anthology* was reprinted in 1968 with a new introduction by Professor R. Bard Shuman of Duke University. (BK)

APOLLO THEATRE, 1934–   . In 1934 Frank Schiffman and Leo Brecher disposed of the Lafayette Theatre* on Seventh Avenue at 132nd Street and acquired Hurtig and Seamon's Music Hall on 125th Street between Seventh and Eighth avenues, renaming it the Apollo Theatre. The downtown Apollo Theatre at Broadway and 42nd Street—Abraham Minsky's notorious burlesque house—had been raided, and burlesque theater managers had been told by the New York City Police Department to clean up or leave town. Schiffman and Brecher seem to have encountered no difficulty in appropriating the name Apollo for their theater, perhaps because their advertisements promised lavish stage extravaganzas that would appeal to cultivated audiences. They opened decorously enough, with a show featuring Aida Ward,* Ralph Cooper, and Benny Carter's orchestra, and the New York *Age** praised "the entire absence of sensuous dancing, salacious jokes, and hokum" (Anderson, *This Was Harlem*, p. 236). In the following years almost every top-ranking black performer played the Apollo, although audiences were capricious and quick to acclaim or reject established artists as well as newcomers. The comedy acts tended to be low down and bawdy, with Jackie "Moms" Mabley* and Dewey "Pigmeat" Markham* as popular favorites.
REFERENCES: Abel Green and Joe Laurie, Jr., *Show Biz*, 1951; Langston Hughes and Milton Meltzer, *Black Magic*, 1967; Jervis Anderson, *This Was Harlem*, 1982. (DA)

APPEARANCES (play), 1925. The history and publicity surrounding Garland Anderson's* optimistic play are probably more significant than its literary merit. Inspired by Channing Pollock's highly moral *The Fool*, Anderson wrote *Appearances* in three weeks and sent it to Al Jolson, the popular Jewish singer who often affected blackface makeup in which to perform. Jolson financed Anderson's trip to New York; black actor Richard B. Harrison* gave a public reading of the play at the Waldorf-Astoria Hotel to raise money for a production; Anderson even had an interview with President Calvin Coolidge. Finally, the play—about a black bellboy falsely accused of rape who conquers his enemies through faith—opened at the Frolic Theatre, 13 October 1925. It closed after twenty-three performances but, following the notoriety of *All God's Chillun Got Wings,** *Appearances* is significant in having had a racially mixed cast in a Broadway production. Later, it toured the country, playing several weeks at a time in Chicago and in various cities on the West Coast. On 30 March 1929, before moving on for a London run, it reopened for twenty-four performances at the Hudson Theatre in New York, still starring black actor Doe Doe Green who was overacting badly. The "dignity of revival," the *New York Times* reviewer observed, should be withheld "for greater works" (2 Apr. 1929, p. 28). Nevertheless, *Appearances* is significant not only for having broken the

color barrier on mixed casts but also because its black protagonist broke from the blackface, foolish stereotype that had commanded the stage since minstrel days.
REFERENCES: Burns Mantle, 1925–1926; NYTTR, 1972; James Hatch, *Black Theater, U.S.A.*, 1974. (BK)

ARCHEY, [JAMES H.] JIMMY (trombonist), 12 October 1902–16 November 1967. Jimmy Archey's childhood nickname identified him in local gigs he played in Virginia from the age of thirteen. He attended Hampton Institute from 1915 until 1919 and began his professional career four years later with Lionel Howard's Band at the Capitol Palace. In 1924 he played regularly at Small's Paradise* and in 1925 at the Alhambra Theatre*; after 1926 he was featured at the Bamboo Inn.* Later, Archey joined the bands of Cab Calloway* and Mezz Mezzrow, and his distinctive trombone playing kept him performing regularly until his death.
REFERENCE: WWJ, 1978. (BK)

ARMSTRONG, [DANIEL] LOUIS "SATCHMO" (trumpeter, singer, composer), c. 4 July 1900–6 July 1971. Louis Armstrong received his first musical training in the band of the Coloured Waifs' Home in New Orleans, where he had been sent for firing a pistol on Rampart Street. In his teens he played in the clubs and sporting houses in Storyville and in 1919 replaced his tutor King Oliver* in Kid Ory's* band. He played the riverboats and New Orleans clubs until 1922, when Oliver asked him to join his orchestra at the Lincoln Gardens in Chicago. Like most New Orleans horn players, Armstrong started on cornet and only later switched to trumpet. His playing was noted for its broad tone, smooth vibrato, and amazing virtuosity in the highest register. His first recorded solo was a chorus of "Chimes Blues" with King Oliver's Creole Jazz Band on the Gennett label in 1923. Armstrong remained with Oliver until 1924 and then went to New York to join Fletcher Henderson's* band at the Roseland Ballroom. He returned to Chicago in 1925 to play in his wife's band, Lil Hardin's* Dreamland Syncopators, and in 1927 led his own band, Louis Armstrong and his Stompers, at the Sunset Cafe. In 1929 he took his band to New York for a residency at Connie's Inn* and at the same time performed on stage in *Hot Chocolates*,* where his husky-voiced rendition of "Ain't Misbehavin' " and his lively scat singing were as much enjoyed as his trumpet playing. After more big band work and solo appearances across the country, he made his first European tour in 1932.

Armstrong's early recordings with his Hot Five and Hot Seven groups helped spread his reputation as a great trumpet soloist and jazz innovator, and in the following decades he achieved extraordinary fame through world tours—notably with his band, the All Stars—and recordings, films, and radio and television appearances. He played Bottom in *Swingin' the Dream* (1939), a musical adaptation of *A Midsummer Night's Dream*, and appeared in many films, among them *Rhapsody in Black and Blue* (1932), *Pennies from Heaven* (1936), *Cabin in the Sky* (1943), *New Orleans* (1947), *A Song Is Born* (1948), *The Glenn Miller Story* (1953), *High Society* (1956), and a documentary produced by Edward R. Morrow, *Satchmo the Great* (1957).

Like other popular black performers such as Fats Waller* and Bill ''Bojangles'' Robinson,* Armstrong was sometimes accused of demeaning the black artist by indulging in stereotyped racial impersonations and dialect humor. Critics failed to realize that performers trained in the early jazz traditions thought of themselves not only as musicians but as entertainers; even in his early days in New Orleans, when he was working with Kid Ory's band, Armstrong had worked out ''a little jive routine with dancing and fooling around between numbers to get laughs'' (Ramsey and Smith, *Jazzmen*, p. 130). His nickname ''Satchmo'' was an abbreviation of an earlier nickname, ''Satchelmouth,'' which indicates that his fellow performers had always recognized him as an amusing, good-natured man.

His first book, *Swing That Music* (1936), was largely the creation of a ghostwriter; his autobiography, *Satchmo: My Life in New Orleans*, was published in 1954.

REFERENCES: Frederic Ramsey, Jr., and Charles Edward Smith, eds., *Jazzmen*, 1939; Albert J. McCarthy, *Louis Armstrong*, 1961; MBA, 1971; WWJ, 1978. (DA)

ASSOCIATED NEGRO PRESS (news service), 1919–   . Founded in 1919 to correlate the growing number of black newspapers in America, the Associated Negro Press made possible the dissemination of news stories among more than 500 newspapers and magazines during the 1920s. Since the turn of the century, their number had more than doubled, and the impact of the black press on its readership mandated an organization. In *The Voice of the Negro in 1919* Robert T. Kerlin* quoted an announcement from the news service to justify its existence: ''today, the average home receives not only one race periodical, but usually two or more, and the exceptional home, office, store, the schools and churches and libraries, receive from six to more than a score.... Through the magnificent advantages of the Associated Negro Press, all important happenings of the race are known regularly in every section of the nation, and by all classes'' (quoted in Vincent, *Voices of a Black Nation*, p. 1).

REFERENCE: Theodore G. Vincent, ed., *Voices of a Black Nation*, 1973. (BK)

ASSOCIATION FOR THE STUDY OF NEGRO LIFE AND HISTORY, 1915–   . Carter Woodson* and four other black men organized the Association for the Study of Negro Life and History on 9 September 1915, in the Wabash Avenue YMCA in Chicago for (as Woodson later wrote) ''the collection of sociological and historical data on the Negro, the study of peoples of African blood, the publishing of books in the field, and the promoting of harmony between the races by acquainting the one with the other'' (''Ten Years of Collecting and Publishing the Records of the Negro,'' *Journal of Negro History*, Oct. 1925,

p. 598). Woodson surprised his cofounders by personally editing, publishing, and funding the first project of the association—the initial issue of *The Journal of Negro History*—in January 1916. The association printed the *Journal* as one of its main tasks and used the *Journal* to publish its news and proceedings and to advertise for funds to finance the numerous research projects it conducted on topics such as free blacks before the Civil War, black urban laborers, rural workers, the church, and the professions. For the first few years the association was bereft of funds and accomplished whatever Woodson managed to do in his spare time. However, contributions from foundations and individuals such as Julius Rosenwald enabled the association to rent an office in 1919, hire a small staff, and free Woodson to give full time to the organization as director. He served in this capacity and as editor of the *Journal* until his death in 1950. His strong dedication to the goals of the organization was instrumental in keeping the group going both during the difficult early years and during the 1930s, when Woodson's uncompromising independence and commitment to the publication of historical and sociological truth as he saw it lost him the financial support of most of the foundations that had paid the bills in the 1920s. Woodson and the association raised the money they needed, after the exit of the foundations (and the major civil rights groups that advised the foundations not to support the group), by obtaining small donations from many individuals. This enabled the association to expand its activities, including the publication of *Negro History Bulletin* beginning in 1937, the further development of Negro History Week (initiated by the association in 1926), the continued collection of important historical collections, and a variety of educational projects.

REFERENCE: *Journal of Negro History*, 1916–1933. (DS)

AS THOUSANDS CHEER (musical revue), 1933. Black entertainers Ethel Waters* and Hamtree Harrington* shared the billing with Marilyn Miller and Clifton Webb in this show by Irving Berlin and Moss Hart. José Limon was a dancer in the chorus, so it portended more than it delivered, although Ethel Waters made a personal success as Josephine Baker* singing "Harlem on My Mind" in a number in which each of the principals did an impression of some other celebrated stage star. *As Thousands Cheer* was the first Broadway musical revue to include what Ethel Waters described as a "dirge." One of her songs, "Supper Time," was about a woman preparing dinner after her husband had been lynched, knowing "that man of mine ain't coming home no more." It made an indelible impression on audiences both in New York during a long run and on the road, in Chicago, through the South, and then to the West Coast, marking the first time black and white performers had appeared onstage together below the Mason–Dixon Line.

REFERENCES: Ethel Waters, *His Eye Is on the Sparrow*, 1951; NYTTR, 1972. (BK)

ATTLES, JOSEPH (entertainer), 3 April 1903– ? Born off the coast of South Carolina, Joseph Attles moved north to Brooklyn when he was twenty-one and, after passing the civil service examinations, expected to find a career with the government. In his free time, however, he sang with the choir of the Abyssinian Baptist Church, where he was discovered and given a job in *Blackbirds [*] of 1928.* He never returned to civil service. Attles toured Europe with the show and then went to work at the Plantation Club* with Cab Calloway.* In later years he went to work for the railroad.

REFERENCE: Hatch-Billops. (BK)

AUSTIN, LOVIE [CORA CALHOUN] (pianist, composer), 19 September 1887–10 July 1972. Lovie Austin was born in Chattanooga, Tennessee, and studied music at Roger Williams University in Nashville and at Knoxville College. She toured with her husband and his partner's act in vaudeville, Austin and Delaney, and with Irvin C. Miller's* *Blue Babies* before coming to New York with the Club Alabam show. She toured the TOBA* circuit with the Sunflower Girls, conducting a group of half a dozen men with her legs crossed, a cigarette in her mouth, leading the band with her left hand while she made new arrangements with her right. Subsequently, she formed her own combo, the Blues Serenaders, with Johnny Dodds, Jimmy Noone, and Tommy Ladnier, which accompanied Ma Rainey* in her first recordings in 1923. Austin wrote "Graveyard Blues" for Bessie Smith* and helped Alberta Hunter* transcribe and copyright her early blues compositions. She served as musical director for the Monogram Theatre in Chicago for twenty years, and she often backed up singers like Ida Cox,* Edmonia Henderson, Viola Bartlette, and Ethel Waters.* During World War II, Lovie Austin was a security inspector in a defense plant, and later she worked as a dancing school accompanist.

REFERENCES: Nat Shapiro and Nat Hentoff, *Hear Me Talkin' to Ya*, 1955; MBA, 1971; WWJ, 1978; BWBO, 1979. (BK)

THE AUTOBIOGRAPHY OF AN EX-COLOURED MAN (novel), 1912. James Weldon Johnson's* only novel, *The Autobiography of an Ex-Coloured Man*, is the fictionalized first-person narrative of a light-skinned black pianist who, after witnessing the burning of a black man in the South, gives up his black identity and his dreams of writing music on black themes and "passes" into white society. It was published in 1912 by a small Boston publishing house—Sherman, French, and Company—that did little to promote it. In fact, aside from a few favorable reviews, the book received little attention, and sales were slow. In addition, Americans were not very interested in black themes before World War I. Fifteen years later, in 1927, with the Harlem Renaissance in full swing, Alfred A. Knopf* republished it, and *The Autobiography* received wide attention and some acclaim. Although the book is not Johnson's life story, the author based much of the work on his own experiences and people he had known. For instance, the book portrays the bohemian life-style of some black New Yorkers in the early twentieth century (which Johnson himself enjoyed during his songwriting days) and black working-class life in Jacksonville, Florida,

Johnson's hometown. Moreover, the protagonist is modeled after a boyhood friend of Johnson's, Judson Douglass Wetmore. *The Autobiography* is perhaps above all an indictment against racism, and although it is written in a restrained style one cannot help but be saddened by the hero's final decision: that racism is too great an obstacle to overcome and that he must sacrifice his identity and dreams of helping his race in order to live a decent life free of the shame and fear that blacks faced in America.

REFERENCE: James Weldon Johnson, *Along This Way*, 1933. (DS)

B

BAKER, GEORGE, FATHER DIVINE (cult leader), c. 1880–7 September 1965. Father Divine, who fashioned and led one of the most successful cults in the twentieth century—Father Divine's Peace Mission—was considered to be God by his myriad followers across the nation in the 1930s. Before coming to Brooklyn in 1915, Baker slowly acquired a few disciples in his native South and made his living by doing odd jobs, such as gardening, in Baltimore. In 1919 he and his twenty disciples moved to the white community of Sayville, Long Island, and during the next ten years his cult gradually expanded. Baker preached peace, brotherhood, cleanliness, and honesty: he had "come" to free people from tyranny, segregation, and hunger. His followers were expected to give all of their loyalty to him, and even husbands and wives were expected to abstain from sex. In return, the squat five-foot Baker provided secular (employment and food) and religious sustenance for his followers. In the late 1920s he began advertising his cult in New York City, and bus loads of blacks and whites would journey out of the city on Sundays to eat sumptuous meals provided by Baker and listen to the charismatic Divine at Sayville. Baker's neighbors, upset at the weekly ruckus that ensued, slapped a public nuisance charge on Divine in November 1931, and a prejudiced judge gave him the maximum sentence in May 1932. The judge, healthy and vigorous, died a few days later, convincing Divine's followers and many previous doubters that the death was Divine retribution. His popularity soared, and on 25 June 1932, a few hours after his release from prison, 7,000 followers swarmed into Rockland Palace at 155th Street and Eighth Avenue for a "Monster Rally to Our Lord" celebration. Divine moved his Mission to Harlem in 1933, and with the death that year of Harlem's leading cultist, George Wilson Becton,* Divine had a clear field for his work. Divine, like Marcus Garvey,* raised the hopes of many blacks with his message that he (a *black* God, after all) would bring peace, plenty, respect, and brotherhood to a people beset by racism and the Great Depression.

REFERENCES: Claude McKay, *Harlem: Negro Metropolis*, 1940; Sara Harris, *Father Divine*, 1971. (DS)

BAKER, JOSEPHINE (singer, dancer), 3 June 1906–12 April 1975. Josephine Baker left her impoverished childhood in Kansas City, Missouri, at the age of thirteen when she joined a travelling show in which Clara Smith* was the headliner. Baker worked as a dresser for the show but occasionally got to dance in the chorus and play small comic parts. When the show closed in Philadelphia in 1921 she auditioned for *Shuffle Along** but was turned down because she was too small, too thin, too dark, and too young. She followed the show to New York where she was eventually hired as a dresser for the second touring company, and while on tour she had the opportunity to substitute for one of the chorus girls. Her comic antics delighted audiences and critics, and she was transferred to the first cast touring company in Boston. The show's producers, Noble Sissle* and Eubie Blake,* wrote a special part for her in their next production, *In Bamville*, which reached New York as *Chocolate Dandies** in 1924; Baker was billed as "That comedy chorus girl," and although her role of an out-of-step, cross-eyed, clowning girl at the end of the chorus line was not an original conception, her realization of it was a comic triumph. She appeared in *Plantation Revue** in 1925, again in the chorus, but replacing Ethel Waters* for one performance. Her success singing "Dinah" was so great that Waters saw to it that she did not have an opportunity to repeat it. In 1925 Baker was picked to go to Paris with Caroline Dudley's *Revue Nègre** and created a sensation. Within a year she was starring at the Folies Bergère and headlining in all of the European clubs that featured *le jazz hot*. She returned to New York in 1936 for a featured spot in the *Ziegfield Follies* but met with a cool reception and returned to France. During World War II she worked for the Resistance movement and served with the women's division of the Free French forces in North Africa, and for her services she was awarded the Legion of Honor, the Rosette of the Resistance, and the seldom-bestowed Medallion of the City of Paris. She and her husband, Jo Bouillon, adopted a dozen children of all races and attempted to bring them up together on a country estate in southwestern France, but the experiment was a personal and financial disaster. Baker made a final, triumphant return to the United States in 1973, performing in concerts at Carnegie Hall and in Harlem. In 1975 she appeared in a new revue in Paris to celebrate her fifty years in show business but died four days after the opening.
REFERENCES: Langston Hughes and Milton Meltzer, *Black Magic*, 1967; Josephine Baker and Jo Bouillon, *Josephine*, 1977; BB, 1980; Donald Bogle, *Brown Sugar*, 1980. (DA)

THE BALLAD OF THE BROWN GIRL (poem), 1927. In the same year that Countee Cullen's* second collection of poems appeared, his publisher issued *The Ballad of the Brown Girl*, with decorations and illustrations to stretch it out to eleven pages. Cullen's homage to the English ballad form is about Lord Thomas, who chooses Fair London, who is white, as his bride instead of the Brown Girl. At the wedding the Brown Girl kills Fair London, then Lord Thomas kills the Brown Girl before killing himself, and the three of them end up in the same grave. The extravagance of the packaging did not entirely succeed in masking the paucity of the allegory. (BK)

BAMBOO INN (cabaret). Located on Seventh Avenue in Harlem, the Bamboo Inn catered to "High Harlem," with elegantly dressed women and professional men, and to visiting white "Babbits." College boys and debutantes went slumming there, and the booths on the balcony were frequently filled with society matrons and their escorts. Chinese waiters served Chinese food under colored spotlights that played on a revolving, mirrored ball on the ceiling, while a tuxedoed black bouncer kept order.
REFERENCES: Wallace Thurman, *Negro Life in New York's Harlem*, 1928; Jervis Anderson, *This Was Harlem*, 1982. (BK)

BAMVILLE CLUB (cabaret). The Bamville Club, at 65 West 129th Street, featured the Fletcher Henderson* Orchestra in its heyday, with specialty acts by Elizabeth Smith and Joe Willis and a frantic Charleston routine danced by a girl billed simply as "Bobbie" whose *café au lait* flapper dress of chiffon and bugle beads matched her skin. Between the acts whites and blacks danced as mixed couples on the tiny floor. The Bamville Club was opened by Broadway Jones, a well-known baritone who appeared in several revues, and who was popularly described as an onyx bullfrog.
REFERENCES: Tom Fletcher, *100 Years of the Negro in Show Business*, 1954; Donald Angus. (BK)

BANANA BOTTOM (novel), 1933. Claude McKay's* *Banana Bottom* tells the story of Bitta Plant, an intelligent and sensitive young Jamaican woman, and her effort to free herself from the morally false identity and strictures of her English Protestant education and upbringing and the impact of these values on her own people. In breaking with the moral influence of the Craigs, a white missionary couple, Bitta's assertion of her own sexual and spiritual independence brings her closer to her pre-English folk heritage and culture. Ultimately, Bitta marries a man of her own choice, Jublan, a proud and moral black peasant, who also respects her intellectual needs and strength. (MH)

BANJO (novel), 1929. Set on the waterfront of Marseilles (Vieux Port) among a band of beach boys from the West Indies, Africa, and America (a microcosm of the black diaspora), Claude McKay's* *Banjo* is the immediate extension of the themes and issues he first presented in *Home to Harlem** (1928). Again, the same symbolic protagonists (Ray—intellect; Banjo—instinct) act and articulate McKay's analysis of the black identity. Only now McKay's canvas is international and his criticism of French racism and moral decadence extends to Western capitalism and the political and cultural imperialism of the West. At the same time, Ray's struggle to be a writer carries McKay's critique of the Harlem Renaissance and his own effort to balance the integrity of the individual artist with the cultural imperatives of a black aesthetic. (MH)

BARBER, J[ESSE] MAX (journalist), c. 1878–September 1949. Involved from their beginnings with the Niagara movement and the National Association for the Advancement of Colored People,* J. Max Barber was president and executive director of the Philadelphia branch of the NAACP during the 1920s. His contributions to early journals and newspapers immediately after the war reinforced the strong activist stance of W.E.B. Du Bois.* Like many black Americans of the period, Barber was obliged to seek income in other fields, and he had a long and successful career as a dentist in Philadelphia.
REFERENCES: WWCR, 1915; DANB, 1982. (BK)

BARBOUR, J. BERNI (composer, director), 22 April 1881–? Billy King* collaborated with J. Berni Barbour on some early touring shows, like *Over the Top*, *They're Off*, and *Exploits in Africa*, but Barbour's own work was more serious. In 1919 he was manager of the Memphis Blues Orchestra for W. C. Handy,* and two years later he began producing his own work, notably an operetta, *Arrival of the Negro*, at the Lutheran Abyssinian Church in New York in 1926. His "musical extravaganza" *Redemption*, an opera called *Ethiopia*, and a military revue called, straightforwardly, *Black Propaganda* all toured the western part of the country. His pageant *Paul Laurence Dunbar's Dream* seems to have played briefly in New York, although he was never reviewed in the white press. Marks published some of Barbour's music: an "Egyptian Intermezzo" and a song that had a brief popularity, "Doan Let Satan Git You on De Judgment Day." In 1927 Barbour assembled the black cast members for the Jerome Kern–Oscar Hammerstein II musical version of Edna Ferber's *Showboat*.*
REFERENCE: WWCA, 1933. (BK)

BARNES, ALBERT C[OOMBS] (art critic and collector), 2 January 1872–24 July 1951. Intelligent, brash, opinionated, Albert Coombs Barnes was a disciple of William James and a friend of John Dewey and William Glackens. Born in Philadelphia and suddenly a millionaire in 1907, Barnes dedicated his life to the collecting and teaching of art, committed, as he said, "to stripping [art] of the emotional bunk [with] which the long-haired phonies and that fading class of egoists, the art patrons, have encumbered it" (quoted in McCardle, "The Terrible Tempered Barnes," p. 93). In 1922 he established the Barnes Foundation in Merion, Pennsylvania, and filled it with the best private collection of Matisse, Monet, Picasso, Cézanne, Renoir, and Degas in the world. It is also filled with African art. This interest, and his zeal to promote the aesthetic properties of African art, led him into intimate contact with several of the most prominent figures of the Harlem Renaissance.

In December 1923 Barnes met Alain Locke* and, soon after, Walter White*

and Charles S. Johnson.* Barnes's articles on African art soon appeared in *Opportunity*.* In addition, his article "Contribution to the Study of Negro Art in America" appeared in the special Harlem issue of *Survey Graphic* in 1925 and in Locke's *New Negro* later in the year, the latter carrying several reproductions of African art objects from the Barnes Foundation. In truth, Locke was dissatisfied with Barnes's unbalanced analysis of the influence of history, culture, and psychology and offered his own interpretation in *The New Negro*, "The Legacy of the Ancestral Arts," to supplement and extend Barnes's disappointing effort.
REFERENCES: Carl McCardle, "The Terrible Tempered Barnes," *Saturday Evening Post*, 21 Mar. 1942; CB, 1945, 1951; Mark Helbling, "African Art," *Phylon*, Mar. 1982. (MH)

BARNES, MAE [EDITH MAE STITH] (singer), 23 January 1907–
Mae Barnes's long and successful career began in 1923 when she was a featured vocalist at Pod's and Jerry's.* She appeared in *Runnin' Wild* that same year and in *Lucky Sambo* in 1925. She then toured in *Shuffle Along* and returned to New York for *Rang Tang* (1927), *The Rainbow Chasers* (1928), and *Hot Rhythm* (1930), and she helped bring the Harlem Renaissance to a close in *Ebony Scandals* (1932), playing in it afterward on the Keith circuit. Like many popular black performers from the twenties, Mae Barnes drifted into obscurity; twenty years later, however, in white musical comedies like *By the Beautiful Sea* and *Ziegfeld Follies of 1956*, she had a decided personal success, and her long series of appearances in nightclubs was well known to many loyal fans.
REFERENCE: BEWW, 1966. (BK)

BARNETT, CLAUDE A. (journalist), 16 September 1889–2 August 1967.
Born in Illinois, Claude Barnett attended Tuskegee Institute and sold ads for the Chicago *Defender* to support himself. He founded and served as director of the Associated Negro Press,* and from 1919 he was widely recognized as an authority on African art.
REFERENCES: NYT, 3 Aug. 1967; DANB, 1982. (BK)

BARNETT, IDA WELLS (humanitarian), 6 July 1862–25 March 1931. Born in Mississippi, Ida Wells studied journalism at Rust College and Fisk University, after which she bought half-interest in the *Memphis Free Speech*, a small black newspaper, with most of her salary as an elementary schoolteacher. Eventually, she bought out her partner and promptly began writing about inequality in education and urged blacks to migrate north. Furthermore, she began to compile "The Red Record," accounting between 1890 and 1900 for 1,217 murders by burning, lynching, and shooting, for none of which had anyone stood trial. In 1895 Ida Wells married a Chicago lawyer, Ferdinand Barnett, and about the same time began to write for the New York *Age*.* Her activities were instrumental in forming the National Urban League* and the NAACP,* and through the halcyon days of the Harlem Renaissance she continued to remind her readers that arts and letters had not yet overcome inequities.

REFERENCES: Charlemae Hill Rollins, *They Showed the Way*, 1964; DANB, 1982. (BK)

BARTHÉ, RICHMOND (sculptor), 28 January 1901– . The sculptures of Richmond Barthé were not only ethnic, they even emphasized primitive qualities in his black subject matter. He is perhaps the best-known sculptor of his race. Born in Mississippi and reared in Louisiana, Barthé began drawing at the age of six, and by the time he was twelve he was selling portraits. He attended the Chicago Art Institute until 1928, at which time he became interested in sculpture, beginning with cuticle sticks, hair pins, and a wooden spatula, and never returned to painting. That same year he received a Harmon Award and the first of two Rosenwald Fellowships. He regularly exhibited after that at the Harmon Foundation and in one-man shows. A casual look at Barthé's work might suggest that he stylized his subjects; instead, he often simply captured their movement, as one of his best-known pieces, *Feral Benga*, illustrates. In clay, marble, or bronze, the work is always recognizable but never photographic. Of abstraction, he said in his oral history, taped for the Hatch-Billops Collection, ''All my life I've been trying to capture the beauty that I've seen in people, and abstraction wouldn't satisfy me.... My work is all wrapped up with my search for God. I am looking for God inside of people. I wouldn't find it in squares, triangles, and circles.'' Barthé's most ambitious project, a bronze monument of a group of James Weldon Johnson's* ''black and unknown bards,'' to memorialize that humanitarian and to stand at the 110th Street entrance to Central Park, just south of Harlem, was never realized. At the time of its planning the government was obliged to confiscate all metal, and art stood aside for World War II. Barthé is widely represented in museum and library collections, notably the Schomburg Collection of the New York Public Library, and the Metropolitan Museum of Art. Carl Van Vechten,* overly enthusiastic as usual, compared him to Donatello.

REFERENCES: Carl Van Vechten, ''*Keep A-Inchin' Along*,'' 1979; Hatch-Billops. (BK)

BASEBALL Although baseball teams remained resolutely segregated until long after the Harlem Renaissance, the activities and achievements of black players were regularly reported in the black press, and the sport itself was popular enough to warrant a Negro World Series. It was held in Kansas City, Missouri, in 1924, between the Kansas City Monarchs for the First National League and the Hilldale Team for the Eastern Colored League. At least five memorable players deserve attention for their efforts in bringing what is usually considered America's national pastime to all Americans, regardless of race. Andrew ''Rube'' Foster (17 September 1879–9 December 1930) pitched for the Leland Giants at the turn of the century and in 1905 won fifty-one out of fifty-five games. Later, the team

was called the Chicago American Giants. Foster founded the National Baseball League, with teams in Indianapolis, Kansas City, Chicago, Detroit, and St. Louis, in an effort to give work to black athletes. A huge man, Foster was 6'4'' tall and weighed more than 200 pounds, protean in his appetites as well as in his energy, although overwork led to his death, following a period of four years in a mental institution. John Henry Lloyd (25 April 1884–19 March 1965) was considered by many players of both races as superior even to Babe Ruth. His long career began with the Young Receivers in his native Florida and continued with the Cuban Giants in Philadelphia, the American Giants in Chicago, and the Buckeyes in Columbus, Ohio, until 1931. Nor was there any marked diminishing of power during his career: in 1911, his batting average was .475; in 1923, it had dropped only to .418. Black players went largely unrecognized at the time, of course, and when Lloyd retired, he was obliged to become a janitor, first in the Atlantic City post office and subsequently in public schools. Well into his seventies, he coached Little League teams and was called, affectionately, ''Pops.'' LeRoy Robert Paige (7 July 1906–8 June 1982) was nicknamed ''Satchell'' because of his big feet. He began playing semiprofessional baseball while working as a porter and an iceman in his native Alabama. In the midtwenties he was a member of the Birmingham Black Barons. In 1933 Paige defeated white baseball celebrity Dizzy Dean in a 1–0 game, and subsequently, Joe DiMaggio called him the best pitcher he had ever faced. Paige joined the Kansas City Monarchs during the forties, and in later years he toured with the Harlem Globetrotters. Cumberland Posey (1891–20 March 1946) was born in Pennsylvania and attended the University of Pittsburgh, Duquesne University, and Pennsylvania State University. At the age of twenty he joined a baseball team composed of steel workers, the Homestead Grays, and worked during the ensuing decade to turn it into a professional organization. Posey negotiated the rights to Forbes Field in Pittsburgh during the off-seasons, and by 1930 the Homestead Grays were the national Negro Championship Team, until felled by Satchell Paige and the Pittsburgh Crawfords. Finally ''Smokey Jo'' Williams (1886–1946) was nicknamed ''The Cyclone'' or ''Cyclone Joe'' when he joined ''Rube'' Foster's Chicago team in 1910, a 6'5'' Texan who became ''Smokey Jo'' two years later with the New York Lincoln Giants. That black team shut out the white National League champions, the Philadelphia Phils, 1–0, in an exhibition game in New York after a World Series game in 1926. Neither that team nor any other black team was ever invited to try again.
REFERENCES: Robert Peterson, *Only the Ball Is White*, 1970; NA, 1976; WWA, 1977; DANB, 1982; *Newsweek*, 21 June 1982. (BK)

BATES, [CLAYTON] PEGLEG (dancer), 11 October 1902– ? At the age of twelve Pegleg Bates lost his leg in a car accident in South Carolina, where he had been born. After an uncle fashioned a crude wooden leg for him, the boy walked two miles to school for three years. The strength he gained through this made it possible for him to take up dancing, and by 1928 when he appeared in Lew Leslie's* *Blackbirds,** he was considered "The Number One Dancer in the Country," a title he maintained for at least the ensuing five years. He was a popular figure in revues at the Cotton Club* and the Apollo Theatre,* and he continued to perform well into the forties in shows such as *Atlantic City Follies* and *Here 'Tis* with Eddie Hunter.*

REFERENCES: Nancy Cunard, ed., *Negro*, 1970; BB, 1980. (BK)

BATOUALA (novel), 1922. René Maran's* sensational story of native life in the French Congo was awarded the Goncourt Prize on publication and created a controversy that carried to Harlem through its immediate English translation by Adele Szold Seltzer. White reviewers were sharply divided over its merits, and it became a *cause célèbre* in the weekly issues of Marcus Garvey's* *Negro World.** Largely plotless, *Batouala* recounts savage life in Africa, often in revolting detail, particularly its sexual initiation rites. The vivid descriptions of superstition, sex, hunting parties, dances, and funeral practices seemed of less interest than the implicit hatred of the white race, however, to readers eager to establish their own racial identity. Strongly phallic in its orientation, laced with strange chants and snatches of songs, and preoccupied with an unself-conscious eroticism, *Batouala* could not fail to either engage or enrage readers in 1922; it still cannot fail to, in its more recent and more accurate translation by Barbara Beck and Alexandre Mboukou, published in 1972 by Black Orpheus Press. (BK)

BEAVERS, LOUISE (actress), 1902–26 October 1962. Although she lived most of her life in California, Louise Beavers was familiar to moviegoers in all parts of the country. Born to musical parents in Cincinnati, Ohio, she moved to Pasadena, California, in 1913, where she graduated from high school. She aspired to become a singer, and from 1923 to 1926 she helped produce and appeared in annual shows with sixteen other women called "The Lady Minstrels." A casting agent spotted Beavers and signed her for her first film, the original *Uncle Tom's Cabin* in 1927. She made her first sound film, *Geraldine*, in 1928 and had featured roles in more than one hundred films thereafter, including *Coquette* (1929), *Wall Street* (1929), *She Couldn't Say No* (1930), *Ladies of the Big House* (1932), *Mr. Blandings Builds His Dream House* (1948), and two black-cast films, *Life Goes On* (1938) and *Reform School* (1939). Her best-known role was that of Fredi Washington's* mother and Claudette Colbert's servant-partner in *Imitation of Life* (1934), in which her acting received high praise from critics. At the same time, however, her part was criticized by those who thought it perpetuated a subservient stereotype of blacks.

Beavers was married to LeRoy Moore. In 1960 she replaced Hattie McDaniel in the radio and television series *Beulah*. Shortly before her death she appeared with Mae West in a nightclub act in Las Vegas.

REFERENCES: BBW, 1977; BDAM, 1982. (PO)

BECHET, SIDNEY (clarinetist, soprano saxophonist), 14 May 1897–14 May 1959. Sidney Bechet displayed a precocious musical talent as a child and played cornet and clarinet in New Orleans bands and orchestras when he was in his early teens. He travelled through the South and Southwest with carnival and touring companies and in 1917 went to Chicago where he performed at the De Luxe Cafe, the Dreamland Cabaret, the Monogram Theatre, and the Pekin Cabaret, with the bands of Lawrence Duhé, Freddie Keppard, King Oliver,* and others. He joined Will Marion Cook's* Southern Syncopated Orchestra in 1919 for its European tour, and during their London engagements Bechet's playing drew enthusiastic praise from diverse critics such as King George V, who particularly enjoyed his playing of "The Characteristic Blues" at a command performance at Buckingham Palace, and the Swiss conductor Ernest Ansermet, who wrote of Bechet's clarinet solos, in an oft-quoted article "On a Negro Orchestra" in *Revue Romande*: "they gave an idea of a style, and their form was gripping, abrupt, harsh, with a brusque and pitiless ending like that of Bach's second *Brandenburg Concerto*" (Ramsey and Smith, *Jazzmen*, p. 306). Bechet was the first jazz soloist to have his work, first on clarinet and later on soprano saxophone, receive serious musical appraisal.

Bechet remained in London for club dates but returned to New York in 1921 to play and act (he was a skillful light comedian) in *How Come?* *Black and White Revue*, and *Seven Eleven*. He also worked with Mamie Smith,* Duke Ellington,* and James P. Johnson* and led his own band, The New Orleans Creole Jazz Band, at the Rhythm Club. He went to Paris with the *Revue Nègre** in 1925 and remained abroad for several years, playing engagements in France and Germany, recording, and making a tour of Russia. He joined Noble Sissle's* band in Paris in 1928 but spent most of the following year in jail in Paris as the result of a shooting incident with another musician, Gilbert McKendrick. After his return to the United States, he worked again with Sissle, toured with Duke Ellington, and then organized a new band of his own, the New Orleans Feetwarmers, which played at the Savoy Ballroom* in New York in 1932. He retired briefly from music in 1934 to run a tailor shop in New York and then rejoined Sissle's band for four years. In the forties he made guest appearances and headed small combos and during World War II played regularly in New York at Nick's, Ryans's, and other clubs. From 1951 he made his permanent home in France; he died in Paris in 1959. He left a prodigious discography; he first recorded in 1923 and continued to make recordings until the year of his death.
REFERENCES: Frederic Ramsey, Jr., and Charles Edward Smith, eds., *Jazzmen*, 1939; EJ, 1960; MBA, 1971; WWJ, 1972. (DA)

BECTON, [GEORGE WILSON] ELDER (evangelist), 15 April 1890–31 May 1933. In Texas, where he was born, Elder Becton had travelled as a boy evangelist before he went to Wilberforce University. In 1922 he returned to this early calling, at the Harlem church of Countee Cullen's* father, as president of the World Gospel Feast Party, Inc. A charismatic and handsome figure, Becton seems to have been more interested in collecting donations than in collecting souls. He owned considerable property, including a fabulously appointed apartment, purchased with the assistance of his parishioners who contributed a dime a day (seventy cents a week) at Sunday services. In pearl gray suit, top hat, malacca cane, and silk gloves, he preached "a square deal for God" from the pulpit and from the quarterly magazine *The Menu*. William A. Jackman served as publisher of the little publication, made up primarily of religious ads and editorials, but to at least one issue Countee Cullen contributed a poem, "If You Should Go," and Becton, in several issues, wrote lengthily about that "consecrated dime" a day, justified regularly as "a revelation of God to me." At the height of his influence, Becton had 200,000 followers. In 1933 he was gunned down by gangsters.

REFERENCES: *WWCA*, 1933; Nancy Cunard, ed., *Negro*, 1970; Jervis Anderson, *This Was Harlem*, 1982; JWJ. (BK)

BENNETT, GWENDOLYN (painter, writer, educator), 8 July 1902–1981. A teacher of art, Gwendolyn Bennett also contributed poetry and short stories to *American Mercury*, *Opportunity*,* *The Crisis*,* *The Messenger*,* and *Fire!!** during the twenties. Bennett was born in Texas, the daughter of a lawyer, and was educated in Washington, D.C., and Brooklyn, where she became the first black elected to the Literary and Dramatic Societies at Girls High School. She studied fine arts at Teachers College, Columbia University, and at Pratt Institute in Brooklyn, where she was the author of two class plays. She received a sorority scholarship to study art in France in 1925 and became acquainted there with a circle of painters who encouraged her work. Upon her return to New York she worked as an assistant editor of *Opportunity* and was associated with Jessie Fauset* in encouraging the literary life of Harlem. She later taught watercolor and design at Howard University and from 1937 to 1940 was director of the Harlem Community Art Center.

REFERENCES: Countee Cullen, ed., *Caroling Dusk*, 1927; BAWPP, 1975; David Levering Lewis, *When Harlem Was in Vogue*, 1981. (PO)

BENTLEY, GLADYS (entertainer), 12 August 1907–18 January 1960. At the Clam House,* Connie's Inn,* and other Harlem cabarets, Gladys Bentley, attired in stiff collar, bow tie, and Eton jackets or full-dress white tails, played her own accompaniments in a lusty style, beating her foot on the floor and ripping out songs in a hoarse voice. Frequently, this heavy singer invented her own scabrous versions of popular songs and once seated at the piano would sing without stopping until dawn. Unidentified by name, she is vividly described in Carl Van Vechten's* *Parties*: "There's a girl up there now you oughta hear. She does her hair so her head looks like a wet seal and when she pounds the piano the dawn comes up like thunder. Say, she rocks the box, and tosses it, you can bet, and jumps it through hoops, and wait till you hear her sing Subway Papa and then go back to the farm and tell the folks and your pappy'll hitch lions to the plough instead o' mules.... Y'oughta hear her yodel. God, she gurgles and coughs and ya-up-i-diddies till you feel ready to push any good enterprise" (p. 33).

After an unhappy childhood in Pennsylvania, where she was made fun of by her family and schoolmates because of her masculine appearance, Gladys Bentley ran away to New York when she was sixteen and got a job at the Mad House, a Harlem nightclub on 133rd Street, using "Bobbie Minton" as a stage name. When Carl Van Vechten and other white visitors from downtown began to popularize the cabarets where she performed, Bentley's pay jumped from $35 to $125 a week. After her success was assured, she dressed openly in tailor-made drag and made no secret of either her name or her homosexuality, even marrying her lover in a civil ceremony in Atlantic City. Weighing in at 400 pounds, she wore a tuxedo for the occasion. In the late twenties Gladys Bentley began to record for OKeh, and during the thirties she owned and performed in Barbara's Exclusive Club. Later, she married a sailor in San Diego and then a Los Angeles newspaper columnist and spent her last years writing her autobiography.

REFERENCES: Carl Van Vechten, *Parties*, 1930; Gladys Bentley, "I Am a Woman Again," *Ebony*, August 1952; Sheldon Harris, BWW, 1979; Eric Garber, "T'ain't Nobody's Bizness," *Advocate*, 13 May 1982. (BK)

BERLACK, THELMA (journalist), 25 September 1906–? At the age of eighteen this Florida high school student won first prize for a "Biggest News of the Week" article sponsored by the *New York World*. That same year, 1924, she won a national oratorical contest; the attendant publicity enabled her to study journalism at New York University, during which time she was society editor for the *Pittsburgh Courier** and assistant managing editor of the *Amsterdam News*,* responsibilities that continued beyond the period of the Harlem Renaissance.

REFERENCE: WWCA, 1933. (BK)

BERNHARDT, [ERIC BARRON] CLYDE (trombonist), 11 July 1905– .
This North Carolina trombonist toured the Midwest until 1928 when he joined Herb Cowens's Orchestra at the Cotton Club* and then C. Luckyeth Roberts's* Band. The following year Clyde Bernhardt moved on to Honey Brown's band, and in 1931 he began his association with King Oliver.* Bernhardt played for several Lafayette Theatre* revues, notably *Spirit of 1929*, and for the *Whitman Sisters Revue** in 1928. He wrote songs as well, but none of them was particularly successful.

REFERENCE: BWW, 1979. (BK)

BETHUNE, MARY McLEOD (educator), 10 July 1875–18 May 1955. Occasionally, a figure far removed from Harlem's geography exerted a powerful influence over the movement of the Renaissance, at least in retrospect. Mary

McLeod Bethune was born in South Carolina to cotton sharecroppers and attended a Presbyterian church school for Negroes, Scotia Seminary in North Carolina, and then won a scholarship to the Moody Bible Institute in Chicago. In 1904 she founded the Daytona, Florida, Normal and Industrial School for Negro Girls, beginning with five children in an abandoned shack and ink that she made from elderberries, selling fish door-to-door to finance the project. Backed by Procter and Gamble (an astonished Harley Procter accepted when Bethune invited him to be on the Board of Trustees for her one-room school), the institution flourished, merging with Cookman Institute in 1922. For the next twenty years Bethune served as president of the Bethune-Cookman College. She was a vice-president of the National Association for the Advancement of Colored People* and recipient of the Spingarn Medal* in 1935. Five years earlier President Herbert Hoover had appointed her to the Conference on Child Health and Protection, and his successor, Franklin Roosevelt, appointed her to the Office of Minority Affairs of the National Youth Administration. Even in old age she was productive, working in the San Francisco Conference for the Organization of the United Nations as a consultant for the Charter for the Declaration of Human Rights. Mary McLeod Bethune died at eighty, the recipient of nine honorary degrees, the Haitian Order of Honor and Merit, the African Star of Liberia, and other acknowledgments of her remarkable career.

REFERENCES: NYT, 19 May 1955; NA, 1976. (BK)

BIBB, JOSEPH DANDRIDGE (editor), 21 September 1891–? Joseph Bibb was born in Georgia and educated at Atlanta University, Livingston College, Harvard University, and Yale University, completing a law degree at the latter in 1918. He was one of the founders of the Chicago *Whip*,* a weekly newspaper that within the decade had a circulation of 67,000. Concurrently, he was its editor and a practicing attorney.

REFERENCE: WWCA, 1927. (BK)

BIRTH OF A RACE PHOTOPLAY COMPANY, INC. (film company), 1916–1918. Emmett J. Scott* was so dismayed by D. W. Griffith's 1915 film *The Birth of a Nation* that he founded a film company to produce a response to it called *The Birth of a Race* and thereby combat its invidious racism. Shortly afterward, Scott was appointed special advisor to the secretary of war and began to devote his attention to the ill treatment of black draftees. With the backing of former president William Howard Taft and others, he sold stock in the company to raise money to finance the film, although some fraudulent activity delayed the project. By the time the film was eventually made the scenario and its intentions had been altered considerably. Elaborate scenes based on Bible stories were incorporated into a war story, and black soldiers whose plight in the army might have been used to positive effect were reduced to familiar black stereotypes. This three-hour catastrophe, advertised as a "Story of a Great Peace"

with "Magnificent Settings / Gorgeous Costumes / Thousands of Actors / Smiles, Tears, Thrills," opened in Chicago in December 1918 to disastrous reviews.
REFERENCES: Daniel J. Leab, *From Sambo to Superspade*, 1975; BBW, 1977; JWJ. (BK)

BIRTHRIGHT (novel), 1922. *Birthright* is the first novel by a white writer to feature a black protagonist since *Uncle Tom's Cabin*. Thomas Stribling, its author, was born in Tennessee in 1881, practiced law in the office of Alabama's governor Emmett O'Neal, and was a reporter for the *Chattanooga News* before turning to fiction. He wrote more than a dozen realistic novels about the South and even won the Pulitzer Prize for *The Store* (1932), but none of them carried the impact of *Birthright*. Stribling's black Harvard student is sensitive and intelligent but thwarted by power, poverty, and racism. Although most black readers applauded Stribling's sympathetic effort, it was too naive for Jessie Fauset,* whose *There Is Confusion** is a black version of the same theme; Walter White* was motivated to write *The Fire in the Flint** because of it. Stribling is therefore only tangentially connected with the Harlem Renaissance but inevitably so.
REFERENCES: Wilton Eckley, *Thomas S. Stribling*, 1975; David Levering Lewis, *When Harlem Was in Vogue*, 1981. (BK)

BLACK AND WHITE (film project), 1932. Through James W. Ford,* shortly to be the first black candidate for national office, the Meschrabpom Film Corporation engaged a number of young black intellectuals to come to Russia to make a film about race problems in Alabama. Organized by Louise Thompson,* the group included Langston Hughes,* who planned to stay on afterward; Taylor Gordon*; Allen McKenzie, a bonafide member of the Communist party; Mollie Lewis, a pharmacist; Dorothy West*; Ted Poston,* younger brother of former Garveyites Robert* and Ulysses; and Harvard graduate Henry Moon, among others. They sailed on the same boat carrying Alain Locke* and Ralph Bunche to Europe. Thompson's recollection of the trip, published in *Freedomways* in 1968, is an excellent account of the undertaking. The black would-be actors were surprised at their affectionate reception and at the strange experience of their color being a badge of honor entitling them to preferential treatment. The Russians were surprised, on their part, that Afro-Americans were not black at all, but various shades of color, and that they were neither working class nor all dancers or actors. Indeed, none of the students, writers, and professionals in the group had ever seen the inside of a steel mill, nor, except for Gordon and Hughes, had they performed professionally. They were paid 400 rubles a month plus a reimbursement of the $90 each had been obliged to put up for transportation, which they spent on good times that most Russians could not afford while waiting for the filming to begin. It soon became evident, however, that few preparations had been made. Hughes, who had been engaged to work on the existing script, discovered that it bore no resemblance to the life of black America or anywhere else at that period. The project was cancelled after a few months, and some members of the company went on to tour Central Asia. Writing about the undertaking later for the *Nation*,* Henry Moon declared that Russia had convinced him that racism in America was essentially a matter of economics. Three members of the company stayed on to become Russian citizens: artist Lloyd Patterson, actor Wayland Rudd, and postal clerk Homer Smith.

REFERENCES: Henry Moon, "A Negro Looks at Soviet Russia," *Nation*, 28 Feb. 1934; Langston Hughes, *I Wonder as I Wander*, 1956; Louise Thompson Patterson, "With Langston Hughes in the USSR," *Freedomways*, Spring 1968; David Levering Lewis, *When Harlem Was in Vogue*, 1981; Louise Thompson Patterson. (PO, BK)

BLACKBERRIES OF 1932 (musical revue), 1932. This imitative show opened at the Liberty Theatre on April 4 and closed before the end of the month. Lee Posner and Eddie Green* wrote the book, and Donald Heywood* and Tom Peluso wrote the music. Jackie Mabley,* Gertrude Saunders,* and Mantan More-land* were the stars. Once again, a black revue traded "not only in the clichés of its own field but in the stereotyped and routine features of Broadway" (NYT, 5 Apr. 1932, p. 27).

REFERENCE: NYTTR, 1972. (BK)

BLACKBIRDS (musical revues), 1926–1939. *Blackbirds* was a periodically annual series of entertainments, staged by Lew Leslie* and usually arranged by Will Vodery,* with skits and songs supplied by a number of people. They repeated a successful formula of racial clichés, but they fostered several careers and introduced some perennially popular songs. After *Blackbirds of 1926* had run for six weeks at the Alhambra Theatre* in Harlem, with Florence Mills* as its star, it played for six months in Paris and, after that, in London where a local reviewer observed that "life in Dixieland must be terribly exhausting" (NYT, 25 Sept. 1926, p. 21). *Blackbirds of 1928*, with songs by the white team Jimmy McHugh* and Dorothy Fields,* including "I Can't Give You Anything But Love" and "Diga Diga Do," opened May 9 for an extended run at the Liberty Theatre. Elisabeth Welch,* Adelaide Hall,* and Tim Moore* were in the cast, joined for a single number called "Doin' the New Low Down" by Bill "Bo-jangles" Robinson,* and with Aida Ward* as a replacement for the recently deceased Florence Mills. McHugh and Fields, abetted by the Hall Johnson* Choir, anticipated George Gershwin's* opera *Porgy and Bess** by seven years with a short musical version of Du Bose Heyward's* recently popular play *Porgy*,* and the song itself later became one of the standard numbers in Ethel Water's* repertory. *Blackbirds of 1929* seems to have been no more than an extension of its predecessor, adding some new songs by Eubie Blake.* *Blackbirds of 1930* opened October 22, but it ran only for twenty-six performances, despite the appearance of Ethel Waters, Buck and Bubbles,* and Flournoy Miller.* Its intent was "glorifying the American Negro," according to the program, but there was little to recommend it except for a haunting song to commemorate the passing of Florence Mills, "Memories of You," by Eubie Blake and Andy Razaf.* A humorless parody of *The Green Pastures*,* then having its great success, may have accounted for the reaction of the *New York Times* reviewer: "Whether Negro musical entertainments should remain faithful to Negro characteristics or should abide by the white man's formula for stage diversion is a question for the anthropologists to discuss among themselves" (23 Oct. 1930, p. 34). "Bojangles" joined Edith Wilson* and Eddie Hunter,* once again as a "guest star," in the "floundering" *Blackbirds of 1933*, patched together in "feeble imitation" of its forerunners. It opened on December 2, but it did not run into the year of its title. *Blackbirds of 1934* and *1936* never even played on Broadway, originating instead in Harlem theaters, although their London runs were fairly successful. The final version, *Blackbirds of 1939*, in a nine-performance run, was notable only for the appearance of Lena Horne. The first *Blackbirds*, which never played on Broadway, had taken on a mythological significance over the years because of the appearance of Florence Mills, her heart-breaking rendition of "I'm a Little Blackbird Looking for a Bluebird," and her Paris and London successes in that 1926 edition. None of the successors, apparently, lived up to their expectations.

REFERENCES: Loften Mitchell, *Black Drama*, 1967; NYTTR, 1972; EMT, 1976. (BK)

BLACK BOY (play), 1926. Paul Robeson* starred in this play by Jim Tully and Frank Dazey of "tawdry theatrical effects and countless dramatic irrelevancies." It opened October 6 and ran for thirty-seven performances at the Comedy Theatre, although Robeson offered a "fine-grained, resilient bit of characterization." He played a roustabout who acts as a sparring partner for a boxer, goes on to become a champion debased by vulgar luxuries and a parasitical mistress, and in defeat returns to his former failed circumstances. The rest of the cast was only notable for "profanities so thick that one suspects them of swearing merely to keep up their courage" (NYT, 7 Oct. 1926, p. 30).

REFERENCES: Burns Mantle, 1926–1927; NYTTR, 1972. (BK)

THE BLACK CHRIST AND OTHER POEMS (poetry), 1929. Countee Cullen's* third collection of poems demonstrated no technical advance on its predecessors; he continued to operate primarily within the confines of conventional English prosodic patterns and to divide his work about evenly among pieces about love, about religion, and about his racial heritage. The title poem is misleading, a long, melodramatic narrative about a lynched boy who appears after death to members of his family, not as some black Messiah but only to implore them to have faith in the mercy of God. As usual, Cullen's work was hindered more than enhanced by his insistence on a poetic diction. (BK)

BLACK CROSS NURSES (women's group) c. 1920–c. 1929. The Black Cross Nurses were, in essence, the women's auxiliary of the Universal Negro Improvement Association (UNIA)* founded by Marcus Garvey* in 1914. The nurses, several hundred strong by the early 1920s, burst onto the public scene as part of the UNIA's first public parade on Monday, 2 August 1920, in Harlem. The women, neatly attired in white, marched together behind the smartly clad African Legion troops of the UNIA. The astonished crowd cheered the nurses and other marchers in the colorful parade. The nurses symbolized the UNIA's commitment to come to the aid of stricken people throughout the world. They remained an important part of the UNIA at least through the 1929 Kingston, Jamaica, Sixth International Convention of the Negro Peoples of the World, which Garvey choreographed as his last great convention. The Black Cross Nurses and the UNIA went into general eclipse in the 1930s.
REFERENCES: E. David Cronon, *Black Moses*, 1955; John Hendrik Clarke, ed., *Marcus Garvey and the Vision of Africa*, 1974. (DS)

THE BLACKER THE BERRY (novel), 1929. The title, taken from the black folk expression, "the blacker the berry, the sweeter the juice," immediately establishes the irony and the theme of Wallace Thurman's* first novel. Unwanted by black or white, both of whom favor blacks with light skin, protagonist Emma Lou's life is a series of rejections. Her own parents' ambivalence toward their darker daughter signals the torment she experiences as a child, a student at the university, and as an adult in Harlem. As she grows not to want herself, outer rejection turns to inner self-hatred. Ultimately, she confronts her dilemma and achieves the challenge implicit in the novel's ironic title. (MH)

THE BLACK KING (film), 1932. Purportedly about Marcus Garvey,* *The Black King* was a Southland production, directed by Bud Pollard, a white man who specialized in black films. Donald Heywood* wrote the script, and Vivian Baber, Harry Gray, and Mary Jane Watkins were featured. By 1932 Garvey had lost much of his following, and the film played upon this by depicting him as an illiterate.
REFERENCES: Daniel J. Leab, *From Sambo to Superspade*, 1975; NA, 1976. (BK)

BLACK MANHATTAN (book), 1930. *Black Manhattan*, published in the spring of 1930 by Alfred Knopf,* was James Weldon Johnson's* attempt "to etch in the background of the Negro in latter-day New York to give a cut-back in projecting a picture of Negro Harlem" (p. vii). Johnson, the overworked executive secretary of the NAACP,* found the time to write *Black Manhattan* only because he had been awarded a Rosenwald Fellowship in 1929–1930 that allowed him to take a leave of absence from his job and concentrate on writing, travel, and restoring his health. Although Johnson did not ignore political and economic issues in *Black Manhattan*, he was particularly interested in chronicling the

cultural history of American blacks with a focus on the New York community. For instance, *Black Manhattan* contains relatively lengthy sections on the development of black theater, the difficulties faced by black athletes, and the contribution of blacks to American music, literature, and art. Indeed, highlights of the book include short sketches of black actors Ira Aldridge and Charles Gilpin* and nineteenth-century pugilist Tom Molineaux. Although the book is (as Johnson intended) impressionistic and written as a popular history, *Black Manhattan* clearly delineates the important events and trends in black history during the first three decades of the twentieth century and is not different in its outline from that of more recent scholarly accounts of that period.
REFERENCE: James Weldon Johnson, *Along This Way*, 1933. (DS)

BLACK NO MORE (novel), 1931. Less a novel than an extended satire, George S. Schuyler's* *Black No More* is supposed to pass between 1933 and 1940. During this period Dr. Crookman dispenses a depigmentation process for small fees and turns the entire black population white. Now members of a majority, they change their names, intermarry, and have their babies bleached. Soon enough, blondes become despised because all of the best people have dark skins. The humor in *Black No More* is crude without being vulgar, and the satire is heavy-handed without much attempt at subtlety. (BK)

BLACK OPALS (periodical), 1927–1928. A group of young Philadelphia black intellectuals published a few issues of *Black Opals* between the spring of 1927 and June 1928, among whom Arthur Huff Fauset,* Nellie Bright,* and Mae V. Cowdery* were most significant. The first issue carried Alain Locke's* enthusiastic if guarded "Hail, Philadelphia" and three poems by Langston Hughes.* Jessie Fauset,* Marita Bonner,* and Lewis Alexander* contributed to later issues; Arthur Huff Fauset, Bright, Cowdery, and other Philadelphians wrote regularly for *Black Opals* during its brief life. Printed through "the desire of older New Negroes to encourage younger members of the group who demonstrate talent and ambition," according to the initial editorial (p. 1), 250 copies of each issue were sufficient for its modest subscription list.
REFERENCES: Vincent Jubilee, "Philadelphia's Afro-American Literary Circle and the Harlem Renaissance," 1980; JWJ. (BK)

BLACK SCANDALS (musical revue), 1928. This "naively and disarmingly amateurish" show by George Smithfield was more like a "pretentious Harlem church or fraternal social" than a Broadway musical. It opened at the Totten Theatre on October 26 and closed almost immediately, notable for "good hoofing"—by 1929 an almost obligatory compliment from the critics—and "mirthless stretches of dialogue" (NYT, 27 Oct. 1928, p. 23). Songs, popular during the period, were appropriated and inserted at random, and the audience tended to laugh at rather than with the proceedings.
REFERENCE: NYTTR, 1972. (BK)

BLACK SOULS (play), 1932. The *New York Times* reviewer believed that Annie Nathan Myer had "thought clearly but written clumsily" in *Black Souls*, her drama about a black poet who has known a white senator's daughter in Paris. When the senator pretends to be interested in a black college because of his lust for the wife of the poet's brother, the college's president, the characterizations grow "unfortunately inept." Eventually, the poet is lynched when he is discovered with the senator's daughter. Rose McClendon* and Juano Hernandez* appeared in the brief run (thirteen performances) at the Provincetown Playhouse, beginning March 30 (31 Mar. 1932, p. 25).
REFERENCES: Burns Mantle, 1931–1932; NYTTR, 1972. (BK)

BLACK STAR LINE (shipping company), 1919–1922. The Black Star Line was the ill-fated shipping line organized by Marcus Garvey* and his Universal Negro Improvement Association* in 1919 as part of their program to "conduct a world-wide commercial and industrial intercourse" with an all-black company (Clarke, *Marcus Garvey and the Vision of Africa*, p. 138). Garvey incorporated the company in Delaware on 26 June 1919 and raised thousand of dollars by selling stock in the company to blacks around the world who were thrilled by the attempt of blacks to enter the all-white world of commerce and shipping. A share of stock cost only $5, and many poor blacks gave away their savings (some mortgaged their houses) in response to Garvey's promise that the Black Star Line would not only uplift the race but also prove highly profitable for its shareholders. Garvey was an outstanding organizer and fund raiser, and he raised more than $600,000 the first year with which to purchase ships and fund voyages.

Unfortunately, money was not enough. Garvey and his associates had absolutely no experience with the complex shipping industry, and he was soon at the mercy of dishonest brokers, venal employees, and his own mismanagement. Within three years the company bought three ships, each of them barely seaworthy, unfit for their intended purposes, and priced so far above their actual value as to be ridiculous. The few voyages of the Black Star Line were, for the most part, incredible fiascos, and ships broke down constantly, were unable to deliver cargoes properly, and spent more time visiting ports to show off to excited black audiences than making a profit. Indeed, the company lost more than $700,000 during its short existence. By early 1922 the press and some shareholders were demanding an investigation, and Garvey was charged with (and indicted on) twelve counts of fraudulent use of the mails (along with three of his company associates). He was found guilty, sentenced to five years in prison in 1925, released in 1927, and deported immediately as an undesirable alien. The towering disappointment in the black community over Garvey's failure was expressed by Captain Hugh Mulzac, a black captain of the Black Star Line: "Thus the great and bold dream of colored resurgence ended in catastrophe. For their hard-won dollars scores of thousands of humble black men and women received in dividends only a transitory inflation of their racial pride. . . . But when the bubble burst as it had to, upon the jagged rocks of incompetence and venality,

the people were left with their dreams of a bright future blighted'' (Clarke, p. 138).
REFERENCES: E. David Cronon, *Black Moses*, 1955; John Hendrik Clarke, ed., *Marcus Garvey and the Vision of Africa*, 1974. (DS)

BLACK SWAN PHONOGRAPH CORPORATION (record company), 1921–1924. Harry H. Pace,* of the Pace and Handy music publishing company, formed the Pace Phonograph Company in January 1921. John Nail* and W.E.B. Du Bois* were on the Board of Directors, Fletcher Henderson* was the recording director, William Grant Still* was the music director, and all of the stockholders and employees were black. It was the company's intention to record only black artists, and Pace hoped to record concert singers, quartets, and glee clubs as well as popular vaudeville and blues performers. The company's label name Black Swan may have been chosen in remembrance of the nineteenth-century concert singer Elizabeth Taylor Greenfield (1809–1876), who toured America and England billed as ''The Black Swan.'' The advertising slogan contained a subtle pun: ''The Only Genuine Colored Record. Others Are Only Passing for Colored.''

The company initially had difficulty in finding a firm to press its recordings but was soon in business with offices in New York City and studios and a pressing plant on Long Island. Their first hit was Ethel Waters* singing ''Down Home Blues'' and ''Oh Daddy,'' and she followed this with ''There'll Be Some Changes Made'' and ''One Man Nan.'' To help advertise Black Swan records, Waters and Henderson and the Black Swan Jazz Masters orchestra were sent on a promotional tour through the South; Lester A. Walton*—later United States consul to Liberia—was the troupe manager. Waters's recordings, and those of Alberta Hunter* and Trixie Smith,* sold so profitably that in 1922 Pace was able to buy out the Olympic Disc Record Company. The Olympic catalog contained items by white as well as black artists, but Pace reissued them anyway on the Black Swan label. Black Swan was soon releasing up to ten recordings a month, at prices as low as seventy-five cents for the popular blues, comic, and hillbilly records. They introduced a classical Red Label series that sold for a dollar, advertising a recording by soprano Antoinette Garnes as ''The First Grand Opera Record Ever Made by a Colored Singer.''

Record companies proliferated in the early twenties, competing for the growing market for ''race'' records and for the services of the most popular artists, and Black Swan soon found itself in financial difficulties. In 1924 the company merged with—a polite business term for ''was sold to''—the powerful Paramount Company. Pace was able to pay his stockholders substantial dividends as Paramount continued to issue the Black Swan catalog.
REFERENCES: Robert M. W. Dixon and John Godrich, *Recording the Blues*, 1970; MBA, 1971. (DA)

BLACK VELVET (play), 1927. After a long run in Chicago, this "strangely diffuse and unsympathetic play" opened at the Liberty Theatre on September 27 for fifteen performances (NYT, 28 Sept. 1927, p. 28). In Willard Robertson's turgid drama an aging Dixie Civil War general approves of the murder of a northern white labor leader who tries to organize black workers in the first act; in the second, he approves of the lynching of a doped-up black boy who had struck his grandson; in the third, he does not approve of the grandson's marrying a black girl and conveniently drops dead before the curtain falls.
REFERENCE: NYTTR, 1972. (BK)

BLAKE, [JAMES HUBERT] EUBIE (pianist, composer), 7 February 1883–12 February 1983. Eubie Blake was the eleventh child (and the only one to survive infancy) of parents who had been slaves. He learned to play the parlor organ as a child and picked up the techniques of early ragtime syncopation and stride bass by listening to the piano sharks who played in Baltimore's taverns and sporting houses. His first job, at the age of fifteen, was playing piano in Aggie Skelton's high-class brothel in Baltimore. He toured with a medicine show, made a brief appearance in New York in 1902 in a plantation-style revue, *In Old Kentucky*, and was resident pianist at the Goldfield Hotel in Baltimore, 1907–1910. Blake teamed up with the singer-lyricist Noble Sissle* in 1915 to form a songwriting and performing vaudeville act—Sissle and Blake, The Dixie Duo—and also played society dates in and around New York booked through James Reese Europe's* Clef Club.* While Sissle and Europe were overseas in World War I (Blake, at the age of thirty-five, was too old to be drafted), he teamed with the baritone Broadway Jones and played the Keith circuit. After the war Blake and Sissle met the equally well-known vaudeville team Flournoy Miller* and Aubrey Lyles.* Miller had been planning to write a musical satire based on two earlier shows, but the four men pooled their talents and financial resources to produce the extraordinarily successful *Shuffle Along** in 1921. The show made the names and fortunes of many performers, and touring companies and revivals appeared throughout the twenties. Blake and Broadway Jones took out a reduced version of the show, *Shuffle Along Junior*, in 1928, but later attempts to revive the initial success failed. A new *Shuffle Along in 1930** closed immediately; *Shuffle Along of 1933** ran only two weeks in New York, and its tab-show version ended up stranded in Los Angeles. An attempted revival of the original *Shuffle Along*, in 1952, lasted only four performances. *Chocolate Dandies** (1924), which Blake considered his finest score, had a respectable run, but *Blackbirds [*] of 1930* was a comparative failure despite Andy Razaf's* lyrics and the performances of Ethel Waters* and Flournoy Miller. Sissle and Blake went to Europe in 1925, touring as "American Ambassadors of Syncopation," and then temporarily dissolved their partnership, Blake returning to America and Sissle returning to Europe with his own band. They performed together again with the USO in World War II, and they worked together off and on thereafter, their last appearance being a documentary film, *Reminiscing with Sissle and Blake*, made at Fisk University in 1974, just a year before Noble Sissle's death. Of their vaudeville act, Blake said: "It ain't much of an act. I play and Sissle sings.... We just come out and do songs.... We were havin' a good time" (Rose, *Eubie Blake*, p. 94).

Blake's first wife, Avis Lee, died in 1939; in 1945 he married Marion Gant Tyler, the granddaughter of Hiram S. Thomas, a celebrated chef who had invented the potato chip called the Saratoga Chip. A showgirl in black musicals in the late twenties, Marion had been married to the musician Willie Tyler, and she had served as business manager of the W. C. Handy* Music Publishing Company. With her administrative skills and understanding of music and musicians, she soon set Blake's tangled business and personal affairs in order, managing them until her death on 26 June 1982. Unwilling to settle into comfortable retirement when he married Marion, he went back to school. He enrolled at New York University to study the Joseph Schillinger system of composition, and he obtained a degree in music in 1950 at the age of sixty-seven. His thesis *Dictys on Seventh Avenue* was published in 1955. Although he remained quietly active through the fifties, Blake was "rediscovered" by the media during the ragtime revival of the sixties and seventies and was in great demand as a performer at jazz festivals, concerts, benefits, and memorial tributes and on television programs. *Eubie*, a production showcasing Blake's music, opened on Broadway in 1978.

Blake wrote about a thousand musical pieces. The earliest, "Charleston Rag"—originally titled "Sounds of Africa" at Will Marion Cook's* suggestion—was written in 1899 although not copyrighted until 1917. His first published pieces were "Chevy Chase" and "Fizz Water" in 1914. His first song with Sissle, "It's All Your Fault," was popularized by Sophie Tucker. He wrote many rags and waltzes; his famous song "I'm Just Wild about Harry" was itself a waltz until Blake turned it into a one-step at the insistence of *Shuffle Along*'s leading lady, Lottie Gee.* Blake was a member of ASCAP from 1922. He appeared in an early De Forest Phonofilm, *Sissle and Blake's Snappy Songs*, in 1923; in a Vitaphone short in 1927; and in a one-reel musical, *Pie Pie Blackbird*, in 1932. He and his orchestra supported Bill Robinson* in the film *Harlem Is Heaven* (1932), and Blake played the role of a musical hall proprietor in *Scott Joplin, King of Ragtime* (1976). The documentary film *Eubie Blake* was produced for French television in 1974. He made hundreds of recordings, the earliest in 1917, and several dozen piano rolls; in 1973, to keep a recording date for a new series of piano rolls, Blake, at the age of ninety, consented to travel by airplane for the first time. He received honorary doctorates and degrees from Brooklyn College, Dartmouth College, Rutgers University, the University of Maryland, the New England Conservatory, Pratt Institute, and Morgan State College. He was

awarded the Medal of Freedom in 1981, and he lived to celebrate his one
hundredth birthday on 7 February 1983.
REFERENCES: Rudi Blesh and Harriet Janis, *They All Played Ragtime*, 1951;
MBA, 1971; WWJ, 1978; Al Rose, *Eubie Blake*, 1979. (DA)

BLANKS, BIRLEANNA (entertainer), 18 February 1889–12 August 1968.
Birleanna Blanks was an Iowa girl who toured widely with Amanda Randolph*
and Hilda Perkins as one of the "Three Dixie Songbirds." She appeared in
many of Billy King's* shows at the Lafayette Theatre,* notably *Over the Top*,
They're Off, and *Exploits in Africa* (1919); and *New Americans*, *A Trip Round
the World*, and *Derby Day in Dixie* (1921). Later, she appeared on Broadway
in *Lucky Sambo** during the 1925–1926 season and made some records for
Paramount.
REFERENCE: BWW, 1979. (BK)

BLEDSOE, [JULIUS] JULES (singer), 29 December 1898–15 July 1943. A
native of Waco, Texas, and a graduate of Bishop College in Marshall, Texas,
Jules Bledsoe went to New York in 1919 to study medicine, but friends persuaded
him to study voice also. Both his parents had fine voices, and he had studied
piano and harmony at home and at school. He made rapid progress, and following
his debut recital at Aeolian Hall in 1924 he was signed by impresario Sol Hurok
to embark on a successful career as a concert baritone in the United States and
Europe. In 1926 he created the role of Tizan in Frank Harling's opera *Deep
River* and also in 1926 sang the first performance of Louis Gruenberg's setting
of James Weldon Johnson's* dramatic poem *The Creation* in a Town Hall concert
sponsored by the League of Composers. He appeared for a short time in a dramatic
role as Abraham McCranie in Paul Green's* *In Abraham's Bosom** (1926) at
the Provincetown Playhouse and created the role of Joe in Jerome Kern's *Showboat** (1928). In 1932 he played the leading role in Shirley Graham's* *Tom-
Tom* in the Cleveland Stadium, Ohio, and sang Amonasro in *Aïda* with the
Cleveland Summer Opera. He repeated the role in the 1933 performances of
Aïda by the Chicago Opera Company at the Hippodrome, New York, which
introduced the prima donna Caterina Jarboro* to America. He sang the title role
in the first European production of Gruenberg's *Emperor Jones** at Amsterdam
in 1934 and later that year repeated the role in the short season given by the
Aeolian Opera Association in New York. In Europe, at Monte Carlo, The Hague,
Amsterdam, Rotterdam, and other cities, he also sang the roles of Rigoletto,
Tonio, and Boris Godunov. He died of a cerebral hemorrhage in Hollywood in
1943.
REFERENCES: NYT, 16 July 1943; Edith J. R. Isaacs, *The Negro in the
American Theatre*, 1947; MBA, 1971; George Shirley, "The Black Performer,"
Opera News, 30 Jan. 1971, pp. 6–13; BCM, 1977. (DA)

BLOODSTREAM (play), 1932. Frederick Schlick's prison drama opened at the Times Square Theatre for twenty-nine performances, beginning March 30, starring Wayland Rudd and Frank Wilson.* The plot would have required "the mad genius of Poe," according to Brooks Atkinson in the *New York Times,* to succeed. A white inmate rebels against prison conditions and kills a guard, after which he is beaten up and shot by the sadistic warden. At the end the two of them are trapped together in a mine when a demented black prisoner, who thinks he is God, dynamites the prison to hasten Judgment Day. "As usual," Atkinson observed, "the Negro performers are the more luxuriant," but Schlick's "imagination [is] richer than [his] technical ability" (31 Mar. 1932, p. 25).
REFERENCES: Burns Mantle, 1931–1932; NYTTR, 1972. (BK)

BLUES Carl Van Vechten,* who first brought the blues out of their Harlem closet for white audiences in the *Vanity Fair** article "The Black Blues" in August 1925, offered an informal assessment of the genre in his manuscript inventory to the James Weldon Johnson* Memorial Collection of Negro Arts and Letters, which he founded at Yale University in 1941:

The Blues are the Negro's prayer to a cruel Cupid. They are songs of disappointed love. There are three major stages in the progress of the Blues. First, they are invented in snatches, sometimes a single line repeated over and over, sung unaccompanied by an individual. Second, they are performed by more or less professional troubadors who accompany themselves on guitars or banjos and purvey their wares on the levee or in a barroom. Third, they are arranged for phonograph or stage performances by well-known composers. The great public became aware of the Blues when W. C. Handy [*] published "The Memphis Blues" in 1912. The impact of the Blues on public consciousness became terrific in the twenties when Bessie Smith [*] often sang them in...the manner of a Southern folk-singer. When she and Clara [Smith*] (no relation) made their most characteristic records, they didn't read from published music. They couldn't, as a matter of fact. They started to sing something somebody remembered; somebody else added a line; another person another, etc. The accompaniment was improvised by a "hot" band or a small group of musicians. The accompaniments were extraordinarily rich and varied and some of the anonymous instrumentalists have since become famous. (pp. 43–44)

Langston Hughes,* however, quoted in Van Vechten's *Vanity Fair* article, identified the genre more succinctly: "The Blues always impressed me as being very sad, sadder even than the Spirituals, because their sadness is not softened with tears, but hardened with laughter, the absurd, incongruous laughter of a sadness without even a god to appeal to" (*"Keep A-Inchin' Along,"* p. 46). The form itself would seem to date from about 1870, according to Stephen Longstreet in *The Real Jazz, New and Old*: "in the farmlands, the cotton and tobacco fields...they were already calling it the blues" (p. 17), although, as Abbe Niles pointed out in his introduction to W. C. Handy's anthology of representative selections, *Blues: An Anthology** "nothing is scarcer when one looks for it than the tune of a folk-blues.... Because the blues were essentially a mold, filled, emptied, refilled, like a child's seashore toy; so easy to fill that little trouble was taken filling it; small pain, short memory. It remained for a musician to take it up'' (p. 18). He was speaking, of course, of W. C. Handy, even though Jelly Roll Morton* claimed to have written ''The Jelly Roll Blues'' in 1905. No one has ever managed a satisfactory explanation of the derivation of the term itself.

REFERENCES: W. C. Handy and Abbe Niles, *Blues*, 1926; Stephen Longstreet, *The Real Jazz, New and Old*, 1956; Carl Van Vechten, *''Keep A-Inchin' Along,''* 1979; CVV. (BK)

BLUES: AN ANTHOLOGY (book), 1926. Albert and Charles Boni published W. C. Handy's* *Blues* as a handsome folio edition at the height of the Harlem Renaissance, in 1926. White musicologist Abbe Niles contributed ''Sad Horns,'' an extensive and informative introduction to Handy's eclectic collection of musical examples. It included his own arrangements of spirituals,* work songs, folk melodies, preceding his ''Jogo Blues,'' ''St. Louis Blues,'' and others; blues* by Will Nash, Clinton A. Kemp, Charles H. Booker, Jr., Ethel Neal, Spencer Williams,* and many others, including Handy's wife, Lucille. He concluded the selection with examples of the bogus blues compositions by white composers Jerome Kern, Irving Berlin, and George Gershwin* and excerpts from Gershwin's *Rhapsody in Blue* and *Concerto in F*. Niles defended inclusion of the latter compositions by pointing out that ''jazz is a thing principally of characteristic melodic figures and of tone-color'' (p. 47). The Mexican caricaturist Miguel Covarrubias* contributed eight half-tone illustrations and several line drawings that served as the nucleus for his full volume, *Negro Drawings*, a year later. (BK)

BOMBOLLA (musical comedy), 1929. This ''strikingly unoriginal'' show by D. Frank Marcus, with music by Bernard Martin, opened at the Royale Theatre on June 26 and closed just over a month later. Isabell Washington* had some personal success as a girl who leaves her southern town to become the star of a show called ''Bombolla'' in New York, singing ''Rub-a-Dub Your Rabbit's Foot'' and ''Hot Patootie Wedding Night.'' Later in the program ''Miss Washington and Her Wild Animals'' had a number called ''African Whoopie.'' In between, the ''laborious comedy routines'' and familiar references to Alabama trains and longings for Mammy undermined the ''fetching speed of strutting and singing'' by the ''Bombolla Dusky Damsels'' and the ''Bombolla Steppers,'' according to the *New York Times* reviewer (27 June 1929, p. 17). *Bombolla*, sometimes referred to as *Bomboola* or *Bamboola*, should not be confused with *Bamboula*, a Salem Whitney* and Homer Tutt* tab show from 1921 in which Jasper Jazz and Raspberry Razz go to Africa in search of music.

REFERENCES: Burns Mantle, 1928–1929; NYTTR, 1972; BB, 1980. (BK)

BONDS, CASCA (personality), c. 1890–? Casca Bonds was adopted by an Englishman with the permission of his laundress-mother when he was seven years old and reared in England. He returned to the United States to avoid conscription when World War I was declared in 1914 and began to study singing with a white music teacher whose secretary he later became. He also became both friend and confidant of A'Lelia Walker* and was usually in attendance during the days of her Dark Tower.* His manner made him the frequent butt of jokes, not without foundation: he spoke in a breathy manner, minced when he walked, and expressed himself with fussy elegance, a homosexual type whom Mme Walker seems to have enjoyed.
REFERENCES: George W. Henry, M.D., *Sexual Variants*, 1948; Eric Garber, "Taint Nobody's Business," *The Advocate*, 13 May 1982. (BK)

BONNER, MARIETA/MARITA ODETTE (writer, teacher), 16 June 1899– 6 December 1971. Marieta or Marita Bonner contributed numerous essays, short stories, and plays to magazines like *The Crisis** and *Opportunity** between 1925 and 1940. Born and educated in Brookline, Massachusetts, she lived in Dorchester, Massachusetts, and graduated from Brookline High School in 1918. That September she entered Radcliffe. She graduated in 1922 having majored in English and comparative literature. She was a member of a number of musical clubs and twice won the Radcliffe song competition. She began teaching after college in the Bluefield Colored Institute in Bluefield, Virginia, 1922–1924. From 1924 until 1930 she taught English at Armstrong High School in Washington, D.C., and began a productive writing career. Her writings include the prizewinning essay "On Being Young—A Woman—and Colored" (*The Crisis*, Dec. 1925); the prizewinning short story "Drab Rambles" (*The Crisis*, Dec. 1927); and plays like "The Pot Maker" (1927), "The Purple Flower" (1928), and "Exit: An Illusion" (1929), which make her part of the little theater movement. In 1927 she won the Wanamaker Prize for Negro Music. In 1930 she married William Occomy, an accountant, and had three children. She taught at Phillips High School in Chicago from 1944 until 1949 and between 1950 and 1963 at the Doolittle School for educationally retarded children. She died at the age of seventy-two from complications after a fire in her Chicago apartment.
REFERENCES: *The Crisis*, Dec. 1925; James V. Hatch, ed. *Black Theater, U.S.A.*, 1974; Radcliff College Archives. (DI)

BONTEMPS, ARNA (writer, librarian), 13 October 1902–4 June 1973. Arna Bontemps was a poet of the Harlem Renaissance who later turned to novels, short fiction, and criticism. Born in Alexandria, Louisiana, Bontemps moved to Los Angeles with his family when he was three. He attended San Fernando Academy (1917–1920) and in 1923 graduated from Pacific Union College. He moved to Harlem in 1924 where he met Langston Hughes,* afterward a lifelong friend with whom he would later collaborate. He taught at private schools in New York and sent his first poems to Jessie Fauset* at *The Crisis*,* where she was literary editor. In 1926 his poem "Golgotha Is a Mountain" won *Opportunity*'s* Alexander Pushkin Award for Poetry. The following year he won this same prize for "The Return" and the first prize in *The Crisis* poetry contest for "Nocturne at Bethesda." Bontemps married Alberta Johnson in 1926, his former student at Harlem Academy, and in 1930 accepted a teaching position at Oakwood School in Huntsville, Alabama. His first novel, *God Sends Sunday*,* appeared that year. During the thirties he wrote two other novels, *Drums at Dusk* and *Black Thunder*, which reflected his interest in slave narratives and rebellions; various short stories; and two children's books, *You Can't Pet a Possum*, and, with Hughes, *Popo and Fifina*.* Bontemps left Alabama in 1932 to devote himself to full-time writing, at his father's house in California, and then, that same year, was appointed to the Illinois Writers Project. In 1936 he studied at the Graduate Library School at the University of Chicago and two years later received a Rosenwald Fellowship for creative writing and travel in the Caribbean. In 1943 he began his twenty-two-year career as head librarian at Fisk University. In 1946 he dramatized *God Sends Sunday* and with Countee Cullen* and white composer Harold Arlen turned it into a successful musical comedy, *St. Louis Woman*. Again in collaboration with Langston Hughes, Bontemps edited two important anthologies: *The Poetry of the Negro, 1746–1949* (1949) and *The Book of Negro Folklore* (1958). His *Story of the Negro* (1956) received the Jane Addams Children's Book Award, and his prolific writings include books about Frederick Douglass, slave narratives, and further volumes of verse. Bontemps was director of university relations at Fisk in 1965, and in 1966 he taught English at the University of Illinois. From 1969 until 1972 he was curator of the James Weldon Johnson* Memorial Collection of Negro Arts and Letters at Yale. Then he returned as writer-in-residence to Fisk until his death. As Charles Nichols noted in his edition of letters exchanged between Bontemps and Hughes, Arna Bontemps was the "keeper of the flame" (p. 7) who both recognized the value of the past and actively carried on the Afro-American heritage through his writings and library work. Among Bontemps's other work relevant to the period was an important collection of contemporary essays by a number of scholars, *The Harlem Renaissance Remembered*. In his introduction he assessed the beginning of the period as "a locus for what I would regard as a more exciting and perhaps more telling assault on oppression than the dreary blood-in-the-streets strategy of preceding years" (p. 5). Of the end of the Harlem Renaissance, he wrote, "The golden days were gone. Or was it just the bloom of youth that had been lost?" (p. 26).

REFERENCES: Arna Bontemps, ed. *The Harlem Renaissance Remembered*, 1972; Arthur P. Davis, *From the Dark Tower*, 1974; Charles H. Nichols, ed., *Langston Hughes-Arna Bontemps Letters*, 1980. (DI)

THE BOOK OF AMERICAN NEGRO POETRY (anthology), 1922, 1931. James Weldon Johnson* edited the first substantial anthology of the Harlem Renaissance, beginning with Paul Laurence Dunbar and concluding with Claude

McKay* and Anne Spencer* in 1922. Nine years later the popularity of the movement occasioned a revision, to which he added those figures whose work had come into prominence during the interim. Johnson's lengthy introduction is perhaps the first assessment of the genre to treat seriously its evolution through the spirituals,* blues,* ragtime, and jazz and the "power of the Negro to suck up the national spirit from the soil and create something artistic and original,...due to a remarkable racial gift of adaptability" (p. 20). His preface to the revised edition in 1931 may stand as an indictment as well as an evaluation of the younger poets of the twenties, observing that they had not "succeeded fundamentally in what they undertook to do." Some of them, in an attempt to "deny intellectually" a race consciousness, either produced "poetry of bombast and braggadocio—or failed to produce anything vital" (p. 6). While acknowledging the obvious talent in the work of Langston Hughes,* Countee Cullen,* Arna Bontemps,* Frank Horne,* and others, Johnson nevertheless failed to "find a single poem possessing the power and artistic finality found in the best poems rising out of racial conflict and contact," and he concluded that the writers "possess a greater self-sufficiency than any generation before them and are freer from sensitiveness to the approbation or deprecation of their white environment" (p. 7). Johnson's own ambivalence underwrites more recent assessments of the period by Nathan I. Huggins in *Harlem Renaissance* (1971) and David Levering Lewis in *When Harlem Was in Vogue* (1981). (BK)

THE BOOK OF AMERICAN NEGRO SPIRITUALS (songbook), 1925. James Weldon Johnson* and J. Rosamond Johnson* edited *The Book of American Negro Spirituals* in 1925. Its success prompted another volume, *The Second Book of Negro Spirituals*, a year later. James Weldon Johnson supplied an extensive introduction to the first; it remains the most succinct analysis of spirituals* both as a musical form and as folk poetry. A briefer introduction prefaced the second collection. For both, J. Rosamond Johnson did most of the arrangements, although Lawrence Brown,* who was at that time giving spiritual recitals with Paul Robeson,* supplied a few additional numbers. *See* Spirituals.* (BK)

BORN TO BE (autobiography), 1929. Taylor Gordon's* autobiography, written at the age of thirty-five, is an account of his childhood in White Sulphur Springs, Montana, where he helped support his family by working as a messenger boy in the local sporting houses; of his adventures as a young man while working as chauffeur, porter, and cook for John Ringling; and of his career as a singer in the middle and late twenties. Muriel Draper* helped Gordon prepare the manuscript of the book and wrote an introduction for the first printing, Carl Van Vechten* contributed a foreword, and Miguel Covarrubias* did the illustrations. The original edition, by Covici-Friede, sold well through two printings. A reprint by the University of Washington Press (1975) had a new introduction by Robert Hemenway.

Hemenway pointed out (p. xxix), quoting several contemporary reviewers of

Born to Be, that Gordon's guileless narrative style, earthy humor, and air of perpetual naivety—that of an "innocent abroad"—appealed to white reviewers who accepted the book as "the straight story" of Gordon's "own gay, irresponsible, happy-go-lucky, sensual, sinful, lyric life" (*New York World*, 24 Nov. 1929) and praised its "unaffected simplicity and child-like frankness" (*Saturday Review of Literature*, 7 Dec. 1929). One of the reviewers quoted by Hemenway was perceptive enough to question whether "this man could have gone through these adventures...and remain so abnormally untouched" (*New Republic*, 1 Jan. 1930), and black reviewers were generally less than enthusiastic, feeling that the book would appeal to prurient tastes and perpetuate black stereotypes. Hemenway dismissed Draper's and Van Vechten's promotions as "condescending" and "patronizing" and attempted to analyze Gordon's literary style and authorial intent. Hemenway also provided a sympathetic account of Gordon's years of mental instability and his peaceful old age.
REFERENCE: Taylor Gordon, *Born to Be, with a new introduction by Robert Hemenway*, 1975. (DA)

BOTTOMLAND (musical play), 1927. Every tenth line was a song cue in this tale about May Mandy Lee who follows her sister Sally north, finds her drinking gin in a Harlem cabaret, and goes back home. *Bottomland* seems to have been compiled rather than written by Clarence Williams* and Eva Taylor,* popular radio entertainers putting on a personal appearance at the request of their public. Donald Heywood,* Spencer Williams,* and Chris Smith,* all experienced composers, contributed additional songs, but *Bottomland* ran for only twenty-one performances, beginning June 27, at the Princess Theatre.
REFERENCE: NYTTR, 1972. (BK)

BOTTOM OF THE CUP (play), 1927. Charles Thompson, educated in the North, returns to found a black college in his hometown. When his brother is killed by their former white missy's beau, Charles takes the blame, sacrificing himself to a lynch mob. Meanwhile, a white girl is giving birth to an illegitimate child in an offstage room of Charles's mother's cabin. The parallel plots in this "well meant but faltering drama" by John Tucker Battle and William J. Perlman suggested that blacks could be more magnanimous than whites, and as if to reinforce that observation, the black actors were judged far superior to the white ones (NYT, 1 Feb. 1927, p. 24). *Bottom of the Cup* lasted for six performances at the Mayfair Theatre, beginning January 31.
REFERENCES: Burns Mantle, 1926–1927; NYTTR, 1972. (BK)

BOWMAN, LAURA (actress, singer), c. 1881–1957. Laura Bowman's career as a popular entertainer took her from vaudeville to radio soap opera. Her remarkable voice was evident when she was a child in Quincy, Illinois, when she began singing at school and church functions. After several years in vaudeville, Bowman became manager of her own group, the Dark Town Entertainers, which included her husband, Sidney Kirkpatrick, and two other men. One of the highlights of their show was Bowman's impersonation of characters from opera, including her favorite, Salome. Following tours of the United States and Europe with the Dark Town Entertainers, Bowman joined the Lafayette Players* and appeared in *His Honor the Mayor* in 1918 and *Shades of Hades* and *That Gets It* in 1922. In 1923 she acted with Sidney Kirkpatrick and Evelyn Preer* in *The Chip Woman's Fortune*,* *Salome*, and *A Comedy of Errors*, a triple bill presented by the Ethiopian Art Players.* She appeared in *Meek Mose*replacing* (1928) and *Sentinels* (1931), of which Brooks Atkinson wrote, "Laura Bowman makes something warm of the monotonously written part of the servant" (NYT, 26 Dec. 1931, p. 15). In 1933 she played in the Negro Theatre Guild production of *Louisiana* on Broadway and went on to appear in the film version, as well as in the Oscar Micheaux* films *Lem Hawkins' Confession* (1935), *God's Stepchildren* (1938), and the first all-black horror film, *Son of Ingagi* (1940). During the thirties she also appeared in the New York productions of *The Tree*reduced* (1932), *Jezebel* (1933), *Yesterday's Orchids* (1934), *Plumes in the Dust* (1936), and others. Bowman had an active career in radio during the forties, working with Rudy Vallee, Fred Allen, and others and in serials such as *Stella Dallas* and *John's Other Wife*. She returned to Broadway in *Jeb* with Ruby Dee and Ossie Davis in 1946 and retired to Los Angeles, where she died at her home in 1957. REFERENCES: NYTTR, 1972; BBW, 1977; DBPA, 1978; BB, 1980. (PO)

BOXING. In addition to the celebrated Jack Johnson,* at least half a dozen singular boxers were prominent during the Harlem Renaissance in the only unsegregated commercial sports arena. Like baseball players and Olympic team contestants, they were reported on regularly in the black press, emblematic of success in a segregated society. The only fighter to hold three titles—featherweight, lightweight, and welterweight—Henry Armstrong (12 December 1912–?), born Henry Jackson and called "Hurricane Henry," began his career as "Melody" Jackson in Braddock, Pennsylvania, in 1931, with a third-round knockout. A popular figure in Harlem as its great days were running out, Armstrong was widely admired for his good looks as well as for his prowess in the ring. "Kid Chocolate" or "The Chocolate Kid" or "The Cuban Bon Bon" was born Eligio Sardinias. He was Cuban by birth but usually identified as a black contender in the ring. He began as a newsboy in Havana and quickly became the country's most colorful boxer. He was undefeated in one hundred amateur bouts before winning twenty-one professional bouts by knockout. His first American fight, in New York in 1928, led to more than forty others, also knockouts. He returned to Cuba at the end of the thirties to become a boxing instructor and, until the Castro regime, received a government pension. Alton Bruce Flowers (12 January 1906–?) was a fighter from the age of eighteen, becoming lightweight champion and the first black to appear in Madison Square Garden, in January 1928. "Tiger" Flowers (5 August 1895–16 November 1927) was born Theo but called "The Georgia Deacon." He won his first fight in 1918 and remained undefeated through fifteen more until 1922. In 1926 he became the first black boxer to win the middleweight title, just after completing the quasi-autobiographical movie *The Fighting Deacon*, in which a dollar-a-week delivery boy becomes a highly paid prizefighter. He was knocked out on 12 November 1927 and died following an operation four days later. "The Boston Tar Baby" was born Sam Langford (4 March 1886–12 January 1956), and although he did not win a world title fight, he was one of the great boxers of the period. He lost the Negro heavyweight title in 1919 to Harry Wills and lapsed into obscurity. Al Laney, a sportswriter for the *New York Herald Tribune*, discovered Langford in 1944, destitute and blind in a Harlem tenement, wrote a story about him that brought in $11,000 to secure his last years in some comfort. Harry Wills himself (15 May 1892–21 December 1958) was called "The Black Panther." He cut an imposing figure in the ring for twenty-two years at 220 pounds on a 6'2" frame. He knocked out his first opponent in 1910 and was rarely defeated thereafter. He lost the title, which he had won from Sam Langford on a foul, in 1922 but continued to contend for it in ensuing fights. He challenged white fighter Jack Dempsey on several occasions, but they never met, which caused considerable controversy among fight enthusiasts of both races. Wills retired in 1932 following his last fight—another knockout—to enter the real estate business.

REFERENCES: WWCA, 1933; WWB, 1974. (BK)

BRADFORD, PERRY "MULE" (composer), 14 February c. 1900–20 April 1970. Touring before the twenties with Jeanette Taylor, Perry Bradford got his nickname from a song called "Whoa, Mule," which he sang while she did an eccentric dance with her eyes crossed. Bradford's own first song, "Harlem Blues," was popularized by Mamie Smith* in a Lincoln Theatre* show called *Maid of Harlem* in which both she and Jeanette Taylor were appearing. Until that time Bradford had been playing his blues* at the Colored Vaudeville Benevolent Association Clubroom, encouraged by Will Marion Cook* but without succeeding in interesting any of the record companies. In 1920 the blues were still considered fairly subversive. OKeh recorded Mamie Smith's number as "Crazy Blues," however, and Bradford's success was insured. Before his first royalty check arrived, he was having to borrow a quarter a day for his lunch and transportation to his office in the W. C. Handy Building, where many black musicians had offices. Three months after the record came out, he got a check for $10,001.01. The following year Ethel Waters* sang his "Messin' Around" on the TOBA* circuit, the title of which later served as a whole show with Bradford lyrics. He ran his own publishing house in New York for a time, printing his "Black Bottom" in 1922. In 1923 the number made a sensation in *Dinah*,* vying in popularity with the Charleston as the latest dance craze. Bradford had known the circle dance from his childhood in the South: the performers clapped their hands and crooned while the preacher called out the steps. Bradford's autobiography *Born with the Blues* is not completely accurate in its details;

it is, nevertheless, a very good account of black theatrical life during the first quarter of the century and, furthermore, a lively one.

REFERENCES: Perry Bradford, *Born with the Blues*, 1965; *ASCAP*, 1966; Al Rose, *Eubie Blake*, 1979. (BK)

BRAINSWEAT (play), 1934. John Charles Bronelle wrote a play about Henry Washington, who gives up work for two years so he can philosophize about a mysterious project for making money. Except for Rose McClendon,* the *New York Times* reviewer found the performers crude and the play itself boring and slow. It ran briefly, beginning November 4.

REFERENCE: NYTTR, 1972. (BK)

BRAITHWAITE, WILLIAM STANLEY (critic, poet, and teacher), 6 December 1878–8 June 1962. Upon his father's death William Stanley Braithwaite left Boston public school in his fourth year. Largely self-educated, he nevertheless became a nationally known anthologist (*Anthology of Magazine Verse*, 1913–1929), critic (editorial staff of the *Boston Transcript*), and professor of creative literature at Atlanta University (1934–1945). In addition, he edited collections of Elizabethan (1906), Georgian (1908), and Restoration verse (1909) and wrote poetry, a biography of the Brontë sisters, and an autobiography, *The House Under Arcturus* (1940). Although Braithwaite appears in *The New Negro** through his essay "The Negro in American Literature" and was a friend of W.E.B. Du Bois* and Alain Locke,* he stands on the creative margins of the Harlem Renaissance. He generously praised the novels of Jessie Fauset* (which portray northern middle-class blacks) and was awe-struck by Jean Toomer's* *Cane**: "a book of gold and bronze, of dusk and flame, of ecstasy and pain, and Jean Toomer is a bright morning star of a new day of the race in literature" (p. 44). But most of what appeared violated his moral and aesthetic sensibility. He denounced Claude McKay* as a "violent and angry propagandist" for his militant poem "If We Must Die" and generally believed that the Harlem writers were pandering to sensationalism in an effort to fulfill white expectations. His advice to McKay, and others, was to submit to magazines only those poems that did not identify the poet as black. In his own considerable poetry Braithwaite was racially neutral, many of his readers never aware that he was black.

REFERENCES: William Stanley Braithwaite, "The Negro in American Literature," *The New Negro*, 1925; Benjamin Brawley, *The Negro in Literature and Art in the United States*, 1929; Richard Bardolph, *The Negro Vanguard*, 1959; Arthur P. Davis and Michael W. Peplow, eds., *The New Negro Renaissance*, 1975. (MH)

BRASS ANKLE (play), 1931. The title of Du Bose Heyward's* drama derives from a southern expression used to describe light-skinned Negroes who laid claim to a strain of Indian blood to avoid the taint of being black. In this play, in which the writing was "hysterically inadequate" (NYT, 24 Apr. 1931, p.

26), a "brass ankle" woman learns that one of her grandparents was black when she gives birth to a black child. Rather than admit to this truth she convinces her white racist husband that she has had a black lover, tricking him in the process into killing her and the child. *Brass Ankle* ran for forty-four performances at the Theatre Masque, opening April 23.

REFERENCES: Burns Mantle, 1930–1931; NYTTR, 1972. (BK)

BRAWLEY, BENJAMIN (critic and teacher), 22 April 1882–1 February 1939. Born in Columbia, South Carolina, Benjamin Brawley attended Morehouse College (of which he wrote a history in 1917), the University of Chicago, and Harvard University. He taught English at Howard University, Morehouse, and Shaw University in Raleigh, North Carolina, and was widely recognized in black colleges as the author of many textbooks and biographies and as editor of anthologies. Two of his studies, *A Short History of the American Negro* (1913), and *The Negro in Literature and Art in the United States* (1919, often revised and enlarged), were early efforts to reveal to America the historical and cultural achievements of black Americans. For Brawley, however, the Harlem Renaissance bordered on abomination. He grudgingly applauded Eric Walrond's* *Tropic Death** and praised Claude McKay* for his command of material, although not for his selection of subject; but Langston Hughes's* *Fine Clothes to the Jew** seemed to him almost depraved and Wallace Thurman's* magazine *Fire!!** outrageous and vulgar. In general, Brawley thought the literary treatment of Harlem to be an unwarranted obsession. Genuine creativity and a true literature would emerge only, he believed, when black writers had experienced life in the South. Other relevant works by Brawley were *Social History of the American Negro* (1921); *Negro Genius* (1936); *Negro Builders and Heroes* (1937).

REFERENCES: Benjamin Brawley, *The Negro in Literature and Art in the United States*, rev. eds., 1925, 1929; WWCA, 1933; Carl Van Vechten, *"Keep A-Inchin' Along,"* 1979. (MH)

BRAXTON, WILLIAM E. (artist), 1878-1932. The first Negro expressionist, as William Braxton was sometimes identified, was born in Washington, D.C., and attended Adelphi College. He had little financial success before the Harlem Renaissance and worked as an office boy, a valet, and a Pullman porter, until his figural studies of the black nineteenth-century actor Ira Aldridge and writer Alexander Pushkin brought him some success. He exhibited at the Harmon Foundation* in 1928 and 1929 and during the latter year at the Smithsonian Institution and the National Gallery of Art.

REFERENCES: Cedric Dover, *American Negro Art*, 1960; NA, 1976. (BK).

BRICKTOP. See SMITH, ADA "BRICKTOP."

BRIGGS, CYRIL (journalist), 28 May 1888–? Best known as editor of the New York *Amsterdam News*,* Cyril Briggs began his newspaper career in the

British West Indies at the turn of the century. He founded the African Blood Brotherhood in the early twenties, which eventually grew to 150 branches and claimed 50,000 members who encouraged active resistance against segregation. Briggs backed Marcus Garvey* for a time but later sued him (and won the case) when the black nationalist accused him of being "white" in his attitudes. From 1914 Briggs's powerful voice was heard frequently in his editorials.
REFERENCES: WWCR, 1915; David Levering Lewis, *When Harlem Was in Vogue*, 1981. (BK)

BRIGHT, NELLIE (teacher, writer), c. 1902–1976. Nellie Bright was born in Savannah, Georgia, of parents from the Virgin Islands, and brought up in Philadelphia, where her father served as an Episcopal clergyman. She attended the Philadelphia School of Pedagogy and the University of Pennsylvania before becoming a teacher. With Arthur Huff Fauset,* also in the Philadelphia school system, Nellie Bright was involved in the local black literary publication *Black Opals*,* contributing several poems to it and generally encouraging Philadelphia's modest version of the Harlem Renaissance.
REFERENCE: Vincent Jubilee, "Philadelphia's Afro-American Literary Circle and the Harlem Renaissance," 1980. (BK)

BROOKS, CLARENCE (actor), 1895–? Clarence Brooks was born in Texas and grew up planning to be a dentist (for which he studied briefly at the University of South Carolina), but before he was twenty he had turned to acting. He appeared on Broadway in the 1929 revival of *Porgy*,* but black audiences knew him better for his performances in many films, beginning with *Realization of a Negro's Ambition* in 1916, the first feature of the Lincoln Motion Picture Company.* When Lincoln's leading actor Noble Johnson* left the organization, Brooks replaced him, in *Love of Nature* (1918), *A Man's Duty* (1919), and *By Right of Birth* (1921). He later acted in *Welcome, Strangers* (1924), *Absent* (1928), and *Georgia Rose* (1930). Subsequently, in the brief list of white films that included favorable appearances by black actors, Brooks played the first legitimate role ever assigned to a member of the race. In *Arrowsmith* (1931), based on Sinclair Lewis's novel about the medical profession, Brooks created the first black character in films not consigned either to comic relief or derision, playing a black doctor in the West Indies.
REFERENCES: Donald Bogle, *Toms, Coons, Mulattoes, Mammies, and Bucks*, 1973; Daniel J. Leab, *From Sambo to Superspade*, 1975. (BK)

BROOKS, JONATHAN HENDERSON (poet), 1905-1945. Born in Mississippi, Brooks attended Tougaloo College before entering the ministry. During his high school years he wrote poetry and short stories and won several writing awards. Three of his poems—"The Resurrection," "The Last Quarter Moon

of the Dying Year," and "Paean"—are present in Countee Cullen's* anthology, *Caroling Dusk** (1927). Most of Brooks's writing has a religious emphasis.
REFERENCE: Countee Cullen, ed., *Caroling Dusk*, 1927. (MH)

BROOKS, SHELTON (composer, singer, actor), 4 May 1886–6 September 1975. Shelton Brooks was born in Amesburg, Ontario, but was brought to the United States in 1901. His first theater work was playing gutbucket piano in cafés in Detroit, but by 1911 he was appearing in vaudeville as a single, playing the piano, singing, and doing imitations. His "Bert Williams"* imitation was especially admired, even by Williams. Brooks worked with Danny Small's Hot Harlem Band as a trap drummer, played in Ken Murray's *Blackouts* for two years, and appeared in the Panama Amusement Company's productions in Chicago of *Canary Cottage* and *September Morn* (1920). In New York he played in *Miss Nobody from Starland* (1920), *K of P* (1923), and Lew Leslie's* *Blackbirds** (1926) and with Florence Mills* in *Dixie to Broadway** (1925). He produced and performed in *Nifties of 1928*; made the vitaphone short *Gayety* in 1929; and performed with "Bird" Allen on CBS radio, billed as Egg and Shell, in 1930. Brooks himself introduced his most famous song, "Some of These Days," at the Majestic Theatre in Chicago in 1910, but Sophie Tucker soon made it her personal specialty. "Darktown Strutters' Ball" (1915) was inspired by a social gathering Brooks attended during the San Francisco Exposition. For Al Jolson, Brooks wrote "You Ain't Talkin' to Me" and "Honey Gal," and among his other popular songs were "Walkin' the Dog," "Jean," and "If I Were a Bee and You Were a Red Red Rose." Brooks died in Los Angeles at the age of eighty-nine.
REFERENCES: Sigmund Spaeth, *A History of Popular Music in America*, 1948; ASCAP, 1980; BB, 1980. (DA)

BROTHERHOOD OF SLEEPING CAR PORTERS   (union), 1925–   .
U.S. Assistant Attorney Perry W. Howard threatened that the railroads would employ Filipinos as porters if black workers tried to organize, in a thwarted attempt to intimidate them. The Brotherhood of Sleeping Car Porters, with strong support from A. Philip Randolph* and *The Messenger,* was founded in 1925 to fight for a 240-hour working month and for more humane conditions. It was the most widely discussed of the black unions, serving as an example for other trade unions in bringing some public dignity to Afro-Americans. The new Pullman porter followed a "creed of independence without insolence; courtesy without fawning; service without servility," and his slogan was "Opportunity not alms," according to Randolph's editorial in *The Messenger* (quoted in Vincent, *Voices of a Black Nation*, p. 236). By 1930 the organization had invited Filipino porters to join for mutual security.
REFERENCES: Theodore G. Vincent, ed., *Voices of a Black Nation*, 1973; Jervis Anderson, *This Was Harlem*, 1982. (BK)

BROWN, ADA (singer), 1 May 1890–31 March 1950. Known as "The Queen of the Blues," Ada Brown came from a musical family and began singing as a child in churches in Kansas City. With a full, rich, and mellow voice, she is said to have sung in clubs in Paris and Berlin during her teens and by 1910 was singing in the Pekin Theatre in Chicago. She had an active career as a blues* singer during the twenties and thirties, playing theater dates steadily on both coasts and recording in Chicago and St. Louis. She toured with Flournoy Miller* and Aubrey Lyles's* *Step on It* in 1922 and with *Struttin' Time* in 1924. She performed at the Lafayette Theatre* in *Plantation Days* (1927), *Bandannaland* (1928), and *Tan Town Tamales* (1930). "Bulging and joyous, she sings the house down repeatedly in 'When a Black Man's Blue' and 'Betty Lou,' " Brooks Atkinson wrote of her performance in *Brown Buddies*￼* with Bill Robinson* at the Liberty in 1930 (NYT, 8 Oct., 1930, p. 29). After *Jangleland* (1931) and *Going to Town* (1932), she appeared at the Apollo Theatre* in *Hawaiian Moon* and *Jungle Drums* in 1934. Brown was one of the incorporators of the Negro Actors Guild of America in 1936. In the late thirties she sang with the Fletcher Henderson* Orchestra in Chicago and at the London Palladium. She sang "That Ain't Right" with Fats Waller* in the 1943 film *Stormy Weather*. After performing in *Memphis Bound* in New York with Bill Robinson* in 1945, Brown retired from music and returned to Kansas City.
REFERENCES: NYTTR, 1972; WWJ, 1978; BWW, 1979. (PO)

BROWN, E. C. (theatrical entrepreneur), ?–? Born in Philadelphia, E. C. Brown began a long and successful career in business, first as a stenographer for the National Railway Company; then as a real estate salesman in Newport News, Virginia; and then as a banker in his hometown by 1915. In 1919, with A. F. Stevens, he purchased the Quality Amusement Company, which controlled the Lafayette Theatre* and the Lafayette Players Stock Company* in New York, with ancillary groups and theaters in Washington, D.C., Chicago, Pittsburgh, and Philadelphia. Under Brown's control, Alex Rogers* and C. Luckeyth Roberts* produced *Baby Blues* at the Lafayette in 1919, in which Wash sells his father's property so he can afford to get married; *An African Prince* in 1920, in which a man gets rich raising hogs, goes to Harlem to get his daughters into society and to buy himself a government nomination as African consul, gets duped, and goes home to his hogs; and a revival in 1921 of *My Friend from Kentucky*, a successful black musical comedy that had played at the Lafayette in 1913.
REFERENCE: BB, 1980. (BK)

BROWN, HALLIE QUINN (educator), 10 March 1849?–16 September 1949. Although her date of birth is unsubstantiated, Hallie Quinn Brown lived to be at least a hundred years old and perhaps four years beyond that. Born in Pennsylvania of freed slaves, she was connected with Wilberforce University for most of her life, first as a student graduating in the 1873 class of six with a bachelor

of science degree and afterward as professor of elocution. The school awarded her an honorary master of science degree in 1890 and an honorary LL.D. in 1936. Before the turn of the century, she had taught in Mississippi, South Carolina, and in Ohio where she began a night school for adult migrant workers. She toured Europe to raise funds for Wilberforce and served briefly as "Lady Principal" at Tuskegee Institute. As president of the National Association for Colored Women, she was responsible for securing preservation of the Frederick Douglass House in Washington, D.C. In 1924 she spoke at the Republican National Convention on behalf of Warren Harding's nomination and civil rights, probably the first black woman to make such a public appearance. Hallie Quinn Brown was widely respected for her work with elocution, public speaking, and the formation of women's clubs for Afro-Americans across the country. Her books usually purport to be about elocution, but more often they speak on behalf of the virtues of a Christian life. She wrote several books, among them a few relevant to the Harlem Renaissance: *Our Women: Past, Present, and Future* and *Tales My Father Told Me* (1925), *Homespun Heroines and Women of Distinction* (1926), and *Pen Pictures of Pioneers at Wilberforce* (1937).
REFERENCES: NAW, 1971; AWW, 1979. (BK)

BROWN, IDA G. (entertainer), 1900–? Ida Brown first appeared onstage at the Lafayette Theatre* in 1919 in a show called *Baby Blues*. Afterward, she carried the title as a nickname during her brief career as a popular singer and dancer on the black theater circuit. She performed in many Lafayette shows: *This and That, Broadway Rastus, Sultan Sam,* and *Alabama Bound*, all in 1920, and later at the Lincoln* and Alhambra* theaters.
REFERENCE: BWW, 1979. (BK)

BROWN, JAMES W. (clergyman), 19 July 1872–? Born in North Carolina, James Brown attended Shaw and Lincoln universities. As a minister of the Mother Zion African Methodist Episcopal Church, first on West 89th Street, then on West 136th Street, and finally in 1925 on West 137th Street, the Reverend Brown denounced liquor from the pulpit. Harlem's cabarets thrived, of course, on the bootleg traffic.
REFERENCE: Jervis Anderson, *This Was Harlem*, 1982. (BK)

BROWN, LAWRENCE (pianist, composer, singer), 29 August 1893–25 December 1972. Lawrence Brown, a native of Jacksonville, Florida, accompanied Roland Hayes* on his concert tours to Europe in the early 1920s. In London, he met Paul Robeson,* who was playing in *Taboo** with Mrs. Patrick Campbell, and the two young men discovered their mutual interest in spirituals* and Negro folk music. According to Carl Van Vechten,* who was instrumental in promoting their first recitals together in New York, Brown's feelings of race pride had been aroused when he heard the recitalist Povla Frizsh sing Ernest Bloch's Psalm settings, in which the composer had "tried to express the soul of the Jewish people as I feel it'' (*"Keep A-Inchin' Along,"* p. 155). Brown was determined to devote his professional life to performing the music of his own people. In New York a few years later he and Robeson prepared a program of spirituals and songs by black composers, which they presented at the Greenwich Village Theatre in April 1925. Brown sang along with Robeson in some of the songs, to the delight of the audience; Van Vechten described Brown's small tenor voice as "quite adequate to the uses to which he puts it, and his spirit in the responses is so accurately just that the effect of Robeson's singing is doubly enhanced by his vital cooperation'' (*"Keep A-Inchin' Along,"* p. 157). Brown's vocal contributions as well as his piano accompaniments may be heard on many of the recordings he made with Robeson, among them "Joshua Fit the Battle of Jericho," "Ezekial Saw the Wheel," "Every Time I Feel the Spirit," and Van Vechten's favorite, "Little David, Play on Your Harp." Brown and Robeson performed together for almost forty years.

REFERENCES: *Black Perspectives in Music,* Fall 1973; Carl Van Vechten, *"Keep A-Inchin' Along,"* 1979. (DA)

BROWN, [LILLIAN] LILLYN (entertainer), 24 April 1885–8 June 1969. "Lillyn" Brown, as she was known, began touring early, sometimes appearing in drag. She was associated with blues* singing at the Lincoln Theatre,* but during the period of popularity for black revues she moved on to Broadway for *Dixie to Broadway,** in 1924. She toured again after that and in 1930 reappeared in New York in *Queen at Home.* Her rich contralto was especially effective in transmitting the blues to a wider audience.

REFERENCE: BWW, 1979. (BK)

BROWN, STERLING A. (writer, teacher), 1 May 1901–   . Sterling Brown may be considered the folk poet of the New Negro Renaissance, although he did not live in Harlem and *Southern Road,* his first book, was not published until 1932. He was born and raised in Washington, D.C., the son of a former slave from eastern Tennessee who became a distinguished minister and professor of theology at Howard University. He attended Dunbar High School in Washington, D.C., and then graduated from Williams College (Phi Beta Kappa) in 1923. The following year he received the M.A. from Harvard where he returned for graduate study in English, 1931–1932. He taught at various colleges before beginning his forty-year tenure at Howard University in 1929. From 1936 until 1939 he was editor of Negro affairs for the Federal Writers' Project as well as a member of the Carnegie-Mydral Study of the Negro. In addition, he was literary editor of *Opportunity** for many years and wrote monthly reviews of new books. In *Southern Road,* he created numerous black folk characters and revealed his understanding and appreciation for black music, especially spirituals,* blues,* jazz, and work songs. His best-known critical works include *Negro Poetry and Drama* (1937), *The Negro in American Fiction* (1937), and *The Negro Caravan* (coedited with Arthur P. Davis and Ulysses Lee in 1941). His

Collected Poems, edited by Michael Harper, appeared in 1980. He has written numerous articles on black literature and folk culture like "A Century of Negro Portraiture in American Literature" (1966). In addition to emphasizing black folk literature, Sterling Brown has "through his many lectures all over the nation, his critical essays and books, and his personal contact with young black writers— probably done more than any other one person to influence and direct the course of Negro American writing," in the view of Arthur P. Davis and J. Saunders Redding (*Cavalcade*, p. 400).
REFERENCES: Arthur P. Davis and J. Saunders Redding, eds., *Cavalcade*, 1971; Richard Barksdale and Keneth Kinnamon, *Black Writers of America*, 1972; Arthur P. Davis, *From the Dark Tower*, 1974; Sterling Brown, *Collected Poems*, 1980. (DI)

BROWN BUDDIES (musical comedy), 1930. Many people contributed to the success of this show about black World War I soldiers in France: Carl Rickman wrote the book; Joe Jordan, Millard Thomas, Shelton Brooks,* J. Rosamond Johnson,* Porter Grainger,* and Leigh Whipper* supplied the lyrics and music; and Bill "Bojangles" Robinson* starred, wearing his arm in a sling because he had been "wounded in a chivalric encounter with the Pittsburgh police," according to the review in the *New York Times* (8 Oct. 1930, p. 29). As usual in black musicals, the plot was superrogatory: soldiers from East St. Louis are followed to France by their girl friends masquerading as YMCA entertainers. The dancing, at "a ruinous pace," kept the show running, however, for 111 performances at the Liberty Theatre, beginning October 7. The *Times* reviewer continued: "It has the exuberance of its race, it dances with carnival wildness, and some of the tunes are appropriately blue. . . . Dancing, which is never lovely and never studied, but bubbling with animal spirits, is the black blood of 'Brown Buddies.' "
REFERENCES: Burns Mantle, 1929-1930; NYTTR, 1972. (BK)

BROWNIES' BOOK (children's magazine), 1921-1922. W.E.B. Du Bois* conducted the production of a magazine for black children, *Brownies' Book*, but the actual editing was carried out by Jessie Fauset* in her capacity as literary editor and Augustus Granville Dill* in his capacity as business manager of *The Crisis.** Five issues carried contributions by Langston Hughes,* but the magazine was not otherwise notable for its content.
REFERENCES: CVV; JWJ. (BK)

BROWNING, IVAN HAROLD (actor), 1891–4 June 1978. Born in Texas, Ivan Browning became a member of the Exposition Four in 1915, first touring in vaudeville under that name and, later, as the Four Harmony Kings. He played the romantic lead, opposite Lottie Gee,* in *Shuffle Along** in 1921, probably the first openly romantic activity between black actors on stage. In 1924 he played the lead in *Chocolate Dandies,** and afterward he toured Europe with

the Four Harmony Kings until 1933. Then in his forties, Browning became a minor actor in films.
REFERENCE: BB, 1980 (BK)

BRUCE, JOHN EDWARD (journalist), 22 February 1856–7 August 1924. A militant black journalist and one of the earliest black nationalists, John Bruce was born a slave in Piscataway, Maryland. After his mother and he were freed in 1860, he lived primarily in Washington, D.C., until the turn of the century when he moved to Albany, New York, before settling in New York City. Although he had a limited formal education, Bruce was extremely well read and wrote prolifically on a wide variety of political and cultural subjects. In 1911 he and his friend Arthur A. Schomburg* organized the Negro Society for Historical Research (the predecessor of the Association for the Study of Negro Life and History,* formed in 1915), which collected many valuable sources used by the black writers and intellectuals of the 1920s. An editor before he was twenty-five, Bruce was a popular contributor to the black press for more than fifty years. Under the pseudonym of "Bruce Grit" he extolled the virtues and beauty of the black race and its heritage, demanded full equality with whites, and urged his readers to avoid integration with a white race he considered bigoted, untrustworthy, and savage. In 1919, after hearing Marcus Garvey* echo Bruce's earlier views on race pride and destiny, Bruce joined the United Negro Improvement Association (UNIA)* and wrote a regular column for Garvey's paper *Negro World.* Garvey appointed Bruce "Duke of Uganda," and when Bruce died in 1924—the first of Garvey's "royalty" to do so—he was accorded a highly memorable sendoff, with three memorial services and a funeral march attended by more than 5,000 UNIA members and foreign black dignitaries dressed in full Garvey regalia. Because Bruce ignored white society and excoriated the views of Booker T. Washington, W.E.B. Du Bois,* and their followers, he has been given little notice by black and white historians. Yet along with T. Thomas Fortune,* he was probably the most respected black journalist of his era.
REFERENCE: Peter Gilbert, ed., *The Selected Writings of John Edward Bruce,* 1971. (DS)

BRYMM, J. TIM (musician), c. 1895–3 October 1946. A Clef Club* rival of James Reese Europe,* Tim Brymm was one of the Seventy Black Devils of the 350th Field Artillery Band during World War I. He made his name through "A Military Symphony Engaged in a Battle of Jazz," but whether this composition was his or an amalgamation has not been ascertained. Before the war he had studied at the National Conservatory with Anton Dvořák, and after it, he began playing regularly in New York. His own orchestra was heard first at the Casino Theatre in May 1919 and later in a number of other locales. Among his compositions are "Camel Walk" and "Zulu Babe," and he wrote other songs with W. C. Handy* and Bert Williams.*
REFERENCES: NYT, 4 Oct. 1946; WWJ, 1972. (BK)

BUBBLE ALONG (musical comedy), 1930. *Bubble Along* at the Garrick Theatre was as derivative as its title, ''a shadowy and nondescript entertainment not
worth the burnt cork fetched to meet the occasion,'' according to the *New York
Times* (3 June 1930, p. 27). Moreover, the dancers were ''enthusiastically out
of step.'' The reviewer listed no authors for this piece, nor cast, since no program
was available. Presumably, it closed immediately.
REFERENCE: NYTTR, 1972. (BK)

BUBBLES, JOHN [JOHN WILLIAM SUBLETT] (dancer), 19 February
1902– . At the age of nine John Sublett convinced his family to move from
Louisville to Indianapolis to further his theatrical career. A year later he was a
star attraction at the Crown Theatre there, and by the time he was seventeen he
had moved to New York with his partner Ford Lee Washington (16 October
1903–?), who became ''Buck'' to his ''Bubbles.'' In 1923, by which time Sublett
had legally adopted Washington, they were billed as ''world famous entertainers'' when they appeared in *Raisin' Cain.** Before their success, they had worked
together as jockeys, janitors, dishwashers, carnival dancers, and even as bat
boys for the Louisville Colonels Baseball Team. Buck and Bubbles was the first
black team to play the Palace Theatre in New York, and they also appeared on
Broadway in *Blackbirds [*] of 1928* and later in some annual editions of the
Ziegfeld Follies. Both of them acted in *Porgy and Bess** in 1935, although not
as a team; Sublett played Sportin' Life. Later, Buck and Bubbles moved to
Hollywood to make a number of Pathé comedies. At the age of eighty, although
confined to a wheelchair, Bubbles was still giving tap-dancing lessons to aspiring
young performers.
REFERENCES: BB, 1980; Hatch-Billops. (BK)

BUCK AND BUBBLES. See BUBBLES, JOHN [JOHN WILLIAM SUBLETT].

BURCH, CHARLES EATON (educator), 14 July 1891–23 March 1948.
Widely recognized as one of the century's leading Defoe scholars, Charles Burch
came to the United States from Bermuda at an early age to study at Wilberforce
University, Columbia University, and Ohio State University, receiving the Ph.D.
in literature from Ohio State. Subsequently, he taught in the English departments
of Tuskegee, Wilberforce, and Howard and was responsible, perhaps, for in-
stituting the first course in the American university system known as ''Poetry
and Prose of Negro Life.'' He began teaching this initial ''black literature''
course during the Harlem Renaissance.
REFERENCE: DANB, 1982. (BK)

BURGOYNE, OLLIE (dancer), 1885–? Although most of her work was in
Europe, Ollie Burgoyne had a brief popular success in New York in 1923 when
she appeared in the show *Follow Me*. This Chicago-born dancer had toured

Europe from the age of six, specializing a few years later in Brazilian and Spanish dances and in a celebrated "snake dance." Like many other talented performers, however, she was more comfortable in Europe than in segregated New York, and after her brief appearance in the midtwenties and another with the Negro Art Theatre* in 1930, Ollie Burgoyne moved permanently to Russia and opened a lingerie shop there.
REFERENCE: BB, 1980. (BK)

BURKE, GEORGIA [GRACIE MALDELL BURKE] (actress), 27 February 1906– . Georgia Burke was born in Georgia and attended Claflin College and New York University before going into show business. She acted in *Blackbirds [*] of 1928*; *Ol' Man Satan*,* *Five Star Final, Savage Rhythm*,* and in two serious dramas of the period, *In Abraham's Bosom** and *They Shall Not Die*.* Subsequently, she played the maid on the popular radio soap opera "When a Girl Marries."
REFERENCE: BEWW, 1966. (BK)

BURLEIGH, ALSTON (musician, actor), ?–? The son of Harry T. Burleigh,* Alston was educated in England and at Howard University. After a stint with the Lafayette Players* in a number of productions between 1918 and 1920, he played with Charles Gilpin* in the Provincetown Playhouse production of *The Emperor Jones** in 1920. Later, Burleigh appeared in *In Abraham's Bosom** and *Harlem** as a featured player, and he sang in the choruses of *Blackbirds [*] of 1928*, *Hot Chocolates*,* and other shows, all between 1926 and 1930. In 1931 he became head of the music and drama department of Virginia State College in Petersburg.
REFERENCE: BB, 1980. (BK)

BURLEIGH, HARRY THACKER (singer, composer), 2 December 1866–12 September 1949. Burleigh received little formal musical training in his native Erie, Pennsylvania, but nevertheless won a scholarship to attend the National Conservatory of Music in New York in 1892. There he studied voice and played double bass and timpani in the orchestra and in his second year became acquainted with the director of the school, Anton Dvořák. Dvořák was interested in Burleigh's singing of spirituals* and Negro songs, since he planned to incorporate American folk themes into his *Symphony from the New World*. Of his work with Dvořák, Burleigh wrote: "I myself, while never a student of Dvořák, not being far enough advanced at that time to be in his classes, was constantly associated with him during the two years he taught in the National Conservatory in New York. I sang our Negro songs for him very often and, before he wrote his own themes, he filled himself with the spirit of the old Spirituals. I also helped to copy parts of the original score" (*Music on the Air*, p. 188).

In 1894 Burleigh was appointed baritone soloist at St. George's Episcopal Church in New York, a post he held for nearly forty years, and in 1900 he joined the choir of Temple Emanu-El in New York, where he sang for twenty-five years. He concertized in Europe and America and sang in the Coleridge-Taylor Festival performances of *Hiawatha* in Washington, D.C., and again in concerts with Samuel Coleridge-Taylor in Chicago in 1906.

Burleigh joined the music publishing firm of Ricordi and Sons in New York in 1900 as editor and arranger. He composed more than ninety ballads and art songs, more than fifty choral pieces, and a number of piano and violin pieces, and he made approximately fifty arrangements of spirituals for solo voice and piano. He made the arrangements of many of the musical examples in H. E. Krehbiel's *Afro-American Folksongs** (1914), and his *Jubilee Songs of the United States of America* (1916), which included the immortal ''Deep River,'' included the first folk-song arrangements in the manner of fine art songs. In 1929 he published *Old Songs Hymnal*, simple arrangements of Negro songs for the use of nonprofessionals. He was a charter member of ASCAP when it was founded in 1914, and in 1941 became the first black to serve on the Board of Directors. Burleigh was awarded the Spingarn Medal* in 1917, received honorary degrees from Atlanta University and Howard University, and had an organization named after him, the Harry T. Burleigh Association, in Indiana, which was devoted to the performance of Negro music.
REFERENCES: H. T. Burleigh, ''The Negro and His Song,'' *Music on the Air*, ed. Hazel Gertrude Kinscella, 1934; John Tasker Howard, *Our American Music*, 1965; MBA, 1971. (DA)

BURLIN, NATALIE CURTIS (musicologist), 26 April 1875–23 October 1921. A pioneer in the field of ethnomusicology, Natalie Curtis Burlin had originally studied to become a concert pianist in her native New York City and in Berlin. After a trip to Arizona in 1900, however, she became interested in Indian culture and its preservation. She convinced President Theodore Roosevelt to remove the ban on the singing of native songs in government schools that had been instituted in the hope of assimilating Indians into the white culture, and that in turn had made the Indians reluctant to permit her to record them. She studied the history and lore and recorded the music of eighteen tribes in the United States, primarily in the Southwest, and in 1907 published *The Indians' Book*, a compilation of folklore, poetry, beliefs, and 200 annotated songs. Her interest in Negro music led her to establish, with white violinist David Mannes, the Music School Settlement for Colored People in Harlem in 1911. To raise funds for the school she organized a concert by black musicians, highly unusual for the period, which was held at Carnegie Hall in March 1914 and introduced the singer Roland Hayes.* To transcribe Negro music undistorted by commercialization, Burlin studied at Hampton Institute and in 1919 published a four-volume collection of songs and spirituals,* *Hampton Series Negro Folk-Songs*. She also recorded the songs and lore of two African students at Hampton, which she published as *Songs and Tales from the Dark Continent* in 1920. She died

at the age of forty-six in a traffic accident in Paris, where she was attending an arts conference.
REFERENCE: NAW, 1980. (PO)

BURNS, SANDY (entertainer), 1884–? Sandy Burns travelled with opera companies and circuses from an early age and then appeared in vaudeville with Irvin C. Miller* and others. He went into partnership with Sam Russell to form a company in 1922, without any title other than "Sandy and Sam," in which they toured widely, Burns playing a one-legged veteran of the Spanish-American War who recruited soldiers. Inevitably, the humor was racially stereotypical, and the actors were obliged to appear in blackface to get work.
REFERENCE: BB, 1980. (BK)

BUSH, ANITA (actress, entrepreneuse), 1883–16 February 1974. A pioneer in the development of the black theater, Anita Bush organized her own performing company in 1915. Her role models were Edna and Cecile Spooner, of the Spooner Sisters Dramatic Company, whom she had seen as a child. Growing up in Brooklyn, the daughter of a tailor who made costumes for the Bijou Theatre near her home, Bush watched performances and met the actors and, after performing small parts herself, decided on a career in the theater by the time she was thirteen. She joined the Williams and Walker Players in 1903 and toured the vaudeville circuit, appearing in *In Dahomey, Abyssinia,* and *Mr. Lode of Koal,* and played in England for a year with *In Dahomey.* When the troupe was disbanded in 1910, Bush organized her own vaudeville touring troupe, "The Hula Hula Dancers." Two years later she returned to New York and, when an injury forced her to give up dancing, organized the Anita Bush Players. The troupe toured the vaudeville circuit, performing dramatic sketches inspired by the Old West. In 1914 the company appeared at the Lincoln Theatre* in New York in the long-running *The Girl at the Fort,* with Charles Gilpin* as the leading man and Dooley Wilson* in a supporting role. Around 1916 Bush moved her company to the Lafayette Theatre* but sold it shortly thereafter due to financial difficulties, and the name was changed to the Lafayette Players Stock Company.* For her roles in two black-cast films, *The Crimson Skull* and *The Bull Doggers,* in 1921 and 1922, Bush renewed her interest in the Old West by learning to shoot, lasso, and ride cowponies. She appeared in the black musical *Swing It* in 1938 and *Androcles and the Lion* in 1939, both productions of the WPA Federal Theatre Project. Bush was executive secretary of the Negro Actors Guild for many years and in 1971 appeared on television in *Free Time.*
REFERENCES: NYT, 19 Feb. 1974; DBPA, 1974; BBW, 1977. (PO)

C

CALLOWAY, BLANCHE (entertainer), c. 1904– . Always overshadowed by her brother Cab Calloway,* Blanche Calloway nevertheless had a successful career. She was born in Baltimore and attended Morgan State College there, but she dropped out to begin performing in local musical revues. She was a featured singer at New York's Ciro Club and in a Chicago show called *Plantation Days*, both during the twenties. In 1931 she formed her own band, Blanche Calloway's Joy Boys, and toured extensively—a single and most glamorous woman surrounded by a group of handsome musicians, elegantly outfitted. In 1938 she filed for bankruptcy, when the vogue for Harlem had passed, and settled in Philadelphia to become active in democratic politics. In later years she founded Afram House, a cosmetics firm, and she served as executive director of WMBM and as disc jockey for WFEC, Miami radio stations.
REFERENCES: BWW, 1979; EBA, 1981. (BK)

CALLOWAY, [CABELL] CAB (singer, bandleader), 25 December 1907– . Cab Calloway was born in Rochester, New York, but raised in Baltimore, where he studied music and voice and first sang in a quartet, the Baltimore Melody Boys. His sister Blanche Calloway* got him into a touring company of *Plantation Days* as a replacement for the first tenor in a vocal quartet. When the company returned to Chicago, Calloway enrolled as a prelaw student at Crane College but soon left to perform at Dreamland Cabaret as drummer and vocalist, and from there he went to the Sunset Cafe where he headed the band The Albanians. He went to New York with this band in 1929, but they flunked their first test at the Savoy Ballroom,* and Calloway left to join Andy Preer's old band The Missourians. When this band filled in for Duke Ellington* at the Cotton Club,* Calloway's energetic conducting, singing, and onstage clowning were a great success. He was hired away briefly by the rival Plantation Club,* which led to the wrecking of that establishment by hired thugs from the mob-owned Cotton Club. He returned to the Cotton Club with his orchestra and played there regularly until 1932. Audiences cheered his singing of "Minnie the Moocher" and his break-away "Hi-de-hi-de-ho" became a national catch phrase. The phrase has been compared to the " 'speaking in tongues' of the slaves during their ring shouts," but its catchy rhythm and endless comic variations suggest that it was more a parody of call-and-answer work songs (Hughes and Meltzer, *Black Magic*, p. 88). Calloway and his band visited England in 1934, and throughout the thirties and early forties they toured the United States and Canada as one of the top ten most popular and highest earning bands in the country. He appeared in many of the shows and revues originating in nightclubs and played Sportin' Life in the revival of *Porgy and Bess** in 1952. Later he toured with the *Harlem Globetrotters Show* and in the late sixties starred in *Hello Dolly* with Pearl Bailey. His films include *The Big Broadcast* (1933), *International House* (1933), *The Singing Kid* (1936), *Stormy Weather* (1943), *Sensations of 1945* and *St. Louis Blues* (1958). *The Cab Calloway Hepster's Dictionary*, a compendium of jive terms, written with Ned Williams, appeared in 1938. His autobiography, *Of Minnie the Moocher and Me*, was published in 1976.

REFERENCES: Langston Hughes and Milton Meltzer, *Black Magic*, 1967; Cab Calloway, *Of Minnie the Moocher and Me*, 1976; Jim Haskins, *The Cotton Club*, 1977; WWJ, 1978; Jervis Anderson, *This Was Harlem*, 1982. (DA)

CALVIN, FLOYD [JOSEPH] (journalist), 13 July 1902–1 September 1939. Floyd Calvin was born in Arkansas and attended City College in New York in the early twenties. He served as associate editor for *The Messenger,** 1922-1923, and the following year became the New York editor of the *Pittsburgh Courier.** He held that position until 1927 and then became special features editor. His syndicated column ran in several black publications, and he was responsible for establishing Calvin's News Service.

REFERENCES: WWCA, 1933; NYT, 2 Sept. 1939. (BK)

CAMPBELL, [CORNELIUS C.] DICK (actor, publicist), 27 June 1903–   . Long active in a number of theatrical ventures during the Harlem Renaissance and afterward, Dick Campbell was born in Texas. He attended Long Island University and Paul Quinn College. Early in his career he performed at the Cotton Club* and Small's Paradise,* in the choruses of *Blackbirds [*] of 1928* and *Hot Chocolates,** and in 1934 in John Bronelle's well-intentioned failure *Brainsweat,** with Rose McClendon.* Later, Campbell cofounded the Rose McClendon Players (1937-1941), served as executive director of the Symphony of the New World, and American National Theater Association (ANTA) representative to Africa, and was active in the American Negro Theatre as a publicist. He was married to the actress Muriel Rahn. In 1970 he was awarded the Harold Jackman* Memorial Award.

REFERENCE: Loften Mitchell, ed., *Voices of the Black Theatre*, 1975. (BK)

CAMPELL, E[LMER] SIMMS (artist, illustrator, cartoonist), 2 January 1906-27 January 1971. Harem girls and their fat sheik, glamour girls with sugar daddies, irate priests and black choirboys, and a bug-eyed "Esky" with a walrus moustache were familiar cartoon figures during the thirties in *Esquire*, all creations of E. Simms Campbell. He studied under the German artist Georg Grosz and at the Chicago Art Institute, and during the last years of the twenties his work appeared in *Judge* and the *New Yorker* as well as in *Opportunity** and *The Crisis.** Campbell rarely dealt with black subject matter, but in later years he delineated the Harlem Renaissance in a series of handsome paintings and cogent essays in *Esquire*: "Home of Happy Feet" and "Blues Are the Negro's Lament," for example. His work was first exhibited in Minneapolis where he had been born, when he was eighteen years old, and five years later the Harmon Foundation* hung some of his paintings. For the ensuing forty years he was one of the country's most successful cartoonists and illustrators. He lived in Switzerland for some time and in New York State.
REFERENCES: *Esquire*, 1934–1938; NYT, 28 Jan. 1971. (BK)

CANE (book), 1923. Jean Toomer's* first book, a gathering and melding of several pieces published in various literary journals, is a series of vignettes, poems, and a concluding prose drama unified through the color and music of its language. The first two sections—six vignettes of rural southern black women and several fragments of northern urban black males—function as cultural tableaus juxtaposed in dramatic tension. The third section, "Kabnis," unifies and gives motion to the first two sections that have been held, as yet, in dramatic suspension, orchestrating and fusing their dramatic juxtaposition. Fear and innocence frame the action as Kabnis, a northern black schoolteacher and would-be poet, journeys south to rural Georgia in an effort to discover and express its meaning. Moral failure is the result as Kabnis is unable to accept, in the cellar of Halsey's workshop, the moral challenge of the past. His despair and his retreat into self-mockery contrast with the person of young Carrie Kate who embraces old Father John while the sun rises from its cradle like a "gold-glowing child . . . and sends a birthsong slanting down gray dust streets and sleepy windows of the southern town" (p. 116). *Cane*, first published by Harper and Brothers in 1923, really the first book of the Harlem Renaissance, is Toomer's own profoundly personal quest as well as his spiritual and aesthetic vision of what black Americans were and were about to become. (MH)

CAROLINA MAGAZINE (periodical), 1844– . The official literary publication of the students of the University of North Carolina devoted its May 1928 issue entirely to writing by black contributors. Lewis Alexander* assembled the materials, beginning with "The Message of the Negro Poets" by Alain Locke * (after James Weldon Johnson's* introduction to *The Book of American Negro Poetry** in 1922, the best essay on the subject as well as an updated one). Charles S. Johnson* contributed an essay on the lyrics to jazz and blues.* The rest of the issue was made up of poems by Langston Hughes,* Waring Cuney,* Lewis Alexander, Sterling A. Brown,* Arna Bontemps,* Edward Silvera,* Jessie Fauset,* Mae V. Cowdery,* Carrie W. Clifford, Nellie R. Bright,* Angelina W. Grimké,* John F. Matheus,* Georgia Douglas Johnson,* James H. Young, Alice Dunbar Nelson,* and Donald Jeffrey Hayes,* some represented by a single selection, others by several. Allan R. Freelon* contributed a pen and ink drawing. The April 1929 issue of *Carolina Magazine* was devoted to four plays by black writers: "The Idle Head" by Willis Richardson,* "Black Damp" by John F. Matheus, "Scratches" by May Sullivan Miller,* and "Undertow" by Eulalie Spence.* (BK)

CAROLING DUSK (anthology), 1927. Countee Cullen* edited "An Anthology of Verse by Negro Poets" five years after James Weldon Johnson's* *Book of American Negro Poetry** appeared in 1922. Johnson had concluded his collection with a handful of poems by members of the younger generation, but the rise of the Harlem Renaissance extended that list in Cullen's collection by nearly two dozen writers. The movement had "awakened to a happy articulation many young Negro poets who had hitherto lisped only in isolated places in solitary numbers," Cullen observed in his foreword to *Caroling Dusk* (p. x). Each writer's group of poems commenced with a detailed biographical—often auto-biographical—note supplying not only professional statistics but often cogent observations about the nature of black poetry and the Harlem Renaissance. Naturally, the collection commenced with work by Paul Laurence Dunbar, whose turn-of-the-century dialect pieces generally mark the advent of a modern, self-aware black literature; it concluded with some poems by nine-year-old Lula Lowe Weeden, a Lynchburg, Virginia, girl. In between, Cullen included substantial selections of representative poems by virtually every poet included in this dictionary.
REFERENCE: Countee Cullen, "Foreword," *Caroling Dusk*, 1927.

CARTER, [BENNET LESTER] BENNY (saxophonist), 8 August 1907–   .
Benny Carter was born in New York, of musical parents. At seventeen, he was playing with June Clark's band and with Billy Paige's Broadway Syncopatos at the Capitol Theatre. He gave up music briefly, a year or so later, to study for the ministry at Wilberforce University, but he seems to have stayed only long enough to join Horace Henderson's Collegians. Later, he played briefly with the orchestras of Duke Ellington* and Fletcher Henderson,* and in 1928 he organized his own orchestra for the Arcadia Ballroom. In 1931 he joined McKinney's Cotton Pickers* and followed that engagement with a long and active career writing film scores, notably for *And Then There Were None* and *The Snows of Kilimanjaro*.
REFERENCE: WWJ, 1972. (BK)

CARTER, ELMER A[NDERSON] (journalist, sociologist), 19 July 1890–16 January 1973. Elmer A. Carter was born in Rochester, New York, and attended Harvard University. He summarized his own career when he retired from the State Division of Human Rights in 1961, quoted in his *New York Times* obituary: "Perhaps it is now safe to say that the old economic custom under which the Negro was the last to be hired and the first to be fired may be passing" (17 Jan. 1973, p. 42). Throughout a long career Carter advocated equal opportunities in employment, housing, and public accommodation. In 1928 he succeeded Charles S. Johnson* as editor of *Opportunity** for which he had written for several years, and he served in that position until 1937. At that time Governor Herbert H. Lehman appointed Carter a member of the Unemployment Insurance Appeals Board.
REFERENCES: Arna Bontemps, ed., *The Harlem Renaissance Remembered*, 1972; NYT, 17 Jan. 1973. (BK)

CARVER, GEORGE WASHINGTON (educator), c. 1861–5 January 1943. Although always associated with an earlier period, George Washington Carver lived well past the Harlem Renaissance. Born of slaves, he was reared by his mother's owner in Missouri. Carver worked his way through Iowa State College, receiving bachelor's and master's degrees there. He then became head of the chemical department at Tuskegee Institute, where his experiments with the peanut, pecan, and sweet potato and in extracting dyes from southern clays became well known. In 1922 Carver was awarded the Spingarn Medal.* Strongly identified with Booker T. Washington, Carver was never in the activist mainstream espoused by W.E.B. Du Bois* and other black leaders during the twentieth century.
REFERENCE: WWCA, 1927. (BK)

CATO, MINTO (opera singer), 4 September 1900–26 October 1979. Born in Little Rock, Arkansas, Minto Cato studied at the Washington Conservatory of Music in Washington, D.C. Before opening a music studio in Detroit she taught music in public schools in Arkansas and Georgia. She began singing professionally during the twenties and appeared with her husband, Joe Sheftal, and his Southland Revue in tours of Europe, Canada, Mexico, Australia, and the Pacific islands. Moving to New York, she appeared in *Keep Shufflin'** in 1928, the Connie's Inn* revue *Hot Chocolates** in 1929, and *Blackbirds [*] of 1930*. During the thirties she sang with opera companies, including the Salmaggi production of Verdi's *Aida* at the New York Hippodrome in 1937. She appeared with the National Negro Opera Company in *Il Trovatore* in 1944 and *La Traviata* in 1947.
REFERENCE: BDAM, 1982. (PO)

CHALLENGE (periodical), 1916–1919. *Challenge* began publication in June 1916, "A Magazine of the People dedicated to the uplift of Negroes and to the

welding of a bond between them and other races that will make the world a decent place to live in,'' according to its regular subtitle. William Bridges, formerly a member of the Black Nationalist Liberty party, was the magazine's managing editor. An avowed ''New Negro'' feeling no loyalty to the American government, as he reiterated in his editorials, Bridges demanded legal action against lynching, questioned the country's disrespect for Germany since blacks were treated better there than here, and voiced strong antiprejudice statements. Elsewhere, issues of *Challenge* carried an occasional poem by Andy Razaf* and ran regular write-in contests for ''favorite'' performer (Evelyn Ellis) and ''most popular'' performers (Abbie Mitchell* and Andrew Brown). Bridges's diatribes, however, calling W.E.B. Du Bois* a ''poor misguided philosopher'' and Fred Moore* a ''political henchman'' (Oct. 1919, pp. 37, 42), sometimes expressed in faulty grammar, give *Challenge* its singular interest. The magazine seems to have died for lack of financial support, since Bridges announced his refusal to accept advertisements of which he did not approve.
REFERENCES: *Challenge*, Oct. 1919; CVV; JWJ. (BK)

CHALLENGE (periodical), 1934-1937. Dorothy West* edited a literary journal called *Challenge* in Boston, beginning in the spring of 1934. Countee Cullen,* Helene Johnson,* and Langston Hughes* contributed to the first issue, and Hughes wrote a note of encouragement: ''All the old timers aren't dead. If they're dozing you ought to wake 'em up'' (March 1934, p. 27). The second issue included contributions by Zora Neale Hurston,* Arna Bontemps,* Claude McKay,* Carl Van Vechten,* Frank Yerby, Cullen, and Hughes. It survived for only a few years, later titled *New Challenge*, until 1937.
REFERENCES: *Challenge*, March 1934; CVV; JWJ. (BK)

CHANGE YOUR LUCK (musical comedy), 1930. This show, with a ''completely enervating and pointless book'' (NYT, 7 June 1930, p. 10) by Garland Howard, and music and lyrics by J. C. Johnson,* ran for eleven performances only, beginning June 6, at the George M. Cohan Theatre, despite good performances by Cora LaRedd, Alberta Hunter,* and Leigh Whipper.* In Evergreen Pepper's Funeral Parlor, the Rat Row Randies and the Uplift League come to grips when the undertaker fills his formaldehyde cans with bootleg booze. According to the program there was a first act ''reprisal'' of a song called ''Religion in Mah Feet''; the *New York Times* reviewer suggested it might not have been a typographical error.
REFERENCES: Burns Mantle, 1929-1930; NYTTR, 1972. (BK)

CHENAULT, LAWRENCE (actor), 1877–? Although he appeared with the Bert Williams* and George Walker Company and with Sissieretta Jones* during the early years of the century, Lawrence Chenault was better known for his work in films. Born in Kentucky, Chenault had typical early theatrical training in that he first sang in the Allen Temple Church in Cincinnati, Ohio, before touring

with various organizations like Ernest Hogan's. He joined the Anita Bush* Company as leading man in her recently formed Lafayette Players* in 1916. Four years later he made his first films, for Oscar Micheaux,* *The Brute* and *Symbol of the Unconquered.* Subsequently, he acted in *The Burden of the Race, The Crimson Skull,* and *Gun Sales Mystery* (1921); *Call of His People, Prince of His Race, Schemes, Secret Sorrow,* and *Spitfire* (1922); *Sport of the Gods,* based on Paul Laurence Dunbar's novel (1923); and *Birthright, House Behind the Cedars,* based on Charles Chesnutt's* novel, and *Son of Satan* (1924); then he took time off from the movies to appear in *Get Set!* a Donald Heywood* Porter Grainger* musical revue for one of the Harlem theaters. Other films followed: *Devil's Disciple* (1926), *Scar of Shame* (1927), *Children of Hate* (1929), *Ten Minutes to Live* (1932), and *Harlem After Midnight* (1934). In these all-black films, designed for black audiences, Chenault was able to escape the invidious racial stereotyping that Hollywood insisted on, although the situation limited his exposure and, therefore, his career. Interestingly, black films used black literature as source material; the black theater did not.
REFERENCES: BAF, 1974; BBW, 1977; BB, 1980. (BK)

CHESNUTT, ALFRED G[EORGE] "SLICK" (actor), 26 Febuary 1900–?
In the movies, after 1932, Slick Chestnutt was called "The Colored Cagney" because of his tough-guy image patterned after the white actor James Cagney, who specialized in thug roles. Chesnutt began his career, however, as one of The Five Cubanolas, playing in many Harlem clubs. Later he appeared in *Seven-Eleven, Watermelons,* and *Chocolate Dandies.**
REFERENCE: BAF, 1974. (BK)

CHESNUTT, CHARLES WADDELL (writer, teacher, lawyer), 20 June 1858–15 November 1932. Born in Ohio, Charles Chesnutt moved with his family in 1866 to Fayetteville, North Carolina, where he attended grade school. He taught school for nine years beginning when he was sixteen. Then in 1883, having taught himself stenography, he moved to New York City and became a stenographer for Dow Jones & Company. He also worked as a reporter for the *Wall Street Gossip* and *New York Mail and Express.* After six months he returned to Cleveland to become a legal stenographer in the accounting department of Nickel Plate Railroad. After studying law he was admitted to the Ohio bar in 1887 and joined a firm there. That same year his first story, "The Gophered Grapevine," appeared in the *Atlantic Monthly.* He published two collections of short stories, *The Conjure Woman* (1899) and *The Wife of his Youth* (1899). He also wrote three novels: *The House Behind the Cedars* (1900), *The Marrow of Tradition* (1901), and *The Colonel's Dream* (1905). A fourth novel, *The Quarry,* was never published, since failing health near the end of his life prevented revision. He worked as a court reporter for the last thirty years of his life. Some critics suggest that his use of folklore and astute analysis of upper class society forecast the artistic awakening of the Harlem Renaissance. In 1928 Chesnutt received the Spingarn Medal,* which cited his "pioneer work as a literary artist depicting the life and struggles of Americans of Negro descent, and for his long and useful career as scholar, worker, and freeman of one of America's greatest cities" (quoted in Barksdale and Kinnamon, *Black Writers of America*, p. 325). He also wrote a biography of Frederick Douglass and various articles and stories for *The Crisis** between 1912 and 1930. In *The Crisis* symposium "The Negro in Art: How Shall He Be Portrayed?"* in November 1926, Chesnutt urged writers to emphasize the story rather than subjectivity or race. His work laid the foundation for the Harlem Renaissance.

REFERENCES: James A. Emanuel, *Dark Symphony*, 1968; Robert A. Bone, *The Negro Novel in America*, 1970; Arthur P. Davis and J. Saunders Redding, eds., *Cavalcade*, 1971; Richard Barksdale and Keneth Kinnamon, *Black Writers of America*, 1972; BAWPP, 1975. (DI)

THE CHINABERRY TREE (novel), 1931. Jessie Fauset's* *The Chinaberry Tree* explores social values in the small New Jersey community of Red Brook. The main character is Laurentine Strange, the daughter of the white Captain Halloway and his former servant Aunt Sal. The chinaberry tree that shades Aunt Sal's house is a symbol of the captain's love for her and offers comfort in the face of community prejudice. Laurentine is ostracized by the community, because she is illegitimate with "bad blood," so she decides to find security and acceptance and respectability. At first her views, like those of the community, are narrow and stultifying. However, deserted by Phil Hackett, befriended by Mrs. Ismay, and loved by Dr. Denleigh, Laurentine along with her cousin Melissa learns to accept herself in spite of white racial discrimination. (DI)

THE CHIP WOMAN'S FORTUNE (play), 1923. Willis Richardson's* one-act play is primarily notable for having been the first serious play by a black writer produced on the white stage. In 1923 the Ethiopian Art Players* went east from Chicago to produce a jazz version of Shakespeare's *Comedy of Errors*, Oscar Wilde's *Salome*, and Richardson's drama. After a brief run in Harlem, it opened on Broadway on May 15. In *The Chip Woman's Fortune*, a porter, who is about to lose his phonograph because he has defaulted on his time payments, plans to rob an old woman who rooms with his family. She has been saving her money, made from selling chips of coal, for her ex-prisoner son. Richardson remembered that the Broadway production closed only because the manager "made a big mistake." In recording his memoirs for the Hatch-Billops Oral Black History Collection, Richardson claimed that when ticket holders arrived after the first week, the manager "put on another play and the people objected so much that they had to give them their money back. The manager left New York and went somewhere and left all the players stranded." The play is probably more significant historically than dramatically.

REFERENCE: Hatch-Billops. (BK)

CHOCOLATE DANDIES (musical comedy), 1924. Many people contributed to the success of this show about horse racing at the Colonial Theatre, opening September 1. Called *In Bamville* during its out-of-town tryout, it had a book by Noble Sissle* and Lew Payton, with music and lyrics by Sissle and Eubie Blake.* The cast included Josephine Baker,* imitating the cross-eyed comedian Ben Turpin; Inez Clough*; Sissle and Payton themselves as the horse owners, with Blake at the piano; Johnny Hudgins*; the Four Harmony Kings; Elisabeth Welch;* Lottie Gee;* Valaida Snow*—all of whom went on to further success. *Chocolate Dandies* was not without its clichés: blackface comedy routines; a sentimental "Mammy's Little Chocolate Cullud Chile"; and some frantic dancing to "There's No Place as Grand as Bandana Land," an opinion unlikely to gain support among the cast members but one fulfilling the expectations of white audiences. Three real horses appeared onstage for a race on a revolving platform.
REFERENCES: NYTTR, 1972; BB, 1980. (BK)

CHRISTIAN, MARCUS B. (educator), 1900–? A self-educated Louisiana writer, Marcus B. Christian became supervisor of Dillard University's Unit of the Federal Writers' Project. He held a Julius Rosenwald Fellowship and was an assistant in the Dillard University Library. From an early age Christian wrote verse, but it displayed little of the excitement often found in the work of other young writers of the period, settling instead for pedestrian versions of conventional forms like the sonnet, faithfully adhered to at the expense of natural syntax.
REFERENCES: PR, 1920; Langston Hughes and Arna Bontemps, eds., *The Poetry of the Negro*, 1949. (BK)

CHURCHES. The influence and power of religious life in Harlem during the period of the Renaissance was as strong as that of the seamier elements. In addition to Marcus Garvey's* African Orthodox Church,* St. Mark's Methodist Episcopal Church,* and St. Philip's Protestant Episcopal Church,* many other churches of lesser dimension were active and prospering. In his *Negro Life in New York's Harlem*＊ Wallace Thurman* contended that people living in Harlem put more of their money into church property than anywhere else; indeed, in 1930 Harlem churches owned property valued at more than $6.5 million, even though many of them were mortgaged and drained their parishioners to meet payments. Among other influential churches of the period were Adam Clayton Powell's* Abyssinian Baptist on 138th Street between Lenox and Seventh avenues; Mother Zion on 136th Street betweeen Lenox and Seventh avenues; Salem Methodist Episcopal Church, where Countee Cullen's* father, Frederick A. Cullen,* was minister, at 129th Street and Seventh Avenue; Metropolitan Baptist at 128th Street and Seventh Avenue; St. Mark's Catholic Church at 138th Street and Lenox Avenue; Mount Olive Baptist, originally a synagogue, at 120th Street and Lenox Avenue; Grace Congregational on 193th Street between Eighth and Edgecombe avenues; the Seventh Day Adventist Church on West 127th Street, where M. C. Strachan denounced moviegoing from the pulpit; and various

churches of "holy roller" groups, like the Saints of God in Christ and Sanctified Children of the Holy Ghost, which seemed to change locations frequently, Black Jews, Black Mohammedans, and various independent spiritualists and store-front churches. The great evangelists of the period, Elder Becton* and George "Father Divine" Baker,* drew such crowds that they held their services in rented ballrooms.
REFERENCES: *Harlem: A Forum of Negro Life*, 1928; Wallace Thurman, *Negro Life in New York's Harlem*, 1928; Jervis Anderson, *This Was Harlem*, 1982. (BK)

CIVIC CLUB DINNER, 1924. Initially designed as a publication party for Jessie Fauset's* novel *There Is Confusion*,* the 21 March 1924 Civic Club Dinner* at its quarters on 12th Street off Fifth Avenue served instead as a dress rehearsal for the Harlem Renaissance. There were 110 guests; Alain Locke* served as master of ceremonies; members of the older black generation, like W.E.B. Du Bois* and James Weldon Johnson,* spoke; and members of the younger one, like Countee Cullen* and Langston Hughes,* read from their works. Several influential white publishers and editors were there, including Carl Van Doren* of the *Century*, Frederick Allen of *Harper's*, Walter Bartlett of Scribner's, Freda Kimberly of *Nation*,* and Paul Kellog of *Survey Graphic*,* the latter of whom was sufficiently impressed to offer to publish an entire issue of his magazine devoted to the "New Negro."
REFERENCE: David Levering Lewis, *When Harlem Was in Vogue*, 1981. (BK)

THE CLAM HOUSE (cabaret). More white patrons than blacks eventually came to the Clam House, a raunchy cabaret on West 133rd Street between Lenox and Seventh avenues. The floor show included Gladys Bentley* in drag, singing her own scatological versions of popular songs. Sometimes called "The Mad House," it was later renamed "Barbara's Exclusive Club" after Bentley's stage name, Bobbie Minton. The floor show also included a male "Gloria Swanson."
REFERENCES: Gladys Bentley, "I Am a Woman Again," *Ebony*, Aug. 1952; Jervis Anderson, *This Was Harlem*, 1982. (BK)

CLAYTON, WILLIAM, JR. (actor), 1897–? William Clayton was born in Virginia and trained at the College of Applied Science in Chicago as a fingerprint expert. Unable to secure work in the field, however, he drifted into black films during the twenties and was shortly identified as a successful villain in films such as *A Prince of His Race* and, with Charles Gilpin* in the lead, *Ten Nights in the Barroom*, both in 1926 for the Colored Players Film Corporation.* Later, he appeared in some of Oscar Micheaux's* films, including *The Wages of Sin* in 1929.
REFERENCES: Daniel J. Leab, *From Sambo to Superspade*, 1975; BBW, 1977. (BK)

CLEF CLUB (musical group), 1911–1924. Around 1910 the basement of the Marshall Hotel, 127 West 53rd Street, became a hangout for black musicians. Within the year they had formed the Clef Club Symphony Orchestra, with headquarters just across the street. James Reese Europe* was president, and Frank Price was vice-president. There were no brasses or reeds in the huge ensemble, but mandolins and guitars joined the usual strings and ten pianos. A Carnegie Hall concert followed, insuring a long success. Later, Will Marion Cook* took over the orchestra when Europe went abroad, and in 1919 Fred "Deacon" Johnson* organized the orchestra for a series of concerts—a "jazz vaudeville show"—at the Selwyn Theatre. Excavation for the IND subway line put an end to the orchestra's headquarters, but changing tastes and the frantic pace of the twenties put an end to the orchestra itself. Still, it served as training ground for many musicians whose later careers were identified with the Harlem Renaissance.
REFERENCES: Tom Fletcher, *100 Years of the Negro in Show Business*, 1954; WWJ, 1972. (BK)

CLOUGH, INEZ (actress, singer), c. 1870–29 November 1933. Inez Clough got her start in the theater in 1896 in John W. Isham's *Oriental America*, the first all-black show to appear on Broadway. She was born in Worcester, Massachusetts, and studied voice and piano in Boston before she went to New York. Clough toured America and England with the cast of *Oriental America*, remaining in England for ten years after the tour ended. She performed as a single throughout the British Isles and worked in London with the English Pantomimes. On her return to America she joined Cole and Johnson's *Shoo Fly Regiment* on tour in 1906 and toured with Bert Williams* and George Walker until 1911. After several years of vaudeville engagements she became a member of the Lincoln Stock Company in New York and later of the Lafayette Players.* In 1917 she appeared in *Three Plays for a Negro Theatre** by Ridgely Torrence and was cited as one of the top ten performers of that year by white drama critic George Jean Nathan. She performed in *Chocolate Dandies** (1924), *Earth** (1927), and *Wanted* (1928) and played the role of the mother in *Harlem** (1929) with "gentleness and dignity," according to the *New York Times* reviewer (21 Feb. 1929, p. 30). Clough also appeared in *De Promis' Lan'** (1930) and *Savage Rhythm** (1932). She died of peritonitis the following year.
REFERENCES: Langston Hughes and Milton Meltzer, *Black Magic*, 1971; NYTTR, 1972; BB, 1980; BDAM, 1982. (PO)

COHEN, OCTAVUS ROY (writer), 26 June 1891–6 January 1959. Octavus Roy Cohen, a popular white writer of detective novels and stories with black characters of crudely racial stereotypes, was born in South Carolina. He flourished during the twenties with works cheaply titled *Polished Ebony* (1919), *Highly Colored* (1921), *Assorted Chocolates* (1922), and *Carbon Copies* (1933).

His best-known character, a southern "darkey" type, appeared in collections such as *Florian Slappey Goes Abroad* (1928).
REFERENCES: William Rose Benét, *The Reader's Encyclopedia*, 1948; James D. Hart, *The Oxford Companion to American Literature*, 1965. (BK)

COLE, LOUIS (entertainer), 5 July 1908–? Born in the South, Louis Cole began to dance in Lenox Avenue clubs when he was nineteen years old. Later, he had a popular success with Elisabeth Welch* at Le Grand Ecart and Le Boeuf sur le Troit in Paris, and in 1934 he became both entertainer and stage manager at Ada "Bricktop" Smith's* club there. When the war broke out, Cole moved to South America.
REFERENCE: CCV. (BK)

COLEMAN, BESSIE (aviator), 20 January 1896–? Born in Atlanta, Georgia, Bessie Coleman was a Chicago woman who became the first licensed airplane pilot of the black race. After an extensive training program in Europe and a series of flying exhibitions in various countries there, she was made a member of the Aero Club of France in 1922. Later that year she returned to America and toured widely, participating in air shows in her Fokker C-2 and giving speeches before various black organizations. For a brief period on the horizon of the Harlem Renaissance, she was taken up by the newspapers as a popular heroine.
REFERENCE: Alexander Gumby Scrapbooks, Columbia University. (BK)

COLOR (poetry), 1925. Countee Cullen's* first collection of poems, *Color*, appeared in 1925, including work that had been first published in seventeen magazines and newspapers, a rare achievement for a writer only twenty-two years old. Nearly all of Cullen's poems are couched in traditional forms: sonnets, ballad stanzas, couplets, carefully rhymed and gracefully turned, sometimes afflicted with nineteenth-century diction and locutions. Although many of them reflect Cullen's racial heritage—the sonnet in which he marveled that God could "make a poet black, and bid him sing" (p. 3) or the long poem dedicated to his friend Harold Jackman* in which he asked, "What is Africa to me" (p. 36)—a nearly equal number seem to reinforce Langston Hughes's* contention that Cullen yearned to be recognized as a poet rather than as a black poet. (BK)

COLORED PLAYERS FILM CORPORATION (film company), 1926–1929. A white organization that specialized in black films, the Colored Players Film Corporation began in 1926 with *A Prince of His Race*. The feature was notable, primarily, for the performance of William Clayton, Jr.,* as the villain. Clayton, a graduate of the College of Applied Science in Chicago, drifted into films when he was unable to get a job in the fingerprinting work for which he had been trained. He played another villain in the company's second feature, *Ten Nights in the Barroom*, with Charles Gilpin* in the leading role. Its third and best-known feature was released in 1927—*The Scar of Shame*, in which a girl frustrated by her "dicty" prospective in-laws takes up with a racketeer, gets disfigured in a fight—her "scar of shame"—and then commits suicide when her former beau marries somebody else. Apparently, it was technically superior to most of the black films of the period. A fourth black feature, *Children of Fate*, was released by the Colored Players Film Corporation in 1929.

REFERENCES: Daniel J. Leab, *From Sambo to Superspade*,1975; BBW, 1977. (BK)

COLUMBIA PHONOGRAPH COMPANY (record company), 1902– . Although the Columbia Phonograph Company had been producing lateral-groove recordings since 1902 and was the major competitor of the powerful Victor Talking Machine Company, it showed little initiative in expanding its catalog to include blues* and race recordings. New companies challenged the patent monopoly on the lateral-cut process and eventually won in the Supreme Court, and by 1920 best-selling recordings by black artists were appearing on OKeh, Pathé, Perfect, Gennett, Starr, and other labels. Somewhat belatedly, Columbia signed up singers such as Mary Stafford* and Edith Wilson* and by 1922 was issuing half a dozen blues recordings a year. Business picked up in 1923 when Frank Walker, a white impresario, was put in charge of Columbia's race list and immediately signed up Bessie Smith* and Clara Smith.* Their first recordings—fourteen by Bessie, eight by Clara—sold well, but the company was in financial trouble and was forced to declare bankruptcy at the end of 1923. A consortium of bankers assumed control and dictated a conservative policy; few new artists were signed and little effort was made to diversify the race list. In 1924 Paramount absorbed the black-owned Black Swan* company and together with OKeh began to dominate the race-records market. In 1925 the English Columbia company bought a controlling interest in the American Columbia company and attempted to expand the catalog by making recordings in the field as other companies were doing. In Atlanta they recorded a gospel group, the Birmingham Jubilee Singers, and a local preacher, the Reverend J. M. Gates, whose "Sermons with Singing" were an instant hit. But Columbia neglected to sign him to an exclusive recording contract, and Gates was taken up by other recording companies. General Phonograph, which owned the OKeh-Odeon company, had been unable to secure rights to electrical recording, and in 1926 they sold OKeh to Columbia, which operated it as an independent subsidiary although gradually reducing its race catalog. Although race records on all labels sold extremely well in the late twenties, the market all but collapsed in the early thirties. In December 1931 English Columbia sold the American Columbia company to Grigsby-Grunow, the makers of Majestic radios, who cut back production, but as the Depression deepened even best-selling Columbia artists such as Bessie Smith* and Blind Willie Smith* were unable to keep the company solvent. In 1934 Grigsby-Grunow sold the Columbia Phonograph Company to the Brunswick Radio Corporation, which in turn was owned by Warner Brothers Pictures.

In 1923 there had been a dozen independent race-record companies; by 1934 more than half of them had been absorbed, through mergers or takeovers, by Consolidated Film Industries.
REFERENCES: Robert M. W. Dixon and John Godrich, *Recording the Blues*, 1970; Giles Oakley, *The Devil's Music*, 1978. (DA)

COMATHIERE, [ABE] A. B. (actor), c. 1890–? A. B. Comathiere was born in New York City about 1890. As one of the original members of the Lafayette Players Stock Company* in 1915, he had played in more than 500 productions before its demise in 1923. He acted in several films for Oscar Micheaux,* notably *Deceit* and *The Brute* in the early twenties, and in 1932 he appeared in *The Black King*,* made by the Southland Picture Corporation. He appeared in many shows during the twenties in a variety of roles.
REFERENCE: BB, 1980. (BK)

COME ALONG, MANDY (musical comedy), 1923. One of the few Harlem shows to receive any attention, *Come Along, Mandy* was a "Charleston-fest" in the view of Theophilus Lewis* in *The Messenger** (Feb. 1924, pp. 42-43). The lively music made up for the plot, which transpired on the islands of Boo-Boo and Poo-Poo where "a cargo of guano [was] unloaded by a detail of sad stevedores." Apparently, this activity also described what was foisted on the audience by the actors. However, *Come Along, Mandy* seems to have run longer than the week usually allotted musical shows at the Lafayette Theatre.* With a cast of black performers who appeared regularly in the shows there—Arthur Taylor, Marie Santos, Ruppert Marks, Lillian Mattison, and John Wilson—the show was notable for its score by Jean Starr, according to Lewis.
REFERENCE: Theophilus Lewis, "Theatre," *The Messenger*, Feb. 1924. (BK)

COMEDY: AMERICAN STYLE (novel), 1933. Jessie Fauset's* *Comedy: American Style* ironically traces the tragic effects of color prejudice in a black family. The novel's six-part dramatic structure emphasizes this theme. "The Plot" introduces Olivia as a child and traces the development of her color mania up to her marriage to Christopher Cary. Although he is light enough to pass, he takes pride in his black heritage. "The Characters," the novel's second section, shows Olivia as the domineering wife and mother of three children who will suffer the consequences of her racial prejudice. The next three sections tell the story of each of Olivia's children. Teresa rejects her true love because he is black and instead marries the white, greedy, small-minded professor her mother selected for her. Oliver, the youngest child, kills himself. Only Phoebe marries and remains true to herself. "Curtain," the novel's final section, shows Olivia Cary in France. Having left her family in Philadelphia, she visits Teresa and her husband but is kicked out. Alone in Paris, Olivia Blanchard Cary has sacrificed human relationships for self-delusion and has, at last, attained the status she sought. (DI)

COME SEVEN (play), 1920. The *New York Times* called this play at the Broadhurst Theatre "distinctly a negro comedy for white folks" (20 July 1920, p. 10). All of the characters were black; all of the actors were white; and Octavus Roy Cohen's* plot was concerned with "recognizable traits": "shiftlessness ... pompousness ... pretensions." A "flashy darkey," a "no-count nigger," and a "high yaller gal" are involved in some tasteless comedy about stealing a paste diamond ring. "Probably a sociologist would find considerable fault," the *Times* reviewer conceded. The play has some historical curiosity as the end of familiar traditions in the white theater, for it opened July 19, less than a year before *Shuffle Along** began to change them. Cohen, however, made a lucrative although undistinguished career, perpetuating racial stereotypes in popular magazines.
REFERENCES: Burns Mantle, 1920–1921; NYTTR, 1972. (BK)

THE CONJURE MAN DIES (novel), 1932. *The Conjure Man Dies* is a mystery story that reveals to the reader the urban social world of Harlem as it carries him through a labyrinth of intrigue to the final surprise ending. Rudolph Fisher's* mystery novel is the first of the genre written by a black American, and his achievement serves to challenge the stereotype roles that blacks played in mystery fiction and films of white writers. After Fisher's death *The Conjure Man Dies* was adapted for the stage as a Federal Theatre Project by Arna Bontemps* and Countee Cullen.* Fisher's book is the distant forerunner of the popular black detective fiction of Chester Himes. (MH)

CONNIE'S INN (cabaret), 1923–1933. Connie's Inn, adjacent to the Lafayette Theatre,* was at first a Harlem delicatessen, with Fats Waller* as its delivery boy. Then in the early twenties Connie (Conrad) Immerman (1894–23 October 1967), a Latvian immigrant, transformed it into one of the most popular clubs, where early morning jam sessions carried out to the Tree of Hope* that stood in front. The white comedian Jimmy Durante thought Connie's Inn was the "swankiest" of Harlem's cabarets, with its red canopy and high prices. Located at Seventh Avenue and 131st Street, it usually catered to predominately white crowds, including not only big spenders but a number of theater people, all of whom cheerfully paid a stiff tab that by 1929 had risen to fifteen dollars a person. The revues *Keep Shufflin'** and *Hot Chocolates** both began as floor shows at Connie's Inn.
REFERENCES: NYT, 24 Oct. 1967; Jervis Anderson, *This Was Harlem*, 1982. (BK)

THE CONSTANT SINNER (play), 1931. Casts were still largely segregated at the time that Lorenzo Tucker* played in Mae West's infamous melodrama about Babe Gordon, a loose lady who has affairs with several men, including Money Jackson, a black boss in a Harlem Resort. Tucker, however, played a subsidiary role, and Mae West's black paramour was played by a white actor

in blackface. *The Constant Sinner* ran briefly, beginning September 14, adding little to Tucker's better-known career in black films, nor to Trixie Smith's,* who was also in the cast.
REFERENCE: NYTTR, 1972. (BK)

CONTEMPO (periodical), 1931–1934. The 1 December 1931 issue of *Contempo*, "A Review of Books and Personalities"—actually, the unofficial student newspaper at the University of North Carolina—was devoted to black subject matter. Lincoln Steffens, the celebrated muckraker of the prewar period, and Carol Weiss King, attorney for the defense, contributed articles about the *Scottsboro* case;* Countee Cullen* contributed "Sleep," a poem guaranteed to offend no one; Langston Hughes* contributed "Christ in Alabama," beginning "Christ is a Nigger, / Beaten and black—O, bare your back," accompanied by a drawing by Zell Ingram of a black male, his palms, upraised as if in surrender, punctured through. Hughes also contributed an article about the *Scottsboro* case, addressed to "Southern Gentlemen, White Prostitutes, Mill-Owners, and Negroes" (p. 1). The issue caused considerable local controversy. When the white publishers Anthony Buttita and Milton Abernathy invited Hughes to stay with them during a campus visit, they were evicted from their apartment.
REFERENCE: JWJ. (BK)

COOK, JEAN LAWRENCE (musician), 14 July 1899–2 April 1976. Born in Georgia, Jean Cook studied first at the Haines Institute and then at Columbia University. From 1922 he began to arrange spirituals* and blues,* and in 1930 he opened the Jean Lawrence Cook Studios to teach popular music pedagogically, that is, to play jazz arrangements of popular music rather than improvise them.
REFERENCE: WWCA, 1933. (BK)

COOK, WILL MARION (composer, conductor, violinist), 27 January 1869–19 July 1944. Will Marion Cook's parents were graduates of Oberlin College, and his father was a law professor at Howard University in Washington, D.C. Cook showed musical talent as a boy, and at the age of thirteen he went to Oberlin Conservatory to study violin and three years later won a scholarship to study with Joseph Joachim at the Hochschule in Berlin. Upon his return to America he attended the National Conservatory of Music, studying harmony and counterpoint with John White and composition with Anton Dvořák. Finding it difficult to make a career as a concert violinist because of racial prejudice, Cook turned to popular music. In 1898 he published his first popular song, "Darktown Is Out Tonight," followed by "Who Dat Say Chicken in Dis Crowd?" with words by Paul Lawrence Dunbar, both under the name of Will Marion. With Dunbar he wrote the musical sketch *Clorindy: The Origin of the Cakewalk* (1898), which introduced Abbie Mitchell,* a young soprano who almost immediately became his wife. Following the success of *Clorindy*, he was composer-in-chief for a succession of musical comedies featuring the popular vaudeville team of

Williams and Walker: *Jes Lak White Folks* (1899); *The Casino Girl* (1900); *The Policy Players* (1900); *In Dahomey* (1902), a satire on the American Colonization Society's "back to Africa" movement; *In Abyssinia* (1906); *In Bandana Land* (1907), noted for its excellent music and singing; *Bon-Bon Buddy* (1909); and *In Darkeydom* (1914). In 1912 he published *A Collection of Negro Songs*, which included the highly popular "Swing Along," "Rain Song," and "Exhortation— a Negro Sermon."

In 1918 he organized the New York (later American) Syncopated Orchestra, which with nine singers toured the United States and Europe. The Swiss conductor Ernest Ansermet, after hearing the orchestra in London, wrote of "the astonishing perfection, the superb taste, and the fervour of its playing" (MBA, p. 368). The orchestra gave a command performance at Buckingham Palace in 1919. Many of the players remained in London at the end of the tour to perform in nightclubs but later assembled for concerts in Paris. Back in New York, Cook organized a Clef Club* Orchestra that played a long engagement at the 44th Street Theatre and served as a core for touring musical show companies.

Cook was an excellent musician and an influential teacher. Although he and Abbie Mitchell separated after the birth of their second child, they continued to work together professionally. Cook composed the music for and conducted the Lafayette Theatre* production *Negro Nuances* (1924), written by and featuring his wife. Their son Mercer Cook, a professor of romance languages at Howard University, wrote the libretto for a Negro folk opera *St. Louis 'Ooman*, which his father set to music in 1929; their daughter Marion married Lewis Douglas, a dancer, choreographer, and director, who directed the *Revue Nègre* * that introduced Josephine Baker* to Paris; their granddaughter Marion Douglas became an actress.

REFERENCES: Edith J. R. Isaacs, *The Negro in the American Theatre*, 1947; Sigmund Spaeth, *A History of Popular Music in America*, 1948; John Tasker Howard, *Our American Music*, 1965; Langston Hughes and Milton Meltzer, *Black Magic*, 1967; MBA, 1971; BB, 1980. (DA)

COOKE, CHARLES L. (arranger), 3 September 1891–25 December 1958. Charles Cooke completed bachelor, master, and doctor of music degrees at the Chicago Musical College. His popular song "Messin' Around" gave its title to a musical comedy of the period, but he was best known as the musical arranger of the Radio City Music Hall shows.
REFERENCE: ASCAP, 1966. (BK)

COPPER SUN (poetry), 1927. Countee Cullen's* second collection of poems was not markedly different from *Color*,* which had preceded it in 1925. Critics tended to chastise Cullen for lacking in "Negro" rhythms and to praise him for his charm and command of conventional English versification. Like its predecessor, *Copper Sun* contained poems about love, religion, and black heritage. (BK)

COTTER, JOSEPH SEAMON (educator, writer), 2 February 1861–1949. Although he could read at the age of four, Joseph Cotter was denied schooling after the age of eight. Born in Bardstown at "My Old Kentucky Home," the illegitimate child of a black and Indian servant, fathered by an unidentified but well-known Louisville citizen, Cotter went to work as a rag picker, then as a worker in the cotton and tobacco fields, and then as a brick maker. At nineteen he was a distiller; at twenty, a teamster, hauling cotton and tobacco; at twenty-one a prize fighter; and at twenty-two he was "discovered" by white educator W. T. Peyton and sent to a ten-month-long night school course to complete the missing years in his education. Cotter went on to become principal of the Samuel Coleridge-Taylor School in Louisville. When as a guest in his home Paul Laurence Dunbar read his own Negro dialect poems for the first time in the South, Cotter was moved to publish his own writings: a book of conventional verses; a quasi-autobiographical, four-act play in blank verse more mathematical than poetical; some folk stories. His poetry appeared in *The Crisis*,* beginning in 1918, and in 1927 he won an *Opportunity** prize for his "Tragedy of Pete." Countee Cullen* anthologized Cotter in his *Caroling Dusk** as the only writer to bridge the gap between Dunbar and James Weldon Johnson.* Although more racially critical than Dunbar, Cotter's work was patently imitative and out of fashion. In his late seventies Cotter published his *Collected Poems*, but the storytelling qualities of his fiction are more likely to survive than his modest verses. His relevant works include *A Rhyming* (1895); *Links of Friendship* (1898); *Caleb, the Degenerate* (1903); *Negro Tales* (1912); *Life's Dawn and Dusk* (1913); *I'm Wondering and Other Songs* (1921); and *Collected Poems* (1938).
REFERENCES: PR, 1920; Countee Cullen, ed., *Caroling Dusk*, 1927; WWCA, 1933. (BK)

COTTER, JOSEPH SEAMON, JR. (writer), 2 September 1895–3 February 1919. Like his father Joseph Seamon Cotter,* Joseph Cotter, Jr., was anthologized in Countee Cullen's *Caroling Dusk** in 1927, eight years after his death from tuberculosis. Some of his poems were published in *The Band of Gideon and Other Lyrics* in 1918; their promise is frail, but Cullen included at least one, "Brother, What Shall You Say," that looks forward to racial tension as subject matter for several other poets of Cotter's generation (p. 103).
REFERENCE: Countee Cullen, ed., *Caroling Dusk*, 1927. (BK)

THE COTTON CLUB (cabaret), c. 1918–1940. Built about 1918 on the corner of 142nd Street and Lenox Avenue, the Douglas Casino was planned as competition with the popular Renaissance Casino* on West 133rd Street. At street level there was a movie and vaudeville theater, and on the second floor a large hall suitable for dances, banquets, and concerts. Jack Johnson,* the former heavyweight champion, rented this hall about 1920 and opened a supper club, the Club Deluxe, but it was not a success, and in 1923 the premises were taken over by the Owney Madden* mob and refurbished as a nightclub to attract white visitors to Harlem. Madden, a notorious gangster and gang leader, was in Sing Sing at the time, serving ten to twenty years for manslaughter, but from prison he supervised the setting up of a corporation to run the nightclub. George "Big Frenchy" De Mange, a bootlegger and life parolee, was in charge, although Walter Brooks, the director of *Shuffle Along*,* served as front man. Decorated in jungle decor, with a proscenium stage, dance floor, and seating capacity of 700, and renamed the Cotton Club, the club opened in the fall of 1923. The staff was imported from Chicago, as were most of the entertainers. Lew Leslie* was the producer and Jimmy McHugh* did the songs; the band was Andy Preer's Cotton Club Syncopators; the chorus girls were uniformly "high-yaller," tall, and under twenty-one. All of the performers were black, but the club enforced a whites-only policy for customers and a $2.50 cover charge to keep out the undeserving poor. The shows were slickly professional and the service was impeccable; the Cotton Club quickly became known as the "Aristocrat of Harlem." A brief closure in 1925 on charges of violating the Prohibition laws necessitated some changes in the administration; the club reopened with a new front man, Harry Block, and with Herman Stack as manager and Dan Healey as producer of the shows. Duke Ellington* and his orchestra, The Washingtons, opened in a new revue in December 1927, with songs by Jimmy McHugh and Dorothy Fields,* singer Edith Wilson,* dancer Earl "Snakehips" Tucker,* and other popular acts. The Columbia Broadcasting System began broadcasting nightly sessions of Ellington's music, spreading his fame, and that of the Cotton Club, across the country. At Ellington's insistence, the club relaxed its whites-only policy, although audiences were still carefully screened, and blacks were usually given the least desirable and least conspicuous tables. Cab Calloway,* fronting Preer's old band The Missourians, filled in temporarily for Ellington at the Cotton Club in 1929 and was such a hit he became a regular alternate to Ellington at the club. Ted Koehler and Harold Arlen replaced McHugh and Fields as songwriters in 1930 and provided a succession of hits for the club's star performers. None was more memorable than "Stormy Weather," which they wrote for Ethel Waters* to sing in the club's eighteenth show in 1933. Jimmy Lunceford and his orchestra took over in 1934 in a show that starred Adelaide Hall,* introduced dancer Avon Long* and gave a young girl from the chorus named Lena Horne her first break, singing "As Long as I Live."

As the Depression deepened and the face of Harlem changed, white audiences no longer flocked to clubs above 110th Street—the Mason-Dixon line in New York. In 1936 the owners closed the Harlem Cotton Club and opened in a new downtown location at Broadway and 48th Street.

REFERENCES: Jim Haskins, *The Cotton Club*, 1977; Jervis Anderson, *This Was Harlem*, 1982. (DA)

COVARRUBIAS, MIGUEL (artist, illustrator, anthropologist), 1904–February 1957. No artist—black or white—captured the Harlem Renaissance so well as Miguel Covarrubias or with such devastating wit and sympathy. In the fall of 1923 he came to New York from his native Mexico. With Ralph Barton and John Held, Jr., Covarrubias was quickly acclaimed one of the most popular caricaturists and illustrators of the twenties. In 1925 Alfred A. Knopf* published his book of caricatures, *The Prince of Wales and Other Famous Americans*, including Florence Mills* in an otherwise white gallery. The following year he supplied a dozen illustrations of black subjects and scenes for W. C. Handy's* *Blues*,* a collection of songs and musical compositions published by Boni and Liveright, and in 1927 Knopf published an expansion of them as *Negro Drawings*. In his introduction Frank Crowninshield* observed that "no draughtsman of our time is better able to indicate mass and cubical content." Moreover, he implied, the incisive line is always humorous but never stereotypical (p. [15]). In his preface to *Negro Drawings*, Ralph Barton was more succinct: "Covarrubias's drawings . . . are bald and crude and devoid of nonsense, like a mountain or a baby" (p. [8]). Covarrubias's work regularly appeared in Crowninshield's *Vanity Fair*,* in the *New Yorker*, and in other popular magazines of the period; he designed dust jackets, illustrated classics like *Uncle Tom's Cabin* and Captain Theodore Canot's *Adventures of an African Slaver*, and designed stage sets. He returned to Mexico during the thirties to teach at the university there, to serve in various governmental capacities connected with the arts, and to write four remarkable archeological, anthropological studies, three about the Americas and one about Bali.

REFERENCES: Carl Van Vechten, Preface to *The Prince of Wales and Other Famous Americans*, 1925; Ralph Barton, Preface to *Negro Drawings*, 1927; Frank Crowninshield, Introduction to *Negro Drawings*, 1927; Virginia Stewart, *45 Contemporary Mexican Artists*, 1951. (BK)

COWDERY, MAE V[IRGINIA] (writer), c. 1909–1953. While still in her teens Mae Cowdery had three poems published in her native Philadelphia's *Black Opals*,* in 1927. After graduating from high school she went to New York to attend the Pratt Institute and was quickly caught up in Harlem's high life. Langston Hughes* encouraged her; Alain Locke* admired her poems; *The Crisis** and *Opportunity** published some of her work, and Charles S. Johnson* chose to include it in his anthology of Harlem Renaissance arts and letters, *Ebony and Topaz*.* Cowdery's influence, however, seems to have been the white poet Edna St. Vincent Millay rather than any of her black confreres, although she lacked Millay's discipline and emulated her romantic bohemianism. In tailored suits and black bow ties, with her hair slicked down to patent leather, Mae Cowdery was one of Harlem's equivalents to F. Scott Fitzgerald's Lost Generation flappers. Her contemporaries were less than convinced of her commitment to a literary career, although her verse carries a valuable period charm. She published a single volume of her work—*We Lift Our Voices and Other Poems*—through the Alpress Company in Philadelphia in 1936.

REFERENCE: Vincent Jubilee, "Philadelphia's Afro-American Literary Circle and the Harlem Renaissance," 1980. (BK)

COX, IDA [IDA PRATHER] (singer), c. 1889–10 November 1967. Ida Cox, the celebrated blues* singer, was born Ida Prather in Knoxville, Tennessee, in 1889, or in Toccoa, Georgia, on 25 February 1896, depending on which account one accepts. She sang with a local church choir as a child and ran away from home to tour as Velma Bradley, Kate Lewis, Julia or Julius Powers, Jane Smith, and various other stage names. She appeared in blackface as an *Uncle Tom's Cabin* Topsy with the White and Clark Black and Tan Minstrels until 1910 and later with the Rabbit Foot Minstrels and the Florida Cotton Blossom Minstrels. In 1920 she married a member of the latter troupe, Adler Cox. During the twenties Ida Cox recorded on the Paramount label and frequently toured the East Coast vaudeville circuit as a featured artist, sometimes billed as "The Sepia Mae West" or "The Uncrowned Queen of the Blues." She appeared with Jelly Roll Morton,* Louis Armstrong,* and other great or soon-to-be-great performers through the decade and at some point shed Cox in favor of a second husband, Jesse "Tiny" Crump, an organist. In the late twenties and early thirties she toured with her own road show versions of *Raisin' Cain** and *Dark Town Scandals*. In 1939 Ida Cox sang in "From Spirituals to Swing," a Carnegie Hall concert, and she continued to perform until a stroke felled her while she was playing in a Buffalo, New York, nightclub, in 1945. In 1961 she returned to New York City to record an album with Coleman Hawkins,* *Blues for Rampart Street*. She died of cancer in 1967, leaving many recordings, some of which were of a number of songs—none of them memorable—she had written herself.
REFERENCES: NYT, 12 Nov. 1967; BWW, 1979. (DS)

CREAMER, HARRY (musician), 21 June 1879–14 October 1930. The co-founder of the Clef Club,* Harry Creamer was born in Virginia and from an early age toured in vaudeville both in this country and abroad. He wrote the score for *Strut Miss Lizzie** in 1922 with Turner Layton and for *Deep Harlem** in 1929 with Salem Whitney* and Homer Tutt.* He contributed songs to various other shows as well, like *Keep Shufflin'** for which Fats Waller* wrote most of the music in 1928. Creamer is best remembered for the perennially popular "After You've Gone."
REFERENCE: ASCAP, 1966. (BK)

CRINER, JOHN LAWRENCE (actor), 19 June 1889–? The Lafayette Players* had a reliable villain in the company in John Lawrence Criner. Later, he appeared in *Dumb Luck* in 1922, an extravagant musical with a cast of ninety and a ten-piece pit orchestra that opened in Connecticut and closed in Massachusetts, stranding the whole company until the producers of *Shuffle Along** put up enough cash to get everybody back to New York. Criner appeared in *Meek Mose** in 1928, but he was better known to black audiences for his appearances in several gangster films.
REFERENCES: BBW, 1977; BB, 1980. (BK)

CRIPPEN, CATHERINE "LITTLE KATIE" (singer), 17 November 1895–
25 November 1929. "Little Kate" or "Katie" Crippen began her career in
Edmond's Cellar* in 1920, about the same time Ethel Waters* was singing there;
like Waters, Crippen was born in Philadelphia. She was one of the first singers
to record for Black Swan,* with Fletcher Henderson* as her accompanist, and
her popularity on records led to engagements at Barron Wilkins's Exclusive
Club,* the Bamboo Inn,* and the Nest.* Subsequently, "Little Katie" Crippen
moved on to appear in many of the revues at the Lafayette Theatre.*
REFERENCE: BWW, 1979. (BK)

THE CRISIS (periodical), 1910– . *The Crisis: A Record of the Darker Race*,
the official monthly publication of the National Association for the Advancement
of Colored People,* was conceived and edited by W.E.B. Du Bois.* Under Du
Bois's direction *The Crisis* became the most prominent monthly magazine in
black America, with a peak circulation of 116,000 copies a month. The magazine
was known for its uncompromising position against lynching, race prejudice,
and the lily-white policies of the major political parties. Du Bois had no patience
for the policies of Booker T. Washington, Woodrow Wilson, and others that he
thought would deny black citizens full access to the promise of American life,
and *The Crisis* mirrored its editor's views. The magazine sold for ten cents a
copy until 1919, when with a circulation of 80,000 copies a month the price
was raised to fifteen cents a copy and $1.50 for an annual subscription. *The
Crisis* did not support Woodrow Wilson for reelection in 1916, but when American involvement in the Great War came in 1917, the journal joined ranks,
declaring that "war is hell but better than slavery." While continuing its crusade
against lynching, *The Crisis* devoted considerable space to the gallant exploits
of black doughboys in the European war. The return of the black veterans in
1919, and especially the "Old 15th" to Harlem, was a cause for celebration in
the magazine and an opportunity for a not-too-subtle statement on the rights of
the returning soldiers. The race riots* in the Red Summer of 1919 proved a
bitter disappointment for Du Bois and was so reflected in his editorials. As might
be expected, *The Crisis* gave much attention to the several Pan-African Congresses* after the war as well as to the growing influence of the Ku Klux Klan
in the Democratic party.
    It was also in the 1920s that the literary contributions to *The Crisis* increased,
and the magazine changed to reflect the creative awakening of the Harlem Renaissance. The poems of Claude McKay,* Langston Hughes,* Countee Cullen,*
and Anita Scott Coleman, to name a few, and the literary criticism of William
Stanley Braithwaite* became more frequent, as did the illustrations and cover
designs of John Henry Adams. In 1925 *The Crisis* began to sponsor its own
annual literary contest. In 1926, acknowledging the artistic awakening afoot,
the magazine published the symposium "The Negro in Art"* involving Vachel
Lindsay,* Sherwood Anderson,* and Sinclair Lewis among others. That same
year Du Bois penned a blistering denunciation of Carl Van Vechten's* *Nigger*

Heaven,* calling it "an affront to the hospitality of black folk and to the intelligence of white" (*The Crisis*, Dec. 1926, p. 81). Du Bois's first interest was always social life, and throughout the decade the magazine continued to emphasize social, economic, and educational matters. In 1924 Du Bois parted company with other black leaders who supported Calvin Coolidge for president and endorsed Robert La Follette instead. In November 1932 *The Crisis* carried Du Bois's indictment of Herbert Hoover and his "lilly white" policies. Du Bois did not go so far as to endorse Franklin D. Roosevelt, but he clearly welcomed the alternative. The 1930s was a trying time for *The Crisis*, as with other publications trying to survive the Depression. Noticeably reduced in size, from fifty to twenty pages an issue, the magazine continued its now familiar editorial stance. Although Marxism and socialism received more serious attention in its pages as economic conditions worsened, *The Crisis* never wavered in its and W.E.B. Du Bois's commitment to the full acceptance of blacks in American life. When Du Bois quit the NAACP in 1934, *The Crisis* continued without its guiding light.

REFERENCES: *The Crisis* 1910–1935; David Levering Lewis, *When Harlem Was in Vogue*, 1981. (DD)

CROWDER, HENRY (composer), c. 1888–1955. Henry Crowder was only peripherally connected with the Harlem Renaissance, but his career and his private life are strongly identified with it. Born in Alabama, he played with Eddie Smith's Alabamians from an early age, and after several years in Chicago he went with the band to Europe. There he met the erratic and gifted white steamship heiress Nancy Cunard* and became her lover as well as her business associate in the Hours Press in Paris. Eager to foster his career as a composer, Cunard published the *Henry Music* in an edition of 150 copies of Crowder's settings for poems by Richard Aldington, Harold Acton, Walter Lowenfels, Samuel Beckett (all English or Irish writers), and Nancy Cunard herself. In Harlem during the early thirties Cunard and Crowder shocked members of both races by openly living together. Shortly afterward, their alliance came to an end.

REFERENCE: Anne Chisholm, *Nancy Cunard*, 1979. (BK)

CROWNINSHIELD, [FRANCIS WELSH] FRANK (magazine publisher), 24 June 1872–28 December 1947. From 1914 until 1936 the French-born Frank Crowninshield published *Vanity Fair*,* the most influential magazine of the twenties for fashion, literature, and the arts. It was the first large-circulation magazine to publish material by black writers and photographs of racial favorites like Florence Mills* and Paul Robeson,* and it gave Langston Hughes* and Countee Cullen* their first publications between slick covers. Several articles by Carl Van Vechten* in *Vanity Fair*—on spirituals,* the blues,* black theater, and the unique gifts of Afro-Americans—did much to popularize the Harlem Renaissance with white readers. Crowninshield's magazine was nothing if not eclectic, publishing the work of writers as diverse as T. S. Eliot and Gertrude Stein and photographs of celebrities as diverse as Mae West and Calvin Coolidge. REFERENCES: Cleveland Amory and Frederick Bradlee, eds., *Vanity Fair*, 1960; CVV. (BK)

CULLEN, COUNTEE [PORTER] (poet), 30 May 1903–9 January 1946. Countee Cullen was still in high school when his gifts were first acknowledged, and at New York University he won the Witter Bynner Poetry Prize, open to all American undergraduate college students. His first book of poetry, *Color** was published in 1925 while he was still in graduate school at Harvard, and *Bookman* and *Poetry* had already published some of his work. That same year his poems reached a wider audience when they appeared in the popular white magazine *Vanity Fair,** and he was shortly taken up by both the black literati and—as Zora Neale Hurston* called white enthusiasts—Negrotarians. Cullen won the Harmon Foundation* Gold Medal Award as well as prizes in *Opportunity** and the endorsements of Alain Locke* and W.E.B. Du Bois,* whose conservative views pushed hard for gentility. In 1927 *The Ballad of the Brown Girl* and *Copper Sun* were published, marking Cullen briefly as Harlem's poet laureate, an unofficial title his contemporary Langston Hughes* would easily usurp in a few years, by default. Even at the peak of the movement Hughes's freewheeling lyrics and painful blues were less comfortable for blacks, eager to establish literary credentials among white critics, than Cullen's pretty sonnets. Indeed, most of Cullen's work openly admits a debt to the English Romantics, notably John Keats, and the genteel tradition to which Cullen clung only weakened his poems eventually. On a Guggenheim Fellowship in 1929 he wrote *The Black Christ*, in which the title poem is a long narrative about lynching, masked in an elaborate biblical metaphor; in 1932 he wrote *One Way to Heaven,** a roman à clef about young black Harlemites during the twenties. Cullen was among the first to call broad attention to contemporary black poets, when he edited *Caroling Dusk** in 1927. During the Depression he became a public high school teacher in New York and spent the rest of his brief life trying to encourage his students to love poetry. One other book of poems, *The Medea and Other Poems* (including his verse and prose translation from Euripides), appeared in 1935, and two juveniles, *The Lost Zoo* and *My Lives and How I Lost Them*, during the forties. Later, he assisted his friend Arna Bontemps* in dramatizing Bontemps's novel as *St. Louis Woman* for the musical stage. None of Cullen's later work carried forward his early promise, and he may have sensed something of that himself in arranging his "collected poems" for publication before his death at forty-two. They appeared as *On These I Stand* in 1945.

Cullen's own genteel upbringing accounts in part for the ambivalence in both his life and work. Born in Kentucky, eleven-year-old Countee Porter was living with a foster family in Harlem when the Reverend Frederick Asbury Cullen* adopted him in 1914. In 1928, following a decorous courtship, he married the daughter of W.E.B. Du Bois*, Nina Yolande Du Bois,* in one of the most spectacular ceremonies Harlem had ever witnessed. A thousand sightseers joined 1,300 invited guests in the Reverend Cullen's Salem Methodist Episcopal Church. There were sixteen bridesmaids; Langston Hughes and Arna Bontemps were among the ushers; Cullen's best friend Harold Jackman* was his best man; Harlem's entire "niggerati" (another Hurston coinage) was in attendance; live canaries sang in gilded cages. After the ceremony Cullen went back to work in the New York office of *Opportunity* and his bride went back to her high school teaching job in Baltimore; two months later he sailed for Europe with the best man; two years later the marriage was dissolved. Cullen's intense friendship with Jackman was in part responsible: they were called by their friends "David and Jonathan"; but the match with Yolande Du Bois was unsuitable intellectually as well as emotionally. A second marriage, to Ida Roberson in 1940, was apparently successful.

Several theories have been offered to explain Cullen's gradual failure as a poet. In a period of experiment he was resolutely formalist, unable or unwilling to abandon traditional forms of English verse; he wanted recognition as a poet rather than as a black poet, as he told Langston Hughes; his race consciousness and his poetic consciousness were simply irreconcilable, as he suggested in his sonnet, "Yet Do I Marvel," that God had done a "curious thing: / To make a poet black, and bid him sing" (*Color*, p. 3). Cullen's reluctance to exploit racial subjects finally defeated him, since unavoidable elements in black life did not easily translate into his view of what an earlier poet had referred to as the "sublime" in the genre. Nevertheless, on occasion Cullen did turn his attention to black subject matter, as in "Black Christ" and "Heritage" and in perhaps his best-known poem "Incident," in which an innocent black child on a holiday in Baltimore is called "nigger" by a white boy and afterward remembers nothing else about the visit. Furthermore, Cullen's poems did much to call attention to other young black artists and writers during the Harlem Renaissance, the period with which his name is always connected and to which it will be, finally, limited. REFERENCES: Countee Cullen, *Color*, 1925; Blanche E. Ferguson, *Countee Cullen and the Negro Renaissance*, 1966; Arna Bontemps, ed., *The Harlem Renaissance Remembered*, 1972; David Levering Lewis, *When Harlem Was in Vogue*, 1981. (BK)

CULLEN, FREDERICK ASBURY (minister), 1868–25 May 1946. One of Harlem's most influential religious leaders was born in Maryland of former slaves. Frederick Asbury Cullen attended Morgan State College there before becoming a teacher for a brief period. After he received an honorary doctor of divinity degree from the Gammon Theological Seminary in Atlanta, Georgia, he served as minister for churches in Maryland for several years. In 1902 the Salem Methodist Episcopal Church on New York's West 53rd Street, serving "Black Bohemia" as the area was called, appointed him minister for its Mission in Harlem. The church itself moved there subsequently and in 1924 relocated in its opulent new quarters at 129th Street and Seventh Avenue. Cullen served

as its minister until 1943 when he retired. During the interim he served the community in many secular capacities as well: with James Weldon Johnson* and W.E.B. Du Bois,* Cullen was instrumental in organizing the Silent Protest Parade* in 1917; he arranged to have the first Afro-American appointed to the New York City police force, in 1911 (Sam J. Battle, who later became parole commissioner); Cullen hand delivered the national executive order to free those blacks imprisoned in Houston, Texas, following the riot there in 1917; he served for some time as president of the Harlem branch of the NAACP*; he assisted in organizing the National Urban League,* holding its first meeting in his home at St. Nicholas Avenue. In 1914 Cullen and his wife adopted eleven-year-old Countee Porter,* who became one of the leading poets of the Harlem Renaissance.
REFERENCES: NYT, 27 May 1946; Jervis Anderson, *This Was Harlem*, 1982. (BK)

CUMBO, MARION (cellist), 1 March 1899–? Marion Cumbo, a student and protégé of Minnie Brown at the Martin-Smith School of Music in New York, also studied at the Institute of Musical Art (now the Juilliard School of Music) with William Willeke and in Chicago with Leonard Jeter and Bruno Steindl. Although he began playing concerts in 1915, Cumbo's talent became widely recognized at the annual convention of the National Association of Negro Musicians* in New York in 1920. He played with the Negro String Quartet from 1919 to 1926 and performed with Johnson's choral groups and with the New Amsterdam and the Harlem orchestras. Active also as a theater cellist, he played for numerous vaudeville shows, at the Amsterdam Theatre in 1929, and with the *Shuffle Along** touring company from 1922–1924. Cumbo also played for the *Chocolate Dandies** (1924), *Brown Buddies** (1930), *Blackbirds [*] of 1938* and the *Hot Mikado* (1939), and he recorded with Fletcher Henderson* and Clara Smith.* He continued to perform with symphony orchestras and in 1950 toured with Eva Jessye's* choral groups. With his wife, Clarissa, he founded Triad Presentations in 1970, an organization dedicated to promoting black concert artists and black composers.
REFERENCE: BDAM, 1982. (PO)

CUNARD, NANCY (editor), 1897–17 March 1965. Connected with the Harlem Renaissance only through her anthology *Negro*, Nancy Cunard rebelled against her wealthy English family by becoming a Communist, living openly with her black lover Henry Crowder,* and publishing subversive and avant-garde materials through her Hours Press in Paris. In the early thirties the steamship heiress took a suite with Crowder in a Harlem hotel when she was refused admittance to the segregated Hotel Theresa and set out to collect material for her anthology. She wrote to Arthur Spingarn* for assistance, even though her antagonism toward the NAACP* and her disapproval of the Harlem Renaissance itself were obvious. Although Eric Walrond* and Claude McKay* refused to contribute without pay, and Jean Toomer* refused to contribute because he no longer considered himself an Afro-American, many others did write for *Negro*, including Cunard herself. She dismissed the NAACP as reactionary and only had use for those blacks who subscribed to the *Negro Liberator*. *Negro* appeared in 1934.

REFERENCES: NYT, 19 Mar. 1965; Anne Chisholm, *Nancy Cunard*, 1979. (BK)

CUNEY, WARING (writer), 6 May 1906–? Born in Washington, D.C., Waring Cuney attended Howard and Lincoln universities and then went on to study at the New England Conservatory of Music and in Rome. His poem "No Images" won first prize in the 1926 *Opportunity** contest, observing in a precious series of images that black writers were unaware of racial beauty, stuck as they were in urban surroundings. Countee Cullen* included half a dozen of his lyrics in *Caroling Dusk** in 1927. Their prosody is casual, and Cuney's attempts at organic forms are not entirely successful, but the content, as in "No Images," sometimes reflects the period from which they developed. Later, Cuney became art and music columnist for *The Crisis.**

REFERENCE: Countee Cullen, ed., *Caroling Dusk*, 1927. (BK)

CUNEY-HARE, MAUD (pianist, lecturer, writer), 16 February 1874–13 February 1936. Maud Cuney, of Galveston, Texas, received her musical education at the New England Conservatory in Boston and studied piano with Emil Ludwig and Edwin Klahre. As an educator she served as director of music in Texas at the Deaf, Dumb and Blind Institute and at Prairie View State College, and as an active folklorist she collected songs in Mexico, the Virgin Islands, Puerto Rico, and Cuba. In her lecture-recitals on black music she was often partnered by the baritone William Howard Richardson. She married William P. Hare of Boston in 1906 and established in Boston the Musical Art Studio and a black little theater movement. She contributed articles on music to *Musical Quarterly, Musical Observer, Musical America,* and *The Christian Science Monitor* and was the editor of the music notes for *The Crisis.** Her book *Negro Musicians and Their Music* (1936) is a valuable source of information about black musicians of the period.

REFERENCES: Maud Cuney-Hare, *Negro Musicians and Their Music*, 1936; MBA, 1971. (DA)

D

DABNEY, FORD T. (musician, producer), 15 March 1883–22 June 1958. Early in life Ford Dabney led his own quartet and owned his own theater in Washington, D.C., where he had been born. He began a talent bureau for black entertainers in the twenties, toured with James Reese Europe,* and for eight years led the orchestra for Florenz Ziegfeld's Midnight Frolics in New York. Dabney's musical comedy *Rang Tang* * ran on Broadway for 119 performances in 1927.
REFERENCE: ASCAP, 1966. (BK)

DAFORA, [HORTON] ASADATA (dancer, choreographer), 4 August 1889–4 March 1965. *Kykunkor*, an African dance-opera, leapt onto the Broadway stage in 1934, "a complete surprise" (NYT, 22 Dec. 1934, p. 31). It had been written, composed, choreographed, and directed by Asadata Dafora, who also danced the central role. Dafora, a native of Sierra Leone, had travelled throughout Africa studying folklore before going to Milan to study voice from 1910 to 1912. He later taught dance in Berlin and Dresden and formed the Asadata Dafora Dance Company, which toured Europe, the United States, and Canada and performed at the White House for Franklin D. Roosevelt. *Kykunkor*, or *The Witch Woman*, was based on African ritual dance and employed authentic costumes and properties. Its slight plot made use of African dialect only. *Zunguru*, an African dance-drama that Dafora wrote and choreographed in 1938, had more plot and less dancing than *Kykunkor* and employed English dialog. The 1940 version of *Zunguru*, however, had African dialog, and John Martin, writing in the *New York Times*, admired its "tremendous gusto. . . . The theatre fairly rocks with vitality," he wrote (21 May 1940, p. 30). Dafora choreographed the voodoo dances in the Orson Welles-Federal Theatre production of *Macbeth* in 1936. He presented African dance festivals and folk operas frequently thereafter, among them *Africana Dance Fest* (1943) and *A Tale of Old Africa* (1946), both performed at Carnegie Hall, and *Batanga* (1952). In 1959 he produced shows with

Les Jazz Modes Quintet. He returned to Sierra Leone to serve as cultural director in 1960 but became ill and returned to Harlem, where he died after a long illness at the age of seventy-five.

REFERENCES: NYT, 22 Dec. 1934, 3 Aug. 1938, 21 May 1940, 7 Mar. 1975; Langston Hughes and Milton Meltzer, *Black Magic*, 1971; DBPA, 1974; BDAM, 1982. (PO)

DANCE. Most of America's dance routines and steps, although certainly not all of them, are Negro in origin. To the natural African rhythms and folk themes, they began in front of slaves' cabins and on the levees, in accompaniment to work or as a relief from it, and moved easily to street corners, then into the cabarets and speakeasies, and finally to the commercial stage in white musical entertainments, claimed by the wrong race, which had some trouble understanding why blacks couldn't come up with anything original. This was the inevitable pattern for the cakewalk, the turkey trot, the bunny hug, various cavortings to ragtime (a musical form appropriated and radically altered by Jewish composers like Louis A. Hirsch and Irving Berlin from Scott Joplin*), and others of briefer duration and less durability. White Hollywood may be blamed for the tango, by way of Cuba, and the maxixe or two-step belongs to Brazil. Nearly all of the others are Afro-American in origin and in conception, including the most celebrated routines from the twenties: the Charleston, the black bottom, and the lindy hop. *Liza** (1922) and *Runnin' Wild** (1923) both lay claim to having introduced the Charleston, the latter by Elisabeth Welch* in a routine in which "knees are used more often than ankles," according to the *New York Times* reviewer (30 Oct. 1923, p. 17). The actual song based on the dance came later, in *George White's Scandals [*] of 1925*, by which time the steps had been firmly set: parallel arms flailed first left and then right, while the feet moved in smaller to larger arcs, back and forth; as a respite from this part of the choreography, the feet remained in place while the knees knocked together and the hands crossed each other, passing from one kneecap to the other. In *Dinah** (1923), the chorus of Honey Girls and Dandy Sambos backed up Ethel C. Ridley when she introduced the black bottom. It had begun as a round dance in the South long before, but in New York its routine more specifically concentrated on illustrating its title, slapping or tweaking the buttocks in syncopation to the rhythm the feet maintained. Again George White appropriated a dance for his *Scandals of 1926* with another song by another white team. The dance was the inspiration for another number as well, sung on records with a good deal of conviction by Ethel Waters,* "I Don't Need Your Black Bottom in My Dance Hall," which made apparent that she was not singing about a dance routine. The lindy hop seems to have made its first public appearance at a Black Dance Marathon at the Manhattan Casino* in 1928. At first it was considered too difficult to gain much popularity, but within the year it had captured Harlem. Based on the fox trot, it employed an improvised series of leaps and contortions, in Carl Van Vechten's* memorable simile, "embroidering the traditional measures with startling varia-

tions, as a coloratura singer of the early nineteenth century would endow the score of a Bellini opera with roulades, runs, and shakes'' (*Parties*, p. 184). None of these three twenties dances was strongly sexual in movement: the Charleston and black bottom were more or less cheerful gyrations, singularly lacking in eroticism; the lindy hop, on the other hand, suggested in its earliest forms a kind of religious rite of pagan ecstasy, as suitable for Igor Stravinsky's *The Rites of Spring* as for the frantic jazz of the Harlem Renaissance. By the thirties the Charleston and black bottom had become as quaint as the minuet; and by the forties the lindy hop had served as a basis for the jitterbug, also black in origin, destined to follow the same pattern.
REFERENCES: NYT, 28 Nov. 1922, 30 Oct. 1923; Theophilus Lewis, ''Theatre,'' *The Messenger*, Nov. 1924; Carl Van Vechten, *Parties*, 1930. (BK)

DANCE WITH YOUR GODS (play), 1934. One of the last entertainments connected with the Harlem Renaissance, Kenneth Perkins's *Dance with Your Gods* opened October 7 and featured Georgette Harvey* and Rex Ingram* in a threatened voodoo seduction of a creole maid. Donald Oenslager designed the opulent sets, but the *New York Times* reviewer would have preferred another ''dim-witted musical'' to such a ''meretricious'' play (8 Oct. 1934, p. 14). *Dance with Your Gods* was notable only for the theatrical debut of Lena Horne as ''a quadronne girl.''
REFERENCES: Burns Mantle, 1934-1935; NYTTR, 1972. (BK)

DANDRIDGE, RAYMOND GARFIELD (editor, poet), 1882–1930. Although one of his arms and both of his legs were paralyzed, Raymond Dandridge served as literary editor of the *Cincinnati Journal* for many years. A disciple of Paul Laurence Dunbar, and given largely to dialect pieces in traditional forms, Dandridge published three volumes of his poems: *Pencilled Poems* (1917), *The Poet and Other Poems* (1920), and *Zalka Peetruza and Other Poems* (1928).
REFERENCE: BAW, 1975. (BK)

DARK LAUGHTER (novel), 1925. *Dark Laughter* traces the journey of Bruce Dudley, who leaves his newspaper work in Chicago, travels to Paris, and ultimately returns to the small town of his youth, Old Harbor, Indiana, as he seeks to replace feelings of alienation with something vital and meaningful. After working in a factory and a friendship with the craftsman Sponge Martin, Bruce becomes the lover of the factory owner's wife and the two ultimately run away together. Throughout the novel Dudley recalls scenes from earlier journeys to the South of carefree, muscular, sexually vital black men and women. Inspired by *Ulysses* and *Lady Chatterly's Lover*, but decidedly inferior, Sherwood Anderson's* *Dark Laughter* is best remembered as one of several novels in the Twenties by white writers that portrayed black Americans as primitive figures of redemptive importance. (MH)

DARK PRINCESS (novel), 1928. W.E.B. Du Bois's* second novel is an attempt to provide the errant writers and intellectuals of the Harlem Renaissance with a serious moral and political direction. The plot concerns a group of African and Asian revolutionaries who plan through the Great Council of the Darker Peoples to liberate the darker peoples of the world from European imperialism. Although *Dark Princess* is poor fare as a novel, it does serve to place American racism in a larger historical context. It also serves to link black racial consciousness with the movements for national independence in Africa and Asia. (MH)

THE DARK TOWER (salon), 1928–1929. In her townhouse at 108 West 136th Street in Harlem, A'Lelia Walker* organized a literary salon in 1928, named after Countee Cullen's* column in *Opportunity**: "The Dark Tower." Its intention was to offer a place for young black artists and writers to discuss their work with each other and where paintings and sculpture might be exhibited. The planning committee was surprised when A'Lelia Walker sent out invitations for a "Grand Opening," about which its members knew nothing. Patrons checked their hats for fifteen cents and then mounted to the top floor to rub shoulders with white café society and indigent black writers. The atmosphere was stiff with dignity, although guests paid for their refreshments while reading poems by Countee Cullen and Langston Hughes* that had been lettered on the walls by a local sign painter. In the beginning young Afro-Americans did make contact with some white publishers there, and one intelligentsia did meet the other intelligentsia; in time, however, The Dark Tower became only another fashionable spot for slumming. It closed briefly when A'Lelia Walker moved to Edgecombe Avenue and then reopened as an entirely redecorated nightclub and restaurant, not only in the house's tower but in the studio below. Geraldyn Dismond,* Harlem's leading social gossip, gurgled in the *Inter-State Tattler** that there was food "just too delicious and music for dancing"; then she devoted the rest of the column to describing the guests (1 Nov. 1929, p. 12). Mayme White, A'Lelia Walker's secretary-companion, sat at the cash register sporting bracelets up each arm to the elbow and greeted white slummers as well as Harlem's elite.
REFERENCES: *Inter-State Tattler*, 1 Nov. 1929; Roi Ottley and William Weatherby, eds., *The Negro in New York*, 1967; CVV. (BK)

DAVENPORT, [CHARLES EDWARD] COW-COW (singer), 23 April 1894–3 December 1955. Nearly all of Cow-Cow Davenport's work was in Chicago, but his distinctive style of singing the blues* made him a popular, if only occasional, figure in Harlem's theaters. He was born in Chicago and planned to go into the ministry, but he was expelled from his theological seminary for playing a processional march in ragtime during a ceremony. For a time, Davenport travelled with Bessie Smith,* doing blackface routines.
REFERENCE: BWW, 1979. (BK)

DAWSON, WILLIAM [LEVI] (composer, conductor), 23 September 1899–? William Dawson, a native of Anniston, Alabama, received the B.A. at Tuskegee Institute; studied at the Horner Institute for Fine Arts, Kansas City, Missouri, and Chicago Musical College; and received the M.A. in music from the American Conservatory of Music in 1927. He taught for a short time in Chicago and played trombone in the Chicago Civic Orchestra and then returned to Tuskegee as director of music. There he formed the Tuskegee Institute Choir, which toured the United States and Europe. Dawson received three Wanamaker Awards, and after his retirement from Tuskegee in 1955 he was sent to Spain by the State Department to train choral groups. He composed *Negro Folksong Symphony* (1934) and various works for solo voices and choruses.
REFERENCES: GD, 1980; EBA, 1981. (DA)

DEAN, [LILLIAN HARRIS] PIG FOOT MARY (entrepreneuse), 1870–July 1929. One of the greatest Harlem success stories belonged to Lillian Harris, a huge southern black woman who turned a $5 investment into a fortune in two decades. She was born in a shanty on the Mississippi Delta in 1870, and, after running away from home as a teenager and wandering from city to city in the North, she hitched a ride to New York City in the fall of 1901. She took $5 she had earned as a domestic and bought a dilapidated baby carriage, a large wash boiler, and some pigs' feet. The proprietor of Rudolph's saloon at 61st Street and Amsterdam Avenue allowed her to boil the feet on his cookstove, and she soon sold all of her delicacy. Business boomed for the hardworking Harris, who was known widely as "Pig Foot Mary." She saved nearly everything she earned and expanded her business to include other southern dishes such as hogmaws, chitterlings, and corn on the cob. After sixteen years at her stall, she moved with the rest of the blacks to Harlem and rented a tiny stall next to John Dean's newspaper and shoe-shine stand on Lenox Avenue and 135th Street. After she married Dean she was less concerned about saving every penny, and she soon was investing in Harlem real estate. In a few years she had amassed a small fortune (her properties at one point were valued at $375,000). Although she was illiterate, she was considered a shrewd businesswoman, and her admonition to tenants and agents who fell behind in rent was legendary: "Send it and send it damn quick!"
REFERENCE: Roi Ottley and William Weatherby, eds., *The Negro in New York*, 1967. (DS)

DEEP HARLEM (musical revue), 1929. *Deep Harlem* attempted to depict "The Progress of the Negro," from Ethiopia's royalty to Harlem's cabarets, with stopovers in both the antebellum and postbellum South. This "unusually inexpert attempt to blend two things which often mix well—the entertainment tastes of Broadway and also of 135th Street" ran only briefly at the Biltmore Theatre, beginning January 7 (NYT, 8 Jan. 1929, p. 35). Homer Tutt* and Salem Tutt Whitney,* the celebrated "Whitney and Tutt" team, wrote the book;

Harry Creamer* contributed the lyrics, and Joe Jordan wrote the music for the show when it opened at the Lafayette Theatre* in Harlem, several months before, minus the "darkey hokum" added between scenes for Broadway, as Bennie Butler called the vaudeville numbers when he reviewed it for the *Inter-State Tattler.* In addition to Whitney and Tutt, the cast included Lena Wilson,* Juanita Stinnette,* and John Mason, the latter made up to look like Al Jolson. In Butler's view a promising Harlem show had been sabotaged by interpolations Broadway demanded of any black offering.
REFERENCES: *Inter-State Tattler*, 7 Jan. 1929; NYTTR, 1972. (BK)

DEFENDER **(CHICAGO)** (newspaper), 1905–   . The Chicago *Defender*, the first black newspaper with a national readership, helped spur the great black migration from the South to the North during and after World War I. Under the leadership of its creator Robert S. Abbott,* the *Defender* grew from a four-page sheet with a press run of 300 at its inception in 1905 to a thirty-two-page weekly paper—proclaimed by Abbott as the "World's Greatest Weekly"—with a national circulation of 200,000 in 1925. The *Defender*'s racially militant stance and flamboyant style endeared it to the black masses; most important, it emphasized the greater opportunities and freedom for blacks in the North and thereby encouraged southern blacks to migrate North to Chicago, New York City, and other northern cities. The *Defender* was undoubtedly the most influential black newspaper in the United States during the period 1915–1925; by the late 1920s, however, the *Pittsburgh Courier*ing* had overtaken the *Defender* in circulation and, according to most, surpassed it in quality.
REFERENCES: Roi Ottley, *The Lonely Warrior*, 1955; Allan H. Spear, *Black Chicago*, 1967; Andrew Buni, *Robert L. Vann of the Pittsburgh Courier*, 1974. (DS)

DELANY, CLARISSA SCOTT (poet), 1901–1927. Clarissa Delany was born in Alabama, the daughter of Emmett Scott,* secretary to Booker T. Washington. She attended Bradford Academy and Wellesley College where she received the Ph.D. in 1923, the year during which her picture appeared on the cover of the July issue of *The Crisis.* She then taught at the Dunbar High School in Washington, D.C., until 1926, when she married Hubert Delany.* Subsequently, she became involved in a study of delinquency among black children in New York City, cut short by her early death in 1927. The modest body of her work indicates a pleasant voice in a series of conventional lyric poems, one of which won fourth place in the first *Opportunity*ing* contest and four of which Countee Cullen* included in his 1927 anthology of verse by black poets, *Caroling Dusk.*
REFERENCES: Countee Cullen, ed., *Caroling Dusk*, 1927; Langston Hughes and Arna Bontemps, eds., *The Poetry of the Negro*, 1949; BAW, 1975. (BK)

DELANY, HUBERT T. (lawyer, judge), 11 May 1901–   . In one of the frequently reproduced photographs of the Harlem Renaissance, made on the rooftop of 580 St. Nicholas Avenue during a party for Langston Hughes,* the guest of honor stands at the front of a line of friends: Charles S. Johnson,* head of the Urban League* and editor of *Opportunity*; E. Franklin Frazier,* social historian; Rudolph Fisher,* medical doctor and fiction writer; and Hubert Delany, handsome young lawyer (City College of New York, 1923; New York University Law School, 1926) and recent husband of Clarissa Scott Delany* who was just beginning her career as a poet. Delany was born in North Carolina, the son of the Reverend Henry Beard Delany, suffragan bishop of the state. When young Delany's wife died a year after their marriage, he drifted from literary circles. His role in the Harlem Renaissance was sufficiently established, however, when in 1929 he was the 121st district Republican candidate for Congress, and in 1935, as city tax commissioner (1934–1942), he was one of six black men appointed by the mayor to investigate the causes of the riots that had broken out in March of that year. In 1942 he was appointed justice of the Domestic Relations Court until Mayor Robert Wagner denied his reappointment in 1955, accusing him of left-wing sympathies. Delany was awarded an honorary doctor of law degree from Lincoln University in 1944.

REFERENCES: WWCA, 1950; *New York Herald Tribune*, 16 Apr. 1954; NYT, 14 Sept. 1955. (BK)

DEPPE, LOUIS (singer), 12 April 1897–26 July 1976. Louis Deppe grew up in Kentucky and Ohio and began singing in local hotels and clubs as a child. He became, at the age of sixteen, a protégé of Sarah Breedlove (Madame C. J.) Walker,* who enabled him to study voice with Buzzi Pecci, Caruso's coach. Before World War I Deppe concertized as a baritone soloist and joined the armed services in 1918. He toured with Anita Patti Brown in South America and the West Indies after the war. Later Deppe moved into jazz, although he continued his career as a concert singer off and on. He formed a long-term association with Earl Hines, after Hines became his accompanist for his first important jazz engagement at the Collins Club in Pittsburgh. During the early twenties he toured with his own group, Louis B. Deppe and His Plantation Orchestra. Deppe sang in nightclubs and with choral groups thereafter and in Broadway musicals such as *Blackbirds [*] of 1928* (in which he sang "I Can't Give You Anything but Love" with Adelaide Hall*), *Great Day* (1929), and *Hello, Paris* (1931). He continued to sing in nightclubs until his retirement in the early fifties.

REFERENCE: BDAM, 1982. (PO)

DE PRIEST, OSCAR (politician), 9 March 1871–12 May 1951. Born in Alabama and reared in Kansas, Oscar De Priest was a United States congressman from 1928 until 1933, standing alone against racial bias. Until 1904 he ran a paint and decorating business in Chicago and simultaneously served as county commissioner. From 1909 he was engaged in a real estate business, and from 1916 he was a member of the Chicago City Council. At a time when black

representation was virtually nonexistent in the federal government, De Priest was a significant figure for Afro-America.
REFERENCES: WWCA, 1933; NYT, 13 May 1951. (BK)

DE PROMIS' LAN' (pageant), 1930. The National Negro Pageant Association of Chicago staged this "Epic of the Negro Soul" at Carnegie Hall on 27 May 1930. Jeroline Hernsley was responsible for the script, and Russell Woodrig arranged the music. A huge cast and a small audience made "a dismal, chilly evening of it," and the single performance, reported the *New York Times*, "leaves something to be said for limited engagements" (28 May 1930, p. 31).
REFERENCE: NYTTR, 1972. (BK)

DETT, R[OBERT] NATHANIEL (composer, conductor), 11 October 1882–2 October 1943. R. Nathaniel Dett was born in Drummondsville, Ontario, where a Negro community had been established by fugitive slaves. He graduated from Oberlin Conservatory of Music in 1908 and subsequently studied at Columbia University, the University of Pennsylvania, the American Conservatory of Music in Chicago, and Harvard University and in France with Nadia Boulanger. He taught at Lane College (1908–1911) and Lincoln Institute in Missouri (1911–1913) and was the director of music at Hampton Institute for eighteen years (1913–1931). At Hampton he developed the famous Hampton Institute Choir, which toured the United States and Europe in the late twenties and early thirties. Dett published three works for chorus and orchestra: *Music in the Mine* (1916), *The Chariot Jubilee* (1921), and *The Ordering of Moses* (1937); five piano suites and other vocal and instrumental works; and two collections of spirituals*: *Religious Folksongs of the Negro* (1927) and *The Dett Collection of Negro Spirituals* (1936).
REFERENCES: MBA, 1971; GD, 1980. (DA)

DILL, AUGUSTUS GRANVILLE (educator, businessman), 1882–10 March 1956. After graduating from Harvard in 1908 Augustus Dill taught for a time at Atlanta University, but his broader interests and personal flamboyance brought him north to become an active member of the NAACP* and to serve as business manager of its magazine *The Crisis.** In 1920 he joined Jessie Fauset* in editing *Brownies' Book,** a magazine for children that W.E.B. Du Bois* had started, and in later years he was organist for his church in New York. Something of a dandy, Dill was recognized by the bright chrysanthemum he wore in his buttonhole; on one occasion, after a lecture by Carl Van Doren* at the Harlem Branch of the New York Public Library, he baited the speaker by curling up on top of the table to ask questions. According to Du Bois's autobiography, Augustus Dill was "suddenly arrested for molesting young men in public places" (p. 282). Du Bois fired him and then regretted having done so for the rest of his life. In the March 1928 issue of *The Crisis* he wrote of Dill's "loyal and efficient service" that had made "hard demands upon his time and strength" and spoke of Dill's

fellow workers as "sympathetic and admiring friends" (p. 96). Augustus Dill retired to Louisville, Kentucky, and died there at the age of seventy-four.
REFERENCES: *The Crisis*, March 1928; W.E.B. Du Bois, *Dawn of Dusk*, 1940; NYT, 10 Mar. 1956; Hugh Murray, "A Movement Begat a Movement," *New York City News*, 23 June 1982; Bruce Nugent. (BK)

DINAH (musical comedy), 1923. Irvin C. Miller* and J. Tim Brymm* produced *Dinah*, a "Harlem musical show" reputed to have appeared "on Broadway," but the *New York Times* failed to account for its appearance. Its chorus of Honey Girls and Dandy Sambos backed up Ethel C. Ridley when she introduced the "black bottom." The dance had such a success that it inspired Ned Wayburn's school, where a thousand students—including white dancer Ann Pennington— came to learn Harlem's version of this southern routine. Three years later, in *George White's Scandals [*] of 1926*, it turned up as a song by Ray Henderson, B. G. De Sylva, and Lew Brown. The plot of *Dinah* was less memorable: a yokel steals his niece's inheritance from a haunted house so he can invest in a dance hall. Gertrude Saunders* played the niece, prompting a catch-phrase in the plot that had a brief popularity in Harlem: "The woman do look good!" Reviewing the show for *The Messenger*,* Theophilus Lewis* thought it was "hoary," but he called Irvin C. Miller the rightful heir to Bert Williams's* mantle as the best black comedian on stage; Flournoy Miller* was his second choice; Eddie Hunter,* Aubrey Lyles,* and Billy Higgins* tied for third place (Jan. 1924, pp. 9–10).
REFERENCES: Theophilus Lewis, "Theatre," *The Messenger*, Jan. 1924; BB, 1980. (BK)

DISMOND, GERALDYN [HODGES] "GERRY MAJOR" (journalist, publicist), 29 July 1894–   . Called variously "the Colored Elsa Maxwell," "Harlem's Hostess," and "Gerry Major," Geraldyn Dismond divorced her Chicago doctor-husband and moved to New York before the twenties to become a familiar figure during the Harlem Renaissance. After graduating from the University of Chicago (Ph.B., 1915), she taught school briefly and then served as a major in the Red Cross during World War I. She found her true vocation, however, in delineating the social scene in a series of columns for a number of black newspapers: "New York Social News" appeared regularly in the New York *Amsterdam News*ered News* in 1925; "Thru the Lorgnette" in *The Pittsburgh Courier*edited in 1926–1927; "In New York Town" in the Chicago *Bee* in 1927; and "Between Puffs by Lady Nicotine" in the *Inter-State Tattler*edited and "New York Social Whirl" in the *Afro-American*edited in Baltimore in 1928. That year she opened the Geraldyn Dismond Bureau of Specialized Publicity on 135th Street in Harlem and advertised herself as a "publicity agent." From 1928 until 1931 she was managing editor of the *Inter-State Tattler*, after which she became associate editor. Over the commercial radio station WABC, for CBS, she became the first black woman announcer, and she hosted a regular program entitled "The Negro

Achievement Hour.'' For many years afterward Gerry Major continued to serve as one of Harlem's social arbiters.
REFERENCES: *Official Theatrical World of Colored Artists*, 1928; WWCA, 1933. (BK)

DITON, CARL ROSSINI (pianist, composer, educator) 30 October 1886–1962. Carl Diton graduated from the University of Pennsylvania in 1909 and studied in Germany before beginning his career as a concert pianist and accompanist. He was the first black accompanist to make a national tour. From 1911 to 1918 he was the director of music at Pain College, Georgia; Wiley College, Texas; and Talladega College, Alabama. Subsequently, he taught at his own studio in Philadelphia. His compositions include *Four Spirituals* (1914), an oratorio *The Hymn of Nebraska* (1921), and songs, choruses, and works for organ.
REFERENCES: MBA, 1971; EBA, 1981. (DA)

DIXIE TO BROADWAY (musical revue), 1924. Lew Leslie* produced this show first in England, in a slightly different format, as *Dover to Dixie* with one holdover from *Shuffle Along*,* ''I'm Just Wild About Harry,'' and one song destined for *Blackbirds [*] of 1926*, ''I'm a Little Blackbird Looking for a Bluebird,'' both sung by Florence Mills.* The rest of the music for *Dixie to Broadway* was by George W. Meyer and Arthur Johnston; Grant Clarke and Roy Turk wrote the lyrics. It opened in New York on October 29, with Cora Green* and Shelton Brooks* as well as Florence Mills in a series of skits and songs, including an homage to Bert Williams* and George Walker; a ragtime version of ''The Parade of the Wooden Soldiers'' from the recently popular European revue *Chauve Souris*; and a chorus line imitating the white ''I Don't Care Girl,'' Eva Tanguay. The *New York Times* noted that the show had ''more precision and polish than most,'' even though it continued the disheartening traditions of light-skinned chorines and blackfaced comedians. One of the songs from the otherwise forgotten score, ''Mandy, Make Up Your Mind,'' later became a staple in the repertoire of Mabel Mercer, doyenne of singers of popular songs (30 Oct. 1924, p. 22).
REFERENCES: NYTTR, 1972; BB, 1980. (BK)

DOMINGO, WILFRED ADOLPHUS (importer), 26 November 1889–?
Wilfred A. Domingo was a Jamaican-born importer of fruits and vegetables who was active in Socialist, Communist, and Garveyite movements in Harlem in the 1920s. Domingo was born in 1889 in Kingston, Jamaica, and began importing fruits and vegetables into Harlem in 1922. He was an active political writer and contributed articles to the radical *Crusader* magazine with anticapitalist themes such as ''Capitalism, the Mother of Colonialism,'' and ''Private Property a Pillar of Prejudice.'' He was editor of Marcus Garvey's* *Negro World** newspaper in 1918–1919, but he left the Garvey movement over political and ideological

differences. He was an important contributor to the radical *Messenger** magazine of A. Philip Randolph* and Chandler Owen* during the period 1917–1922 and even supported their early efforts to discredit Garvey, after Garvey had dealt with the Ku Klux Klan. By 1923, however, he broke with *The Messenger*, claiming their "Garvey Must Go" campaign was much too anti–West Indian for his tastes. He founded his own weekly magazine, the *Emancipator,** and later joined the Communist party, as well as handling publicity and propaganda for the African Blood Brotherhood. Little is known of his later life.
REFERENCES: WWCA, 1933; Theodore Kornweibel, Jr., *No Crystal Stair*, 1974. (DS)

DOUGHERTY, [ROMEO] LIONEL (journalist), 24 December 1906–9 December 1944. Born in New Jersey, Romeo Lionel Dougherty dropped his first name and became a cub reporter for the *Brooklyn Eagle* during the twenties and then sports and drama editor for the *Amsterdam News** for thirty-five years. He then served as editor and manager of the *Washington Sun* until 1941. Dougherty was instrumental in securing entry into the American Federation of Labor in New York for black movie house operators.
REFERENCE: WWCA, 1933. (BK)

DOUGLAS, AARON (artist), 26 May 1898–22 February 1979. Aaron Douglas was the best-known painter of the Harlem Renaissance and, during his long career, one of the best black painters of his generation. He completed a bachelor of fine arts degree at the University of Kansas, in which state he had been born, when he was twenty-four. After teaching in Kansas City high schools for two years, he began to study under Winold Reiss,* the white artist who influenced a number of young black painters. Douglas held a Barnes Foundation fellowship in 1928, and he exhibited his work at the Harmon Foundation* that same year. Douglas designed the poster for the Krigwa Players,* painted a series of murals in the Harlem Branch of the New York Public Library, and illustrated the publicity for Carl Van Vechten's* *Nigger Heaven,** but he is probably better known for his work in many periodicals: *Vanity Fair,** *Theatre Arts, The Crisis,** *Sun, Opportunity,** *Boston Transcript,* and *American Mercury.* Furthermore, he illustrated books and their advertisements by Countee Cullen,* James Weldon Johnson,* Langston Hughes,* and Alain Locke.* In later years Douglas was a member of the faculty at Fisk University.
REFERENCES: AAB, 1972; Romare Bearden, "A Final Farewell to Douglas, *Amsterdam News*, 24 Feb. 1979; CVV. (BK)

DRAPER, MURIEL (hostess, writer), 1891–26 August 1956. The wife of baritone Paul Draper (whom she divorced in 1916) was first known for her London salon "Edith Grove," where musicians like Pablo Casals and writers like Henry James called regularly. During the twenties Draper returned to her native America and established a salon in New York, this time frequented by many of the young Harlem artists and writers. In a renovated stable on 40th Street, she gave impoverished teas every Tuesday, with sufficient refreshments—usually supplied by friends—for about a third of the guests. With an old acquaintance from her years abroad, Carl Van Vechten,* she persuaded Taylor Gordon* to write his autobiography, *Born to Be*,* and in 1929 she took on the "pleasurably hazardous" task of editing it for publication. In her introduction she claimed that the book was "exactly his," lacking only his "enchanting quirks and sworls accent[ing] the vowels that sang in his ear" and "crabbed little thick black marks indicat[ing] the consonants that choked in his throat" (pp. xi–xii). Muriel Draper's memoir *Music at Midnight* (1929) gives no hint of her later social conscience that manifested itself through her various interests in psychoanalysis (she was responsible for introducing Karen Horney to the American public), Gurdjieff's teachings (a passion she shared with Jean Toomer* and Dorothy Peterson*), and Marxism (in connection with which she lectured widely). She will be remembered for her support of Afro-Americans connected with the arts, her strange beauty, and her unconventional clothing and hats, some of which are preserved with her papers at Yale. In connection with her dress, Taylor Gordon wrote of her in *Born to Be*: "She knows how to drape her shapely figure in all materials—window curtains, silk bedspreads, satins, Spanish shawls—so that no matter where or how big the party may be people always ask, 'Who is that woman?' " (p. 189).

REFERENCES: Muriel Draper, *Music at Midnight*, 1929; Taylor Gordon, *Born to Be*, 1929; Carl Van Vechten, "Ma Draper," *Yale University Library Gazette*, Apr. 1963; Virgil Thomson, *Virgil Thomson*, 1966. (BK)

THE DREAM KEEPER (poetry), 1932. Selected by Langston Hughes* "expressly for young people," according to Effie L. Power's introductory note (p. [xvii]), *The Dream Keeper* contains a number of poems from his two earlier collections, *The Weary Blues** and *Fine Clothes to the Jew*,* as well as some few newer pieces. Often identified as a children's book, it is nevertheless an excellent introduction to Hughes's poetry. The book is enhanced with illustrations by Helen Sewell. (BK)

DRESSING ROOM CLUB, INC. (black theater organization), 1923. The Dressing Room Club may have served the same purposes as Actors' Fund performances, staging shows for peers to raise money. At the Lafayette Theatre,* on 25 November 1923, for example, with Leigh Whipper* as "chairman," various acts from the *Runnin' Wild** company, Florence Mills,* Tom Fletcher,* Will Vodery* and the Plantation Club Orchestra, and Hamtree Harrington,* all joined forces for a one-night variety show.

REFERENCE: Tom Fletcher, *100 Years of the Negro in Show Business*, 1954. (BK)

DU BOIS, [NINA] YOLANDE (teacher), c. 1900–December 1960. Yolande Du Bois, only surviving child of W.E.B. Du Bois,* was born in Atlanta in 1900. She did well, if not spectacularly, at the prestigious Bedales Preparatory School in London and at Fisk University, where she graduated in 1924. She was, as David Lewis said in *When Harlem Was in Vogue*, "outstandingly ordinary—a kind, plain woman of modest intellectual endowment" (p. 201). Although Du Bois loved his daughter deeply, he was undoubtedly disappointed in her mediocre accomplishments, not to mention her inability to sustain either of two ill-fated and short marriages. On 9 April 1928 she married the poet Countee Cullen* in a posh ceremony that was the social event of the year in Harlem. The marriage dissolved in a year. Later she married Arnett Williams and bore her only child by him, Du Bois Williams, in 1932. Again, the marriage folded, and she taught school in Baltimore until her death by a sudden heart attack several weeks before Christmas in 1960. A distraught Du Bois buried his daughter in the family plot in Great Barrington, Massachusetts, beside his wife and his son, who died as an infant in Atlanta in 1906 when no hospital would admit him because of his color.

REFERENCES: W.E.B. Du Bois, *Dusk of Dawn*, 1940; Shirley Graham Du Bois, *His Day Is Marching On*, 1971; David Levering Lewis, *When Harlem Was in Vogue*, 1981. (DS)

DU BOIS, W[ILLIAM] E[DWARD] B[URGHARDT] (sociologist), 23 February 1868–27 August 1963. W.E.B. Du Bois was perhaps the greatest black activist-intellectual of the twentieth century. Historian, sociologist, publicist, journalist, poet, novelist, and editor are just some of the labels that fit this multitalented black leader. Born in Great Barrington, Massachusetts, in rural white New England, Du Bois was left a penniless orphan after his mother died following his graduation from the local high school. Still, he managed to work his way (with scholarship aid) through Fisk University (A.B., 1888), Harvard University (A.B., 1890, *cum laude*; and M.A., 1891), two years at the University of Berlin (1892–1894), and again at Harvard (Ph.D., sociology, 1896).

His superior education and opportunities to travel and study in Europe provided Du Bois with a strong foundation for the life of an intellectual, and he pursued an academic career during the period 1894–1910 as a professor and researcher at Wilberforce University (1894–1896), University of Pennsylvania (1896–1897), and Atlanta University (1897–1910). During his year in Philadelphia he spent much of his time completing his monumental study *The Philadelphia Negro*, one of the first scientific sociological studies compiled in the United States. His work impressed President Horace Bumstead of Atlanta University, who offered him an appointment in sociology and directorship of the newly formed conferences that produced the Atlanta University Studies of the Negro Problem. During his tenure at Atlanta Du Bois began to realize that the race problem could not be solved completely by revealing true conditions through systematic investigation; rather, organized and determined protest efforts were also necessary to awaken black and white America to the problem.

Du Bois published his beautiful *Souls of Black Folk* in 1903, which, in addition to showing his incredible range of talents, revealed his strong support of black social equality in opposition to the conservative views of Booker T. Washington. Du Bois was founder and general secretary of the Niagara movement, a group that opposed Washington and his followers from 1905 to 1909 and that evolved into the National Association for the Advancement of Colored People (NAACP)*, an organization Du Bois also helped to found and for which he served as director of publicity and research from 1910 to 1934. During those years Du Bois *was* the NAACP to most people. He founded and edited the group's magazine, *The Crisis*,* during all of that time and was the most visible spokesman for the organization.

Still, Du Bois managed to remain somewhat independent of the predominantly white leadership of the Board of Directors of the NAACP, and he initiated projects that did not always meet their liking, including the Pan-African Congresses* he organized in 1919, 1921, 1923, and 1927. He found time to write *Dark Princess*,* a novel, in 1928, and began a black theater group in Harlem, Krigwa Players,* in 1927. Yet his contribution to the Harlem Renaissance went far beyond that: he opened the pages of *The Crisis* to many young black writers, and he personally encouraged and helped hundreds of blacks trying to make a contribution to the artistic and intellectual life of black America.

Although he had superb intellectual talents and ideological instincts, Du Bois, unlike many great modern leaders, was haughty, remote, and aloof, and he lacked the necessary interpersonal skills, diplomacy, and tact to build a strong popular following. He came across, personally and in his writings, as an elitist, unlike two of his major black opponents, Marcus Garvey* and Washington, both of whom attracted a large following with a more populist manner and message. James Weldon Johnson,* who as executive secretary of the NAACP often helped protect Du Bois from antagonistic coworkers and members of the Board of Directors, wrote that only a few "particular friends" of Du Bois saw the "light-hearted" man who was "so abundantly endowed with the gift of laughter." Johnson admitted that Du Bois lacked the "ability to unbend in his relations with people outside the small circle" of his friends, and this "gained him the reputation of being cold, stiff, supercilious, and has been a cause of criticism amongst even his adherents" (*Along This Way*, p. 203). Others, less kindly, might have used more negative adjectives to describe Du Bois, such as arrogant, puritanical, condescending, and uncompromising. On the other hand, he was not—as *The Messenger** satirized—"the well-known astrologer who erstwhile dwelt apart from the world in an ivory tower," without human faults and humane feelings (quoted in Lewis, *When Harlem Was in Vogue*, p. 213). He could occasionally let his hair down with friends and drink and dance a bit raucously, and it was well known that Du Bois pursued women somewhat aggressively in his private life. Moreover, he showed his sense of humor and proportion when he applauded George Schuyler's* satire *Black No More*,* which contained probably the most vitriolic and bitter lampooning of Du Bois ever printed.

Yet Du Bois was undoubtedly an angry and frustrated man, angry at his race's position as one of the "rejected parts" of "European Civilization" and frustrated perhaps that much of his prodigious professional and intellectual effort often went unnoticed and had done little to change the world's racial situation (*Dusk of Dawn*, p. 3). In 1934 he resigned from the NAACP and *The Crisis* when he decided that the best route for blacks was no longer the slow search for social equality with whites; rather, blacks should support "purposeful segregation for economic defense" and the strengthening of the black community (*Autobiography of W.E.B. Du Bois*, p. 298). It sounded too much like a step backward to Walter White* and the other NAACP leaders, and they parted company with Du Bois. He returned to Atlanta University from 1934 to 1944 as chairman of the sociology department and founded and edited *Phylon* magazine until 1944. At the age of seventy-six he renewed his work with the NAACP but began to take an even more active interest in world peace and justice. He turned to left-wing ideology increasingly as the best possible solution to racism, war, and poverty; after extensive trips to Russia and China in 1958–1959 and harassment from American officials throughout the 1950s for his left-wing views, Du Bois formally joined the American Communist party in 1961. At the invitation of President Nkrumah, Du Bois took up residence in Ghana in 1961 and became a citizen of Ghana in 1963. He died there later that year at the age of ninety-five, the author of twenty-one books and editor of fifteen others.
REFERENCES: James Weldon Johnson, *Along This Way*, 1933; W.E.B. Du Bois, *Dusk of Dawn*, 1940, and *The Autobiography of W.E.B. Du Bois*, 1968; Shirley Graham Du Bois, *His Day Is Marching On*, 1971; Rayford W. Logan and Michael R. Winston, eds., *W.E.B. Du Bois*, 1971; David Levering Lewis, *When Harlem Was in Vogue*, 1981. (DS)

DUDLEY, SHERMAN H. "MULE" (entertainer, theater owner), 1864?–March 1940. One of the Smart Set comedians, Mule Dudley got his nickname with the Georgia Minstrels at the turn of the century, singing a song called "Hey, Mule!" (Perry "Mule" Bradford* is said to have got his nickname from singing a song called "Whoa, Mule!") In 1913 Dudley organized the first black theater circuit, and during the twenties it controlled twenty-eight playhouses across the country. With the stock market crash the Texas-born entrepreneur was obliged to sell his holdings, but his pioneering efforts anticipated the Theatrical Owners and Bookers Association,* in which he became a major stockholder in 1920.
REFERENCE: BB, 1980. (BK)

DUNBAR APARTMENTS, 1927– . Named for Paul Laurence Dunbar, the late-nineteenth-century black poet, the five-acre Dunbar apartment complex of cocoa-brown brick rose in 1927 between 149th and 150th streets, spanning Seventh to Eighth avenues. More than 500 units surrounded a Florentine court-

yard with grass walks and flower gardens. A four-room apartment rented for $67.50, and a six-room apartment (with two baths) rented from $84.00 to $99.00, although the Depression dropped those rates by $20.00 or more. In 1929 the complex began printing its own *Dunbar News*, a biweekly paper that carried not only social notes and obituaries but poems, including at least one by Langston Hughes.* Although it was primarily inhabited by Harlem white-collar workers, various celebrities of the period made their homes there: W.E.B. Du Bois,* Countee Cullen,* E. Simms Campbell,* Rudolph Fisher,* Fletcher Henderson,* Paul Robeson,* and Leigh Whipper.* Constructed by Roscoe Conkling Bruce, son of the black Mississippi senator, the Dunbar Apartments was one of Harlem's showplaces.
REFERENCES: *Dunbar [Apartment] News*, 7 Oct. 1931, 30 Nov. 1932; David Levering Lewis, *When Harlem Was in Vogue*, 1981; JWJ. (BK)

DUNBAR GARDEN PLAYERS (little theater group), 1929. One of the small theatrical groups that flourished briefly, the Dunbar Garden Players (named after the poet) opened 30 July 1929 with Alice Brown's *Joint Owners of Spain* and Eugene O'Neill's* *Before Breakfast*, directed by Eulalie Spence,* at St. Mark's Theatre on Lower Second Avenue.
REFERENCES: CVV; JWJ. (BK)

DUNN, BLANCHE (actress), ?–? Although this serenely beautiful Jamaican girl appeared with Paul Robeson* in the film version of *The Emperor Jones*,* she was a widely recognizable figure in the social life of the Harlem Renaissance, not only in New York but in Saratoga and Atlantic City. Unconcerned with racial matters, Blanche Dunn did nothing, apparently, but attend first nights, parties at A'Lelia Walker's* Villa LeWaro, and floor shows in speakeasies. Her startling glamour, moreover, was enhanced by a massive calm on which she travelled from lover to lover and finally to a husband of noble birth with whom she went to live in Capri.
REFERENCES: David Levering Lewis, *When Harlem Was in Vogue*, 1981; Donald Angus. (BK)

DUNN, JOHNNY (cornetist), 19 February 1897–20 August 1937. First with Perry Bradford* and then with Mamie Smith,* Johnny Dunn was largely responsible for the popularity of the blues* during the twenties. "The World's Greatest Cornetist," as he billed himself, took credit for having created the familiar "wah-wah" sound produced by placing a toilet plunger over the mouth of his instrument, and he recorded the first blues with orchestra for Columbia Records, "Jazzin' Babies Blues." Born and reared in Memphis, Tennessee, Dunn got his early training from other musicians in local gigs, and then, at an early age, he moved to New York to accompany shows at the Lafayette Theatre.* Until Louis Armstrong* took over in popularity in 1924, Dunn was widely

recognized for his playing. He was also recognized as a Harlem dandy, sporting elegant clothes and stylish accessories. He went abroad with Lew Leslie's* *Blackbirds [*] of 1926*, and he died in Paris.
REFERENCE: WWJ, 1972. (BK)

E

EARTH (play), 1927. In this melodrama that swayed between Christianity and voodoo "through long festoons of rhetoric," playwright Em Jo Basshe was often "beyond her artistic depth," according to the *New York Times* after the first of twenty-four performances on March 9 at the 52nd Street Theatre. Inez Clough* played Deborah, mother of six dead children, who prays first to God for the return of her favorite and then at a voodoo shrine with the aid of Blind Brother Elijah. When a fire in the forest is blamed on Deborah's evil beliefs, she strangles the voodooist and is then struck dead as a sinner, while the rest of the cast sings "Free at Last." "In its most primitive aspects," the *Times* reviewer observed of this production, "negro acting has a tremendous depth that is not so much artistry as frankness. And through negro culture our novelists and playwrights hope to find the colorful folklore that our starved literature needs most of all" (10 Mar. 1927, p. 23). In his monthly theater column in *The Messenger*,* Theophilus Lewis* referred to *Earth* as the "latest Broadway forgery of Negro drama," further observing that Em Jo Basshe was a male (Apr. 1927, p. 157). REFERENCES: Burns Mantle, 1926–1927; Theophilus Lewis, "Theatre," *The Messenger*, Apr. 1927; NYTTR, 1972. (BK)

EASTON, SIDNEY (actor, composer), 2 October 1896–24 December 1971. Sidney Easton's career as an actor—in carnivals, minstrel shows, burlesque, and films—was unmemorable, but he wrote many songs, among them "Go Back Where You Stayed Last Night," one of the staple numbers in Ethel Waters's* early scabrous repertoire.
REFERENCE: ASCAP, 1966. (BK)

EBONY AND TOPAZ (anthology), 1927. *Ebony and Topaz*, "a collecteana," was Charles S. Johnson's* farewell effort on behalf of the National Urban League* to encourage and display the intellectual and literary talent of black Americans. In the following year he began an academic career at Fisk University.

Whereas Alain Locke's* *The New Negro** heralded the Harlem Renaissance in 1925, and Johnson's own editorial "An Opportunity for Negro Writers" in *Opportunity** in September 1924 blazed with anticipation and promise, *Ebony and Topaz* was more quietly a summing up and a relaxation of vigilance, a sense that the Renaissance had matured, and that self-assurance, not self-consciousness, presently marked black literary expression. The arrangement of materials was meant to reflect the shift in mood that Johnson detected in that present generation: Negro folk life, "free from the wrappings of intricate sophistication"; historical figures of heroic stature, "who flashed like bright comets across a black sky"; racial problems and attitudes, "rather coldly in the hands of students"; essays of self-appraisal and self-criticism without "the familiar tears of self-pity and apology" (p. 14). Stories by Arthur Huff Fauset* and John Matheus*; a play by Zora Neale Hurston*; essays by George Schuyler,* Arthur Schomburg,* Theophilus Lewis,* and Locke, and poems by a dozen young black poets and a group of undergraduates from Fisk, Howard, and Lincoln universities—all appeared in *Ebony and Topaz*; white writers Julia Peterkin*, Guy B. Johnson, Dorothy Scarborough, and Paul Green* also contributed; Aaron Douglas,* Charles Cullen, and Richard Bruce Nugent* supplied a variety of illustrations. Issued in a handsome three-color cover and well printed on sturdy stock in 1927, *Ebony and Topaz* was issued in a facsimile edition in 1971. (BK)

EDMONDS, RANDOLPH (playwright), 1900–? Randolph Edmonds's plays about historical black figures Desmond Vesey and Nat Turner deserve resurrection. His forty-seven plays were later collected in three anthologies: *Shades and Shadows* (1930), *Six Plays for the Negro Theatre* (1934), and *The Land of Cotton and Other Plays* (1943). His work has been produced primarily in schools and colleges in the South, where he worked in the American Educational Theater Association, the Department of Health, Education and Welfare, and other organizations. He retired as chairman of the drama department at Florida A & M University to write a history of black theater.
REFERENCE: James V. Hatch, ed., *Black Theater, U.S.A.*, 1974. (BK)

EDMOND'S CELLAR (cabaret). Edmond "Mule" Johnson's cabaret at 132nd Street and Fifth Avenue, in the words of its most celebrated entertainer Ethel Waters,* was "the last stop on the way down in show business"; a performer who ended up there had "no place to go but into domestic service," as she reported in her 1951 autobiography *His Eye Is on the Sparrow* (p. 124). The low ceiling was covered with artificial flowers and the walls were hung with old photographs of earlier entertainers. About 150 people—most of them various underworld figures, prostitutes, drug dealers, thieves, and transvestites—crowded in nightly for the three-piece band and various entertainers. Other than Ethel Waters, none of them seems to have made a successful career, although Edna Wilson was well known for her specialty, a comic dance during which she revealed her underwear, called "showing your laundry." Ethel Waters's celebrated shaking to her "Shim Me Sha Wabble" and her risqué songs ("Go Back Where You Stayed Last Night," "Shake That Thing") and her blues ("St. Louis Blues") were first heard at Edmond's Cellar during eleven- or twelve-hour stints, beginning nightly at 9 P.M.

REFERENCE: Ethel Waters, *His Eye Is on the Sparrow*, 1951. (BK)

EDWARD, H.F.V. (playwright), 1898–1973. Influenced by a temporaray job with the New York State Employment Service, H.F.V. Edward wrote "Job Hunters," a one-act play about unemployment in Harlem after the stock market crash. It clearly anticipated the Chicago riots of 1935. Edward was a bookkeeper and later an advertising manager for *The Crisis*,* in which "Job Hunters" was published in December 1931.

REFERENCE: James V. Hatch, ed., *Black Theatre, U.S.A.*, 1974. (BK)

EDWARDS, JODIE "BUTTERBEANS" and SUSIE HAWTHORNE (entertainers), c. 1896–1967. Popular from 1917, when they got married onstage as a publicity stunt, Susie and Jodie Edwards toured the country as Butterbeans and Susie in a series of husband-and-wife sketches. "Butterbeans," who took his name from an earlier performer named Butler "Stringbean" May, did an "itch" dance called "Heebie Jeebies," and Susie sang the blues.* Following their comedy routines they concluded their act with an old-fashioned cakewalk. Their popularity continued through the twenties, at the Lincoln Theatre* in 1924, in *Black and White Revue* at the Columbia Theatre in 1926, occasionally at the Lafayette Theatre,* but more often on tour. On the theater circuit they sometimes joined Trixie Smith* or Ethel Waters* in semi-integrated shows, the first half exclusively white and the second half exclusively black. Butterbeans and Susie died in the sixties, largely forgotten, but their marital sketches may well have been the genesis of later film and television family shows and situation comedies, from *I Love Lucy* to *The Jeffersons*.

REFERENCE: BB, 1980. (BK)

ELLINGTON, [EDWARD KENNEDY] DUKE (composer, musician), 29 April 1899–24 May 1974. Duke Ellington picked up his nickname as a schoolboy in Washington, D.C., because he was always so well dressed. As the son of fairly affluent parents—his father was employed by the Department of the Navy—Duke was given piano lessons from the age of six or seven. At nineteen he organized his own five- or six-member band, and two years later he was playing professional engagements with Duke's Washingtonians. He moved to New York in 1920 with his wife and son Mercer and took a job playing with Barron Wilkins. Later Ellington played an extended engagement at the Hollywood Café on Broadway, and when Irving Mills became manager and renamed it the Kentucky Club in 1927, he featured "Duke Ellington and the Kentucky Club Orchestra." The swelling popularity of the Harlem Renaissance among white patrons carried Duke Ellington on to the Cotton Club,* with Mills as his manager. The white starched collars and ill-fitting black tuxedos of the Washingtonians gave way to satin-trimmed beige tails for the eleven members of the Cotton Club Orchestra and a white lounge suit for its handsome, elegant leader. They began the long floor show with a bravura piece and then played two or three other numbers at intervals, including the popular "Harlem River Quiver," which they had already recorded for Victor. Divorced from his wife by that time, Ellington fell in love with and married Mildred Dixon, Henri Wessells's partner in a dancing team. The popularity of the orchestra gave Ellington sufficient clout to have the color barrier against black patrons relaxed somewhat, although the audience remained predominantly white and the entertainment was designed to cater to its tastes. When the popularity of the Harlem Renaissance began to wane, Duke Ellington made his first European tour in 1933. His later career, well known and well documented, marks him as one of the genuine giants in black music. His most significant compositions stem from this later period, but during the years he was known primarily as a band leader and pianist, he was already writing: "Blind Man's Buff" (1922); "Pretty Soft for You" (1924); "Jig Walk," "Jim Dandy," and "With You" (1925); "Check and Double Check" (1930); and one of his most enduring songs, "Mood Indigo" (1931).

REFERENCES: Stanley Dance, *The World of Duke Ellington*, 1970; Duke Ellington, *Music Is My Mistress*, 1973; Jim Haskins, *The Cotton Club*, 1977. (BK)

ELLIS, EVELYN (actress), 2 February 1894–5 June 1958. Although most of her acting career was spent on the New York stage, Evelyn Ellis also appeared in the Hollywood films *The Lady from Shanghai* (1948), *The Joe Louis Story* (1953), and *Interrupted Melody* (1955). She was born in Boston and joined the short-lived New Lincoln Stock Company in Harlem around 1914. Her first major role was in *Othello* at the Lafayette Theatre* in 1919, and she subsequently appeared in *The Unloved Wife, Roseanne,** and the revival of *Goat Alley,** a drama about black life in the slums of Washington. In 1927 she played the role of Bess in *Porgy,** produced by the Theatre Guild. Ellis was also seen in the Orson Welles staging of *Native Son* in 1941 and its 1942 revival and in *Deep Are the Roots*, directed by Elia Kazan in 1945. Ellis directed an all-black production of *Tobacco Road* in 1950, in which she portrayed the mother with "a certain pathetic beauty," according to Brooks Atkinson in the *New York Times* (7 Mar. 1950, p. 23). Ellis later appeared in several off-Broadway plays and in the 1951 revival of *The Royal Family*. Her last Broadway performance was in *Touchstone* in 1953. She died at her home in Saranac Lake, New York, at the age of sixty-four.

REFERENCES: NYT, 6 June 1958; NYTTR, 1972; DBPA, 1974; BB, 1980. (PO)

EMANCIPATOR (periodical), 1919. Founded and edited by W. A. Domingo,* a West Indian Socialist and racial militant, the *Emancipator* was one of several radical weekly magazines that appeared in New York after World War I. Domingo had been editor of Marcus Garvey's* newspaper *Negro World** in 1918–1919, but broke with Garvey in 1919 over a variety of issues and personal conflicts. With the financial help of several left-wing labor unions, Domingo began publishing the *Emancipator* in 1919, and he used some of the ten issues of the *Emancipator* (a short-lived periodical) to reveal the contradictions and shortcomings of Garvey and his movement.

REFERENCES: Richard B. Moore, "The Critics and Opponents of Marcus Garvey," in *Marcus Garvey and the Vision of Africa*, ed. John Henrik Clarke, 1974. (DS)

THE EMPEROR JONES (play), 1920. Eugene O'Neill's* dramatic version of panic opened at the Provincetown Playhouse in Greenwich Village in November 1920, to fleeting attention in the *New York Times*. In a series of "long, unventilated intermissions interspersed with fragmentary scenes," *The Emperor Jones* proved, nevertheless, effective theater, with Charles Gilpin* in a powerful performance. Described as a "burly darky from the states," Jones is an escaped convict who has set himself up as ruler of an island in the West Indies. Once he has bled the island of its wealth, he attempts to leave, only to discover that the jungle is stronger than he is. Always accompanied by the relentless beat of tom-toms, he stumbles in the darkness until, at dawn, some Jungian memory drives him back to his starting place where the natives calmly wait to "shoot him down with bullets they have been piously molding according to his own prescription" (7 Nov. 1920, sec. 7, p. 1). A month later, Alec Woollcott covered a Broadway run of matinées at the Selwyn Theatre when the Provincetown Players moved on to the next play in their repertory, devoting all of his attention to Gilpin's "amazing and unforgettable performance" (28 Dec. 1920, p. 9). Paul Robeson* played the role during the London production of *The Emperor Jones*, and before returning with it for another run at the Provincetown Playhouse in 1924, there were productions in France and Germany. The *New York Times* reviewer called attention to Robeson's "stirring and frequently exciting performance" but, remembering Gilpin's equal success in the role, had "fleeting suspicions that it is the play rather than the player that so holds an audience" (7 May 1920, p. 18). The play was less successful with black audiences during a Lafayette Theatre* production; they razzed the actor to get out of the jungle, because he was in Harlem.

REFERENCE: NYTTR, 1972. (BK)

THE EMPEROR JONES (film), 1933. Paul Robeson* repeated his stage success in *The Emperor Jones*,* produced by John Krimsky and Gifford Cochran with a much expanded scenario. Scenes in a nightclub, in a Pullman car, and on a chain gang were included to account for the protagonist's rise to power, and according to at least one reviewer, "crap-shooting, gin-guzzling, immorality, cutting, killing, fear of ghosts and other supposed Negro characteristics are dragged [in], in heavier quantities than usual" (quoted in Leab, *From Sambo* *to Superspade*, p. 111). Moreover, Robeson was obliged to interpolate several songs into the film, including "Water Boy" and "John Henry," and a scene requiring him to strike a white man was edited out. Fredi Washington* as a Harlem prostitute, Frank Wilson,* and Rex Ingram* were featured in the cast, and Dudley Moore was the director.

REFERENCES: Donald Bogle, *Toms, Coons, Mulattoes, Mammies, and Bucks*, 1973; BAF, 1974; Daniel J. Leab, *From Sambo to Superspade*, 1975. (BK)

THE EMPEROR JONES (opera), 1933. Louis Gruenberg's* opera *The Emperor Jones*, with a libretto by Kathleen de Jaffa adapted from Eugene O'Neill's* play of that name, was first performed 7 January 1933 at the Metropolitan Opera in New York. The popular white baritone Lawrence Tibbett played Brutus Jones; Mark Windham was Smithers, the cockney trader; the conductor was Tulio Serafin. The opera, in one act and seven scenes, was generally well received since it reflected in some measure the sensational success of the original play. Olin Downes judged Gruenberg's score "the first American opera by a composer whose dramatic instinct and intuition for the theatre seem unfailing" (Howard, *Our American Music*, p. 417), but other observers thought that the score "is secondary—it is incidental music to O'Neill's play" *(Opera News*, 10 Feb. 1979, p. 18). Gruenberg incorporated into his score the relentlessly accelerating drum beat that had accompanied the play, but Randall Thompson pointed out that "unfortunately his screaming interludes by the chorus and orchestra far surpass the drum's sonority" *(Opera News*, p. 19). The opera was given nine times in two successive seasons at the Metropolitan, sometimes coupled with *Pagliacci* and sometimes—incongruously—with *Hansel and Gretel*. The first European production was at Amsterdam in 1934, with Jules Bledsoe* in the title role.

REFERENCES: May Silva Teasdale, *Handbook of 20th Century Opera*, 1938; GD, 1955; John Tasker Howard, *Our American Music*, 1965; Hans Heinsheimer, "Emperor Resurrexit," *Opera News*, 10 Feb. 1979. (DA)

ETHIOPIAN ART PLAYERS (little theater group), 1923. Raymond O'Neill founded the Ethiopian Art Players in Chicago in 1923 and, with Oscar Wilde's *Salome* produced by Mrs. Sherwood Anderson, brought the company to New York for a brief run, first at the Lafayette Theatre* (where the company was called "The Negro Folk Company") and then at the Frazee Theatre on Broadway. The bill also included a jazz version of Shakespeare's *Comedy of Errors*. The endeavor was unsuccessful, but it was notable for having staged Willis Richardson's* *Chip Woman's Fortune*.* This one-act play became, then, the first serious dramatic work by a black writer to appear on a Broadway stage.

REFERENCES: Loften Mitchell, *Black Drama*, 1967; James V. Hatch, ed., *Black Theater, U.S.A.*, 1974. (BK)

EUROPE, JAMES REESE (conductor, composer), 22 February 1881–9 May 1919. James Europe was born in Mobile, Alabama, but grew up in Washington, D.C., where he learned piano as a child and studied violin with Enrico Hurlei, an assistant director of the United States Marine Band. From 1904 he served as musical director of black musical comedies in New York, including *The Shoo-Fly Regiment* (1906) and *Mr. Lode of Kole* (1908). In 1910 he formed the Clef Club,* a chartered organization that served as a central hiring place and booking office for black musicians. The Clef Club Orchestra, under his direction, first performed at the Manhattan Casino in 1910 and in 1912 gave a concert at Carnegie Hall. The orchestra consisted of more than a hundred players and included dozens of mandolins, harp guitars and banjos, and ten pianos, as well as strings, reeds, brass, and timpani. The steady strumming accompaniment, infectious rhythms, and rich harmonies delighted the audience, although some conservative critics thought that the orchestra should concentrate on more "serious" music. Europe responded: "We have developed a kind of symphony music that, no matter what else you think, is different and distinctive, and that lends itself to the playing of the peculiar compositions of our race" (MBA, p. 349). The Clef Club booking offices provided orchestras and dance bands of all types and sizes for club and society dates in the New York area. Eubie Blake,* who worked with Europe in those years, venerated his memory: "To colored musicians he was as important— he did as much for them as Martin Luther King did for the rest of Negro people. He set up a way to get them jobs—the Clef Club—and he made them get paid more. . . . And all the rich white people loved him" (Rose, *Eubie Blake*, p. 57).

In 1914 Europe formed a smaller orchestra, the Tempo Club Orchestra, which played for Vernon and Irene Castle in New York and on extended tours. When America entered World War I, Europe organized the 369th Infantry Band, known as the Hell-Fighters,* whose "syncopated rhythms" (Europe disliked the term *ragtime*) and technical polish amazed and delighted military and civilian audiences abroad. The band played an eight-week engagement in Paris and after the war toured widely. In 1919, with a new band called James Europe's Hellfighters, Europe began an American tour playing jazz concerts but was killed by one of his bandsmen during a concert in Boston.
REFERENCES: MBA, 1971; WWJ, 1978; Al Rose, *Eubie Blake*, 1979; Jervis Anderson, *This Was Harlem*, 1982. (DA)

EVANS, ORRIN CROMWELL (journalist), 5 September 1902–6 August 1971. Orrin Cromwell Evans attended Drexel University in Philadelphia, where he was born, and then became city editor of the *Philadelphia Tribune* for six years. Afterward, he was first managing editor and then general editor of the *Philadelphia Bulletin*, a weekly tabloid. Evans was active in both the National Urban League* and the NAACP* and proved a strong Socialist spokesman at their conventions.
REFERENCES: WWCA, 1933; NYT, 8 Aug. 1971. (BK)

EVANTI, LILLIAN [LILLIAN EVANS] (opera singer), 1891–6 December 1967. Like other serious black singers, Lillian Evanti found little work in America and was obliged to make her career in Europe. Born Lillian Evans, she married her music teacher at Howard University, Roy W. Tibbs, and combined her last name with his at the suggestion of Jessie Fauset* to give it an operatic ring: Evanti. From 1925 she sang in France, England, Germany, Italy, South America, finally making her New York debut at Town Hall in 1932. After other concert tours she founded the National Negro Opera Company in 1943.
REFERENCE: DANB, 1982. (DA)

EXCLUSIVE CLUB (cabaret). Barron Wilkins had long had a solid-citizen reputation when he opened his Exclusive Club at Seventh Avenue and 134th Street. As early as 1910 he had owned other cabarets: Little Savoy, Astoria Club, Executive Club. During the interim period he sponsored black baseball teams and financed Jack Johnson's* claim to the heavyweight title. At his private Exclusive Club predominately white patrons were admitted only after 11:00 P.M. and then were allowed to toss fifty-cent pieces at the performers, for whom Duke Ellington* conducted the orchestra for a brief period. Wilkins carried some political clout, apparently by paying graft to the police, but in 1924 he was murdered by Yellow Charleston, a business associate, gunned down near his own club.
REFERENCE: Jervis Anderson, *This Was Harlem*, 1982. (BK)

F

FARROW, WILLIAM McKNIGHT (artist), 13 April 1885–? William Farrow immortalized one of the forerunners of the Harlem Renaissance in his 1923 portrait of Paul Laurence Dunbar. Born in Ohio, Farrow studied at the Chicago Art Institute intermittently between 1908 and 1917, working at the same time in the post office. Afterward, he became assistant curator at the institute, until 1922, when he was put in charge of labelling and then printing. In 1926 he became curator of the Egyptian collection. Farrow's regular column, "Art in the Home," appeared in the Chicago *Defender*,* and he wrote articles and essays for *The Crisis* * and *Homesteader*. He exhibited widely in Chicago, New York, and Washington, D.C., and regularly at the Harmon Foundation,* beginning in 1928. Farrow is best known for the series of posters he designed for Pathé phonographs and Kimball pianos.
REFERENCE: WWCA, 1933. (BK)

FAST AND FURIOUS (musical revue), 1931. J. Rosamond Johnson,* Porter Grainger,* Zora Neale Hurston,* and others contributed to this brief catastrophe. Tim Moore,* Juano Hernandez,* Jackie "Moms" Mabley,* and Etta Moten* appeared in the cast, and both the "John Henry" legend and the "East Coast Blues" were introduced in an atmospheric beginning. Later, there was a *Macbeth* sketch. Nothing seems to have helped. It opened on September 15 and died in less than a week, but *Fast and Furious* is worth recording because of the stage appearance of Zora Neale Hurston who acted in two skits and even, apparently, sang a song in one of them.
REFERENCES: Burns Mantle, 1931–1932; NYTTR, 1972. (BK)

FAUSET, ARTHUR HUFF (folklorist), 20 January 1889– . Arthur Huff Fauset, half-brother of writer Jessie Fauset,* was an important, if not central, figure in the Harlem Renaissance. Fauset was born in 1889 in Flemington, New Jersey, and went on to earn the B.A., M.A., and Ph.D. from the University of

Pennsylvania while he taught and was a principal in the Philadelphia public schools between 1918 and 1946. His particular interest was folklore, and he studied and wrote about the folklore of Nova Scotia and about blacks in Philadelphia, the West Indies, and the South. He also was a gifted writer, and he contributed numerous stories, essays, articles, and reviews to *Opportunity** and *The Crisis** and especially to *Black Opals.** A close friend of Alain Locke,* Fauset contributed the article "American Negro Folk Literature" to Locke's *New Negro** compilation. Fauset, the winner of a 1926 *Opportunity* prize, also contributed an article to the ill-fated *Fire!!**; he was one of several young black scholars to be aided by Charlotte Mason,* the enormously wealthy white patron of Locke and others. Fauset contributed often to the Harlem Renaissance, but he also sounded its death knell in a 1933 *Opportunity* essay in which he argued that even if blacks demonstrated equal ability with whites in the arts, it would not ensure social and economic recognition for the race. Relevant works include *For Freedom: A Biographical Story of the American Negro* (1927) and *Black Gods of the Metropolis* (1944).

REFERENCE: David Levering Lewis, *When Harlem Was in Vogue*, 1981. (DS)

FAUSET, JESSIE REDMON (writer, editor), 26 April 1882–30 April 1961. Jessie Fauset was both a prolific Harlem Renaissance writer and an influence on other writers as literary editor of *The Crisis** (1919–1926) and an editor of the *Brownies' Book,** a children's magazine (1920–1921). She was born in Camden County, New Jersey, the seventh child of Redmon Fauset, an African Methodist Episcopal minister, and Annie Seamon Fauset. Named "Jessie Redmona," she was the only black student in her classes at Philadelphia's High School for Girls; she graduated Phi Beta Kappa from Cornell in 1905, one of its first black women graduates. (Earlier, she had been denied admission to Bryn Mawr because of her race.) From 1906 to 1919 she taught Latin and French at the M Street High School (after 1916 called Dunbar) in Washington, D.C. After taking summer school courses at the Sorbonne in Paris and a year of study she received the M.A. from the University of Pennsylvania in 1919. As literary editor of *The Crisis* she encouraged the work of George Schuyler,* Jean Toomer,* Countee Cullen,* Langston Hughes* (whose first work appeared in the *Brownies' Book*), and Claude McKay,* among others, which indicates her impact on the Harlem Renaissance. In addition, she wrote poetry, essays like those discussing the 1921 Pan-African Congress,* which she attended, and perceptive critical articles like "The Gift of Laughter" in *The New Negro** (1925). Between 1924 and 1933 she wrote four novels: *There Is Confusion** (1924); *Plum Bun** (1929); *The Chinaberry Tree** (1931); and *Comedy: American Style** (1933). They were highly praised by critic William Stanley Braithwaite* (*Opportunity,** Jan. 1934, pp. 24–28) as an innovative contribution to the literature of black America. In 1929 she married Herbert Harris, a businessman. From 1927 to 1944 she taught French at De Witt Clinton High School in New York City. In the early 1950s she moved to Montclair, New Jersey, with her husband, where she remained

until his death in 1958, although she spent a brief time teaching at Hampton Institute in 1949. After her husband's death, Jessie Fauset moved to Philadelphia where she died two years later.
REFERENCES: Robert A. Bone, *The Negro Novel in America*, 1970; Arthur P. Davis, *From the Dark Tower*, 1974; Barbara Christian, *Black Women Novelists*, 1980; Carolyn Wedin Sylvander, *Jessie Redmon Fauset*, 1981. (DI)

FERRIS, WILLIAM H. (journalist), 20 July 1874–23 August 1941. William Ferris graduated from Yale in 1895, in New Haven, Connecticut, where he was born, and completed a master's degree at Harvard in 1900, although his early training at the latter was in the Harvard Divinity School. He wrote for the *Boston Guardian* and was employed by the Negro Society for Historical Research before allying himself with Marcus Garvey* and the UNIA.* When Garvey founded *Negro World*,* Ferris began his long tenure as its literary critic and was largely responsible for encouraging his readers to submit their attempts at poetry for publication. Ferris himself wrote an inflated, pontificating prose, and his literary judgment was limited, but he must be credited for much of the interest in black arts and letters that *Negro World* fostered among its readers. When he resigned as literary editor in 1923, he began his service in a similar capacity for *The Spokesman*.* He was acting chancellor of the UNIA in 1920, and at the organization's second convention, the following year, he was elected assistant president general. Ferris's early book *The African Abroad*, published in two volumes in 1913, is an informative account of the subject at a time when black Americans were still largely invisible in a white society.
REFERENCE: WWCA, 1927. (BK)

FETCHIT, STEPIN (actor), 30 May 1892–   . His real name was Lincoln Theodore Monroe Andrew Skeeter Perry, but to a wide popular audience (about which hindsight leads to some ambivalence) Stepin Fetchit was the first black actor in films to carve for himself a recognizable personality and style. He appeared in many motion pictures, beginning in 1927 in *In Old Kentucky*, but he had his first substantial success in *Hearts in Dixie** two years later. In dozens of films that followed (and as recently as *Amazing Grace* in 1974), his characterization never varied: an invidious racial stereotype, dull witted, easily frightened, bone-lazy. Nevertheless, Stepin Fetchit brought to these roles—the only roles available to him—a comic timing that other actors might well envy. With a fine irony, Stepin Fetchit contradicted the roles he played with a spendthrift, flashy private life: cashmere suits, a pink Cadillac with his name in neon on its side, and extravagant parties. In later years he identified himself with Charlie Chaplin, another actor who played a simple and honest character whom audiences loved for tolerating those who mistreated him, so he, in turn, could help others. Once he claimed to have taken his name from a second-rate racehorse; on another occasion he said he had begun as half of a comedy team called "Step and Fetch It." That same ambiguity informs his screen performances: despite their obvious perpetuating of ugly racial clichés, their popularity instigated the long journey black actors have made toward equality in white films; maligned by civil rights advocates, the roles, nevertheless, are marked by an innocence that, out of its comic context, becomes familiarly stoic and, therefore, not unfamiliar in black history.

REFERENCES: Donald Bogle, *Toms, Coons, Mulattoes, Mammies, and Bucks*, 1973; Daniel J. Leab, *From Sambo to Superspade*, 1975; WWH, 1976. (BK)

FIELDS, DOROTHY (lyricist), 15 July 1905–28 March 1974. Daughter of vaudevillian Lew Fields, Dorothy Fields was a white girl who wrote floor show material for the Cotton Club* when she was barely twenty-one. The following year she teamed up with another white writer, Jimmie McHugh,* and contributed the score for *Harry Delmar's Revels of 1927*. Her first notable success in a long, subsequent career came with *Blackbirds [*] of 1928*. It included the perennially popular "I Can't Give You Anything but Love" (which she and McHugh had written for the Delmar show) and "Diga Diga Do." Fields wrote a few numbers for later black revues, but most of her work with McHugh, Jerome Kern, Cole Porter, and Sigmund Romberg was for the white musical comedy theater.

REFERENCE: NYT, 29 Mar. 1974. (BK)

FINE CLOTHES TO THE JEW (poetry), 1927. Langston Hughes's* second collection of verse, *Fine Clothes to the Jew*, is composed almost entirely of urban poems. (A brief group is titled "From the Georgia Roads," but even some of those pieces reflect the rest of the book.) Many of the poems are deliberate imitations of the blues,* based less on the three-line structure customarily used in those songs than on organic prosodies of Hughes's own devising, although that "strict poetic pattern," as he referred to it in an introductory note, informs them, and they are constructed "after the manner of the Negro folk-songs known as *Blues*" (p. [13]). The poems in the section "Glory! Halleluiah!" are strongly religious in theme, powerfully turned because of the juxtaposition of the devout and the ecstatic attitudes expressed in religious fervor. (BK)

FIRE!! (periodical), 1926. There was a single issue of *Fire!!* in November 1926, launched by Langston Hughes,* Zora Neale Hurston,* and Wallace Thurman* as editors; John P. Davis as business manager; and Richard Bruce Nugent* in charge of distribution, with assistance from Gwendolyn Bennett* and Aaron Douglas.* Its intention was to publicize the young writers' break with the older black literary establishment, "to burn up a lot of old, dead conventional Negro-white ideas of the past," according to its own publicity. Published when the Harlem Renaissance was at its peak, the issue contained work by all three editors as well as by Countee Cullen,* Arna Bontemps,* Helene Johnson,* Waring Cuney,* Lewis Alexander,* Bennett, and Edward Silvera,* with drawings by Douglas and Nugent. Rean Graves, editor of the Baltimore *Afro-American*,* told his readers he had burned his copy after decrying most of the contributions, including Thurman's story about a sixteen-year-old prostitute, Nugent's nudes, and Hughes's "usual ability to say nothing." The reaction pleased Hughes enough to move him to quote it in his 1941 autobiography *The Big Sea* (p. 237). Extant copies of *Fire!!* are rare; ironically, much of the initial run was burned during a fire in an apartment house where it had been stored. It was reprinted in facsimile by the Fire!! Press in 1982.

REFERENCES: Langston Hughes, *The Big Sea*, 1940; David Levering Lewis, *When Harlem Was in Vogue*, 1981; *Fire!!* 1982; CVV, JWJ. (BK)

THE FIRE IN THE FLINT (novel), 1924. Walter White's* *Fire in the Flint* offers a stinging indictment of southern racism. A black physician, Kenneth B. Harper, returns with a northern medical degree to his Georgia hometown and hopes that competence might overcome prejudice. Instead, he encounters a climate of hostility and fear. His modern professional skills invite suspicion from the town's resident doctors, one white, the other black. Ku Klux Klan members resent his efforts to help black farmers improve their lot, and an influential white patriarch, although sympathetic, hesitates to defend him publicly. In a climactic series of brutal events, a white gang rapes his sister, his brother dies in a wild attempt at revenge, and with the sheriff's concurrence Harper is lynched to prevent his impending disruption of established interracial customs. (RZ)

FISHER, RUDOLPH (medical doctor, writer), 1897–26 December 1934. Born in Washington, D.C., Rudolph Fisher grew up in Harlem and Providence, Rhode Island. After receiving B.A. and M.A. degrees from Brown University, he attended Howard University Medical School and interned at Freedman's Hospital. In 1925 he moved to New York where he pursued a double career: medicine and literature, in both of which he accomplished distinguished work. After two years as a research fellow at Columbia University's College of Physicians and Surgeons, specializing in roentgenology, Fisher established a successful practice as an X-ray specialist. His other career began with the short story "City of Refuge," written while in medical school and published in *Atlantic Monthly* in February 1925, about the dreams and ironies of experience that confront those who left the South for the promise of adventure and success in Harlem. "The Promised Land," published in the *Atlantic Monthly*, January 1927; and "Miss Cynthie," published in *Story*, June 1933, are more successful treatments of this same theme, since, with time, Fisher saw more deeply the emotional complexity and moral ambiguity of the new cultural experience. The year his first story appeared, however, he won the first prize for fiction in the literary contest that Joel Spingarn's* wife, Amy, esablished; also, in 1925, Carl Van Vechten* proclaimed Fisher "the most promising" of the "new school of Negro authors" ("*Keep A-Inchin' Along*," p. 58). Other stories by Rudolph Fisher are more centrally concerned with Harlem itself, the dynamics and disruptions of racial and social life and the ingenious and devious ways individuals present themselves to the world about them: "The South Lingers On" (*Survey Graphic*,* Mar.

1925), "Ringtail" (*Atlantic Monthly*, May 1925), "High Yaller" (*The Crisis*,*
Oct. 1925),. "Blades of Steel" (*Atlantic Monthly*, Aug. 1927), and "Common
Meter" (Baltimore *Afro-American*,* Feb. 1930). Fisher's "Caucasian Storms
Harlem" in H. L. Mencken's* *American Mercury*, in August 1927, is his shocked
response upon discovering that certain cabarets in Harlem banned blacks so as
to cultivate a white clientele. This article prefigures Fisher's satiric first novel
The Walls of Jericho,* in 1928. *The Conjure Man Dies*,* a detective novel,
appeared in 1932. Fisher died two years later of an intestinal cancer caused by
his work with radiation, four days after the death of Wallace Thurman,* the first
of the Harlem Renaissance writers to die. Curiously, Fisher's short fiction was
never collected for publication during the period, although in both quantity and
quality it deserved to be.
REFERENCES: Robert Bone, *Down Home*, 1975; Carl Van Vechten, "*Keep
A-Inchin' Along*," 1979; David Levering Lewis, *When Harlem Was in Vogue*,
1981. (MH)

FISHER, WILLIAM ARMS (music editor, composer), 27 April 1861–18 December 1948. Fisher was born in San Francisco and studied in Oakland, London,
and in New York at the National Conservatory of Music with Anton Dvořák.
In 1897 he joined the music publishing firm of Oliver Ditson in Boston as editor
and director of publications, and from 1926 to 1937 he served as vice-president
of the firm. He edited anthologies of New England psalm tunes and spirituals*
and in 1926 published *Seventy Negro Spirituals*. His song "Goin' Home " is
based on the theme of the second movement of Dvořák's *Symphony from the
New World*.
REFERENCES: MBA, 1971; GD, 1980. (DA)

FLETCHER, TOM (entertainer, writer), 1873–12 October 1954. A popular
TOBA* performer, Tom Fletcher was travelling with an *Uncle Tom's Cabin*
show at the age of fifteen. His memoirs were published on the day that he died,
an invaluable account of the various hardships as well as the history of the Afro-
American performer in America.
REFERENCE: Tom Fletcher, *100 Years of the Negro in Show Business* (1954).
(BK)

FLIGHT (novel), 1926. In *Flight* Walter White* explored the struggles of a
young mulatto woman, Annette Angela ("Mimi") Daquin, who must survive
in sharply different worlds. The harsh, mechanical efficiency of European-Amer-
ican ways contrasts with the warmer, humane tendencies of an Afro-American
heritage. Within the latter there are distinctions between the relaxed customs of
a New Orleans Creole life-style and the striving of Atlanta's black middle class.
In the dreadful Atlanta race riot of 1906, however, Mimi discovers her own
black loyalties. Shortly thereafter, she is alone and vulnerable when her father
dies of a coronary and as the result of an unhappy love affair that leaves her

pregnant. Mimi flees to Philadelphia and New York City, where she passes for white. Despite success in the fashion industry and marriage to an affluent white man, a terrible longing nags at Mimi. Harlem beckons, her affinity for black culture prevails, and she deserts her husband to reestablish her racial ties. (RZ)

FLORENCE MILLS THEATRICAL ASSOCIATION, INC., 1927. With Jessie A. Shipp* as president and Florence Mills's* widower U. S. Thompson* as treasurer, a group of people connected with the theater sponsored a campaign for a Florence Mills Memorial Fund to build a home and recreation center for black performers. There was an advertising campaign and letters were sent out to prospective subscribers, but nothing seems to have come of the project. REFERENCES: CVV; JWJ. (BK)

FOLIES BERGERE REVUE (musical revue), 1930. The *New York Times* predicted a big success for this show at the Gansevoort Theatre, but it ran only briefly, beginning 15 April 1930, despite its tuneful musical score by Eubie Blake* and Will Morrissey.* The integrated cast included Helene and Cortez, apache dancers from the Paris Folies Bergères, which explains the title. REFERENCE: NYTTR, 1972. (BK)

FOLK BELIEFS OF THE SOUTHERN NEGRO (book), 1926. Newell Niles Puckett's book is one of a series issued by the University of North Carolina Press, including *The Negro and His Songs* and *Negro Workaday Songs.* The burst of interest in black music during the Harlem Renaissance, and notably James Weldon Johnson's* collections of spirituals* as well as Carl Van Vechten's* adulatory essays about such matters in *Vanity Fair,* must account for part of their success. Puckett's book investigates voodoo but also burial customs, control songs, and superstitions from more than 400 informants. At the time of its publication it was compared favorably with the work of Sir James Frazer, and, one reviewer hazarded, it might be titled *The Ebony Bough.* The origin of the majority of the superstitions, Puckett contended, lies in southern white people, going back in many instances to European sources, but their transformation into a unique folklore of their own demonstrates that it is probably impossible for one race to understand another by way of its beliefs. The Mississippi-born professor of sociology at Western Reserve University further asseverated, after twenty years of study and several years experience as a voodoo doctor in New Orleans, that whites knew blacks only in a very superficial way. As was characteristic of the work of a generation of southern white anthropologists and folklorists, Puckett emphasized the European roots of black folk culture. In contrast, black and largely northern-born white scholars emphasized the African or pluralist origins of black music and folklore. REFERENCES: WWA, 1950; Carl Van Vechten, *"Keep A-Inchin' Along,"* 1979. (MH, BK)

FOLLY TOWN (musical revue), 1920. In one of the earliest integrated casts, ten black performers in "a riot of jazz" joined a California trio, Oriental acrobats, and "a host of comedians, vaudevillians, singers, dancers and show girls" on May 17 for one of the "most ambitious productions ever attempted on the burlesque stage" (NYT, 18 May, 1920, p. 9). Ralph Dunbar's Tennessee Ten made a particular hit in this Bert Lahr revue, but they are unaccounted for afterward.
REFERENCE: NYTTR, 1972. (BK)

FORD, ARNOLD JOSIAH (religious leader), 1876–1935. Born in Barbados, Arnold Josiah Ford began his career as a music teacher and musician in the British Royal Navy. Subsequently, as a member of the Clef Club,* he was assistant to James Reese Europe,* and after World War I he composed several songs for the Universal Negro Improvement Association* and that organization's "Universal Ethiopian Anthem." They were collected in his *Universal Ethiopian Hymnal*, published by the organization in 1920. He was director of its orchestra, of the Band of the African Legion, and of the Liberty Hall Choir. During the twenties, however, his interests changed and he founded the Congregation Beth B'nai Abraham, a synagogue for Ethiopian Jews, serving as its rabbi from 1924.
REFERENCE: WWCA, 1933. (BK)

FORD, JAMES W. (politician), 22 December 1893–21 June 1957. James W. Ford was the first Afro-American to run for national public office, as vice-presidential candidate to William Foster, representing the Communist party, in 1932. Born the grandson of a lynched black, Ford joined the army after three years at Fisk University and served in the 92nd Division of the 325th Signal Corps. He actively protested military segregation during the period of his service, to little avail. In 1919 he was a leader in the Chicago Federation of Labor, and in 1926 he became a member of the Central Committee of the Communist party and organized the American Negro Labor Congress. In 1935 he wrote the pamphlet *The Right to Revolution for the Negro People*, published by the NAACP.*
REFERENCES: Theodore J. Vincent, ed., *Voices of a Black Nation*, 1973; David Levering Lewis, *When Harlem Was in Vogue*, 1981. (BK)

FORSYNE, IDA (dancer), 1883–? Like Inez Clough,* Georgette Harvey,* and many other talented black performers who had difficulty finding work in America, Ida Forsyne, a diminutive dancer with a captivating smile, lived in Europe for several years, touring England, France, and Russia to great acclaim. Born in Chicago, she learned to dance by watching rehearsals at a local theater, and, when she was sixteen, joined the Black Patti Troubadours as a singer and dancer. She toured the West Coast with the Patti troupe and went with them to New York, where she performed in the original *Smart Set* in 1903 and in Will Marion Cook's* *Southerners* in 1904. As "Topsey, the Famous Negro Dancer" in a show billed as *Abbie Mitchell[*] and her Coloured Students*, Forsyne

travelled to London with the Tennessee Players in 1906. She performed in Europe for the next five years, becoming the "cakewalking toast of Russia" (Hughes and Meltzer, *Black Magic*, p. 92), and learning Russian-style dancing in St. Petersburg and Moscow. On her return to America she performed the "Scay-a-Da-Hootch" dance in Flournoy Miller* and Aubrey Lyles's* *Darkydom* at the Lafayette Theatre* in 1915. Although she appeared in the Billy King* productions *They're Off* and *Over the Top* in 1919, and *Strut Your Stuff, Town Top-Piks*, and Will Mastin's *Holiday in Dixie* in 1920 and 1921, Forsyne found leading roles hard to come by. She worked as a maid for Sophie Tucker for two years, toured the TOBA* circuit on and off, and toured the South with *The Smart Set*. She was not hired by the major nightclubs because she was too dark skinned, but she continued to get small parts featuring her Russian dancing in various touring shows and in *Rainbow Chasers* (1926) and *Darktown Strutters* (1925), and in *Malinda** (1929) she did a "Zulu" dance. She played the part of Mrs. Noah in *The Green Pastures** on Broadway in 1932 and in the 1936 film version and appeared in the Oscar Micheaux* film *The Underworld* in 1935 and on Broadway in *The Emperor Jones** in 1936. She advised Ruthanna Boris on the choreography of *Cake Walk* for the New York City Ballet in 1951.
REFERENCES: Langston Hughes and Milton Meltzer, *Black Magic*, 1971; BB, 1980. (PO)

FORTUNE T[IMOTHY] THOMAS (journalist), 3 October 1856–2 June 1928. T. Thomas Fortune seems to have coined the word *Afro-American* during his long and productive career in newspaper work. At the age of seventy-two, he was still writing regularly for *Negro World.** Born in Florida of slaves, he attended Howard University for two years. He first became a printer for the New York *Sun* but was quickly elevated to staff writer. He served as editor of *The Globe* and *Negro World*, beginning in 1923, after serving briefly in the same capacity for the *Daily Negro Times*. Fortune wrote two books before turning to full-time newspaper work: *Black and White: Land, Labor, and Politics in the South* (1884) and *The Negro in the South* (1885). He is best remembered, however, for having founded the New York *Age*,* one of the earliest and most influential black newspapers, in 1883, and for his incisive editorials in *Negro World*. He suffered a nervous collapse and died in 1928.
REFERNCES: NA, 1976; DANB, 1982. (BK)

FOSTER, WILLIAM (actor, journalist), ?–19 April 1940. William Foster began making all-black films as early as 1913 and writing about them in the Chicago *Defender*,* for which he was circulation manager, in 1915. He believed that a black film industry, catering exclusively to black audiences, could be a solid business venture, even though it required white backing. The Foster Photoplay Company failed after a few productions, but he continued to write about the possibilities in such an industry under his pseudonym Juli Jones, Jr. In 1925 Foster became associated with the Haitian Coffee Company and, two years later,

with the Chicago *Daily Times*. In 1928 he attempted to reestablish his film company, but it completed no productions. As a visionary, however, Foster anticipated the career of Oscar Micheaux.*
REFERENCE: Daniel J. Leab, *From Sambo to Superspade*, 1975. (BK)

FOUNTAIN, WILLIAM E. (actor), ?–? William E. Fountain (sometimes Fountaine) began appearing in Salem Whitney* and Homer Tutt* shows in 1918 and later in Harlem revues like *Alabama Bound* and *Chocolate Brown*, both in 1921. The following year he joined the Eddie Hunter* Company and toured. As tenor with the Strutt Payne Quartet he recorded for Black Swan* and appeared at the Plantation Club.* Fountain acted in at least one Oscar Micheaux* film, *The Dungeon*, and appeared in at least one Broadway musical, *Brown Buddies*,* but his best-known appearance was as the snaky villain "Hot Shot" in the 1929 film *Hallelujah!**
REFERENCES: BBW, 1977; BB, 1980. (BK)

FOUR LINCOLN UNIVERSITY POETS (pamphlet), 1930. Lincoln University issued a pamphlet devoted to the work of four of its students, Waring Cuney,* William Allyn Hill, Edward Silvera,* and Langston Hughes.* President William Hallock Johnson contributed a foreword, noting that "intellectual interest is not confined to the routine of the classroom, and that undergraduate enthusiasm is not monopolized by athletics and campus politics" (p. 4). Some of Cuney's and Silvera's poems had appeared in Countee Cullen's* *Caroling Dusk*,* in *Opportunity*,* and in *The Crisis*;* some of Hughes's poems had appeared in his collections published by Alfred A. Knopf.* Hill, the last of four brothers and a third generation to attend Lincoln, was born in Maryland, graduated in 1929, and went on to study singing in Boston. His career as a poet seems not to have progressed beyond this pamphlet. (BK)

FOUR NEGRO POETS (pamphlet), 1927. Published as one of "The Pamphlet Poets," a series that included Edna St. Vincent Millay, Emily Dickinson, Witter Bynner, and Ralph Waldo Emerson, *Four Negro Poets* opened with an essay by Alain Locke,* pointing out that "race poetry does not mean dialect but a reflection of Negro experience true to its idiom of emotion and circumstance" (p. 3). Claude McKay* was represented by ten poems; Jean Toomer* by five; Countee Cullen* by nine; and Langston Hughes* by twenty-one, all of which had appeared in print earlier in various books and magazines. (BK)

FOUR SAINTS IN THREE ACTS (opera), 1934. In Hartford, Connecticut, in 1934, the Friends and Enemies of Modern Music produced the Virgil Thomson–Gertrude Stein collaboration *Four Saints in Three Acts*, "an opera to be sung," with an all-black cast. In his introduction to the published text Carl Van Vechten* recalled that Thomson had accompanied him to a performance of Hall Johnson's* *Run, Little Chillun** the previous year, saying at intermission, "I am going to have Four Saints sung by Negroes. They alone possess the dignity and the poise, the lack of self-consciousness that proper interpretation of the opera demands. They have the rich, resonant voices essential to the singing of my music and the clear enunciation required to deliver Gertrude's text'' (p. 7). *Four Saints in Three Acts* was a *succès d'estime* and went on to play for six weeks on Broadway and then briefly in Chicago, with its original cast of more than forty black singers and dancers. The opera has been infrequently revived, always with a black cast in its professional reincarnations.

REFERENCE: Carl Van Vechten, ''A Few Notes About Four Saints in Three Acts,'' in *Four Saints in Three Acts*, by Gertrude Stein, 1934. (BK)

FRANK, WALDO (novelist and cultural critic), 25 August 1889–9 January 1967. Born of wealthy and cultured white parents, Waldo Frank was a brilliant student at De Witt Clinton High School (New York); Les Chamettes Pensionnat (Lausanne, Switzerland), and Yale University, where he was Phi Beta Kappa and graduated with a Ph.D. in 1911. While at Yale Frank won two literary awards, wrote theatrical reviews for the *New Haven Courier-Journal* (1910–1911), and graduated, determined to be a playwright and drama critic. However, after living in Paris (1913) Frank returned to New York City and settled into his life's work: cultural critic, lecturer, editor, and novelist. Along with Van Wyck Brooks, Floyd Dell, and James Oppenheim, Frank founded *Seven Arts** (1916), one of the most exciting magazines of the day, and helped to launch Sherwood Anderson* (''Emerging Greatness''), to introduce the French avant-garde to America, and to let America experience the moral and political electricity of Randolph Bourne. For the remainder of the decade and to the end of the twenties, Frank wrote six novels; three works of cultural history and criticism; three books of literary criticism; and one play, ''New Year's Eve'' (1928), and served as contributing editor to *The New Republic* (1925) and *New Masses* (1926). In *Our America* (1919) Frank argued, as had Van Wyck Brooks in *America's Coming of Age* (1915), that America was culturally split between genteel idealism (high brow) and material obsession (low brow). In Frank's words, man was ''externalized.'' What America most needed was a collective identity, a sense of cohesion and purpose. Ten years later, in the *Rediscovery of America* (1929), Frank singled out various ethnic and professional groups as examples of social fragmentation. Only southern rural blacks approximated true group wholeness. It was the task of the artist to make conscious and thus permanent what southern blacks only possessed as if by chance. Jean Toomer* possessed this genius.

Toomer was Frank's most direct contact with the writers of the Renaissance. They first met in 1919 and became intimate friends, linked by a common aesthetic and philosophic purpose. In 1922 they travelled to Spartanburg, South Carolina. *Holiday** (1923) and *Rediscovery of America* (1929) were the direct result of Toomer's criticism and friendship.

REFERENCES: William Bittner, *The Novels of Waldo Frank*, 1958; Paul J. Carter, *Waldo Frank*, 1967; Mark Helbling, ''Jean Toomer and Waldo Frank,'' *Phylon*, June 1980. (MH)

FRAZIER, E[DWARD] FRANKLIN (sociologist), 24 September 1894–17 May 1962. E. Franklin Frazier, one of the outstanding sociologists of the twentieth century and the first black to be elected president of a major scholarly association (American Sociological Association in 1948), was born in Baltimore in 1894. He excelled in his high school studies and won a scholarship that allowed him to attend Howard University, where he graduated in 1916. He had several high school teaching positions, received an M.A. at Clark University in Worcester, Massachusetts, in 1920, and was a research fellow at the New York School of Social Work in 1921. He moved to Atlanta in 1922 to teach sociology at Morehouse College; he also helped organize and later directed the Atlanta School of Social Work. During his Atlanta years Frazier wrote essays and articles for a number of books and journals, including *Journal of Social Forces, Opportunity,* * *Nation,* * *The Crisis,* * *The Messenger,* * *Southern Workman* and *Howard Review*, and contributed the essay "Durham: Capital of the Black Middle Class" to Alain Locke's* *New Negro.* * His articles and research during the 1920s and 1930s concerned a wide variety of racial issues such as social equality for blacks, the plight of the black family, and race prejudice. His candid work on the latter angered whites in Atlanta, and he was forced to leave the city in 1927. He decided to complete his education and received a Ph.D. at the University of Chicago in 1931; his dissertation was later published as *The Negro Family in Chicago* (1932). He was a research professor and, later, professor of sociology at Fisk University (1929–1934), before he was named chairman of the sociology department at Howard University, where he stayed from 1934 to 1959. After the 1935 Harlem race riot,* Frazier was named to direct a survey for Mayor LaGuardia's Commission on Conditions in Harlem. He produced several pathbreaking works on blacks in America, including *The Negro Family in the United States* (1939), *The Negro in the United States* (1949), and *Black Bourgeoisie* (1957).

REFERENCES: WWCA, 1933; NYT, 22 May 1962; G. Franklin Edwards, ed., *E. Franklin Frazier on Race Relations*, 1968; Jason E. Blackwell and Morris Janowitz, eds., *Black Sociologists*, 1974. (DS)

FREDERICK DOUGLASS FILM COMPANY, 1916–1918. One of the earliest black movie organizations, the Frederick Douglass Film Company produced *The Colored American Winning His Suit* in 1916, a six reeler cut to four for distribution. The work of educated, professional men with little dramatic experience, this film was about "Bob Winall" and "Jim Sample," rivals for a girl whose father is falsely accused by a villainous white named "Mister Hinderus" until another white, "Colonel Goodwill" steps in. This morality play had a script by a Jersey City black pastor. Later, the company produced *The Scapegoat*, with Abbie Mitchell,* based on a story by Paul Laurence Dunbar, and a documentary called *The Heroic Black Soldier of the World*, but it did not survive into the twenties.

REFERENCE: Daniel J. Leab, *From Sambo to Superspade*, 1975. (BK)

FREELON, ALLAN [R.] (painter), 1895– . Born in Philadelphia, Allan Freelon attended the Pennsylvania Music School of Art and the University of Philadelphia. He exhibited his work at the Harmon Foundation* in 1928, 1929, and 1930. In Cézanne-like blocks of color, his work suggests the paintings of the early impressionists, but he was also capable of turning out a fairly inept *Crisis** cover in June 1928. His Windy Crest Studio in Telford, Pennsylvania, later became a haven for young black painters.
REFERENCE: Cedric Dover, *American Negro Art*, 1960. (BK)

FREEMAN, HARRY LAWRENCE (composer, conductor), 9 October 1869–21 March 1954. Freeman studied music as a child in Cleveland and was an assistant organist at the age of ten. In the early 1900s he conducted musical comedies with the Pekin Theatre Company in Chicago and the Cole and Johnson Brothers companies in New York. He composed fourteen operas, five of which have received stage or concert performances. The first, *The Martyr*, was produced in Denver in 1893 and again at Carnegie Hall in New York in 1947. *Valdo* was given in Cleveland in 1906, *The Tryst* in New York in 1911, *Vendetta* at the Lafayette Theatre* in 1923, and his most famous *Voodoo* at the 52nd Street Theatre in 1926. *Voodoo* was also heard in an abridged version over station WCBS that year. Freeman composed the ballet *Zulu King* (1934), the symphonic poem *The Slave*, cantatas, and songs. He received the Harmon Foundation* Award in 1930.
REFERENCES: MBA, 1971; GD, 1980. (DA)

FRIENDS OF NEGRO FREEDOM (trade union), 1920–1923. A. Philip Randolph* founded the Friends of Negro Freedom to combat Marcus Garvey's* rise to prominence and the Universal Negro Improvement Association.* A number of radicals joined him in this endeavor to unionize migrant workers. It disbanded in 1923.
REFERENCE: Jervis Anderson, *This Was Harlem*, 1982. (BK)

FULLER, META VAUX WARRICK (sculptor), 9 June 1877–13 March 1968. Meta Fuller was a prolific sculptor and an influential teacher for most of her long creative life. She was born in Philadelphia to parents who cultivated her interest in the arts. She won a three-year scholarship to the School of Industrial Art of the Pennsylvania Museum of Fine Arts and then went to Paris in 1899 for further study. She experienced financial difficulties and racial discrimination there, but during her second year Auguste Rodin offered to become her master, advising her in her work. Fuller opened a studio in Philadelphia upon her return to America, but she found it difficult to sell her work. Although dealers claimed that domestic sculpture wouldn't sell, she thought her race was the issue. In 1907, however, she was commissioned to sculpt 150 Negro figures for the Jamestown Tercentennial Exposition. In 1910 a fire in a Philadelphia warehouse destroyed her sculpting tools and all of the work she had done in Paris and

Philadelphia; temporarily, then, she devoted herself to raising her three sons. She was inspired to return to sculpture when W.E.B. Du Bois* asked her to produce a piece for the fiftieth anniversary celebration of the Emancipation Proclamation in New York. Her sculpture of a black boy and girl was effectively the beginning of her use of the Negro as subject matter and of her development toward more realistic and intimate work. From 1929 on Fuller had her own studio near her home in Framingham, Massachusetts, where she exhibited annually and taught private pupils. She became well known in the Boston area during the thirties and forties, and she received commissions nationally thereafter. She was elected a fellow of the American Academy of Fine Arts, and her work received special honor at Howard University in 1961. Fuller's work may be seen today in the Arthur Schomburg* collection in the New York Public Library and in the Boston Museum of Afro-American History, the Palace of the Legion of Honor in San Francisco, Howard University, the Cleveland Museum of Art, the Atlanta YMCA, and the Boston University School of Medicine, which houses a bronze bust of her husband, psychiatrist and neurologist Solomon G. Fuller.

REFERENCES: NAW, 1980; BDAM, 1982. (PO)

G

GARVEY, MARCUS [AURELIUS] (racial nationalist), 17 August 1887–10 June 1940. Marcus Garvey, still considered by many the most extraordinary black leader of the twentieth century, excited and galvanized blacks in the United States and Latin America with his program of self-help, race pride, and African nationalism in the post–World War I era. Garvey was born 17 August 1887 in St. Ann's Bay, Jamaica, a small town on the beautiful northern coast of the island, the youngest of eleven children. From his cold and formal father Garvey gained his love of learning and books as well as his stubbornness; from his mother he inherited a respect for religion. He was mostly self-educated, and he read widely throughout his life. When he was fourteen, in fact, he was forced to leave school and go to work; he was apprenticed as a printer in Kingston and learned the trade so well that he was made foreman by the age of twenty. Garvey left Jamaica in 1910 after losing his job due to his leadership in a strike and after his efforts to publish his own newspaper and begin his own reform movement had both failed. He worked and travelled the next few years in Central America and Europe, where he learned firsthand how blacks throughout the world were oppressed. In London he came under the influence of Duse Mohammed Ali,* a Pan-Africanist, and he read for the first time the work of Booker T. Washington. When Garvey returned to Jamaica in the summer of 1914 he was burning with a desire to start an organization that would "promote the spirit of race pride and love," uplift blacks in Africa and elsewhere, and promote black self-help on the lines of Washington's work at the Tuskegee Institute. He was not very successful in this regard, although he organized the Universal Negro Improvement Association* as a vehicle for achieving his goals.

In 1916 Garvey decided that he needed to raise funds in the United States to further his work, and on March 23 he landed in Harlem. Slowly, he built a small following with the help of his *Negro World** weekly, founded in 1918. More important, his superb oratorical style caught people's attention as he competed with other soapbox orators in Harlem, and his message struck a responsive chord—racial self-respect—in black Americans. In 1919 he began to attract larger crowds, and a widely publicized but unsuccessful attempt on his life brought him hundreds of new followers. Garvey and his UNIA reached the peak of their popularity in the early 1920s, when he held an international convention in Harlem (1920) that attracted delegates from around the world, founded an all-black shipping company—the Black Star Line*—to compete in the all-white shipping industry, and announced an ambitious project to colonize Africa with New World blacks. None of his programs and goals was realized. A combination of poor management on Garvey's part, an inability to choose proper subordinates, and opposition from influential American blacks destroyed Garvey's chances. He was found guilty of mail fraud in connection with the collection of money for the shipping company; the Liberian government blocked his efforts at African colonization; and his UNIA orgainization split into separate factions after Garvey was deported in 1927, having served more than two years in the Atlanta Federal Penitentiary. He settled in Jamaica for several years, serving in local government and organizing another of his colorful and triumphant international conventions. Still, he felt isolated from the main currents of political life, and he moved to London in 1935. He continued to preside over the activities of a declining UNIA; edited the monthly magazine *Black Man*, which had replaced the *Negro World* in the mid-1930s; and never stopped his worldwide campaign to win "Africa for the Africans," until his death from a stroke on 10 June 1940.

Marcus Garvey was a man of great contrasts. On the one hand, he had a dynamic personality that made him the most charismatic black leader of the twentieth century: thousands of blacks were drawn to him and gave up their life savings for the causes he invoked. On the other hand, his inability to manage this money and choose his associates, along with his difficult personality, proved his downfall. His wife, Amy, edited two volumes of his writing as *The Philosophy and Opinions of Marcus Garvey* in 1923, and he subsequently wrote much bad verse.

REFERENCES: E. David Cronon, *Black Moses*, 1955; John Hendrik Clarke, ed., *Marcus Garvey and the Vision of Africa*, 1974, (DS)

GAY HARLEM (musical comedy), 1927. *Gay Harlem* was one of the few Lafayette Theatre* shows to which Theophilus Lewis* gave serious attention in his monthly theater column in *The Messenger*,* an "intelligent and highly entertaining lampoon of the more picturesque phases of life as it is lived in this community of rooming houses and hot-dog stands" (June 1927, p. 193). Lewis's intention, however, was to criticize reviewers of other black publications like the *Amsterdam News** for feigning shock over *Gay Harlem* as "a medley of loose morals and lasciviousness blended with a wanton display of female flesh" and for suggesting that Irvin C. Miller,* the author, should be writing about dignified home life in Harlem. That, in Lewis's view, was "not gay but tragic" and hardly likely to run successfully at the Lafayette. *Gay Harlem* was at least

an attempt to avoid racial clichés like ghosts and chicken stealing that afflicted so many popular entertainments of the period.
REFERENCE: Theophilus Lewis, "Theatre," *The Messenger*, June 1927. (BK)

GEE, LOTTIE (entertainer), ?–? Lottie Gee, whose dates of birth and death and whose activities other than during a few years are unknown, began her popular career as one of Aida Overton Walker's dancing girls early in the century. She appeared in *The Red Moon*, James Weldon Johnson's* 1905 musical comedy, and some other shows of the period. Subsequently Lottie Gee formed a trio with Effie King and Lillian Gillman and then a sister act with the former to tour in vaudeville. She was soloist with the Southern Syncopated Orchestra until *Shuffle Along** brought her to stardom in 1921, singing "I'm Just Wild about Harry." She appeared in other revues during the twenties, notably *Chocolate Dandies** in 1924, and in 1928 she teamed up with Edith Spencer, the two of them advertising themselves as "Harlem's Sweethearts."
REFERENCES: *Official Theatrical World of Colored Artists*, 1928; BB, 1980. (BK)

GEORGE, MAUDE ROBERTS (musician, journalist), c. 1892–c. 1945. Maude Roberts George studied music at Walden University and afterward taught there. From 1922 she was music critic for the Chicago *Defender*,* and from 1929 she served as director of the National Association of Negro Musicians.*
REFERENCE: WWCA, 1933. (BK)

GEORGE WHITE'S SCANDALS (musical revue), 1921–1931. Two months after *Shuffle Along** opened with its all-black cast, *George White's Scandals of 1921* featured white comedian Lou Holtz in blackface makeup and Theresa Gardella as "Aunt Jemima," the hit of the show in a protracted skit with songs about the good life on the old plantation. Ten years later *George White's Scandals of 1931* (the eleventh edition of this series) included a "Negro Fantasy" entitled "That's Why Darkies Were Born," sung by Everett Marshall, a white tenor in blackface, accompanied by white showgirls decked out in wings and halos. According to the lyrics, *somebody* was obliged to plant cotton, hoe corn, and still sing songs. This number was followed by Ethel Merman singing "Life Is Just a Bowl of Cherries." Burns Mantle's annual chronology of the Broadway season only reinforced white myopia toward racial slurs through a proofreader's unfortunate error: The number was called "That's Why Darkies Are Born" (p. 390).
REFERENCES: Burns Mantle, 1931–1932; NYTTR, 1972. (BK)

GEORGIA NIGGER (novel), 1932. One of several novels with black subject matter by white writers, *Georga Nigger* by John Spivak describes in sordid but never sensational detail the grim life of prisoners in a chain gang. The nearly flat narrative of such implacable horrors gives the book its power, like long-suppressed documents suddenly made public. (BK)

GERSHWIN, GEORGE [JACOB GERSHVIN] (composer, pianist), 26 September 1898–11 July 1937. Brooklyn-born George Gershwin published his first song when he was sixteen and had written a full-length musical score before he was twenty-one. In 1919 he wrote his first hit song, "Swanee," with lyrics by Irving Caesar, which the Jewish entertainer Al Jolson introduced—wearing blackface—in the musical *Sinbad*. For *George White's Scandals[*] of 1922*, Gershwin composed a one-act opera with a Harlem setting, using ragtime recitatives, blues,* and spirituals* cast as operatic arias, called "Blue Monday." One critic called it "The most dismal, stupid, and incredible blackface sketch that has probably ever been perpetrated," and another called it "the first gleam of a new American musical art" (quoted in Jablonski and Stewart, *The Gershwin Years*, p. 66). The producers dropped "Blue Monday" after the opening night performance, but the show's conductor, Paul Whiteman, encouraged Gershwin to employ its jazz idioms in symphonic writing and commissioned *Rhapsody in Blue* for a concert to be called "Experiment in Modern Music" at Aeolian Hall in 1924. With an orchestration by white composer Ferde Grofé, and Gershwin at the piano, this work led to commissions from Walter Damrosch, conductor of the New York Symphony Society, for a full-length concerto in 1925 and *An American in Paris* in 1928. During this period Gershwin not only studied harmony and composition with Rubin Goldmark in order to do his own orchestration, but he turned out at least a dozen successful musical comedies. Gershwin's crowning achievement, however, was the opera *Porgy and Bess** in 1935, with a libretto by Du Bose Heyward,* on whose novel and play it was based, and additional lyrics by Ira Gershwin, George's brother, who had written and would continue to write most of the lyrics for their musical comedies. Many of the arias in *Porgy and Bess* were immediately taken up as hit songs, but Gershwin not only incorporated into the score genuine folk material, such as the street cries of the Strawberry Woman, the Honey Man, and the Crab Man, but composed music of authentic Negro character, such as the call-and-response numbers "It Takes a Long Pull to Get There" and "Gone, Gone, Gone" and the spirituals "Oh, Doctor Jesus" and "My Man's Gone Now." *Porgy and Bess*, produced by the Theatre Guild at the Alvin Theatre, New York, at the heart of the Depression and the tail end of the Harlem Renaissance, gave employment to some of the finest black singers of the day: Todd Duncan, a Washington, D.C., music teacher, and Anne Wiggins Brown in the leading roles; John W. Bubbles,* of Buck and Bubbles, as Sportin' Life, even though he could not read music; Ruby Elzy; Eva Jessye*; Georgette Harvey*; Warren Coleman; and Edward Matthews. The many revivals of *Porgy and Bess* in this country and abroad ensure it a lasting place in the operatic repertoire. Its composer died of a brain tumor in Hollywood shortly before his thirty-ninth birthday.

REFERENCE: Sigmung Spaeth, *A History of Popular Music in America*, 1948; Gilbert Chase, *America's Music*, 1955; GD, 1955; Edward Jablonski and Lawrence D. Stewart, *The Gershwin Years*, 1958; John Tasker Howard, *Our American Music*, 1965. (DA, BK)

GIBSON, JOHN T. (entrepreneur), 14 February 1878–12 June 1937. During a long and successful career the 5'3" John T. Gibson was called the "Little Giant." He was born in Philadelphia where, in 1911, he bought the North Pole, a movie house, and in 1920 he traded it for the Standard Theatre. During the twenties he featured shows with Ethel Waters,* Buck and Bubbles,* Bessie Smith,* and even entire New York productions imported for brief runs, all for white audiences. Gibson served as a trustee to Morgan State College in Baltimore, turned philanthropist for various black organizations, and lived in baronial splendor until the stock market crash forced him to sell everything but a modest house in West Philadelphia.
REFERENCE: BB, 1980. (BK)

GILPIN, CHARLES (actor), 20 November 1878–6 May 1930. Born in Richmond, Virginia, Charles Gilpin quit school when he was about twelve years old to do a song-and-dance act with some travelling fairs. Subsequently, he toured with the Williams and Walker Company and was one of the original members of the Pekin Stock Company in Chicago while still in his teens. For a time Gilpin sang with the Canadian Jubilee Singers and, from 1911 until 1914, with the Pan American Octette. In 1914 he appeared in *The Girl at the Fort* with the Anita Bush* Company, directed by the white actess Billie Burke, and stayed on with the company to organize the Lafayette Players* in 1916. Aside from a single scene in John Drinkwater's *Abraham Lincoln*, a British biographical drama on Broadway in December 1919, Gilpin had no opportunity to demonstrate his substantial talent to an audience that might bring him to public attention. Even in Drinkwater's play he was obliged to speak in a bogus dialect as the Reverend William Custis. *Abraham Lincoln* was only mildly successful, but Gilpin was singled out for praise, and in 1920 when he was working as an elevator operator at Macy's, he was solicited for the leading role in Eugene O'Neill's* *The Emperor Jones*.* Legend claims the offer came as the elevator was going up. "Going down," said Gilpin. The *New Republic* ranked him with the greatest artists of the American stage after his performance, and critic Heywood Broun called it heroic. The following year Gilpin was received at the White House, and he was awarded the Spingarn Medal*; furthermore, the Drama League named him as one of ten people who had done most for the American theater during the year, even though there was controversy over Gilpin's invitation to the banquet. O'-Neill used Paul Robeson* for the London run of *The Emperor Jones*, because Gilpin's drinking sometimes showed in his performances and because he had begun to alter lines in the script that would be offensive to blacks. Gilpin appeared in several other plays, helped to start the now distinguished Karamu House* in

Cleveland, Ohio, and in 1926 starred in a film version of *Ten Nights in the Barroom* produced in Philadelphia by the Colored Players Film Corporation.* The assignment had come at the right time—he had suddenly lost his voice and returned to operating an elevator in desperation—but he refused the leading role in a 1927 Hollywood version of *Uncle Tom's Cabin*, a decision that ended his career. Gilpin died when he was only fifty-two.
REFERENCES: NYTTR, 1972; BB, 1980. Jervis Anderson, *This Was Harlem*, 1982; James Haskins, *Black Theater in America*, 1982. (BK)

GINGERSNAPS (musical revue), 1929. Salem Whitney* and Homer Tutt's* New Year's Eve offering with music and lyrics by Donald Heywood,* and George Morris, *Gingersnaps* was a "glum and inept" series of "snapshots" of black life, in "humorless and pointless sketches" by "accordion-voiced singers." But, as the *New York Times* reviewer continued, "Negro frolics, no matter how bad, invariably contain some dance numbers that stand out by the speed and precision of their 'hoofing' " (1 Jan. 1930, p. 30).
REFERENCE: NYTTR, 1972. (BK)

GINGERTOWN (short stories), 1932. A dozen stories comprise Claude McKay's* single venture into the genre, six about Harlem and six about Jamaica. Although Rudolph Fisher* complained in his *New York Herald Tribune* review about inaccuracies in dialect and Harlem residents sometimes lapsing into Jamaican phraseology, he praised the skillfulness of the structure. The Harlem stories, notably "Mattie and Her Sweetman," are evocative introductions to social and sexual mores among displaced people who find "Living...harder than working" (*Gingertown*, p. 65). On the other hand, in the Jamaican stories, highly colored with local customs, the people draw strength from their common roots.
REFERENCES: Rudolph Fisher, *New York Herald Tribune Books*, 27 Mar. 1932; Claude McKay, *Gingertown*, 1932. (BK)

GLORY HOLE (cabaret), c. 1928. The Glory Hole was typical of several "social parlors" in Harlem, a musty basement room behind a trucking company, about ten feet square, with a plank floor, a library table, some chairs, and a piano. Here, according to Wallace Thurman* in his *Negro Life in New York's Harlem*,* unskilled laborers and their girls "swear, drink and dance as much and as vulgarly as they please. Yet they do not strike the observer as being vulgar. They are merely being and doing what their environment and their desire for pleasure suggest" (p. 29). Such "intimate lowdown civic centers" could be found "all over the so-called bad lands of Harlem," Thurman contended, more colorful and typical than the posh places where thrill-seeking whites came to slum.
REFERENCE: Wallace Thurman, *Negro Life in New York's Harlem*, 1928. (BK)

GOAT ALLEY (play), 1921. Ernest Howard Culbertson's play about black life in Washington, D.C., opened at the Bijou Theatre, 19 June 1921, with a pre-performance endorsement from the *Medical Review of Reviews*, but the *New York Times* reviewer called it "crude and inexpert" (21 June 1921, p. 20). Six years later the Toussaint Players revived it at the Princess Theatre, on April 20, but it was still "crude and uneven" (NYT, 21 Apr. 1927, p. 24). The first reviewer thought it would have been just as realistic "played by professional actors in blackface" and noted that denying entrance to anyone under the age of twenty was no more justified than to deny entrance to women under the age of forty-five to Avery Hopwood's popular farce *Ladies' Night in a Turkish Bath*. The second reviewer observed that the sociological problem in the play was "neither confined exclusively to the negro race nor new to the theatre" and added that the cast dispelled the "prevalent illusion...that all negroes are good actors." *Goat Alley* is about a sincere girl who tries but fails to remain faithful to her jailed lover. After his release, when he learns of her prostitution, he abandons her and their child.
REFERENCES: Burns Mantle, 1920–1921, 1926–1927; NYTTR, 1972. (BK)

GOD SENDS SUNDAY (novel), 1931. In Arna Bontemps's* early novel *God Sends Sunday*, Little Augie is a racing jockey during the southern black hey-day of the 1890s in big cities. The colorful life among racetrack habitués and their elegant ladies forms an evocative background for Little Augie's good luck and fortune, both of which he loses in the course of the story. *God Sends Sunday* served in part as the basis for *St. Louis Woman*, a 1945 musical comedy on which Countee Cullen* collaborated with Bontemps, with music and lyrics by white writers Harold Arlen and Johnny Mercer. (BK)

GOD'S TROMBONES (poetry), 1927. James Weldon Johnson's* series of folk sermons, written in the manner of an old-time preacher, have never been out of print since their first publication in 1927. Beginning with a "Prayer," they proceed through sermons about the Creation, the Prodigal Son, Moses, Noah, the Crucifixion, and Judgment Day, to "Go Down, Death," a funeral sermon. Johnson eschewed dialect because the speakers he was imitating—part "orator" and part "actor"— were "saturated with the sublime phraseology of the Hebrew prophets and steeped in the idioms of King James English" (p. 9). Line arrangements approximate speech tempos and rolling rhythms evoke Old Testament rhetoric in these deeply moving monologues. Johnson himself frequently "intoned" them—his word for his delivery—at social gatherings during the twenties. Aaron Douglas* supplied the illustrations for *God's Trombones*. (BK)

GOIN' HOME (play), 1928. Two years before it opened at the Hudson Theatre on August 24 for a run of seventy-six performances, Ransom Rideout's play was voted a special prize by the Pasadena Community Players. Neither they nor other little theater groups had been able to cast it because of the number of

people required. The *New York Times* reviewer found it intelligent, despite a "flat conclusion and theatrical sentimentality" but questioned the insertion of what had become obligatory comedy and dancing into any Afro-American offering since, in this case, such elements diverted attention from "the deeply penetrating quandary" (24 Aug. 1928, p. 23). Israel, a black war hero, opens a café with his French wife, Lise, who believes that he comes from a wealthy American family. The white son of the family that raised Israel stops with his black troops en route to America, and a small race war begins to fester. Lise seduces the white boy; Israel mistakenly kills his black friend, an African who cannot comprehend the "instinctive loyalty" of a black for a white who destroys his own "racial authority" by sleeping with a black girl. Most of the action transpires in the atmosphere of a black *What Price Glory?*, Maxwell Anderson's war play, and a few days later, in a follow-up notice, the *New York Times* suggested that "coincidence strains credibility" (2 Sept. 1928, sec. 7, p. 1).
REFERENCE: NYTTR, 1972. (BK)

THE GOLDFRONT STORES, INC. (play), 1924. Caesar G. Washington's three-act comedy, *The Goldfront Stores, Inc.*, was staged at the Lafayette Theatre* by the Ethiopian Art Players,* one of the first nonmusical, serious efforts by a black playwright. Theophilus Lewis,* in his monthly column in *The Messenger* about theatrical matters, praised it for its plot construction and its pioneering effort as a black play by a black writer about a black subject, despite inconsistencies in dialect and some self-conscious exposition. Edna Thomas* and Abbie Mitchell* appeared in the cast, directed by Raymond O'Neill. The plot concerned a not-very-bright fellow duped by a gold digger.
REFERENCE: Theophilus Lewis, "Theatre," *The Messenger*, Apr. 1924. (BK)

GORDON, EUGENE (newspaperman), 23 November 1890–? Eugene Gordon was born in Florida and attended Howard University intermittently from 1910 until 1917 and Boston University from 1921 until 1923. From 1919 he was an editorial writer for the *Boston Post*, and he later contributed articles to both *Opportunity** and *The American Mercury*.
REFERENCE: WWCA, 1933. (BK)

GORDON, [EMMANUEL] TAYLOR (singer, writer), 29 April 1893–5 May 1971. Taylor Gordon was the youngest child in the only black family in the mining town of White Sulphur Springs, Montana, where his widowed mother worked as a laundress. As a youth he became a driver-mechanic and worked for several years for John Ringling as chauffeur, porter, and cook. Encouraged to exploit his fine natural tenor voice, he studied for a short time in New York and then joined a vaudeville act, The Inimitable Five, organized by J. Rosamond Johnson.* When Johnson's *Book of American Negro Spirituals** was published in 1925, Gordon joined Johnson for a series of concerts of spirituals* in America and Europe. His pleasing voice, extrovert personality, and seemingly ingenuous character made him popular with the cultural smart set in the twenties, and his autobiography *Born to Be** was published in 1929 when he was at the height of his professional and social success. After a falling out with Johnson in the early thirties, Gordon's career suffered a sharp decline, leading to many years of professional and psychological frustration. He became convinced that his unpublished novel *Doanda*, written in 1935–1936, had been stolen by John Steinbeck for *The Grapes of Wrath*, and his increasing paranoia led to a mental breakdown in 1947. He was in and out of New York mental hospitals until 1959, when he was released to the care of his sister, with whom he lived in White Sulphur Springs until his death.

REFERENCES: Taylor Gordon, *Born to Be*, 1929, reprint, *with a new introduction by Robert Hemenway*, 1975; David Levering Lewis, *When Harlem Was in Vogue*, 1981. (DA)

GRAHAM, SHIRLEY [MRS. W.E.B. DU BOIS] (writer, composer), 11 November 1904–27 March 1977. Shirley Graham was born in Indianapolis, Indiana, where she studied music as a child. When she was in her teens, her father, a Methodist minister, became head of a school in Monrovia, Liberia, and while the family was in Africa she went to school in Paris. From 1929 to 1931 she taught music at Morgan State College and then enrolled at Oberlin College, where she obtained the B.A. and M.A. While a sophomore at Oberlin she wrote the music-drama *Tom-Tom*, which was produced by the Cleveland Opera Company in 1932. She was supervisor of the Negro Unit of the Federal Theater in Chicago, which produced *Little Black Sambo* and *Swing Mikado* (1939). Her books include *George Washington Carver, Scientist* (1944, with George D. Lipscomb), *Paul Robeson, Citizen of the World* (1946), *Frederick Douglass: There Was Once a Slave* (1949), and *The Story of Phillis Wheatley* (1949). She married W.E.B. Du Bois* in 1951 and accompanied him to Ghana in 1960 where she was active in television. She died in Peking, China, in 1977.

REFERENCES: Unsigned jacket note to Shirley Graham, *Paul Robeson, Citizen of the World*, 1946; TCA, 1955; BCM, 1977. (DA)

GRAINGER, PORTER (actor, writer), ?–? Porter Grainger appeared in many shows during the twenties, and he contributed to the scripts of several of them, notably *Get Set* with Donald Heywood,* in 1923; *Lucky Sambo** with Freddie Johnson* and *De Board Meeting* with Leigh Whipper* in 1925; *We'se Risin'*, also with Whipper, in 1927; and *Brown Buddies** in 1930. At the height of her popularity with white audiences Bessie Smith* sometimes sang at private parties to Porter Grainger's accompaniment.

REFERENCES: Chris Albertson, *Bessie*, 1972; BAF, 1974. (BK)

GRANGER, LESTER B. (sociologist), 16 September 1896–9 January 1976. Lester B. Granger served for twenty years as executive director of the National Urban League* (1941–1961), but he had an earlier career as well, first in the

92nd Division of the 167th Brigade during World War I. He graduated from Dartmouth in 1917 and attended New York University (1921–1922) and the Social Work School (1925), at all three of which he distinguished himself in athletics. He organized the New Jersey Urban League in 1919 and subsequently became a social worker there, participating in choir contests and state amateur basketball conferences.
REFERENCES: WWCA, 1933; NA, 1976; NYT, 10 Jan. 1976. (BK)

GREAT DAY (musical play), 1929. The extravagant production of *Great Day*, with music by Vincent Youmans and a libretto by William Cary Duncan, had several delays before opening on October 17 and then ran for only thirty-six performances. The plot summaries offered in two contemporary accounts suggest that the book underwent drastic changes along the way. In one version Emmy Lou works in a New Orleans gambling casino to raise money for Chick Carter who wants to succeed with a sugar plantation. When he falls for a French chanteuse, Emmy Lou falls to the oldest profession. In another version Emmy Lou sells her old plantation to Carlos, who turns it into a casino. Jim Brent, who loves Emmy Lou, throws Carlos into a Mississippi River flood. In both versions the levee breaks and the plantation faces ruin. Three memorable songs—"More Than You Know," "Great Day," and "Without a Song"—all of which retained their popularity, were "shouted at you with considerable vehemence by an energetic chorus," according to the *New York Times* (18 Oct. 1929, p. 24). White actress Mayo Methot appeared as Emmy Lou, and Flournoy Miller* and Aubrey Lyles* did their usual turn in blackface.
REFERENCES: Burns Mantle, 1929–1930; NYTTR, 1972. (BK).

GREELY, AURORA (dancer), 1905–? While still a Wadleigh High School student in Harlem, Aurora Greely was a chorus girl in *Liza** in 1922. She appeared in *Broadway Rastus*, *Runnin' Wild,** and other shows until 1927, when she teamed with LeRoy Bloomfield to tour. She danced at the Los Angeles Cotton Club until 1931.
REFERENCE: BB, 1980. (BK)

GREEN, CORA (singer), ?–? Cora Green was a member of the famed Panama Trio, along with Florence Mills* and Ada "Bricktop" Smith,* which toured throughout the United States on the Pantages Circuit for three years beginning in 1916. She had a rich contralto voice and sang in school productions in Baltimore before beginning her career in vaudeville at the age of fourteen with an act known as Green and Pugh. She performed in Irvin C. Miller's* *Put and Take** (1921) and *Strut Miss Lizzie** (1922) and in *Dixie to Broadway** (1924). Her co-star in several shows was Hamtree Harrington,* with whom she appeared in *Nobody's Girl* (1926) and *Vaudeville at the Palace* (1927) and on tour in Europe. She starred in *Ebony Showboat* (1929) and later appeared in *Policy

Kings on Broadway (1938) and in the Oscar Micheaux* films *Swing* (1938) and *Moon over Harlem* (1939).
REFERENCES: BBW, 1977; BB, 1980. (PO)

GREEN, EDDIE (actor, composer), 1901–September 1950. Best remembered as the composer of "A Good Man Is Hard to Find," Baltimore-born Eddie Green began his career as a self-taught magician at the age of twelve. He went into vaudeville at sixteen and eventually began to appear at the Apollo Theatre.* He was in *Hot Chocolates** and *Blackbirds[*] of 1932*, in blackface and surrounded by a bevy of light-skinned chorines. After the Harlem Renaissance Green went into radio work, notably as a cast member of the popular show *Duffy's Tavern.* He founded the Sepia Arts Picture Company in the thirties.
REFERENCES: BBW, 1977; BB, 1980. (BK)

GREEN, PAUL (playwright), 17 March 1884–May 1981. A North Carolina farmer's son, Paul Green went to the University of North Carolina and taught for a time before going into the army in 1917. He emerged as a second lieutenant, returned to college to finish his degree in 1921, and went on to Cornell University for graduate work. The folk plays of this white writer—almost exclusively dealing with black subject matter—began to be produced by the Carolina Folk Players in 1923: "White Dresses" and "Granny Bolling." The following year four more one-act plays were printed in *Poet Lore*, and in 1925 the Dallas, Texas, Little Theatre produced *The No'Count Boy. In Abraham's Bosom** brought him the Pulitzer Prize in 1927. Later, Green attempted to fuse music and symbols in his plays with open staging in emulation of the German expressionists of the twenties, but except for *Roll Sweet Chariot** they failed to reach Broadway. These "symphonic dramas," as Green called them, were interrupted in 1941, when he collaborated with black novelist Richard Wright on a dramatization of *Native Son.*
REFERENCES: Raul Walser, ed., *Paul Green of Chapel Hill*, 1951; *Time*, 18 May 1981. (BK)

GREENLEE, RUFUS (entertainer), c. 1895–1963. Rufus Greenlee teamed with Thaddeus Drayton while they were both in their teens and toured Russia with Ida Forsyne.* They were the only black actors to play with Bert Williams* at the Palace Theatre during World War I, and in 1922 they appeared in the ill-fated *Liza.** Afterward, they toured again with their own show, *Lovin' Sam from Alabam'*, returned to Russia, and broke up during the Depression.
REFERENCE: BB, 1980. (BK)

THE GREEN PASTURES (musical play), 1930. White playwright Marc Connelly based his enormously successful play on white novelist Roark Bradford's *Old Adam and His Chillun*, a retelling of the Old Testament stories in terms of the devout beliefs of southern Afro-Americans in a more innocent age where angels have wings and fish fries are popular in heaven. More than one black audience member could have agreed, however, that *The Green Pastures* is only one white writer's version of another white writer's version of one black preacher's version of religion. Brooks Atkinson, the influential critic for the *New York Times*, called it "drama of great pith and moment," "a play of surpassing beauty," and even "the divine comedy of the modern theatre" (27 Feb. 1930, p. 26). In retrospect, *The Green Pastures* is patronizing and full of familiar stereotypes. The transformation of conventional black comedy into universal themes is always apparent, however, and the later film version gives some credence to Atkinson's further assertion that "the beauty of the writing, the humility of the performance, put the theater to its highest use." In a huge cast of Afro-Americans, many of whom had appeared in plays and musicals during the preceding decade, Richard B. Harrison* as "De Lawd" had the greatest triumph, reflecting in his performance what Atkinson called "the fusion of all the dumb, artless hopes of an ignorant people whose simple faith sustains them." REFERENCES: Burns Mantle, 1929–1930; NYTTR, 1972. (BK)

GREGORY, T. MONTGOMERY (writer), 31 August 1887–21 November 1971. T. Montgomery Gregory, writer and educator, was born in Washington, D.C., in 1887. He attended Harvard University (1906–1910), where he came under the influence of George Pierce Baker and the 47 Workshop. He received his undergraduate degree from Howard University in 1910 and taught English, drama, and public speaking there from 1910 to 1924. While at Howard Gregory organized the Howard Players as an experimental theater; directed the college's debating team; and, as chairman of an intercollegiate committee, led a successful campaign at the opening of World War I to create an Officers' Training Camp for blacks at Fort Des Moines, Iowa. Gregory entered the service at that time and was commissioned a first lieutenant; he worked primarily with the Bureau of Military Intelligence during the war. In 1924 he accepted a supervisory position with the Atlantic City public schools, and he worked there as a supervisor and principal until his retirement in 1956. Gregory, an active writer, contributed literary reviews to *Opportunity** (including a review of *Cane**), wrote an essay on Negro drama for Alain Locke's* *New Negro** (1925), coedited with Locke *Plays of Negro Life** (1928), and penned "The Negro in Drama" for the fourteenth edition of *Encyclopedia Britannica* (1937). He was eighty-four at his death in 1971.
REFERENCES: WWCA, 1933; NYT, 25 Nov. 1971. (DS)

GRIMKÉ, ANGELINA WELD (poet), 27 February 1880–10 June 1958. Angelina Grimké was the only child of Archibald Grimké,* a slave of mixed blood who became a distinguished journalist and diplomat. Brought to Boston by his white abolitionist aunts, he married white Sara E. Stanley, although she died when their three-quarters white daughter was eighteen. Angelina Grimké had grown up as the only black student in her several excellent preparatory schools and the Boston Normal School of Gymnastics, from which she graduated in 1902. She then began her long career in education, eventually teaching at the Dunbar High School in Washington, D.C. In 1916 she wrote *Rachel*, a full-length play of strongly racial propaganda couched in arch sentimentality. It was presented at the Myrtill Minor Normal School that year and published four years later. By that time Grimké had already published the short story "The Closing Door" in Margaret Sanger's *Birth Control Review* in 1919, and later she published a number of poems in various anthologies, including Alain Locke's* influential *New Negro** in 1925. She had been writing verse since the turn of the century, much of it deliberately self-suppressed, according to her recent biographer Gloria T. Hull because it was "explicitly woman-identified" ("Under the Days," p. 17). Grimké's attraction to other women was strong, to her sister poets Clarissa Scott Delany* and Georgia Douglas Johnson* through their work, and especially to her fellow teacher Mamie (or Mary) Burrill. Their intense relationship between 1896 and 1903 left her somewhat withdrawn and solitary. Her father's intellectual demands and smothering love, which continued until his death in 1930, further undermined her emotional equilibrium, and she resigned her teaching position in 1933 to live in semiseclusion. Ironically, Mary Burrill's only published work also appeared in the *Birth Control Review* in the same year as Grimké's story. "The Closing Door" deals with infanticide and sexual prejudice; Burrill's one-act play is about a woman beaten down by poverty and too many children, titled "That They Sit in Darkness." Angelina Grimké's verse, most of it still unpublished in the Moorland-Spingarn Research Center at Howard University, suggests that she may be one of the most interesting of the Harlem Renaissance poets.

REFERENCES: WWCA, 1933; NYT, 11 June 1958; James V. Hatch, ed., *Black Theater, U.S.A.*, 1974; Gloria T. Hull, "Under the Days," *Conditions Five*, Autumn 1979. (DS, BK)

GRIMKÉ, ARCHIBALD HENRY (editor, lawyer), 17 August 1849–25 February 1930. Although his important work was accomplished long before the Harlem Renaissance began, Archibald Grimké spent his old age enjoying a period for the success of which he was partly responsible. Born in South Carolina, the son of a slave and her white owner, and a slave himself to his own half-brother, Grimké left the South after the Civil War to complete his work toward bachelor's and master's degrees at Lincoln University and, in 1874, a law degree at Harvard. He then served as editor of the *Boston Hub* (1883–1885) and wrote for the *Boston Traveler*, *Boston Herald*, and *Atlantic Monthly*, until he was engaged in 1894 to serve as U.S. consul to Santo Domingo, a position he held for four years. From its beginnings he was connected with the NAACP,* serving as its early president, with the Author's League, and with the American Negro Academy. He wrote biographies of William Lloyd Garrison (1891), Charles Sumner (1892), and Denmark Vesey (1901); his influential *Shame of America; or The Negro's Case Against the Republic* was issued and widely distributed by the American

Negro Academy Occasional Papers in 1924. Grimké's forebears included his great-aunts Sarah M. Grimké and Angelina Grimké Weld, the white abolitionist-feminists, and his daughter was Angelina Grimké,* a poet and playwright whose verses often appeared in black magazines during the Harlem Renaissance.
REFERENCES: Janet Stevenson, *Spokesman for Freedom*, 1969; David Levering Lewis, *When Harlem Was in Vogue*, 1981; Jervis Anderson, *This Was Harlem*, 1982. (BK)

GRUENBERG, LOUIS (composer), 3 August 1884–10 June 1964. Louis Gruenberg was born at Brest-Litovsk in Russia, but after an early career in Europe as a pianist he settled in the United States to devote himself to composition. He became interested in incorporating American musical idioms—jazz, spirituals,* and Indian tunes—into symphonic music; the most successful of these works were *Daniel Jazz* (1926), for tenor voice and eight instruments; *The Creation* (1926), a "Negro sermon" for baritone and eight instruments, based on one of James Weldon Johnson's* pieces from *God's Trombones**; *Jazz Suite* (1930); and his opera (1933) based on Eugene O'Neill's* *Emperor Jones.** Gruenberg arranged four volumes of Negro spirituals. He was one of the founders of the League of Composers and won Academy Awards for his film scores.
REFERENCES: GD, 1955; John Tasker Howard, *Our American Music*, 1965; *Opera News*, 17 Oct. 1964, 10 Feb. 1979. (DA)

THE GUARDIAN **(BOSTON)** (newspaper), 1902–1960. *The Guardian*, a weekly newspaper published in Boston, was the brainchild of William Monroe Trotter* and George Washington Forbes. The idea to start his own newspaper came to Trotter in the winter of 1901–1902, and by late 1904 *The Guardian* enjoyed a circulation of some 2,500 copies a week. That year Forbes left the enterprise, and Trotter continued with the invaluable aid of his wife, Geraldine Pindell Trotter. Not by accident the editorial offices of *The Guardian* were located on the very floor of the same building that housed William Lloyd Garrison's *Liberator.** From its first issues Trotter used *The Guardian* to support his personal campaigns, principally a relentless attack on Booker T. Washington and his "Tuskegee Machine," as the institute was popularly called because of its political clout. The paper's early motto reflected Trotter's more militant stand on the issue of racial equality: "Segregation of the Colored Is the Real Permanent Damning Degradation in the U.S.A.—Fight It!" Fight it the paper did, in campaigns against Washington, Jim Crow, the Ku Klux Klan, the movie *Birth of a Nation*, and civil rights organizations that Trotter found too accommodationist for his liking. It was Trotter's strident militancy that kept him and his newspaper from attaining the national prestige and influence he so badly desired. By 1920 *The Guardian* lagged behind newer black newspapers that had grown up in large urban centers like New York and Chicago. A 1928 survey of the Negro press observed that "the Boston *Guardian* is revered, by a few faithful perennials, because of its consistently uncompromising insistence upon absolute citizenship rights for the Negro.'' That same survey did not rate *The Guardian* among the best black-owned newspapers in the country. Trotter had difficulty keeping *The Guardian* publishing during the Great Depression. With the editor ill the paper missed an issue in the summer of 1933. Supported by a small group of ardent admirers, Trotter kept editing *The Guardian* until his death on 7 April 1934, his sixty-second birthday. The paper continued to be published, although without its creator who had given it a direction for more than thirty years.

REFERENCES: Eugene Gordon, "The Negro Press," *The Annals*, Nov. 1928; Charles W. Puttkammer and Ruth Worthy, "William Monroe Trotter," *Journal of Negro History*, 43, 1958; Stephen R. Fox, *The Guardian of Boston*, 1970. (DD)

GUION, DAVID (composer) 15 December 1895–? David Guion, of Ballinger, Texas, was largely self-taught, although he studied piano with Leopold Godowsky at the Vienna Conservatory. He taught music at several colleges in Texas and at the Chicago College of Music and founded the David Guion Choral and Fort Worth Harmony Clubs. He made many piano transcriptions and concert arrangements of Negro and cowboy songs, including "Turkey in the Straw," "The Arkansas Traveller," and "Home on the Range," and composed *Imaginary Early Louisiana Songs of Slavery*, *Negro Lament*, *Pickaninny Dance*, *Southern Nights Suite*, and the primitive African ballet *Shingandi*.

REFERENCES: GD, 1955; John Tasker Howard, *Our American Music*, 1965. (DA)

GUMBY, [LEVI SANDY] ALEXANDER (personality, collector), 1885–16 March 1961. Like A'Lelia Walker,* or Casca Bonds,* or Blanche Dunn,* Alexander Gumby was better known in Harlem for the flamboyance of his personality than for his achievements. Nevertheless, he compiled a remarkable series of scrapbooks detailing various matters about the American Negro from about 1890 to 1950, through magazine and newspaper articles, programs, flyers, letters, and similar ephemera, arranged by subject matter rather than by chronology. This extraordinary collection, now at Columbia University, includes more than 140 scrapbooks, 14 boxes of clippings, and letters from many people connected with the Harlem Renaissance as well as from Booker T. Washington and Abraham Lincoln; moreover, it contains valuable documents connected with slavery and abolition. Gumby was born in Maryland, attended Dover College in Delaware for a year, and then worked in various capacities, at the Peekskill Military Academy, as a Pullman porter and as "best butler" with the Burghardt Steiner family at Riverdale on the Hudson. In New York he became a bellhop and saved his tips; by the time of the Harlem Renaissance he had developed an unmistakable identity as one of its reigning dandies. Richard Bruce Nugent,* in an unpublished memoir in the Arthur Schomburg* collection in the New York Public Library, remembered him well: "Fancy clothes, a perennial walking stick, pale yellow kid gloves and a diamond stick-pin helped make him the Beau

Brummel of his particular little group." Gumby's friends called him "The Count." Concurrently, he developed a passion for rare books and first editions. "Gumby's Bookstore," as his second-floor, Fifth Avenue apartment near 125th Street was called, became a familiar hangout for many Afro-American artists and writers of the period between 1926 and 1930. Painters hung their work there, young composers and musicians performed in semiformal recitals; Countee Cullen* was guest of honor at a reception when one of his books was published. Gumby collected Chinese vases, cloisonné samovars, and handsome protégés as well as books; he had a rosewood square grand piano (under which Nugent remembered sleeping more than once); he employed a white male secretary, Edward Kolchin, for a time; there was always ample food and drink. To finance these additional extravagances, Gumby claimed, he became a postal clerk, although how that income supported his profligacy remains a mystery; his *New York Times* obituary refers to a wealthy friend who underwrote these expenses. Gumby's tuberculosis closed the door to his Harlem salon—"the first unpremeditated interracial movement in Harlem," according to his autobiographical scrapbook—and halted publication of the handsome *Gumby Book Studio Quarterly** he had begun. The entire Cotton Club* floor show, joined by Aida Ward,* Roy Atkins, Cora Green,* and others, joined forces to stage a Gumby Fund Benefit dance and entertainment in October 1931 to help defray the expenses for the five years he spent in the hospital to effect a partial cure. Alexander Gumby returned to Harlem to spend his remaining years at work on his scrapbooks, which he presented to Columbia University in 1950, afterward keeping them up to date with further deposits until his death at the age of seventy-six.
REFERENCES: NYT, 18 Mar. 1961; Eric Garber, "Taint Nobody's Bizness," *The Advocate*, 13 May 1982; Alexander Gumby Scrapbook Collection, Columbia University; Bruce Nugent, "On Alexander Gumby," undated; Bruce Nugent, 1980. (BK)

GUMBY BOOK STUDIO QUARTERLY (periodical), 1930–1931. During the winter of 1930–1931, Alexander Gumby* finally issued his long-delayed literary quarterly. Money, more than editorial problems, seemed to have held it up. Handsomely printed on heavy, deckle-edged paper, the *Gumby Book Studio Quarterly* included George Schuyler,* Arthur Schomburg,* and Richard Bruce Nugent* among its contributors. Its challenging editorial observation—"Disagreement is salutary; eager approbation or sterile imperviousness abortive"—had no opportunity to develop, since the *Gumby Book Studio Quarterly* ceased publication after its first issue (p. 3). Indeed, it may never have been distributed. Gumby was felled by ill health, and both his salon and his magazine came to a sudden halt.
REFERENCE: Alexander Gumby Scrapook Collection, Columbia University. (BK)

H

HAGAN, HELEN E. (composer, pianist), 1893–1964. At the age of thirteen Helen Hagan went to Yale University to study with Horatio Parker. Two scholarships provided funds for two years' study in Europe. The outbreak of the war brought her home to America, but she returned to give recitals for soldiers in France. She made her New York debut at Aeolian Hall in 1921, causing Theophilus Lewis* to "urge the white people who have been to see *Shuffle Along*[*]. . .to put off going to this trash one evening and take a night at the feet of a real Negro artist. And then shuffle along back home with something uplifting from the Negro soul" (*The Messenger*, Oct. 1921, p. 260). After her Aeolian Hall recital Hagan concertized widely. Also, she wrote a full concerto for piano and orchestra.

REFERENCES: Theophilus Lewis, "Theatre," *The Messenger*, Oct. 1921; MBA, 1971. (BK)

HALL, ADELAIDE (singer), 20 October 1910–   . With a singing style that was vivacious as well as sultry, Adelaide Hall was a popular performer on stage, on tour, and as a recording artist. Of the two recordings she made with Duke Ellington,* Barry Ulanov said that her "measured amatory acrobatics" made the 1927 recording of "Creole Love Call" a jazz classic. In it "the saxes played lovely obbligatos for the lovely soprano voice of Adelaide Hall, whose wordless vocal was almost an obbligato in itself" (*History of Jazz in America*, p. 178). The daughter of a music teacher at Pratt Institute, Hall appeared in *Shuffle Along** and *Runnin' Wild** in the early twenties, toured Europe with *Chocolate Kiddies* and, back in New York, appeared in *Desires of 1927*. Her career went into high gear as the star of *Blackbirds [*] of 1928*, Brooks Atkinson commenting in the *New York Times* that "Adelaide Hall introduces the customary high-calorie diversions with a style that fairly steams, whether she is singing 'Diga, Diga, Do' in Jungle-land or recounting the varied accomplishments of her man" (10 May 1928, p. 31). Of *Brown Buddies*,* in which she appeared with Bill Robinson* in 1930, Atkinson wrote, "grinning with pleasure [she] turns music into exclamation.... 'Give me a man like that,' she shouts, making wicked eyes" (*NYT*, 8 Oct. 1930, p. 29). During the early thirties she made frequent tours of the United States with accompanists such as Art Tatum, Joe Turner,* and Bernard Addison and also appeared in France and England. In the midthirties she moved to London, where she starred in *The Sun Never Sets* and had her own radio program. Although she remained in England she continued to tour throughout the world and in 1957 appeared on Broadway with Lena Horne in *Jamaica*. She recorded as late as 1970, and in 1983 she spelled Alberta Hunter* at The Cookery. REFERENCES: Barry Ulanov, *History of Jazz in America*, 1955; WWJ, 1978; BB, 1980. (PO)

HALL, JUANITA [LONG] (actress, singer), 6 November 1901–28 February 1968. The "Bloody Mary" of Rogers and Hammerstein's *South Pacific* began her career with club dates in New Jersey during the twenties. She appeared in *Showboat** and *The Green Pastures*,* and subsequently became assistant director for the Hall Johnson* Choir and director of the WPA Chorus Group. REFERENCES: BAF, 1974; EMT, 1976. (BK)

HALLELUJAH! (film), 1929. Metro-Goldwyn-Mayer Studios released *Hallelujah!* based on a novel by Wanda Tuchock and directed by King Vidor, following the first all-black feature produced by a white studio, *Hearts in Dixie,** by only a few months. Shot on location in Arkansas and Tennessee, the film perpetuated a number of stereotypes: Zeke, a good country boy, falls in love with Chick, a bad girl, who gets him mixed up in a crap game with her lover Hot Shot; Zeke kills his own brother accidentally, gets religion, converts Chick, kills Hot Shot, goes to prison, and then returns home to his patient girlfriend Missy Rose. Daniel Haynes,* Nina Mae McKinney,* William E. Fountain,* and Victoria Spivey* played these roles, respectively, and with a good deal of conviction. At the joint premiere on Broadway (where blacks were refused admission) white audiences hailed it enthusiastically, but in Harlem the response was more circumspect. Scenes of southern black church services, abetted by rousing spirituals* from the Dixie Jubilee Chorus, exaggerated and even seemed to poke fun at the religious services and the fervor they evoked. Still, Alain Locke* and Sterling A. Brown,* reviewing the film in "Folk Values in a New Medium" in 1930, praised *Hallelujah!* because, like *Hearts in Dixie*, it had "taken Negro life out of the conventional rut and advanced it almost to a point of vital realism," even though it relied on the "usual claptrap"(Patterson, *Black Films and Film Makers*, pp. 27-29). REFERENCES: Daniel J. Leab, *From Sambo to Superspade*, 1975; Lindsey Patterson, *Black Films and Film Makers*, 1975. (BK)

HAMID, SUFI ABDUL (cultist), ?–1938. Sufi Abdul Hamid led campaigns in Chicago and New York in the 1930s to convince white businessmen in black

neighborhoods to hire blacks in their stores. Although he claimed his birthplace as the Egyptian Sudan and his alma maters as the Islamic University of Cairo and University of Athens, most likely Hamid was born in the American South and spent much of his early years travelling around the world. He was a cultist in Chicago in the late 1920s with the name of Bishop Conshankin when a group of "Negro Moslems" convinced him that his talents could be better used to bring jobs to the black community. He was a highly charismatic figure with his strong voice and unusual wardrobe—bright colored cape, Russian long boots, and Sikh-type turban—gracing a powerfully built body. Moreover, he had significant assistance from the black press and pulpit in Chicago to make his campaign slogan a reality: "More Jobs for Negroes: Buy Where You Can Work." In 1930 the campaign was highly successful as Black Belt businesses and stores gave in to his demands; soon there were black clerks employed in many locations. Hamid moved to Harlem in 1932 and tried to repeat his Chicago success. This time without significant help from the black upper class or community leaders he was able to excite and mobilize some of the black masses in Harlem to join him in picketing those businesses that refused to hire blacks in Harlem. He was somewhat successful at first; yet he faced fierce opposition from the Left, conservative blacks, and finally the police after he formed the Negro Industrial and Clerical Alliance. He was arrested and jailed in 1935 for ten days and, discouraged, moved back into the business of the occult. In 1938 he was operating a Buddhist Temple of Tranquillity, in competition with "Father Divine" Baker's* Peace Mission. According to Claude McKay,* Sufi "went aloft in an airplane in which he intended to demonstrate his mystic powers. It crashed, and ended his career" (*Harlem*, p. 228). Still, Sufi should be remembered for originating two of the first consumer boycotts by blacks in the United States and demonstrating the potential power of the black community to determine its economic fate.
REFERENCE: Claude McKay, *Harlem*, 1968. (DS)

HAM'S DAUGHTER (musical comedy), 1932. Notable for the appearance of the popular singer Trixie Smith,* Dennis Donoghue's *Ham's Daughter* ran briefly at the Lafayette Theatre,* one of the many musical shows unsuccessful in making a bid for a Broadway run. In the plot Eliza (played by "Dr. Mary Jane Watkins") is lured north by a city slicker, appropriately called Slick, only to be deserted by him. A smart detective returns her to the bosom of her psalm-singing family and her beau.
REFERENCE: BB, 1980. (BK)

HANDY, W[ILLIAM] C[HRISTOPHER] (composer, publisher), 16 November 1873–28 March 1958. W. C. Handy, the son of a minister in Florence, Alabama, learned solfeggio at the Florence District School for Negroes, studied organ as a child, and learned to play the cornet from a white bandmaster who had been stranded in the town when a touring circus had folded. As a youth he played with the Bessemer Brass Band and sang in quartets and then toured for seven years with Mahara's Minstrels as cornet soloist and, later, director. He taught briefly at the Teacher's Agricultural and Mechanical College for Negroes in Huntsville, Alabama, and led bands and dance orchestras in and about Memphis, Tennessee, before forming a music publishing company with Harry Pace,* a lyricist and singer, in 1907. Handy had had a sound musical education and his early band orchestrations were conventional, but he began to incorporate into his arrangements elements of the folk music, particularly the blues,* that was sung and played in the Mississippi Delta about the turn of the century. The title "Father of the Blues" that was later bestowed upon him is not be be taken literally; the blues did not originate with him, nor was his "Memphis Blues" (1912) the first blues publication; "Baby Seal Blues," by Artie Matthews, and "Dallas Blues," by Hart A. Wand, a white composer, preceded "Memphis Blues" by some weeks. Handy could be said to have formalized the blues, establishing the twelve-bar musical structure and the three-line lyric pattern of a repeated opening line followed by a third, rhyming line.

"Memphis Blues" was tremendously popular, and Handy followed it with "Jogo Blues" (1913), "St. Louis Blues" (1914), "Jo Turner Blues" (1915), and "Beale Street Blues" (1917). Alberta Hunter* introduced "Beale Street Blues" in Chicago in 1917, together with another Pace-Handy publication, Eddie Green's* "A Good Man Is Hard to Find." Pace and Handy moved their company to New York in 1918, and when Pace withdrew in 1921 to found a pioneering race recording company, Handy's brother C. E. Handy became president of the firm, W. C. serving as secretary-treasurer. Handy was stricken with an eye disease in the early twenties that left him almost blind, but he continued to work at his successful publishing business and to lead bands, organize concerts, and occasionally play cornet. A gala concert by W. C. Handy's Orchestra and Jubilee Singers at Carnegie Hall in 1928 presented music by Handy, James A. Bland, Samuel Coleridge-Taylor, R. Nathaniel Dett,* J. Rosamond Johnson,* Will Marion Cook,* H. T. Burleigh,* and other notable black composers; the finale was "St. Louis Blues" played by Fats Waller* at the organ, with full orchestra and chorus.

Handy continued active through the thirties, working at his business, touring with bands, conducting at the Apollo Theatre,* making recordings, and occasionally playing cornet at the Cotton Club.* He was injured in a subway accident in 1943, but although he was a semi-invalid for the rest of his life he remained active in the music business. His publications include *Blues: An Anthology** (1926), *Book of Negro Spirituals* (1938), *Negro Authors and Composers of the United States* (1936), his autobiography *Father of the Blues* (1941), and *Unsung Americans Sung* (1944). A statue of W. C. Handy was erected in Memphis, Tennessee, in 1960, and a commemorative stamp was issued in 1969. The film *St. Louis Blues* (not to be confused with the Bessie Smith* 1929 two-reeler) was based loosely on Handy's life.

REFERENCES: Sigmund Spaeth, *A History of Popular Music in America*, 1948; MBA, 1971; Jim Haskins, *The Cotton Club*, 1977; Giles Oakley, *The Devil's Music*, 1978; WWJ, 1978. (DA)

HAPPY RHONE'S CLUB (cabaret), c. 1922. Arthur Rhone's cabaret at 143rd Street and Lenox Avenue set a style for later clubs in Harlem. His was the earliest to hire waitresses and offer a floor show. Alberta Hunter* sang there, and Noble Sissle* served as master of ceremonies, to entertain a mixed clientele. On occasion, Rhone rented the place out to the NAACP* for one of its frequent parties where influential white patrons could meet Harlem's fledgling poets. The plush black and white decor underscored the integration.
REFERENCES: Carl Van Vechten, *"Keep A-Inchin' Along,"* 1979; David Levering Lewis, *When Harlem Was in Vogue*, 1981. (BK)

HARDIN, LIL[LIAN] (musician), 3 February 1898–27 August 1971. After three years of musical training during her teens at Fisk University in her native Tennessee, Lil Hardin moved to Chicago. She was a song demonstrator in a music store there until 1918, a band member in various Chicago gigs until 1921, and then intermittently with King Oliver's* Band until 1924. She married Louis Armstrong* that year, separated from him in 1931, and divorced him in 1938. During the interim years they made records together as well as separately for OKeh, Paramount, Gennet, and Black and White, and she organized and toured with Madame Lil Armstrong's Dream Syncopaters. "Miss Lil," as she preferred to be called, received a teaching degree from the Chicago College of Music and did postgraduate work at the New York College of Music. Her All-Girl Band played at the Harlem Opera House in 1931 and the following year her All-Boy Band played there as well. She wrote a number of songs, including the briefly popular "Struttin' with Some Barbeque," and she served as Decca Records' house pianist for other performers. Lil Hardin was still playing as late as 1968 when a group of Chicago jazz musicians got together for a concert in New York. She died of a heart attack while performing in a memorial concert in Chicago for Louis Armstrong in 1971.
REFERENCES: WWJ, 1978; BDAM, 1982. (BK)

HARLEM (play), 1929. Wallace Thurman* and white writer William Jourdan Rapp* coauthored "An Episode of Life in New York's Black Belt," as the subtitle to *Harlem* read. It ran briefly at the Apollo Theatre at Broadway and 42nd Street beginning February 20, and after Burns Mantle chose it as one of the best plays of the 1928–1929 season for his annual volume, it reopened for a shorter run at the Eltinge Theatre the following October 21. Inez Clough,* Lew Payton, and Isabell Washington* appeared in the initial production; the revival had an almost completely new cast. The *New York Times* reviewer observed: "Not for some time have the natural processes become so firmly entangled in the warp and woof of the dramatic art. It is a rag-bag drama and

high-pressure blow-out all in one'' (21 Feb. 1929, p. 30). Between the rent parties of the first and third acts, given by a southern family struggling to survive in a New York railroad flat, the plot included rival lovers, white racketeering in Harlem, the numbers* game, and murder. The reviewer predicted a long run if the police censors didn't close the play for its "pungent vocabulary." In his weekend essay for the *New York Times*, Brooks Atkinson questioned *Harlem* as *drama* but found it "deep rooted in elemental playmaking...as a medley of local customs and traits." Comparing it with white versions of black life, he thought it lacked the "poetic exorcism" of *In Abraham's Bosom** and the "bizarre pornography" of *Lulu Belle** but possessed "the ring of authenticity that comes from the negro influence in its authorship" (3 Mar. 1929, sec. 8, p. 1). Originally called ''Black Belt,'' and advertised under that title before its opening, *Harlem* proved successful enough for a second company to play in Detroit and then move on for a run in Chicago.
REFERENCES: Burns Mantle, 1928–1929, 1929–1930; NYTTR, 1972. (BK)

HARLEM: A FORUM OF NEGRO LIFE (periodical), 1928. One issue of *Harlem* appeared in the fall of 1928. It included a story by Langston Hughes,* an essay about voting rights by Walter White,* and other work by several black artists and writers. Richard Bruce Nugent* and Aaron Douglas* contributed illustrations, and Nugent criticized Afro-Americans who were overly sensitive to ethnic stereotyping in plays like *Porgy** and white patrons who indiscriminately endorsed everything about Harlem. Other contributors included Richmond Barthé,* Esther Hyman, Georgia Douglas Johnson,* Helene Johnson,* Theophilus Lewis,* Alain Locke,* and George S. Schuyler.* Wallace Thurman* edited the magazine, setting its tone by encouraging blacks to write about themselves rather than for outmoded standards of an earlier generation or for the current white vogue for Harlem. It sold for twenty-five cents a copy, one-fourth the price of its predecessor *Fire!!** Even a cursory reading makes clear that both publications died from a lack of funds rather than from a lack of talent among their contributors.
REFERENCE: JWJ. (BK)

HARLEM GENERAL HOSPITAL 1907–   . Founded in 1907, the Harlem General Hospital was a white stronghold until 1919 when Dr. Louis Wright, fourth in his class at the Harvard Medical School, was appointed clinical assistant in the outpatient clinic. In 1923 a formal investigation of the unethical practices in the hospital resulted in the appointment of five black doctors by 1925, and by 1930 the medical staff of forty-six had nineteen black members. Three hundred beds served a potential 200,000 patients, however.
REFERENCE: David Levering Lewis, *When Harlem Was in Vogue*, 1981. (BK)

HARLEM GLOBETROTTERS (basketball team), 1927–   . The internationally famous Harlem Globetrotters first played during the 1927–1928 season, organized by a five-foot Englishman named Abe Saperstein. Born in London in

1900 and reared in Chicago, he was coaching the "Chicago Reds" when he was hired to train the Giles Post American Legion black team. He named it the "Savoy Big Five," because they played exhibition games at Chicago's Savoy nightclub. In January 1927 three of the "Big Five" went on the road as the Harlem Globetrotters: Walter "Toots" Wright, Byron "Fat" Long, and Willis "Kid" Oliver, picking up Bill Tupelo and Andy Washington to complete the team. They travelled by automobile to their engagements and, inevitably, experienced much of the segregation in hotels and restaurants that black actors had suffered for many years. In the beginning their playing was more or less orthodox; then in 1929 Inman Jackson joined the group, became its first adept clown, and the collective personality of the group began to form.

REFERENCES: Dave Zinkoff and Edgar Williams, *Around the World with the Harlem Globetrotters*, 1953; NA, 1976. (BK)

HARLEM: NEGRO METROPOLIS (history), 1940. Claude McKay's* *Harlem: Negro Metropolis* is perhaps the most fascinating general portrait of Harlem in the 1920s and 1930s. In particular, McKay addressed the question of how "the Aframericans as a minority" can "fit into the frame of the American composite" (p. 31). Although McKay examined many aspects of Harlem life in this book—entertainment, cultists, the numbers* game, businessmen, labor organizing—it is politics and mass movements that most interested him, and he related in depth the activities of Father Divine (George Baker*), Marcus Garvey,* and Sufi Abdul Hamid.* At times the book is as much a personal statement as an informal history. For instance, McKay attacked the elite black leaders of the NAACP* and other black intellectuals who were, he argued, "supinely abdicating their prerogatives to white leaders", and who were so concerned with "segregation" that they could not grasp what Booker T. Washington, A. Philip Randolph,* and others were doing in building a black economic and community power base (p. 255). He also criticized constantly the white Communists who, he claimed, tried to use blacks for their own ends. Indeed, McKay had little good to say about whites and, as an aside, blasted those whites who were involved in the twenties' movement: "The Harlem Renaissance movement of the antic nineteen twenties was really inspired and kept alive by the interest and presence of white bohemians. It faded out when they became tired of the new plaything" (p. 248). For Claude McKay the place of the black community in America must not be determined by whites or black intellectuals but by the "Negro people's instinctive urge to group themselves, to distinguish themselves as a responsible, integral part of the American commonwealth as against the intellectuals' resistance to this effort, which they combat as a measure of Segregation" (p. 255).

REFERENCES: Claude McKay, *Harlem*, 1940; James R. Giles, *Claude McKay*, 1976. (DS)

THE HARLEM ROUNDERS (musical revue), 1925. One of the dozens of shows that opened and closed, usually after a week's run, at the Lafayette

Theatre,* *The Harlem Rounders* proved a popular success and ran somewhat longer. "All Harlem is enthused and thrilled by the cleverest combination put together here since the days of Lubrie Hill," the *Inter-State Tattler*'s* reviewer exclaimed (6 Mar. 1925, p. 7). J. Leubrie Hill had had an astonishing success twelve years before, when his Darktown Follies offered a three-act comedy, *My Friend from Kentucky*, at the Lafayette. *The Harlem Rounders* featured J. Rosamond Johnson*; Abbie Mitchell*; Billy Higgins*; Dewey Markham*; Frank Montgomery and his wife, Florence McClain; and the "Musical Aces."
REFERENCES: *Inter-State Tattler*, 6 Mar. 1925; Carl Van Vechten, *"Keep A-Inchin' Along,"* 1979. (BK)

HARLEM SHADOWS (poetry), 1922. Most of the reviewers of Claude McKay's* *Harlem Shadows* were astonished to discover that none of it was written in Negro dialect. The *Bookman* reviewer was sufficiently overwhelmed to declare McKay not only a great black poet but a great poet, praising the subtlety and beauty of his love lyrics and protests. *Harlem Shadows* included some poems from *Spring in New Hampshire*, which McKay had published in England in 1920, and others that had appeared in a number of American magazines, notably "If We Must Die," his sonnet written in response to the horrors of the Red Summer of 1919. It also included a selection of evocative lyrics about Jamaica. Max Eastman contributed a sympathetic introduction. (BK)

HARLESTON, EDWIN A. (painter), 1882–21 April 1931. Born in Charleston, South Carolina, Edwin A. Harleston exhibited at the Harmon Foundation* in 1931. He is best known for *The Old Servant* (1928), a painting notable for its realistic modelling. Like the work of several other artists of the period, Harleston's paintings are imitative and academic, lacking the imaginative design of Aaron Douglas* or the rhythm of Richmond Barthé.*
REFERENCE: Cedric Dover, *American Negro Art*, 1960. (BK)

HARMON, PAPPY (entertainer, junk dealer) c. 1860–1929. During the twenties a genial old man—one of the legendary eccentrics in Harlem—with a horse named Maude who pulled his junk wagon was a well-known figure along 131st Street. He hawked fresh vegetables or fish or other people's castoffs, depending on the day's inventory. Pappy Harmon had been born in Greenwich Village around the time of the Civil War, and he sang and danced in various shows until 1910. In his old age, with his wife and children dead, he lived alone but kept pigeons on his Fifth Avenue rooftop.
REFERENCE: Loften Mitchell, *Black Drama*, 1967. (BK)

HARMON FOUNDATION (philanthropic trust), 1922–   . In 1922 William Elmer Harmon, a wealthy white real estate magnate, founded the Harmon Foundation, and by late 1925 he and his foundation had been convinced by black leaders Alain Locke* and George Edmund Haynes* to give a considerable sum

to endow the William E. Harmon awards for black achievement in the United States. In December 1925 the foundation announced that it would award annually to blacks two prizes—a gold medal and $400 to the winners and a bronze medal and $100 to the runners-up—in each of seven categories: literature, fine arts, science, education, industry, religion, and music. In addition, an eighth prize of $500 (for which whites would also be eligible) would be awarded to a person who helped improve race relations in the country. The first awards, which were announced in December 1926, included a gold medal in literature for Countee Cullen* in recognition of his first volume of poetry, *Color*.* In January 1928 the foundation began its long and generous support of black art by sponsoring the first all-black art exhibition in the United States at the International House in New York City. By 1933 five such exhibitions had been held, and travelling exhibits of the work of nearly 150 artists had been carried to fifty cities and an audience of more than 150,000 people. Although the Harmon Foundation was applauded by most blacks for its strong support of black art, there were a few artists such as Aaron Douglas* and Romare Bearden who criticized the foundation for exhibiting mediocre work and, by primarily accepting work that imitated white artists, stifling black expression. Still, by 1931 the Harmon Foundation was widely considered, along with the Rosenwald Fund, as the most influential organization contributing financial support to blacks in the United States.
REFERENCES: NYT, 21 Dec. 1925, 8 Dec. 1926; Cedric Dover, *American Negro Art*, 1960; David Levering Lewis, *When Harlem Was in Vogue*, 1981. (DS)

HARPER, LEON (entertainer, entrepreneur), 1899–1943. Leon Harper was born in Alabama but began work at Connie's Inn* in Harlem before World War I. In 1923 he teamed up with Osceola Banks and appeared with her in some of the early Shubert shows. Later, he danced in *Blackbirds[*] of 1926* in England, and eventually he became producer of revues at the Apollo Theatre* and organizer of the popular line of Harlem chorines "The Harperettes."
REFERENCE: BB, 1980. (BK)

HARRINGTON, [JAMES CARL] HAMTREE (comedian), 1889-1956. A popular TOBA* performer for many seasons, James Carl Harrington got his stage name from an early skit in which he stole a ham and hid it in a tree. He was born in South Carolina and ran away to join a carnival while still in his teens. In between touring shows with Edna Murray, Maude Mills, and Cora Green,* Harrington made his living as a barber. He went to New York from Chicago in *Strut Miss Lizzie*,* in 1922; subsequently, he appeared on Broadway in *Plantation Revue*,* *Dixie to Broadway*,* and *Blackbirds[*] of 1929*. Later, the "vest-pocket Bert Williams,"* as he was frequently billed, appeared in a few films, but during the thirties, when work was scarce, he opened a photography studio in Harlem. His last appearance seems to have been in an ill-fated

revival of *Shuffle Along** in 1952; Hamtree Harrington died in Harlem, in obscurity, four years later.
REFERENCES: NYTTR, 1972; DANB, 1982. (BK)

HARRIS, GEORGE WESTLEY (journalist), 1 August 1884–? When George Harris joined the New York State Assembly in 1919, he was well known as a distinguished newspaper editor. He attended Tufts and Harvard universities, completing his work toward his bachelor's degree at Harvard in 1907. He was first associate editor of the New York *Age** and then editor of the *Amsterdam News.** Subsequently, as an editor for the *New York News*, he organized the first charity bureau for the indigent in New York.
REFERENCE: PR, 1920. (BK)

HARRISON, HAZEL (pianist), 1881–1968. Hazel Harrison was one of the first black musicians to have a successful concert career in the United States. She began her musical studies in her native town of Laporte, Indiana, and later studied piano with Victor Heinze in Chicago and with Ferruccio Busoni and Egon Petri in Germany, where she appeared as soloist with the Berlin Philharmonic Orchestra in 1904. She concertized widely in the United States in the 1920s and performed with the Chicago Symphony, Minneapolis Symphony, and Los Angeles Symphony. She had a brilliant keyboard technique, and in her concert programs she featured Busoni-Bach transcriptions and pieces by Lizst as well as music by contemporary composers. In later years she taught at Howard University.
REFERENCES: MBA, 1971; BCM, 1977. (DA)

HARRISON, HUBERT [HENRY] (radical), 27 April 1883–December 1927. Hubert Harrison has been called by his contemporaries "perhaps the foremost Afro-American intellect of his time," "a plain black man who can speak more easily, effectively, and interestingly on a greater variety of subjects that any other man I have ever met even in the great universities," and "the most brilliant street orator" New York ever produced (Rogers, *World's Great Men of Color*, pp. 440, 441, 433). Harrison was born in St. Croix, Virgin Islands, in 1883. In 1899 he made a tour of the world with a yachting party of young scientists— he was the cabin boy—and settled in New York the next year. He held a variety of odd jobs while he spent the rest of his waking hours studying and attending night school. He graduated with a perfect examination—his teacher called him the most remarkable Negro he had ever met—and easily passed the Post Office examination test. He worked there for four years, until Booker T. Washington and his New York cronies, unhappy with Harrison's radical politics, were able to win his dismissal. By sleeping only two or three hours a day, Harrison was able to read an incredible amount, and he soon had mastered many disciplines; still, his first loves were politics, economics, and sociology. He was looking for the best social system in which his race could rise; he thought socialism would

be the answer, and he was one of the first blacks in America to embrace socialism seriously. He joined with Elizabeth Gurley Flynn, Bill Haywood, Morris Hilquitt, and other white party leaders in organizing workers and speaking out against capitalist oppression. By 1917, however, he noticed that many Socialists were not sincerely trying to address the race issue, and he left the party to form his own Liberty League, which would emphasize race before class. Although he was best-known for his oratory on Harlem streetcorners, he also was a prolific writer. As early as 1906 he was writing book reviews for the *New York Times*. He was assistant editor of *Masses* and editor of Marcus Garvey's* *Negro World* (1920–1922); he edited his own journal, *The Voice of the Negro*, as the mouthpiece of the Liberty League and compiled some of his essays into two powerful and provocative volumes: *The Negro and the Nation* (1917) and *When Africa Awakes* (1920). Joel A. Rogers* claimed that Harrison was a powerful influence on black economic radicals such as A. Philip Randolph* and *The Messenger* group and black racial radicals such as Marcus Garvey (who first won over Harlem residents at inauguration ceremonies for Harrison's Liberty League in 1917). Until just before his death in 1927 Harrison was ignored by the white education establishment. Finally, recognizing his genius and knowledge, the New York Board of Education appointed him a lecturer, and New York University brought him in to give lectures as well. Still, Harrison could never find enough work to lift him out of poverty, and during his later years he was nearly penniless. He died owning only some old clothes and his precious books. All of his published work is relevant to the period: *The Negro and the Nation* (1917), *The Voice of the Negro* (1927, editor), and *When Africa Awakes* (1920).
REFERENCE: J. A. Rogers, *World's Great Men of Color*, 1973. (DS)

HARRISON, RICHARD B[ERRY] (actor, educator), 28 September 1864–14 March 1935. Richard B. Harrison, the son of escaped slaves, was born in London, Ontario. His education was sketchy, but when working as a bell-boy in Detroit as a young man he began to be interested in the theater. He trained in elocution and toured on the Chautauqua circuits giving recitations from Shakespeare, Poe, Kipling, and Paul Laurence Dunbar; taught drama and elocution at North Carolina Agricultural and Technical State University; and organized festivals for black schools and churches. He was directing a church festival in Harlem when he was chosen to play De Lawd in Marc Connelly's *Green Pastures* (1930). It was his first major acting role on stage, although he had appeared briefly in the play *Pa Williams' Gal* by Frank Wilson* in 1923 at the Lafayette Theatre.* He was sixty-five years old when he first appeared in *The Green Pastures*. To master the southern dialect he had to be coached by a speech instructor, and he was concerned about the responsibility of playing such a demanding role; but he had a magnificent speaking voice and great personal dignity, and from the moment he first appeared on stage—in response to perhaps the most extraordinary entrance cue ever written: "Gangway! Gangway for de Lawd God Jehovah!"— he was in complete command. Brooks Atkinson wrote that he played the role

"with the mute grandeur of complete simplicity" (NYT, 27 Feb. 1930, p. 26). Harrison played De Lawd 1,657 times, in New York and on tour, and died at the age of seventy during the return run of the play in New York. He received the Spingarn Medal* in 1931. An auditorium is named for him at North Carolina Agricultural and Technical State University.
REFERENCES: Marc Connelly, *Voices Offstage*, 1968; NYTTR, 1972; EBA, 1981. (DA)

HARVEY, GEORGETTE (actress, singer), 1883–17 February 1952. At the age of eighteen Georgette Harvey came to New York from St. Louis, where she had sung in choirs, and formed a singing quartette called "The Creole Belles," which performed in New York and toured Europe for sixteen years. Harvey remained in Europe after the breakup of the quartette, playing in cabarets and clubs with great success, particularly in St. Petersburg, where she lived for over a decade, immensely popular with members of Czar Nicholas's court. She fled the Russian Revolution and performed in Japan before returning to New York, where she acted in *Runnin' Wild* in 1923, in *Solid South*, and in *Five Star Final* in 1930. She played a "bellowing, arms-akimbo alley oracle" in the original cast of *Porgy** and appeared frequently on Broadway during the thirties in plays such as *Savage Rhythm** and *Ol' Man Satan** (1932), *The Party's Over* (1933), *Dance with Your Gods** (1934), *Stevedore** (1934 and 1939), *Lady of Letters* and *The Hook-up* (1935), *Pre-Honeymoon* (1936), *Brown Sugar* (1937), and *Morning Star* (1940) (NYT, 11 Oct. 1927, p. 26). In *Mamba's Daughters*, according to the *New York Times*, she conveyed "with superb skill [Mamba's] alert and unconquerable determination" (4 Jan. 1939, p. 24). She played in *Porgy and Bess** (1935) and *Anna Lucasta* both in New York and on tour. Harvey was active in the Negro Actors Guild. Her last New York stage appearance was in *Lost in the Stars* in 1949.
REFERENCES: NYT, 18 Feb. 1952; NYTTR, 1972. (PO)

HATHAWAY, ISAAC SCOTT (artist), 4 April 1874–? Isaac Hathaway was born in Lexington, Kentucky, and educated at the New England Conservatory of Music from which he graduated in 1894 and the Cincinnati Art Academy in 1898–1899. He was responsible for making the death masks of W.E.B. Du Bois,* Paul Laurence Dunbar, Booker T. Washington, and Frederick Douglass; his work is in the collections of the Smithsonian Institution, Ward's Museum in Rochester, New York, and the National History Museum in Chicago.
REFERENCE: PR, 1920. (BK)

HAWKINS, COLEMAN (jazz saxophonist), 21 November 1904–19 May 1969. "The father of the tenor saxophone," Coleman Hawkins was an innovator in developing the role of this instrument in a jazz ensemble and, as such, enormously influenced the saxophonists of his own and succeeding generations. He won many music awards and recorded extensively throughout his career. Hawkins began studying music early in his native St. Lous, Missouri. His mother started him on the piano when he was five years old, and by the time he was ten he was proficient on the cello and the tenor saxophone. He continued his musical studies at Washburn College in Topeka, Kansas, and in Chicago. He had begun playing with bands professionally at the age of sixteen and in 1921 joined Mamie Smith's* Jazz Hounds. He toured with Smith until 1923 and then left to work in New York, where he appeared at the Garden of Joy, a popular cabaret, with Ginger Jones. In 1924 he began a ten-year association with the Fletcher Henderson* Orchestra, and in Henderson's arrangements Hawkins's rich, full tone (obtained, he said, by using a stiff reed) set a new standard for tenor saxophone playing.

Hawkins began recording in 1922 with the Jazz Hounds and in 1933 made his first recording with his own orchestra. He made numerous film soundtracks and recordings thereafter, becoming particularly well known through his recording of "Body and Soul" and his album "The Hawk Flies." In 1944 he made the first bebop recording, "Woody 'n You," with the composer Dizzy Gillespie.

Hawkins went to Europe in 1934 and remained for five years, playing in Great Britain, France, Holland, Switzerland, Belgium, and Scandinavia. He returned to America in 1939 and formed his own big band, which played at all major New York clubs and ballrooms, and later toured with smaller bands and his own sextet as well as appearing as a soloist with other orchestras. He appeared with Jazz at the Philharmonic from 1946 to 1967.

REFERENCES: Nat Shapiro and Nat Hentoff, eds., *Hear Me Talkin' to Ya*, 1955; WWJ, 1978; BDAM, 1982. (DA, PO)

HAWTHORNE, SUSIE. See EDWARDS, JODIE "BUTTERBEANS" and SUSIE HAWTHORNE.

HAYDEN, PALMER (artist), 1893–1973. Palmer Hayden studied at the Cooper Union, beginning in 1925, where he worked as a janitor to pay for canvas and paint as well as for room and board. In the first Harmon Foundation* contest in 1926, he won the Gold Award, and the following year he went to Paris to study. His painting *Midsummer Night in Harlem* is in the permanent collection of the Harmon Foundation. Its crowded canvas is typical of his work at the time: lively action, strong contrast in light, and topical subject matter.

REFERENCES: Cedric Dover, *American Negro Art*, 1960; NA, 1976. (BK)

HAYES, DONALD JEFFREY (writer), 16 November 1904–? At the age of five Donald Hayes moved to New Jersey from North Carolina where he had been born. In high school, according to his own biographical note in *Caroling Dusk*,* Countee Cullen's* anthology of black poetry, he "was awarded, after a near student strike, court action and the dismissal of a member of the faculty— the highest debating honors" (p. 188). He completed his education in Chicago and then wrote a number of Broadway revues and a number of poems, none of the latter of which had racial themes and most of which were weakened by exclamation points and ellipses. Later, he worked for the New Jersey State Employment Service as a counsellor for retarded citizens.

REFERENCES: Countee Cullen, ed., *Caroling Dusk*, 1927; *Ebony*, Feb. 1949. (BK)

HAYES, ROLAND (singer), 3 June 1887–31 December 1976. Roland Hayes, the son of former slaves, was born into dire poverty on a farm in Curryville, Georgia, but learned the rudiments of music through the local church choir. He managed to be accepted at Fisk University, although he had only a fifth-grade education. He studied voice there with Jennie A. Robinson but left after four years and went to work as a waiter in Louisville, Kentucky, singing occasionally in a movie theater—behind the screen—to accompany silent operatic ''shorts.'' In 1911 he joined the Fisk Jubilee Singers for a series of concerts in Boston and remained there to study with Arthur Holland, working as a messenger at the John Hancock Insurance Company to support himself and his mother. He gave his first recital at Steinhart Hall in Boston in 1912 and shortly thereafter formed the Hayes Trio, with baritone William Richardson and pianist William Lawrence, and toured on the Chautauqua Concert circuit. In 1914 he teamed with Harry T. Burleigh* to sing duets on one of Booker T. Washington's lecture tours. He gave a recital at Jordon Hall, Boston, in 1915 and succeeded in filling Boston's prestigious Symphony Hall in 1917 with an audience composed largely of his black supporters and fellow employees at John Hancock.

He made his New York debut at Aeolian Hall the same year; sang there again in 1919, with Burleigh at the piano, in a program that included songs by Burleigh and Samuel Coleridge-Taylor; and gave a recital in that hall in 1920. The critic of the *New York Times* was condescending: ''one of those whose music is a natural gift that 'just grows' and whose voice has the clear, ringing appeal traditional with his race'' (quoted in BCM, p. 77). Undaunted, Hayes studied in England for a year and for another on the Continent, perfecting his languages, finding influental patrons, and singing public and private concerts. A solo recital in Town Hall, New York, on 1 December 1923 was a turning point in his career. The critics—alerted, perhaps, by reports of his European success—showered him with praise. The *New York Times* capitulated: ''He astounds by virtue of both natural and cultivated beauty of voice'' (quoted in BCM, p. 75). He gave a second sold-out recital at Town Hall and a third at Carnegie Hall and then set out on his first American tour under professional management. He toured constantly thereafter, giving up to 125 concerts a year throughout the United States and Europe, opening the doors for black singers who would come after him. The doors did not always open easily; he was the first black to sing before mixed audiences in the South, even at Constitution Hall in Washington, D.C. (thirteen years later, the Daughters of the American Revolution roused public outrage by refusing that hall to Marian Anderson*), but despite his increasing fame white critics and audiences were often reluctant to accept him. Even in Europe he sometimes met with initial resistance from the xenophobic press for presuming to sing lieder and arias in the original languages.

Hayes's voice was a small, light tenor; Olin Downes described it as "unforgettable for tonal beauty and poetic illusion...for sentiment that was never affected or exaggerated and a simplicity that few singers attain" (quoted in BCM, p. 80.). His programs were uncompromisingly formal but always ended with a group of spirituals.* "These songs," he wrote, "have become a part of me. They speak to me clearly, echoing the dim past—our ancient African ancestry and tribal memories" (quoted in BCM, p. 79). His had been a "great family for singin' " he was told, when he went back to Georgia in 1926 to buy the farm where his mother had been a slave; songs such as "Steal Away" and "He Never Said a Mumbalin' Word" were believed to have been sung originally by his great-grandfather, a high born chief who had been brought as a slave from the Ivory Coast in 1790. Although Hayes's first professional and financial success had come from singing for "rich and famous people," he found that "walking softly in white society used to be, by and large, a somewhat melancholy adventure" (Helm, *Angel Mo' and Her Son, Roland Hayes*, p. 241).

His collection of arrangements of spirituals, *My Songs: Aframerican Religious Folksongs*, was published in Boston in 1948. His biography by MacKinley Helm, written in the first person in the form of an autobiography, *Angel Mo' and her Son, Roland Hayes*, was published in 1942. He was given the Spingarn Medal* in 1924 and received honorary degrees from various colleges and universities. In 1950 he joined the faculty of Boston University. He sang his final concert on his seventy-fifth birthday in 1962 at Carnegie Hall and died at his home in Brookline, Massachusetts, at the age of eighty-nine.

REFERENCES: MacKinley Helm, *Angel Mo' and Her Son, Roland Hayes*, 1942; WWA, 1945; GD, 1955; MBA, 1971; BCM, 1977. (DA)

HAYNES, DANIEL (actor), 1894–29 July 1954. Daniel Haynes was born in Georgia and attended Atlanta University there. Subsequently, he studied at the University of Chicago, the City College of New York, and the Turner Theological Seminary. His stage credits include *The Bottom of the Cup** and *Earth** in 1927, in the latter of which he appeared as Brother Elijah. He played musical roles in *Rang Tang** (1927), *Showboat** (1929), and *The Green Pastures** (1930). He played the role of Zeke in the 1929 film *Hallelujah!** and he appeared with Spencer Tracy in *The Last Mile* in 1932. When *The Green Pastures* was filmed a few years later, he recreated his original part.

REFERENCE: BAF, 1974. (BK)

HAYNES, GEORGE EDMUND (sociologist), 11 May 1880–9 January 1960. Born in Arkansas, George Haynes completed work toward his bachelor's degree at Fisk University in 1903 and went on to receive the first Ph.D. degree awarded to an Afro-American at Columbia University in 1912. He then became head of the social science division at Fisk and later headed the Negro Division of the Department of Labor, called "Department of Negro Economics." In 1910 he launched the National Urban League,* with the assistance of Frances Kellor and Ruth Baldwin, and was active in its work until 1918, and from 1921 he served as executive secretary for the Federal Council of Churches. Haynes wrote *The Negro at Work in New York City* (1912) and "Wanted: A Fair and Square Chance" (*Southern Workman*, Feb. 1919).

REFERENCES: PR, 1920; WWCA, 1933; NYT, 10 Jan. 1960. (BK)

HEARTS IN DIXIE (film), 1929. Twentieth Century Fox Studios produced the first all-black talking film, directed by Paul Sloane and featuring Clarence Muse*; Zack Williams; Gertrude Howard*; Mildred Washington; Eugene Jackson, who had recently appeared in some of the *Our Gang* comedies; and in the role of the slow-witted but sly "Gummy," Stepin Fetchit.* According to Alain Locke* and Sterling A. Brown,* the "story and production do not perpetuate the old libels and the hackneyed caricatures" (Patterson, *Black Films and Film Makers*, pp. 27-29); more recent evaluations, however, sharply disagree. First designed as a short comedy, then expanded to epic proportions, and finally reduced to a series of episodes to separate the songs and dances, *Hearts in Dixie* is about an "Uncle Tom" type named Nappus whose daughter marries Gummy and has two children by him. When strong prayer and spirituals* fail to save her and the daughter from voodoo spells, Gummy marries a shrew and Nappus sells his farm to finance his grandson's education in the North. White critic Robert Benchley, while decrying the racism in the film, called Stepin Fetchit "one of the great comedians" and observed that the quality of the voices of black actors and their sense of timing made them ideal performers for the then novel medium of talking films (*Opportunity*, Apr. 1929, pp. 122–23).

REFERENCES: Robert Benchley, "Hearts in Dixie," *Opportunity*, Apr. 1929; Daniel J. Leab, *From Sambo to Superspade*, 1975; Lindsey Patterson, *Black Films and Film Makers*, 1975. (BK)

HEGAMIN, LUCILLE (singer), 29 November 1894–1 March 1970. Known as "Harlem's Favorite" in the early twenties, Lucille Hegamin sang in a refined, "torch-blues" style reminiscent of Ethel Waters* and white singer Ruth Etting, with a "vigorous, powerful voice, deep and resonant, youthful and exuberant" (BWW, p. 222). She began singing in local churches and theaters as a child in Georgia and performed with the Leonard Harper Minstrel Stock Company in tent shows throughout the South. In 1914 she began singing in clubs in Chicago accompanied by her husband, pianist Bill Hegamin, and later, backed up by her own band, sang in Seattle and Los Angeles. Her recording career began after their move to New York in 1919. She opened the Shuffle Inn in 1921, toured with her own groups the "Blue Flame Syncopators" and the "Dixie Daisies," and worked with the "Sunnyland Cotton Pickers" in 1926–1927. As the "Cameo Girl" she appeared in several shows at the Lafayette* and Lincoln* theaters,

among them *Creole Follies* (1923), *Lincoln Frolics* with Adelaide Hall* (1926), *Shufflin' Feet* (1927), *Midnight Steppers* (1928), and *New Year's Revels* (1930). After the 1933 and 1934 seasons at the Paradise in Atlantic City, Hegamin gave up her musical career and became a registered nurse, coming out of retirement on the Spivey label only in 1962.
REFERENCES: WWJ, 1978; BWW, 1979. (PO)

"HELL FIGHTERS" REGIMENT (World War I unit), 16 June 1916–1919. The "Hell Fighters," the popular name given to the black 15th New York regiment from Harlem (later renamed the United States 369th Regiment), were under shell fire in France for 191 days during World War I, held one trench without relief for 91 days, never retreated, and, for their bravery, received the Croix de Guerre from the French government and were selected by the French High Command to be the first Allied unit to set foot on enemy territory. The Germans (or the French, depending on which story you believe) grudgingly gave them their nickname of "hell fighters." The regiment was first organized on 16 June 1916 as a National Guard unit under the command of a white colonel, William Hayward. Four months after war was declared by the United States, the unit was shipped to South Carolina and later New Jersey for training and, after they endured the usual Jim Crow treatment, embarked for France on 12 November 1917. The Hell Fighters were attached to the Eighth Corps of the Fourth French Army as a combat regiment and were the only American unit allowed to carry its state colors. In April 1918 the men from Harlem had their first taste of fighting in the Champagne region. They returned home as heroes, and on 17 February 1919, 1,300 black soldiers and 18 white officers of the 369th, led by Hayward, marched through Manhattan to Harlem, cheered by more than a million excited onlookers. The only black officer, Lieutenant James Reese Europe,* led his famous regimental band along the route as well.
REFERENCES: Arthur Little, *From Harlem to the Rhine*, 1936; David Levering Lewis, *When Harlem Was in Vogue*, 1981. (DS)

HENDERSON, [JAMES] FLETCHER [HAMILTON] "SMACK" (musician), 18 December 1897–28 December 1952. Fletcher Henderson was as well known as any musician during the twenties and the leader of one of the most popular orchestras. He had begun studying piano at the age of six in his native Georgia, avoiding the jazz and ragtime that his educator-father disparaged. He majored in chemistry at Atlanta University College and then went to New York to work in a chemistry laboratory in 1921, moonlighting as a song demonstrator for the Pace and Handy Music Company. When Harry Pace* started the Black Swan Phonograph Corporation,* Henderson became its recording manager as well as its full-time accompanist for Bessie Smith* and Ethel Waters,* and leader for instrumental selections. He organized the Black Swan Troubadors, a band to accompany Ethel Waters on one of the first promotional tours sponsored by a record company. In 1924, he married Leora Meoux, a classical trumpet player he had met on a Hudson River boat. She had had some experience as a member of the Musical Spillers in vaudeville and, later, with the Lafayette Theatre* Orchestra, but she credited her husband for her jazz training and Louis Armstrong* for teaching her to play "hot trumpet." Also in 1924 Henderson formed his own ten-piece band, emulating the instrumentation in Paul Whiteman's jazz band and performing first at the Club Alabam and shortly afterward, having expanded his group to sixteen pieces, at the Roseland Ballroom. Louis Armstrong and Coleman Hawkins* were among his instrumentalists, and Fats Waller* and Leora Meoux sat in from time to time. Not surprisingly, Henderson's orchestra was in great demand. The house he and his wife shared on 139th Street in Harlem became a hangout for many musicians of the period: Bessie Smith, Clara Smith,* and Cab Calloway,* for example. Some of them took room and board there from time to time; some came to eat, some to rehearse, as Fletcher Henderson's group continued to grow in popularity. His orchestrations and those of his sideman-arranger Don Redman,* reflected the spontaneous character of classic early jazz combos but called for tighter, more controlled sectional playing as well as solo improvisation; his Roseland Orchestra was probably the first to have the "big band" sound usually identified with the thirties. Duke Ellington* said, "Musicians mostly remember that band, during those years, as the greatest dance band anyone ever heard. They played some formidable music" (Shapiro and Hentoff, *Hear Me Talkin' to Ya*, p. 202). The debacle of Vincent Youmans's *Great Day,* for which Henderson had signed, plus the stock market crash and the sudden collapse of the recording business, brought the first phase of Henderson's career to an end. Later, he made arrangements for Tommy and Jimmie Dorsey, while his wife formed her own music group, the Vampires. Henderson joined Benny Goodman's band in 1939 as arranger and sextet-pianist, and he arranged for other orchestras for many years as well as heading his own bands on tour and in residencies in New York and Chicago. He was actively performing with his sextet at Café Society, a New York nightclub, until two years before his death at fifty-five, following a series of strokes.

REFERENCES: Nat Shapiro and Nat Hentoff, eds., *Hear Me Talkin' to Ya*, 1955; MBA, 1971; Walter C. Allen, *Hendersonia*, 1973; *Fletcher Henderson: Developing an American Orchestra*, 1977; WWJ, 1978; BWBO, 1981; BDAM, 1982. (DA)

HENDERSON, KATHERINE (actress), 23 June 1909–? One of the great beauties of the period, Katherine Henderson worked with Eva Taylor's* tours and on her radio program. She had begun her career at the age of eight, however, touring with musical revues. She first appeared on Broadway in Taylor's ill-fated *Bottomland* in 1927. The following year she worked with the Kathleen Kirkwood Underground Theatre in Greenwich Village, and in 1929 she acted in *Keep Shufflin'.*

REFERENCE: BWW, 1979. (BK)

HENDERSON, ROSA (singer) 24 November 1897–6 April 1968. Rosa Henderson toured in southern vaudeville with her husband, the comedian Slim Deschamps. She appeared in many black revues at the Lafayette,* Alhambra,* and Lincoln* theaters and was a popular singer with black audiences. Her only Broadway show seems to have been *Yeah Man!* a 1932 failure.
REFERENCE: BWW, 1979. (BK)

HERNANDEZ, JUANO [JUAN G.] (actor) c. 1896–17 July 1970. Juano Hernandez, who had a distinguished career in sound motion pictures, began his career as an acrobat in a circus in his native Puerto Rico. After an engagement at the Cotton Club* he sang in the chorus of *Showboat* in 1929. In later years he taught dramatics at the University of Puerto Rico.
REFERENCE: BAF, 1974. (BK)

HERSKOVITS, MELVILLE (anthropologist), 10 September 1895–25 February 1963. Melville Herskovitz, a white, Jewish anthropologist, was the first Africanist in the United States and was the originator of Afro-American Studies. Born in Bellefontaine, Ohio, in 1895, Herskovits served in the Medical Corps in World War I before attending the University of Chicago, where he graduated in 1920. He went to Columbia to study with Franz Boas and earned the Ph.D. in 1923. He lectured at Columbia for several years, taught at Howard University for two years, and finally accepted a position at Northwestern University, where he stayed from 1927 until his death in 1963. Herskovits's research in Africa and with blacks in the United States in the 1920s and 1930s revolutionized the study of Afro-Americans. Most importantly, he demonstrated that American blacks were not a people without a past; on the contrary, they came to the Americas with a strong African cultural heritage. As much as Carter Woodson* and W.E.B. Du Bois,* Herskovits awakened blacks to the fact that they had a history worth knowing before slavery. He was one of five white contributors to the famous March 1925 *Survey Graphic* issue on Harlem and wrote an annual assessment of race relations in the United States for the *American Journal of Sociology*, beginning in 1929.
REFERENCES: Melville Herskovits, *The Myth of the Negro Past*, 1941; George Simpson, *Melville Herskovits*, 1973. (DS)

HEYWARD, DOROTHY [KUHNS] (playwright), 6 June 1890–19 November 1961. Born in Wooster, Ohio, Dorothy Kuhns attended Radcliff (1919–1923) and enrolled in George Pierce Baker's 47 Workshop at Harvard. Her play *Nancy Annit* (1924) won the Harvard Prize and was produced on Broadway. Soon after her marriage to Du Bose Heyward,* she was inspired to dramatize his novel *Porgy,* set among the Gullah-speaking blacks on the waterfront of Charleston, South Carolina. Produced by the Theatre Guild, *Porgy* had a successful run in 1927 and, a decade later, was transformed into George Gershwin's* opera *Porgy and Bess*.* In 1939 Dorothy Heyward again collaborated with her husband to

bring his novel *Mamba's Daughters* to the stage. Again set among the Gullah blacks, the play was a popular success with Ethel Waters.* Dorothy Heyward's last play, *Set My People Free*, in 1948 was a return to Charleston and a dramatization of Denmark Vesey's aborted slave rebellion in 1882.
REFERENCES: AAB, 1972; AWW, 1979. (MH)

HEYWARD, DU BOSE (novelist, playwright), 31 August 1885–16 June 1940. Born in Charleston, South Carolina, Du Bose Heyward quit school when he was fourteen to support his family by working first in a hardware store and then on the Charleston waterfront. He published his first book, *Carolina Chansons*, in 1922, shortly before his marriage to Dorothy Kuhns Heyward,* a young playwright. In 1925 his novel about the Gullah natives in Charleston, *Porgy*,* was a popular and critical success, leading to its dramatization by the husband and wife team two years later; a decade later he collaborated with Ira Gershwin on the libretto for George Gershwin's* opera based on the play, *Porgy and Bess.* Heyward wrote other novels after *Porgy*, notably *Mamba's Daughters* in 1929, which he and his wife dramatized, with Ethel Waters* in the leading role, in 1939. Like Julia Peterkin,* also born and reared in South Carolina, Heyward was sensitive and sympathetic in his portrayals of indigent and ignorant black Americans, but to white readers and theatergoers, the characters may encourage some invidious stereotyping.
REFERENCES: NYT, 17 June 1940; William Rose Benét, ed., *The Reader's Encyclopedia*, 1948. (BK)

HEYWOOD, DONALD (composer), 24 September 1901–13 January 1967. After attending Fisk University, Northwestern Medical School, and the Mordkin Moser Conservatory, Donald Heywood joined the Will Marion Cook* Orchestra. He composed the score for *Get Set* with Porter Grainger* in 1923, featuring "the treat of the evening," Ethel Waters,* and *Miss Calico* in 1926, again with Ethel Waters, but featuring also a parody of *Lulu Belle*,* the popular white play about an infamous Harlem woman, then running on Broadway. Although she repeated the number in later shows, Ethel Waters first sang Heywood's "I'm Coming, Virginia" in this Lafayette Theatre* show. For the Broadway stage Heywood wrote *Hot Rhythm*,* both versions of *Africana*,* and *Blackberries of 1932.*
REFERENCE: WWJ, 1972. (BK)

HIGGINS, [WILLIAM WELDON] BILLY (composer, comedian), 1888–? Best remembered as the composer of the perennial "There'll be Some Changes Made," Billy Higgins was a ballad singer, first in his native South Carolina and later, from 1912 until 1917, with the Billy King Company. He served in the 805th Pioneer Infantry Division as a sergeant during World War I but saw no action. Usually in blackface, he appeared in a number of shows, both in New York and on tour: *Exploits in Africa* and *Over the Top* (1919), *Keep It Up* (1922),

Gold Dust and *Follow Me* (1923), *The Harlem Rounders** (1925), and *Hot Chocolates** (1929), among others. He was married to the popular black performer Valaida Snow,* apparently briefly, since he is never mentioned in accounts of her glamorous if melodramatic career.
REFERENCE: BB, 1980. (BK)

HILL, [BERTHA] CHIPPIE (singer), 15 March 1905–7 May 1950. The owner of LeRoy's gave Chippie Hill her nickname when she began dancing in his cabaret chorus line at the age of fourteen. In 1922 she appeared at Edmond's Cellar,* where Ethel Waters* got her start in New York. Most of Chippie Hill's work was in Chicago, although she performed from time to time in New York. Rudi Blesh remembered her deep contralto voice as richly expressive. There was a revival of interest in her during the forties, but it was cut short when she was killed by a hit-and-run driver in New York.
REFERENCE: BWW, 1979. (BK)

HILL, CLIFTON THOMPSON (artist), 1902–? Like a number of other young black painters of the period, Virginia-born Clifton Hill studied under Winold Reiss* at the Cooper Union. He exhibited at the Harmon Foundation* in 1929, 1930, and 1933 and at the Smithsonian Institution in 1929. His work shows the marked influence of his teacher.
REFERENCE: AAB, 1972. (BK)

HILL, LESLIE PINCKNEY (educator), 14 May 1880–16 February 1960. Leslie Hill, born in Virginia, received the bachelor's and master's degrees at Harvard and was awarded a Litt.D. degree at Lincoln University. He taught at Tuskegee Institute and then was long active in Pennsylvania educational organizations as principal of the Cheyney State Teacher's College. Hill wrote *The Wings of Oppression*, a collection of verse, in 1921 and the historical drama *Toussaint L'Ouverture* in 1928.
REFERENCES: PR, 1920; WWCA, 1933. (BK)

HITE, MATTIE (singer), c. 1890–c. 1935. Although Mattie Hite has been called "one of the greatest cabaret singers of all time" (BWW, p. 231), very little is known about her life. She grew up in New York City and moved to Chicago about 1915, where she worked with Florence Mills* and Alberta Hunter* at the Panama Club. She returned to New York in 1919, sang in clubs, and recorded with Fletcher Henderson.* She appeared at the Lincoln* and Lafayette* theaters during the late twenties in *Hot Feet, Tip Top Revue, Chocolate Blondes*, and *The Temple of Jazz*. She recorded with Cliff Jackson in 1930, but her whereabouts are unknown after that time. Along with blues* shouters like Lucille Hegamin* and Mary Stafford,* who could "sing louder than any nightclub

band,'' Hite sang in a style old-timers called "throwing it from the velvet"
(Hughes and Meltzer, *Black Magic*, p. 97).
REFERENCES: Langston Hughes and Milton Meltzer, *Black Magic*, 1971; BWW,
1979. (PO)

THE HOBBY HORSE (bookshop), c. 1928–1930. At 205 West 136th Street
Douglas Howe ran his Hobby Horse shop, advertising in the window and on
calling cards, "Howe About Books?" Young black writers of the period con-
gregated there and could always count on finding their works on display and in
stock. Occasionally Howe also mounted painting and photographic exhibitions
by black artists such as James Allen (1907–?), whose popular photographic
portraits of Harlem Renaissance luminaries, both black and white, were frequently reprinted in the black press.
REFERENCE: Alexander Gumby Scrapbook Collection, Columbia University.
(BK)

HOBOKEN BLUES (play), 1928. Michael Gold's *Hoboken Blues* was produced by The New Playwrights' Theatre, "the only avowedly die-hard radical
theatre in the city," according to the *New York Times* (18 Feb. 1928, p. 10).
A white cast in burnt cork enacted its version of corruption in Harlem, revival
meetings, and cakewalks, unrelieved by a dull script and a boring plot. Experimental staging did not help.
REFERENCE: NYTTR, 1972. (BK)

HODGES, JOHNNY "RABBIT" (saxophonist), 25 July 1907–11 May 1970.
In 1920, when he was fourteen, Johnny Hodges began studying with Sidney
Bechet* whose style he emulated, and in 1924 he began to play professionally.
He appeared successively, and always successfully, in the Rhythm Club, the
Basha, the Paddock Club, and at the Savoy Ballroom.* In 1927 he joined Duke
Ellington's* Kentucky Club Orchestra. Hodges wrote the popular "I'm Begin-
ning to See the Light" and many other songs.
REFERENCE: ASCAP, 1966. (BK)

HOLIDAY (novel), 1923. Waldo Frank's *Holiday* is set in the town of Nazareth,
a decayed and decaying southern town split into two worlds—black and white.
Each world is separate and yet seeks wholeness in terms of the other. This stasis
of desire is played out to its murderous climax in the persons of John Cloud
(black) and Virginia Hade (white). Their passion galvanizes the town, and John
is lynched. Throughout, the tramp steamer *Psyche*, which docked at Nazareth
to open the novel, remains tied to an empty pier as the townsmen search for
John and execute their justice. (MH)

HOLLOWAY, JOHN WESLEY (minister, poet), 28 July 1865–? As a poet
John Wesley Holloway was clearly from another time and generation, but he

published his only collection of verse in 1919, *From the Desert*, made up of devotional, moral, and religious subjects, nearly all of them in dialect. He was born in Georgia and began writing poetry at the age of eight. After attending Clark and Fisk universities he was ordained in 1900 and then served in various churches in Alabama, Georgia, New Jersey, and Oklahoma.
REFERENCE: BAWPP, 1975. (BK)

HOLLOWAY, LUCY ARIEL WILLIAMS (poet, musician), 3 March 1905– ? When she was a senior at Fisk University, Alabama-born Lucy Williams won the *Opportunity** prize in 1926 for her dialect poem ''Northboun'.'' Other poems of hers appeared in *Opportunity* in 1929 and 1935. She attended Emerson Institute and Talladega College and after graduating from Fisk went on to study music at Oberlin College. Subsequently, she became director of music at North Carolina College, Durham. She is the author of *Shape Them into Dreams: Poems*, published in 1955 by Exposition Press, New York.
REFERENCES: Countee Cullen, ed., *Caroling Dusk*, 1927; Langston Hughes and Arna Bontemps, eds., *The Poetry of the Negro,* 1949. (PO)

HOLSTEIN, CASPAR (businessman), 6 December 1877–9 April 1944. With Jessie Fauset,* Alain Locke,* Charles S. Johnson,* James Weldon Johnson,* and Walter White,* Caspar Holstein was cited by David Levering Lewis as one of the six most influential people who, in Langston Hughes's* phrase,''midwifed the so-called New Negro literature into being'' (*When Harlem Was in Vogue*, p. 121). Holstein was a bolito king, the numbers* racket that both made and broke Harlem success. Holstein devised a system for betting on three-digit numbers drawn from the daily stock market reports. The odds were 600–1. At the height of his power, the ''King of Policy,'' as he was popularly called, owned three apartment buildings, a Long Island house, and property in Virginia as well as a modest fleet of automobiles. By 1926 his Turf Club at 111 West 136th Street began to sponsor staid balls; he was an Elk; he stood tall in his West Indian community. Moreover, he wrote for *Negro World** about repression in the Virgin Islands, where he had been born, and also for *Opportunity*,* where he was tolerated largely because of the money he paid out for its annual contest. In March 1925, after what had been conceived as a one-time-only competition, James Weldon Johnson read Holstein's astonishing letter at the awards dinner: ''Having been all my life a firm and enthusiastic believer in the creative genius of the Black Race, to which I humbly belong, OPPORTUNITY'S Prize Contest to foster artistic expression among Negroes has been a source of breathless interest to me.'' It would go far, Holstein continued, in ''bridging the gap between the black and white races in the United States today, and particularly will it encourage among our gifted youth the ambition to scale the empyrean heights of art and literature.'' He enclosed a check for $55, ''with a heart bursting with joy and appreciation,'' so another contest could be conducted the following year. *Opportunity* published the letter in its June 1925 issue (p. 177). Annually, Caspar

Holstein gave huge sums of money to various other charities as well, but his obituary concentrated on more nefarious events in his life. In September 1929, for example, he was kidnapped for $50,000 ransom but released a few days later, badly beaten up. In the thirties he went to prison for three years for a minor infraction in the numbers game that had made him flush in the twenties. Dutch Schultz and his bootleg liquor and other white encroachments ended Holstein's reign. The character Randolph Pettijohn in Carl Van Vechten's* *Nigger Heaven*￼ is an unflattering portrait of the bolito king.

REFERENCES: Carl Van Vechten, *Nigger Heaven*, 1926; *Opportunity*, May 1925; NYT, 10 Apr. 1944; David Levering Lewis, *When Harlem Was in Vogue*, 1981. (BK)

HOLT, NORA [LENA DOUGLAS] (music critic, singer), 1890?–25 January 1974. Best known as a nightclub singer, Nora Holt was the first black woman to earn a master of music degree at the Chicago Musical College in 1918. Born Lena Douglas in Kansas City, she was educated at Western University in Quindaro, Kansas. Briefly, beginning at the age of fifteen, she was married successively to musician Sky James, politician Philip Scroggins, and barber Bruce Jones, before going on to graduate school in Chicago. There, she worked on "The Line," the infamous red-light district, singing in various clubs, including the celebrated establishment of the Everleigh Sisters, and during this period she was music critic for the Chicago *Defender*￼ as well. After completing her master's degree she founded the National Association of Negro Musicians*￼ and served for three years as its vice-president, and she edited and published the magazine *Music and Poetry* while continuing to write music. For three years she was married to George Holt, an elderly hotel owner, during which time she changed her name to Nora. At thirty she was a wealthy widow, holding the largest single block of stock in the Liberty Life Insurance Company. In the middle of an apparent affair with Gordon Jackson, a local doctor, she met and quickly married Joseph L. Ray, who controlled the food concession in Bethlehem, Pennsylvania, in his role as Charles Schwab's private car man. The wedding, in 1923, was the most brilliant social event of the black season. Clarence Cameron White,*￼ the violinist-composer, performed before the vows, and Chicago's black blueblood line was in attendance. The bride, wearing over six carats in diamonds in each ear and a pearl-encrusted gown, also sported a black eye, by rumor from Dr. Jackson. During the brief marriage—nineteen months, of which Nora Holt had spent thirty-two days in Bethlehem—she was discovered in New York with Leroy Wilkins, brother of Barron Wilkins, owner of the Exclusive Club,*￼ after which Ray brought suit for adultery.

One of the remarkable personalities of the Harlem Renaissance, Nora Holt then moved to New York with a sizable legacy from her fourth husband, a provocative reputation from her fifth, a solid musical background, and a rowdy repertoire that she sang in a voice ranging from "deepest bass to shrillest piping," according to her publicity releases. She became one of the reigning glamor queens of the period and served as model for the steamy courtesan Lasca Sartoris in Carl Van Vechten's* *Nigger Heaven** in 1926. The portrait was not without foundation: while he was writing his novel she was discovered by a detective agency *in flagrante delicto* with W. L. Patterson, a Harlem lawyer, and named by his wife in an adultery suit. Gossip columnists adored Nora Holt: "She can't behave" became a familiar tag when her name was mentioned. During the thirties she travelled widely in France, England, Japan, and China, singing and playing many of her own compositions. On her return to the United States in 1938 she studied at the University of Southern California, taught school, operated a beauty parlor, and served on the Board of Education in Los Angeles. She returned to New York in 1943 to become music critic for the *Amsterdam News** until 1956, when she became music critic for the *New York Courier*. She conducted a radio program, the *Nora Holt Concert Showcase*, on WLIB from 1953 until 1964, when she retired to California, a highly respected, articulate and still glamorous figure in musical circles.

REFERENCES: Roger Didier, "(Little Lena) The Mamma Who Can't Behave," *Heebie Jeebies*, 1 Aug. 1925; *Inter-State Tattler*, 22 Jan. 1926; NYT, 30 Jan. 1974; Carl Van Vechten, "*Keep A-Inchin' Along*," 1979; David Levering Lewis, *When Harlem Was in Vogue*, 1981; Nora Holt. (PO, BK)

HOME TO HARLEM (novel), 1928. *Home to Harlem* details the adventures of the elemental, hedonistic Jake, who has recently returned to Harlem after deserting the war in France, and the efforts of the West Indian Ray to make intellectual and moral sense of the world. Although each character represents a separate mode of existence, each is dependent on the other as they work together on the railroad; enjoy the cabarets, house parties, bars, and women of Harlem; and confront the power and exploitation of the larger white society. Thus "instinct" and "intellect" are meant to be joined, complementary elements in Claude McKay's* search for an authentic and viable black identity. (MH)

HOPKINS, CLAUDE (musician), 24 August 1903?–? Claude Hopkins began studying piano in his native Washington, D.C., at the age of seven. After receiving the bachelor and master of music degrees at Howard University, he played briefly with Wilbur Sweatman's* Orchestra and then formed his own band for a summer's engagement in Atlantic City. Afterward, playing in an all-black cabaret in Asbury Park, Hopkins and his six-piece group were hired by Caroline Reagon for her *Revue Nègre** in Paris. A European tour followed, and when Hopkins returned to the United States in 1927, he toured in *Gingersnaps*.* Engagements at the Cotton Club* and at Roseland followed during the thirties. Hopkins and his band appeared in a few musical films in that period. None of his own compositions seems to have had any marked success, but among them are "Vamping a Cold," "Low Gravy," and "I Would Do Anything for You." Hopkins was still performing with small combos as late as 1970.

REFERENCES: ASCAP, 1966; WWJ, 1978; Donald Angus. (BK)

HORNE, FRANK (poet), 18 August 1899–? In Arna Bontemps's* *Harlem Renaissance Remembered*, a collection of essays by various contemporary critics on literary figures from the twenties, Ronald Primeau refers to Frank Horne with a number of other writers—Gwendolyn Bennett,* Waring Cuney,* Angelina Grimké,* Donald Jeffrey Hayes,* Georgia Douglas Johnson,* Helene Johnson,* Anne Spencer,* and Bontemps himself—as the "Second Echelon Poets" (p. 247). After the twenties, they were largely ignored by the anthologists until fairly recently, although Sterling Brown* had found in their work something of the "temporal roots in the past and spatial roots elsewhere in America" that put the poetry of the Harlem Renaissance in a "continuing tradition" (quoted in *Harlem Renaissance Remembered*, p. 248.) Frank Horne was born in Brooklyn and educated at the City College of New York, where he excelled as an athlete, primarily in track events. Later he completed a degree at the Northern Illinois College of Ophthalmology and practiced as an optometrist in both Chicago and New York. He taught school for a brief period in Fort Valley, Georgia, before going to work for the U.S. Housing Authority in Washington, D.C. From his undergraduate days, however, he continued to write poetry. His first success came in 1925 when his "Letters Found Near a Suicide" won the poetry competition prize in *The Crisis*.* Other poems appeared in *Opportunity** and the sesquicentennial edition of William Stanley Braithwaite's* annual anthology of magazine verse, and he was anthologized in both Countee Cullen's* *Caroling Dusk** in 1927 and James Weldon Johnson's* revised edition of *The Book of American Negro Poetry** in 1931. Horne had no success, however, in reaching a wider audience, and he was even ignored in black literature collections issued during the Black Arts movement of the sixties, during which time he had continued to write strong and effective verse that appeared occasionally in *The Crisis*.

From the beginning, Horne's work has fallen into three groups: poems in a Christian syntax, exploring the passionate connections between religion and politics; poems about black heritage; poems growing from athletic metaphors and themes. Although Horne often demonstrated his ability to write in conventional forms, their restrictions often hampered him, and his best work was always cast in loose, organic patterns.

REFERENCES: Countee Cullen, ed., *Caroling Dusk*, 1927; James Weldon Johnson, ed., *The Book of American Negro Poetry*, 1931; Arna Bontemps, ed., *The Harlem Renaissance Remembered*, 1972. (BK)

HOT CHOCOLATES (musical revue), 1929. At Connie's Inn* the floor show was so successful that Connie Immerman expanded it to a full-length revue at the Alhambra Theatre* and then at the Hudson Theatre on Broadway, where it ran for 216 performances. Fats Waller* and Harry Brooke wrote the music, and Andy Razaf* wrote the lyrics. Virginia Wheeler, Edith Wilson,* dancer Paul Meeres, and Eddie Green* were in the cast that later included Cab Calloway,* who replaced Paul Bass. Six weeks after the opening Louis Armstrong* was

featured during the intermissions. In addition to featuring the hit tune, "Sweet Savannah Sue," the show included what the *New York Times* reviewer called "a synthetic but entirely pleasant jazz ballad" called "Ain't Misbehavin' " (21 June 1929, p. 17). Geraldyn Dismond,* using her pseudonym "Lady Nicotine" in the *Inter-State Tattler*,* thought parts of *Hot Chocolates* would "make even a flapper blush" and noted that a particularly scabrous number, "Pool Room Papa," had been removed after opening night (28 June 1929, p. 12).
REFERENCES: *Inter-State Tattler*, 28 June 1929; NYTTR, 1972. (BK)

HOT RHYTHM (musical revue), 1930. Will Morrissey,* Ballard MacDonald, and Edward Lanley wrote the sketches, and Don Heywood* and Porter Grainger* wrote the music and lyrics for "a pretty tasteless, pointless and soggy rehash of preceding white and negro entertainments" (NYT, 22 Aug. 1930, p. 18). It included parodies of *Othello* and Spencer Tracy's currently popular *Last Mile*, but only Mae Barnes's,* "Who Boop Boop a Dooped a Lotta Boops Before Helen Kane Ever Heard of Boop" made an impression. Johnny Hudgins,* Eddie Rector,* Edith Wilson,* and Dewey "Pigmeat" Markham* were also featured in this Time Square Theatre offering that ran briefly after its August 21 opening.
REFERENCES: NYTTR, 1972; BB, 1980. (BK)

HOWARD, GERTRUDE (film actress), 13 October 1892–30 September 1934. Gertrude Howard's career in motion pictures began in 1914. She appeared in *The Circus Cyclone* (1925); *River of Romance, South Sea Love*, and *Uncle Tom's Cabin* (1927); *Synthetic Sin, Mississippi Gambler*, and *Showboat* (1929); and *Great Day* and *Conspiracy* (1930). Although consigned to play domestics most of the time, she was assured of some minor immortality as Beulah, the maid of whom Mae West requested, in *I'm No Angel* (1933), "peel me a grape."
REFERENCES: Donald Bogle, *Toms, Coons, Mulattoes, Mammies, and Bucks*, 1973; BAF, 1974. (BK)

HOW COME? (musical comedy), 1923. *How Come?* played on Broadway at the downtown Apollo Theatre for a brief run. Eddie Hunter* wrote it, but it was praised more for his "funny moments" than for the show itself. Alberta Hunter* and Sidney Bechet* were featured in the cast for this thin plot about a crooked secretary who steals funds from a bootblack parlor that serves as a front for bootlegging. Black musicals, the *New York Times* reviewer suggested, were "dark clouds" in which *Shuffle Along** had been a "silver lining." *How Come?*, on the other hand, reduced such matters to an "absurdity," a "poor burlesque show" presented by an "undistinguished and incapable cast" (17 Apr. 1923, p. 26).
REFERENCES: Burns Mantle, 1922–1923; NYTTR, 1972; BB, 1980. (BK)

HUDGINS, JOHNNY (dancer), ?–? Billed as a "wah-wah" comedian, Johnny Hudgins appeared regularly at the Alhambra Theatre* and was an occasional headliner at the Lafayette Theatre.* He played on Broadway in *Blackbirds[*] of 1928* and in *Broadway Scandals*. After the twenties he toured South America. Throughout his career Hudgins pretended to be mute, engaging in dance and pantomime but never speech.

REFERENCES: Nancy Cunard, ed., *Negro*, 1970; CVV. (BK)

HUGHES, LANGSTON (writer), 1 February 1902–22 May 1967. Langston Hughes, poet laureate of Harlem, read and discussed in most of the world's major languages, is a legend whose work runs like a creative avalanche from early poems like "The Negro Speaks of Rivers" to his death in 1967. His creative range (poetry, fiction, opera, drama, translation, gospel song-plays, history and biography, anthology, humor) is staggering, and his influence on individuals such as Léopold Senghor, Aimé Césaire, Jacques Roumain, and Nicolás Guillén is testament to the quality of his expression and vision. His work during the years of the Harlem Renaissance is an important but small part of his life's work.

Born in Joplin, Missouri, Hughes early gave promise of his creative abilities— elected class poet of his grammar school (1915) and senior editor of his class yearbook. After breaking with his despised father, who then lived alone and well in Mexico City, Hughes returned to America and attended Columbia University (1922). Columbia proved disappointing, but nearby Harlem and glittering Broadway proved irresistible. By spring 1925 he had published several poems in *The Crisis*,* met W.E.B. Du Bois* and Jessie Fauset,* given his first public reading, and aroused the distant interest of Alain Locke.* Soon after, he shipped out on the S.S. *Malone* and encountered, in the words of one of his poems, "My Africa: Motherland of the Negro peoples!" He put into ports from Dakar, Senegal, to Luanda, Angola, and his experiences and inspiration were expressed in stories such as "Luani of the Jungle" and "Burutu Moon" and poems such as "Danse Africaine," "Liars," and "Fog." Six months later, in Paris, he met Locke, who obtained permission to use ten poems for the special Harlem issue of *Survey Graphic** in 1925. He also met Paul Guillaume, Albert C. Barnes,* and René Maran.* In November 1924 Hughes was back in Harlem and then moved to Washington, D.C., to live with his mother.

Throughout the next year Hughes made several trips to New York and soon met the full range of individuals, black and white, who collectively comprise the Harlem Renaissance. "Discovered" by Vachel Lindsay* (in December 1925), who read three poems—"Jazzonia," "Negro Dancers," and "The Weary Blues"—that Hughes had slipped beneath his plate at the Wardman Park Hotel, Langston Hughes soon became the best-known black poet in America. He won poetry prizes in contests held by *Opportunity** and *The Crisis* and appeared in *Vanity Fair** and twenty other journals by the end of the decade. In 1926 Alfred Knopf,* alerted by Carl Van Vechten,* who greatly admired both Hughes and Hughes's poetic use of the mood and rhythm of the blues* and jazz as well as his identification with the language and life of "low-down folks," published

*The Weary Blues** and a second volume of poetry, *Fine Clothes to the Jew*,* in the following year. Although still a student at Lincoln University (B.A., 1929), Hughes gave poetry readings in several northern cities and in 1927 made a poetry reading tour in the South. He also began a novel in his junior year, *Not without Laughter*,* that was published in 1930. Hughes's trip south was soon followed by another; this time he travelled with Zora Neale Hurston* to search out folklore materials. Unfortunately, their friendship was shattered, as their effort to coauthor "Mule Bone," a three-act comedy, ended in bitter recriminations. More shattering was his break in 1930 with Charlotte Mason,* who had provided full financial support since their first meeting in 1928. According to Hughes, at least, the Renaissance was over. He would later return to this period of his life in his autobiography *The Big Sea* (1940).

But in 1931, with money received from the Harmon Foundation* Gold Award for Literature for *Not without Laughter*, Hughes sailed for Cuba and Haiti. In the years that followed his work took several directions, more of it devoted to fiction and drama than to verse. He flirted briefly with Marxism during the thirties (the resulting poems largely unpublished until after his death) but spent more time writing plays for little theater groups in Los Angeles, Cleveland, and Harlem. During the forties and fifties he turned to autobiography as well as to further novels and stories, and in a series of dialogs in the Chicago *Whip** he evolved his "Jesse B. Semple," better known as "Simple," a street-smart, canny, compassionate voice to speak in the words of as well as for an ordinary Afro-American. Four volumes of "Simple" stories eventually resulted. Hughes also wrote dozens of essays, translated works by others, and edited volumes of poetry, folklore, African literature, humor, and stories by other black writers. In 1961 he telegraphed his old friend from the twenties, Carl Van Vechten: "I SEE IN THE PRESS YOU AND I ARE TO REPRESENT THE RACE IN THE NATIONAL INSTITUTE OF ARTS AND LETTERS" (JWJ). The recognition had been a long time in coming. Early black critics would have preferred Afro-Americans presented less authentically, and white critics until the sixties at least gave scant attention to black writers.

Langston Hughes's major contribution to the Harlem Renaissance was his fresh, often earthy, bittersweet, racially sensitive poetry. But he was also an assistant editor on Wallace Thurman's* short-lived literary magazine *Fire!!** and his manifesto "The Negro Artist and the Racial Mountain" in the *Nation* (23 June 1926) served powerful notice that the younger generation of black writers was determined to create its own art.

REFERENCES: Robert Bone, *The Negro Novel in America*, 1958; James Emanuel, *Langston Hughes*, 1967; David Levering Lewis, *When Harlem Was in Vogue*, 1981; CVV, JWJ. (MH, BK)

HUMMIN' SAM (musical revue), 1933. Ellen Nutter wrote this torpid show, with music and lyrics by Alexander Hill. Gertrude "Baby" Cox was the lead, supported by Lorenzo Tucker* and Lionel Monogas.* Characters were named

Hot Cakes, Miss Jitters, Yellow George, and Harlem Dan, but the whole show lacked vitality, even in its dancing—an automatic invitation for a black revue to fail—and it seemed to the *New York Times* reviewer largely the work of amateurs. It opened April 8 and closed immediately.
REFERENCES: Burns Mantle, 1932–1933; NYTTR, 1972. (BK)

HUNTER, ALBERTA (singer, composer), 1 April 1895– . Alberta Hunter ran away from her home in Shelby County, Memphis, Tennessee, at the age of eleven and worked briefly as a cook in Chicago until she found she could earn more money running errands and singing in sporting houses. She started performing in Dago Frank's Club, moved on to Hugh Hoskins's, then to a featured spot at the Panama Club, and finally to the Dreamland Cabaret, where she earned the title "The Idol of Dreamland." She quickly "developed the persona of a tough little cookie who could take care of herself," but Eubie Blake said of her, "you felt so sorry for her you wanted to kill the guy she was singing about" (Bogle, *Brown Sugar*, p. 27). She was one of the first singers to record the blues,* sometimes using her sister's name, Josephine Beatty, as a pseudonym and sometimes the name May Alix (not to be confused with Mae Alix,* who also recorded early blues and jazz), and from the early twenties through the thirties she was a best-seller on Black Swan,* Paramount, Gennett, OKeh, Victor, Decca, and Bluebird labels. Her early song "Downhearted Blues," which she wrote and recorded for Paramount, was taken up by Bessie Smith* and made even more popular. At the Dreamland Cabaret she also introduced Eddie Green's* "A Good Man Is Hard to Find," which was picked up and immortalized by Sophie Tucker, and W. C. Handy's* "Loveless Love" and "Beale Street Blues."
    By the time she got to New York in the early twenties, Hunter had become a sophisticated cabaret and show performer. She appeared in *How Come?** and in the ill-starred *Dumb Luck* (1922), which folded on the road, stranding the cast, which included Ethel Waters,* in Massachusetts. In 1928 she went to London to play Queenie in *Showboat,** with Paul Robeson,* and from there went to Paris where she replaced Josephine Baker* at the Folies Bergères and appeared at Chez Florence. She was popular with the Prince of Wales, and Noel Coward wrote the song "I Travel Alone" for her. In the thirties she played a series of residencies in New York and became a popular NBC radio star. She appeared with Ethel Waters in *Mamba's Daughters* in 1939. During World War II she toured with the USO, and she continued performing in Europe, the United States, and Canada until her retirement in 1956. She worked as a practical nurse for twenty years, although occasionally making records, until her "rediscovery" in 1977. In recent years she has performed regularly at The Cookery in Greenwich Village and has made many personal and television appearances. Her recordings, reissued, are once again best-sellers. Her songs can be wistful, raunchy, sophisticated, mournful, funny, or earthy, but of her own blues singing she has said, "The blues? Why the blues are part of me. To me, the blues are—well, almost religious. . . . When we sing the blues, we're singin' out our hearts. . . . When

I sing...what I'm doing is letting my soul out" (Shapiro and Hentoff, *Hear Me Talkin' to Ya*, pp. 246–47).

REFERENCES: Nat Shapiro and Nat Hentoff, eds., *Hear Me Talkin' to Ya*, 1955; Robert M. W. Dixon and John Godrich, *Recording the Blues*, 1970; WWJ, 1978; BWW, 1979; Donald Bogle, *Brown Sugar*, 1980; Jarvis Anderson, *This Was Harlem*, 1982. (DA)

HUNTER, EDDIE (comedian), 4 February 1888–? Eddie Hunter was the elevator operator in an apartment building frequented by Enrico Caruso, and he performed his skits and songs while taking the celebrated tenor up or down. Caruso is said to have encouraged him, so Hunter abandoned the elevator for the stage. He wrote *Going to the Races* for the Lafayette Theatre,* one of the first shows to use stage and screen simultaneously. He toured Europe with another show of his own devising, *Good Gracious*, and he played there with the original version of *Blackbirds** in 1926. He wrote *The Eddie Hunter Company*, in which a forger is captured at an aristocratic party (1922); *Darktown Scandals* (1927), in which a salesman for a southern steamship company runs a gin mill; and *Struttin' Hannah from Savannah* (1927), in which a hen-pecked husband spends his wife's money resulting in her having him arrested. His single Broadway show, a flop called *How Come?** got its title from Caruso who, according to legend, asked "How come you are always on duty when I take the elevator?" It ran only briefly, in 1923, but it led to a successful recording contract for Hunter. Stories of his tours of the United States are not material for legends, however; they are too easily authenticated: in Phoenix, Arizona, for example, Hunter said the men in the company were obliged to sleep on the stage of the theater simply because there were no accommodations available within commuting distance, although the women were sometimes put up in churches. (It was Ethel Waters's* experience that they were put up in a town's brothels.) In the thirties Eddie Hunter went into real estate, and, well into his own eighth decade, he was still managing about twenty buildings in Harlem.

REFERENCES: Loften Mitchell, ed., *Voices of the Black Theatre*, 1975; NA, 1976; BB, 1980; Hatch-Billops. (BK)

HUNTER, MAURICE (model), 1898–? Born Cokas Kwaba near Johannesburg, South Africa, Maurice Hunter adopted the name of the missionary who took him to Dutch Guiana when he was a child. In 1910 he moved to the United States with his parents, and after working as a shoe-shine boy, an elevator operator, and a waiter, he became one of the most widely employed—although not usually recognized—models in America. This handsome, muscular Zulu posed not only for illustrations in most of the popular white magazines of the period, like *Saturday Evening Post* and *Colliers*, but for their most successful artists, like Norman Rockwell, Robert Henri and Charles Dana Gibson. Hunter, who advertised himself as "The Man Behind the Mask," posed for advertisements as well, as Indian chiefs and Cream of Wheat cooks, as white soldiers and Pullman porters. He was the subject of stories and interviews in the black press, appeared infrequently as a supernumerary with the Metropolitan Opera in *Aïda*, gave programs of historical "living statues," as they were called, and continued modelling well into his sixties.

REFERENCE: Alexander Gumby Scrapbooks, Columbia University. (BK)

HURSTON, ZORA NEALE (writer), 7 January 1901–28 January 1960. Born in an all-black town, Eatonville, Florida, and one of eight children, Zora Neale Hurston early gave notice that her mother's admonition, "jump at the sun," would translate into a vivid imagination, a powerful personality, and an inexhaustible will to survive. Upon her mother's death in 1904 Hurston was essentially on her own, living with various relatives and drifting from job to job. Driven to have an education, she spent two years at Morgan Academy in Baltimore (1916–1918) and a year at Howard University (1918–1919), where she studied with Alain Locke* and was first published in the campus literary magazine *Stylus** where her story "John Redding Goes to Sea" appeared in 1921. It caught the attention of Charles S. Johnson,* and two stories, "Drenched in Light" (1924) and "Spunk" (1925, which won second prize in the first *Opportunity** awards competition), and a play, "Color Struck" (1925), were published in *Opportunity*. In January 1925 Hurston was in New York City, her career as a writer just beginning and her rich personality marking her as one of the period's most singular figures. Her career as a folklorist was also about to take off.

In 1925 Hurston attended Barnard College on a scholarship and graduated with a bachelor of arts degree in 1928. Her work in anthropology gained the attention of Franz Boas at Columbia University, and he immediately sought her assistance. At his urging Hurston was awarded a fellowship by the Association for the Study of Negro Life and History to collect folklore—songs, jokes, dances, games, superstitions, customs, tales—in the South. A follow-up trip, this time financed by wealthy, white Charlotte Mason,* took her from Florida to Louisiana and deep into the practice and cult of voodoo. Out of this Hurston published six essays in Nancy Cunard's* *Negro* in 1934: "Characteristics of Negro Expression," "Conversations and Visions," The Sermon," "Mother Catherine," "Uncle Monday," and "Spirituals and Neo-Spirituals." Furthermore, she wrote articles for the *Journal of Negro History* (1927) and the *Journal of American Folklore* (1931) and the book of folktales and voodoo practices *Mules and Men* (1935), with an introduction by Boas.

Earlier Hurston had contributed sketches to *Fast and Furious*,* a black revue that ran briefly on Broadway in 1931; a second revue, *Jungle Scandals*, failed to open. A month later, however, she began to shape a theater entertainment, tentatively titled *Spunk*, more ethnic and less in imitation of the popular shows in Harlem. Hall Johnson* expressed some interest in the project but rejected it to work on his own *Run, Little Chillun*,* the finale of which he staged in frank imitation of the conclusion to Hurston's work. Underwritten by Mason, the entertainment—titled *The Great Day*—had a single performance on 10 January

1932 at the Broadway Theatre, where *Savage Rhythm** was playing, putting to use the sets of that unsuccessful melodrama.

In 1934 Hurston received a Rosenwald fellowship (hopefully for study that would lead to a Ph.D. in anthropology and folklore at Columbia), and in 1936 and 1937 she received two Guggenheim fellowships to study magic practices (*obeah*) in Haiti and Jamaica. Her book *Tell My Horse*, based on her research, was published in 1938. In addition to writing, Hurston was a member of the American Folklore Society, Anthropological Society, Ethnological Society, the New York Academy of Sciences, and the American Association for the Advancement of Science. Her final effort of an academic nature, *The Florida Negro*, written for the Florida Federal Writers Project in 1938, was never published.

If anthropology provided her with an analytical perspective, a means to conceptualize the significance of her own and her people's existence, it also served to stimulate her already profound and playful imagination. Beginning with "Drenched in Light," her short stories and plays of the twenties are set in southern black communities, often named as Eatonville. While adding to the creative lore of the Harlem Renaissance a rich sense of the southern folk roots of black Americans, Hurston was also intimately involved in the personal lives of the Renaissance. Beyond the fact of Mason's and Boas's intellectual companionship, she was a close friend for a time of white writers Fannie Hurst and Carl Van Vechten.* More important were her relationships with Alain Locke, who immediately recognized her brilliant talents; Langston Hughes,* with whom a deep friendship ultimately foundered over questions about their unpublished play "Mule Bone"; and Wallace Thurman,* with whom she shared a biting wit and helped establish the literary journal *Fire!!** Thurman's portrait of her as Sweetie Mae Carr in his novel *Infants of the Spring** is doubtless exaggerated but probably accurate in spirit: "a short story writer, more noted for her ribald wit and personal effervescence than for any actual literary work. She was a great favorite among those whites who went in for Negro prodigies" (p. 229).

In the thirties Hurston wrote three novels: *Jonah's Gourd Vine* (1934),* *Their Eyes Were Watching God* (1937), and *Moses, Man of the Mountain* (1939), all of which are deepened expressions of the folk consciousness she fashioned into art in the previous decade. Subsequently, she wrote a not entirely reliable autobiography, *Dust Tracks on a Road* (1942), and a final novel, *Seraph on the Suwanee* (1948). Zora Neale Hurston disappeared from New York at that time and died twelve years later, in obscurity, in Florida. Presently, however, the University of Florida offers a Zora Neale Hurston fellowship in anthropology.

REFERENCES: Wallace Thurman, *Infants of the Spring*, 1932; Hugh Gloster, *Negro Voices in American Fiction*, 1948; Robert E. Hemenway, *Zora Neale Hurston*, 1977; Lillie P. Howard, *Zora Neale Hurston*, 1980; David Levering Lewis, *When Harlem Was in Vogue*, 1981. (MH)

I

IMES, WILLIAM LLOYD (clergyman), 29 December 1889–? William L. Imes was a clergyman who fought racial discrimination and segregation during a long career as a minister and writer. Imes was born in 1889 and earned the B.A. at Fisk University in 1910 and the M.A. at both Fisk (1912) and Columbia universities (1915). While he was at Columbia he also attended Union Theological Seminary and was awarded the B.D. in 1915. He was a minister in Plainfield, New Jersey (1915–1919), Philadelphia (1919–1925), and St. James Presbyterian Church in New York City (1925–1943). Imes was a member of the NAACP* Board of Directors from 1925 to 1945, and he fought against school segregation and in favor of black employment during the Depression. He was made vice-president of the NAACP in 1945. His relevant works are "The Status of Free Negroes and Slaves," *Journal of Negro History*, 1919; *The Way of Worship in Everyday Life*, 1947; and *The Black Pastures*, 1957.
REFERENCES: WWCA, 1933; WWBA, 1976. (DS)

IMITATION OF LIFE (novel), 1933. One of several novels with black subject matter by white writers, *Imitation of Life* by Fannie Hurst is about a nineteen-year-old white widow, Bea, who joins business forces with a black widow, Delilah. Bea manufactures maple syrup and Delilah makes waffles; they rise to success in public but suffer mightily in private. Delilah's problems with her light-skinned daughter who wants to pass are far more interesting than Bea's problems with her own daughter and some puerile love affairs. The novel is long on sentimentality and concludes with Delilah's funeral, as elaborate as any actual Harlem extravaganza. *Imitation of Life* was taken up immediately by Hollywood, offering Louise Beavers* and Fredi Washington* opportunities at serious roles. (BK)

IN ABRAHAM'S BOSOM (play), 1926. Just before it closed at the Province-town Playhouse, *In Abraham's Bosom* was considered for the Pulitzer Prize.

When it opened on December 30 it had been either casually reviewed or simply dismissed. According to the *New York Times* reviewer, Paul Green's* "powerful tragedy" was written with "courage, understanding, logic and humor"; moreover, Rose McClendon,* Julius Bledsoe,* and Abbie Mitchell* in the central roles added "an instinctive and intense quality of dramatic action and speech" (31 Dec. 1926, p. 10). Six weeks later, when it moved to the Garrick Theatre, Frank Wilson* replaced Bledsoe, on thirty minutes' notice, and became a star, however briefly it blazed. Brooks Atkinson, reviewing the play a second time, called it "the most penetrating, unswerving tragedy in town" (20 Feb. 1927, sec. 7, p. 1). At the time, however, New York audiences, primarily white, had come to expect little more in Afro-American offerings than fast dancing and blackface comedy, and the positive response from reviewers did not insure financial success. *In Abraham's Bosom* covers a thirty-year period in seven scenes. In 1885 Abe, the young black son of a white plantation owner, is motivated to read and study to escape the lynching horrors inflicted on his race. He names his son after Frederick Douglass and offers him to God in exchange for help in establishing a school for black children. Because of Abe's righteous discipline, the school fails, and fifteen years later he finds himself working in a mine, with his son turned juvenile delinquent. Back home three years later, hoping to start his school again, he disowns his son who then betrays him to white racists. The play won the Pulitzer Prize in May 1927 and was revived for six weeks.

REFERENCES: Burns Mantle, 1926–1927; NYTTR, 1972. (BK)

INCHIN' ALONG (novel), 1932. One of several novels with black subject matter by white writers, *Inchin' Along* by Kelley Welbourn is about Dink Britt, an Alabama farmer struggling for his economic independence and emotional dignity in the face of southern racial prejudice. Like the hero of Thomas S. Stribling's *Birthright*,* Dink is probably too perfect a person to be entirely believable. (BK)

INFANTS OF THE SPRING (novel), 1932. *Infants of the Spring*, Wallace Thurman's* second novel, suffers many of the same defects he perceived to be fatal to the literature of the Harlem Renaissance: too much exposition, too much talk, too little concern for character. This farewell indictment to the period, however, is oddly and tragically appropriate. The central character, Raymond Taylor, who challenges, lacerates, and presides over the various inhabitants of "Niggerati Manor," his Harlem salon, is both an acute critic and painful projection of Thurman's own intellectual ambivalence, artistic ambitions, and personal frustrations. Thurman is not the only familiar face in this thinly veiled roman à clef: Langston Hughes,* Countee Cullen,* Zora Neale Hurston,* and especially Richard Bruce Nugent* appear in its pages, gathering for a variety of encounters, sexual as well as social. (MH)

INGRAM, REX (actor), 20 October 1896–19 September 1969. Rex Ingram was born on the *Robert E. Lee*, a Mississippi riverboat on which his father was a stoker. At an early age Ingram became a cook on the Union Pacific Railroad and subsequently started a window-washing business, but by the age of twenty-four he was the first black to make Phi Beta Kappa at Northwestern University, where he graduated from the medical school in 1919. Ingram appeared in the original film version of *Tarzan* (1918) and in many other movies after that: *The Ten Commandments* (1923), *The Big Parade* and *Beau Geste* (1926), Cecil B. DeMille's *King of Kings* (1927), *Hearts in Dixie** (1929), *Trader Horn* (1931), and *King Kong* (1934). In many of his films Ingram appeared in roles stereotyped for black actors: slaves, native chieftains, African savages. His good looks and rich voice always overcame that obstacle, and even when cast as a servant he was never subservient. In 1937 Ingram was able to demonstrate his full talents, in the role of De Lawd in the film version of *The Green Pastures**, and three years later he commanded $2,500 a week as the genie in *The Thief of Bagdad*. He continued to act in films until his death, although after 1948, when he pleaded guilty to a morals charge, his career suffered markedly. Ingram's only stage work seems to have been in San Francisco where he appeared in productions of popular plays during the twenties.
REFERENCES: Dan Bogle, *Toms, Coons, Mulattoes, Mammies, and Bucks*, 1973; BAF, 1974; Daniel J. Leab, *From Sambo to Superspade*, 1975. (BK)

INTERNATIONAL CONVENTION OF THE NEGRO PEOPLE OF THE WORLD , 1920. During the month of August in 1920, 25,000 delegates met in Madison Square Garden, sponsored by Marcus Garvey's* Universal Negro Improvement Association* for the largest black solidarity demonstration to that date. Garvey sparked the imagination of the race as no individual had theretofore done, dubbing Ethiopian counts and Nile dukes for the occasion. It was headed by His Grace, Archbishop, Primate of the African Orthodox Church, and Chaplain General George Alexander McGuire.*
REFERENCE: David Levering Lewis, *When Harlem Was in Vogue*, 1981. (BK)

THE INTERNE (novel), 1932. Wallace Thurman's* third novel, *The Interne*, is a collaboration with white author Abraham L. Furman and deals largely with white characters. It is a story of despair set in the context of a big city hospital and the ambitions and conflicts of young interns and nurses. Carl Armstrong, the central character, strives to be a surgeon. His ideals, however, are quickly shattered. In his disillusionment he barely avoids the temptation to engage in illegal practices. Reviewers of the novel generally thought *The Interne* to be obvious and overstated. (MH)

INTER-STATE TATTLER (newspaper), 1925–1932. Published in New York, the *Inter-State Tattler* carried accounts of black social life in large cities like Philadelphia, Chicago, and Kansas City, as well as in small ones like New

Haven, Connecticut, and of course in Harlem. The weekly issue carried theatrical and sports news; want ads; a lonely hearts column; photographs of show-business personalities, boxers, and pretty nonentities from various parts of the country; and topical editorials. Bennie Butler and Geraldyn Dismond* served as its successive managing editors before moving on to write the paper's theater reviews and society columns. George B. Jones followed them as editor. The *Inter-State Tattler* included among its writers, usually on an intermittent basis, familiar figures such as T. Thomas Fortune,* William Monroe Trotter,* Ulysses Poston, Theophilus Lewis,* and Mary White Ovington.* Toward the end of its run the paper became more political in its interests, featuring, for example, a four-part story on Marcus Garvey,* beginning 3 March 1932, based on letters and journals of Robert L. Poston,* the UNIA* official who had died several years before. Primarily, however, the *Inter-State Tattler* seems to have been devoted to superficial matters, old-fashioned gossip, and advertisements for cabarets, restaurants, entertainments, and an astonishing number of skin-lightening products. (BK)

ISAACS, EDITH [JULIET RICH] (editor, critic), 27 March 1878–10 January 1956. Editor for many years of *Theatre Arts* magazine, Edith Isaacs combined her interest in the theater with an interest in black culture. Two years after her death, as a tribute to her support of Afro-Americans in the arts, and to her belief in the importance of the theater as a force for social progress, a Theatre Arts Project for East Harlem was established in her honor at the James Weldon Johnson Community Center.

Born Edith Juliet Rich in Milwaukee, Isaacs graduated from Milwaukee-Downer College in 1899 and became a reporter for the *Milwaukee Sentinel*, of which she was made literary editor in 1903. She married Lewis M. Isaacs, a New York lawyer and composer in 1904, and moved to New York where she wrote for the *Ladies' Home Journal* and became drama critic for *Ainslee's Magazine*. She became editor of *Theatre Arts* in 1918, and within a few years had become an influential voice in the world of theater. She saw the American theater as undemocratic, commercial, inartistic, and dull, and in her capacity as editor and critic sought to correct these faults by focusing attention on the theater outside of New York; on college, regional, and community groups; and by promoting dance, music, and art as significant factors in the theater. She fostered new talent, publishing for the first time many writers who were later to become well known, and opened her home as a center for artists of varying backgrounds, ages, and nationalities. She worked for the creation of the National Theatre Conference in 1925 and the American National Theatre and Academy and strongly supported the Federal Theatre Project during the thirties.

Isaacs worked with Alain Locke* on the exhibition of the Blondiau-Theatre Arts Collection of Primitive African Art in the twenties. So that the collection would not be scattered after the exhibition closed, Isaacs bought it and eventually divided the works between Howard University and the Arthur Schomburg* Center of the New York Public Library. In August 1942 *Theatre Arts* published an issue totally devoted to the Negro in the American theater, for which Isaacs wrote the narrative. Although she became crippled with arthritis in the early thirties she continued to edit *Theatre Arts* from her wheelchair and later wrote and edited books on the theater when she became confined to her home.

REFERENCES: NYT, 11 Jan. 1956; NAW, 1980. (PO)

J

JACKMAN, HAROLD (teacher), c. 1900–1960. Winold Reiss's portrait of Harold Jackman was included in the "New Negro" issue of *Survey Graphic** in March 1925, less for his achievements than for his good looks. Born in London and reared in Harlem, Jackman was a junior high school history teacher whose intimate friendship with Countee Cullen* brought him into contact with most of the leading figures of the Harlem Renaissance. He was a frequent guest at Carl Van Vechten's* soirées and A'Lelia Walker's* Dark Tower,* and he was regularly involved in the intellectual ferment of the period. In the late twenties Jackman—an inveterate collector—began sending materials by and about black Americans to Atlanta University; when Cullen died in 1947, he requested that his various gifts there be called the Countee Cullen Memorial Collection, and when Jackman himself died in 1960, the name was changed to the Countee Cullen-Harold Jackman Memorial Collection. Jackman was the physical model for the protagonist in Van Vechten's *Nigger Heaven,** and he turned up—equally thinly veiled—in Wallace Thurman's* *Infants of the Spring.** His more lasting contribution to the Harlem Renaissance, however, is a series of day books that he kept, beginning in 1926, detailing many of its significant events. Jackman's sister Ivie deposited them in the Atlanta collection.
REFERENCES: David Levering Lewis, *When Harlem Was in Vogue*, 1981; Hatch-Billops. (BK)

JACKSON, [CLIFTON LUTHER] CLIFF (pianist), 19 July 1902–24 May 1970. One of the more popular pianists of the period, Cliff Jackson left his native Virginia before he was twenty to play in New York. He first appeared at Happy Rhone's Club in 1925; then in the pit for *Musical Aces*, a black theater revue, in Harlem in 1926; and then as pianist-conductor for his own show, *Krazy Kats*, in 1927. He also played semiregularly at the Lenox Club, at Roseland, and at the Capitol Palace.
REFERENCE: WWJ, 1972. (BK)

JACKSON, JAMES A. (journalist), 20 June 1878–? James Jackson got his early training on his hometown newspaper, the *Bellefonte Daily Gazette*, in Pennsylvania, but he also worked as a railroad policeman and manager for minstrel and touring musical comedy companies. By 1919 he had become the most widely read black show-business newspaperman in America, as a member of the staff of *Billboard*, a position he held until 1925. During the same period he wrote feature articles for both the *New York Herald* and *Sun* and served as theatrical editor for the *Washington Tribune*. Jackson's reviews and statistics of Afro-American entertainment ran regularly in *Billboard*, but in 1925 they were dropped because of a lack of black advertising in the paper. From 1927 until 1933 Jackson was special agent in the U.S. Department of Commerce. He also had the distinction of being the first black bank clerk in Illinois and one of two black agents in the U.S. Military Intelligence for the army.
REFERENCES: WWCA, 1933; BBW, 1977. (BK)

JACKSON, MAY HOWARD (sculptor), 1887–12 July 1931. Known for her portrait busts of Afro-American leaders, May Howard Jackson was born in Philadelphia and educated at the Pennsylvania Academy of Fine Arts. She maintained her own art studio in Washington, D.C., from 1902 to 1931, lectured, and taught sculpture at Howard University. A pioneer in the depiction of Negro subjects in sculpture, Howard deliberately broke away from the academic conventions she had been taught. Her "Mulatto Mother and Her Child" and "Head of a Child," for example, suggest the burdens of blacks in a white society. Her portrait busts of Paul Laurence Dunbar, Kelly Miller* of Howard University, Archibald Grimké,* and W.E.B. Du Bois* brought her recognition among blacks. She exhibited at the New York Emancipation Exposition in 1913, the Corcoran Gallery in 1915, and the National Academy of Design in 1916 and in 1928 received the Harmon Foundation* Bronze Award in Fine Arts, but "full maturity and freedom of her talent were denied her because of the isolation imposed by...prejudice" (Butcher, *The Negro in American Culture*, p. 221).
REFERENCES: Margaret J. Butcher, *The Negro in American Culture*, 1956; AAA, 1970. (PO)

JARBORO, CATERINA [CATHERINE YARBOROUGH] (singer), 24 July 1903–? Caterina Jarboro's mother, Elizabeth Harris Yarborough, had been a choir singer, and Caterina gained her first musical experience in the choir of St. Thomas Catholic School, Wilmington, North Carolina. At the age of thirteen she went to Brooklyn to live with an aunt and study music, and at the age of eighteen she joined the company of *Shuffle Along.* * She worked mostly backstage since she was too young and her skin was too dark for a regular position in the chorus, although she understudied one of the principals and did perform occasionally on stage. Determined to have a serious musical career, she went to Paris to study voice and then to Milan, where she studied with Nini Campino and began to win student competitions and get private engagements. She made her debut as Aïda at the Puccini Opera House in Milan in 1931, and this was followed by engagements in *The Queen of Sheba* and *L'Africaine* in Belgium. In 1933 she returned to New York to sing the title role in *Aïda* with Alfredo Salmaggi's Chicago Opera Company at the Hippodrome, 22 July 1933. She scored a personal triumph, and the opera had to be repeated two days later. She sang the role again in a special outdoor performance of *Aïda* at Ebbets Field in September 1933 and opened the Hippodrome season with it again that fall. But black singers were not accepted in American opera companies at that time, and she received no contract offers. Jarboro was unwilling to compromise her art; she refused to appear in vaudeville, and although she was willing to perform without fee at the poorer black colleges, she insisted upon being paid for benefits sponsored by wealthy individuals. After a short concert tour she returned to Europe for opera engagements in Latvia, Lithuania, and Russia. She served as an interpreter with the United States Army in World War II until she was injured while travelling with a convoy and returned to America.

REFERENCES: Maud Cuney-Hare, *Negro Musicians and Their Music*, 1936; Langston Hughes and Milton Meltzer, *Black Magic*, 1967; MBA, 1971; Hatch-Billops. (DA)

JESSYE, EVA (choral director, composer), 1895–?   Eva Jessye showed musical talent as a child, and when Will Marion Cook* brought a touring musical show to her hometown of Coffeeville, Kansas, in 1907, he was impressed by her enthusiasm and skill and encouraged her to continue with her musical studies. She studied choral music and musical theory at Western University, Kansas, and after a period of teaching in public shools in Oklahoma became director of the music department at Morgan State College in Maryland. She worked on the staff of the Baltimore *Afro-American** in 1922 and then went to New York to seek an active career in music. Her first work there was singing in theaters as a warm-up act before films, but in 1926, with Cook's encouragement, she formed a choral group, the Original Dixie Jubilee Singers—later called simply the Eva Jessye Choir—which quickly became popular in stage appearances and on radio, on the *Major Bowes Family Radio Hour* and the *General Motors Hour*. In 1929 she trained a choir to sing in the King Vidor film *Hallelujah!** which had an all-black cast. In 1931 NBC broadcast her folk oratorio *Paradise Lost and Regained*, based on Milton's poem. In 1934 she served as choral director for the Virgil Thomson-Gertrude Stein opera *Four Saints in Three Acts** and in 1935 as choral director for George Gershwin's* *Porgy and Bess.** She was associated with the Thomson and Gershwin operas in all subsequent revivals.

Her published works include *My Spirituals* (1927), *The Life of Christ in Negro Spirituals* (1931), *Paradise Lost and Regained* (1934), and *The Chronicle of Job* (1936). Eva Jessye has received honorary degrees from Wilberforce University, Ohio, and Allen University, South Carolina. Her papers are housed at Pittsburg State University, Kansas.

REFERENCES: MBA, 1971; *Ebony*, May 1974, p. 162; NYT 7 Oct. 1979. (DA)

JOHNSON, CHARLES S[PURGEON] (educator), 24 July 1893–27 October 1956. Charles S. Johnson's list of achievements caused Langston Hughes* to distinguish him as one of the three "midwives" of the Harlem Renaissance, along with Jessie Fauset* and Alain Locke,* declaring that Johnson had done more for young black intellectuals than anyone else. Arna Bontemps* echoed that opinion, believing that Johnson was more aware of the positive impact of the movement than others. Born the son of a Baptist minister who had learned to read not only English but Latin, Greek, and Hebrew from his former master, Johnson began his intellectual training under his father's tutelage on the Virginia-Tennessee border where the family lived. He first attended Wayland Academy in Virginia and last served as president of Fisk University in Tennessee, but in between, his influence on the rest of black America was profound. He graduated from Virginia Union and then attended the University of Chicago for graduate work, which he completed in 1917. After serving in the 103rd Pioneer Infantry he returned to Chicago where, appalled by the poverty in which the race continued to languish, he embraced the "sociological positivism" then familiar and popular among black intellectuals. Its intention was to call attention to the best attributes and achievements of the race, thereby leading eventually to the end of segregation and bigotry. The problem, Johnson believed, was not only economic but a matter of isolation and misunderstanding. The 1919 race riot gave him ample proof of that, but as a result of it, Chicago's Race Relations Commission was founded, with Johnson as member. His work in that organization led to the book he coauthored with a white member of the commission, Graham R. Taylor, *The Negro in Chicago: A Study in Race Relations and a Race Riot.* In 1921 Johnson became executive director of research and publicity for the National Urban League,* and in that capacity he edited the *Urban League Bulletin,* financed by the Carnegie Foundation. In 1923 he founded *Opportunity,* not to compete with *The Crisis** but to supplement its more international interests and coverage with a magazine directed toward Harlem's cultural activities, which in turn reflected the cultural activities of the rest of black America. The following year— spurred on by Jessie Fauset, whose novel *There Is Confusion** was about to be published; by his own secretary Ethel Nance*; and by Regina Anderson,* who was a librarian in the Harlem branch and a strong supporter of young black artists and writers—Johnson organized the Civic Club Dinner.* That now legendary gathering motivated *Survey Graphic** to devote an entire issue (March 1925) to the work of Afro-Americans. In 1925 Johnson organized the literary contests in *Opportunity* and its awards banquets that, in effect, encouraged white publishers to take on black writers. Believing that "literature has always been a great liaison between races," as he declared in *Opportunity* (Aug. 1925, p. 227), Johnson was pragmatic enough to realize that the race pride manifested through Marcus Garvey* and his UNIA* would thrive only in practical terms with respect and assistance from the majority—that is, white—in America. After Alain Locke's *New Negro** was published in 1925, the anthology designed to introduce black writers and subjects to a broader audience, Johnson edited *Ebony* *and Topaz,** a "collectanea" of drawings, poetry, stories, imaginative sketches, as a companion volume. It appeared in 1927. The following year Johnson resigned from *Opportunity* and the Urban League to join the faculty at Fisk University as head of its social science department, to direct its Race Relations Institute, and eventually to become its first black president. Death at sixty-three ended a career that included honorary degrees from the University of Glasgow in Scotland, Harvard University, and Columbia University and the Harmon Foundation* Gold Medal in 1930. Charles Johnson left few papers behind him, although his list of publications is impressive. His influence on other black writers was powerful, if only because he nurtured and encouraged them. More recent critics are wont to disparage the validity of a black literature dependent on a white patronage, but Johnson's work in the Harlem Renaissance surely made possible, in part at least, the Black Arts movement of the succeeding generation. His relevant works are *The Negro in Chicago: A Study in Race Relations and a Race Riot* (1922, with Graham R. Taylor), *The Negro in American Civilization* (1930), *Shadow of the Plantation* (1934), *Negro College Graduates* (1937), *Patterns of Negro Segregation* (1943), and *Education and the Cultural Crisis* (1951).

REFERENCES: *Opportunity*, Aug. 1925; WWCA, 1933; Arna Bontemps, ed., *The Harlem Renaissance Remembered*, 1972; David Levering Lewis, *When Harlem Was in Vogue*, 1981; EBA, 1981. (BK)

JOHNSON, EDWARD AUSTIN (lawyer), 23 November 1860–24 July 1944. Edward Austin Johnson, the first black elected to the New York State legislature, was born near Raleigh, North Carolina, the son of slaves. He graduated from Atlanta University in 1883, earning his way through school by teaching summers and working as a barber. He taught as well, while studying law at Shaw University in Raleigh. He earned the LL.B. degree in 1891 and became dean of the Law School in 1893. Along with many other prominent black southerners Johnson headed north in response to the frightening increase in white violence toward blacks and the passage of Jim Crow laws. In 1917 he was elected to the New York legislature and served one term, failing in his bid for reelection. Still, during his years in Albany he was able to assist in the passage of a bill that created free state employment bureaus, and he secured an amendment to the Civil Rights Act of 1913, making it a misdemeanor to discriminate on the basis of race, color, or nationality in public employment or in most public facilities. He resumed his law practice in 1919. Blinded in 1925, he ran (unsuccessfully), nevertheless, for Congress in 1928 and continued his leadership in the 135th Street YMCA Branch, Harlem Board of Trade and Commerce, Upper Harlem Taxpayers Association, and Congregational Church. He also wrote several books, including the utopian novel *Light Ahead for the Negro* (1904) and *Adam vs. Ape-Man in Ethiopia* (1931), in which he argued that black Ethiopians were the first people to evolve and that they developed an advanced civilization long before white Europeans. In his earlier *School History of the Negro Race in*

America from 1819 to 1890 (1891) he emphasized self-help and race pride as a means to improve the black citizen's position in American life.
REFERENCES: WWCA, 1933; DAB, 1935. (DS)

JOHNSON, FENTON (writer), 7 May 1888–17 September 1958. Fenton Johnson was born in Chicago and attended its university as well as Northwestern. At nineteen he had plays produced by the stock company of the Old Pekin Theatre in Chicago, and a few years later began to publish his own work. He taught English briefly at Louisville State University and later was special editor to the Eastern Press Association and acting dramatic critic for the *New York News*. During the twenties he edited the small literary magazine *Correct English*, and his own work began to be included in anthologies of black poetry. James Weldon Johnson* called him "one of the first Negro revolutionary poets" in *The Book of American Negro Poetry** (p. 140). The themes in Johnson's work were concurrently racial and religious, but their prosodies were conventional, their diction often arch, and their content not always free of sentimentality. In a note for Countee Cullen's* anthology *Caroling Dusk,** Johnson promised a complete autobiography "when I am able to realize that I have done something," but only three of his poems were included, in part because he had written none during the Harlem Renaissance (p. 62). His relevant works are *A Little Dreaming* (1912), *Visions of Dusk* (1915), *Songs of the Soil* (1916), and *Tales of Darkest Africa* (1920).
REFERENCES: James Weldon Johnson, ed., *The Book of American Negro Poetry*, 1922; Countee Cullen, ed., *Caroling Dusk*, 1927; Benjamin Brawley, *The Negro Genius*, 1937. (BK)

JOHNSON, [FRED] DEACON (music contractor, entertainer), 12 August 1878–29 March 1944. Fred Johnson, known as "Deacon," studied music in his native Arkansas and at McGill University in Montreal. He entertained professionally at the Chicago World's Fair in 1893 and performed in Montreal until 1900. He toured with minstrel and vaudeville companies until 1903, when he settled in New York and set up a music contracting company, the Deacon Johnson Musical Exchange. This enterprise functioned successfully until his death. Johnson was active with the Clef Club* from its beginning, serving as president from 1915 to 1919, and wrote a theatrical news column for the New York *Age** during the twenties.
REFERENCE: BDAM, 1982. (PO)

JOHNSON, GEORGIA DOUGLAS (writer, teacher), 10 September 1886–May 1966. Born in Atlanta, Georgia, Georgia Douglas Johnson became a prominent poet and playwright whose home in Washington, D.C., which she called "Halfway House," became a meeting place for black writers for more than forty years. She was educated at Atlanta University and Oberlin Conservatory of Music in Ohio. She married Henry Lincoln Johnson, who also trained at Atlanta University and taught in Alabama and Washington, D.C. Then she worked for the government. She published three volumes of poetry during the Harlem Renaissance: *The Heart of a Woman* (1918), *Bronze: A Book of Verse* (1922), and *An Autumn Love Cycle* (1928). Erlene Stetson in *Black Sisters* described the way these volumes are modeled on the sonata form and trace the development of womanhood from youth through motherhood to maturity. Johnson's last book, *Share My World: A Book of Poems*, was privately published by the author in 1962. In addition to writing poetry. she wrote the words for the song "I Want to Die While You Love Me" and various one-act plays, including "Plumes: Folk Tragedy," which won the *Opportunity** magazine contest for best play in 1927, and "A Sunday Morning in the South" (1924), which protests against racial injustice. Proud of her heritage, Johnson continued to write until her death at the age of eighty.

REFERENCES: WWCA, 1933; James V. Hatch, ed., *Black Theatre, U.S.A.*, 1974; BAWPP, 1975; Erlene Stetson, *Black Sisters*, 1981. (DI)

JOHNSON, HALL (choral director, composer), 12 March 1888-30 April 1970. Hall Johnson received his musical education in Athens, Georgia, where his father was an elder in the African Methodist Episcopal Church, and at Knox Institute, Georgia; Atlanta University; Allen University, South Carolina; and the Hahn School of Music. After graduating from college he attended the University of Pennsylvania, the Institute of Musical Art, and the University of Southern California. After he arrived in New York in 1914 he played violin in James Reese Europe's* Tempo Club Orchestra in performances with Vernon and Irene Castle. He played in the *Shuffle Along** orchestra in 1921 and was the violist in the Negro String Quartet (Felix Weir, 1st violin; Arthur Boyd, 2nd violin; Marion Cumbo,* cello), which gave concerts in New York and appeared with Roland Hayes* at Carnegie Hall in 1925.

In 1925 he organized a choral group to sing spirituals* in an authentic manner—that is, with "conscious and intentional alterations of pitch...individual improvisation...absolute insistence upon the pulsing, overall rhythm" (MBA, p. 430). The choir was soon in great demand for concerts and theater and radio appearances and was recorded by the RCA Victor Company in 1928. Johnson was appointed choral director for Marc Connelly's *Green Pastures** in 1930 and arranged the spirituals that the Celestial Choir sang offstage or in the orchestra pit throughout the play. The Hall Johnson Choir also appeared in the Warner Brothers film of *The Green Pastures* in 1936. Johnson's folk play *Run, Little Chillun,** for which he wrote both book and score, played in New York in 1933 for 126 performances and was revived in Los Angeles in 1935.

Johnson organized the Negro Festival Chorus of Los Angeles in 1941 and the Festival Chorus of New York City in 1946. The Hall Johnson Choir represented the United States at the International Festival of Fine Arts in Berlin in 1951. Johnson's compositions include the cantata *Son of Man*; the operetta *FiYer*; *The Green Pastures Spirituals*; and art songs and spiritual arrangements, including

the popular "Honor, Honor," "Ride on, King Jesus," and "Crucifixion." He received the Caspar Holstein* Prize for composition (1925, 1927), the Harmon Foundation* Award (1931), the New York Handel Medal (1970), and an honorary doctorate of music from the Philadelphia Academy of Music.
REFERENCES: MBA, 1971; BCM, 1977; GD, 1980. (DA)

JOHNSON, HELENE (poet), 1907–? Born in Boston, Helene Johnson attended Boston University and, in 1926, Columbia University Extension. Her poems appeared in *Opportunity*,* *Vanity Fair*,* and *Fire!!*　as well as in *The New Negro*.* William Stanley Braithwaite included her work in the sesquicentennial edition of his annual *Anthology of Magazine Verse*, and her name was otherwise linked with various literary matters of the period. Johnson's work was usually concerned with ghetto life and a fierce identification with her racial heritage. She seems to have disappeared from the New York scene some years before the end of the Harlem Renaissance.
REFERENCES: Countee Cullen, ed., *Caroling Dusk*, 1927; Langston Hughes and Arna Bontemps, eds., *The Poetry of the Negro*, 1949; BAWPP, 1975. (PO, BK)

JOHNSON, HENRY (war hero), c. 1897–1929. Henry Johnson, a private in the 15th New York Infantry (renamed the 369th United States Infantry)—Harlem's "Hell Fighters"*—became the most famous black soldier in World War I when he almost single-handedly repulsed an attack by about twenty-four Germans. Johnson and another private, Needham Roberts, were on watch at a small observation point early in the morning of 14 May 1918, when the Germans attacked and wounded both men, Roberts seriously. Johnson, a small redcap porter from Albany, New York, was able to kill the first Germans with his rifle, and when he ran out of ammunition, he used his rifle butt and a bolo knife to kill several more, including one who was trying to carry Roberts away as a prisoner. Although Johnson was shot and seriously wounded again at this point, the Germans retreated before his continued ferocity, and a nearly exhausted Johnson was still able to kill at least one more German with a grenade as they left. For their bravery Johnson and Roberts were awarded the Croix de Guerre by the French government—the first American privates to receive that honor—in what quickly became known in the United States as "The Battle of Henry Johnson." The incident immediately made the black volunteers from Harlem one of the most well-known fighting groups in the war. Johnson, who was crippled somewhat in the action, apparently disappeared into obscurity after the war.
REFERENCE: Arthur W. Little, *From Harlem to the Rhine*, 1936. (DS)

JOHNSON, [JOHN ARTHUR] JACK (prize fighter), 31 March 1878–10 June 1946. Jack Johnson was the subject of the powerful and popular play *The Great White Hope* by Howard Sackler in 1968, about the first black heavyweight champion of the world and the campaign of hatred and bigotry waged against him by whites eager to regain the title. As a stable boy in Galveston, Texas, where he was born, Johnson was called "Li'l Artha" because he was so small, but as a janitor and cotton picker he grew to six feet in height and weighed 200 pounds. He won the heavyweight title in 1908 and defended it against many challengers until 1915. Before that time he had engaged in various matches abroad, because he was wanted in America for violation of the Mann Act. In 1919 Johnson advertised in several issues of *The Messenger** a land company in Mexico, where property was available at five dollars an acre and up, and where neither race prejudice, censorship, espionage, or conscription could afflict Afro-Americans. He sold out his "Jack Johnson's Land Company" in 1921 and turned to acting, in two black films for the Andlauer Production Company,* *As the World Turns* and *For His Mother's Sake*, playing himself and giving boxing lessons to the heroes. After returning permanently to the United States in 1928 he fought exhibition bouts until his death in a car accident in 1946. Johnson was admitted to the boxing hall of fame in 1954, acclaimed by many boxing enthusiasts of both races as the greatest heavyweight fighter in history.

REFERENCES: Theodore G. Vincent, *Voices of a Black Nation*, 1973; WWB, 1974; BBW, 1977. (BK)

JOHNSON, J[AMES] C. (musician), 14 September 1896–27 February 1981. J. C. Johnson began writing songs at an early age. He was pianist-conductor for the Army Ambulance Corps Band and later wrote revues with Fats Waller,* Nat Burton, and Andy Razaf.* Among his familiar songs are Bessie Smith's* "Empty Bed Blues" and Ethel Waters's* "Guess Who's in Town?" and "You Can't Do What My Last Man Did."

REFERENCES: ASCAP, 1966; BDAM, 1982. (BK)

JOHNSON, JAMES P. (musician), 1 February 1891–17 November 1955. James P. Johnson was a professional pianist from the age of thirteen, playing in summer resorts and clubs along the New Jersey coast where he had been born. He joined the Clef Club* Band briefly in the early twenties, toured Europe with *Plantation Days*, and often served as accompanist for many of the Smith* singers—Bessie,* Mamie,* Trixie,* and Laura—and for Ethel Waters.* Innovator of "stride piano" style, with its insistent and strong left hand, Johnson was influential in helping Fats Waller* develop his own style. In addition to Johnson's popular songs, "If I Could Be with You One Hour Tonight," "Runnin' Wild," and "Charleston," he wrote a piano concerto, a suite based on W. C. Handy's* "St. Louis Blues," an opera based on Eugene O'Neill's* *The Dreamy Kid*, and the symphony *In Brown*.

REFERENCES: ASCAP, 1966; NYT, 18 Nov. 1955. (BK)

JOHNSON, JAMES WELDON (writer, civil rights leader), 17 June 1871– 26 June 1938. James Weldon Johnson was perhaps the most versatile and accomplished black person in twentieth-century America. Author, diplomat, popular songwriter, lawyer, educator, and powerful advocate of civil rights and black artistic expression, Johnson was a leading figure during the Harlem Renaissance. He was born in Jacksonville, Florida, the eldest child of educated parents, and grew up in a secure and happy, cultured, middle-class environment surrounded by books and music. After completing his undergraduate degree at Atlanta University in 1894, he returned to serve as principal of Stanton, Jacksonville's black grammar school, his own alma mater, where he gradually developed the high school program that had not been available for him a few years before. Also, he edited his own short-lived newspaper there and, in 1897, after studying law with a white attorney, became the first Afro-American to be admitted to the Florida bar, through examination in a state court. Additionally, he collaborated with his brother, J. Rosamond Johnson,* an accomplished musician, as lyricist for about 200 songs, including the perenially popular "Under the Bamboo Tree" and what has come to be called the "Negro National Anthem": "Lift Every Voice and Sing".

At the turn of the century the brothers took their comic opera *Tolosa* to New York in an unsuccessful bid for commercial production, but they met many important entertainers there, including Bob Cole with whom they joined forces. By 1905, however, James Weldon Johnson had grown increasingly discontent with the popular musical theater, despite his success, and began searching for a more appropriate way to use his talents. With the assistance of the New York Republican party he secured a position as U.S. consul to Venezuela (1906–1908) and then to Nicaragua (1909–1912). Toward the end of this successful period he wrote the novel *The Autobiography of an Ex-Coloured Man*,* published in 1912. He had married Grace Nail in 1910, and he hoped to obtain a more prestigious and comfortable diplomatic post. However, the Democratic victory in the 1912 election, and his realization that a black in the diplomatic service (even under a Republican administration) had little hope for advancement, moved him to look elsewhere for a career. Beginning in 1914 he worked as an editorial writer for the New York *Age** and published some of his poems in *Fifty Years and Other Poems* (1917). His knowledge of Spanish enabled him to translate into English the F. Periquet libretto of *Goyescas* by Enrique Granados, which was performed at the Metropolitan Opera House in 1916.

The writing, editing, and translating did not pay the bills, however, and when Joel Spingarn,* chairman of the board of the NAACP,* asked Johnson in late 1916 if he wanted to be considered for the position of field secretary of the fledgling organization, Johnson replied: "I find it difficult to think of any other field which would allow me so large an opportunity to do something for the advancement of the race" (15 Nov. 1916, quoted in Levy, *James Weldon Johnson*, p. 170). He was a resounding success in his job. He increased the number of NAACP branches fivefold in three years and even made major inroads into the South. He helped organize the 1917 Silent Protest Parade,* investigated lynchings and peonage, and led a delegation of black leaders who sought clemency from President Wilson for black soldiers who had been condemned for their alleged activities in the Houston Riot of 1917. He was constantly on the road, speaking to groups, organizing new branches, and sparking interest in the NAACP and racial justice. In 1920 he was named the first black Secretary of the NAACP, a position he held until 1930. In a way, it was almost the perfect job for Johnson, and it allowed him to use many of his talents and abilities to the fullest. Above all, Johnson was a gentleman, and he conducted himself with a quiet dignity and cultured manner that enabled him to move easily among the elite of both races. He was a superb public speaker and organizer, a tireless worker, and an extremely tactful and diplomatic man. He managed to keep the peace at the NAACP during the 1920s when a number of large egos threatened to disrupt things from time to time, Walter White* and W.E.B. Du Bois,* for example. Mary White Ovington,* who originally opposed his selection as field secretary (due to his ties to the Republican party and Booker T. Washington) admitted soon after that she had misjudged him badly. ''He's a fine worker and his quiet way accomplished a great deal,'' she wrote to Spingarn in 1917 (quoted in Levy, *James Weldon Johnson*, p. 188). Years later, she described Johnson as ''a slender figure with long, delicate, musician's hands. A man of much dignity, who never shows a sense of inferiority either by shrinking back or by pushing himself forward'' (*Portraits in Color*, p. 2).

He had a magnificent self-confidence, due, no doubt, to his comfortable upbringing, and this allowed him to react calmly and with ''sweet reasonableness'' to dangerous racial situations, according to a contemporary (quoted in Lewis, *When Harlem Was in Vogue*, p. 143). As executive secretary he continued to expand the membership of the NAACP as the group became increasingly enmeshed in a wide variety of legal, constitutional, and legislative issues. One of Johnson's greatest accomplishments was his almost single-handedly cajoling the House of Representatives to pass the Dyer Anti-Lynching Bill in 1921. Although the Senate refused to go along Johnson's efforts had brought the issue before the public as never before. In addition to his outstanding work for the NAACP, Johnson also found time during his fourteen years with that group to write and publish several significant works. In 1922 he edited *The Book of American Negro Poetry** (later enlarged in 1931), which became a standard anthology, and in 1925 and 1926 he and Rosamond assembled two collections of American black spirituals.* In 1927 he published *God's Trombones—Seven Negro Sermons in Verse*,* where he tried to recapture the imagery, style, and fervidness of the old black preachers he had heard. In doing so he tried to demonstrate (as he had attempted in his work on the spirituals) the contribution of blacks to American culture, for Johnson strongly believed that the ''final measure of the greatness of all peoples is the amount and standard of the literature and art they have produced'' (quoted in Lewis, *When Harlem Was in Vogue*, p. 149). In this regard Johnson successfully convinced the Julius Rosenwald Fund to grant fellowships to blacks engaged in artistic and creative endeavors. Indeed, they granted the first one to Johnson in 1929–1930, which allowed him a year's sabbatical to write *Black Manhattan*,* an informal history of black New York published in 1930.

Near the end of his year off Johnson, who was nearing sixty, decided that a more contemplative and less rigorous existence might be better for his physical and psychological well being. Therefore, he resigned from the NAACP and accepted a teaching appointment at Fisk Univeristy. He also taught several fall terms at New York University after 1934 and published *Negro Americans: What Now?** (1934) one year after the successful appearance of his autobiography *Along This Way*. Johnson enjoyed his last few years, writing, teaching, and spending summers in Maine. He died in 1938 in a car accident near his summer home.

Shortly thereafter, plans began to erect a memorial, designed by Richmond Barthé,* at the 110th Street entrance to Central Park, where Harlem began. When metal proved unavailable at the outbreak of World War II, funds that had been collected were donated to Yale University, where one of Johnson's warmest friends, Carl Van Vechten,* founded the James Weldon Johnson Memorial Collection of Negro Arts and Letters in 1941. Johnson's widow eventually turned over all of her husband's papers to Yale.

REFERENCES: Mary White Ovington, *Portraits in Color*, 1927; James Weldon Johnson, *Along This Way*, 1933; Eugene Levy, *James Weldon Johnson*, 1973; Carl Van Vechten, *"Keep A-Inchin' Along,"* 1979; David Levering Lewis, *When Harlem Was in Vogue,* 1981. (DS)

JOHNSON, J[OHN] ROSAMOND (composer, singer), 11 August 1873–11 November 1954. J. Rosamond Johnson, brother of James Weldon Johnson,* was born in Jacksonville, Florida, and received his music degree from the New England Conservatory of Music in Boston. He taught music in Jacksonville, toured in vaudeville, and appeared with John W. Isham's Octoroon Company in *Oriental America* (1897) before going to New York about 1900. With his brother he wrote several songs, including "Li'l Gal," "Since You Went Away," and "Lift Every Voice and Sing," which became known as "The Negro National Anthem." In 1901 the brothers signed a contract with Joseph W. Stern and Company guaranteeing them monthly payments against future royalties, the first such contract between black song writers and a Tin Pan Alley publisher. Their first popular hit was "My Castle on the Nile" (1901), and this was followed by winning songs such as "The Maiden with the Dreamy Eyes," "The Old Flag Never Touched the Ground," "Didn't He Ramble," and the amusing ragtime song "Under the Bamboo Tree," the melody of which is a syncopated inversion of the spiritual "Nobody Knows the Trouble I've Seen." The brothers teamed with Bob Cole to write a suite of six songs, "The Evolution of Ragtime" (1903), and the musicals *Shoo-Fly Regiment* (1906) and *The Red Moon* (1908). When James Weldon Johnson was appointed a United States consul to Venezuela, J. Rosamond continued working with Cole in vaudeville and wrote the music for *Mr. Lode of Kole* (1909), which starred Bert Williams.* After Cole's death in 1911 Johnson teamed briefly with another vaudevillian, Charlie Hart, and then went to England where he served as music director at Hammerstein's Opera House in London in 1912 and 1913. Upon returning to America he taught at the Music School Settlement in New York and concertized with the J. Rosamond Johnson Quintet. He toured at home and abroad with the tenor Taylor Gordon* in the mid and late twenties, in programs of spirituals and folk songs. He served as musical director of *Harlem Rounders** (1925), and for *Fast and Furious** (1931) he contributed the music and appeared wih his J. Rosamond Johnson Quartet. He created the role of Frazier in *Porgy and Bess** (1935) and trained the choir and played the role of Brother Green in *Cabin in the Sky* (1941).

Johnson's compositions include art songs; popular songs; a work for chorus and orchestra, "Walk Together Children" (1915); and two song collections, *Shout Songs* (1936) and *Rolling Along in Song* (1937). With his brother he collaborated on two collections of spirituals, *The Book of American Negro Spirituals** (1925) and *The Second Book of Spirituals* (1926).

REFERENCES: Sigmund Spaeth, *A History of Popular Music in America*, 1948; Langston Hughes and Milton Meltzer, *Black Magic*, 1967; MBA, 1971; BB, 1980. (DA)

JOHNSON, MALVIN GRAY (painter), 1896–October 1934. Gray Johnson, as he was usually called, was born in Greensboro, North Carolina, and began his academic studies at the National Academy of Design. His early work was conventional, but soon he became influenced by the impressionists, and his major work—all depictions of black life in its various facets—experimented with light and color. Throughout most of his life he was obliged to work at commercial art or at a number of menial jobs, devoting himself to serious work when he was able to save money for supplies and to find time. He received his first public recognition in 1929 when he won the Otto H. Kahn Prize at the Harmon Foundation* Exhibit. Subsequently, his work was shown in a number of minor galleries and museums. Six months after his early death the Harmon Foundation in cooperation with the Delphic Studios mounted an exhibition of his paintings with some sculpture of Richmond Barthé* and Sargent Johnson*; the show ran in New York in the spring of 1935.

REFERENCE: *Negro Artists: An Illustrated Review of Their Achievements*, 1971. (BK)

JOHNSON, MORDECAI WYATT (educator), 12 January 1890–11 September 1976. Mordecai Johnson, who delivered the Harvard Commencement Address in 1922 on postwar racism, was born in Tennessee, educated at Morehouse College, Harvard University, and the University of Chicago. For some time he was minister at the First Baptist Church in Charleston, West Virginia, and in 1926 he was appointed president of Howard University.

REFERENCE: Philip S. Foner, ed., *The Voice of Black America*, 1972. (BK)

JOHNSON, NOBLE (actor), 18 April 1881–? Noble Johnson appeared in more than 120 motion pictures, most of them white productions, beginning in 1914. Before that, in his native Colorado, he had been a cowboy, a cook, and a horse trainer, following the racing circuit with his father. With his brother George, Johnson became allied with the Lincoln Motion Picture Company* in 1916 and starred in its first feature, *Realization of a Negro's Ambition*, a tale of moral uplift that Horatio Alger might have invented. In two subsequent features, *Trooper of Troop K* (1917) as a black cavalryman rescuing a white officer and *The Law of Nature* (1918) as a stalwart rancher, he grew popular enough to be offered a contract by the white Universal Pictures. Tall and muscular, handsome and fair-skinned, Johnson appeared in a number of popular films that continue to draw audiences in revival: *The Four Horsemen of the Apocalypse* with Rudolph Valentino (1921), *Ben Hur* (1926), Cecil B. DeMille's *King of Kings* (1927), and *King Kong* (1933), for example. Noble Johnson played African chiefs and Indian braves, Pacific savages, Egyptian charioteers, Eastern slaves, Bagdad eunuchs, and toward the end of his long career even a zombie, in *The Ghost Breakers*, with Bob Hope.
REFERENCES: Daniel J. Leab, *From Sambo to Superspade*, 1975; BBW, 1977. (BK)

JOHNSON, SARGENT (artist), 7 October 1888–10 October 1967. A Boston-born painter and sculptor, Sargent Johnson studied at the School of Fine Arts there and exhibited annually, from 1929 until 1931, through the San Francisco Art Association. He won the Otto Kahn Award at the Harmon Foundation* in 1928 and the Bronze Award there in 1929. His interest was always in what he described as the natural beauty of the Afro-American, but he observed as well that without the interest and support of his own race his work would not survive.
REFERENCES: Cedric Dover, *American Negro Art*, 1960; NA, 1976. (BK)

JOHNSON, WILLIAM (artist), 1901–? Born in North Carolina, William Johnson began studying early at the National Academy of Design in New York and then in Paris. He won the Harmon Foundation* Gold Medal in 1929 and subsequently exhibited his work in New York, Chicago, and Denmark. His subject matter ranged from black American life to abstract figures reminiscent of the work of Georges Rouault and Vincent Van Gogh.
REFERENCES: Cedric Dover, *American Negro Art*, 1960; NA, 1976. (BK)

JONAH'S GOURD VINE (novel), 1934. *Jonah's Gourd Vine* is the story of John Buddy Pearson, preacher and former field hand and carpenter, who inspires his congregation as much as he causes them pain for his philandering, irresponsible ways. Forced to leave town (Eatonville, Florida) for beating his wife and misreading the temperament of his fellow townsfolk, John rebuilds his life in Plant City as a respectable and prosperous preacher. Returning to Eatonville to strut his wealth, he is seduced by a young prostitute and killed by a train. In this first novel by Zora Neale Hurston,* John's frustrations, his individual weaknesses, and his vitality and eloquence serve to symbolize the moral and cultural tensions in the collective folk life of black men and women who are simultaneously people of the land, of Africa, and of God. (MH)

JONES, EUGENE KNICKLE (sociologist), 30 July 1885–11 January 1954. Eugene Knickle Jones's long and distinguished career began with his bachelor's degree from Virginia Union and his master of arts degree from Cornell University. In 1910 he organized the National Urban League* and the following year became its field secretary. In 1918 he succeeded George Haynes* as its executive director, a position he held until 1941. During the thirties Jones served as advisor on Negro affairs to the State Department and in the forties as a Civil Service commissioner.
REFERENCES: WWCA, 1933; NYT, 12 Jan. 1954. (BK)

JONES, JOSHUA (poet, novelist), 1876–1953. Born in South Carolina, Joshua Jones served as city editor of the *Boston Advertiser* and the *City Record* and, after graduating from Brown University, as secretary to May or James Curley. Anthologized in Robert Kerlin's* *Negro Poets* (1923) and James Weldon Johnson's* *Book of American Negro Poetry** (1922), Jones also wrote two volumes of verse: *The Heart of the World and Other Poems* (1919) and *Poems of the Four Seas* (1921). His novel *By Sanction of Law* (1924) is unique in that interracial marriage, built upon pride in one's individuality as well as family heritage, is offered as a solution to America's racial paranoia.
REFERENCES: Hugh Gloster, *Negro Voices in American Fiction*, 1948; Arthur P. Davis and Michael W. Peplow, eds., *The New Negro Renaissance*, 1975. (MH)

JONES, LAURENCE C. (educator), 21 November 1882–14 July 1975. Laurence C. Jones founded the Piney Woods Country Life School near Braxton, Mississippi, and presided over its successful growth from 1909 until just before his death in 1975. Jones was born in St. Joseph, Missouri, of middle-class parents, attended the State University of Iowa—the only black student there— and graduated in 1909. Strongly influenced by the efforts of Booker T. Washington, he rejected lucrative offers of employment to teach in Mississippi, where, legend has it, he started with three illiterate boys, $1.65 in capital, and a large stump for a desk. During the next sixty years Jones almost single-handedly raised funds to build a school that stressed, at first, survival skills: for boys—how to sharpen plows, shoe horses, and raise stock; for girls—how to iron, sew, plan a proper diet, and practice personal hygiene. Academic subjects were added later. Jones slowly won the support of local whites, and his students eventually included thousands of trained mechanics, farmers, and teachers, many of whom settled in rural areas. Jones and his Piney Woods School are not, of course, ordinarily identified with the Harlem Renaissance; like Mary McLeod Bethune,*

however, Jones was able to achieve his goals in part because the national atmosphere made it possible for Afro-Americans to assert themselves. A renaissance—a humanistic revival of learning—is not confined by geography.
REFERENCES: Beth Day, *The Little Professor of Piney Woods*, 1955; NYT,
15 July 1975. (DS)

JONES, MAGGIE [FAE BARNES] (singer), c. 1900–? "The Texas Nightingale," as she was billed, began her career in New York clubs in 1922. She
toured for TOBA* for several seasons and recorded for Black Swan,* Victor,
and Parke Record companies, with Louis Armstrong and others. Her only Broadway appearance may have been in *Blackbirds[*] of 1928*. After the stock market
crash Maggie Jones went back to Texas, but admirers from the twenties remembered her big voice and varied repertoire.
REFERENCE: BWW, 1979. (BK)

JONES, MAUDE (elocutionist), ?–3 June 1940. Maud Jones was well along
in years and had only a parochial celebrity during the Harlem Renaissance. She
was called, or called herself, "The Colored Ellen Terry" after the well-known
white actress, and the record of her performance at Mother Zion Church on 9
March 1922 was probably typical. She recited Paul Laurence Dunbar's "Ode
to Ethiopia," Edgar Allan Poe's "The Bells," Robert Service's "The Cremation
of Sam McGee," and a selection from *Romeo and Juliet*, playing both parts.
REFERENCE: JWJ. (BK)

JONES, SISSIERETTA "BLACK PATTI" (singer), 1869–24 June 1933.
Sissieretta Jones was born Matilda Joyner in Portsmouth, Virginia, and studied
at the New England Conservatory in Boston. Her singing at the Grand Negro
Jubilee at Madison Square Garden in New York in 1892 created a sensation,
and one critic was so impressed by her brilliant soprano voice that he dubbed
her the "Black Patti," comparing her to the reigning Italian prima donna of the
day, Adelina Patti. She then went off to sing at the Pittsburgh Exposition for
$2,000 a week; at the White House for President Harrison; and left for an extended
concert tour of Europe in 1893. The Black Patti Troubadours, organized in 1896
to present her to her best advantage, set the pattern for future Black Patti Troubadours programs: an opening farce performed by the supporting company,
followed by a buck-dancing contest and an olio, and then the finale, an Operatic
Kaleidoscope, featuring Sissieretta Jones in arias and scenes from popular operas
and operettas. Considerable versatility was required of the supporting artists,
who had to sing in the operatic ensembles as well as play in the knock-about
farces. In later years the company offered more conventional musical shows and
was called the Black Patti Musical Comedy Company; Jones took on small
speaking parts as well as singing her operatic selections. Sissieretta Jones toured

for more than twenty years. She retired about 1920 to her home in Providence, Rhode Island, where she died in 1933.

REFERENCES: Langston Hughes and Milton Meltzer, *Black Magic*, 1967; MBA, 1971; BB, 1980. (DA)

JOPLIN, SCOTT (pianist, composer), 24 December 1868–11 April 1917. Scott Joplin, "The King of Ragtime," left his Texarkana, Texas, home in his early teens to play in honky-tonks in the river towns of the Mississippi Valley and by the age of seventeen was established as a popular piano player at Honest John Turpin's Silver Dollar saloon in St. Louis. He took a small band to Chicago for the World's Columbian Exposition in 1893 and in 1895 organized the Texas Medley Quartet (actually an octet), which toured in vaudeville. When Joplin enrolled at George Smith College for Negroes in courses in harmony and composition in 1896, he had already published a couple of sentimental Victorian ballads and three conventional piano pieces, but his *Original Rags* (1899) was his first attempt at notating the syncopated piano style he had perfected. "The Maple Leaf Rag" (1899), issued by the white music publisher John Stillwell Stark, was a runaway best-seller, but Joplin aspired to larger musical forms than piano rags and in 1903 produced his first opera, *A Guest of Honor: A Ragtime Opera* (the score of which has been lost), and *The Ragtime Dance*, a folk ballet with narrative soloist. In 1908, when ragtime was sweeping the country, Stark published Joplin's teaching book "The School of Ragtime—Six Exercises for Piano," which contained his famous instruction, "Play slowly until you catch the swing, and never play ragtime fast at any time." Joplin settled in New York about 1909 to teach and compose, concentrating on his major work *Treemonisha*, a folk opera in ragtime. He published the score at his own expense in 1911 but could find no producer for it. He became obsessed with the idea of having the opera performed and in 1915 succeeded in staging it in a hall in Harlem, with a full cast of eleven but no scenery or orchestra. The audience was unimpressed; as music historian Rudi Blesh put it, "The listeners were sophisticated enough to reject their folk past, but not sufficiently to relish a return to it in art" (Blesh and Janis, *They All Played Ragtime*, p. 249). Joplin never recovered from the disappointment of the opera's failure. He had suffered fits of depression for several years, and his mind gave way completely; he died in the Manhattan State Hospital on Ward's Island on April 11, 1917. Harlem gave him an impressive funeral.

In 1975, at the height of the ragtime revival, *Treemonisha* received its first fully staged production, by the Houston Grand Opera, and scored a tremendous success.

REFERENCES: Rudi Blesh and Harriett Janis, *They All Played Ragtime*, 1951; MBA, 1971; Jervis Anderson, *This Was Harlem*, 1982. (DA)

JORDAN, JOE (ragtime pianist, composer), 11 February 1882–11 September 1971. Composer of the scores for the Broadway shows *Strut Miss Lizzie** (1922),

Deep Harlem* (1929), and *Brown Buddies** (1930), Joe Jordan began his long musical career playing piano by ear as a young child in Cincinnati. He attended Lincoln Institute in Jefferson City, Missouri, for a time but by 1900 was playing ragtime piano in cafés and brothels in St. Louis. He remained in Chicago after the vaudeville show *Dandy Coon*, for which he was musical and stage director in 1903, folded and became musical director for the Pekin Music Hall the next year. He composed the score for the first production of the Pekin Stock Company, *The Man from Bam*, starring Flournoy Miller* and Aubrey Lyles.* For the next ten years Jordan was active as a musical director, composer, and arranger for shows both at the Pekin Theatre in Chicago and in New York, including *The Mayor of Dixie*, *Rufus Rastus*, and *The Red Moon*. He organized and wrote the music for *The Memphis Students*, the first "syncopated music" concert, starring Abbie Mitchell* and Ernest Hogan, in 1905 and wrote for the second edition in 1908 as well. His song "Lovely Joe" made a star of Fanny Brice in the Ziegfeld Follies in 1910.

Jordan toured widely in Europe on the vaudeville circuit from 1915 to 1920, returning occasionally for work in the United States. In 1926 he made his first recording with his group, Jordan's Ten Sharps and Flats. In addition to writing scores for Broadway musicals during the twenties, he arranged music for prominent entertainers of the time and was musical director of *Keep Shufflin'** in 1928. He conducted the Negro Unit Orchestra of the WPA Federal Theater Project during the thirties and became the first black to be elected to the Board of Directors of the American Federation of Musicians Local 208. During World War II he entertained servicemen as a member of the Special Services Division of the U.S. Army. Retiring to Tacoma, Washington, after the war, he continued to write songs and to teach private students for the rest of his life. Jordan's best-known songs include "Pekin Rag," "J.J.J. Rag," "Morocco Blues," "Rise and Shine," "Teasin' Rag," and "These Eyes of Mine."
REFERENCE: BDAM, 1982. (PO)

JOURNAL OF NEGRO HISTORY (periodical), 1916–   . The *Journal of Negro History*, the first historical magazine written expressly to treat black history seriously and in a scientific manner in the United States, was first published in January 1916 by the newly organized Association for the Study of Negro Life and History.* The driving force behind the Association and the *Journal* was Carter G. Woodson,* a professionally trained black historian, who spent $400 of his own money to publish the first issue. The *Journal* was well received by other American historians and the public; still, Woodson and his fledgling association operated on a tiny budget until 1919, when support from men such as Julius Rosenwald allowed the organization and *Journal* to move into their own offices and retain a limited staff. The *Journal* modeled itself after other scientific historical journals published in the United States. It printed scholarly articles, some of which had been written by researchers subsidized with money from the association's research funds; impressive historical documents, which otherwise would not have been easily available to scholars; and annual reports of the association's officers and records of the organization's annual convention. The *Journal*'s articles improved substantially during the 1920s in both documentation and literary quality, and more than 300 libraries (75 of them in the South) had subscribed to the *Journal* by 1926. Because of its strongly academic tone, it never reached a wide public audience.

REFERENCES; WWCA, 1933; Charlemae Hill Rollins, *They Showed the Way*, 1964. (DS)

JULIAN, HUBERT FAUNTLEROY (pilot), 1897–? Standing 6'2'' tall and as dashing and glamorous as any matinée idol, "The Black Eagle" was born Hubert Fauntleroy Julian in Port of Spain, Trinidad, probably in 1897. In March 1921, having invented the "parachutta gravepreresista," with a helicopter blade that went into action when a parachutist was in trouble, he arrived in Harlem driven by a white chauffeur all of the way from Canada, where he had been learning to fly. For some time he simply cut a handsome figure around town, in a black velvet cape, serving as sweetman to a brothel keeper. In April 1923, however, he began his spectacular career by selling tickets at a dollar apiece for his proposal to parachute into a vacant lot between Seventh and Eighth avenues from 138th to 139th streets. He sold the viewing rights to his body to a local undertaker, just in case he didn't survive, descended in a red jumpsuit with a streaming banner that advertised "Hoenig Optical Open Today," and landed on the roof of the United States Post Office two blocks off course. Harlem went wild with enthusiasm, carrying Julian to the UNIA's* Liberty Hall, where he was served with a summons for inciting a riot. Marcus Garvey* hired him on the spot. Six months later he made another jump, this time playing "Runnin' Wild" on a saxophone as he descended for a local music company, landing six blocks south of his goal, flipping over a flag pole into the police station, and blaming the bad landing on a failed test for his "saxophona parachutta gravepreresista." In January 1924 he proposed flying to Ethiopia in a hydroplane, solicited donations to underwrite the project, and was finally forced by law to take off in July or forfeit what money he had collected. A huge crowd gathered for the departure of "The Black Eagle" for Africa, but his right pontoon dropped off and he nose-dived into the bay at Flushing. Haile Selassie engaged him as head of Ethiopia's Imperial Air Force in 1930. Julian lost the job when he cracked up one of its three planes, so he returned to Harlem, in pink shirt, white riding breeches, a monocle, and a pith helmet, to lecture on his adventures in jaw-breaking sentences peppered liberally with French. Few figures captivated the imaginations of Harlem residents so thoroughly; nor did Julian's exploits cease with the end of the period. A decade later he was flying in the Russo-Finnish war, challenging Hermann Goering to an aerial duel at 10,000 feet over the English Channel, serving as a triple agent in Cuba, and at the age of about seventy still retaining much of his good looks and glamour.

REFERENCE: John Peer Nugent, *The Black Eagle*, 1971. (BK)

JUNGLE ALLEY (cabaret district). Between Lenox and Seventh avenues 133rd Street was called Jungle Alley because of the number of cabarets and nightclubs there. The Clam House,* Tillie's Chicken Shack,* Pod's and Jerry's,* and Mexico's* were only the better known places on a much longer list. Nora Holt* recalled that the names of many others seemed to change from week to week in the free-wheeling exchange of properties of owners, even though the entertainment and decor and bootleg liquor rarely did.

REFERENCES: Bruce Kellner, *Carl Van Vechten and the Irreverent Decades*, 1968; Jervis Anderson, *This Was Harlem*, 1982. (BK)

K

KARAMU HOUSE (little theater group), 1916– . Two Oberlin College graduates, Rowena and Russell Jelliffee, both white social workers, founded Karamu, a playhouse, in 1916 in Cleveland, Ohio, in an abandoned pool hall, as the Neighborhood Association. Langston Hughes,* then in his early teens, worked backstage and got his first exposure to theater and even his first training for plays he would later write. During the ensuing years the Jelliffees were responsible for staging virtually every play by every black writer of merit. Originally devoted to staging work only by Afro-Americans, Karamu is now an interracial, sophisticated playhouse that continues to give hearings to young black actors and writers.

REFERENCES: Langston Hughes and Milton Meltzer, *Black Magic*, 1971; Faith Berry, *Langston Hughes*, 1983. (BK)

KEEP SHUFFLIN' (musical comedy), 1928. A canvas banner stretched across West 63rd Street to welcome Flournoy Miller* and Aubrey Lyles* back to Daly's Theatre, where *Shuffle Along** had opened seven years before *Keep Shufflin'*. Andy Razaf,* Henry Creamer,* Con Conrad, and Clarence Todd wrote the lyrics, and James P. Johnson* and Fats Waller* wrote the music, arranged by Will Vodery.* Last-minute revisions and alterations were obvious on opening night, February 27, however, in this tale of Steve Jenkins and Sam Peck—Miller and Lyles in blackface—who plan to blow up a bank in Jimtown (where these shows frequently occurred) for the benefit of the "Equal Got League." A dancer named Billie Yarborough was singled out for commendation as "a wide-eyed, shiny haired, stomping grotesque" in an otherwise forgettable evening (NYT, 28 Feb. 1928, p. 18).

REFERENCE: NYTTR, 1972. (BK)

KELLEY, WILLIAM MELVIN, SR. (journalist), 22 April 1894–? Born in Tennessee, William Melvin Kelley dropped out of Wilberforce University to

become circulation manager of the *New York News* in 1913. Three years later he became business manager of the *Amsterdam News** and the following year business manager of the *Champion Magazine* in Chicago. He served as industrial secretary of the National Urban League* in 1917 and 1918, and from 1919 to 1921 he was assistant business manager for *Pearson's Magazine* and then circulation manager for the *New York Dispatch*; in 1922 he began his long tenure as editor of the *Amsterdam News*. During the Black Arts movement of the sixties his son William Melvin Kelley, Jr., became widely recognized as a novelist.
REFERENCE: WWCA, 1933. (BK)

KENNEDY, ROBERT E[MMETT] (writer) 1877–1941. A southern white who spent his childhood in Louisiana, Robert E. Kennedy wrote several books that present the color and flavor of black life in the villages and small towns of the South. *Black Cameos* (1925) is a transcription of twenty-eight anecdotes through which are interwoven words and music of seventeen spirituals.* *Gritny People* (1927) is a record of the daily lives of those who gather in Aunt Susan Smiley's "cook-shop" in the village of Gretna, Louisiana. *Red Bean Row* (1929) creates the daily life and ceremony of those who live in the Negro quarter of a small southern town. Among his other works were several collections of songs: *Mellows: A Chronicle of Unknown Singers* (1925); *Runes and Cadences* (1927); and *More Mellows* (1931).
REFERENCE: NYT, 5 Mar. 1925. (MH)

KERLIN, ROBERT T. (poet, anthologist), 22 March 1866–21 February 1950. Born in Missouri, Robert T. Kerlin was a professor of literature at several universities and colleges, most notably Lincoln and Virginia Military Institute, after receiving the Ph.D. from Yale (1906). He also wrote poetry and fiction, contributed articles to *Southern Workman* and *Nation*,* and anthologized the poetry of black poets: *Contemporary Poetry of the Negro* (1921) and *Negro Poets and Their Poems* (1923). In addition, Kerlin sought to awaken whites to what average black men and women really thought about their life in America. His book *The Voice of the Negro* (1919) is a compilation from the black press of the various responses both to the riots* in Washington (1919) and the general postwar disillusionment.
REFERENCES: WWW, 1963; BIA, 1971; AAB, 1972. (MH)

KING, [WILLIAM] BILLY (entertainer, producer), 1875–? Billy King fled the Alabama farm where he was born, when he was still a youngster, and toured in vaudeville. In the 1890s he organized the King & Bush Wide Mouth Minstrels and then joined the Georgia Minstrel Company, then the King & Marshall (called "Garbage" Marshall) Company, and finally, the Rogers All-Star Revue, before starting his own company about 1916 with Gertrude Saunders.* Primarily at the Chicago Grand Theatre, he staged weekly shows, many of his own devising, until 1923, featuring a number of people who went on to successful careers in

New York, several popular songs, innovative stage devices, and plots that were later widely imitated. A representative list is of some historical interest: in 1918—*Catching the Burglar*, in which a burglar escapes when the detective (King) captures the fellow being robbed; *The Board of Education*, with Gertrude Saunders, in which two hustlers get free room and board by joining that organization; *The Con Man*, in which a hustler disguises his friend first as a scarecrow, then as a statue, and then as a mongrel dog, because a rich widow wants to spend her money on a pet; *The Heart Breakers*, in which a girl's parents hire King to spy on their daughter and her beau; in 1919—*Exploits in Africa*, with the popular song "Bleeding Moon"; *Over the Top*, in which a black sea captain goes to the Paris Peace Conference and makes speeches about the mistreatment of blacks in America, starring Gertrude Saunders, Ida Forsyne,* and Marcus Slayter; *They're Off*, again with Gertrude Saunders and Ida Forsyne, but featuring Theresa Burroughs singing "Up in My Aeroplane," during which she somehow flew out over the audience; in 1920—*Hello Dixieland!* featuring "Hey Hey," a song whose title became one of the catch-phrases of the Harlem Renaissance; *The New American*, about the status of blacks in the United States, apparently a serious musical play; *Chinatown*, featuring the perennially popular song "After You've Gone," played by an orchestra conducted by a woman, Marie Lucas;* and in 1922—*Moonshine*, in which a bootlegger pursues Billie Booker, featuring the Magnetic Maids and the Incomparable Steppers.
REFERENCE: BB, 1980. (BK)

KIRKPATRICK, SIDNEY (actor), ?–? Sidney Kirkpatrick played the title role in *Captain Rufus* produced by the Pekin Stock Company in Chicago in 1914 and toured the United States and Europe with the Dark Town Entertainers, a troupe managed by his wife, Laura Bowman.* He appeared with Bowman in the New York productions of *His Honor the Mayor* (1918), *That Gets It* (1922), and as Satan in *Shades of Hades* (1922–1923). In 1923 he appeared with Laura Bowman and Evelyn Preer* in a triple bill presented by the Ethiopian Art Players,* which included *Salome*, *A Comedy of Errors*, and *The Chip Woman's Fortune*,* the first drama by a black writer produced on Broadway. John Corbin wrote in the *New York Times*, "The Herod of Sidney Kirkpatrick was essentially and powerfully tragic. Mr. Kirkpatrick was thoroughly the artist. Seldom on any stage has there been a more torrential flood of words more deeply felt and justly phrased than in his final entreating of Salome. In his other roles he is equally admirable . . . [and] has revealed the sure touch not only in his Herod but as Silas in *Chip Woman* and the merchant in *Comedy of Errors*" (20 May 1923, sec. 7, p. 1). Kirkpatrick also appeared on Broadway in *Meek Mose** in 1928.
REFERENCES: NYTTR, 1972; BB, 1980. (PO)

KNOPF, ALFRED A. (publisher), 12 September 1892–11 August, 1984. With his wife, Blanche, Alfred Knopf founded his celebrated Borzoi Books in 1915, with H. L. Mencken* and Carl Van Vechten* two of his earliest (and, later,

best-known) writers. In 1923 Mencken recommended the manuscript for Walter White's* novel *The Fire in the Flint.* * In 1925 Van Vechten recommended publication of Langston Hughes's* first collection of poems, *The Weary Blues.* * Furthermore, Knopf republished *The Wooings of Jezebel Pettyfer*, Haldane McFall's turn-of-the-century novel about Negro life in Barbados; and James Weldon Johnson's* *Autobiography of an Ex-Coloured Man,* * which had been out of print since 1912; and he issued Miguel Covarrubias's* *Negro Drawings* in 1927. Knopf's most notable success in the field, however, occurred when he published Van Vechten's *Nigger Heaven* * in 1926, the novel that did more to publicize black Harlem to white readers than any other work of the period.
REFERENCE: WWA, 1981. (BK)

KRIGWA PLAYERS (little theater group), 1926–1928. Fearing the death of the Afro-American folk play because of the popularity of the black Broadway revues, W.E.B. Du Bois* organized a "little Negro theatre" through *The Crisis* * in 1926. First called Crigwa Players, for *Crisis* Guild of Writers and Artists, the spelling was soon changed to Krigwa. The basement of the Harlem Branch of the New York Public Library, at 135th Street, was home base, but the company regularly appeared in one-act play competitions elsewhere. Its first program included Willis Richardson's* *Compromise* and Eulalie Spence's* *Fool's Errand*, giving weekend performances with simple stage sets that Aaron Douglas* helped decorate. By January of the following year the program had been expanded to include interpretive dancing on occasion, and the organization gave rise to other Krigwa Players Little Negro Theatres in other parts of the country. The Negro Experimental Theatre,* which followed in 1928, was a natural descendant of this initial attempt to create a theater, as Du Bois put it in *The Crisis*, "about us . . . by us . . . for us . . . near us" (July 1926, p. 134).
REFERENCES: *The Crisis*, July 1926; Loften Mitchell, *Black Drama*, 1967. (BK)

L

LAFAYETTE PLAYERS STOCK COMPANY (theater group), 1914–1932. When Lester A. Walton* brought the Anita Bush* Company from the Lincoln Theatre* to the Lafayette Theatre* in 1914, Charles Gilpin* joined the group and organized a new stock company, the first in Harlem. Few if any plays by black writers were available, so the Lafayette Players regularly staged works that had proven successful on the white stage. Between 1916 and 1923 a new play went on every Monday, with rehearsals in the morning and matinee and evening performances. Among the offerings were *Madame X* and *Within the Law*, both popular white melodramas; *Very Good Eddie*, a Jerome Kern musical play; and several classics: *The Count of Monte Cristo*, *Faust*, *Othello*, and *Dr. Jekyll and Mr. Hyde*, the latter with Clarence Muse* in whiteface makeup. Writing in *The Messenger** after the company was firmly established, George S. Schuyler* lamented that no plays by Ibsen, Strindberg, or Shaw were ever offered to acquaint Harlem audiences with serious modern drama. Just before the company collapsed, however, Theophilus Lewis,* in his monthly column in *The Messenger*, praised it for having staged Frank Wilson's* *Pa Williams' Gal.** This black family drama by a black playwright, for all its faults, at least attempted to contribute to a serious black aesthetic. Mismanagement led to the company's demise, apparently. Walton sold out to Robert Levy who, in turn, sold the Lafayette to the Quality Amusement Company. By 1923, however, there was an increasing call with better salaries for black performers in the musical revues that had become popular downtown. At the Lafayette a show like *Follow Me*, a "hodge-podge small time vaudeville," could run for three weeks, but a play like *Pa Williams' Gal* survived for one week (Dec. 1923, p. 923). In addition to Clarence Muse and Charles Gilpin, many black actors performed with the Lafayette Players, among them E. Rich Abrahams, Mrs. Charles H. Anderson, Laura Bowman,* Tom Brown, Inez Clough,* A. B. Comathiere,* Will A. Cook, Opal Cooper, Charlotte Freeman, Alice Gorgas, Abbie Mitchell,* Lionel Monogas,* J. Frances Mores, Charles Moore, Charlie Olden, Evelyn Preer,* Arthur

Ray, Charles T. Taylor, and Dooley Wilson,* among others, many of whom went on to successful careers on Broadway. The company's real beginnings lay with Bush, Bishop, Freeman, Gilpin, and Wilson in *The Girl at the Fort* at the Lincoln. Seven years later, when the Lafayette disbanded its stock company, after 250 productions, the remaining members moved to Los Angeles and continued to perform until 1932.

REFERENCES: *The Messenger*, Mar., Nov. 1917, Oct., Dec. 1923; Langston Hughes and Milton Meltzer, *Black Magic*, 1971; BB, 1980; Errol Hill, ed., *The Theatre of Black Americans*, 1980; Jervis Anderson, *This Was Harlem*, 1982. (BK)

LAFAYETTE THEATRE, 1912–1934. The "House Beautiful," as the Lafayette Theatre was called, stood at 132nd Street and Seventh Avenue, probably the first New York theater to desegregate, as early as 1912, allowing blacks judged as respectable to sit in the orchestra. By 1916 the theater had its own stock company and played before almost exclusively black audiences in popular plays as well as classics from the white theater repertory. The Lafayette seated 2,000 patrons and for nearly seven years offered an uninterrupted diet of Broadway successes like *Madame X* and *Within the Law*, Shakespeare, and dramatizations of *Dr. Jekyll and Mr. Hyde* and other well-known novels. When Frank Schiffman took over the management in 1923, he turned the Lafayette into a vaudeville house, with continuous performances from early afternoon until midnight, except on Fridays when a midnight show went on until four A.M. A new revue or play began each week, often in frank imitation of something on Broadway: when *Artists and Models* opened downtown, *Brownskin Models* opened at the Lafayette. Shows like *Aces and Queens* played there in 1925, with music and lyrics by Porter Grainger* and Freddie Johnson;* and Bessie Smith* starred in *Mississippi Days* in 1928. Wallace Thurman* contended that the Friday midnight show was always best, with catcalls and hisses, gin bottles passed around, and a congenial atmosphere. Later, the Lafayette became a movie house and finally a church. It is notable also for having first offered Willis Richardson's* *Chip Woman's Fortune** in 1923, even though it failed there. The brief Broadway run a month later marked the first play by a black writer dealing with black characters to appear in a white commercial theater.

REFERENCES: Wallace Thurman, *Negro Life in New York's Harlem*, 1928; Loften Mitchell, *Black Drama*, 1967; BB, 1980; Jervis Anderson, *This Was Harlem*, 1982. (BK)

LARSEN, NELLA (writer, librarian, nurse), 1893–1963. An active member of the Harlem Renaissance, Nella Larsen wrote two important novels dealing with identity and marginality. These themes emerged from her life, which began in Chicago when she was born to a white Danish woman and a black West Indian father. Two years later, after her father died, her mother married a Dane. Educated in Chicago, at sixteen Larsen travelled to Denmark for three years.

After a year of study at Fisk University in Nashville, Tennessee, she attended the University of Copenhagen and then returned to the United States once again. She graduated from the Lincoln Hospital Training Program in New York in 1915. For a year she worked as a nurse at Tuskegee Hospital in Alabama. Then she enrolled in the New York Public Library Training School. She had a career as children's librarian at the 135th Street Branch in New York from 1922 until 1929. During this period she married Elmer Imes (1883-1941), a Fisk graduate and physicist, widely recognized for his work in infrared absorption bands. He was an infrequent figure with his wife at black as well as white parties during the Harlem Renaissance but more at home in the laboratory than the salon. During the same period Larsen wrote her only two novels, *Quicksand** (1928) and *Passing** (1929). In 1929 she received the Harmon Foundation's* bronze medal. In 1930 she became the first black woman to win a Guggenheim for creative writing, and that same year her story "Sanctuary" was published in *Forum*. She then travelled to Spain to work on a third novel, but it was never completed. Divorced in 1933, she spent her last thirty years as a supervising nurse at Bethel Hospital in Brooklyn in relative obscurity.
REFERENCES: WWCR, 1915; Robert A. Bone, *The Negro Novel in America*, 1970; Arthur P. Davis, *From the Dark Tower*, 1974; Barbara Christian, *Black Women Novelists*, 1980; Mary Helen Washington, "Lost Women," *Ms*, Dec. 1980. (DI)

LATIMER, CATHERINE ALLEN (librarian), c. 1895–? The first black woman to be employed by the New York Public Library, Catherine Allen Latimer was born in Tennessee and educated at Howard University and in Europe. In 1920 she became an assistant in the library, and in 1926 she was appointed reference librarian in charge of the Division of Negro Literature and History, working in the 135th Street Branch. It was here, under her direction, that the Arthur Schomburg* Center for Research in Black Culture had its genesis.
REFERENCE: WWCA, 1933. (BK)

LAWRENCE, WILLIAM (pianist), 20 September 1895–17 March 1981. William Lawrence, of Charleston, South Carolina, was the pianist in the Hayes Trio that toured the eastern states in 1917, and he served as Roland Hayes's* accompanist on his European tours in the twenties. Subsequently, he had his own music studio in New York; during the thirties he was codirector of the Symphonette Orchestra.
REFERENCES: MacKinley Helm, *Angel Mo and her Son, Roland Hayes*, 1942; *Black Perspectives in Music*, Fall 1981. (DA)

LEE, CANADA [LEONARD LIONEL CORNELIUS CANEGATA] (actor), 3 May 1907–9 May 1952. Born in New York, one of the most celebrated actors of his generation gave up seven years of violin study with J. Rosamond Johnson* to become a jockey. Before he was twenty years old he had changed his name

to Canada Lee and become a boxer, winning a national amateur lightweight competition in addition to 90 out of 100 fights. He won 175 out of the 200 that followed, but a detached retina brought his boxing career to an end in 1933. He began acting almost immediately, first in WPA productions. In 1941 Lee starred in Richard Wright's *Native Son* and later in many plays and films.
REFERENCE: NYT, 10 May 1952. (BK)

LEE, GEORGE (novelist, businessman), 1894–1976. After serving in World War I (92nd Division) George Lee returned to America and became a successful businessman and politician in Memphis, Tennessee, insisting that blacks must be proud of their history and themselves. In 1930 he decided to become a writer and his first novel, *Beale Street: Where the Blues Began* (1934), endorsed for publication by James Weldon Johnson,* documented the pride and self-respect of the respectable middle class as well as the lives of dope peddlers, whores, gamblers, blues* players and easy riders. It was the first book by a black writer to be advertised by the Book of the Month Club. Lee's second novel, *River George* (1937), is the expansion of a chapter in *Beale Street* and there, briefly, Lee criticized Harlem and those who presume that spiritual emancipation will originate in the North and not the South.
REFERENCES: WWCA, 1938; Hugh Gloster, *Negro Voices in American Fiction*, 1948; David M. Tucker, *Lieutenant Lee of Beale Street*, 1971. (MH)

LEMONIER, TOM (composer), 29 March 1870–14 March 1945. Tom Lemonier was one of several black musicians who contributed songs to the musical comedies and revues that ran briefly in Harlem and occasionally on Broadway. He was an active member of the American Society of Composers, Authors, and Publishers, although none of his songs seems to have survived beyond their initial hearing.
REFERENCE: ASCAP, 1966. (BK)

LENOX CLUB (cabaret). Located on Seventh Avenue at 143rd Street, the Lenox Club catered to a 90 percent black clientele, although the newspapers could report of both races in attendance for the suggestive dancing in the floor shows. There were three shows each night, with a chorus line of eight; the first went on at 11 P.M. and the last one ended at 7 A.M. A sign in the window read: "WE POSITIVELY DO NOT SELL INTOXICATED DRINKS OF ANY KIND"; it even appeared in advertisements briefly.
REFERENCES: *Inter-State Tattler*, 5 July 1929; Jervis Anderson, *This Was Harlem*, 1982. (BK)

LESLIE, LEW [LEV LESSINSKY] (theatrical producer), c. 1886–10 March 1963. Lew Leslie began his successful career as a producer of black revues with a show at the Plantation Club.* He expanded that into a Broadway musical in the summer of 1922. The following year he took Florence Mills* and others from the cast to England for a new revue called *Dover to Dixie*, and in 1924 he brought it back home as *Dixie to Broadway*. His *Blackbirds[*] of 1926* began as a short run at the Alhambra Theatre* before going on to Paris and London but failed to open on Broadway because of the death of its star Florence Mills. Other installments followed, notably *Blackbirds of 1928*, but none of the subsequent versions was a success.

REFERENCES: EMT, 1976; BB, 1980. (BK)

LEWIS, THEOPHILUS (drama critic), 4 March 1891–? For a period of four years at the heart of the Harlem Renaissance, Theophilus Lewis contributed thoughtful theater criticism to *The Messenger*,* the only regular evaluations of black drama during the period. Born in Baltimore, Lewis had little formal schooling, served overseas in the army during World War I, and took a job in the post office in New York in 1922. He began to write for *The Messenger* simply because of his interest in the theater when he submitted a review of a Lafayette Theatre* show to A. Philip Randolph.* That editor was sufficiently impressed to engage Lewis for a regular column, and even though *The Messenger* could offer no salary, it did at least pay for Lewis's theater tickets. His monthly reviews reflect his own ambivalence about the coarse musical revues, acknowledging their vulgarity and stereotyping and at the same time the "spiritual craving" they satisfied: "Whether that craving is refined or ethical is beside the point, so long as it's human. Since these shows satisfy a very definite and intense desire they are sound theater. So let us enjoy their verve, beauty and sin while we may, for the drear and inevitable day is coming when they will be against the law" (Mar. 1927, p. 85). He decried the use of blackface, light-skinned chorus girls, actors unwilling or unable to hold out for serious roles, and white ownership of black theaters; he praised little theater groups like the Krigwa Players* and the National Ethiopian Art Theatre,* regularly staging serious black plays by black playwrights, and he urged establishing a race theater that could educate its audiences. Lewis published a few stories in *The Messenger*, and he reviewed new books from time to time, but his controlling interest was theater criticism, and he left *The Messenger* to write occasional articles for *Catholic World*, *Commonweal*, and the *Pittsburgh Courier*.* He continued to work for the post office until his retirement. Writing about Lewis in Arna Bontemps's* anthology *The Harlem Renaissance Remembered*, Theodore Kornweibel, Jr., rightly assessed his contribution: "Mere criticism was not his end; rather, he intended to help provide an ideology for the development of a national black theater which would be both a source of a racial ethos and a repository of the race's genius" (p. 171).

REFERENCES: *The Messenger*, Mar. 1927; Anna Bontemps, ed., *The Harlem Renaissance Remembered*, 1972. (BK)

LIBERATOR (periodical), 1918–1924. The *Liberator* was founded, owned, and edited in its first years by the well-known writer and Socialist Max Eastman, who began the magazine as a successor to the government-banned *Masses*. The

Liberator was an avant-garde, bohemian sheet, which gave space to economic and political news and views, as well as art, poetry, fiction, and criticism. Eastman would not tolerate "dogma and rigidity of mind," so a wide spectrum of left-center views could be found in the *Liberator* in its early editions; moreover, Eastman proclaimed that the *Liberator* would be completely free of any censorship in its literary selections. Eastman, however, soon left the magazine in the hands of coeditors Michael Gold and Claude McKay.* Gold and other left-wing Marxists pushed the magazine toward Marxist purity, and McKay was unsuccessful in either obtaining assurances that at least 10 percent of the space in each issue would be devoted to racial issues or that good writing would still be prized over mediocre left-wing propaganda pieces. Disappointed over the magazine's policies and eager to see the Bolshevik Revolution in person, McKay left for Russia in late 1922. The *Liberator*, which had a circulation of 50,000 in its first years and 60,000 under Gold and McKay, continued to veer toward the Communist line until, in October 1924, it merged with several Communist periodicals to form the *Communist Monthly*, a propaganda piece owned by the Communist party and edited by Earl Browder, a leading American Communist party member.

REFERENCES: Milton Cantor, *Max Eastman*, 1970; David Levering Lewis, *When Harlem Was in Vogue*, 1981. (DS)

LINCOLN MOTION PICTURE COMPANY (film company), 1915–1923. Organized in 1915 to take advantage of the growing audience for movies, the Lincoln Motion Picture Company was headed by Noble Johnson* as its president and leading actor. His brother George Perry Johnson was business manager and they were joined in the venture by actor Clarence Brooks,* druggist James T. Smith who lent financial support, and white cameraman Harry Gant. Operating with little money and unpaid performers, the company released its first effort in 1916, a two-reeler entitled *Realization of a Negro's Ambition*, advertised as "A two-part drama of love and adventure, pictured with a good moral, a vein of clean comedy and beautiful settings" (quoted in BAF, 1974, pp. 142–43). Noble Johnson starred as a Tuskegee Institute graduate who rescues a rich white man's daughter, makes his fortune in oil, and returns to his southern home to marry his fiancée and live happily ever after, having realized his ambitions. *Trooper of Troop K* was released the following year, again with Johnson in the leading role, featuring "gripping scenes [of] . . . unflinching bravery" in which black cavalry soldiers "sacrificed their blood and life for their country" (p. 143). *The Law of Nature* followed in 1918, "a virile production full of human interest and realistic western atmosphere " (p. 143), after which Noble Johnson resigned as president and signed a contract with Universal Studios. Clarence Brooks took over as Lincoln's leading actor in *A Man's Duty*, made in 1919 but apparently not released until 1921, a melodrama in which the hero, believing himself guilty of murder, becomes "practically a wreck on the shoals of dissipation," according to the plot summary released for publicity (p. 144). Lincoln's last film, *By Right*

of Birth, also featured Brooks in 1921, dealing with California blacks being cheated out of their oil rights by a Mexican-American stockbroker. Even white newspapers gave some favorable notice to this fourth venture, but Johnson's defection, distribution problems, and lack of funds forced the Lincoln Motion Picture Company to disband in 1923.
REFERENCES: BAF, 1974; Daniel J. Leab, *From Sambo to Superspade*, 1975; BBW, 1977. (BK)

LINCOLN THEATRE, 1909–1932. Sources disagree about the first theater in Harlem. Two seem to have opened in 1909: the Crescent at 36–38 West 125th Street and the Lincoln at 56–58 West 125th Street, named after the white emancipator of the growing numbers of Afro-Americans who had begun moving into the area a few years before. Early movies at low rates and popular stage shows at the Lincoln managed to put the Crescent out of business, however. The Lincoln seated more than a thousand patrons, and it featured exclusively black performers for exclusively black audiences. Until its defection to the Lafayette Theatre* in 1914, the Anita Bush* Players Company staged plays at the Lincoln. Musical revues, however, continued to draw audiences because they included so many familiar stars, Fats Waller* among them, at the Lincoln's elaborate pipe organ as the accompanist for silent films, and Jules Bledsoe* in a Harlem revival of *The Emperor Jones.** Legend has it that, during more than one performance of the Eugene O'Neill* play, black audiences cried out to Bledsoe, "Get out of that jungle! This is Harlem!" Wallace Thurman* reported that nearly all performers at the Lincoln were openly razzed, the audience's spontaneous remarks often proving funnier than the jokes onstage. Chorines were openly courted during the three-hour-long shows, patrons joined in on the songs, and nobody seemed particularly aware of how bad the shows were or of the stench in the theater.
REFERENCES: Wallace Thurman, *Negro Life in New York's Harlem*, 1928; Loften Mitchell, *Black Drama*, 1967; Jervis Anderson, *This Was Harlem*, 1982. (BK)

LINDSAY, [NICHOLAS] VACHEL (poet), 1879–5 December 1931. Vachel Lindsay was a white, performing poet, born in Illinois. He had an early popularity through his incantatory work on African themes, *The Congo* (1914), strongly influenced by the rhythms of black dancing and revival singing. He came from a fundamentalist background with a mystic faith in nature, often living as a vagabond, trading poems for shelter during summer tours. During the twenties his popularity as a poet waned, but his opinions, as a supporter of young black writers, were widely sought. In 1925, for example, he was including Langston Hughes's* poems in his own public lectures, and he served as a judge for various literary contests and was one of several white writers represented in the 1926

Crisis symposium "The Negro in Art: How Shall He Be Portrayed?"* Lindsay died in 1931, probably a suicide, following the decline of interest in his work. REFERENCES: William Rose Benét, ed., *The Reader's Encyclopedia*, 1948; NYT, 6 Dec. 1931. (BK)

LIZA (musical comedy), 1922. Irving C. Miller* wrote the book, and Maceo Pinkard* wrote the music and lyrics for a "rehash of white concepts" patterned after *Shuffle Along.** It had its origins in Chicago, where the influential Chicago *Whip** thought the material was unsuitable: a series of scenes in Jimtown again, a jail, a barbershop, a graveyard, on the levee, a ballroom, with an apparently extemporaneous plot. The *New York Times* reviewer regretted that black revues were "so unbelievably crude and rough hewn" and that "blackface makeup on black actors was "a custom of the trade" (28 Nov. 1922, p. 24). *Liza* was one of the first "speed shows," as they were often called, relying on their frantic dancing for success, and was notable at least for introducing "the Charleston" to Broadway for the first time on November 27. The dance became a twenties trademark, and even today it is probably the first visual image that comes to mind when the decade is referred to. Shortly into its brief run *Liza* gave a midnight benefit for the NAACP,* with some help from cast members of *Shuffle Along*, and raised $900.
REFERENCES: Burns Mantle, 1922–1923; NYTTR, 1972; BB, 1980. (BK)

LOCKE, ALAIN (critic, educator), 13 September 1886–9 June 1954. Born into the elite of Philadelphia's black community (his father had a law degree from Howard University and taught at the Philadelphia School of Pedagogy), Alain Locke was a brilliant student at Central High School, the School of Pedagogy, and Harvard University, where he was Phi Beta Kappa and graduated *magna cum laude* (1907). He was also the first Afro-American Rhodes Scholar (1907–1910) and studied for a year in Berlin and the Collège de France in Paris. In 1912 he returned to the United States and served as an assistant professor of philosophy and education at Howard (1912–1916). His first work was published as "Race Contacts and Inter-Racial Relationships" in 1916, and he returned to Harvard to complete work toward a doctorate degree in philosophy. After completion of his dissertation "The Problem of Classification in Theory of Value" (1918), he returned to Howard to chair the philosophy department and to teach until 1953.

In 1925 Locke helped edit the special Harlem issue of *Survey Graphic** "Harlem: Mecca of the New Negro"; eight months later Locke's *New Negro*,* built upon the nucleus of writing in the *Survey Graphic*, dramatically announced that the younger generation of black Americans was "vibrant with a new psychology" and that "the new spirit was awake in the masses" (p. 3). Although Locke is best known for this celebrated collection of writers, essayists, and poets, his role in helping to generate a cultural renaissance was more complex and more widespread than this specific achievement.

Always alert to help promote and support talented individuals, Locke sought to introduce young writers, artists, and singers to his own patron, the wealthy and influential Charlotte Mason,* who was willing to provide financial support for young black intellectuals. Zora Neale Hurston,* Langston Hughes,* Claude McKay,* Richmond Barthé,* and Aaron Douglas* were some of the most notable people under Locke's careful nurturing to find their way to "Godmother's." In addition, Locke, along with George Edmund Haynes,* counseled the Harmon Foundation* as it began in 1926 to give annual awards for literature, music, fine arts, industry, science, education, and race relations to black artists, writers, and professionals. Also, under the auspices of the Harmon Foundation, Locke and Haynes assembled the enormously successful all-Negro art exhibition at New York's International House in 1928.

More visibly, Locke was busy throughout the twenties seeking to celebrate and to guide critically the artistic and intellectual efforts of black Americans as well as to inform and interest a supportive white audience. He published works on art, music, and African art. He established, with T. Montgomery Gregory,* the Howard Players, one of the first little theater groups, and also edited with Gregory the first anthology of black drama, *Plays of Negro Life** (1927). Finally, Locke regularly wrote reviews of contemporary literature for *Opportunity** and appeared in numerous magazines throughout the twenties. Consistently, it was Locke's understanding that through art itself, through a conscious forging of a cultural expression, both blacks and whites would achieve a new sense of identity and a commitment to social and political justice.

At the same time Locke was especially active in helping to promote the interests and fame of the "New Negro" in Europe, especially France, which Locke believed was uniquely free of racial prejudice. In 1924 he met the Martiniquian writer René Maran,* winner of the Prix Goncourt (1921) for his novel *Batouala,** and became a close friend. Through Maran, Locke helped to make available to black Americans the writers and intellectuals of the French black Third World. He also found in Maran a helpful ally who helped publish in French some of the leading figures of the Renaissance.

In 1936, in the article "Harlem: Dark Weather Vane," Locke had severe reservations about his earlier enthusiasm and what, in fact, was new about the New Negro. Although Locke was especially concerned about the need for economic and political reform, he never abandoned his belief in the essential worth of intellectual and artistic expression. Until the end of his life he criticized and celebrated black arts and literature.

REFERENCES: CB, 1944, 1954; Alain L. Locke, ed., *The New Negro*, 1968; Margaret Just Butcher, *The Negro in American Culture*, 1972; Nathan Irvin Huggins, *Harlem Renaissance*, 1971; Arthur P. Davis, *From the Dark Tower*, 1974; David Levering Lewis, *When Harlem Was in Vogue*, 1981. (MH)

LOGGINS, VERNON (educator, writer), 10 January 1893–3 October 1968. Vernon Loggins, a leading white scholar in the field of American literature, was

an instructor and, later, professor at Columbia University from 1925 until 1960, where he earned the Ph.D. in 1931. His doctoral dissertation, the first careful scholarly analysis of black literature before the turn of the century, was published by Columbia University Press in 1931 as *The Negro Author: His Development in America to 1900*. The book stands up well today, and the author made wise and generous use of the Arthur Schomburg* collection in the New York Public Library in completing it. Loggins also wrote *Chansons du Midi*, privately printed in 1924, and seven scholarly books in his field.
REFERENCE: AAB, 1972. (DS)

LONG, AVON (singer, dancer), 18 June 1910–15 February 1984. Born in Baltimore, Avon Long migrated to New York in his late teens and began dancing in nightclub shows, notably at Connie's Inn* and the Cotton Club* in 1931. His long career in the theater began when he replaced John Bubbles* as Sportin' Life in George Gershwin's* *Porgy and Bess*ytes in 1936. Subsequently, he acted in several plays and films.
REFERENCES: Langston Hughes and Milton Meltzer, *Black Magic*, 1971; DBPA, 1974. (BK)

A LONG WAY FROM HOME (autobiography), 1937. Divided into six sections, each a major phase of Claude McKay's* intellectual and artistic experiences and growth, *A Long Way from Home* traces his life from early childhood in Jamaica to his return to America from Europe and Morocco in the mid-thirties. McKay's commitment to the ideal of the racial power and integrity of the artist and his art serves to unify man and event, his own inner spiritual quest and his complex social and political experiences. This commitment also serves to establish McKay's profound disagreements with Alain Locke* (in particular) and most of the white and black intellectuals directly involved in the Harlem Renaissance. (MH)

LOUISIANA (play), 1933. J. Augustus Smith's play about a Christian minister confronting voodoo opened with Trixie Smith* and Laura Bowman* in the cast, staged by the Negro Theatre Guild at the 48th Street Theatre, on February 27. Had it been put on in Harlem, the *New York Times* reviewer suggested, its defects would have been acceptable, but on Broadway they came off as simple incompetence (NYT, 28 Feb. 1933, p. 15).
REFERENCE: NYTTR, 1972. (BK)

LOVEJOY, ALEC (actor), c. 1893–19 April 1946. After early tours of Europe with Mamie Remington's Pickaninnies, Alec Lovejoy appeared in many Harlem musical shows but never, apparently, on Broadway. He acted with the Eddie Hunter* Company for a period during the twenties and with Ethel Waters* in

Miss Calico in 1926. Also, he appeared in several Oscar Micheaux* films as well as the film version of *The Green Pastures** in 1936.
REFERENCES: BBW, 1977; BB, 1980. (BK)

LOVINGGOOD, PENMAN (writer, concert singer), 25 December 1895–? Born in Austin, Texas, Penman Lovinggood began musical training at an early age. He later studied at Samuel Houston College, which his father had founded, and privately in Philadelphia and with J. Rosamond Johnson* in New York. He made his debut as a tenor at Town Hall in New York in November 1925 and was active thereafter as a teacher, church soloist, and music columnist. During the thirties he sang in J. Rosamond Johnson's quartet and played with the W. C. Handy* orchestra. His opera *Menelek* was produced by the American Negro Opera Association in 1936. He was the recipient of a Wanamaker Prize for composition and a Griffith Music Foundation Medal. Lovinggood wrote a study of black artists of the Harlem Renaissance, *Famous Modern Negro Musicians*, published in Brooklyn in 1921.
REFERENCE: BDAM, 1982. (PO)

LOWE, JAMES (actor), 1880–1963. James B. Lowe was the first black actor publicized by a white studio, when he appeared as Uncle Tom in Universal's 1927 version of *Uncle Tom's Cabin*. Lowe had acted in two earlier films, both westerns, *Demon River* and *Blue Blazes*, but he only came to public attention when he replaced Charles Gilpin.* That well-known actor had been signed to play Uncle Tom, only to quit when he discovered that the director Harry Pollard intended to perpetuate the old racial stereotypes. In retaliation Universal sent out publicity releases to attest that Lowe was looked upon at the studio as "a living black god" and that "a heavenly power" had brought him to play the role (quoted in Bogle, *Toms, Coons, Mulattoes, Mammies, and Bucks*, p. 6). Lowe bided his time, waiting until sufficient footage had been shot before protesting against the characterization forced on him. Universal never used him again, nor did he ever make another film. Five years later James B. Lowe was working as a tailor in Paris.
REFERENCES: Donald Bogle, *Toms, Coons, Mulattoes, Mammies, and Bucks*, 1973; Daniel J. Leab, *From Sambo to Superspade*, 1975; WWH, 1976. (BK)

LUCAS, MARIE (dance-orchestra leader), 1880s–26 April 1947. Marie Lucas was a pianist and trombonist as well as an arranger and a conductor. She was the daughter of Sam Lucas, a well-known minstrel, and Carrie Melvin Lucas, a violinist and cornetist. She began musical studies with her parents and continued them in Nottingham, England, and at the Boston Conservatory. She made her debut in *The Red Moon* in 1909, a show in which her father had a leading role. She was well known by 1915 as the leader of the Ladies Orchestra at the Lafayette Theatre* in Harlem. The next year she became musical director as well of the Quality Amusement Corporation, which managed several black theaters in the

East. During the twenties Lucas was the leader of a male dance band that played at the Howard Theatre in Washington, D.C., and she later toured widely with her own orchestra, the Merry Makers.
REFERENCE: BDAM, 1982. (PO)

LUCKY SAMBO (musical play), 1925. *Lucky Sambo* seems to have had two runs, first at the Colonial Theatre beginning June 6 and then a year later at the Columbia Theatre beginning May 26. Porter Grainger* and Freddie Johnson* wrote the music and lyrics. Joe Byrd as Rufus Johnson and Tim Moore,* replaced in the second run by Billy Higgins,* as Sambo Jenkins—familiar types long before their first Broadway incarnation in *Shuffle Along*—supplied the comedy. Amanda Randolph* and Lena Wilson* also appeared in this thin comedy about selling phoney oil stock in a rural slum area where eventually oil really is discovered. As usual, the dancing received the most praise. The later reviewer for the *New York Times* noted: "The first essential, of course, is that they shall appear in artificial blackface—the paler hues are all very well for heroes and chorus, but comedians must be definitely black." Still, *Lucky Sambo* was an "excellent specimen" of an "amusing and agile entertainment" rapidly gaining popularity with white audiences at the time (26 May 1926, p. 24)
REFERENCES: Burns Mantle, 1925–1926; NYTTR, 1972. (BK)

LULU BELLE (play), 1926. In retrospect, *Lulu Belle* is a lurid melodrama by white playwrights Charles McArthur and Edward Sheldon, notable only because of its mixed cast: 97 out of 114 actors were black. White stars Leonore Ulric and Henry Hull played the leads in dark makeup, but Evelyn Preer,* later succeeded by Edna Thomas,* was prominent in the cast. David Belasco lavished "his entire stock of goods" on the production, according to the *New York Times* reviewer, with "huge mobs of colored actors," although the plot and characters were lost in "decorative bricabrac and colorful atmosphere" (10 Feb. 1926, p. 20). Lulu Belle is a Harlem prostitute who gets George Randall to desert his wife and children, only to desert him for a prize fighter whom she then discards for a degenerate French count. Randall follows her abroad and strangles her. The play had a considerable vogue with white audiences newly fascinated by tales of Harlem lowlife, and there was a concurrent production in San Francisco. *The Crisis*,* always conservative in its view of depictions of the steamy side of Harlem, was circumspect: "The Negro has emerged as a human being who is not a caricature and not a comedian" (May 1926, p. 34).
REFERENCES: Burns Mantle, 1925–1926; *The Crisis*, May 1926; NYTTR, 1972. (BK)

LUNCEFORD, JIMMIE (musician), 6 June 1902–13 July 1947. Jimmie Lunceford, born in Missouri, took his musical training at Fisk University and City College of New York, after which he taught high school for a short time. He was flutist with George Morrison's Orchestra, Fletcher Henderson's* Orchestra, and Wilbur Sweatman's* Orchestra, although probably only briefly with Henderson, since he is unidentified in phonograph recordings of the period. Lunceford formed his own group in 1929, and he played regularly at the Lafayette* and Apollo theaters* in the early thirties.

REFERENCES: *Fletcher Henderson: Developing an American Orchestra*, 1977; ASCAP, 1980. (BK)

LYLES, AUBREY (playwright, comedian, producer), 1882–4 August 1932. Aubrey Lyles was born in Jackson, Tennessee, where he met his future vaudeville partner Flournoy Miller.* The friends attended Fisk University together and then joined the Pekin Stock Company in Chicago as writers and comedians. (For the history of their work together as the vaudeville team Miller and Lyles, see MILLER, FLOURNOY.) After the unsuccessful *Keep Shufflin'* * (1928) the team separated. Lyles went to Africa for a year and on his return to New York produced *Runnin' de Town*, which was not a success. He rejoined Miller in 1930 to make two talking shorts for RKO pictures, and the team resumed touring in vaudeville. Their last show together was *Sugar Hill* * (1931). Lyles died in New York in 1932.

Lyles was the "little man" of the team, and the character he portrayed, Sam Peck, was a mixture of timidity and bravado. In their famous fight routine, puny Sam challenged the much larger Steve (Miller), and the pugilistic travesty that developed became a vaudeville classic. Late in his career Lyles became convinced that Amos 'n' Andy had fashioned their act after Miller and Lyles routines, Amos copying Miller, Andy copying Lyles. He sued, and although he lost the suit, Miller and Lyles were given a chance to appear on radio with their act. It did not go over well.

REFERENCES: Maud Cuney-Hare, *Negro Musicians and Their Music*, 1936; BB, 1980. (DA)

M

MABLEY, JACKIE "MOMS" (comedienne), 19 March 1897–23 May 1975. In the late sixties, "Moms" Mabley's comedy record albums made her "an overnight success" after almost fifty years in show business. Born Loretta Mary Aiken in North Carolina, she began in vaudeville as a teenager with the team of Buck and Bubbles (Ford Lee Washington and John Bubbles*). Influenced by the act of Butterbeans and Susie (Jodie Edwards and Susie Hawthorne*), she developed her talent as a comic monologist on the black vaudeville circuit, creating the character of a world-weary old woman wearing funny hats, runover shoes, and baggy stockings, whose stories were a "mix of sassy folk-wisdom and sly insights" (NA, p. 833). Her first big New York success was at Connie's Inn* in 1923. She played in clubs during the twenties and appeared in shows such as *Miss Bandanna* and *Look Who's Here* (1927), *Devil's Frolics* (1929), and *The Joy Boat* and *Sidewalks of Harlem* (1930). Along with Zora Neale Hurston* and others, Mabley wrote some sketches for *Fast and Furious* in 1931, in which she and Hurston appeared as cheerleaders in a skit of Hurston's called "Football Team." She was one of the great favorites at the Apollo Theatre,* where, according to Jervis Anderson in *This Was Harlem*, the demanding, discriminating, and merciless audience recognized almost no popular entertainer until he or she had appeared and excelled there. Although her act was "garrulously naughty," he wrote, "she was seldom coarse" (p. 238). *Moms Mabley at the U.N.*, which sold more than a million albums in 1960, was her first recording to achieve commercial success and was followed by *Moms Mabley at the Geneva Conference* and others. She appeared at Carnegie Hall with Nancy Wilson and Cannonball Adderley in 1962 and at the Kennedy Center in 1972. Her first television appearance was with Harry Belafonte in 1967, and she was a frequent guest on comedy and talk shows thereafter.

Although she had played minor parts in films such as *The Emperor Jones* and *Boarding House Blues*, Mabley's first starring role came in 1974, a year before her death. *Amazing Grace* was delayed after Mabley suffered a heart attack, but after the implantation of a pacemaker, she returned to work on the film she hoped would make her grandchildren proud of her. In it she played her usual toothless, rubber-faced old woman full of grit and gumption. "The movie, like Mabley, sort of shambles along," according to Vincent Canby, reviewing it in the *New York Times*, "but we laugh with Moms in appreciation of her implacable, firmly unbudgeable stand in favor of common sense" (2 Nov. 1974, p. 16).

REFERENCES: *Ebony Success Library*, vol. 2, 1973; NYT, 2 Nov. 1974, 24 May 1975; NA, 1976; DBPA, 1978; BB, 1980; Jervis Anderson, *This Was Harlem*, 1982. (PO)

McCALL, JAMES EDWARD (journalist), 2 September 1880–? The "New Negro" was a phrase coined by James Edward McCall, who was himself an example. He attended Alabama State Normal School and then Howard University until he went blind as a result of typhoid fever just after the turn of the century. For a time he wrote regularly for the Montgomery, Alabama, *Advertiser* as "The Blind Tom of Literature." In 1907 he graduated from Albion College in Michigan, with the assistance of his sister who attended with him, returning afterward to continue a career in journalism in Alabama. There he founded the *Emancipator*,* a weekly "race paper," as such news organs were called at that time. In 1920 he became city editor and editorial writer for the Detroit, Michigan, *Independent*.

REFERENCE: WWCA, 1933. (BK)

McCLENDON, ROSE (actress), 12 August 1884–12 July 1936. Rose McClendon was a distinguished actress and crusader for the advancement of blacks in the theater. She grew up in New York City where she directed and acted in plays and cantatas for her church. For ten years after her 1904 marriage to Dr. Henry Pruden McClendon, a chiropractor and Pullman porter, she continued her church work but had no professional involvement in the theater. In 1916 she studied at the American Academy of Dramatic Art on a scholarship and devoted the rest of her life to acting and the teaching of acting. Her first role was in *Justice* in 1919, followed by *Roseanne** in 1924, but she received her first critical acclaim in *Deep River* in 1926, in a performance that Ethel Barrymore called "one of the memorable, immortal moments in the theatre" (NAW, p. 450). She appeared in Paul Green's* Pulitzer Prize-winning play *In Abraham's Bosom** in 1926 and played the role of Serena in the original production of *Porgy** in 1927, with which she toured the United States and Europe. She played in *The House of Connelly* in 1931, and of her role as the mother in *Never No More*,* the grim study of a lynching, Brooks Atkinson wrote, "She is both majestic and humble. She acts from the inside out" (NYT, 8 Jan. 1932, p. 17). She also appeared in *Black Souls** (1932), *Brainsweat** (1934), and *Roll Sweet Chariot** (1934). At the time she was playing Cora Lewis in Langston Hughes's* play *Mulatto*,* Atkinson wrote, "Rose McClendon is an artist with a sensitive personality and a bell-like voice. . . . It is always a privilege to see her adding fineness of perception . . . to her parts'' (NYT, 25 Oct. 1935, p. 25). She became ill with pleurisy during the run of *Mulatto* and died of pneumonia six months later.

A dynamic and sparkling woman, McClendon had also directed plays at the Negro Experimental Theatre,* and her goal was to establish a permanent Negro theater for the training of actors and the production of plays by black writers. Toward this end she and actor Dick Campbell* organized the Negro People's Theatre in 1935, which produced a black version of Clifford Odets's *Waiting for Lefty*. After her death the Negro People's Theatre was incorporated into the Negro Unit of the Federal Theatre Project, but in 1937 Dick Campbell founded the Rose McClendon Players, dedicated to carrying out her vision of a community group for training in all aspects of the theater. In 1946 Carl Van Vechten,* who had himself photographed McClendon dozens of times, presented a collection of one hundred of his photographs of black artists and writers to Howard University to be known as the Rose McClendon Memorial Collection.

REFERENCES: Loften Mitchell, *Black Drama*, 1967; NYTTR, 1972; DBPA, 1974; Carl Van Vechten, "*Keep A-Inchin' Along*," 1979; NAW, 1980; Jervis Anderson, *This Was Harlem*, 1982. (PO)

McCOY, VIOLA [AMANDA BROWN] (entertainer), c. 1900–? Viola McCoy appeared regularly in shows at the Lafayette,* Lincoln,* and Alhambra* theaters as well as in cabarets and nightclubs. In 1927 she owned, operated, and performed in Jack's Cabaret. When the Harlem Renaissance ran down, and business with it, she opened her own nightclub in Saratoga in 1930.

REFERENCE: BWW, 1979. (BK)

McDOUGALD [AYER], [GERTRUDE] ELISE JOHNSON (essayist, educator), 1885–1971. Elise Johnson McDougald, was the daughter of Peter Johnson, a founder of the National Urban League.* After graduating from Columbia University she taught in the New York City elementary school system from 1905 to 1911, when she resigned to marry and raise a family. McDougald remained active in various endeavors. She worked as head of the women's department of the United States Employment Bureau and as social investigator and vocational guidance expert for the New York City Board of Education; she was strongly involved in the Henry Street Settlement and for a time worked with the Manhattan Trade School and the New York Branch of the U.S. Department of Labor. During the halcyon days of the Harlem Renaissance she contributed essays to *The Crisis,* *Opportunity,* and, notably, Alain Locke's* *New Negro* where she published "The Double Task," an article that first appeared in the March 1925 Harlem Renaissance issue of *Survey Graphic* as "The Task of Negro Womanhood." She later married a second time and as Gertrude E. (Mrs. Vernon) Ayer became the first black principal in the New York City public school system, a position she retained until her retirement in 1954. Although not part of the mainstream of the Harlem Renaissance, many were familiar with the surpassing

beauty of Elsie Johnson MacDougald [*sic*] through Winold Reiss's* pastel portrait of her reproduced in the "New Negro" issue of *Survey Graphic*.
REFERENCES: Alain Locke, ed., *The New Negro*, 1925; *Newsweek*, 22 Oct. 1954; National Portrait Gallery, Smithsonian Institution, Washington, D.C. (MH, BK)

McGUIRE, GEORGE ALEXANDER (clergyman), 26 March 1866–10 November 1934. Born in Antigua, George Alexander McGuire assisted Marcus Garvey* in founding the African Orthodox Church* after serving in various parishes in Ohio, Virginia, Pennsylvania, and Arkansas. He joined Garvey in 1918 to become chaplain general of the Universal Negro Improvement Association* and, at the 1921 convention, bishop of the African Orthodox Church. He broke with Garvey some time later, but the church continued to flourish, and at the time of McGuire's death it boasted 30,000 members.
REFERENCE: DANB, 1982. (BK)

McHUGH, JIMMIE (composer), 10 July 1894–23 May 1969. White composer Jimmie McHugh began his long and successful career by writing the music for the Cotton Club* revues for a period of seven years, many of the songs with white lyricist Dorothy Fields.* He and Fields teamed to write the score for *Blackbirds[*] of 1928*, borrowing some songs for it from an earlier show they had done. Later, McHugh composed two songs deeply associated with Ethel Waters,* "Porgy" and "Don't Blame Me," before he moved on to his more celebrated career as a Hollywood composer.
REFERENCES: ASCAP, 1966; NYT, 25 May 1969. (BK)

MACK, CECIL [RICHARD CECIL McPHERSON] (composer, music publisher), 1883–1 August 1944. Richard McPherson, who used the professional name of Cecil Mack, was born in Norfolk, Virginia. He attended Lincoln University in Pennsylvania, left in his junior year, went to New York to earn enough money to enter the University of Pennsylvania Medical School, and left there after one semester. Back in New York, about 1905 he began to work with the team of Bert Williams* and George Walker and composed the song "I'm Miss Hannah from Savannah" for Walker's wife, Aida Overton Walker. With Walker he formed the Gotham-Attock Music Publishing Company, the first black enterprise of its kind in the United States. He collaborated with James Reese Europe* on *The Black Politician* (1907) and wrote the popular songs "Down Among the Sugar Cane," "That's Why They Call Me Shine," and the Nora Bayes special "You're in the Right Church but the Wrong Pew." He provided the lyrics for James P. Johnson's* score of *Runnin' Wild** (1923) and formed and directed Cecil Mack choirs that appeared in *Blackbirds[*] of 1928* and *1929* (in the latter show the choir performed a *Porgy** travesty), *Bombolla** (1929), and *Rhapsody in Black** (1931). For the Federal Theatre Project he wrote *Swing*

It (1937). His wife, Gertrude Curtis McPherson, was the first black woman dentist to practice in New York City.
REFERENCES: NYT 2 Aug. 1944; BB, 1980. (DA)

McKAY, CLAUDE (writer), 15 September 1889–22 May 1948. Born in the hill country of Jamaica (Clarendon Parish), Claude McKay was a published poet (*Songs of Jamaica* and *Constab Ballads*, 1912) by his twenty-third birthday and was awarded the medal of the Jamaica Institute of Arts and Science. This recognition, plus government encouragement for younger men to acquire a scientific agricultural education, led McKay to Tuskegee Institute (1912) and soon after to Kansas State University (1913). However, determined to be a writer, he left for Harlem in 1914.

Once in New York McKay published two poems in *Seven Arts* ("The Harlem Dancer" and "Invocation") and then burst upon the public with "If We Must Die," his angry response to the race riots* that convulsed Chicago in 1919. In the same year he travelled to London, became deeply immersed in the writings of Marx and Lenin, and joined the staff of Sylvia Pankhurst's Communist newspaper *The Worker's Dreadnought* (1920). One year later McKay returned to New York and at Max Eastman's invitation joined his radical magazine the *Liberator** as an associate editor. However, in June of the next year, at odds with Michael Gold and the general political-literary emphasis of the journal, McKay resigned as coeditor and left for Russia. Although McKay's reception in Moscow was a great personal success—he met Trotsky, Zinoviev, and Bukharin and addressed the Fourth Congress of the Third Communist International—he gradually became disenchanted with communism and was ultimately baptized a Roman Catholic four years before his death.

After six months in Russia McKay left for Berlin (1923) and then went to France (1923–1928) and North Africa (1931–1934). When McKay left America, he had published two volumes of poetry, *Spring in New Hampshire* (1920) and *Harlem Shadows** (1922), and was the most famous poet among black Americans. But he was determined to write prose. His first novel, *Color Scheme* (1925), went unpublished, and from a subsequent series of short stories (later published as *Gingertown**) grew *Home to Harlem** (1928). This was the first novel by a Harlem writer to be a best-seller, and despite the criticism of W.E.B. Du Bois*— "[it] nauseates me"—won the Harmon Foundation* Gold Medal Award for literature. In the following year McKay wrote *Banjo** (1929). While in Tangiers he completed *Gingertown** (1932) and wrote his chef d'oeuvre *Banana Bottom** (1933).

It is impossible to discuss the Harlem Renaissance without mentioning Claude McKay; however, his relationship with many of the most notable figures was both strained and distant, and he was extremely critical of its general scope and thrust. Although McKay thought Marcus Garvey* was a "curious blend of bourgeoise obsolescence and utopian fantasy," according to his 1941 *Harlem: Negro Metropolis*, he was impressed by the mass response that Garvey was able to generate (p. 9). Likewise, McKay saw his own work and his own role as an artist saturated with the color, the laughter, the anger, and the passion of the man in the street. On this basis he criticized Alain Locke's *New Negro** as a "remarkable chocolate soufflé of art and politics," and he thought the writings of the Renaissance too greatly resembled "an uplift organization and a vehicle to accelerate the pace and progress of smart Negro society," according to his autobiography *A Long Way From Home* (p. 322). What he believed was needed was a literature and an art rooted in the black experience. McKay's emphasis reflects his more general understanding that history is the story of group power and group achievement.

REFERENCES: Claude McKay, *A Long Way From Home*, 1937, and *Harlem: Negro Metropolis*, 1941; Nathan Irvin Huggins, *Harlem Renaissance*, 1971; Wayne F. Cooper, ed., *The Passion of Claude McKay*, 1973; Allison Gayle, Jr., *The Way of the New World*, 1975; James R. Giles, *Claude McKay*, 1976. (MH)

McKINNEY, NINA MAE (singer, actress), 1909 or 1913–May 1967. Nina Mae McKinney is best known for her role as the beautiful temptress Chick in King Vidor's film *Hallelujah!** She came to New York from Philadelphia with her parents at the age of twelve and taught herself to dance by imitating performers she saw on stage and in films. She began her career dancing in chorus lines, appearing in *Blackbirds[*] of 1928* and *Gingersnaps** (1929). After her success in *Hallelujah!* in 1929 she was signed to a five-picture contract by MGM but was actually cast in only two. In *Safe in Hell*, according to Mordaunt Hall reviewing it in the *New York Times*, McKinney was "about the most entertaining item in the film" (19 Dec. 1931, p. 5). She had a small part in *Reckless* and dubbed Jean Harlow's songs. She also appeared in the classic black musical short *Pie Pie Blackbirds*, with Eubie Blake* and the Nicholas Brothers in 1932. She toured Europe as a café singer, billing herself as "The Black Garbo," and costarred with Paul Robeson* in *Sanders of the River*, filmed in England in 1935. Later she toured with her own band and played in many black-cast films. McKinney appeared in minor roles in several Hollywood films of the forties, including *Together Again*, *Dark Waters*, *Danger Street*, and *Pinky*.

REFERENCES: NYTTR, 1972; WWH, 1976; BBW, 1977; BB, 1980. (PO)

McKINNEY'S COTTON PICKERS (dance band), 1927–1930. During the most frantic craze for black jazz, from 1927 until 1930, William McKinney's band was the best known for college and fraternity dances. His was one of the first groups to turn popular songs into instrumental jazz numbers suitable for the wild dances of the period. McKinney's Cotton Pickers toured much of the country, concentrating on the Midwest, avoiding the South, but still encountering the inevitable segregation that plagued black artists, even in college towns.

REFERENCES: Nancy Cunard, ed., *Negro*, 1970; Donald Angus. (BK)

MADDEN, [OWEN VINCENT] OWNEY (businessman), 1892–23 April 1965. More candidly identified as a mobster and bootlegger, English-born Owney Madden was head of the Gopher Gang in New York's infamous "Hell's Kitchen" on Ninth Avenue. He was eighteen years old at the time; at twenty-three, he was in Sing Sing state prison for murder but in control of his syndicate from inside, financing the Club DeLuxe with Madden's No. One Beer; and at thirty, he was paroled for good behavior. The Club DeLuxe became the Cotton Club* that same year, 1923, redecorated with a primitive motif to please the tastes of whites who had begun to go slumming in Harlem. Champagne was about thirty dollars a bottle, but Madden's No. One Beer was considerably less. At the height of his notoriety the white racketeer rode around Harlem in a bulletproof Duesenberg. The Depression and the end of Prohibition put an end to Madden's empire, and he died in obscurity in Arkansas.
REFERENCES: NYT, 24 Apr. 1965; Jim Haskins, *The Cotton Club*, 1977; Jervis Anderson, *This Was Harlem*, 1982. (BK)

MAKE ME KNOW IT (play), 1929. D. Frank Marcus, Roland Irving, and Earl B. Westfield collaborated on a comedy that ran for four performances, beginning on November 4, subtitled "A Panorama of Negro Life." It only dealt with politics and racketeering, however. Bulge Bannon, played by A. B. Comathiere,* and his henchmen try to elect a black politician to office, thereby ousting a white one who has been discriminating against Negroes. The action included a gun battle, blowing up a safe, and the title song "Make Me Know It," sung by Vivienne Baber.
REFERENCE: NYTTR, 1972. (BK)

MALINDA (musical comedy), 1929. Ida Forsyne* was featured in this show about a Miami schoolmarm who goes to Harlem to be a singer. Her suitor, a detective, saves her from the clutches of a city slicker. Sandwiched between scenes involving gun fights in cabarets and spirituals* in church socials, there were flashbacks to the old plantation, all of which made for "too much book" despite good music, according to the *New York Times* reviewer. He called it a combination of Joel Chandler Harris, Du Bose Heyward,* and Carl Van Vechten* (4 Dec. 1929, p. 37). Dennis Donoghue wrote the book, and Roland Irving and Earl B. Westfield wrote the music and lyrics.
REFERENCES: Burns Mantle, 1929–1930; NYTTR, 1972. (BK)

MALONEY, ARNOLD HAMILTON (educator), 4 July 1888–? Born in Trinidad, Arnold Maloney studied at Naparima College and then went to the United States to study medicine at the invitation of his father's brother. Maloney discovered, however, that he was expected to serve an apprenticeship for some time in exchange for his uncle's sponsorship. A period of virtual slavery followed, during which his health was permanently damaged. Eventually, he arranged to attend Lincoln University and teach elementary school in exchange for his tuition.

Afterward, Maloney attended the General Theological Seminary, and in 1915 he became a clergyman in Syracuse, New York, using much of his income to put his brother Clarence through the Dalhousie Law School. In 1919 Maloney attended the August Convention of the Universal Negro Improvement Association* and seems to have been directly connected with its subsequent administration for a time. In 1922 he became professor of psychology at Wilberforce University, serving simultaneously as one of the regular Sunday evening speakers at the UNIA Liberty Hall. Although Maloney played down his association with Marcus Garvey* in his autobiography, he served as assistant and acting chaplain general for the organization, and he regularly contributed essays and editorials to Garvey's newspaper *Negro World*,* a selection of which Maloney edited with his brother and published in 1924. The following year Maloney entered the medical school at the University of Indiana, financing his studies by writing a political column for the *Indianapolis Recorder*. In 1931 he became head of pharmacology at Howard University. Relevant works include *Some Essentials of Race Leadership* (1924, with Clarence MacDonald Maloney), *Pathways to Democracy* (1945), and *Amber Gold* (1946).

REFERENCES: Arnold Hamilton Maloney, *Amber Gold* (1946); E. David Cronon, *Black Moses*, 1955. (BK)

MANHATTAN CASINO [ROCKLAND PALACE] (dance hall). On Eighth Avenue at 155th Street, the Manhattan Casino had housed concerts by James Reese Europe* and dance exhibitions by Vernon and Irene Castle before the war. Afterward, the dance palace was often rented out to the NAACP* for its annual charity balls and whist tournaments and, still later, to other organizations for various large functions. By that time its name had been changed to the Rockland Palace, and Fletcher Henderson's* orchestra was often engaged there. Owned by a syndicate of West Indians and operated by Jewish entrepreneurs, its income was funneled back into Harlem only through salaries paid to the janitors and doormen. In its decadence, at the height of the Harlem Renaissance, it staged integrated transvestite costume balls (in competition with the Savoy Ballroom*) for which the management engaged white judges like Carl Van Vechten* and playwright Avery Hopwood.

REFERENCES: Wallace Thurman, *Negro Life in New York's Harlem*, 1928; Bruce Kellner, *Carl Van Vechten and the Irreverent Decades*, 1968. (BK)

MARAN, RENÉ (writer), 15 November 1887–9 May 1960. At the age of thirty-four, while at Fort Archambaud in the region of Lake Tchad, René Maran learned that his novel *Batouala** had won the Prix Goncourt, the most prestigious award France has to offer a young writer. Although celebrated as a member of "a race which is loyal to France," his scathing preface to *Batouala* strained official understanding. Fifteen months later (1923) he was forced to resign his administrative duties in the French Colonial Empire.

Born in Fort de France, Martinique, Maran moved with his parents to Gabon in 1890 and, because of the climate, to Bordeaux in 1894 where he was enrolled at the Lycée Talence and the Grand Lycée Michel Montaigne while his parents remained in West Africa. Upon graduation in 1909 he entered the French Colonial Service and served until he resigned. Back in France he took up residence in Paris and soon became involved in the various pan-African movements beginning to emerge in the French capital. He joined the editorial staff of Tovalou Houénou's *Les Continents*, the journal of the Ligue Universelle de la Défense de la Race Noire. Later, in 1930 he joined Dr. Léo Sajous, founder of the Comité Universel de l'Institut Nègre de Paris, and his literary journal *La Revue du Monde Noir*, in which would appear writings from important black writers in the Antilles, Haiti, Africa, France, and the United States.

Batouala was highly praised by black Americans who expressed strong feelings of racial pride and marvelled at the evidence Maran provided of Africa's artistic potential. In turn, Maran took notice of the Harlem Renaissance writers and began to appear in *Opportunity** as well as bringing the New Negro movement to the attention of the French public through his essay "Le Mouvement Negro-Litteraire aux Etats-Unis." In addition to several articles celebrating black American writers, Maran helped to have Walter White's* *Fire in the Flint** translated into French and made several unsuccessful efforts to get Alain Locke's* *New Negro** translated as well. Locke in turn attempted (equally unsuccessfully) to interest Alfred A. Knopf* in Maran's work, none of which seems to have had any direct impact on the Harlem Renaissance, except for *Batouala*.

In 1924 Maran met Locke in Paris, the beginning of a close friendship, and soon Maran's salon became a meeting place for most of the major figures of the period. At the same time, through Maran, writers such as Léon Damas (French Guiana), Léopold Senghor (Senegal), and Aimé Césaire (Martinique) either met in person or were encouraged to read the work of America's black intelligentsia.

REFERENCES: Lilyan Festeloot, *Les Ecrivains Noirs de la Langue Française*, 1965; Michel Fabre, "Autour de René Maran," *Présence Africaine*, 1973; Michel Hausser, *Les Deux Batouala de René Maran*, 1975; Femi Ojo-Ade, *René Maran, Ecrivain Negro-Africain*, 1977. (MH)

MARINOFF, FANIA (actress), 21 March 1887–7 November 1971. With her husband, white author Carl Van Vechten,* the Russian-born Fania Marinoff played frequent hostess for many of the first racially mixed parties in New York. Almost integrated revues in themselves, these gatherings at 155 West 55th Street often included Paul Robeson* singing, James Weldon Johnson* reciting, Bill Robinson* dancing, or George Gershwin* playing the piano. On other occasions the Peruvian contralto Marguerite D'Alvarez and Bessie Smith* came as guests and stayed to entertain. Black countertenor Taylor Gordon* first sang spirituals* in New York there, before his first concert. Ethel Waters* was a frequent guest as well as performer. Walter White* called the Marinoff-Van Vechten apartment "the mid-town office of the NAACP."*

REFERENCES: Bruce Kellner, *Carl Van Vechten and the Irreverent Decades*, 1968; Carl Van Vechten, *"Keep A-Inchin' Along,"* 1979. (BK)

MARKHAM, DEWEY "PIGMEAT" (comedian), 18 April 1906–? In Gansel White's Minstrel Show, in which Dewey Markham first appeared, the song "Sweet Papa Pigmeat" gave him his nickname. Born in North Carolina, he began touring as a child with the Gillis carnivals. After an engagement at the Alhambra Theatre* in New York in 1928 he moved to the Standard Theatre in Philadelphia and later into films and radio during the thirties. Markham toured in A. D. Price's *Sugar Cane* from 1925 to 1927 and then played in *Hot Rhythm*￼* in 1930 and in *Cocktails of 1932*.
REFERENCES: BAF, 1974; BB, 1980. (BK)

MARTIN, ELDER CLAYBORN (religious leader), 1851–July 1937. "The barefoot prophet," as Clayborn Martin was widely known in Harlem, strode into bars and dives, quoted scripture, took up a collection, and moved to other dens of iniquity. As a youth in Virginia, where he was born, he had a vision in which he was told, "Take off your shoes, for this is holy ground. Go teach my Gospel," so Roi Ottley and William Weatherby reported in their "informal social history" *The Negro in New York* (p. 252). Elder Martin died indigent in the Harlem Hospital, with his handwritten message pinned to his body: "Help bury the prophet."
REFERENCE: Roi Ottley and William J. Weatherby, eds., *The Negro in New York*, 1967. (BK)

MARTIN, MRS. GEORGE MADDEN (novelist), 3 May 1866–30 November 1946. In 1920 Mrs. George Madden Martin began a fourteen-year term on the board of the Committee on Inter-racial Cooperation in the city of her birth, Louisville, Kentucky, and in the 1930s she was chairwoman of the Association of Southern Women for the Prevention of Lynching. In addition to undertaking efforts to abolish racial discrimination, Martin urged women to be more politically active. She also wrote several novels and short stories. *March On* (1921) explores the character of the "new woman." Her collection of eight sketches, *Children in the Mist* (1920), drawn from observations of black life throughout the South and structured as a chronology from Emancipation to the present, is simultaneously a critique of white racism and of economic exploitation. Among her other works was the play *The Lion's Mouth* (1924).
REFERENCES: *Nation*, Dec. 1914; WWW, 1950. (MH)

MARTIN, SARA [SARA DUNN] (singer), 18 June 1884–24 May 1955. Described variously as "dramatic" and "heavy," this handsome singer was born in Kentucky and began performing in vaudeville as a single when she was in her teens. She toured for TOBA* in some revues, on one occasion with Fats Waller,* and appeared in many shows at the Lincoln Theatre* and the Lafayette Theatre.* Her Broadway appearances were undercut by the failure of her single

show, *Bottomland*,* in 1927. She made many recordings, however, giving permanent evidence of her rich talent.
REFERENCES: BWW, 1979; JWJ. (BK)

MASON, CHARLOTTE [MRS. RUFUS OSGOOD] (patroness), 18 May 1854–15 April 1946. As Agatha Cramp in Rudolph Fisher's* *Walls of Jericho*,* as Dora Ellsworth in Langston Hughes's* *Ways of White Folks*,* and as "Godmother" in Zora Neale Hurston's* memoir *Dust Tracks on a Road*, Charlotte Louise Vandervere Quick Mason has been immortalized but with marked ambivalence. Married in 1886 to Rufus Osgood Mason and widowed at the age of fifty-one in 1905 when her physician husband was seventy-three, she first used her vast wealth in some preliminary anthropological studies of American Indians, even making some field trips. She was interested as well in psychology and psychic phenomena, through the influence of her late husband, and in 1907 she wrote "The Passing of a Prophet," published in *North American Review*. By the twenties her interests had shifted to the primitive and, therefore, innocent elements in Afro-American arts and letters. From her regal penthouse on Park Avenue the old dowager ruled over a stable of protégés that included both Hughes and Hurston as well as Aaron Douglas,* Richmond Barthé,* Hall Johnson,* Claude McKay,* Louise Thompson,* and especially Alain Locke.* None of them was permitted to divulge her identity as the source of their good fortune, even though one or another of them would serve as escort on several occasions. She paid Langston Hughes's living expenses while he was writing his first novel, *Not without Laughter*,* and she underwrote the single performance on Broadway of Zora Hurston's music drama *The Great Day*.* Mason invested more than $75,000 in young black artists, but she broke off the alliances when her charges proved disloyal by abandoning what she considered the purity in their work: its primitivism. Because she believed in the cult of primitivism and disliked social protest, the breaks were frequent. An eccentric with a strong bias about what Negro art was supposed to be, Charlotte Mason remains a shadowy figure, denied by accident or intention an obituary in the *New York Times* and, in the work of her own protégés, given cautious attention.
REFERENCES: Langston Hughes, *The Big Sea*, 1940; Zora Neale Hurston, *Dust Tracks on a Road*, 1942; Robert Hemenway, *Zora Neale Hurston*, 1977; David Levering Lewis, *When Harlem Was in Vogue*, 1981; Jervis Anderson, *This Was Harlem*, 1982; Louise Thompson Patterson. (DI, BK)

MATHEUS, JOHN FREDERICK (writer), 10 September 1887–? John Frederick Matheus, an award-winning writer and a professor of modern languages, was born in Keyser, West Virginia, in 1887. After graduating from high school in Steubenville, Ohio, in 1905 he completed his collegiate studies at Western Reserve University in 1910, graduating *cum laude*. He taught languages at Florida A. & M. College in Tallahassee (1910–1922) and earned the A.M. degree at Columbia in 1921. In 1922 he began a long career as professor and head of the

Department of Romance Languages at West Virginia State College. In addition, he authored more than fifty short stories, plays, and articles, the most famous of which was his short story "Fog," which appeared in *Opportunity** in May 1925 and later in Alain Locke's* *New Negro** and was placed on the honor list in Edward J. O'Brien's *Best Short Stories of 1925*. "Fog" won Matheus an *Opportunity* award in 1925, and he was a winner in 1926 in the Personal Experience Sketch category. He is also known for his one-act play, " 'Cruiter" (1927), and *Ouanga*,* an opera for which he wrote the libretto (1929; premiere performance, 1949). In 1930 he acted as secretary to Charles S. Johnson,* the American member of the League of Nation's International Commission of Inquiry to investigate charges of slavery and forced labor in Liberia. In the 1930s Matheus published several scholarly articles in journals such as *Modern Language Journal*, *Journal of Negro History*, and *Quarterly Review of Higher Education Among Negroes*.

REFERENCES: WWCA, 1933, 1950. (DS)

MATTHEWS, RALPH (journalist), c. 1904–30 August 1978. For more than forty years Ralph Matthews was one of the leading black journalists in the United States. Born in Harford County, Maryland, around 1904, Matthews began his newspaper career as a reporter with the *Afro-American** in Baltimore in 1924. After eleven years there he was named editor of the *Afro-American* paper in Washington, D.C., and later edited papers in Philadelphia, Newark, Cleveland, and again in Washington. Most of them were with the *Afro-American* chain papers. Matthews covered some of the leading stories of his time, including important civil rights issues, the coronation of King George VI of Britain in 1936, and the Korean War. In 1977, one year before his death, the National Newspaper Publishers Association cited him for his writing and his ability to establish newspapers dedicated to Afro-American civil rights.

REFERENCE: CA, 1967. (DS)

MEEK MOSE (play), 1928. When Frank Wilson's* *Meek Mose** opened at the Princess Theatre on February 6, the building seemed destined to become a black repertory house, at least briefly. Mayor Jimmy Walker and the European theatrical producer Max Reinhardt both made speeches at the opening, the former a patronizing one about black achievements and overcoming racial handicaps, the latter about the fertile material available to black playwrights. In Wilson's play a pacifist leader urges his black neighbors to accept their lot when the white community moves them from "Blacktown" to "Badtown." A period of disease and death follows, during which Meek Mose is chastized, but he discovers oil in the new ghetto and everybody lives happily ever after. This "childishly naive endeavor" ran for twenty-four performances. The *New York Times* reviewer might have added that the plot was no more than a variation on a device popular in blackface comedies of the crudest kind just a few years earlier. Instead, he observed that perhaps "the negro, in writing about himself, sees himself, not

as he is, but in the vivid reds, blues, and greens of the comic strip. He becomes, in brief, a caricature, and such a caricature as even few whites make him out to be" (7 Feb. 1928, p. 30). If the Princess Theatre chose to devote itself to entertainment rather than to realistic drama, the reviewer concluded, it belonged in Harlem rather than on Broadway.
REFERENCES: Burns Mantle, 1927–1928; NYTTR, 1972. (BK)

MENCKEN, H[ENRY] L[OUIS] (critic, editor), 2 September 1880–29 January 1956. Critic, curmudgeon, sometime bon vivant, H. L. Mencken represents for many the spirited iconoclasm of the 1920s. In the pages of the *American Mercury*, the magazine he edited with theater critic George Jean Nathan, Mencken launched his scathing critique of Americans and American culture, pillorying almost everyone and everything within his intellectual reach, which was considerable. But, as he protested, the *American Mercury* was more than lampoon and presentation of the absurd. For Mencken also opened its pages to those whose views were seldom acknowledged: urban immigrants, autobiographical experiences of ghetto children, and the critical viewpoints of and by black Americans. In addition, Mencken was vitriolic in his contempt for groups such as the Ku Klux Klan. His most direct contact with the Harlem Renaissance came through the person of Carl Van Vechten,* who placed Mencken (as Russet Durwood) in his novel *Nigger Heaven*,* but he was friendly, too, with Walter White,* James Weldon Johnson,* and other Afro-Americans. In 1926 *The Crisis** asked various writers and publishers to respond to several questions, all grouped under the heading "The Negro in Art: How Shall He Be Portrayed?"* The questions were Van Vechten's, and Mencken appeared in the first installment, in March. He replied, "The artist . . . should be free to depict things exactly as he sees them." The brevity of his remarks matched his general feeling that the Harlem Renaissance was "pathetically pale, like a candle in the sunlight" (p. 129).
REFERENCES: *The Crisis*, March 1926; Bruce Kellner, *Carl Van Vechten and the Irreverent Decades*, 1968; Carl Bode, *Mencken*, 1969; W.H.A. Williams, *H. L. Mencken*, 1977. (MH, BK)

THE MESSENGER (periodical), 1917–1928. *The Messenger*, considered by many the best radical magazine published by and for blacks in the era of the Harlem Renaissance, was founded and coedited by Socialists A. Philip Randolph* and Chandler Owen* in the fall of 1917. Originally it was called the *Hotel Messenger* and was the semiofficial organ of the headwaiters union in New York; however, Randolph and Owen soon parted company with the union and published their own magazine—*The Messenger*—described by the editors in an early edition as "The Only Radical Negro Magazine in America." Indeed, before 1923 the magazine took consistently radical stands: opposition to black participation in World War I; sharp criticism of so-called race leaders such as Marcus Garvey,* W.E.B. Du Bois,* Emmett Scott,* Kelly Miller,* and R. R. Moton* for their acceptance of white racist practices and/or their procapitalist attitudes; and bitter attacks on capitalism and the two major political parties.

Above all, though, Randolph, Owen, and the rest of the periodical's staff— W. A. Domingo,* George Frazier Miller,* and William N. Colson—tried to find a way out for American blacks who, as a group, were mired in poverty and oppressed by racism. After 1923 socialism lost its hold on even the small minority of blacks it had attracted after World War I, and *The Messenger*'s circulation dwindled from 26,000 in 1919 to 5,000 at best. Randolph and Owen began to doubt whether a Socialist revolution (which they assumed would be the salvation of the race) could occur in the foreseeable future, and *The Messenger* began to tout black capitalism as a possible avenue for black economic improvement. In fact, from 1923 to 1925 *The Messenger* printed an increasing number of favorable (and uncharacteristically uncritical) appraisals of black business leaders.

With Owen's departure from the magazine in 1923 and Randolph's deep involvement after 1925 in organizing the Brotherhood of Sleeping Car Porters,* George Schuyler* kept the magazine going, for the most part, between 1925 and its demise in 1928. Schuyler's "Shafts and Darts" was a popular column in the magazine, as was the excellent theatrical criticism penned by Theophilus Lewis* from September 1923 to July 1927. Abram Harris, Joel A. Rogers,* James Ivy, and Wallace Thurman* all wrote for *The Messenger*, and Thurman brought in young writers and poets such as Langston Hughes,* who published his first short stories and sixteen early poems in *The Messenger*.

By 1928 the magazine, which had lost much of its readership and was growing more heavily in debt with every issue, survived mainly as an organizing tool for the Brotherhood of Sleeping Car Porters, which itself was at its lowest ebb. Finally, after desperate attempts to keep the periodical going, Randolph and Schuyler reluctantly ended publication after the June 1928 issue.

REFERENCE: Theodore Kornweibel, Jr., *No Crystal Stair*, 1974. (DS)

MESSIN' AROUND (musical revue), 1929. Perry Bradford* wrote the lyrics and Jimmy Johnson wrote the music for *Messin' Around*. It opened April 22 and featured a female boxing match. Aurelia Wheedlin and Emma Maitland, both licensed boxers, sparred nightly at the Hudson Theatre during a brief run, the winner varying from performance to performance. Cora LaRedd and some "fairly good hoofing" got less play in the *New York Times* review than the show's "outstanding claim to distinction: more gold teeth than any other group of similar size in New York, perhaps on the whole Atlantic seaboard" (23 Apr. 1929, p. 26). As usual, the review was condescending but, by 1929, deservedly so, since so many of the familiar clichés continued to be perpetuated, not the least of which was a black comic wearing blackface.

REFERENCE: NYTTR, 1972. (BK)

MEXICO'S (cabaret). In Mexico's, a Harlem cabaret named for the owner who had been a Mexican mercenary, there were regular "cutting contests" for

musicians during the early morning hours after the regular house jam sessions. The audience voted on the winners by applause, as new musicians challenged older ones. Mexico's was located at 133rd Street and Seventh Avenue.
REFERENCE: Jervis Anderson, *This Was Harlem*, 1982. (BK)

MICHEAUX, OSCAR (filmmaker), 2 January 1884–1 April 1951. Oscar Micheaux's remarkable career in pioneering the black film industry had several beginnings. This son of former slaves began work as a Pullman car porter in his native Illinois, but when he saw an advertisement for cheap land on the Rosebud Indian Reservation, he took up farming and ranching and within five years had expanded his South Dakota homestead to 500 acres. He lost his land to dishonest in-laws while he was still in his twenties, so he turned to writing black pulp fiction, using his own experiences for subject matter. Micheaux was a talented publicist and seems to have had no trouble selling stock to midwestern farmers in the Western Book and Supply Company, which published his *Conquest* in 1913, *The Forged Note* in 1915, and *The Homesteader* in 1917.

When the Lincoln Motion Picture Company* wanted to make a film version of *The Homesteader*, Micheaux refused because he could not get the company to let him direct it himself; instead, he founded the Micheaux Film Corporation in 1918, selling shares for $75 each, and made his own movie. *The Homesteader*, which appeared in 1919, was not untypical of the lurid melodramas that followed: A black boy loves a white girl named Agnes but marries the daughter of a villainous black minister who plots with his other daughter to drive the new bride mad and steal the groom's homestead. The bride stabs her father, kills herself, and Agnes turns out to be black, leading to a quick second marriage and a happy ending. Micheaux made it for $15,000, with virtually no retakes.

Over two dozen feature films followed *The Homesteader*, all designed for black audiences, even in the South, where the ingratiating Micheaux convinced white movie house owners to run special matinees for segregated showings. Film clips from these films reveal amateurish acting, crude lighting, makeshift sets (Micheaux frequently filmed in the homes of friends and business associates), and lurid action that invariably includes scenes in Harlem cabarets with chorus lines of pretty girls. Micheaux used actors from the Lafayette Players Stock Company* in the beginning—Evelyn Preer,* for example, played Agnes in *The Homesteader*—but shortly, he had developed his own stable of performers, usually light skinned and usually in emulation of Hollywood stars: Lorenzo Tucker,* the romantic lead in many Micheaux films, was billed as "the Black Valentino," and a Micheaux vamp named Bee Freeman was called "the Sepia Mae West." A few of the films are notable for ancillary reasons: *Within Our Gates* (1920) is about lynching; in *Birthright* (1924) a black Harvard student returns to his southern hometown to start a black college, only to be opposed by both black and white members of the community; Paul Robeson* played in *Body and Soul* (1924); and *The House Behind the Cedars* (1923) was based on

Charles W. Chesnutt's* novel, probably the first film translation of a novel by a black writer.

None of Micheaux's films had any critical reputation, but their popularity was considerable, largely because of their maker's ability to sell himself. He must have been an imposing figure, travelling around the country from movie house to movie house in flashy automobiles, wearing big hats and full-length fur coats. He always operated on a shoestring, and bankruptcy caught up with his extravagant risks in 1928. He reorganized the following year, largely with backing from white investors, but during the thirties the criticism of his work grew stronger because of his insistence on light-skinned performers and depictions of invidious stereotypical behavior. He wrote some additional novels, and he made a final film, which opened in a white movie house in New York in 1948.

Micheaux's novels include *Conquest* (1913), *The Forged Note* (1915), *The Homesteader* (1917), *The Wind From Nowhere* (1941), *Masquerade* (1947), and *The Case of Mrs. Wingate* (1944). Among his films are *The Homesteader* (1919); *Within Our Gates*, *The Brute*, and *Symbol of the Unconquered* (1920); *Gunsaulus Mystery* and *Deceit* (1921); *The Dungeon*, *The Virgin of the Seminole*, and *Son of Satan* (1922); *Jasper Landry's Will* and *The House Behind the Cedars* (1923); *Birthright* (1924); *Body and Soul* (1925); *The Spider's Web* and *Devil's Disciple* (1926); *Millionaire* (1927); *When Men Betray* and *East Street* (1928); *Wages of Sin* (1929); *Thirty Years Later*, *The Broken Violin*, *The Fool's Errand*, and *Daughter of the Congo* (1930); *Dark Princess*, *The Exile*, and *Darktown Revue* (1931); *Veiled Aristocrats*, *Black Magic*, and *Ten Minutes to Live* (1932); *The Girl From Chicago* and *Ten Minutes to Kill* (1933); *Harlem After Midnight* (1934); *Lem Hawkin's Confession* (1935); *Temptation* and *Underworld* (1936); *God's Stepchildren* (1937); and *Betrayal* (1948).

REFERENCES: WWCA, 1933; Donald Bogle, *Toms, Coons, Mulattoes, Mammies, and Bucks*, 1973; Daniel J. Leab, *From Sambo to Superspade*, 1975; BBW, 1977. (BK)

MILES, JOSEPHINE (entertainer) 1900–1965. After touring with *Shuffle Along** in 1922 Josephine Miles played in *Runnin' Wild** in 1923, but she was best known for her radio work in the Midwest. During the late twenties she had some wide appeal as Evangelist Mary Flowers.

REFERENCE: BWW, 1979. (BK)

MILES, LIZZIE (singer), 31 March 1895–17 March 1963. Lizzie Miles did not often perform in New York, but her distinctive style strongly influenced other singers, and her association with the Harlem Renaissance is sufficient. Born in New Orleans, she toured in vaudeville, with circuses (often riding on an elephant), and with minstrel shows. She sang with King Oliver,* first in New Orleans, then in Chicago, and eventually in Los Angeles. In 1921 she appeared at the Club DeLuxe in Harlem, shortly before it was transformed into the Cotton Club,* a year or so later at the New Star Casino, and in 1924 at the Nest.* Then she began a series of European tours. Most of Lizzie Miles's work, however, was in New Orleans, where she was still singing until shortly before her death. REFERENCES: BBW, 1977; CVV; JWJ. (BK)

MILLER, FLOURNOY (playwright, comedian, producer), 1889–1971. Flournoy Miller and his brothers Irvin Miller* and Quintard Miller,* who also spent their lives in the theater, were born in Columbia, Tennessee, sons of the editor of the black weekly newspaper the *Nashville Globe*. Flournoy and his future partner Aubrey Lyles,* were childhood friends; they attended Fisk University together and produced and performed in amateur shows before joining the Pekin Stock Company in Chicago, where they wrote shows and played small parts. In 1909 Miller and Lyles and Flournoy's brother Irvin starred in *The Colored Aristocrats*, in which they introduced the comic characters Steve Jenkins (Miller) and Sam Peck (Lyles) about whom many of their vaudeville skits and show plots were to revolve. Miller left Chicago in 1908 to form the Bijou Stock Company with Marion A. Brooks, but it folded after one season in Montgomery, Alabama, and Miller went back to touring with Lyles in vaudeville. They had a long run in Yonkers in 1910, followed by a great success at Hammerstein's Victoria Theatre in New York, and in 1915 they starred in *Darkydom* at the Howard Theatre in Washington, D.C., and the Lafayette Theatre* in New York. They had become a star comedy act on the Keith Circuit, and in 1921 they joined forces with Noble Sissle* and Eubie Blake* to create and perform in the extraordinary hit *Shuffle Along*.* The plot of *Shuffle Along* and some of the characters were based on two earlier Miller and Lyles vaudeville sketches, *Mayor of Dixie* (1905) and *Who's Stealin'?*.* (1918), and they introduced into the show their famous comic fight routine. In 1922 two of Miller's straight plays, *The Flat Below* (written with Lyles) and *Going White*, were produced at the Lafayette Theatre. The successful Broadway musical *Runnin' Wild*.* (1924), which introduced the Charleston, was followed by two flops, *Backbiters* and *Honey* (both 1925), but they succeeded again in 1927 with *Rang Tang*.* *Keep Shufflin'*.* (1928), an attempt to duplicate the success of *Shuffle Along*, was not a success, and the team broke up temporarily, Miller wrote and appeared in *Blackbirds[*] of 1930* and a 1930 version of *Shuffle Along* and in the same year rejoined Lyles to make two talking shorts for RKO pictures and resume touring on the Columbia circuit. Their last show together was *Sugar Hill*.* (1931), with music by James P. Johnson.* After Lyles's death Miller teamed with Mantan Moreland;* they toured in vaudeville, appeared in the first all-black western sound movie, *Harlem on the Prairie* (1936), and were featured in other black-cast films. *Sugar Hill* was revived in Los Angeles in 1951. REFERENCES: Maud Cuney-Hare, *Negro Musicians and Their Music*, 1936; Langston Hughes and Milton Meltzer, *Black Magic*, 1967; BB, 1980. (DA)

MILLER, GEORGE FRAZIER (religious leader), 28 November 1864–1948. Born in South Carolina, George Miller completed his bachelor's degree in 1888 and his master's degree in 1893 at Howard University and then went on for a doctor of divinity degree at the New York Theological Seminary in 1912. From the turn of the century until his death he was minister at the St. Augustine Protestant Episcopal Church in Brooklyn. A frequent agitator for open unions, he was long active in the NAACP,* having been one of its founding members. In 1918 his speech from his pulpit against "legal lynchings" stirred sufficient controversy to merit printing in the *Brooklyn Daily Eagle*, 15 May 1918.

REFERENCES: WWCA, 1933; Roi Ottley and William J. Weatherby, eds., *The Negro in New York*, 1967. (BK)

MILLER, IRVIN C. (playwright, comedian, producer), 1884–1967. Irvin Miller, Flournoy Miller's* older brother, was born in Columbia, Tennessee, and after attending Fisk University he worked with Flournoy in the Pekin Stock Company in Chicago. He wrote for and toured with the John Rucker Company of New Orleans and appeared with Flournoy Miller and Aubrey Lyles* in *Who's Stealin'?** (1918). His *Alabama Bound* (1920) at the Lafayette Theatre* starred Ida Brown;* *Bon Bon Buddy, Jr.* (1922), so named in deference to the famous Bert Williams* and George Walker show of twenty years earlier, had music by Maceo Pinkard* and starred Gertrude Saunders.* *Put and Take** (1922) was a failure at Town Hall, but *Dinah** (1923), with music and lyrics by Tim Brymm* and with Mae Barnes,* Ethel Ridley, and Gertrude Saunders in the cast, was a success; it introduced the black bottom to New York two years before George White* featured it in his *Scandals[*] of 1925*. *Liza** (1924) was the first show to be backed entirely by black capital. *Broadway Rastus* (1925) was a revival of a 1915 endeavor, with music by Pinkard and Miller and his second wife, Blanche Thompson, in the cast. Miller produced a series of revues that he toured through the South, among them *Blue Baby*, *Tokio*, and *Brownskin Models* of whatever year it happened to be.

REFERENCES: *Official Theatrical World of Colored Artists*, 1928; BB, 1980. (DA)

MILLER, KELLY (educator), 23 July 1863–29 December 1939. Kelly Miller, a leading black educator, sociologist, and conciliator among black political factions, was born in Winnsboro, South Carolina, in 1863. He graduated from Howard University in 1886, working his way through school with a job at the United States Pension Office, and attended graduate school in mathematics and physics at Johns Hopkins (1887–1889). He was named professor of mathematics at Howard in 1890, and he remained at the school until his retirement in 1934, serving as dean of the College of Arts and Sciences (1907–1918) and a professor of sociology (1918–1934). Although he was a very successful dean and professor, he is best remembered for his writing and leadership in race relations. Miller was a frequent contributor to magazines and journals, wrote numerous books and pamphlets, and contributed a weekly letter to more than one hundred newspapers. He consistently attempted to bridge the gap between warring ideologies

expressed by blacks; indeed, in the 1920s he could be considered a friend by both NAACP* supporters and the Booker T. Washington circle. His antilabor, anti–women's suffrage, and other conservative views angered radicals such as A. Philip Randolph,* and his intellectual life-style and approach kept him (as it did W.E.B. Du Bois*) a distant figure in the eyes of the black masses; thus he never attained his goal of becoming a race leader such as Washington had been. Relevant works include *From Servitude to Service* (1905), *Race Adjustment* (1908), *Out of the House of Bondage* (1914), and *An Appeal to Conscience* (1918).
REFERENCES: DAB, 1928; WWCA, 1933; NYT, 30 Dec. 1939; Theodore Kornweibel, Jr., *No Crystal Stair*, 1974. (DS)

MILLER, QUINTARD (playwright, comedian, producer), ? – ? Quintard Miller was the third of the talented brothers from Columbia, Tennessee, and like Flournoy Miller* and Irvin Miller* he got his start with the Pekin Stock Company in Chicago. As writer, performer, or producer he was engaged in shows such as *Broadway Gossips* (1920); *Darktown Scandals* and *Some Baby* (1921); *The Devil, Bon Bon Buddy, Jr.*, *This Way Out*, and *Liza** (1922); *Tunes and Topics* (with Bessie Smith*) and *The Mayor of Jimtown* (1923); *Annie Oakley, Take It Easy*, and *The Flat Above* (1924); *Broadway Brevities, Charleston Fricassee, Dixie Brevities*, and *Harlem Butterflies* (1926); *Shuffle Along of 1926* (a Kansas City version), *Miss Dinah of 1926*, and *Bare Facts* (1927); and *Dixie Brevities* (1927 and 1928) and *Get Lucky* (1934). Quintard Miller and Marcus Slayter, a native of Ohio who had been a dance director for a troupe in Philadelphia, met in 1919 and formed a producing team. They took touring shows through the South, including many of the shows listed above, and in their company at various times were performers such as Adelaide Hall,* Eddie Green,* Jimmie Basquette, Greenley and Drayton, Florence and Willie Covan, and Monette Moore. Miller and Slayter retired in the late forties, and Miller ran a catering business in Los Angeles.
REFERENCES: *The Official Theatrical World of Colored Artists*, 1928; *Negro Digest*, July 1951; BB, 1980. (DA)

MILLER SULLIVAN, MAY (playwright), ?– . Born in Washington, D.C., May Miller graduated from Howard University and taught speech and drama at the Frederic Douglass High School in Baltimore. Her 1929 play *Riding the Goat* examines the conflicts between the educated black and the primitive black and was published, along with four of her other plays, in *Negro History in Thirteen Plays*, which she edited with Willis Richardson* in 1935. *Graven Images* (1929) is a play designed for eighth grade students, based on the Old Testament story of Moses's marriage to a black woman. Her other works include a short story in *Opportunity** (1945), *Into the Clearing* (1959), *Poems* (1962), and *Clearing and Beyond* (1983).
REFERENCES: BAWPP, 1975; Hatch-Billops. (PO, BK)

MILLS, FLORENCE (singer, dancer), 25 January 1895–1 November 1927. Florence Mills was winning dance contests at the age of five and made her first stage appearance at the age of eight in *Sons of Ham* in Washington, D.C., billed as Baby Florence Mills and singing "Miss Hannah From Savannah," a song that she had learned from Aida Overton Walker, wife of George Walker. She toured with the Bonita Company as one of the "picks"—the singing and dancing "pickaninnies"—and then in the Mills Sisters trio with her sisters Olivia and Maude. When Olivia dropped out the trio became a duo, and when Maude left Florence teamed with Kinky Clark to be billed as Mills and Clark. Later, she teamed with "Bricktop" (Ada Smith*) and Cora Green* as the Panama Trio* and toured with the Tennessee Ten in a trio with her husband, the comedian and dancer U. S. Thompson* and another man, Fredi Johnson.

Her big break came when she replaced Gertrude Saunders* in *Shuffle Along** in 1921; Harlem and all New York took her to its heart. She left the show the next year to star in Lew Leslie's* *Plantation Revue,** which was enlarged into *From Dover to Dixie* when it went to London and retitled *Dixie to Broadway** when it returned to New York in 1924. It was the first musical show built around a singing and dancing female star rather than a comedy team. She starred again in *Blackbirds[*] of 1926*, which played at the Alhambra Theatre* in New York and then ran five months in Paris and six months in London. (When Mills left the show in London, she was replaced by the young black American-English singer Mabel Mercer.) Mills returned to New York an international star but died suddenly of appendicitis in the autumn of 1927. She was still a young woman and at the peak of her fame, but she had spent all of her life in the grueling routine of show business; onstage, she was a dainty, captivating, pixieish figure, but audiences seemed to sense a quality of wistfulness beneath her theatrical sparkle, especially when she sang her theme song, "I'm a Little Blackbird Looking for a Bluebird." Harlem gave Florence Mills one of its most spectacular funerals, causing a flock of blackbirds to be released from a plane as it passed over the cortege.

REFERENCES: Maud Cuney-Hare, *Negro Musicians and Their Music*, 1936; Langston Hughes and Milton Meltzer, *Black Magic*, 1967; BB, 1980. (DA)

MITCHELL, ABBIE (singer, actress), 1884–16 March 1960. Abbie Mitchell was born in New York City but educated in Baltimore. She studied voice in New York with H. T. Burleigh* and Emilia Serrano, and at the age of fourteen she auditioned for Will Marion Cook's* *Clorindy: the Origin of the Cakewalk*. Although she was at first considered too young, she eventually took over the leading role and married the composer. She played the leads in many of the Williams and Walker shows and other musicals composed or conducted by her husband and was one of the principal singers in Joe Jordon's Nashville Students (none of whom were from Nashville and none of whom were students), a playing-singing-dancing troupe that appeared at Hammerstein's Victoria Theatre in New York in 1905 and later toured Europe as the Tennessee Students, winning great acclaim. Mitchell studied voice in Paris with Jean de Reszke and concertized in Europe and the United States. She developed her talents as a dramatic actress at the Lafayette Theatre* and in 1924 collaborated with Flournoy Miller,* Aubrey Lyles,* and her husband Will Marion Cook to create *Negro Nuances*, a musical history of blacks from Africa to the Reconstruction period. In 1926 she appeared as the Mother in Paul Green's* Pulitzer Prize play *In Abraham's Bosom*.* After another period of vocal study in Paris in 1931 she resumed her concert and operatic career to excellent notices, appearing as Santuzza in the Aeolian Opera Association's production of *Cavalleria Rusticana* and as Clara in the original cast of *Porgy and Bess** in 1935. She played Addie in *The Little Foxes* in 1939, and in later years she taught at Tuskegee Institute.

REFERENCES: Maud Cuney-Hare, *Negro Musicians and Their Music*, 1936; Edith J. R. Isaacs, *The Negro in the American Theatre*, 1947; MBA, 1971; BCM, 1977; BB, 1980. (DA)

MOHAMMED ALI, DUSE (journalist), 1867–? Duse Mohammed Ali was the leading Pan-African thinker before World War I and personally influenced the ideas of Marcus Garvey.* Duse Mohammed Ali, half-Sudanese and half-Egyptian, was educated in London just before the war and made his early living as a touring actor. In 1911 he published *In the Land of the Pharoahs*, probably the first history of Egypt written by an Egyptian. In 1912 he began publication of the monthly magazine *Africa Times and Orient Review*, to give expression to his and other writers' strong feelings in favor of independence and home rule for black, brown, and yellow people under colonial rule. The magazine folded in 1914, reappeared in 1917, and became the *Africa and Orient Review* in 1920. In 1912, when young Marcus Garvey was in London, Duse Mohammed Ali took him on as a messenger. Garvey's later political ideas were heavily influenced by Duse Mohammed Ali, although the latter dismissed Garvey from his job after three months for indolence and a belief that he was essentially shallow. In 1917, when Garvey was first attempting to organize his followers in Harlem, an opponent used Duse Mohammed Ali's character assassination of Garvey to hurt his chances of developing strong support. Still, Garvey hired Duse Mohammed Ali in 1922 as a foreign affairs specialist for his own newspaper *Negro World*.* Eventually, Duse Mohammed Ali immigrated to Nigeria where he edited the *Nigerian Comet*.

REFERENCES: E. David Cronon, *Black Moses*, 1955; John Hendrik Clarke, ed., *Marcus Garvey and the Vision of Africa*, 1974. (DS)

MONAGAS, LIONEL (actor), 1903–1945. Born in Venezuela, Lionel Monagas began acting with the Lafayette Players Stock Company* toward the end of its seven-year tenure in Harlem. Like many other members of that troupe, he went on to Broadway, notably Garland Anderson's* 1925 *Appearances*,* where he played the black bellboy hero falsely accused of rape. Two years earlier Monagas had appeared in Willis Richardson's* *Chip Woman's Fortune*,* the first play by a black writer to be produced in a Broadway theater. Most of his subsequent performances were in the strident black musicals of the period: *Runnin' Wild** (1923), *My Magnolia** (1926), *Ol' Man Satan** (1932), *Louisiana,** and *Hummin' Sam** (1933) among others. In 1936 Monagas acted in his first straight play since *Appearances*, a dramatization of Rudolph Fisher's* *The Conjure Man Dies.** He also acted with the Federal Theatre Project and subsequently appeared in some Hollywood films.

REFERENCES: *The Messenger*, Mar., Nov. 1917; NYTTR, 1972; Allen Woll, *Dictionary of the Black Theatre*, 1983. (BK)

MOORE, FRED RANDOLPH (journalist), 16 June 1857–3 March 1943. Fred Moore was born in Washington, D.C., and served there as a messenger to five secretaries of the U.S. Treasury. In 1907 he purchased the New York *Age*,* a newspaper for which he had written for twenty years. During the twenties Moore organized his own antiliquor campaign, and when insufficient response came in to his editorials, he printed rumors without mentioning names in an attempt to reinforce Prohibition. As a founding member of the National Urban League* Moore was eager to improve the social environment of Afro-Americans, a difficult endeavor in view of the increasing white bootleg business that went on in Harlem. Moore may be faulted for recruiting his newspaper staff from his own family but not for organizing the Citizens' League for Fair Play. In 1933, in the face of growing unemployment, Moore and John H. Johnson, an Episcopal clergyman, founded the league to encourage white merchants in the area to hire blacks, since their trade was largely among black citizens. Pickets and boycotts accounted for some modest improvement. Moore continued to write for the New York *Age* well into his eighties, always in deference to middle-class virtues in what he considered Harlem's best society, never fully comprehending the "New Negro" of the twenties.

REFERENCES: WWCR, 1915; Roi Ottley and William J. Weatherby, eds., *The Negro in New York*, 1967; Jervis Anderson, *This Was Harlem*, 1982. (BK)

MOORE, MONETTE (pianist), 19 May 1902–21 October 1962. While still in his teens Monette Moore was playing the piano in Kansas City nightclubs. He first appeared in New York at Clara Smith's* Theatrical Club in 1924. In 1925 he supplied the piano music for *Lucky Sambo.** For a time he was the featured pianist at Small's Paradise, and then from 1927 until 1932 he played regularly at Connie's Inn.* He also played for *Messin' Around** (1929) and *Brown Buddies** (1930).

REFERENCE: BWW, 1979. (BK)

MOORE, TIM (comedian), c. 1880–1952. Best known in his later career as the Kingfish in the television version of *Amos and Andy*, Tim Moore ran off to join a medicine show when he was about twelve years old. He and Romeo Washburn were the original Gold Dust Twins, touring widely before the turn of the century, with Cora Miskel and Her Pickaninnies. Later, he became a jockey for a time and then a featherweight boxer. In 1908 Moore toured in a one-man show version of *Uncle Tom's Cabin*, half his face made up to look white and the other half made up to look black. For several years he toured with his wife in *Tim Moore's Chicago Follies* and in subsequent revues called *Rarin' to Go* and *Southland Revue*. He made his Broadway debut in *Blackbirds[*] of 1928* and later appeared in *Harlem Scandals* and in *Blackberries of 1932*.* Television brought him a new career that ended only because of his death when he was about seventy-two; the Black Power movement that finally did away with the racial stereotypes perpetuated on shows like *Amos and Andy* was another decade ahead.

REFERENCE: BB, 1980. (BK)

MORAND, PAUL (writer), 13 March 1888–23 July 1976. Two of French writer Paul Morand's books had a considerable vogue during the Harlem Renaissance, *New York*, a travel book, and *Magie noire* ("Black Magic"), both published in 1929. The Harlem section of the former was both informative and evocative; the latter reflected Morand's general interest in exotic peoples and places. *Magie noire*, illustrated with drawings by Aaron Douglas,* consists of eight stories of black life set in the United States, Africa, and the West Indies; their common theme is atavism and the primitive savagery just beneath the surface of cultural and social life. Consequently, Morand has often been criticized as a decadent attempting to titillate his readers, particularly by black revisionists skeptical of white patronage during the twenties.

REFERENCE: *Encyclopedia of World Literature in the Twentieth Century*, 1969 (MH, BK)

MORELAND, MANTAN (comedian), 1902–28 September 1973. Mantan Moreland was a familiar moon-face in more than 300 movies, including 15 Charlie Chan features, as a terrified chauffeur, bug-eyed in fright, and crying a line of his own invention, "Feets, do yo' stuff!" He ran away at the age of twelve from his home in Monroe, Louisiana, to become a dancer in travelling shows and circuses, and for a time he toured with Tim Moore's* *Chicago Follies*. During the twenties Moreland was a staple in black musical entertainments at the Apollo Theatre,* and he appeared in *Connie's Inn Frolics* (1927) and *Blackbirds[*] of 1928*, *1930*, and *1932*, teaming up with Tim Moore again in *Harlem Scandals* (1932). One all-black film, *One Dark Night* (1939), allowed him to break away from the stereotype he followed in the thirties and honed to perfection in the forties. Finally, in 1957 he was able to demonstrate what a gifted performer he really was, with a sense of timing that far greater actors might envy, as the hilarious and touching Estragon in an all-black version of Samuel Beckett's

Waiting for Godot. During the brief Broadway run more than one reviewer reminded readers what the white theater had missed out on for so long.
REFERENCES: Donald Bogle, *Toms, Coons, Mulattoes, Mammies, and Bucks*, 1973; Daniel J. Leab, *From Sambo to Superspade*, 1975. (BK)

MORRISON, FREDERICK ERNEST (actor), c. 1912–? Frederick Morrison was still a baby when his father—a cook for a movie producer—got him into films. As "Sunshine Sammy" or "Pickanniny Sam" the youngster appeared in a number of Hal Roach shorts starring Snub Pollard and Harold Lloyd, popular white comedians of the period. Later, in the *Our Gang* comedies Morrison was the highest paid black performer in the movies at $250 a week. His parents took him into vaudeville for a period during the twenties; afterward, his popularity in films diminished.
REFERENCE: Daniel J. Leab, *From Sambo to Superspade*, 1975. (BK)

MORRISSEY, WILL (producer), 19 June 1887–17 December 1957. According to a *New York Times* reviewer in 1930, Will Morrissey was "addicted to the production of shows which are invariably inferior to the jests he personally contributes to them" (22 Aug. 1930, p. 18). Born in New York, Morrissey wrote special material for many vaudeville performers and several popular songs, notably "Loving You the Way I Do." He was cofounder of the Overseas Theatre League.
REFERENCES: ASCAP, 1966; NYTTR, 1972. (BK)

MORTON, JELLY ROLL [FERDINAND JOSEPH LaMENTHE] (musician), 20 September 1885–10 July 1941. In New Orleans, where he was born, this celebrated pianist changed his name from LaMenthe to Morton and early acquired his lifelong nickname "Jelly Roll." As a child he studied piano and guitar, and he was familiar with Spanish, French, and African music from his earliest years. At sixteen he played the piano in various cafés there, but from 1917 until 1922 he worked in California, already recognizable by his unique piano style and by the diamond filling he sported in a front tooth. In 1923 he moved to New York to play at Roseland, afterward touring with the Red Hot Peppers or the Chicago Syncopators. Morton's earliest recordings were made in Chicago with the New Orleans Rhythm Kings, but he rarely performed there during the tours that occupied him and his band until about 1930. After that, he was at the Checker Club in Harlem, the Lido Room, and Pod's and Jerry's.* Like many black performers from the twenties, Jelly Roll Morton went into an eclipse with the Depression and concluded his career running a modest nightclub in Washington, D.C.
REFERENCES: Langston Hughes and Milton Meltzer, *Black Magic*, 1967; WWJ, 1972. (BK)

MOSES, ETHEL (actress), ?–? Called "The Harlem Harlow" during the thirties when she appeared in several films for Oscar Micheaux,* Ethel Moses had already had a long career in silent black films. She appeared in revues at the Cotton Club,* Connie's Inn,* and the Ubangi Club, as well as in several shows: *Dixie to Broadway** (1924), *Blackbirds[*] of 1926*, *Showboat** (1927), and *Keep Shufflin'** (1928).
REFERENCE: BAF, 1974. (BK)

MOTEN, ETTA (actress), 1902– ? Etta Moten was born in San Antonio, Texas, and moved with her family to Kansas City when she was sixteen to attend Western University. An early marriage ended in divorce, but she supported her three children singing on the midwestern Chautauqua circuit until Eva Jessye* engaged her as guest soloist. Moten's command of French, German, and Italian eventually brought her work in the white theater in 1932, playing a voodoo girl in a Broadway bomb called *Zombie*. This appearance followed those in two other failures, *Fast and Furious** and *Sugar Hill*,* both black music shows.
REFERENCE: *Inter-State Tattler*, 25 Feb. 1932. (BK)

MOTION PICTURES AND MOTION PICTURE COMPANIES. Many minor film companies sprang up at the outset of the Harlem Renaissance in addition to those of more substantial stature like the Lincoln Motion Picture Company,* Reol Motion Picture Corporation* (white-owned but exclusively black in content and casting), Andlauer Production Company,* Birth of a Race Photoplay Company,* Frederick Douglass Film Company,* Colored Players Film Corporation,* and the organization of Oscar Micheaux.* More than two dozen companies of lesser significance flourished briefly, a few of which produced films of some minor interest. Ebony Film Company produced *A Black Sherlock Holmes* (1918) and *Spying the Spy*, a ghost story (1919), with white backing and scripts by white writer Leslie T. Peacock. Royal Gardens Motion Picture Company produced *In the Depths of Our Hearts*, about prejudice in the race over variations in skin color (1919). Maurice Film Company produced *Nobody's Children*, about a stepfather who gives his daughter to the underworld, starring the organization's founders, Richard and Vivian Maurice (1920). The Democracy Film Corporation, to combat the racism in D. W. Griffith's *Birth of a Nation*, made *Injustice*, about a Red Cross Nurse whose black butler rescues her on the battlefield during World War I (1919). Ben Strasser Productions made *His Great Chance*, advertised as a "dramatic comedy" (1923), with Tim Moore* who later played the Kingfish in the popular television series based on the Amos and Andy radio show; the company also made the first all-black murder mystery, *A Shot in the Night*. Norman Film Company made *The Bull Dogger*, a western with Anita Bush* and the black rodeo star Bill Pickett (1923). Tono Films was organized in New York as an all-black corporation including Paul Robeson,* Noble Sissle,* Maceo Pinkard,* Earl Dancer, James C. Johnson,* and Will Vodery.* Rosebud Film Corporation made *Absent* with Clarence Brooks* (1927).

Paragon Pictures Corporation made three features (1928–1932): *The Crimson Fog*, *The Dusky Virgin*, and *Dixie Love*. Aristo Films produced the first black-cast sound film, *Georgia Rose* (1930), a musical comedy with Clarence Brooks, Dora Dean Williams, and Spencer Williams,* about a farm girl who goes to Harlem cabarets for some high life and returns in the nick of time. Other companies of the period include the following: Ben Roy Productions (1921), Blackburn Velde Producers (1921), C. B. Campbell Studios (1921), Colored and Indian Film Company (1917), Colored Motion Picture Producers of America (1926), Del Sarte Film Company (1921), D.W.D. Film Corporation (1921), Dunbar Film Corporation (1928), E. S. and L. Colored Feature Productions (1921), Midnight Productions (1928), North State Film Corporation (1921), Progress Pictures Association (1921), Sherman Dudley, Jr. (1926), Southland Productions (1932), Supreme Arts Productions (1921), Trio Production Company (1922), Western Pictures Production Company (1922), White Film Corporation (1921), and Young Producers Filming Company. Edward Mapp's *Blacks in American Films* carries an excellent index of individual films by and about Afro-Americans.

REFERENCES: BAF, 1974; Daniel J. Leab, *From Sambo to Superspade*, 1975; BBW, 1977; Valerie Shaw, *Black Hollywood Yesterday*, 1983. (BK)

MOTLEY, ARCHIBALD, JR. (artist), 1891–? From the beginning of his career Archibald Motley painted in the rounded, stylized masses that marked the work of white painters Thomas Hart Benton and Grant Wood a decade later. In 1923 in Motley's "Mending Socks" the flattened surfaces are already obvious, and by 1928, when "Old Snuff Taker" won the Harmon Foundation Gold Medal Award, his technique and his style already anticipated the look of American artists during the thirties. "Stomp" and "The Jockey Club," both from the late twenties, indicate Motley's depiction of larger groups, stylizing the activities of his figures with the spill of light against dark. Motley was the first black artist to have a one-man show in New York, and in 1929 he was awarded a Guggenheim scholarship.

REFERENCE: Cedric Dover, *American Negro Art*, 1960. (BK)

MOTON, ROBERT RUSSA (educator), 26 August 1867–31 May 1940. Robert Moton was, in a real sense, the successor to Booker T. Washington as a southern black leader with strong support from whites in government and business. Moton grew up on a plantation in Prince Edward County, Virginia, the son of former slaves. He was educated by his mother at home and at a free school for blacks that opened nearby. He attended school whenever he could but spent much of his youth working hard at a variety of odd jobs. In 1885, at the age of eighteen, he entered Hampton Institute. He was a popular student, and he stayed on after graduation in 1890 to be commandant in charge of military discipline. He worked at the school for the next twenty-five years, and his responsibilities increased to include fund raising in the North and representing the institute on a variety of boards, commissions, and conferences. By the time Booker T. Washington died in 1915 Moton was the obvious choice to replace him as principal of Tuskegee Institute. In most ways Moton, who had been a disciple of Washington, kept Tuskegee an unthreatening place to whites, and he was able to use their money to increase greatly the endowment and physical plant. Still, he added a "college department" in the 1920s (which proved controversial) so that the college could produce better-trained black teachers and employees.

Moton was successful in arguing for a camp to train black officers in World War I, as well as for the establishment of a black combat division. Emmett Scott's* appointment as assistant to the secretary of war was also attributable to Moton's influence. Late in the war Moton was sent to France by President Wilson to report on the condition of black troops. After the war he became embroiled in a dispute over whether black doctors and other supervisory personnel would be allowed to work at a veterans' hospital for blacks in Tuskegee. Moton wanted a black professional staff at the hospital because, as he put it, "Negroes have a right above all other people to serve their own"; yet he was aware of "the necessity of preserving intact those relations of goodwill and mutual helpfulness between white people and black people at Tuskegee, in the South, and all over the country—which latter was the outstanding achievement of Booker [T.] Washington" (quoted in Hughes and Patterson, *Robert Russa Moton of Hampton and Tuskegee*, p. 172). In the end Moton won.

Like Washington, Moton was a member of dozens of important organizations and boards, such as the National Negro Business League,* the National Urban League,* the Dunbar National Bank in New York City, and the Negro Rural School Fund Board. He contributed numerous articles to dozens of magazines, and he has an essay in Alain Locke's* *New Negro.** He was a recipient of the Harmon Foundation* Award for contributions to better race relations in 1930 and was awarded the Spingarn Medal* in 1932. He resigned from Tuskegee in 1935 and died five years later. His relevant works include *Racial Good Will* (1916), *Finding a Way Out* (1920, autobiography), and *What the Negro Thinks* (1929).

REFERENCES: WWCA, 1933; DAB, 1937; Graham Werden Hughes and F. D. Patterson, *Robert Russa Moton of Hampton and Tuskegee*, 1956. (DS)

MULATTO (play), 1935. Langston Hughes's *Mulatto* was the first full-length play by a black writer to have a Broadway production. It opened 24 October 1935 at the Vanderbilt Theatre to cautious reviews. Brooks Atkinson, covering it for the *New York Times*, admitted to its "fatal weaknesses as a drama." The short story on which it was based, "Father and Son," had suffered some fatal weaknesses as well when it appeared in *The Ways of White Folks** the year before. Hughes's obvious commitment to demonstrate the subject as demoralizing for the race—in Atkinson's apt rendering, "the casual begetting of illegitimate children who are denied the prerogatives of their paternity, scorned by the whites,

hated by the blacks''—resulted in heavy-handed melodrama. Rose McClendon*
starred as Cora, mother of three children by her white master, one of whom is
college educated. In a violent argument he strangles his father and subsequently
commits suicide just before a lynching mob arrives. ''The sympathies evoked
by Hughes's story are muddled and confused,'' Atkinson concluded, even though
he admired ''a playwright who is flaming with sincerity'' (NYT, 26 Oct. 1935,
p. 25). Hughes was not entirely to blame: he had returned from his trip to Russia
to write the screenplay for *Black and White** to find the play already in rehearsal,
and with several changes in the script, most of them designed to further sen-
sationalize the melodrama.
REFERENCE: NYTTR, 1972. (BK)

MURPHY, CARL J. (editor, publisher), 17 January 1889–26 February 1967.
Carl Murphy was born in Baltimore and returned there, after his education at
Howard and Harvard universities and after teaching German at Howard from
1913 to 1918, to become editor of the powerful weekly newspaper *Afro-American.**
REFERENCE: WWCA, 1933. (BK)

MUSE, CLARENCE (actor, writer), 7 October 1889–November 1979. Clarence Muse was born in Baltimore, but his forebears came from Virginia, South
Carolina, and Martinique. Muse received a degree in international law from
Dickinson College in 1911, but from that time on his heart belonged to the
theater. He began his career as a member of a quartet in Florida, and he acted
with a stock company there in an early forerunner of the twenties musical shows,
Stranded in Africa. Shortly after, he was stranded in New York, with a wife
and child to support through occasional jobs in vaudeville. He formed a stock
company with Billy Pugh called *The Two Muses* and then joined the Crescent
Players, the Anita Bush* Company at the Lincoln Theatre,* and the Lafayette
Players* from its inception as cofounder with Charles Gilpin.* In 1921 Muse
appeared in *The Custard Nine*, made by the Del Sarte Film Company, foreshadowing his later career in more than 150 movies. During the early twenties
he appeared in whiteface makeup with the Lafayette Players in their production
of *Dr. Jekyll and Mr. Hyde*, and under circumstances not entirely clear he
appeared similarly in the opera *Thais* with an otherwise white cast. When the
Lafayette Theatre turned to vaudeville, Muse went on to appear in several Chicago revues, *Hoola Boola*, for example, and *Ramblin' Around*, which do not
seem to have come into New York. However, two other New York productions
deserve some mention. In 1922 Flournoy Miller* and his partner Aubrey Lyles*
sandwiched in a straight melodrama, *The Flat Below*, about a corrupt church
deacon. Clarence Muse produced it. In 1927 he produced *Miss Bandanna*, with
Jackie ''Moms'' Mabley* in what may have been her first starring role, as a
stage-struck Mississippi girl who goes to New York. Muse acted in the second
all-talking film, *Hearts in Dixie** (1929); in *Huckleberry Finn* (1931); and in

Broadway Bill (1934), all of which explain his absence from the frantic black musical revues of the twenties.

Despite his small stature Muse moved naturally with considerable dignity, and his voice was incantatory; the style was only suitable at the time to subservient roles in Hollywood's product. (His absence from the film version of *The Green Pastures*,* however, is surprising.) In later years, criticized for playing docile servants, despite the fact that he had humanized one of the oldest stereotypes, Muse retorted: "A lot of you people called me Uncle Tom, but I have something to call you. You were as dumb as I was. You were the audience and you laughed at what I did" (quoted in *WWH*, 1976, p. 273). Clarence Muse also wrote songs, among them "When It's Sleepy Time Down South," and frequent articles for the *Pittsburgh Courier*,* usually about the activities of various members of TOBA.* In 1973 he was admitted into the Black Film Makers Hall of Fame, and he was further acknowledged by his alma mater through two honorary degrees: doctor of humanities in 1972 and doctor of laws in 1978, just a year before his death at ninety.
REFERENCES: ASCAP, 1966; NA, 1976; WWH, 1976; BBW, 1977. (BK)

M. WITMARK & SONS (music publishers), ?– . Julius, youngest of the Witmarks and one of the founders of the American Society of Composers, Authors, and Publishers,* was responsible for signing up Eubie Blake* and Noble Sissle.* In addition to publishing the music of white composers like Victor Herbert, Sigmund Romberg, and Ernest K. Ball, the music publishers M. Witmark & Sons also published Paul Laurence Dunbar, James Weldon Johnson* and J. Rosamond Johnson,* and Harry T. Burleigh.*
REFERENCE: ASCAP, 1966. (BK)

MY MAGNOLIA (musical comedy), 1926. Although *My Magnolia* closed after four performances at the Mansfield Theatre, it differed slightly from earlier all-black shows in trying to carry through a serious story line. Although inept and underrehearsed, it was notable for its almost continuous dancing, executed with "frenzied expertness," according to the *New York Times* reviewer. Eddie Hunter* wrote the "not even moderately amusing" book and Alex Rogers* and C. Luckyeth Roberts* wrote the music and lyrics. Like many similar entertainments, its action occurred in and around contemporary Harlem, stringing a series of "lopsided and ambling" sketches and songs on a thin plot about a girl who goes north to be on the stage (13 July 1926, p. 19).
REFERENCES: Burns Mantle, 1926–1927; NYTTR, 1972. (BK)

N

NAIL, JOHN E. (realtor), 1883–5 March 1947. Jack Nail was the most successful real estate man in New York City in the early twentieth century. He and his partner Henry Parker managed the sale of Saint Philip's Protestant Episcopal Church* properties in the Tenderloin section of Manhattan in 1909 and then managed the real estate affairs of the church as it bought more than $640,000 worth of Harlem properties with some of the money gained from the sale of its Tenderloin property. Nail and Parker also acted as agents for the YMCA when it decided to join most other black organizations and move to Harlem from midtown Manhattan in the second and third decades of the twentieth century. Nail, the son of well-known saloon owner John B. Nail, was brought up in New York City and was a friend of James Weldon Johnson* and other members of the black cultural and business elite. Johnson, who married Nail's sister, described him as "the most popular boy in New York, an exceedingly handsome boy" (*Along This Way*, p. 172). Nail was successful as well as popular. He was the first president of the Negro Board of Trade in Harlem, the first black elected to the Real Estate Board of New York, a member of the Mayor's Housing Committee, and vice-president of the Republican Business Men's Club of New York City (an exclusive and predominantly white organization). He was also active in support of the National Urban League.*

REFERENCES: WWCR, 1915; "John E. Nail," *The Crisis*, Mar. 1924; James W. Johnson, *Along This Way*, 1938; Gilbert Osofsky, *Harlem*, 1966. (DS)

NANCE, ETHEL RAY (secretary), ?– . From 1923 Ethel Nance served as Charles S. Johnson's* secretary. She worked on the *Survey Graphic** issue, "The New Negro"; she encouraged young black intellectuals to go to Harlem; she volunteered for various duties at the Harlem Branch of the New York Public Library; and she kept dossiers on young members of the Harlem Renaissance. With Regina Anderson* and Louella Tucker, she shared an apartment that became a meeting place for many aspiring artists and writers. Any play requires its stage

crew: Ethel Nance was a tireless worker on *Opportunity*,* its editing, its literary contests, its awards banquets. When Johnson resigned from the National Urban League* to join the faculty at Fisk University, Ethel Nance accompanied him to Tennessee. She retired later to San Francisco.
REFERENCES: David Levering Lewis, *When Harlem Was in Vogue*, 1981; CVV; Louise Thompson Patterson. (BK)

NATION (periodical), 1865– . The *Nation* was founded by abolitionists at the end of the Civil War to further the freedmen's interests. Yet from its first issue on 6 July 1865, under the editorial guidance of E. L. Godkin, the *Nation* quickly retreated from its abolitionist heritage by tacitly accepting white racism and ignoring black needs and causes. In 1881 Henry Villard, a railroad magnate and son-in-law of William Lloyd Garrison, bought the *Nation* and the *New York Evening Post* and turned the *Nation*, in effect, into the weekly edition of the *Post*. When Villard died in 1900, his son Oswald Garrison Villard* assumed control of both papers and within a few years had radically changed their editorial policy to coincide with his liberal, antiracist, pacificist ideals. In 1918 Oswald sold the *Evening Post* but held onto an independent *Nation* magazine that remained a forthright and crusading liberal weekly even after Villard relinquished control in 1932. Under Villard, a founder and later vice-president of the NAACP,* the *Nation* (circulation 25,000–30,000) presented blacks and black causes in a more favorable light than nearly any other national journal.
REFERENCES: Oswald Garrison Villard, *Fighting Years*, 1939; Dollena Joy Humes, *Oswald Garrison Villard*, 1960; James M. McPherson, *The Abolitionist Legacy*, 1975. (DS)

NATIONAL ASSOCIATION FOR THE ADVANCEMENT OF COLORED PEOPLE (NAACP), 1909– . An outgrowth of the 1905 Niagara movement, the National Association for the Advancement of Colored People originated in a 1909 National Negro Congress, which followed the issuance of a "Call" authored by Oswald Garrison Villard* to commemorate the hundredth anniversary of Abraham Lincoln's birth. By May 1910 a permanent organization was established, known as the NAACP. Morefield Storey served as the first president of the association and William English Walling as chairman of the biracial Executive Committee. Oswald Garrison Villard was elected treasurer, and W.E.B. Du Bois* was persuaded to leave Atlanta University to become director of publicity and research as well as editor of *The Crisis*,* the association's monthly magazine, which first appeared in November 1910. It was Mary White Ovington,* another of the founders, who suggested the name of the publication to Du Bois, taken from James Russell Lowell's poem "The Present Crisis." In 1910 Joel Spingarn* joined the Executive Committee, beginning a long career with the NAACP that culminated in his succeeding Storey as president in 1929. Spingarn's brother Arthur Spingarn* served as the first chairman of the influential

Legal Committee. In 1916 James Weldon Johnson* was hired as field secretary; he became national secretary in 1920.

By 1919, its tenth anniversary, the association was established as the largest and most influential civil rights organization in America. Its membership had grown to more than 90,000 persons in 310 branches across the country. *The Crisis*, which ran to fifty pages and sold for fifteen cents a copy, had a monthly circulation of more than 100,000, its all-time high. It was also in 1919, as the association celebrated the return of black veterans from World War I, that southern membership exceeded that in the North for the first time. That year Villard resigned from the organization after numerous disputes with Du Bois. On its tenth anniversary the association had published the results of its exhaustive study into lynching in America, *Thirty Years of Lynching*. James Weldon Johnson, Walter White,* and others made frequent trips into the South to investigate incidents of lynching and other violations of civil rights. The Legal Committee joined in several highly publicized legal suits, and the association made numerous appeals to the federal and state governments to protect the rights of black citizens. Congress's failure to pass a national antilynching bill after 1919 was a bitter disappointment to Du Bois and the leadership.

In 1915 the association began presenting annually the Spingarn Medal,* as the inscription read, for "the highest and noblest achievement of an American Negro." Ernest Everett Just of Howard University was the first recipient of the award for his scientific research. The medal was awarded every year except 1938, when the recipient refused to accept the honor for personal reasons. In 1924, through *The Crisis*, the association presented awards given by Amy (Mrs. Joel) Spingarn in literature and the arts, to acknowledge the creative awakening that had begun among a younger generation of American blacks. Du Bois opened the pages of the magazine to the poetry of James Weldon Johnson, Countee Cullen,* Claude McKay,* Langston Hughes,* and others. There were regular articles about black actors and painters; book reviews and pieces of literary criticism were common. The focus of *The Crisis* remained, though, the programs and policies of the association and the accomplishments of blacks in education, the professions, and the arts.

In politics the association came increasingly under the influence of Du Bois. In 1916 the NAACP counseled support of Republican Charles Evans Hughes to protest Woodrow Wilson's segregation of departments of the federal government. In the twenties the association continued its political activities on behalf of black citizens on the national level and through its several hundred branches. In 1924 Du Bois broke with other leaders in supporting Progressive candidate Robert La Follette over Calvin Coolidge, and in 1932 the association refused to endorse Herbert Hoover for reelection, condemned by Du Bois for his "lilly-white" policies. Although no official endorsement came, the association clearly welcomed the election of Franklin D. Roosevelt.

By the early thirties, the NAACP had changed considerably from its first years. No longer a fledgling organization straining for recognition against Booker

T. Washington and the political machine his Tuskegee Institute had become, the association now struggled against the hard realities of the Great Depression. Membership declined dramatically in the economic crisis, and the circulation of *The Crisis* fell to one-tenth its postwar high. The NAACP also witnessed the passing of the old guard. James Weldon Johnson resigned as executive secretary in 1928, for reason of health, and accepted a position at Fisk University. He was succeeded by Walter White. Morefield Storey died in 1929. Gone too was Du Bois, admittedly the association's most important figure. He left the NAACP and *The Crisis* in 1934. Although *The Crisis* printed more articles on Marxism and socialism as the Depression worsened, the association embraced the New Deal and its possibilities for black citizens. Under the direction of Walter White, the Spingarns, and a young Roy Wilkins, the NAACP survived the Great Depression to remain the single most important civil rights organization in twentieth-century America.

REFERENCES: *The Crisis*, 1910–1938; Langston Hughes, *Fight for Freedom*, 1962; Charles Flint Kellogg, *NAACP*, 1967. (DD)

NATIONAL ASSOCIATION OF NEGRO MUSICIANS (union), 1919–? Organized by Carl Diton* in Washington, D.C., in 1919, the National Association of Negro Musicians had 1,000 members within four years. Henry Grant served as president of the organization that R. Nathaniel Dett* had tried to begin years before.

REFERENCE: *The Crisis*, May 1923. (BK)

NATIONAL BROTHERHOOD WORKERS OF AMERICA (labor union), 1919–   . The National Brotherhood Workers of America was one of the early attempts to organize black skilled labor for better wages and conditions as well as for shorter working hours. Thirteen states were represented at the first—and presumably single—conference in New York.

REFERENCE: *The Messenger*, Sept. 1919. (BK)

NATIONAL COLORED PLAYERS (little theater group), 1929. In the autumn of 1929, at the West End Theatre off 125th Street at St. Nicholas Avenue, Ida Anderson's National Colored Players opened a season of serious drama. Despite positive notices in the *Inter-State Tattler*,* the company seems to have received scant attention and folded after three productions: *Seventh Heaven*, *Crime*, and *The Gorilla*, each given a week's run beginning October 7.

REFERENCE: *Inter-State Tattler*, 11 Oct. 1929. (BK)

NATIONAL ETHIOPIAN ART THEATRE (little theater group), 1924–1925. First organized as a school from which a genuine black theater ensemble might emerge, the National Ethiopian Art Theatre began with a dance recital in the summer of 1924. It drew little attention, although Theophilus Lewis,* writing about it in *The Messenger*,* noted that it would be necessary to conscript black

playwrights for the endeavor, and he suggested Frank Wilson,* whose *Pa Williams' Gal** at the Lafayette Theatre* had made such a favorable impression the preceding year (Aug. 1924, p. 250). On 15 October 1924, NEAT, as Lewis coined it in his columns, gave an initial performance of three one-act plays at the Lafayette: *Being Forty*, by Eulalie Spence*; *Bills*, a comedy not even dignified by an identification of the author; and *Cooped Up*, a rooming house drama of sexual passion by one of NEAT's students, Eloise Bibb Thompson. Ardelle Dabney, F. Eugene Corbie, Lillian Creamer, G. Alfred Woods, Joseph A. Steber, and Helmsley Winfield were among the cast members. Winfield went on to become the director of the Sekondi Players, a group of Yonkers, New York, high school students, whose performances and productions three years later, in 1927, drew some attention in the black press, according to Lewis (Apr. 1927, p. 121). For its second season, during the summer of 1925, NEAT presented *The Maker of Cremona, The Florist Shop*, and a revival of Ridgely Torrence's *Rider of Dreams*. Clarissa and Carey D. Blue, Sybil Poston, and J. W. Jackson had joined the company by that time, although Lewis singled out only F. Eugene Corbie for praise. His appearance in *Cape Smoke*, a recent, mixed-cast, downtown flop, had given him enough experience to set him apart from the others. Despite the amateurish aspects of NEAT, however, Lewis praised its producer Anne Wolter and welcomed any respite from the "smutty imbecilities of the Lafayette and the sex saturnalia of the Lincoln"* (July 1925, p. 268).
REFERENCES: Theophilus Lewis, "Theatre," *The Messenger*, Aug., Nov. 1924, July 1925, Apr. 1927; George S. Schuyler, "Theatre," *The Messenger*, Nov. 1924. (BK)

NATIONAL NEGRO BUSINESS LEAGUE (organization), 1900–1933. Founded by Booker T. Washington, in Boston, the National Negro Business League had 400 delegates from thirty-four states and held annual conventions until the Depression brought about its demise. At the height of its influence it had 40,000 members, and from its power base secretary Albon L. Holsey organized the Colored Merchants' Association in 1930.
REFERENCE: David Levering Lewis, *When Harlem Was in Vogue*, 1981. (BK)

NATIONAL URBAN LEAGUE (organization), 1911–   . The National Urban League was organized by prominent blacks and whites in New York City on 16 October 1911 in response to the needs of the growing number of blacks migrating from the rural South to the cities. Not unlike other reform organizations formed to aid immigrant groups in the Progressive Era just before World War I, the Urban League offered help to newcomers in finding housing and jobs and protection to them (particularly the women) from exploitation. Among other things, the league also fought for better housing, sanitary services, recreational facilities, and job opportunities for blacks; engaged in intensive research that revealed the dimensions of the urban problems blacks faced; and worked to improve cooperation among the races, although in a more quiet and conservative

manner than the NAACP.* In 1923 the league began publication of *Opportunity*,* a magazine that publicized the research findings of the organization but also served as a showcase for many young black writers who emerged during the 1920s. Although the national headquarters was in New York City the goal of the league was to establish self-supporting professionally staffed local affiliates in as many cities as possible.
REFERENCE: Nancy J. Weiss, *The National Urban League*, 1974. (DS)

NEGRO AMERICANS: WHAT NOW? (book), 1934. James Weldon Johnson's* brief tract summarizing the position of the Afro-American citizen at the conclusion of the Harlem Renaissance offered nothing new in its assessment, but the eloquence of its plea for black readers to look forward as a result of the race's achievements thus far in the century led to a number of positive reviews. Only W.E.B. Du Bois* in one of his first post-*Crisis** reviews, for the *New York Herald Tribune*, chided Johnson for ignoring the economic issues of the Depression and the crucial questions dealing with segregation and integration practices in the country.
REFERENCE: W.E.B. Du Bois, review of *Negro Americans, What Now?* by James Weldon Johnson, *New York Herald Tribune Books*, 18 Nov. 1934. (BK)

THE NEGRO AND HIS SONGS (book), 1925. Howard W. Odum and Guy B. Johnson, white faculty members at the University of North Carolina, compiled a volume of religious, social, and work songs of Afro-Americans to illustrate the Negro character. No music was reprinted, so the concentration was on the language of the text and its poetic value. Furthermore, it considered the influence of white songs on black and vice versa, assuming that language reveals an important level of cultural interaction between the races. (BK, MH)

NEGRO ART INSTITUTE (learned society), 1924–? The American Negro Academy, founded in 1897 to refute charges of black inferiority, published annual papers by a number of respected scholars. When it disbanded in 1924, The Negro Art Institute was founded by Alain Locke,* based on an idea of Walter White.* When the Charles Garland American Fund for Public Service rejected the proposal, Charlotte Mason* agreed to underwrite it, provided its "primitive purity" was maintained.
REFERENCE: David Levering Lewis, *When Harlem Was in Vogue*, 1981. (BK)

NEGRO ART THEATRE (little theater group), 1929. Founded in the Abyssinian Baptist Church at the close of the twenties, the Negro Art Theatre was a short-lived endeavor that began auspiciously with Adam Clayton Powell, Jr., and Laura Bowman* in *Wade in the Water* on June 20.
REFERENCE: Loften Mitchell, *Black Drama*, 1967. (BK)

NEGRO EXPERIMENTAL THEATRE (little theater group), 1929–1931. Sometimes referred to as the "Harlem" rather than "Negro" Experimental Theatre, the group was founded in February 1929 at the 135th Street Branch of the New York Public Library. Inez Wilson and Andrew Brown had just had some success in a serious play or sketch called "Retribution" at the Lincoln Theatre*; as a result, a number of young Harlem intellectuals banded together to form a company devoted to straight dramatic presentations. Dorothy Peterson* and Regina Anderson* seem to have spearheaded the idea, joined by Theophilus Lewis,* Ira De Augustine Reid,* Jessie Fauset,* Harold Jackman,* and the Lincoln actors. Four months later the company gave what the *Inter-State Tattler*™ reviewer called "an unusually brilliant" performance of Georgia Douglas Johnson's* one-act play "Plumes," directed by Jackman (5 July 1929, p. 12). Two years later, in February 1931, the company moved to Saint Philip's Protestant Episcopal Church* Parish House and staged George Calderon's "Little Stone House," Ridgely Torrence's "Rider of Dreams," and (written by Regina Anderson under the pseudonym "Ursala Trelling") "Climbing Jacob's Ladder." REFERENCES: *Inter-State Tattler*, 5 July 1929; Loften Mitchell, *Black Drama*, 1967; Loften Mitchell, ed., *Voices of the Black Theatre*, 1975. (BK)

"THE NEGRO IN ART: HOW SHALL HE BE PORTRAYED? A SYMPOSIUM," 1926. White writer Carl Van Vechten* ghostwrote the questionnaire for Jessie Fauset* to run in *The Crisis*™ during a period of several months in 1926. The "artists of the world" were asked to respond about an author's responsibility in depicting black characters, his culpability in delineating negative aspects, criticism of publishers who insist on stereotypes and sensationalism, and the dangers of pandering to low tastes. Among the respondents were, in addition to Van Vechten himself, Sherwood Anderson,* Benjamin Brawley,* Charles W. Chesnutt,* Countee Cullen,* W.E.B. Du Bois,* John Farrar, Jessie Fauset, John Herbert, Du Bose Heyward,* Langston Hughes,* Georgia Douglas Johnson,* Robert Kerlin,* Alfred A. Knopf,* Sinclair Lewis, Vachel Lindsay,* H. L. Mencken,* Haldane McFall,* Julia Peterkin,* William Lyon Phelps, Joel Spingarn,* and Walter White.* REFERENCE: Carl Van Vechten, *"Keep A-Inchin' Along,"* 1979. (BK)

NEGRO LIFE IN NEW YORK'S HARLEM (monograph), 1928. Wallace Thurman's* extended essay *Negro Life in New York's Harlem* is seminal to any study of the Negro Renaissance, as the movement was familiarly called during the twenties. Subtitled "A Lively Picture of a Popular and Interesting Section," it was published as Little Blue Book No. 494 by Haldeman-Julius Publications in Girard, Kansas, one of a series of paperbound pamphlets on a wide variety of subjects. *Negro Life in New York's Harlem* is divided into sections on social life, cabarets, rent parties* and the numbers* racket, churches,* journalism, and the emerging "New Negro." It is not only witty and informative but unique in having been written during the period by one of its leading members. Originally, it had appeared in the *Haldeman-Julius Quarterly* in 1928; it has not been reprinted. (BK)

THE NEGRO MOTHER AND OTHER DRAMATIC RECITATIONS (poetry), 1931. The Golden Stair Press issued five dramatic monologues by Langston Hughes,* with illustrations by the white artist Prentiss Taylor*: "The Colored Soldier," "Broke," "The Black Clown," "The Big Timer," the title piece, and "Dark Youth of the U.S.A." The twenty-page booklet was also issued in a limited edition of seventeen copies, each of which Taylor painted in full color; they were signed by both artist and author. Four of the six pieces were also issued as broadsides. (BK)

NEGRO WORKADAY SONGS (book), 1926. Unlike their *Negro and His Songs** (1925), *Negro Workaday Songs*, by professors Guy B. Johnson and Howard W. Odum of the University of North Carolina, included musical examples and recordings, demonstrating the difficulty in transcribing black melodies with existing musical notation. Furthermore, they demonstrated that the blues* had derived from folk songs. The book gives special attention to melody and convincingly shows the need for phonographic records as a means to preserve and study this rich source of cultural tradition. (MH, BK)

NEGRO WORLD (newspaper), 1918–1933. The *Negro World* was for sixteen years the weekly organ of Marcus Garvey* and his Universal Negro Improvement Association.* Based in New York City, the *Negro World* was circulated throughout the United States, Africa, the West Indies, and much of the world until it was banned by most colonial governments for its strident black nationalist message. At its peak it may have had a circulation reaching as many as 200,000 readers, and it helped spread Garvey's message of black pride, self-help, and black independence. As it said on its masthead, the *Negro World* was "A Newspaper Devoted Solely to the Interests of the Negro Race," and it ran news stories, features, Garveyite editorials, and literary efforts as well. Claude McKay* called it the best edited black news organ in New York, which is not surprising, given the outstanding editorial staff that Garvey attracted. W. A. Domingo,* Hubert Harrison,* T. Thomas Fortune,* John Edward Bruce,* Eric Walrond,* William H. Ferris,* and other eminent black writers and intellectuals edited or wrote for the *Negro World*. Garvey himself was an editor and driving force in the publication of the newspaper at various times, particularly in the late 1910s and 1930s. The paper also carried news of the activities of the UNIA and acted as a unifying force for the worldwide efforts of that group; indeed, sections of the paper were printed in Spanish and French for the convenience of readers outside the United States. In late 1933 Garvey suspended publication of the paper and began printing the monthly *Black Man* instead.

REFERENCES: E. David Cronon, *Black Moses*, 1955; Tony Martin, *Race First*, 1976. (DS)

NELSON, ALICE [MOORE] DUNBAR (writer, educator), 19 July 1875–19 September 1935. Alice Dunbar Nelson worked actively in the fields of education, journalism, politics, and social work to advance the cause of equal rights for Afro-Americans. She grew up in New Orleans, the daughter of a middle-class family, and graduated from Straight College with a teaching degree in 1892. Her first book of poetry and sketches, *Violets and Other Tales*, was issued while she was teaching in New Orleans. One of her poems, appearing in the Boston *Monthly Review*, came to the attention of the poet Paul Lawrence Dunbar, whom she married two years later. After her marriage she taught in Brooklyn public schools and contributed her time as a teacher of evening classes on New York's East Side. She served as secretary of the National Association of Colored Women from 1897 to 1899. Her second book, *The Goodness of St. Rocque and Other Stories*, tales of French and Creole characters set in New Orleans, was published in 1899.

In 1902, having separated from Dunbar, who died four years later, she became a teacher of English at Howard High School in Wilmington, Delaware, a position she held for eighteen years. During this time she wrote articles on Negro history for various journals and edited two anthologies for students, *Masterpieces of Negro Eloquence* (1914) and *The Dunbar Speaker and Entertainer* (1920). She worked on loan drives and for the Red Cross during World War I and was an advisor to the Woman's Committee of the U.S. Council of National Defense. During the twenties Dunbar contributed poems, sketches, and a play to *Opportunity** and *The Crisis*.* Despite the esteem in which she was held by her students and colleagues, Dunbar was dismissed from her teaching post at Howard for political activity. She became the first black woman to be a member of the Delaware Republican State Committee to which she was elected in 1920. She had married newspaper publisher John Robert Nelson in 1916 and became associate editor of his *Wilmington Advocate*, a newspaper devoted to the advancement of blacks, in 1920. She also wrote a column on race relations for the *Washington Eagle* and was editor of the *A.M.E. Church Review*. In 1924, concerned about the problems of delinquent black girls, she helped to found the Delaware Industrial School for Colored Girls and volunteered there for many years as teacher and parole worker. She became involved with the American Interracial Peace Committee of the Friends Service Committee in 1928, serving as its executive secretary, and lectured on the cause of world peace at colleges and universities around the country.

REFERENCES: BAWPP, 1975; NAW, 1980. (PO)

THE NEST (cabaret). Just around the corner to the right from Small's Paradise, the Nest was located in the basement apartment of a brownstone house on West

134th Street. Owned and operated by Johnny Cobb, this tiny haven was a popular after-hours spot for Nora Holt,* Walter White,* Carl Van Vechten,* and other intellectuals of the period. It was rarely patronized by whites slumming from downtown, who preferred the frantic pleasures of places like the Cotton Club.* Blues singer Marjorie Sipp performed regularly at the Nest and, like her boss, enjoyed sitting at the tables with neighborhood regulars and occasional white visitors who themselves became regulars in time. Like the Glory Hole*—though for different reasons marked by clientele, entertainment, and ambience—the Nest was largely unknown during the Harlem Renaissance, but it was typical, again like the Glory Hole, of many intimate clubs that catered to exclusive audiences.

REFERENCES: Bruce Kellner, *Carl Van Vechten and the Irreverent Decades*, 1968; Donald Angus. (BK)

NEVER NO MORE (play), 1932. James Knox Millen's melodrama closed after twelve horrifying performances. Rose McClendon* played the mother in an ambitious and God-fearing family of six. The youngest, a juvenile delinquent played by Leigh Whipper,* strangles a white girl in panic in the first act; in the second act an angry white mob burns him alive outside the door of his mother's cabin; in the third act the mother threatens the mob with a bomb when it plans to destroy the whole family. This single night of "bloodlust and horror in the South" and "sheer nervous torture" was more than the play could adequately cope with, although Rose McClendon, according to the *New York Times*, as usual, was praised for her performance (8 Jan. 1932, p. 27).

REFERENCES: Burns Mantle, 1931–1932; NYTTR, 1972. (BK)

THE NEW NEGRO (anthology), 1925. Building upon the nucleus of writings and poetry he had arranged for the special Harlem issue of *Survey Graphic** (March 1925), Alain Locke's* more comprehensive anthology of black writers, poets, and artists boldly announced to the world that a new spirit of self-awareness, artistic consciousness, and racial pride now existed among the "advance guard of the African peoples in their contact with Twentieth Century civilization" (p. 14). Especially significant is the focus on Harlem as the symbol of a new era—"the laboratory of a great race-welding" (p. 8). In addition to including the contributions of thirty-three others, Locke himself wrote four essays and the foreword: "The New Negro," "Negro Youth Speaks," "The Negro Spirituals" (the second extended discussion by a black critic after W.E.B. Du Bois's* "Of the Sorrow Songs"), and "The Legacy of the Ancestral Arts." Reviewing the book for *The Messenger** in April 1926, former Garveyite Ulysses Poston observed that the "virile, insurgent, revolutionary spirit peculiar to the Negro is missing" (p. 119). Other reviews were favorable.

REFERENCE: U. S. Poston, "Books," *The Messenger*, Apr. 1926. (MH)

NEW NEGRO ART THEATRE (little theater and dance group), 1931. On April 29 the Theatre-in-the-Clouds in the Chanin Building served as the site for the first serious recital of black dancing in New York. The white doyenne of modern dance Ruth St. Denis was one of the sponsors of the program, staged by the New Negro Art Theatre. It included numbers based on African themes and on Negro spirituals,* as well as a group of novelties featuring Hemsley Winfield (later, with his own company, to stage a ballet at the Metropolitan Opera House when *The Emperor Jones** was given its musical incarnation there) and Ollie Burgoyne* in a company of eighteen dancers. Four months later, in an evening made up largely of variety acts, Winfield appeared in drag in the leading role in Oscar Wilde's *Salome*, a production he directed himself, under the auspices of the New Negro Art Theatre.
REFERENCES: Langston Hughes and Milton Meltzer, *Black Magic*, 1971; Alexander Gumby Scrapbooks. (BK)

NEWSOME, [MARY] EFFIE LEE (writer), 19 January 1885–? Born in Philadelphia, Effie Lee Newsome attended Wilberforce University, Oberlin College, the Philadelphia Academy of Fine Arts, and the University of Pennsylvania between 1901 and 1914. She conducted a regular children's column in *Opportunity** and contributed to children's magazines.
REFERENCE: WWCA, 1927. (BK)

NICHOLAS, FAYARD (dancer), 1914– . Fayard Nicholas with his younger brother Harold (1920–) performed as The Nicholas Brothers, first at the Lafayette Theatre* in 1928. In top hats and tails they evolved a series of elegant and acrobatic routines that kept them popular for half a century. Their routine usually ended in a startling series of leaps, each of which terminated in full splits, over each other's heads down a flight of tall stairs. At the Cotton Club* they danced with the orchestras of Duke Ellington* and Cab Calloway,* and before moving to Hollywood for their later, more spectacular career in films, they danced in *Pie Pie Blackbird*, a short movie musical offering of the era, in 1932. Fifty years later they were still performing—minus the splits—successfully and with much of their exuberance intact on a Public Broadcasting System program called *G.I. Jive*.
REFERENCE: BBW, 1977. (BK)

NICHOLAS, HAROLD. See NICHOLAS, FAYARD.

NIGGER (novel), 1923. One of several novels with black subject matter by white writers, Clement Wood's *Nigger* covers three generations of an Afro-American family. Sentimental, honest Jake raises seven grandchildren: one girl becomes a white man's mistress, another a prostitute, and another a kitchen drudge; one boy is killed during a robbery, another is paralyzed, a third dies during the war, and a fourth survives his grim background to get a steady job.

Curiously, the title seems to have caused no difficulty among black readers, although three years later many Harlem readers turned in outspoken wrath against the title of Carl Van Vechten's* novel *Nigger Heaven.** (BK)

NIGGER HEAVEN (novel), 1926. Set against the welter and complexity of life in Harlem, Mary Love, a prim librarian, and Byron Kasson, an aspiring writer recently graduated from the University of Pennsylvania, fall in love and plan their future. However, Byron, unable to overcome feelings of inadequacy and consumed with self-pity, rejects Mary's quiet support and abandons himself to the erotic and sadistic attentions of Lasca Sartoris. *Nigger Heaven* concludes with Byron attempting to shoot Randolph Pettijohn, Lasca's new lover. Approximately a third of the novel is devoted to lurid scenes of cabaret life and Byron's steamy affair; the rest concentrates on Harlem's intellectual pastimes and concerns and Byron's pallid romance with Mary. *Nigger Heaven* created an initial furor because of its title; still controversial, Carl Van Vechten's* novel is defended as art and condemned as exploitation. (MH, BK)

NORTH AIN'T SOUTH (musical comedy), 1923. George S. Schuyler* demolished this Salem Whitney* and Homer Tutt* show at the Lafayette Theatre,* because it contended that the South was a preferable locale for blacks rather than the North; because the score was "tuneless"; because of its chorus of "pale, homely girls"; because Maude DeForest's singing was "painful"; because of the "bad dancing"; and because of skits perpetuating racial stereotypes, like "The Cave of Alabama and the Sporty Thieves," which took place in a graveyard. Moreover, he charged, "someone very early deceived Mr. Whitney into believing he possessed the ability to become a comedian" (23 Nov. 1923, p. 863).
REFERENCE: George S. Schuyler, "Theatre," *The Messenger*, Nov. 1923. (BK)

NORTH HARLEM COMMUNITY COUNCIL (reform group), 1918–? One of forty or fifty social service agencies organized by blacks in the 1910s and 1920s, the North Harlem Community Council (along with the North Harlem Vocational Guidance Committee) worked to improve the condition of the neighborhood, particularly in education, housing, and health.
REFERENCE: Gilbert Osofsky, *Harlem*, 1966. (DS)

NOT WITHOUT LAUGHTER (novel), 1930. Set in a small Kansas town, Langston Hughes's* *Not without Laughter* is focused on Aunt Hager Williams and her three daughters: Harriet who is a whore and becomes a blues* singer, Tempy who is married and from the respectable middle class, and Anjee who is married to fun-loving yet wandering Jim boy. Their three lives strongly contrast with their mother's folk wisdom and profound religious beliefs. However, it is through the eyes and efforts of the young son of Anjee to find his way that the various conflicting family values and experiences are weighed. Although Sandy does not resolve for himself the conflicting values of his extended family, he is Langston Hughes's symbol of the challenges young blacks of his generation will have to confront in attempting to live in a racist, competitive society. (MH)

NUGENT, RICHARD BRUCE (illustrator, writer), 2 July 1906– . Enfant terrible of Washington, D.C., and Harlem in the twenties, self-consciously decadent—he affected the manners of Carl Van Vechten's* Peter Whiffle—Bruce Nugent (who called himself "Richard Bruce") sprinkled the Harlem Renaissance with perfumed prose and satiric illustrations. He first appeared in Alain Locke's* *New Negro** with "Sahdji," a pseudo-African ritual peppered with ellipses. Later, he collaborated with Locke in writing the scenario for the choral entertainment *Sahdji—An African Ballet*, first staged in 1932 at the Eastman School of Music, with a score by William Grant Still.* Nugent was also an associate editor of Wallace Thurman's* *Fire!!** and contributed drawings along with those by Aaron Douglas,* as well as a story, "Smoke, Lillies and Jade," a deliberately impressionistic piece, again punctuated with ellipses, and vaguely pornographic and homosexual. He also contributed illustrations to Thurman's second magazine, *Harlem,** and served again as associate editor. Because of his wit and striking good looks, Nugent was a popular figure during the twenties in New York. He had arrived there at the age of thirteen and discovered Harlem by working as an errand boy, a bellhop in an all-women's hotel, a "secretary and confidence man for a modiste," an ornamental iron worker, a designer, and an elevator operator, so he reported in his autobiographical sketch for Countee Cullen's* anthology of black poetry, *Caroling Dusk,** in 1927 (p. 206). Two poems appeared there and another in *Opportunity.** Most of his work remained unpublished, however. During the years that followed he began to amass a large collection of Afro-Americana, and to many scholars and writers he has proven an invaluable source of information.
REFERENCES: Alain Locke, ed., *Plays of Negro Life*, 1927; Countee Cullen, ed., *Caroling Dusk*, 1927; David Levering Lewis, *When Harlem Was in Vogue*, 1981; Hatch-Billops; Richard Bruce Nugent. (MH, BK)

NUMBERS (gambling game). Often called "Harlem's favorite indoor sport," the numbers gambling game originally was based on winning numbers derived from the New York Clearing House bank exchanges and balances published in the newspapers: reading from the right, the seventh and eighth digits of the exchanges and the seventh of the balances; another way of putting it, the second and third digits in millionth figures opposite the exchanges and the third digit in millionth place opposite the balances. (In Bolito, a similar popular pastime, one bet only on two figures.) The runners were out before 10 A.M., collecting cash in exchange for slips from clients, as middlemen between the betters and the bankers. Runners were paid commissions on all of their collections, and then they reimbursed the winners, keeping a percentage for themselves. Not surpris-

ingly, since the game was illegal anyway, both runners and bankers would disappear on occasion, especially when receipts were heavy. A $1 bet could yield $540 on a hit, but the odds were 1,000–1. The actual numbers on which people bet—and nearly everybody in Harlem played the numbers—came from dreams, streetcar numbers, church hymn numbers, birthdays, and death dates.
REFERENCES: Carl Van Vechten, *Nigger Heaven*, 1926; Wallace Thurman, *Negro Life in New York's Harlem*, 1928. (BK)

O

THE OCTOROON (play), 1929. Probably revived because of the popular interest in black entertainment, Dion Boucicault's vivid antislavery melodrama of 1859 was given a straight and sincere production at the Maxine Eliott Theatre, beginning March 12. The fact that the cast was mixed—still a fairly unique circumstance in 1929—added to the interest of *The Octoroon*, although its run was brief.
REFERENCES: Burns Mantle, 1928–1929; NYTTR, 1972. (BK)

OH JOY (musical revue), 1922. At the Bamboo Isle at 57th Street and Eighth Avenue *Oh Joy* ran for four weeks, with Blanche Thompson, Ethel Williams, and the authors, Salem Whitney* and Homer Tutt.* It was notable for the song "Georgia Blues," with which Ethel Waters* had had a personal success during the out-of-town run in Boston. When she learned that the Bamboo Isle was not a theater but a tent set up in a vacant lot that doubled as a tennis court, Waters refused to appear, even though the producers had cushioned the spectators' benches.
REFERENCES: Ethel Waters, *His Eye Is on the Sparrow*, 1951; BB, 1980; Allen Woll, *Dictionary of the Black Theatre*, 1983. (BK)

OLIVER, [JOSEPH] KING (cornetist), 11 May 1885–8 April 1938. King Oliver got his nickname after an open musical combat contest with other cornet players in 1917, in the legendary Storyville, Louisiana, where he had been born thirty-two years before. Afterward, he formed the leading jazz band in New Orleans with Kid Ory,* and his own Creole Jazz Band was the first black group to make records, beginning in 1922. King Oliver's Syncopaters played at the Savoy Ballroom* from 1925 until 1927, but by 1928 his style of playing had gone out of fashion, and he spent his last years as a poolroom attendant back

in the South. King Oliver's "West End Blues" and "Sugar Foot Stomp" were among his more popular compositions.
REFERENCES: WWJ, 1972; NA, 1976. (BK)

OL' MAN SATAN (musical pageant), 1932. This "allegory" was given twenty-four performances at the Forrest Theatre beginning October 3, but the program indicated no author for *Ol' Man Satan*. Donald Heywood* arranged the music for what had evolved through the experiments of a troupe of black actors who rehearsed for several years without pay, hoping for a successor—financially as well as critically—to *The Green Pastures.** In what the *New York Times* reviewer referred to as the "childish crudity" of Heywood's "artless script," Mammy Jackson tells some youngsters a number of stories from the Bible, through which Satan's influence is demonstrated. It was "confused, overambitious, and somewhat repetitious," and a noisy stage crew did not contribute to a professional production (4 Oct. 1932, p. 26).
REFERENCE: NYTTR, 1972. (BK)

OLYMPIC TEAMS, UNITED STATES, 1924, 1928, 1932. Black Harlem took pride in those athletes who represented the race in the International Olympic Games. Photographs and interviews appeared regularly in the black press, and briefly a number of young men were touted as celebrities. In Paris in 1924 Hubbard Dehart won first place in the running broad jump, and Edward Gourdin won second place in the same event. In Los Angeles in 1932 Gourdin won first place in the running broad jump, and Ralph Metcalf won second place in the 100-meter dash and third place in the 200-meter dash. But the real star was Eddie Tolan (1900–31 Jan. 1967), "The Fastest Human Being," as he was regularly identified. Born in Denver, Colorado, he attended the University of Michigan where his natural gifts were developed. In 1932 he set a new record in the 100-meter dash and won a first gold medal, at 10.3 seconds. He also performed in the 1936 Olympics and then retired from competition to teach physical education in Michigan high schools.
REFERENCES: NYT, 1 Feb. 1967; NA, 1980. (BK)

O'NEILL, EUGENE (playwright), 16 October 1888–27 November 1953. America's premiere playwright began his career with at least three dramas in which black material was of paramount importance. "The Dreamy Kid," about superstition and gangster life, appeared in 1920. Both Charles Gilpin* and Paul Robeson* had personal successes in *The Emperor Jones** (1922), and it was this play that moved O'Neill from the Provincetown Playhouse to Broadway and his later, commercial success in the theater. In 1924 his play about miscegenation, *All God's Chillun Got Wings,** with a mixed cast, caused a furor.
REFERENCE: Arthur and Barbara Gelb, *O'Neill*, 1962. (BK)

ONE WAY TO HEAVEN (novel), 1932. Countee Cullen's* only novel, *One Way to Heaven*, begins promisingly as a love story between Sam and Mattie, two attractive Harlem lower-middle-class people. Sam is a con artist who proclaims his sinful ways at revivals; Mattie is a domestic servant who tries to reform him after they marry. The central section of the book, an unsuccessful satire of Harlem's upper crust, has little to do with Cullen's protagonists beyond Mattie's working for Constantia Brandon, a wealthy hostess. Joel Spingarn,* Carl Van Vechten,* Nora Holt,* and other familiar figures appear in thin disguise. At the novel's conclusion Sam dies of pneumonia, pretending for Mattie's sake that his desire for salvation is sincere. (BK)

OPPORTUNITY (periodical), 1923–1949. *Opportunity: A Journal of Negro Life* succeeded the *Bulletin* of the National Urban League* in 1923 and remained the association's official monthly publication until 1949. Edited in its early years by Charles S. Johnson,* the league's director of research, *Opportunity* ran to thirty-two pages an issue and sold for fifteen cents a copy. Johnson resigned in 1928 to take a position in the sociology department at Fisk University, replaced by Elmer A. Carter.* The magazine directed its message at an urban, educated, middle-class audience concerned with the problem of race relations in American society. One of *Opportunity*'s ancillary purposes was to promote the programs and policies of the Urban League. In addition to a report of pertinent news, the magazine's regular departments included "Social Progress," "Our Negro College," "Labor," and the "Survey of the Month," as well as notes on black accomplishments in the arts and professions. Although *Opportunity* sought to inform and instruct its readers on the social and economic condition of the race, and only secondarily on political issues, there was a decidedly literary character to the publication. James Weldon Johnson,* Helene Johnson,* Alain Locke,* Langston Hughes,* and, for a short time, Claude McKay* were but a few of the frequent contributors to the magazine. Countee Cullen* and Gwendolyn Bennett* each served for a period as literary critic in the 1920s, and in the 1930s Sterling Brown* of Howard University wrote the monthly column "The Literary Scene." Among his first contributions to *Opportunity* was a stinging critique of the twelve Southern poets—John Crowe Ransom and Allen Tate among them—who published their racist diatribe as *I'll Take My Stand*. A typical issue carried several poems, book reviews, and pieces of literary criticism, and there were occasional pieces of fiction from the leading figures of the Harlem Renaissance. Carl Van Vechten's* controversial *Nigger Heaven** was the subject of numerous articles and a lengthy review by James Weldon Johnson in the autumn 1926 issues. In 1925 *Opportunity* began sponsoring its own literary contest to encourage the creative talents of a younger generation of black Americans. The first poetry prize was given to Langston Hughes for "The Weary Blues"; Countee Cullen was the runner-up. The contest was suspended in 1927 for financial reasons but was resumed in 1934. *Opportunity* occasionally published the results of special investigations into the conditions of blacks in major American cities.

Its first issue contained a lengthy analysis of the Chicago Commission on Race Relations's report on the 1919 race riot*; the entire March 1929 issue, edited by E. Franklin Frazier,* addressed "Negro life in Chicago." Like other publications of its kind, *Opportunity* struggled to survive during the Great Depression and afterward. From 1944 it appeared four times a year until it ceased publication in 1949. Although a 1928 survey of the Negro press rated *Opportunity* the best of the postwar magazines, its monthly circulation never exceeded 11,000 copies. For a quarter-century *Opportunity* remained for black Americans a source of information and an outlet for creative expression, a voice for the Urban League's motto: "Not Alms, but Opportunity."
REFERENCES: *Opportunity*, 1923–1949; Eugene Gordon, "The Negro Press," *The Annals*, 140 (November 1928); David Levering Lewis, *When Harlem Was in Vogue*, 1981. (DD)

ORY, [EDWARD] KID (trombonist), 25 December 1886–23 December 1973. Kid Ory was a tailgate trombonist in his own New Orleans band from 1919 until 1924, after which he joined King Oliver* in Chicago. With Louis Armstrong's* band after 1926, Kid Ory wrote one of the great musical hits of the twenties, "Muskrat Ramble," as well as other popular songs. After the twenties he moved to the West Coast and started a chicken ranch, but during the forties he started another orchestra and toured with it. His original New Orleans group was the first to broadcast or record in that city so alive with jazz music. He died in Hawaii at eighty-seven.
REFERENCES: ASCAP, 1966; NA, 1976. (BK)

OUANGA (opera), 1932. Librettist John Frederick Matheus* and composer Clarence Cameron White* based their opera *Ouanga* upon the life of Jean Jacques Dessalines, the liberator and ruler of Haiti at the beginning of the nineteenth century. White and Matheus were colleagues at West Virginia State College, and in 1928 they had gone to Haiti to do field research into the folklore and folk music of the island. This led to their collaboration on a play with incidental music, *Tambour*, and a year or so later to their major work, the four-act opera *Ouanga*. (The word means "charm" or "talisman" in Haitian creole.) *Ouanga* was presented in concert form by the American Opera Society in Chicago in November 1932; the first stage performance was given by the H. T. Burleigh* Music Association in South Bend, Indiana, in June 1949, with the composer conducting. A local critic wrote: "This is a rich score. The themes are on a rhythmic pattern that jolts and sways with a jungle beat and often sweeps to majestic, terrifying heights" (quoted in MBA, p. 290). The Negro opera company Dra-Mu produced *Ouanga* at the Academy of Music in Philadelphia in 1950, and the National Negro Opera Company gave concert performances of it in 1956 at the Metropolitan Opera House and at Carnegie Hall in New York.
REFERENCE: MBA, 1971. (DA)

OVINGTON, MARY WHITE (political activist, writer), 11 April 1865–15 July 1951. Born in New York of abolitionist parents, Mary White Ovington dedicated her life to the social and political equality of black Americans and the elimination of racism. She is best known for her work with the NAACP,* which she helped found in 1909 and worked for until her death. Her autobiography *The Walls Came Tumbling Down* (1947) details her involvement as well as her early efforts in New York to establish model housing projects for blacks: The Tuskegee and the Lincoln Settlement for Negroes. Somewhat less remembered is her wide range of writings. Her first work, *Half a Man: The Status of the Negro in New York* (1911), is a sociological study of the different roles available to white and black women in the first decade of the century. *Portraits in Color* (1927) is a biographical rendering of twenty black men and women. In addition, Ovington wrote fiction—"White Brute," which appeared in *The Masses* (1915), and *The Shadow* (1920)—and two plays, *The Awakening* (1923) and *Phillis Wheatley* (1932). Finally, she wrote two novels for children—*Hazel* (1913) for girls and *Zeki: A School Boy at Tolliver* (1931) for boys—and helped to edit *The Upward Path: A Reader for Colored Children* (1920), a collection of poems and stories by black writers. Ovington also contributed to *The Crisis** symposium "The Negro in Art: How Shall He Be Portrayed?"* in April 1926. Her response reflected her lifelong effort to achieve human equality for all: that stereotyping and propaganda in art should be condemned.

REFERENCES: B. Joyce Ross, *J. E. Spingarn and the Rise of the NAACP*, 1972; Leonard Courtney Archer, *Black Images in the American Theatre*, 1973; NAW, 1980. (MH)

OWEN, CHANDLER (journalist), 5 April 1889–November 1967. Chandler Owen collaborated with A. Philip Randolph* in publishing, Socialist, and union activities. Owen was born April 5, 1889, in Warrenton, North Carolina, of parents affluent enough to send him to a private high school and Virginia Union University. In 1913 he gained admission to the New York School of Philanthropy, the social work arm of Columbia University. He completed his work there with the help of one of the first social work fellowships granted by the National Urban League.* In 1915 Owen met Randolph, and the two spent hours together studying and discussing politics, working-class history, and socialism. They joined the Socialist party during World War I, became part of the legion of soapbox orators and philosophers who spoke on Harlem street corners, and founded together and coedited the impressive radical periodical *The Messenger** from 1917 to 1923. Owen was a brilliant writer and analyst and possessed a marvelous memory; yet he was still less impressive both physically and as an orator than his friend Randolph. According to George S. Schuyler* in his autobiography *Black and Conservative*, Owen "was a facile and acidulous writer, a man of ready wit and agile tongue endowed with a saving grace of cynicism" (p. 137). In the early 1920s Owen lost some of his zeal for socialism and for publication of the magazine, and he left New York to take a position with the Chicago *Bee* in

1923. For the next forty-five years Owen involved himself in local Republican politics and public relations ventures; in both he was at best modestly successful. He and Randolph remained on excellent terms until Owen's death in November 1967.

REFERENCES: George S. Schuyler, *Black and Conservative*, 1966; Jervis Anderson, *A. Philip Randolph*, 1973; Theodore Kornweibel, Jr., *No Crystal Stair*, 1974. (DS)

P

PACE, HARRY H. (music publisher, record company and insurance executive), 6 January 1884–1943. Harry Pace was a professor of Greek and Latin at Lincoln University, Jefferson City, Missouri, and a sometime lyricist and singer when he met W. C. Handy* in 1908. The two young men formed the Pace and Handy Music Company, the first black music publishing firm in the country and one of the first to issue blues* compositions. Pace left the firm in 1913 to become secretary-treasurer of Standard Life Insurance Company in Atlanta, rejoined Handy when the firm moved to New York in 1918, and left the firm again in 1921 to form the Pace Phonograph Company. This company—almost immediately renamed the Black Swan Phonograph Corporation*—was the first black-owned recording company in the country, and Pace helped pioneer blues recordings by signing up artists such as Ethel Waters,* Alberta Hunter,* and Trixie Smith.* Pace sold the company to the Paramount Record Company in 1924 and returned to the insurance business, as founder and first president of Northeastern Life Insurance Company of Newark, New Jersey. Northeastern later combined with two other insurance companies to form Supreme Liberty Life Insurance Company, with Harry H. Pace as first president.
REFERENCES: "Biggest Northern Business," *Ebony*, Aug. 1946, p. 43; MBA, 1971; BB, 1980. (DA)

PADMORE, GEORGE [MALCOLM IVAN MEREDITH NURSE] (political activist, editor), 1902 or 1903–1959. Born in Trinidad, George Padmore was educated at Columbia, Fisk, and Howard universities, where he pursued premedical study, and then at New York University Law School. In 1927 he abandoned education in favor of the Communist party and, in the following year, began editing the *Negro Champion*, later known as *Harlem Liberator*. In 1929 he went to Russia as head of the Negro Bureau of the Red International of Labor Unions, and in 1931 he headed the International Trade Union Committee of Negro Workers in Germany. He edited *Negro Worker* during this period, but

in 1933 he resigned from the Communist party because of ideological differences. Later, he was involved in various Pan-African organizations.
REFERENCE: James R. Hooker, *Black Revolutionary*, 1967. (BK)

PALMS (periodical), 1923–1929. Published six times a year, initially in Guadalajara, Mexico, and then in Aberdeen, Washington, *Palms* was a poetry journal edited by Idella Purnell. Countee Cullen* served as editor for the October 1926 issue, devoted entirely to the work of black poets, including Lewis Alexander,* Gwendolyn Bennett,* Arna Bontemps,* William Stanley Braithwaite,* Waring Cuney,* W.E.B. Du Bois,* Jessie Fauset,* Langston Hughes,* Georgia Douglas Johnson,* Helene Johnson,* Richard Bruce Nugent,* Albert Rice,* Clarissa Scott (Delany),* Anne Spencer,* and Cullen himself. Walter White* contributed the introductory essay "The Negro Renaissance," tracing the influence of African arts on twentieth-century music and painting; Alain Locke* reviewed Langston Hughes's *Weary Blues*;* and brief biographies concluded the issue. (BK)

PAN-AFRICAN CONGRESSES, 1919, 1921, 1923, 1927, 1947. The brainchild of W.E.B. Du Bois,* the Pan-African Congresses were an attempt to bring blacks from around the world together to pressure white leaders for greater freedom and opportunities for development. In 1919 the NAACP* asked Du Bois to investigate the racist treatment of black troops in Europe. While there, Du Bois organized the first Pan-African Congress, he later wrote, to give blacks a chance to express their concerns to the conferees at the Versailles Peace Conference. Fifty-seven delegates—sixteen Americans, twenty West Indians, and twelve Africans among them—answered Du Bois's call and met in Paris in February 1919 at the Grand Hotel. Although Du Bois and the delegates were able to confer with officials of the leading colonial countries, Du Bois termed the results of the Congress "small," as he encountered "the real crux of the problem of my time . . . the widespread effort of white Europe to use the labor and material of the colored world for its own wealth and power" (*Dusk of Dawn*, p. 261). Still, Du Bois found it useful for blacks to sit together with white world leaders and try to reach broad cooperation that might lead to a more "peaceful and accelerated development of black folk" (p. 275). Therefore, he organized a second Congress, 29 August–6 September 1921, which met successively in London, Brussels, and Paris with 113 delegates present. The effectiveness of the congress was nullified by both the unpromising postwar European political climate and the fact that many people confused the activities of Marcus Garvey* with the Pan-African Congresses of Du Bois (much to the chagrin of the latter). Du Bois nonetheless attempted a Third Pan-African Congress in 1923 in London, Paris, and Lisbon, but it was not well attended; a fourth Congress in New York in 1927 met a similar fate, and a fifth Congress scheduled for Tunis in 1929 was cancelled. Du Bois did preside over a Fifth Pan-African Congress in Manchester, England, in 1947.

REFERENCES: W.E.B. Du Bois, *Dusk of Dawn*, 1940; Rayford Logan and Michael R. Winston, eds., *W.E.B. Du Bois*, 1971. (DS)

THE PANAMA TRIO (theatrical act), c. 1912–1915. The Panama Trio— Florence Mills,* Ada Smith* ("Bricktop"),* and Cora Green*—toured coast-to-coast on the Pantage vaudeville circuit in the 1910s. They may have adopted the name Panama Trio when they performed at the Panama Club in Chicago; Alberta Hunter* remembers that when she was singing at the club sometime after 1910, in the rough and noisy room upstairs, the Panama Trio was playing downstairs in the room that featured "more of a quiet reserved type of entertainment" (Shapiro and Hentoff, *Hear Me Talkin' to Ya*, p. 87.) Mills, Bricktop, and Green all achieved individual fame later.

REFERENCES: Nat Shapiro and Nat Hentoff, eds., *Hear Me Talkin' to Ya*, 1955; BB, 1980. (DA)

PANASSIÉ, HUGHUES (jazz historian and critic), 27 February 1912–8 December 1974. Forced into physical inactivity due to poliomyelitis at the age of five, Hughues Panassié became a devotee of jazz and by the age of eighteen knew as much about this form of music—especially Dixieland—as anyone in his native France. In 1932 he founded the Hot Club de France and in 1934 wrote the first of his seventeen books on jazz, *Le Jazz Hot*. In his manuscript inventory to the James Weldon Johnson* Memorial Collection of Negro Arts and Letters at Yale University, Carl Van Vechten* wrote: "This is the first *important* book to deal solely with this subject. As the material is all highly controversial there is not a single statement herein about which there could be no argument" (p. 188). *Le Jazz Hot* was translated into English and issued by Witmark in America, in an extremely small and therefore rare edition, the following year when Panassié came to the United States to give his Sorbonne lectures. In 1948 he organized the first jazz festival in Nice.

REFERENCES: EJ, 1970; NYT, 10 Dec. 1974; CVV. (MH, BK)

PANSY (musical comedy), 1929. An "All-Colored Musical Novelty," *Pansy* had a book by Alex Belledna and songs by Maceo Pinkard,* but for Brooks Atkinson, reviewing it in the *New York Times* after its opening on May 14, it was a "nightmare of lost cues, forgotten words, embarrassed performers and frantic efforts backstage to avoid complete collapse behind the footlights" (15 May 1929, p. 36). No plot summary is extant, but the cast of characters included a dean of students and some "campus cut-ups." The hisses and boos gradually subsided into stunned disbelief at this "worst show of all time," but its three performances are worth documenting because of the appearance of Bessie Smith* in the cast: "Obese and wickedly orbed," Atkinson concluded, she reappeared

at infrequent intervals through the evening to "break the shock of complete defeat."
REFERENCES: Burns Mantle, 1928–1929; NYTTR, 1972. (BK)

PASSING (novel), 1929. Nella Larsen's* *Passing* contrasts two women who are light enough to pass. Clare Kendry, the central character, is married to a white man and is passing in order to escape the poverty of her childhood. At tea one day she meets her former friend Irene Redfield, who is married to a black physician and lives in Harlem. Clare Kendry wants to return to the world she left behind but fears that she will be discovered. Nonetheless, she does participate in Harlem's social life. At the end, after her husband finds out her identity, she falls to her death from a seventeenth-floor apartment. The author leaves the conclusion unresolved, for the reader does not know if she fell accidentally or if, in jealous anger, Irene Redfield pushed her. Larsen reveals the hypocrisy and pretentiousness of the black middle class as well as the psychic price paid by those who seek security and status through passing. (DI)

PA WILLIAMS' GAL (play), 1923. F. H. Wilson, who later, as Frank Wilson,* had some success as a dramatic star in the leading role in *Porgy*,* had his first play produced at the Lafayette Theatre* in September 1923, just at the end of the seven-year tenure of the Lafayette Players Stock Company.* Richard B. Harrison,* later to play "De Lawd" in The Green Pastures,* and Rose McClendon,* later to appear in several serious roles on Broadway, were in the cast of *Pa Williams' Gal*. This family drama about a girl who disobeys her father was long on coincidence and apparently mediocre in its structure, but Theophilus Lewis,* in his monthly theater column in *The Messenger*,* thought it was the most valuable contribution to black theater of the year, because despite its limitations it was the first attempt by a serious black author to write a serious play. *Pa Williams' Gal* ran for a week; at the Lafayette, after that length of time, a show continued only on the basis of audience response, and in 1923 a "hodge-podge of smalltime vaudeville" with Billy Higgins* called *Follow Me* proved far more popular and lasted for three weeks (*The Messenger*, Dec. 1923, p. 929).
REFERENCES: Theophilus Lewis, "Theatre," *The Messenger*, Oct., Dec. 1923. (BK)

PAYTON, PHILIP A., JR. (realtor), 27 February 1876–? Philip A. Payton, Jr., sometimes called the "Father of Colored Harlem," was instrumental in opening up apartments in Harlem for black occupancy. Born in Westfield, Massachusetts, in 1876, Payton went south for his education, graduating from Livingstone College in North Carolina in 1898. He arrived in New York City in 1899, and after suffering through odd jobs and several unsuccessful years as a fledgling realtor, he began to do well by managing black tenements for white landlords. By 1904 he was the leading black realtor in the city, and he had founded his own company, The Afro-American Realty Company, to buy, build, or lease homes. Although he had strong community support—financial and moral— and the help of Booker T. Washington and his associates, Payton did not have sufficient experience to handle his growing capital properly, and the company went bankrupt by 1907. Still, Payton had moved hundreds of blacks into formerly all-white buildings and had laid the foundation for black Harlem. Apparently, Payton continued to do business in Harlem even after his company folded, although his activities after 1910 cannot be easily determined today.

REFERENCES: WWCR, 1915; Claude McKay, *Harlem*, 1940; Gilbert Osofsky, *Harlem*, 1966. (DS)

PETERKIN, JULIA [MOOD] (writer), 31 October 1880–10 August 1961. One of the few white writers admired by black intellectuals like W.E.B. DuBois* and Walter White,* Julia Peterkin introduced readers to the lives of the Gullah natives in South Carolina. She first came to prominence in 1924 with *Green Thursday*, a volume of sketches. *Black April*, a tragedy built around events on her own plantation, Lang Syne, where 400 to 500 blacks lived and worked, made a commercial and critical success in 1927. In the following year her rich folk comedy *Scarlet Sister Mary*, with its memorable, free-spirited heroine and her nine children (eight of them illegitimate), won the Pulitzer Prize. *Bright Skin*, however, proved unconvincing in 1932. Peterkin concluded her career as a writer in 1933 with *Roll, Jordan, Roll*, a nonfiction work about plantation life prepared in collaboration with Doris Ullman, the white photographer. The strong support she received from Carl Sandburg and H. L. Mencken,* as well as from influential black writers, was later contradicted by Black Arts movement critics and others who accused her of ignoring social and economic problems in favor of lurid local color. To any objective reader Peterkin's best work is clearly sympathetic to black Americans; moreover, she is a sorely underrated writer.

REFERENCES: Emily Clark, *Innocence Abroad*, 1930; John M. Bradbury, *Renaissance in the South*, 1963; Thomas H. Landess, *Julia Peterkin*, 1976. (BK)

PETERSON, DOROTHY [RANDOLPH] (teacher, sometime actress, promoter), c. 1900–? "One of the best known and most social of Negroes in Greater New York," Dorothy Peterson was born around the turn of the century and by 1925 had become a strong force in the literary matters of the Harlem Renaissance, according to Carl Van Vechten* (CVV, p. 37). The daughter of Jerome Bowers Peterson,* she turned their family home in Brooklyn into a modest literary salon for a time. Later, she and her brother Sidney shared an apartment that served as an East Side equivalent to the Regina Anderson*–Ethel Nance* haven on Harlem's West Side. In 1930 Dorothy Peterson took a leave of absence from her teaching position in a public high school to play Cain's girlfriend in Marc Connelly's *Green Pastures*,* but this seems to have been her only foray onstage, although she was active in some of Harlem's little theater groups. Many friends recognized her as the model for Van Vechten's heroine in his Harlem novel

Nigger Heaven,* a beautiful and cultured woman intensely interested in her racial heritage. In later years Dorothy Peterson taught in the Wadleigh High School for Girls in Harlem, devoting much of her time to gather materials for the James Weldon Johnson* Memorial Collection of Negro Arts and Letters at Yale University.
REFERENCES: Carl Van Vechten, "*Keep A-Inchin' Along*," 1979; CVV. (BK)

PETERSON, JEROME BOWERS (journalist), 12 September 1859–19 February 1943. At fourteen Jerome Bowers Peterson left his Brooklyn school to become a messenger for Freedman's Savings and Trust Company. After putting himself through night school, he joined the staff of the New York *Globe* and then founded the New York *Age*,* becoming with T. Thomas Fortune* a contributing editor before the turn of the century. In 1904 he was appointed U.S. consul to Venezuela. His daughter Dorothy Peterson* was a popular figure during the Harlem Renaissance and worked at the Harlem branch of the New York Public Library. His son Sidney became a medical doctor and served at Seaview Hospital on Staten Island and in the New York City Department of Health. Jerome Bowers Peterson's home in Brooklyn was a meeting place for young black intellectuals and one of the first to encourage mixed gatherings. The locale is memorialized in Carl Van Vechten's* *Nigger Heaven*ted* as the home of Aaron Summers and its ambience fully described.
REFERENCE: CVV. (BK)

PICKENS, WILLIAM (educator, writer), 15 January 1881–6 April 1954. Educated at Yale (Phi Beta Kappa, 1904) and Fisk universities (M.A., 1905), professor of classics at Talladega College until 1914 and Wiley College in Marshall, Texas, until 1918, when he was given an honorary doctorate there, and dean and subsequently vice-president at Morgan State College in Maryland, William Pickens combined scholarship with a life of political activity. He resigned from Morgan in 1920 to become field secretary of the NAACP.* With Joel Spingarn,* Pickens established the Negro Officers Training Corps during World War I, and he may have coined the phrase "The New Negro," having given one of his books that title fully nine years before Alain Locke* used it for his own anthology of writings by and about contemporary Afro-Americans. Although critical of the UNIA,* Pickens understood that Marcus Garvey's* success reflected a deep and real need on the part of black Americans for racial pride and a political voice. Pickens's major work in the twenties, *The Vengeance of the Gods and Three Other Stories of Real American Color*,* reflects this attitude. Other relevant works are *Abraham Lincoln: Man and Statesman* (1910), *Frederic Douglass and the Spirit of Freedom* (1912), *Heir to Slaves* (1911, autobiography), *The New Negro* (1916), *Bursting Bonds* (1923, a revision of

his 1911 autobiography), and *American Aesop: The Humor of the Negro, the Jew, the Irishman, and Others* (1926).
REFERENCES: PR, 1920; Hugh Gloster, *Negro Voices in American Fiction*, 1948; NYT, 7 Apr. 1954; WWW, 1963. (MH)

PIERCE, BILLY (dancing teacher), 14 June 1890–1934? Billy Pierce ran the Broadway Dancing School in 1923 and tutored whites in how to do the Charleston and the black bottom, both of which had originated in black shows; the sugar foot strut, from *Rio Rita*; and the varsity drag, from *Good News*. Fred and Adele Astaire, Helen Morgan, Libby Holman, Marilyn Miller, Ramon Navarro, Louise Brooks, Ann Pennington, Clifton Webb, Ed Wynn—all of them well-known white performers—and, by rumor, Lillian and Dorothy Gish, Carl Van Vechten,* Fania Marinoff,* and Anita Loos were among his more celebrated pupils. Billy Pierce received a master's degree from Howard University and then worked as a reporter on the *Washington Eagle*, the Chicago *Defender*,* the *Originator*, the *Inter-State Tattler*,* and other black papers. Briefly, he was manager of the Attucks Theatre in Washington, D.C., before opening his dance studio. In the thirties he staged and danced in Charles Cochran's *Evergreen* by Rogers and Hart in London and seems to have stayed on there afterward.
REFERENCES: WWCA, 1933; Nancy Cunard, ed., *Negro*, 1970; CVV. (BK)

PINKARD, MACEO (musician), 27 June 1898–21 July 1962. The composer of "Sweet Georgia Brown" was born in West Virginia, and toured with his own orchestra in the early twenties. He founded his Maceo Pinkard Publication Agency and the Omaha Theatrical Company to assist young black performers in a segregated marketplace. He wrote the score for *Liza*,* a 1922 failure, and contributed to other musicals of the period, counting among his popular songs "Gimme a Little Kiss, Will You, Huh?" and Ethel Waters's* "Sweet Man."
REFERENCE: ASCAP, 1966. (BK)

PITTSBURGH COURIER (newspaper), 1910– . The *Pittsburgh Courier* grew from a tiny sheet (500 copies on its maiden run on 15 January 1910) to become the leading black weekly in the nation by the late 1920s, with a circulation of 250,000. During the *Courier*'s first year of publication Robert L. Vann,* an attorney who initially served as the paper's lawyer, took over as editor. Under Vann's leadership the *Courier* consistently addressed the major problems blacks faced in Pittsburgh and the nation: inadequate housing, few job opportunities, inferior education and health care, and misrepresentation by the white press, to name a few. Still, the *Courier* was not a left-wing paper. It championed black capitalism and, in general, held a conservative-to-moderate stance compared with more forthright or radical publications such as the Chicago *Defender** and *The Messenger** on economic issues, racial accommodation, and loyalty of blacks to the United States. The one exception in this area was the *Courier*'s strong support, for several years, of the efforts of A. Philip Randolph* to organize the

Brotherhood of Sleeping Car Porters* in the 1920s. At that time the *Courier* developed a truly national circulation, since Vann attracted national advertisers and excellent writers who wrote interesting material.

One study of the black press in the late 1920s claimed that the *Courier* was read chiefly because of its feature stories, sports coverage, editorials, and special columns such as George Schuyler's* "Views and Reviews," one of the most popular and controversial offerings in black American journalism. Schuyler, who also was writing editorials for the *Courier* by 1926, attacked Marcus Garvey* unmercifully as "America's Greatest Comedian" and was not particularly sympathetic to the Harlem Renaissance, one segment of which he dubbed "Negro Art Hokum." Among the other feature writers who joined the *Courier* in the mid-1920s were John C. Clark, Joel A. Rogers,* Julia Bumbrey Jones, and many more, including Floyd Calvin,* who managed the *Courier*'s New York office and began weekly broadcasts of the *"Pittsburgh Courier* Hour" over station WGBC in New York. By the end of the decade the *Courier* had supplanted the *Defender* as the best black paper in America, according to several experts. Vann's personal attacks in the *Courier* on James Weldon Johnson* and W.E.B. Du Bois* in the mid-1920s also increased the paper's circulation. Vann and the *Courier* switched to the Democratic party in 1932, a move that may have encouraged many blacks to end their traditional attachment to the Republicans.
REFERENCES: Eugene Gordon, "The Negro Press," *The Annals*, 1928; Andrew Buni, *Robert L. Vann of the "Pittsburgh Courier,"* 1974. (DS)

PLANTATION CLUB (cabaret), 1922–1924. In 1929 Cab Calloway* was seduced away from the Cotton Club* for a new cabaret that attempted to duplicate it, but the Cotton Club was run by Owney Madden* and his gang, and the result of the theft was a brawl in which, in the memory of one witness, the bar was physically uprooted and transplanted out in the gutter. Cab Calloway went back to the Cotton Club. All of this occurred at the end of the decade. Also called the Plantation Club, Sam Salvin's cabaret at 50th Street and Broadway had flourished earlier (1922–1924) with black song and dance acts appearing during supper hours. Florence Mills* was there in 1922, followed by Ethel Waters* for a summer run, and Josephine Baker* did a comedy routine with a trombone about the same time. The *Plantation Revue** began as a floor show there.
REFERENCES: Ethel Waters, *His Eye Is on the Sparrow*, 1951; Jim Haskins, *The Cotton Club*, 1977. (BK)

PLANTATION REVUE (musical revue), 1922. Lew Leslie* and Will Vodery* expanded the Plantation Club* floor show into a full-length revue that opened at the 48th Street Theatre on July 17 in a "spontaneous outburst of song, dance, color and buoyant spirits," even though the *New York Times* reviewer regretted "several rough jokes" and some Broadway imitations. Florence Mills,* her

husband U. S. Thompson,* Edith Wilson,* and Shelton Brooks* were in the
cast (18 July 1922, p. 18).
REFERENCE: NYTTR, 1972. (BK)

PLAYS OF NEGRO LIFE (anthology), 1927. Alain Locke* and T. Montgomery Gregory* edited the first book devoted exclusively to black subject matter
in dramatic form. Subtitled "A Sourcebook of Native American Drama," these
twenty plays "of the Contemporary Negro Theatre" include works by Willis
Richardson,* Frank Wilson,* John Matheus,* Eulalie Spence,* Jean Toomer,*
Georgia Douglas Johnson,* and Richard Bruce Nugent,* among other young
black playwrights, many of which were available only in back issues of *Opportunity* and *The Crisis.* Plays by white dramatists Eugene O'Neill,* Paul Green,*
and Ridgely Torrence, among others, completed the collection. Locke contributed a preface and compiled a bibliography; Gregory compiled a chronology
with cast lists; Aaron Douglas* added decorations and illustrations; and a fine
selection of photographs from productions was included as well. At the time
Plays of Negro Life was published, not one serious play by a black playwright
had yet been given a Broadway production. (BK)

PLUM BUN (novel), 1929. Jessie Fauset's* *Plum Bun*, subtitled "A Novel
without a Moral," focuses on the psychological development of Angela Murray.
The five-part structure of the novel shows the stages of her growth and echoes
the title's allusion to the nursery rhyme:

> To Market, to Market
> To buy a Plum Bun;
> Home again, Home again,
> Market is done.

After her parents' death Angela moves from Philadelphia to New York to study
painting. Although she first succumbs to romantic illusion she eventually learns
honesty, independence, and love. With Anthony Cross she does not need to pass
nor does he. Poor and light skinned, Anthony with Angela can accept who he
is despite racial discrimination and violence. In contrast to her sister Virginia,
who teaches music to black children in Harlem and marries her true love, Angela
must journey to that courageous self-definition that enables her to flourish cre-
atively as an artist as well as a whole person. The novel ends happily and
instructively, despite its subtitle. (DI)

POD'S AND JERRY'S (cabaret). Also called The Catagonia Club, Pod's and
Jerry's was a hangout for Broadway stars like Paul Whiteman, Beatrice Lillie,
Mae West, and Tallulah Bankhead, according to some memories, although none
of these people allude to this place in their autobiographies or for that matter to
other Harlem cabarets. The clientele was predominantly white, however, and

celebrities did sometimes drop by to hear Willie-the-Lion Smith* entertain. It was located on 133rd Street.
REFERENCES: David Levering Lewis, *When Harlem Was in Vogue*, 1981; Jervis Anderson, *This Was Harlem*, 1982. (BK)

POPO AND FIFINA (children's novel), 1932. Arna Bontemps* and Langston Hughes* collaborated on *Popo and Fifina*, a story about two black children in Haiti whose family moves from the village to a farm, where their father, Papa Jean, becomes a fisherman. E. Simms Campbell,* soon to become one of the leading cartoonists for *Esquire* magazine, contributed illustrations. (BK)

PORGY (novel), 1925. Du Bose Heyward's* *Porgy* is set among the Gullah-speaking blacks on the Charleston, South Carolina, waterfront. Porgy, a silent and generally aloof black cripple, begs in the day and in the evening gambles what little he has collected. His life is sad until he meets Bess who brings him both love and a renewed sense of youth. His happiness, however, is broken once Bess begins to try "happy-dus," and she is taken back by Crown, her former lover. (MH)

PORGY (play), 1927. Based on his successful novel, Du Bose Heyward's* dramatic version of *Porgy** written in collaboration with his wife, Dorothy Heyward,* was "a chocolate covered lithograph strip, splashed with color, disorderly, unwieldly, heavy and spontaneous by turns, yet always true," according to the *New York Times* reviewer after its Theatre Guild opening on October 10 (11 Oct. 1927, p. 26). The sordid atmosphere that in the novel had served as background took over the plot that ran "timidly through a sprawling production." It featured a number of popular performers of the period, and Frank Wilson* was especially effective in the leading role, although the acting, on the whole, was pronounced "undisciplined." Part of its popular success was surely attributable to a white audience's demand for "an ebony carnival of crap-shooting, murders, blaring picnics, comedy bits, passionate spirituals, a hurricane" (11 Oct. 1927, p. 26). A few days later, in a Sunday editorial follow-up, the *Times* said the play was "ruder, deeper, franker, coarser than it is between book covers" and blamed that on the black acting which "expressed those qualities of human nature" (16 Oct. 1927, sec. 9, p. 1).
REFERENCES: Burns Mantle, 1927–1928; NYTTR, 1972. (BK)

PORGY AND BESS (opera), 1935. *Porgy and Bess* by George Gershwin* was the last large-scale Broadway production to make use of an all-black cast during the thirties, too late to be considered as part of the Harlem Renaissance, yet deeply involved with people and works inextricably identified with the twenties. Du Bose Heyward* based the libretto on his 1925 novel and 1927 play *Porgy,** but he "cut out the conventional Negro vaudeville stuff that is authentic and plenty 'hot' as well," as he wrote to Gershwin during preparations (quoted in

Jablonski and Stewart, *The Gershwin Years*, p. 196). The popularity of black entertainments during the twenties had motivated Gershwin as early as 1926 to consider a serious undertaking based on Carl Van Vechten's* *Nigger Heaven,** but the following year he read *Porgy* and immediately wrote to suggest a collaboration. Heyward and his wife Dorothy Heyward* were already collaborating on the dramatic version, so the opera was delayed temporarily. With lyrics by his brother Ira, Gershwin composed the score between 1933 and 1935, and the full production, cut from four hours to a conventional playing time, opened at the Alvin Theatre on October 10. Todd Duncan and Anne Brown sang the leading roles, with Georgette Harvey* and Ruby Elzy in subsidiary parts; Eva Jessye* conducted the choir; and John Bubbles,* who read no music, was Gershwin's hold-out choice for Sportin' Life. Audiences were briefly enthusiastic but critics were not. It went on tour after only 124 performances and closed five months later in Washington, D.C., at a loss of $70,000. In part, the country's economy explains the failure; in part, the avant-garde nature of the work was the cause; but a falling off of interest in black subject matter explains it too.
REFERENCES: Edward Jablonski and Lawrence D. Stewart, *The Gershwin Years*, 1958; GD, 1980. (BK)

PORTER, JAMES A[MOS] (painter), 1905–28 February 1970. James A. Porter was an outstanding artist and head of Howard University's art department for more than forty years. Born in Baltimore in 1905, Porter attended Washington's Armstrong High School, where he graduated in 1923. He received a B.S. degree in art with honors from Howard in 1927 and later earned an M.A. in art history from the Fine Arts Graduate Center of New York University in 1936. Porter's paintings have been shown in almost every important exhibition of Negro art in this country since 1927. He received honorable mention in the Harmon Foundation* Exhibition of 1928 for the portrait "Sarah," and in 1933 he won the Arthur Schomburg* Portrait Prize for the figure painting "Woman Holding a Jug." His intense interest in African art did not begin until 1935, when he spent a summer at the Sorbonne in Paris and then travelled through Europe studying African art and European painting. In 1943 he published *Modern Negro Art* (later reprinted by Arno Press), which became a standard reference work for that field. He also wrote a historical monograph, a catalog-brochure, and prizewinning book reviews. In addition, he illustrated books for others. Still, he should be most remembered for his skill as a portrait artist.
REFERENCE: *Negro History Bulletin*, Apr. 1970. (DS)

POSTON, ROBERT L[INCOLN] (journalist), 1890–1924. With his brother Ulysses, Robert Poston was one of the active leaders in the Universal Negro Improvement Association.* Born in Kentucky, he joined the staff of *Negro World** after an apprentice career with newspapers in Louisville and Detroit. While the African Blood Brotherhood vied with the UNIA for members, Poston clearly distinguished between them in *Negro World*, insisting that the latter "does not link up with white organizations, to quote the words of the *Crusader Bulletin*, 'whose interests are identical with our interests' '' (4 Mar. 1922). In 1923 he married the young sculptor Augusta Savage,* an alliance cut short by Poston's death six months later, when enroute to Europe he contracted pneumonia. His brother continued to write for *Negro World*, condemning journalists like George S. Schuyler* and H. L. Mencken* for their antireligious attitudes. A younger brother, Ted Poston,* became a well-known journalist after the Harlem Renaissance.

REFERENCES: *Negro World*, 4 Mar. 1922; NYT, 27 Mar. 1962; Theodore G. Vincent, ed., *Voices of a Black Nation*, 1973; Andrew Buni, *Robert L. Vann of the Pittsburgh Courier*, 1974. (BK)

POSTON, [T. R.] TED (journalist), 1907–? The younger brother of *Negro World** writers Ulysses Poston and Robert Poston,* Ted Poston was born in Kentucky and took a cattle boat from Savannah, Georgia, to New York when he was still in his teens. He worked as a dining-car waiter and free-lance reporter and at other odd jobs until 1932, when he joined a number of other young black artists and writers for the ill-fated *Black and White** film project of the Meschrabpom Film Corporation in Russia. He returned from the journey, strongly anti-Communist, to begin work as a reporter for the *Amsterdam News** and later as a sports writer for the white *New York Post*. A successful story about George "Father Divine" Baker's* process server being beaten up by some of that popular religious leader's "angels" secured Poston a position as full-time staff reporter. He became the first black general-assignments writer on a large-circulation daily. His earlier work for the black press on the *Scottsboro* case* and the March on Washington, D.C., on behalf of the defendants is eloquent testimony to his talent as a journalist.

REFERENCES: New York *Amsterdam News*, 10 May 1910; *Newsweek*, 11 Apr. 1949; Theodore J. Vincent, ed., *Voices of a Black Nation*, 1973. (BK)

POWELL, ADAM CLAYTON, SR. (clergyman), 5 May 1865–12 June 1953. Adam Clayton Powell, Sr., was perhaps the most famous black clergyman in the United States during the first half of the twentieth century. Born in Franklin County, Virginia, the son of a German planter and a part black, part American Indian woman, Powell had only a few years of schooling in his youth. He worked at a variety of odd jobs and lived a carefree and (what he would later consider) immoral life until he was converted at a revival meeting in March 1885. After his conversion he resolved to enter politics and study law, and from 1888 to 1892 he attended Virginia Union University, graduating from both the theological department and the normal/academic department. After holding successful pastorates in St. Paul, Philadelphia, and New Haven, Powell was named pastor of the venerable Abyssinian Baptist Church in New York City in December 1908. Powell combined superb business sense with an impressive preaching style, and he managed to enrich his congregation both materially and spiritually. He was one of the first black leaders to buy land in Harlem (for the church); by 1923 a new building for the Abyssinian Baptist congregation had been constructed on 138th Street and the church had realized a fine profit on the real estate transactions. Powell turned the church into a community center that dispensed aid of various kinds to needy persons, and he railed against immorality, profligacy, and racism.

There were few important religious, interracial, or civil rights activities in which Powell was not involved between 1908 and the outbreak of World War II. For example, he was a founder of the National Urban League,* an early leader of the NAACP,* an organizer of the Silent Protest Parade* of 1917, and a proponent of race pride. The few goals he did not attain in his life—to enter politics and be elected to Congress—were reached by his son Adam Clayton Powell, Jr., who was the first black to represent New York City in Congress. Even after his retirement in 1937, the elder Powell continued to be a community leader in Harlem. His relevant works are *Patriotism and the Negro* (1918) and *Against the Tide* (1938).

REFERENCES: WWCA, 1933; DAB, 1937. (DS)

PREER, EVELYN (actress), 26 July 1896–18 November 1932. Born in Mississippi, Evelyn Preer began acting in high school in Chicago and subsequently toured the Orpheum Circuit as a leading lady with Charley Johnson's vaudeville troupe. For several years she acted with the Lafayette Players* in New York, appearing in *Why Wives Go Wrong* and *The Good Li'l Bad Girl* and on Broadway in *Lulu Belle,* *Rang Tang,* and *Porgy.* In 1923 she played the title role in *Salome*, part of a triple bill presented by the Ethiopian Art Players,* which also included *The Chip Woman's Fortune* and *A Comedy of Errors*, in which Preer showed "excellent comedy talent," according to the *New York Times* reviewer (8 May 1923, p. 22). She met and married her husband, actor Edward Thompson, when they appeared together in *The Warning* in 1924. During this period she also began her career in films, with *The Homesteader* in 1918. She starred in numerous Oscar Micheaux* films during the next decade, including *Within Our Gates* and *The Brute* (1920); *The Gunsaulus Mystery* (1921); *Birthright* (1924); *The Spider's Web*, *The Devil's Disciple*, and *The Conjur Woman* (1926); *Melancholy Dame* (1929); and *Georgia Rose* (1930). Her last picture was *Blonde Venus* (1932) with Marlene Dietrich.

Reminiscing about her film experiences for a series of articles in the *Pittsburgh Courier** (11, 18, 25 June 1927), Preer described the realistic fights the actors staged for the camera, resulting in real tears, black eyes, and scars, such as the scene in *The Brute*, where the villain chopped down her bedroom door with an axe, yanked her out, and dragged her around the room by her hair. Since that scene she had worn bobbed hair, she commented. In *Birthright*, the bloodhounds who were supposed to chase her took a liking to her, and she had to call them with a piece of meat to get them to follow her. In the same film she had to run across a swinging log bridge, roll down a long hill, and end up in a pond that

turned out to be much deeper than she had expected. Evelyn Preer died at the height of her career, and in 1933 Clarence Muse* originated an annual radio program in her memory on station KRKD in Los Angeles.
REFERENCES: NYTTR, 1972; BBW, 1977; DBPA, 1978; BB, 1980. (PO)

PRICE, FLORENCE (composer), 9 April 1888–3 June 1953. Born in Little Rock, Arkansas, Florence Price received her musical education at the New England Conservatory of Music, Chicago Musical College, and the American Conservatory of Music in Chicago; she taught at Shorter College, Clark University, Memphis, Tennessee. She was the first black woman to win recognition as a composer and received the Wanamaker Award for her *Symphony in E minor* in 1932. Other works include *Concert Overture on Negro Spirituals*; *Piano Concerto in F minor*; *Negro Folksongs in Counterpoint*, for string quartet; three works for chorus and orchestra: *Three Little Negro Dances*, *The Wind and the Sea*, and *Lincoln Walks at Midnight*; an arrangement of the spiritual* "My Soul's Been Anchored in the Lord"; and "Songs to the Dark Virgin," which was introduced by Marian Anderson.*
REFERENCES: MBA, 1971; BCM, 1977; ASCAP, 1980. (DA)

PUT AND TAKE (musical revue), 1921. All of the actors were seasoned performers, but none had appeared in New York before *Put and Take* opened at Town Hall on August 23, full of "simple pep" and "about twice as much energy as is needed to run the average Broadway revue" (NYT, 24 Aug. 1921, p. 12). Irvin C. Miller,* whose more celebrated brother Flournoy Miller* had coauthored *Shuffle Along* three months before, wrote the book, and Spencer Williams,* Tim Brymm,* and Perry Bradford* wrote the music. Irvin Miller himself appeared in the cast, doing blackface comedy routines with Emmett Anthony, and Andrew Tribble had some personal success in drag. The chorus, the *New York Times* further noted, was "attractive though dusky."
REFERENCE: NYTTR, 1972. (BK)

Q

QUICKSAND (novel), 1928. Nella Larsen's* *Quicksand* is the story of Helga Crane, who cannot find a place for herself with either race. Born of mixed parentage, like Larsen herself, she is educated by a white uncle. She becomes a teacher at Naxos, a southern black college, where she is disillusioned by the hypocrisy she sees. She then goes to Harlem where Mrs. Hayes-Rore, a wealthy Negro patron, introduces her to the comforts of upper-middle-class life. To avoid a romance and ease her feelings of suffocation, Helga Crane moves to Denmark, where she is treated as a curiosity. She falls in love with a painter but rejects the idea of intermarriage. Lonely for black people, she returns to Harlem. Denying her own sensuality, she marries the Reverend Green and moves to rural Alabama, where, through continuous childbearing, she is trapped in a life without freedom. Thus she is caught in the metaphorical quicksand she had struggled to escape. Larsen uses elements from her life to illuminate the psychological development of a woman stifled in Negro society, in upper-class European society, and in rural, southern, black folk culture. (DI)

R

RAINEY, MA [GERTRUDE MALISSA NIX PRIDGETT] (singer), 26 April 1886–22 December 1939. The daughter of minstrel troupers, Gertrude Pridgett began performing as a young girl in *A Bunch of Blackberries* in the Springer Opera House in her hometown of Columbus, Georgia, in 1900 and first toured with Fat Chappelle's Rabbit Foot Minstrels in 1902. She married Pa (William) Rainey, a singing comedian, in 1904, and they travelled with tent shows through the early years of the century, billed as "Assassinators of the Blues." The title "Mother of the Blues," later bestowed on Ma Rainey, is somewhat misleading. She claimed that about 1902, after she had heard a girl in Missouri sing a song about a woman deserted by her man, she added it and similar numbers to her act, calling such songs "the blues"*—a claim refuted by many old-time musicians. Some form of the "blues" was being sung and played throughout the South well before the turn of the century, probably evolving from spirituals* and Afro-American folk music. Ma Rainey developed a blues style that bridged the never entirely congenial gap between the early, primitive, rural blues and the later, more sophisticated, urban blues. During these early years Ma Rainey toured with many travelling circuses and tent shows, but from 1917 she toured with her own show, *Madame Gertrude Rainey and Her Georgia Smart Sets*. After 1924 she toured with her Georgia Wild Cats Jazz Band, and in 1927 she toured with her *Louisiana Blackbirds* revue. In 1930, when touring became difficult, she closed her show *The Arkansas Swift Foot* on the road and joined Boise de Legge's *Bandana Babies*. Her final tours were with Al Gaines's Carnival from 1933 until 1935.

Ma Rainey made her first recording in 1923 with Lovie Austin* and her Blues Serenaders for Paramount, and in the next five years she made about ninety recordings for that company, with supporting artists such as Louis Armstrong* and Coleman Hawkins,* and with the Tub-Jug Wash Band. Most of her recordings were made in Chicago, and she seems never to have performed in New York City, although her songs and her style were familiar and admired in Harlem, at least until 1928, when Paramount decided that her down-home material had gone out of fashion and dropped her contract.

Ma Rainey had a big, rough, penetrating voice; she could moan a blues softly or holler in a raucous shout. She was an extraordinary looking woman: short, squat, heavy, with a broad face and a mouth full of big, gold-filled teeth. "Ma, there are two things I've never seen," vaudeville performer Billy Gunn once told her, "an ugly woman and a pretty monkey." "Bless you, darling," was her reply (Albertson, *Bessie*, p. 101). Dressed flamboyantly in silks and satins; bedecked in sequins, gold chains, and diamonds; and carrying a large ostrich-feather fan, Ma Rainey would make her stage entrance through the doors of a large replica of a Victrola, blowing kisses—and her fans would go wild. Pa Rainey seems to have died or dropped out of her life fairly early, but an adopted son Danny sometimes appeared as a dancer in the shows. She was big hearted and generous toward her fellow performers, particularly the girls in her troupes, in whom she took a more than motherly interest. Bessie Smith* once had to bail her out of jail in Chicago, following a particularly indecent drinking and stripping party with a group of young women.

Ma Rainey was astute in business, and when she retired in 1935 she owned and operated two theaters in Georgia, the Lyric in Rome and the Airdrome in Columbus. She lived with her brother Thomas Pridgett, Jr., a deacon, and was an active member of the Friendship Baptist Church in Columbus until her death in 1939. Her connection with the Harlem Renaissance was only tangential, but the powerful impact of the blues on the period mandates inclusion of the "Mother of the Blues."

REFERENCES: Robert M. W. Dixon and John Godrich, *Recording the Blues*, 1970; Derrick Stewart-Baxter, *Ma Rainey and the Classic Blues Singers*, 1970; Chris Albertson, *Bessie*, 1972; Giles Oakley, *The Devil's Music*, 1978; BWW, 1979. (DA)

RAISIN' CAIN (musical revue), 1923. Frank Montgomery wrote the music and lyrics for *Raisin' Cain*, a musical tour of Negro history from Africa to New York, featuring Buck and Bubbles (Ford Lee Washington and John Bubbles*) as Bert Williams* and George Walker. The year before, Montgomery had choreographed *How Come?*,* which enjoyed an equally brief Broadway run. Both shows seem to have been based on a series of "Hello" revues—"Hello Harlem," "Hello Frisco," "Hello Dixie," for example—that Montgomery and his wife, Florence McClain, produced and toured in from 1919 until 1921.

REFERENCES: *Official Theatrical World of Colored Artists*, 1928; BB, 1980. (BK)

RANDOLPH, AMANDA (actress), c. 1902–24 August 1967. Amanda Randolph was the leading actress at the Alhambra Theatre* during the twenties, appearing in weekly programs of a wide variety. Born in Louisville, Kentucky, she and her sister Lillian worked in show business from the time they were small

girls. When the Alhambra closed, she teamed with W. C. Handy's* daughter Catherine as The Dixie Nightingales in 1932, and a few years later she began her long career in the movies. Amanda Randolph was best known, however, for her work on radio and television, where she played the cantankerous, meddling mother-in-law on the *Amos and Andy Show* and the maid on the *Danny Thomas Show*.
REFERENCES: NYT, 24 Aug. 1967; DBPA, 1978. (BK)

RANDOLPH, A[SA] PHILIP (labor leader), 15 April 1889–16 May 1979. A. Philip Randolph, the foremost black labor leader of the twentieth century, was a central figure in the civil rights movement from World War I until his death in 1979. His protégé, civil rights leader Bayard Rustin, claimed that "no individual did more to help the poor, the dispossessed and the working class in the United States and around the world than A. Philip Randolph" (NYT, 17 May 1979, p. 1). Randolph was born in Crescent City, Florida, of a poor family but one that imbued in him the traits that would separate him from most other men of his time: a strong love of learning, a belief that race was (or should be) unimportant in the affairs of the world, and a driving concern for the welfare of all people in the world. He received a diploma from nearby Cookman Institute before heading for Harlem in 1911. He worked at a series of menial jobs while attending evening classes at City College. He befriended Chandler Owen,* and the two young men spent endless hours discussing intellectual topics, the future of their race, and socialism (which both embraced during World War I). Just before he met Owen he married Lucille Green, a Howard graduate, who supported Randolph throughout much of his life by working as a beautician and later as the first black municipal social worker in New York City. In 1917 Randolph and Owen began publishing the radical *Messenger*,* which for twelve years was the organ for Randolph's political and union activities and ideas. Randolph also became known at this time as one of the great soapbox orators in Harlem. His father had taught him to speak beautifully articulated English, and Randolph's polished style and deep, melodious voice assured him of audiences whenever he spoke. He and Owen spoke across the country in 1917–1918 in opposition to black participation in World War I; indeed, they were jailed briefly in Cleveland for their activities. By the mid-1920s Randolph had come to doubt that socialism was the wave of the future or the salvation of his race and the world.

Randolph threw himself completely by 1925 into the organization of a union for sleeping car porters and maids. The Brotherhood of Sleeping Car Porters* was founded August 25, 1925. It took four years for Randolph's union to gain recognition from the all-white leadership of the AFL, and not until 1937 was he able to bring the powerful Pullman Company to agree to sign a bargaining contract with his union. Throughout this thirteen-year period Randolph worked tirelessly, even though he was fiercely opposed by Communists, the white labor hierarchy, and many blacks who saw his union as a segregated (and therefore unworthy) organization. His unflappable dignity, good humor, high integrity, and refusal to quit even in the face of intimidation and bribery by the Pullman Company enabled him to be the first black leader of a union in the AFL-CIO. His prominence in this role pushed him to the leadership of the civil rights movement, and he was highly instrumental in convincing Franklin Roosevelt to allow blacks to obtain jobs in defense plants in World War II, as well as in pushing Harry Truman to integrate the armed forces in 1948. When he spoke at the Washington March in 1963, many people knew that his lifelong efforts had made that day possible. He retired as president of his union in 1968, but remained active in his Harlem community, living a simple life of reading, writing, and attending an occasional show (he had always loved the theater). He was ninety years old when he died in 1979 in Harlem.

REFERENCES: Jervis Anderson, *A. Philip Randolph*, 1973; Theodore Kornweibel, Jr., *No Crystal Stair*, 1974; NYT, 17 May 1979. (DS)

RANDOLPH, RICHETTA (secretary), ?–? Richetta Randolph was a secretary for the NAACP* from its beginnings and privy to many of the important decisions made by her superiors. In his autobiography *A Man Called White* Walter White* claimed that Randolph served "as stenographer, confidante, and mentor to all of us" (p. 39), and in his autobiography *Along This Way* James Weldon Johnson* called her "the best confidential secretary I have known or know of" (p. 309).

REFERENCES: James Weldon Johnson, *Along This Way*, 1933; Walter White, *A Man Called White*, 1948. (DS)

RANG TANG (musical comedy), 1927. Two barbers (Flournoy Miller* and Aubrey Lyles,* still performing as a blackface team) fly from "Jimtown, U.S.A." to Africa in a stolen airplane in this "extravagant and entertaining" show by Kaj Gynt. Jo Trent wrote the lyrics and Ford Dabney* wrote the songs for Mae Barnes* and Evelyn Preer,* both of whom were praised in the *New York Times* review, but Miller and Lyles seemed uneasy with some new material (13 July 1927, p. 20).

REFERENCE: NYTTR, 1972. (BK)

RAPP, WILLIAM JOURDAN (playwright), 17 June 1895–12 August 1942. Born in New York City, white playwright William Jourdan Rapp was both a feature writer for the *New York Times* and editor of *True Story Magazine* from 1926. In 1928 he collaborated with Wallace Thurman* to write *Harlem**, which opened at the Apollo Theatre* on 2 February 1929. It was revived, on Broadway at the Eltinge Theatre eight months later, on 21 October 1929 but ran for only sixteen performances, less than a fifth the length of its Harlem run. Nevertheless, Burns Mantle chose it for his annual volume of condensations of the "best plays" of the season, and most reviews were generally impressed with the vitality of the cast. Rapp wrote other plays as well, and his contribution to *Harlem* may

have been one of molding Thurman's characters and situations into a dramatic form.
REFERENCES: Burns Mantle, 1928–1929; WWW, 1950; AAB, 1972. (MH)

RAZAF, ANDY (lyricist), 16 December 1895–3 February 1973. Andreamenentania Paul Razafinkeriefo was the son of Malagasy nobility, and John R. Walker, U.S. consul to Madagascar, was his maternal grandfather, but by 1924 Andy Razaf was a popular lyric writer in Harlem. He supplied the words for about a thousand songs by Eubie Blake,* Fats Waller,* J. C. Johnson,* and many others for more than twenty years, and he was then a newspaper columnist until his death at the age of seventy-seven. He began by writing some verse under his real name for *Negro World* in 1922, but soon he was supplying Ethel Waters* with fairly salacious lyrics for songs like "My Handy Man." Later, Razaf wrote "Honeysuckle Rose," "Memories of You," "Ain't Misbehavin'," "Stompin' at the Savoy," and, some time afterward, "In the Mood." Among his musical librettos were *Keep Shufflin'* (1928), *Hot Chocolates* (1929), and *Blackbirds [*] of 1930*.
REFERENCES: NYT, 5 Feb. 1973. (BK)

RECTOR, EDDIE (actor), 12 December 1898?–1962. After touring the South as a pickaninny in several troupes Eddie Rector made his New York debut in J. Leubrie Hill's *My Friend from Kentucky* at the Lafayette Theatre* in 1913. Afterward, he toured in vaudeville for TOBA* until *Dixie to Broadway*,* where he had a personal success with a "Bambousa" dance. In 1928 Rector replaced Bill Robinson* for the tour of *Blackbirds [*] of 1928*, but he returned to New York for *Hot Rhythm* (1930) and *Yeah Man* (1931). Eddie Rector's full significance has never been entirely recognized. In dapper tap and soft-shoe dancing he was a strong influence on his peers and on those dancers who followed him, not only through his work in shows but in various clubs in Harlem: Connie's Inn,* the Plantation Club,* and the Cotton Club.*
REFERENCE: BB, 1980. (BK)

REDDING, J[AY] SAUNDERS (teacher, essayist, novelist, critic), 13 October 1906– . An elegant man, Jay Saunders Redding lived in a richly varied, richly accomplished life. Born in Delaware and educated at Lincoln, Brown, and Columbia universities, Redding has been a teacher, editor, critic, novelist, essayist, and short-story writer. Awards and honors have been numerous: Rockefeller Grant (1940), Guggenheim (1944–1945 and 1959–1960), director of the Division of Research and Publications of the National Foundation on the Arts and Humanities (1966–1967), and the distinguished service award of the National Urban League* (1945).

Redding's first major work, *To Make a Poet Black*, an appraisal of the work of various black writers throughout American history, was published in 1938 and has been followed by a long list of distinguished works. His only publication

in the twenties came when he was a student at Brown, "Delaware Coon," which Eugene Jolas accepted for *Transition*, one of the few black contributions to that international publication.
REFERENCES: CB, 1969; AAB, 1972. (MH)

REDMAN, DON (composer, arranger), 29 July 1900–30 November 1964. Born in West Virginia, Don Redman was at first a saxophone player during the twenties, but he had played the trumpet at the age of three and had even organized his own band at the age of six. He studied at Storer College when he was just eleven and then went on to study theory and composition at the Boston Conservatory. Redman played with Billy Paige's Broadway Syncopates in 1923, and with Fletcher Henderson's* orchestra from 1924 to 1926, serving as its primary arranger; he afterward was with Paul Whiteman's orchestra for thirty-five years. Redman wrote a number of songs, none of them memorable, but he recorded widely as an accompanist for Bessie Smith,* Louis Armstrong,*, and, later in his career, Pearl Bailey.
REFERENCES: ASCAP, 1966; NA, 1976. (BK)

REED, GEORGE (actor), 1867–1952. In 1920 George Reed played the role of Jim in the first film version of *Huckleberry Finn* and was on screen in minor roles afterward. He broke from his familiar family-retainer role at least once: as the Reverend Deshee in the film version of *The Green Pastures*. Usually, however, he was cast as a caretaker, butler, stable hand, or servant.
REFERENCE: WWH, 1976. (BK)

REID, IRA DE A[UGUSTINE] (sociologist), 2 July 1901–16 August 1968. Ira Reid was educated at Morehouse College and Atlanta University. He completed his master's degree at the University of Pittsburgh, at which time he became industrial secretary of the Urban League in New York. Reid wrote for *Opportunity** and prepared a large number of government pamphlets and monographs on social, economic, and educational issues; his thesis *Negro Immigration, His Background, Character, and Social Adjustment, 1899–1937* was published in England in 1939, and the following year he wrote a study of Afro-American youth called *In a Minor Key*. His far-reaching research, now preserved on microfilm, is part of the Arthur Schomburg* collection in the New York Public Library.
REFERENCE: NYT, 17 Aug. 1968. (BK)

REISS, WINOLD (painter), 1887–29 August 1953. Winold Reiss was a pioneer in the depiction of blacks as individuals rather than as either ethnic stereotypes or dark-skinned whites, and as such he influenced the work of his student, the painter Aaron Douglas,* and other black artists. The son of a Bavarian landscape painter, Reiss studied at the Kunstgewerbe Schule in Munich and painted folk groups of Sweden, Holland, and Germany before moving to the United States.

He became fascinated with the American Indian and travelled extensively in the American West, Canada, Mexico, and Central America, painting Indians and scenes of tribal life. In 1925 he was selected to illustrate the Harlem number of the *Survey Graphic** and subsequently Alain Locke's* *New Negro*.* In addition to painting or drawing in pastels the artists and scholars of the Harlem Renaissance, among them Alain Locke, Jean Toomer,* Countee Cullen,* Paul Robeson,* Roland Hayes,* and W.E.B. Du Bois,* he painted a series on Afro-Americans living on the Carolina coast. Alain Locke wrote of him in *The New Negro*, "without loss of naturalistic accuracy and individuality, he somehow subtly expresses the type, and without being any the less human, captures the racial and local" (p. 420). Reiss was a professor of mural painting at New York University. Known as "The Holbein of the Humble," he painted many murals in hotels, restaurants, theatres, and railroad stations with ethnic groups as subjects. His work can be seen in the National Portrait Gallery and the Whitney Gallery of Western Art.

REFERENCES: Alain Locke, ed., *The New Negro*, 1925; NYT, 31 Aug. 1953; Margaret Butcher, *The Negro in American Culture*, 1956; AAD, 1973; David Levering Lewis, *When Harlem Was in Vogue,* 1981; *Portfolio Magazine of the Fine Arts*, Sept.–Oct. 1982. (PO)

RENAISSANCE CASINO (dance hall and theater), ?–? The Renaissance Casino was a two-story structure at 133rd Street and Seventh Avenue, operated by the black-owned Sares Realty Company for several purposes. On the ground floor a spacious auditorium showed first-run movies in the Renaissance Theatre. The second-floor ballroom was rented out for dances, banquets, concerts, and even Sunday night basketball games. The name of the organization making use of it was always spelled out in flashing lights over the entrance.

REFERENCES: Wallace Thurman, *Negro Life in New York's Harlem*, 1928; BB, 1980. (BK)

RENT PARTIES. The fund-raising tradition of the rent party seems to have begun in the South, but it quickly became an established event in the life of Harlem. Houses renting for $185 to $250 a month, apartments for about $20 a room, and even squalid tenements at $10 a room often obliged the average black family to supplement its income by holding open house. An admission fee of twenty-five cents was usually standard, followed by nominal charges for food and drink. There was always music, sometimes a three-piece ensemble and sometimes only improvised rhythms and singing for dancing that occurred in the cleared front rooms. Boiled pig's feet, ham hocks, cabbage, and a mixture of peas and rice called "Hopping John" made up the standard menu; the booze was strictly rot-gut, whether bootlegged or homemade. If rent parties were a necessary economic evil, they were nevertheless social events as well, as essential to Low Harlem as literary receptions were to High Harlem. "The Wayside Printer" travelled back and forth across Harlem with his equipment in tow to

prepare on-the-spot advertisements for rent parties masquerading in various disguises. Ira De A. Reid,* industrial secretary for the National Urban League,* gathered several of them for *Ebony and Topaz** (1927, pp. 145–146), all beginning with cheerful invitations: "Papa is mad about the way you do, / So meet the gang and Skoodle um Skoo at / A Social Whist Party"; "If you cant Charleston or do the Pigeon Wing / You sure can shake that thing at a / Social Party"; "Save your tears for a rainy day, / We are giving a party where you can play / With red mammas and too bad She-bas / Who wear their dresses above their knees / And mess around with whom they please." Sometimes rhyme was abandoned in favor of a more straightforward approach: "Come and get fixed." These "parlor socials," "too terrible parties," "matinée parties," "social entertainments"—as many as twelve to a single block and five to an apartment building, simultaneously, on any night of the week—were called "shin-digs" in the South. The name was appropriate for their northern versions as well.
REFERENCES: *Ebony and Topaz*, 1927; Wallace Thurman, *Negro Life in New York's Harlem*, 1928; Langston Hughes, *The Big Sea*, 1940. (BK)

REOL MOTION PICTURE ORGANIZATION , 1921–1922. The success of the Lincoln Motion Picture Company* led to the formation of several other film organizations, none of them—with the exception of Oscar Micheaux's*—of marked significance. In 1921 Robert J. Levy, a white entrepreneur with Harlem connections, founded the Reol Motion Picture Corporation and produced, among other features, *The Burden of Race, The Simp, Sport of the Gods* (based on Paul Laurence Dunbar's novel), and *Ties of Blood*, all in the first year. *The Jazz Hounds, Schemers,* and *Spitfire* followed in 1922. *The Call of His People*, also made in 1922, featured Edna Morton, billed as "the colored Mary Pickford," and was typical of Reol's work: a successful black businessman passes for white until his fiancée persuades him to confess to his boss, only to learn that his color makes no difference. Other Reol features included *Easy Money* and *Secret Sorrow*. The company seems not to have lasted beyond 1922.
REFERENCES: Daniel J. Leab, *From Sambo to Superspade*, 1975; BBW, 1977. (BK)

REVUE NÈGRE (musical revue), 1925. An all-black revue opened at the Théâtre des Champs-Elysées in Paris in the fall of 1925 and created a sensation. It was the brainchild of Caroline Dudley Reagon, a rich, white socialite, who during her formative years in Chicago at the turn of the century had fallen under the spell of black music and musicians. Married to a wealthy American in the foreign service, she seized on the idea of transporting something of the Harlem Renaissance to Paris, where she and her husband were stationed. Reagon had first thought to engage Gertrude Saunders,* the star of the 1921 *Shuffle Along.** Saunders demurred, however, and Reagon went to the Plantation Club* to audition Ethel Waters,* only to hire Josephine Baker* instead. (More than once, Ethel Waters refers to Caroline Dudley Reagon as Mary Louise Howard, in her autobiography.) Then, through Carl Van Vechten,* she engaged twenty-five-year-old Donald Angus, an inexperienced but reliable white youth, to serve as a kind of regisseur for a company of twenty. Angus began his duties by hiring Claude Hopkins* and his six-piece band from an all-black nightclub in Asbury Park, while Reagon collected a chorus line, including Maude de Forest and Hazel Valentine, as well as some comedians and other dancers. They sailed on the S.S. *Berengaria*; none of them spoke any French and none of them had been to Europe before; but on arrival Reagon simply turned them all over to Angus. He put them up in a number of small hotels near Montmartre, mustered them around for daily rehearsals, doled out their salaries like allowances to keep them from going broke, took Josephine Baker out for her fittings, and even got Sidney Bechet* to sit in with the band during the intermission riffs. From her first appearance onstage, wearing a girdle made out of bananas, Josephine Baker was one of the brightest black stars of the century, although the Harlem Renaissance was long dead before she returned to America to perform. A year or so later, Reagon thought to repeat her success with Clara Smith* as her star, but nothing came of the venture.

REFERENCES: Carl Van Vechten, *"Keep A-Inchin' Along,"* 1979; Lynn Haney, *Naked At the Feast*, 1981; Donald Angus. (BK)

RHAPSODY IN BLACK (musical revue), 1931. As a kind of mistress of ceremonies, Ethel Waters* (who was "inclined to attenuate her act beyond its endurance") explained that all the world was a rhapsody and that Harlem was a "rhapsody in black." This "jazz concert," as the program termed it, featured fewer black clichés than usual, but the result was often "soggy and monotonous," according to the *New York Times*, rather than the "simple, unpretentious show" it tried to be (5 May 1931, p. 33). Among the offerings were W. C. Handy's* "St. James Infirmary"; Ethel Waters singing "Eli Eli" in Hebrew; a song that went on to become a standard, "I Found a Million Dollar Baby at the Five and Ten Cents Store"; and a choral version—with words by J. Rosamond Johnson*—of George Gershwin's* *Rhapsody in Blue*. Other numbers were by Jimmie McHugh* and Dorothy Fields,* Mann Hollinger and Alberta Nichols, Ken Macomber, and Cecil Mack.* Earl "Snakehips" Tucker* and Eddie Rector* were in the cast.

REFERENCES: NYTTR, 1972; BB, 1980. (BK)

RICE, ALBERT (poet), 1903–? Albert Rice was born in Washington, D.C., and left government work in 1926 to turn himself into a poet when he met Richard Bruce Nugent,* "the bizarre and eccentric young vagabond poet of High Harlem," as Rice described his new friend. Rice's own work had a studied archness, an abhorrence of "all things Anglo-Saxon," he claimed, but it suffered a superficial surface because of what must be described as camp mannerisms and nineteenth-century diction. His poem "The Black Madonna" was included in Countee Cullen's* *Caroling Dusk*,* but Rice's autobiographical note for that 1927 anthology is far more lively and sets the jaunty tone for many of the writers of the Harlem Renaissance:

I'd rather live in the squalor of Mulberry Street, N.Y. (Little Italy) than at Irvington-on-the-Hudson. I love bull fights and dislike baseball games. I like dancing and dislike prayer meetings. I love New York because it is crowded and noisy and an outpost of Europe. . . . I like Washington because it has such a large share of Babbits, both white and black. And I like it because Georgia Douglas Johnson[*] lives there and on Saturday nights has an assembly of likable and civilized people, and because it was from this Saturday night circle that Jean Toomer,[*] Richard Bruce [Nugent], and Richard Goodwin, the artist, went forth to fame and infamy. (p. 177)

REFERENCE: Countee Cullen, ed., *Caroling Dusk*, 1927. (BK)

RICHARDSON, WILLIS (playwright), 5 November 1889–1977. Willis Richardson is remembered as the first serious black writer to have a play produced on Broadway, *The Chip Woman's Fortune*,* in 1923. He was born in North Carolina and reared in Washington, D.C., where he attended Dunbar High School and came under the encouragement of Mary Burrill, an aspiring playwright as well as one of his teachers. Encouraged also by Angelina Grimké's* play *Rachael*, which he had seen in 1916, presented under the auspices of the NAACP,* Richardson began to write plays, first contributing some dramatic sketches for children to W.E.B. Du Bois's* *Brownie's Book** in 1920 and during the same year a one-act play, "The Deacon's Awakening," to *The Crisis*.* When the Howard Players at Howard University were denied permission to stage some of Richardson's one-act plays—the school's white president feared that dramatized propaganda might prove deleterious to Howard's reputation—W.E.B. Du Bois encouraged the young writer to submit his work to the Ethiopian Art Players* in Chicago. That company's triple offering—Oscar Wilde's *Salome*, Shakespeare's *Comedy of Errors*, and Richardson's *Chip Woman's Fortune*—opened in Harlem and then on Broadway in May 1923. The Howard Players staged his *Mortgaged* in 1924, the Karamu House* staged his *Compromise* in 1925, and in 1926 *The Crisis* awarded him first prize for drama in its annual contest for *Broken Banjo*, which its Krigwa Players* then produced. Many other plays followed, published in several issues of *The Crisis*, but Richardson had little commercial success (six full-length plays went unpublished as well as unproduced). From 1910 he supported himself as a clerk in the U.S. Bureau of Printing and Engraving until his retirement in 1955. In "The Hope for Negro Drama," an article in *The Crisis* in November 1919, Richardson expressed the interests that continued to motivate his writing: black drama's educational value. Other relevant works are *Plays and Pageants of Negro Life* (1930) and *Negro History in Thirteen Plays* (1935).
REFERENCES: James V. Hatch, ed., *Black Theater, U.S.A.*, 1974; James Haskins, *Black Theatre in America*, 1982. (BK)

RIOTS. During the period of the Harlem Renaissance volcanoes of racism continued to erupt in various parts of the country. No consideration of the period is accurate without an accounting of them. Since the Emancipation Proclamation, nearly 3,000 Negroes had been lynched without trial; fifty-four years later, on 2 July 1917 in East St. Louis, Illinois, 6,000 black citizens were driven from their homes and 200 of them were murdered by shooting, lynching, or burning. Large numbers of Afro-Americans had migrated to northern cities like East St. Louis, angering many whites who feared that blacks would take their jobs by working for lower wages. Trade unions apparently egged white workers on, and during the riot that ensued the perpetrators motivated a Silent Protest Parade* in New York four weeks later, one of the most famous events in the history of Harlem and one that showed not only a rising black militancy in the North but a first public demonstration by Afro-Americans.

Less than a month after the parade another riot broke out in Houston, Texas. Black troops in the Twenty-fourth Regiment, already angered by Jim Crow* laws, went on a rampage when a black woman was arrested in their camp, firing indiscriminately and killing seventeen or eighteen white people, including some women and children. In the aftermath sixty-three of the black soldiers were court-martialed and thirteen were hanged, denied the right to appeal. Another forty-one were sentenced to life imprisonment. The Red Summer of 1919 came two years afterward. James Weldon Johnson* gave this bloody season its name, following riots in Washington, D.C., Chicago, and several small southern towns. In June 1919 the Washington, D.C., Provost Guard was called out to restore order when whites burned the black Longview section of the city. Concurrently, twenty-three blacks and fifteen whites were killed in Chicago when a black boy went swimming in Lake Michigan and may have inadvertently drifted into a segregated area. Hundreds of others were injured and left homeless. In Elaine, Arkansas, one hundred blacks were killed when they tried to organize a union to get an equal payment for their cotton, and twelve others were sentenced to death, although the NAACP* was able to have those judgments overruled. Another riot occurred in Knoxville, Tennessee, in September, when blacks and whites fired directly on each other.

Two years hence, writing in the *Washington Bee* on 11 June 1921, five days after the fact, Calvin Chase called the Tulsa, Oklahoma, race riot the ''worst in history'' and appalled his readers with the news that some of the bodies were still lying where they had fallen. The entire black quarter of the city had been leveled by fire; twenty-six black citizens had been killed, and a thousand others had fled to the Osage Hills. Ten white citizens had been killed as well. The riot began after two black men were arrested for ''impudence and assault,'' having been rude to a white girl in an elevator. In fear of a possible lynching, a dozen black men asked to be sworn in as deputies; instead, white law officers confiscated their guns. Blacks, outnumbering whites three to one, opened fire, and in retaliation whites set fire to buildings including a church in which fifty blacks had taken refuge. The state militia was called out to establish martial law.

Writing in the Baltimore *Afro-American** on June 10, Hubert Harrison* urged blacks to arm and contribute to the president's Liberal League, predicting at least three other riots over the summer, for which they should be prepared (Vincent, *Voices of a Black Nation*, p. 138). Other skirmishes continued to occur over the years, minor by comparison with those that had gone before. Then on 19 March 1935 a riot brought the Harlem Renaissance to an ugly and violent conclusion on its home turf. A sixteen-year-old black youth, Lino Rivera, stealing a knife from a white store was an excuse rather than the actual cause for the riot. Since the stock market crash and the ensuing Depression, increasing numbers of Afro-Americans had been living on the edge of poverty, sometimes over the edge, paying double what white tenants paid for rent, denied employment solely because of their race, women surviving on a domestic slave market, facing double the rates of pneumonia and venereal disease, even double the death rate of children. "In the very citadel of America's new Negro," Roi Ottley later wrote, "crowds went crazy like the remnants of a defeated, abandoned, hungry army" (Ottley and Weatherby, *The Negro in New York*, p. 275). Ten thousand black Americans swept through Harlem, destroying the property of white merchants. A few were killed; many were injured; hundreds of thousands of dollars of damage resulted from the first major riot to occur in Harlem.

REFERENCES: James Weldon Johnson, *Black Manhattan*, 1930, and *Along This Way*, 1933; Roi Ottley and William J. Weatherby, eds., *The Negro in New York*, 1967; J. Paul Mitchell, ed., *Race Riots in Black and White*, 1970; Theodore G. Vincent, ed., *Voices of a Black Nation*, 1975; David Levering Lewis, *When Harlem Was in Vogue*, 1981; Jervis Anderson, *This Was Harlem*, 1982; Alexander Gumby Scrapbooks, Columbia University. (BK)

ROBERTS, C[HARLES] LUCKYETH "LUCKEY" (pianist, composer), 7 August 1887–5 February 1968. Born in Philadelphia, Luckey Roberts made his stage debut at the age of three in a production of *Uncle Tom's Cabin* and as a child toured with Gus Seekes's Pickaninnies and Mayme Remington's Ethiopian Prodigies. He studied music in New York with Eloise Smith and Melville Charlton and from 1910 was resident pianist at Barron Wilkins's Little Savoy Club and toured in vaudeville as a singer, dancer, pianist, and leader of his own band. His first published work, "Junk Man Rag" (1913), was a popular hit, and his "Pork and Beans" became a favorite piano "shout" at Harlem rent parties* and improvisational jazz sessions. A pianist of prodigious technical skill, Roberts is considered to be the founder of the Harlem piano school, and his playing greatly influenced the styles of Fats Waller,* James P. Johnson,* Willie-the-Lion Smith,* and Duke Ellington.* During the twenties and thirties he was extremely popular as a society pianist and band leader in America and Europe. He worked with lyricist Alex Rogers* from 1913 until Rogers's death in 1930, a partnership that produced many fine songs and musical shows—usually written for the Quality Amusement Company—and the radio scripts for George Moran and Charles Mack's *Two Black Crows*. Roberts wrote or collaborated on fourteen

musical revues; among them were *My People* (1917); *Baby Blues* and *This and That* (both 1919); *Go-Go* and *Sharlee*, both produced by John Cort at Daly's 63rd Street Theatre in 1923; *Steppin' Time* (1924); and *My Magnolia** (1926). His piano rag "Ripples of the Nile" (1912), rewritten in slow tempo, became the 1940s popular song "Moonlight Cocktail." His concert works include "Whistlin' Pete—Miniature Syncopated Rhapsody" for piano and orchestra.
REFERENCES: Rudi Blesh and Harriet Janis, *They All Played Ragtime*, 1951; MBA, 1971; WWJ, 1978; BB, 1980. (BK)

ROBERTS, WALTER ADOLPHE (writer), 1886–? A prolific journalist for New York and San Francisco newspapers, Walter Adolphe Roberts was born in Jamaica but came to the United States at an early age. During World War I he was correspondent for the *Brooklyn Daily Eagle*, writing regular dispatches from the front. Afterward, until 1921 Roberts was editor for *Ainslee's Magazine*, and in 1922 he became an associate editor for *Hearst's International Magazine*. There are virtually no black themes in his verse, but *Pierrot Wounded and Other Poems* (1919) and *Pan and Peacocks* (1928) both show some influence of his Jamaican background. In later years he wrote a number of travel books and histories about various areas in the West Indies but seems to have forsaken verse. During the Harlem Renaissance—with which movement he was never strongly identified—he wrote a number of mystery and detective novels, rarely with black themes or characters and sometimes under pseudonyms, like *The Mind Reader* (1929) and *Top Floor Killer* (1935).
REFERENCE: Langston Hughes and Arna Bontemps, eds., *The Poetry of the Negro*, 1949. (BK)

ROBESON, ESLANDA [CARDOZA GOODE] (chemist), 15 December 1896–13 December 1965. Eslanda Cardoza Goode, who later married Paul Robeson,* studied at the State University of Illinois but completed a bachelor of science degree from Columbia University. As the first Afro-American citizen employed on the staff of Presbyterian Hospital in New York, she was in charge of the Surgical Pathological Laboratory. In 1925 she resigned to become her husband's business manager for his first European tour, and she continued in that capacity for the duration of his career in theater and concert work.
REFERENCES: WWCA, 1933; DANB, 1982. (BK)

ROBESON, PAUL (actor, singer), 9 April 1898–23 January 1976. Paul Robeson, a minister's son from Princeton, New Jersey, achieved his first fame at Rutgers University, where he won twelve varsity letters, earned Phi Beta Kappa membership in his junior year, and was twice named to Walter Camp's All-American Football Team. After graduation with a B.A. in 1919 he studied law at Columbia University, received a degree, and joined a law firm. But his theatrical talents were undeniable, and in 1921 he made his first stage appearance in a revival of Ridgely Torrence's *Simon the Cyrenian* at the 135th Street YMCA.

In 1922 he appeared as Jim in Mary Hoyt Wilborg's *Taboo** at the Sam Harris Theatre and the next year made his first appearance in England in the same play, retitled *The Voodoo*, with Mrs. Patrick Campbell at the Opera House, Blackpool. The Provincetown Players' 1924 production of *All God's Chillun Got Wings*,* which Eugene O'Neill* had written with Robeson in mind, caused a controversy when the black actor appeared opposite the white actress Mary Blair. In 1925, *The Emperor Jones** was revived for Robeson at the 52nd Street Theatre; in 1926 he appeared in the title role of *Black Boy** at the Comedy Theatre; in 1928 he took over the role of Crown in *Porgy** at the Republic Theatre, and later that year he went to London to play Joe in *Showboat** at the Drury Lane Theatre.

His magnificent singing voice had been recognized even in his college days, although he was turned down by the Rutgers Glee Club. While still in law school he substituted for the bass with the Four Harmony Kings in *Shuffle Along** and appeared at the Plantation Club* singing J. Rosamond Johnson's* "Li'l Gal." In *Taboo* he sang a song by H. T. Burleigh,* and in *The Emperor Jones*, in the scene where Jones is lost in the jungle, he sang a spiritual* instead of whistling to keep up his courage. He met the pianist-arranger Lawrence Brown* in London during the run of *Taboo* and later in New York prepared with him a program of spirituals and songs by black composers. This they presented at the Greenwich Village Theatre 19 April 1925, and it was so successful that it had to be repeated a week later. During and after the London run of *Showboat* Robeson gave recitals of spirituals in England, and in 1929, following two sold-out concerts at Carnegie Hall, he undertook his first European concert tour.

In May 1930 he made his first appearance as Othello at the Savoy Theatre in London: "For nobility of mind and rich beauty of utterance it is difficult to think the part could be better played" (NYT, 20 May 1930, p. 33). In the next decade he appeared in London as Yank in *The Hairy Ape* (1931), Balu in *Basilisk* (1935), and Toussaint in *Toussaint L'Ouverture* (1936); and in New York in revivals of *Showboat* (1932) and *All God's Chillun Got Wings* (1933) and in *John Henry* (1940). In 1943 *Othello*, directed by Margaret Webster, with Robeson, Uta Hagen, and Jose Ferrer, opened at the Shubert Theatre in New York for a record-breaking American Shakespearean run of 296 performances, followed by a long tour.

Robeson's first film *Body and Soul* (1924), produced and directed by Oscar Micheaux,* was shown only in black communities. Subsequently, he starred in box-office successes such as *The Emperor Jones*,* *Saunders of the River*, *King Solomon's Mines*, *Jericho*, *Showboat*, and *The Proud Valley*, in which he played a miner in a Welsh village. In 1942 he appeared in *Tales of Manhattan*, with Ethel Waters* and Eddie Anderson* but thereafter refused to portray stereotyped roles in films.

From the beginning of his career he accepted the responsibility, as one of the most talented members of his race, of working for civil rights and civil liberties. Despite his great popular success, certain professional and social doors remained closed to him. When the Metropolitan Opera presented Louis Gruenberg's operatic realization of *The Emperor Jones** in 1933, Robeson was not even considered for the title role. (He sang excerpts from the opera in concert with the Philadelphia Orchestra under Eugene Ormandy at Carnegie Hall in 1940, however.) Racial prejudice even followed him to England, where he had enjoyed social acceptance, and in 1930 he was turned away from the Grill Room at the Savoy Hotel in London because of complaints from American tourists. The matter was brought up in the House of Commons, but the prime minister announced, regretfully, that there was nothing the government could do about it.

In the forties Robeson took an increasingly militant stand on civil rights and became an outspoken supporter of the Soviet Union, which he had first visited in 1934. In 1950 his American passport was revoked, and for eight years he was effectively silenced at home and abroad. He sang again at Carnegie Hall in 1958 and made a final tour of Europe, but advancing age and poor health brought his performing career to a close. He was honored in a tributory concert at Carnegie Hall on his seventy-fifth birthday in 1973 but was too ill to attend. He died in Philadelphia in 1976.

Robeson made about 300 recordings, ranging from the blues* with Count Basie's orchestra, through spirituals, folk songs and "songs of the people" in all languages, classical songs, popular songs, ballads, and show tunes, to concert pieces such as Earl Robinson's *Ballad for Americans*, which he introduced on national radio in 1939. Robeson's voice was distinctive and unforgettable. Carl Van Vechten,* his early promoter, described it as "clear, resonant, and of exceptionally pleasant quality and of considerable range" (*"Keep A-Inchin' Along,"* pp. 155–156); the critic of the *New York World* coined the phrase "a voice in which deep bells ring." But he had little formal voice training and was uninterested in perfecting his technique and musicianship. Of his own singing, he said, "I am essentially a folk singer . . . I have never been much interested in vocal virtuosity" (BCM, p. 91).

Much has been written about Robeson, beginning with the biography *Paul Robeson, Negro* (1930) by his wife, Eslanda Cardoza Goode Robeson,* whom he married in 1921. His autobiography *Here I Stand* appeared in 1976; a pictorial biography, *The Whole World in His Hands*, by his granddaughter Susan Robeson followed in 1982. Presently, white scholar Martin Dubermann is writing a definitive biography.

REFERENCES: WWT, 1947; GD, 1955; NYTTR, 1972; Paul Robeson, *Here I Stand*, 1976; BCM, 1977; Carl Van Vechten, *"Keep A-Inchin' Along,"* 1979; David Levering Lewis, *When Harlem Was in Vogue*, 1981. (DA)

ROBINSON, BILL "BOJANGLES" [LUTHER ROBINSON] (dancer), 25 May 1876–25 November 1949. Born in Richmond, Virginia, and orphaned young, Bill Robinson was raised by his grandmother. From the time he was eight years old they lived in Washington, D.C., where he worked in a racing stable and danced in taverns and beer gardens for pocket money. His first stage appearances were with Mayme Remington for fifty cents a night as a "pick"—

one of a troupe of singing and dancing "pickaninnies" who came on to enliven the finale to a stage act. In 1891, when he was twelve years old, he went to New York from Louisville, Kentucky, in the travelling show *The South Before the War*, which featured Eddie Leonard. He tried to enlist in the Spanish-American War, was turned down, but travelled with a regimental company anyway until he was accidentally shot in the knee. He teamed with George Cooper in a vaudeville act for five years and then started working as a single and quickly became a favorite on the Keith circuit. He had a lively, expressive face, was a competent singer, and kept up a line of patter and jokes while dancing. Despite his success in vaudeville, where he earned up to $2,000 a week, he did not have a New York theater hit until late in life. He had tried out his famous stair-dance at the Palace as early as 1921, but not until he introduced it in the *Pepper Pot Revue* (1927) did it attract attention. The faltering *Blackbirds[*] of 1928* brought him in as an "Extra Added Attraction" three weeks after the opening, and he was a sensational hit. He was fifty years old. He went on to star in *Brown Buddies** (1930) and *Hot from Harlem* (1931) and headlined at the top New York clubs. He returned to Broadway in *The Hot Mikado* in 1939.

He made an independent film, *Harlem Is Heaven*, in 1932 but scored his first great movie success with Shirley Temple in *The Little Colonel* (1935) for 20th Century Fox. Other films with Temple followed: *The Littlest Rebel* (1936) and *Rebecca of Sunnybrook Farm* (1938). He also staged the dances for the Temple film *Dimples* (1936).

Robinson acquired the nickname "Bojangles" from a racetrack pal when he was a young man, and in his late career it became the general term of affection for a much-loved public personality. But everything was not as "copacetic" as he professed. Although he was enormously popular with white audiences, some blacks thought that his movie roles presented him as a stereotype of the comic, acquiescent, faithful black servant, and he was accused of being an "Uncle Tom." Nor was he universally liked by other black performers; he was sometimes difficult to work with, and his detractors pointed out that the stair-dance was not a new act, and that his routine of tap dancing on a drum in the film *Stormy Weather* (1943) had been originated by Eddie Rector.* All agreed, however, that he was a superb dancer. Also, he was extremely generous: he played more benefits than any other entertainer and gave lavishly to charity. He was on good terms with the New York Police Department and was known for years as the "Mayor of Harlem." Although he earned approximately $3 million in his sixty-three years in show business, he died almost penniless.

REFERENCES: Marshall and Jean Stearns, *Jazz Dance*, 1968; Jim Haskins, *The Cotton Club*, 1977; BB, 1980; Lynne Fauley Emery, *Black Dance in the United States from 1619 to 1970*, 1980. (DA)

ROBINSON, WARREN (religious leader), ?–? Warren Robinson, elder of the Beth B'nai Abraham Synagogue at 29 West 131st Street, hired a Jewish teacher to tutor him in "Jewish mannerisms and Yiddish" before proclaiming himself "the Messiah." "Rasputin" might have been more appropriate. His love cult involving voodoo rites with four- and five-year-old children resulted in a notorious trial in 1926. He served eight months of a three-year sentence, returned to Harlem, and found his church still going strong.

REFERENCE: Howard Brotz, *The Black Jews of Harlem*, 1970. (BK)

ROCKLAND PALACE. See MANHATTAN CASINO.

ROGERS, ALEX[ANDER CLAUDE] (lyricist), 1876–14 September 1930. Alex Rogers, from Nashville, Tennessee, arrived in New York about 1900 and began to work with Bert Williams* and George Walker, writing lyrics for *The Sons of Ham* (1900), *In Dahomey* (1903), *Abyssinia* (1906), *Bandanna Land* (1908), and *Mr. Lode of Kole* (1909). He wrote *In the Jungles* (1911) for the Black Patti Troubadours and with Harry Creamer* produced *The Old Man's Boy* (1913) for the Negro Players Company in Philadelphia. He collaborated with C. Luckyeth Roberts* on *Baby Blues* and *This and That* (1919), *Go-Go** (1923), and *My Magnolia** (1926), and he and Roberts wrote many songs together. In all, Rogers wrote the lyrics for about 2,000 songs, beginning with early hits such as "Bon Bon Buddy," with music by Will Marion Cook,* and Bert Williams's great song "Nobody," the music of which Williams wrote himself.

REFERENCES: Sigmund Spaeth, *A History of Popular Music in America*, 1948; BB, 1980. (DA)

ROGERS, JOEL AUGUSTUS (writer), 1880 or 1883–6 September 1966. Joel A. Rogers, through his books and newspaper columns, may have done more than any other person to popularize black history during the first half of the twentieth century. Rogers was born in Negril, Jamaica, in either 1880 or 1883, one of eleven children of a schoolteacher who later became a plantation manager to support his large family. Rogers, a light-skinned black, met little racial prejudice in Jamaica where only dark-skinned blacks were overtly discriminated against. However, when he came to the United States in 1906, he quickly found out that prejudice against blacks extended to light-skinned blacks as well. He constantly heard Americans say that blacks had never accomplished anything, and he vowed to prove them wrong; much of his life was spent in demonstrating the contributions of black people throughout history, thereby eliminating one of the major bases for racial prejudice. He outlined his arguments against prejudice in his book *From Superman to Man*, a fictionalized conversation between a young educated black porter and a southern legislator, which he published privately in 1917. At this time Rogers was himself a porter in Chicago and was studying art there. It was writing, however, that took much of his time.

He published *As Nature Leads* (1919), *The Approaching Storm and How It May Be Averted* (1920), *The Maroons of the West Indies and South America* (1921), *The Ku Klux Spirit* (1923), *This Mongrel World; A Study of Negro-Caucasian Mixing Throughout the Ages, and in All Countries* (1927), and *The*

World's Greatest Men of African Descent (1931). Although biographical details about Rogers are sketchy, he apparently made a living between 1917 and 1933 from his work as a newspaper writer and columnist. His friend George S. Schuyler* helped arrange for Rogers to write a column for the popular *Pittsburgh Courier** and the *Illustrated Feature Section*, distributed weekly to many black newspapers. Rogers's column "Your History" consisted of short vignettes of Afro-American history, and it was read by thousands of enthusiastic readers. He also penned another column, "Rambling Reminiscences," and was assigned to cover the coronation of the Ethiopian Emperor Haile Selassie in 1930. Although Rogers was self-educated and an amateur historian, his work, which also includes six books written after 1933, is an outstanding contribution to Afro-American history. More important, perhaps, he gave many blacks a feeling of race pride through his countless examples of black achievement in history. He died in New York City in 1966.
REFERENCE: W. B. Turner, "Joel Augustus Rogers," *Negro History Bulletin*, February 1972. (DS)

ROGERS, MARSHALL "GARBAGE" (comedian), ?–1934. Garbage Rogers got his nickname from a routine about a garbage collector when he was with the Billy King* Stock Company before World War I. He appeared with Ethel Waters* in *Miss Calico* and in a 1924 film with Paul Robeson,* *Body and Soul*, made by Oscar Micheaux.* Rogers was married to the entertainer Gladys Mike, and he appeared with Noble Sissle* in *Harlem on Parade*.
REFERENCE: BB, 1980. (BK)

ROLL SWEET CHARIOT (play), 1934. Paul Green's* "Symphonic Play of the Negro People" featured Frank Wilson* and Rose McClendon* and purported to treat the disintegration of the South. Opening 2 October 1934, it was a disappointment after the success of his *In Abraham's Bosom*,* and it closed in short order. Perhaps Broadway was growing weary of the familiar theme and materials.
REFERENCES: Burns Mantle, 1934–1935; NYTTR, 1972. (BK)

ROPE AND FAGGOT: A BIOGRAPHY OF JUDGE LYNCH (cultural and social history), 1929. *Rope and Faggot* was Walter White's* first book-length effort at nonfiction. This involves a social-scientific explanation of lynching, the practice whereby a mob with no legal authority acts simultaneously as prosecutor, jury, judge, and executioner. An instrument of white control in America's southern and border states, lynching claimed the lives of more than 3,400 black men and women from 1882 to the late 1930s. White sought to expose and analyze this brutal form of racism. Separate chapters explore the history of mob violence; the social, psychological, and economic climate that made it possible; the religious fundamentalism and sexual mythologies that perpetuated it; and the prospects that more diligent law enforcement, including federal intervention, might prevent lynching. (RZ)

ROSEANNE (play), 1923. Nan Bagby Stephens's highly charged drama about religious hypocrisy was first presented on Broadway on 29 December 1923 with a white cast, and it failed. Three months later, on March 8, it was revived at the Greenwich Village Theatre with Rose McClendon* and Charles Gilpin.* As the title character, McClendon played a devout laundress who having raised an orphan then entrusts her to the Reverend Brown, played by Gilpin, for religious training. When Brown seduces the girl, her foster mother denounces him from his own pulpit, urging that he be lynched—a punishment always associated with white mob violence. Roseanne retracts her demand, choosing instead to leave the minister to God's wrath. McClendon was much admired, but Gilpin proved disappointing enough to receive scathing reviews. Theophilus Lewis,* reviewing the play with some inevitable misgivings in *The Messenger*ings in March 1924, conceded that a white actress "without sentimentality or exaggeration" was successful in the "most significant dramatic work on black life" to that date (pp. 73–74).
REFERENCES: *The Messenger*, Mar. 1924; NYTTR, 1972; Arna Bontemps, ed., *The Harlem Renaissance Remembered*, 1972 (BK)

RUN, LITTLE CHILLUN (musical show), 1933. Hall Johnson's* "folk drama" had a cast of 200 Harlem residents and songs of which the *New York Times* said "some of them deserve—without the usual equivocation—[to be called] superb, and all of them are more than good" (2 Mar. 1933, p. 21). The plot of *Run, Little Chillun* dealt with the conflict between a cult of "new day pilgrims" and a Baptist community, contrasting the strength of religion and of savagery. Edna Thomas,* Alston Burleigh,* Fredi Washington,* Ollie Burgoyne,* Olive Bell, and Walter Price were among the actors.
REFERENCES: Burns Mantle, 1932–1933; NYTTR, 1972. (BK)

RUNNIN' WILD (musical revue), 1923. J. P. Johnson* and Cecil Mack* supplied the lyrics and music and Flournoy Miller* and Aubrey Lyles* wrote the book for a loose series of skits about the adventures of Sam Peck and Steve Jenkins. The cast included Lionel Monagas,* Adelaide Hall,* Georgette Harvey,* and George Stamper. George White, well known for his semi-annual *George White's Scandals*,* was given credit for much of its success, and for a new dance to a song introduced by Elisabeth Welch*: "The Charleston," the *New York Times* reviewer observed, was a routine in which "knees are used more often than ankles" (30 Oct. 1923, p. 17).
REFERENCES: Burns Mantle, 1923–1924; NYTTR, 1972. (BK)

RUSHING, [JAMES ANDREW] JIMMIE (singer), 26 August 1903–8 June 1972. In the forties white writers Don Raye and Gene de Paul wrote a popular song in tribute to Jimmie Rushing, "Mr. Five By Five." Rushing—as rotund in youth as in old age—left Wilberforce University for the West Coast, and by 1925 he was well known as a jazz vocalist there. He moved to New York two years later to sing with Walter Page's band. In 1929 he joined Benny Moten, appeared in some of the variety shows and revues at the Lafayette Theatre,* and from 1935 until 1940 sang with Count Basie. He was still performing and recording well into his sixties.

REFERENCES: ASCAP, 1966; WWJ, 1972; BWW, 1979. (BK)

S

ST. LOUIS BLUES (film), 1929. Warner Brothers Studios financed a two-reel short directed by Dudley Murphy that more or less dramatized W. C. Handy's* celebrated "St. Louis Blues." Bessie Smith* starred, preserving on film the strong combination of sensuality and despair that marked her success with black audiences during the twenties. In *St. Louis Blues* Bessie Smith played a blues* singer whose pimp deserts her for another woman. She then sings, with a good deal of conviction and searing pain, the title song, backed up by an overblown choir more suitable for church services. After twenty years in obscurity the film was resurrected by the Museum of Modern Art for inclusion in its catalog of American film classics.
REFERENCE: Donald Bogle, *Toms, Coons, Mulattoes, Mammies, and Bucks*, 1973. (BK)

SAINT MARK'S METHODIST EPISCOPAL CHURCH, 1927– . Built in 1927 on a triangular block between 137th and 138th streets, where Edgecomb and St. Nicholas avenues fanned to the north, Saint Mark's Methodist Episcopal Church held elaborate services, with more ceremony than sermon, apparently, including a liturgy strongly influenced by Roman Catholicism, elegant robes on all participants, and Handel oratorios rather than familiar hymns from the choir. The charismatic clergymen of the period, however, were affiliated elsewhere. Saint Mark's featured a gymnasium, a swimming pool, and several club rooms for local organizations. During the opening week the Elks, the Masons, the Knights of Pythias, and the Odd Fellows donated their collections to the church. Three years later Saint Mark's carried a $275,000 mortgage into the Depression.
REFERENCES: Wallace Thurman, *Negro Life in New York's Harlem*, 1928; Jervis Anderson, *This Was Harlem*, 1982. (BK)

SAINT PHILIP'S PROTESTANT EPISCOPAL CHURCH, 1818– . Founded in New York in 1818, Saint Philip's moved to Harlem in 1911, erecting a new

building on 133rd Street between Seventh and Eighth avenues at a cost of $200,000. It was a leading influence in getting Afro-Americans to buy up property in Harlem and did so itself; by the twenties it was the wealthiest church with the wealthiest congregation, largely mulatto, "dicty," or high-toned in the eyes of others. The parish house became a familiar social center, serving as backstage space for the $60,000 wedding A'Lelia Walker* produced for her adopted daughter in 1923 and as the stage itself for the Negro Experimental Theatre* in 1931. The church had a large gymnasium and a successful basketball team; between games the space was used for art classes and, during the Depression, for a soup kitchen. As for the religious services, there was usually standing room only.
REFERENCES: Wallace Thurman, *Negro Life in New York's Harlem*, 1928; Jervis Anderson, *This Was Harlem*, 1982. (BK)

SATURDAY EVENING QUILL (periodical), 1928–1930. The Boston Quill Club, a group of young black intellectuals with literary interests in Boston during the twenties, published the first issue of its *Saturday Evening Quill* in June 1928. President Eugene Gordon* was largely responsible for its editing, assisted by Florence Harmon, who also worked with him on the Boston *Post*, and Grace Vera Postles, a student at the Emerson School of Oratory. Members of the organization were regular contributors: Waring Cuney,* George Reginald Margetson, Florida Ridley, Alvirah Hazzard, Helene Johnson,* and Dorothy West,* some of whom were later involved in publishing *Challenge** in Boston. The *Saturday Evening Quill* printed selections in every genre, as well as illustrations. Far more conservative in its content and attitude than other black little magazines like Wallace Thurman's* *Fire!!** and *Harlem,** for example, it attracted the attention of conservative writers like W.E.B. Du Bois,* who thought it "by far the most interesting and the best" (*The Crisis*, Sept. 1928, p. 301). Two subsequent, annual issues of the *Saturday Evening Quill* appeared in 1929 and 1930 before publication ceased.
REFERENCES: *The Crisis*, Sept. 1928; Abby Ann Arthur Johnson and Ronald M. Johnson, "Forgotten Pages," *Journal of American Studies* 8, no. 3 (1974). (BK)

SAUNDERS, GERTRUDE (singer), ?–? A popular performer of the twenties, Gertrude Saunders was also noted for her talent as a comedienne. She left Benedict College in Columbia, South Carolina, to join the Billy King* Company, remaining with it several years. She introduced King's hit songs: "Wait Till the Cows Come Home," from *The Board of Education* (1918); "Little Lump of Sugar," from *The Heart Breakers* (1918); and "Hot Dog," from *They're Off* (1919). In *Town Top-Piks* in 1920 she sang the perennial "Rose of Washington Square." She came to the attention of Eubie Blake,* Noble Sissle,* Flournoy Miller,* and Aubrey Lyles* in 1921, who cast her as the original star of *Shuffle Along.** She was replaced by Florence Mills* when she left this successful show to take advantage of an offer by the Hertig and Seamon Music Hall to join a new company, which, however, soon failed. Vaudeville engagements and roles in several New York musicals and revues followed, including *Liza** (1922), *Dinah* (1923), *Cotton Land* (1924), and later *Rolling On, Jazzbo Regiment, Midnight Steppers*, and *Club Hollywood Review*. She appeared in *Blackberries of 1932,** and one of her last stage roles was in *Run, Little Chillun,** when it was revived in Los Angeles in 1938, five years after its Broadway run. REFERENCE: BB, 1980. (PO)

SAVAGE, AUGUSTA [FELLS] (sculptor), 29 February 1882–26 March 1962. Augusta Savage, who had struggled much of her life to develop her talent as a sculptor, ultimately devoted herself, at the expense of her own career, to the teaching and encouragement of talented young blacks and to the fight for recognition of black artists. She worked in several mediums but was noted primarily as a sculptor of portraits in bronze and plaster and for her wood carvings. Born Augusta Fells in Florida, one of fourteen children of a house painter, she had begun modeling figures from the local clay as a child, despite opposition from her father, who considered such activities sacrilegious. She attended Tallahassee State Normal School briefly, married and had a daughter; later she married James Savage. When one of her clay models won a prize at a county fair, she realized she might be able to make a living with her talent. Determined to obtain training, she raised enough money to get to New York and entered the four-year, tuition-free art program at Cooper Union in 1921, supporting herself as an apartment caretaker and laundress, with extra grants from Cooper Union.

In 1923 she became a *cause célèbre* when she was turned down for a summer art school sponsored by the French government at Fontainebleau. One hundred American women, to be selected by a committee of eminent American artists and scholars, were to receive free tuition and expenses. When she learned that she had been rejected because of her color, she made the story public. A storm of editorials and letters in newspapers followed; her outraged supporters urged the committee to reconsider and appealed to President Harding and the French government to put pressure on the committee. Although she never received the scholarship, she did receive an offer to study with sculptor Hermon MacNeil, and the incident brought her to the attention of the art world and made the public aware of the discrimination against black artists. To her disadvantage, however, she was seen as a troublemaker by certain critics and gallery owners who could have helped advance her career.

In the meantime, Savage was becoming known as a portrait sculptor, having done busts of W.E.B. Du Bois* and Marcus Garvey*. Later she did busts of many other black leaders such as Frederick Douglass and James Weldon Johnson.* She exhibited at the Philadelphia Sesquicentennial Exposition in 1926 and at the Harmon Foundation* Exhibitions of 1928, 1930, and 1931. She continued to have financial difficulties, however, and the necessity of working, usually as a laundress to support herself and her family, took time away from the practice

of her art. Her third husband, Robert L. Poston,* a journalist and associate of
Garvey, had died six months after their marriage in 1923. In 1925 she was
financially unable to take advantage of a scholarship to study at the Academy
of Fine Arts in Rome. Savage finally got her chance to study abroad in 1929
when she won the first of two Julius Rosenwald Fellowships for her sculpture
"Gamin," a study of a Harlem boy. She studied for three years in Paris at the
Grande Chaumière, winning citations for her work at the Salon d'Automne and
the Salon Printemps and a medallion at the Colonial Exposition of the French
government.

Upon her return to New York in 1932, she established the Savage Studio of
Arts and Crafts. The exhibitions of her students' work were favorably received,
and she influenced several artists who later became nationally recognized. A
dedicated teacher, she put her own work aside and encouraged gifted children
to study with her regardless of their ability to pay. In 1934 she became the first
black woman to be elected to the National Association of Women Painters and
Sculptors and that year exhibited at the Architecture League. She was appointed
the first director of the Harlem Community Art Center in 1937, where she
organized programs in recreation and other areas of education as well as art. As
an assistant supervisor of the Federal Arts Project of the WPA for New York
City, she became a spokesperson for black artists, fighting to increase the number
of blacks employed by the WPA and for their right to become supervisors on
WPA projects. She was an organizer of the Harlem Arts Guild and established
the Vanguard Club to develop an awareness of political and social issues among
the artists of Harlem. In 1939 Savage headed a corporation that opened the Salon
of Contemporary Negro Art, devoted to the exhibition and sale of works of black
artists, which, unfortunately, had to close after a few years for lack of funds.
One of Savage's major works was a sculpture commissioned for the New York
World's Fair of 1939–1940. Called "Lift every voice and sing," it was a sixteen-
foot-tall harp with singing figures, representing the musical gifts of blacks to
the world. Although the statue received wide publicity, it was destroyed after
the fair was over. Shortly thereafter, she left the New York art scene for a rural
life.

From 1945 until her death, she maintained a studio in Saugerties, New York,
continuing her teaching and producing a few portrait sculptures. Savage down-
played the significance of her own artistic production, but of her work with
children she said, "If I can inspire one of these youngsters to develop the talent
I know they possess, then my monument will be in their work" (NAW, p. 629).
REFERENCES: NYT, 27 Mar. 1962; Romare Bearden and Harry Henderson,
Six Black Masters of American Art, 1972; AAD, 1973; NAW, 1980; Jervis
Anderson, *This Was Harlem*, 1982. (PO)

SAVAGE RHYTHM (play), 1931. Harry Hamilton and Norman Foster with
James P. Johnson* and Cecil Mack* wrote this melodrama in which Inez Clough*
appeared as Orchid, a Harlem musical star who returns to her home in the South

where her mother and grandmother are "conjure women." Jealousy leads to murder, and Orchid falls in a trance, having inherited the power to conjure, to accuse the killer. The "shapeless and uneven acting" and "aimless" direction in *Savage Rhythm* brought about its demise after twelve performances (NYT, 1 Jan. 1932, p. 30). Georgette Harvey* appeared as Orchid's slatternly sister encumbered with some illegitimate children, and Juano Hernandez* appeared as Orchid's hometown beau. In the middle of the brief run, on 10 January 1932, the scenery for *Savage Rhythm* served as a background for a single, concert performance of Zora Neale Hurston's* ethnic entertainment of music and dance, *The Great Day.**

REFERENCES: Burns Mantle, 1931–1932; NYTTR, 1972. (BK)

SAVOY BALLROOM (dance hall), March 1926– . "The Home of Happy Feet," at 140–141 Lenox Avenue, opened in March 1926 on a $100,000 cash investment by white backers, with a marble staircase, huge cut–glass chandelier, a 50– by 200–foot dance floor of polished maple, and a soda fountain. The instant success of the Savoy Ballroom led to a duplicate version in Chicago, only slightly less opulent, in less than a year. A young Afro–American, Harold Parker, managed the staff of one hundred that offered twelve hours of continuous dancing to two bands; on weekends there might be three or even four bands to spell one another. The Savoy could hold 4,000 people, at fifty cents apiece on weeknights and seventy–five cents on weekends, who came not only for the regular dancing but for special occasions as well. There were costume balls, surprise entertainers, cash prizes for lindy hop contests, and even a "Savoy 400 Club" for wealthy patrons. At the grand opening Fletcher Henderson's* orchestra supplied the music and Eddie Rector* led the floor show. Subsequently, nearly every celebrated black performer in Harlem turned up at the Savoy in one capacity or another.

REFERENCES: Carl Van Vechten, *Parties*, 1930; Nancy Cunard, ed., *Negro*, 1970; WWJ 1972. (BK)

SCHOMBURG, ARTHUR A. (bibliophile), 24 January 1874–10 June 1938. Arthur Alphonso Schomburg was perhaps the greatest collector of books on the history of blacks in the United States, Spain, and Latin America. Born in 1874 in San Juan, Puerto Rico, he was educated in San Juan and the Danish West Indies, before going to the United States on 17 April 1891. He read law for five years and worked as a researcher with the New York firm of Pryor, Mellis, and Harris; later he worked for the Bankers Trust Company of Wall Street (1908– 1929) as head of the mailing department with a large staff of white subordinates. Although he was active in the movement for Puerto Rican independence, almost all of his time away from work was spent collecting books, pamphlets, manuscripts, and other sources related to the history of blacks throughout the world. In addition, he travelled to Europe in 1924 to do research and collect more materials. While in Spain he definitely established that two famous Spanish painters, Juan Pareja and Sebastian Gomez, were black. His passion for establishing a history for his race was unquenchable, and he endured innumerable personal sacrifices to make his inestimable contributions. "The American Negro must remake his past in order to make his future," he wrote. "For him, a group tradition must supply compensation for persecution, and pride of race is the antidote for prejudice. History must restore what slavery took away, for it is the social damage of slavery that the present generation must repair and offset" (quoted in Spero and Harris, *The Black Worker*, p. 426).

Schomburg was one of the founders of the Negro Society for Historical Research and president of the American Negro Academy. In 1925 he contributed "The Negro Digs Up His Past" to the famous *Survey Graphic** issue on Harlem, later reprinted in Alain Locke's* *New Negro.** In 1926 the Carnegie Corporation bought his collection for $10,000 (only one–fifth of its inherent value, according to Joel A. Rogers*) and placed it in the New York Public Library's 135th Street Branch. With Schomburg's continued guidance that collection grew to more than 10,000 volumes by the end of the 1930s and is today one of the great collections of Afro–Americana in the world. In his own bibliography are several relevant works: *Placido* (1905), *The Collected Poems of Phillis Wheatley* (1915, editor), *A Bibliographical Check List of American Negro Poetry* (1916), and *A Plea for Negro History* (1918).

REFERENCES: Sterling Denhard Spero and Abram L. Harris, *The Black Worker*, 1931; WWCA, 1933; J. A. Rogers, *World's Great Men of Color*, 1973. (DS)

SCHUYLER, GEORGE S[AMUEL] (writer), 25 February 1895–31 August 1977. George S. Schuyler, a prominent black journalist and satirist, was born in Providence, Rhode Island. He moved to Syracuse, New York, when he was three and attended public schools there. He later wrote that as a child he read books about famous blacks and their accomplishments, including the participation of blacks in American wars: "This was a fascinating revelation, and no colored child could harbor any feeling of inferiority afterward" (*Black and Conservative*, p. 13). He dropped out of school when he was seventeen and enlisted in the army. He spent the next seven years (1912–1919) with the black Twenty–Fifth U.S. Infantry and was discharged as a first lieutenant.

After working at menial jobs in Syracuse for several years, he moved to New York City in the winter of 1922–1923. He lived as a hobo for several months until he was "discovered" by A. Philip Randolph* and Chandler Owen,* the editors of the radical magazine *The Messenger.** Schuyler helped edit and write the magazine from 1923–1928 and at the same time penned columns for the popular black weekly the *Pittsburgh Courier,** including his long–running "Views and Reviews," which he launched in October 1924. He published numerous articles in black and white magazines and periodicals during the 1920s and 1930s, the most famous of which, "The Negro–Art Hokum," appeared in the 16 June 1926 *Nation.** In that essay Schuyler argued that the black man in the United States was "merely a lampblacked Anglo–Saxon" and therefore should create art in the mainstream of the Western European culture in which his consciousness had been shaped. In the next issue of the *Nation* Langston Hughes* published a rebuttal of Schuyler in which he urged black writers and artists not to ignore their racial heritage and to search within themselves for their creative powers, rather than looking to whites or blacks for approval or the criteria for what is acceptable. Schuyler appears in this debate and elsewhere as tending toward an assimilationist view; yet he was proud of his race and only wanted to speed acceptance by whites in part by limiting the tendency of blacks to segregate themselves through a "racial" art separate from the Western mainstream.

Schuyler published a number of essays on racial themes in *The American Mercury*, and wrote a series of articles for the *Pittsburgh Courier* based on his 1925 assignment to tour 200 southern communities and report on conditions there. In 1931 he published his first novel (and his best–known work today), the lively *Black No More.** In this work, the first full–length satire by a black American, Schuyler managed to lampoon most of the major black figures of the 1920s while making great fun of both white and black racial attitudes. In January 1931 Schuyler was hired as a secret foreign correspondent by the *New York Evening Post* to investigate the modern slave trade in Liberia. He returned to write a series of articles on the trade and based his second novel, *Slaves Today* (1932), on his investigations. Schuyler turned increasingly conservative after World War II and became a virulent opponent of communism and the civil rights revolution. He died 31 August 1977 in New York City.

REFERENCES: George S. Schuyler, *Black and Conservative*, 1966; Michael W. Peplow, *George S. Schuyler*, 1980. (DS)

SCOTT, EMMETT JAY (publicist), 13 February 1873–12 December 1957. Emmett Jay Scott wrote for the *Houston Post* before becoming an associate editor of a new black Houston paper, the *Texas Freeman*, in 1894, in which he strongly endorsed the ideas of Booker T. Washington. For eighteen years, after they met in 1897, Scott and Washington worked in perfect tandem as they successfully gained control of most national black organizations, newspapers, and political patronage. They organized the National Negro Business League* in 1900, and Scott administered the group as secretary until 1922. In 1909 President Taft appointed Scott to the American Commission to Liberia, and in 1912 Scott was secretary of the International Conference on the Negro, held at Tuskegee Institute. When Washington died in 1915, Scott continued as secretary of Tuskegee, a position he had assumed in 1912. The new Tuskegee president, Robert Russa Moton,* helped Scott gain an appointment as assistant to Secretary of War Newton D. Baker, and Scott advised Baker on issues relating to black soldiers and civilians.

REFERENCES: WWCA, 1933; NYT, 14 Dec. 1957; DAB, 1980. (DS)

SCOTT, WILLIAM EDOUARD (painter), 1884–1964. William Scott's *The Lord Will Provide*, depicting the travails of his race, hangs in the Harmon

Foundation,* but this Indiana painter was best known for portrait painting. He studied at the Chicago Art Institute from 1904 to 1908 and then in Paris under Henry O. Tanner,* dean of the former generation of black painters. Scott won the Harmon Foundation* Gold Medal in 1927.
REFERENCE: Cedric Dover, *American Negro Art*, 1969. (BK)

SCOTTSBORO CASE (lawsuit), 1931–1933. In Scottsboro, Alabama, nine black boys ranging in age from thirteen to nineteen were accused of raping two white prostitutes in a railroad boxcar and were sentenced to death. Probably no event in the period sparked more legal and emotional controversy for black America. The trials followed the lynchings of forty black citizens during 1930 and fifteen more during the first four months of 1931. In April the Communist International Labor Defense Fund engaged the powerful white criminal lawyer Clarence Darrow to represent the defendants, but he withdrew on the advice of Walter White,* who feared that the NAACP* might become identified as revolutionary or Marxist, claiming that the black organization had the case under control. The nine boys were sentenced to die on July 10, but worldwide protests— from Albert Einstein, Thomas Mann, George Bernard Shaw, and other influential white voices—as well as demonstrations around the country delayed any action. White novelist John Dos Passos characterized the flaws in both prosecution and procedure that led to the wide public outcry; he was later quoted in Nancy Cunard's* *Negro* anthology in 1934:

Reading the testimony of the Scottsboro case, you feel all that—the band outside the courthouse, the mob starved for joy and sex and power hanging around, passing from mouth to mouth all the juicy details of the raping. You feel that filthy prurient joy in the court room, the stench of it is in the badly typewritten transcript of the court procedure, in the senseless ritual, the half illiterate, poorly phrased speeches of the judge and the solicitor, the scared answers of the two tough girls, evidently schooled for days in their story, sometimes seeming to enjoy the exhibitionism of it. Evidently the court stenographer didn't take the trouble to put down what the colored boys said in their own words; what they said didn't matter, they were going to burn anyway. (p. 162)

In May 1933 3,000 people marched on Washington, D.C., to demand the release of the Scottsboro Boys, as they had come to be called. President Franklin Roosevelt refused to meet with a committee of twenty-five, including James W. Ford,* vice-presidential candidate for the Communist party the previous year; Louise Thompson,* secretary of the Scottsboro Action Committee; and Ruby Bates, one of the white prostitutes who by that time had admitted her own perjury. They presented petitions with signatures variously estimated between 145,000 and 200,000. The case, which inspired Langston Hughes's* one-act play *Scottsboro Limited** and John Wexley's Broadway drama *They Shall Not Die*,* was finally settled as one by one the convictions were overturned.
REFERENCES: Nancy Cunard, ed., *Negro*, 1970; Dan T. Carter, *Scottsboro*, 1969. (BK)

SCOTTSBORO LIMITED (poetry, drama), 1932. The Golden Stair Press printed Langston Hughes's* verse drama about the *Scottsboro* trial in a pamphlet entitled *Scottsboro Limited*, with four poems on similar themes. The play had first appeared in *New Masses*, and the poems in *Contempo*,* *Opportunity*,* and the Associated Negro Press. Prentiss Taylor,* the white artist who had illustrated Hughes's *Negro Mother and Other Dramatic Recitations*ize* the year before, also published by the Golden Stair Press, contributed four lithographs. Even on the printed page, the play deals a swift blow, strongly Marxist in its attitudes, highly charged in its poetry. (BK)

THE SECOND COMIN' (play), 1931. George Bryant's religious melodrama was markedly less successful than *The Green Pastures*,* running for only eight performances from December 8, but Brooks Atkinson, in his *New York Times* review, thought it strove "to present an authentic study of the emotional phases of the Negro as they are expressed in their search for religion" (9 Dec. 1931, p. 32). Nicodemus, a doubting member of the black congregation, challenges the white Reverend Wilbur to save the church from failure by performing a miracle: a black Jesus. Wilbur then privately hypnotizes Nicodemus's sweetheart, Glory, impregnates her, and publicly predicts a virgin birth. When a white son is born to Glory at Christmas, Wilbur dies of a stroke during a fight with Nicodemus. "It takes a good white actor to hold his own against a troupe of psalm-singing Negroes," Atkinson concluded.
REFERENCES: Burns Mantle, 1931–1932; NYTTR, 1972. (BK)

SEVEN ARTS (periodical), 1916–1917. James Oppenheimer and Waldo Frank,* white editors of this literary and political magazine, published "The Harlem Dancer" by "Eli Edwards" in 1917. This early poem by Claude McKay* marked the first substantial one in print since the dialect pieces by Paul Laurence Dunbar at the turn of the century and may, with the Silent Protest Parade,* mark the beginning of the movement that came to be known as the "Harlem Renaissance." After its single year of publication *Seven Arts* merged with *Dial*. (BK)

THE SHEIK OF HARLEM (musical comedy), 1923. Irvin C. Miller* and Donald Heywood* fabricated *The Sheik of Harlem*, a popular Lafayette Theatre* show, in which a girl falls in love with a macho type who disguises himself as an overdressed sissy. Reviewing it in *The Messenger*,* Theophilus Lewis* decried the unfunny comedians who were unrelated to the plot, but the show itself "rises to the ranks of light opera or the calibre of George Bernard Shaw's 'Arms and the Man' " (Sept. 1923, p. 819). Lewis, not usually given to such enthusiasm for Harlem's shows, also admired Hattie King Reavis singing Miller's song to Will Marion Cook,* "It Don't Pay to Love a Northern Man in from the South."
REFERENCE: Theophilus Lewis, "Theatre," *The Messenger*, Sept. 1923. (BK)

SHELTON, RUTH [ADA] GAINES (playwright), 8 April 1872–? Ruth Gaines Shelton graduated from Wilberforce University in 1895, and after assisting her father, the Reverend George W. Gaines, in overseeing construction of the Old Bethel A.M.E. Church in Chicago, she went back to teach in her native Missouri. She wrote many plays for clubs, schools, and churches during a period of about twenty years, culminating with "The Church Fight," which won second prize in the Amy Spingarn Contest sponsored by *The Crisis*,* in 1925. One of the few comedies of the period, her play treats in-fighting among the parishioners and is only incidentally racial in its theme.
REFERENCES: WWCA, 1927; James V. Hatch, ed., *Black Theater, U.S.A.*, 1974. (BK)

SHIPP, JESSE A. (actor), 1859–1 May 1934. Jesse A. Shipp co-authored *In Dahomey* in 1902, *Abyssinia* in 1906, and other Bert Williams* and George Walker extravaganzas. He was active in the black musical organization The Frogs and toured in vaudeville as one of "The Tennessee Ten" until 1917. When an attempt was made at that time to establish a Negro theater, with productions of Ridgely Torrence's three one-act plays, Shipp played a leading role in *Simon, the Cyrenian*, but the Negro theater did not continue beyond that initial production, and Shipp had no marked success until he was cast as Abraham in *The Green Pastures** thirteen years later, ironically, another play by a white playwright. Apparently, Shipp was a greatly gifted actor for whom roles simply were unavailable at a time when fast dancing and quick comedy were more likely to engage the attention of Broadway audiences.
REFERENCE: Loften Mitchell, *Black Drama*, 1967. (BK)

SHIPP, OLIVIA [SOPHIE L'ANGE PORTER] (dance-band bassist), 17 May 1880–18 June 1980. Born in New Orleans, Olivia Shipp was a self-taught church organist. She joined her sister in New York about the turn of the century and began playing in vaudeville shows. She began the study of cello with Leonard Jeter and played in the school orchestra at the Martin-Smith School of Music, where she was also a teaching assistant. She took up the study of the string bass with various teachers in 1916, and in 1917 began playing this instrument in Marie Lucas's* Lafayette Theatre* Ladies Orchestra. She organized Olivia Shipp's Jazz-Mines during the twenties and founded the Negro Women's Orchestral Civic Association. Married to the son of actor Jesse Shipp,* she continued to play with dance orchestras as a free-lance performer for many years.
REFERENCE: BDAM, 1982. (PO)

SHOWBOAT (musical play), 1927. Oscar Hammerstein's stage adaptation of Edna Ferber's novel *Showboat*, with a score by Jerome Kern, opened at the Ziegfield Theatre on 27 December 1927. The tragedy of the miscegenous union of Julie and Frank was sensitively enacted, and blacks were presented as characterful individuals rather than racial stereotypes. The plot was unusually dramatic for a musical comedy of the day, and the first, unsigned, review in the *New York Times* noted "perhaps a slight lack of one kind of comedy, and an overabundance of another, and a slight slowness in getting under way" (28 Dec. 1927, p. 26). Charles Winnager's Cap'n Andy was declared the "outstanding hit of the evening," although Norma Terris's Magnolia was considered "a revelation." Howard Marsh, "one of the more facial tenors," was judged "satisfactory" as Ravenal, the comedy team of Eva Puck and Sammy White was "reliable," and Edna May Oliver played Parthy Ann Hawks with "requisite austerity." "Old Man River," as sung by Jules Bledsoe* (Joe) and the black chorus, was "remarkedly effective." Helen Morgan (Julie) "purveyed two numbers in her distinctive style." All in all, the *Times*'s anonymous critic thought that *Showboat* was "an excellent musical comedy; one that comes perilously close to being the best the town has seen in several seasons." Brooks Atkinson, in a follow-up piece in the *Times* a week later, had no such reservations; he proclaimed *Showboat* "one of those epochal works about which garrulous old men gabble for twenty-five years after the scenery has rattled off to the storehouse" (8 Jan. 1928, sec. 8, p. 1).

A London company of *Showboat*, with Paul Robeson* as Joe and Alberta Hunter* as Queenie, opened in May 1928. *Showboat* had an original run in New York of 572 performances; a revival in 1932 ran 180 performances; another in 1946 ran 572 performances. It was made into a movie twice: in 1936 with Robeson as Joe and in 1951 with William Warfield in the role.
REFERENCES: WWT, 1947; Sigmund Spaeth, *A History of Popular Music in America*, 1948; NYTTR, 1972. (DA)

SHUFFLE ALONG (musical comedy), 1921. As the first black show of the twenties, *Shuffle Along* is often credited with having sparked the Harlem Renaissance, on 22 May 1921. Apparently, it was not very original, but it set a pace and style during a period eager for novelties. After the first week's run business was so heavy that the street on which it was playing had to be designated for one-way traffic only. Aubrey Lyles* and Flournoy Miller* based the book on two earlier works: *The Mayor of Dixie*, a 1905 Pekin Stock Company vaudeville skit, and *Who's Stealin'?* a show that had toured briefly in 1918. In the thin plot of *Shuffle Along*, grocery-store owners Jenkins and Peck (played in blackface by Miller and Lyles) run for mayor against the reform candidate Harry Walton, about whom everybody is eventually "wild" in the best-known song from the score. The comedians sneak funds from their stores to finance their individual campaigns and hire the same detective to spy on each other. When Jenkins wins, he appoints Peck as chief of police; then Walton runs them both out of town. The score, by Noble Sissle* and Eubie Blake,* accounted strongly for the success of *Shuffle Along*: Gertrude Saunders,* soon replaced by Florence Mills,* sang the big hit "Love Will Find a Way," and everybody else, including Josephine Baker* and Mae Barnes* in the road company chorus line, sang "I'm Just Wild about Harry." Originally, that song had been a waltz, until Lottie

Gee* took over to give it the frantic stridency that identifies it with the twenties. Paul Robeson* appeared briefly during the run as one of the Four Harmony Kings; Caterina Jarboro,* later to sing in opera, was kept backstage because she was considered too dark for the chorus and understudied the female leads; Ulysses "Slow Kid" Thompson* performed his undulating dances; and Hall Johnson* on viola and William Grant Still* on oboe were in the pit with Eubie Blake, who played his own songs on the piano.

Shuffle Along had opened first at the Howard Theatre in Washington, D.C., and then had a run at the Dunbar Theatre in Philadelphia, each time with some success. When it opened at Daly's 63rd Street Music Hall in New York, a seedy lecture hall in need of renovation and well out of the Broadway area, no one anticipated much chance of a long run. Nor was the report in the *New York Times* encouraging. The reviewer noted that Miller and Lyles demonstrated "no marked comic talent" and that the "principle asset" of the show was its having been "written, composed, and played entirely by negroes. . . . Little or none of it," the reviewer continued, "is conspicuously native and all of it is extremely crude—in writing, playing and direction." In his opinion *Shuffle Along* was no more than a "fair-to-middling amateur entertainment" (23 May 1921, p. 16).

For his 1971 study of the period, *Harlem Renaissance*, however, Nathan Irvin Huggins drew together some contrary opinions. Alan Dale, writing for the *New York American* on May 25, recognized the dancing as something absolutely unique: "They revelled in their work; they simply pulsed with it, and there was no let-up at all. . . . How they enjoyed themselves! How they jigged and pranced and cavorted, and wriggled and laughed. . . . Every sinew of their bodies danced; every tendon in their frames responded to their extreme energy" (p. 289). For an anonymous reviewer in the *New York Sun*, on May 23, the chorus was full of "dash and ginger" (p. 290). On May 24 the *New York Herald* reviewer encapsulated the success of *Shuffle Along* in one sentence: "the world seems a brighter place to live in" (p. 290). Eubie Blake's own memories of the show—particularly its preparation—enhance these observations: there was a constant struggle for funds and backing; at the time few professional girls were available for the chorus line; Flournoy Miller kept arguing that they had to keep the show clean; lacking money for costumes they appropriated the sweat-stained cast-offs from *Frank Fay's Fables*, a recently failed Broadway revue.

Shuffle Along had a long Broadway run, strongly patronized by white audiences, and including a benefit performance that raised $1,000 for the NAACP,* road company versions, subsequent editions in 1930 and 1933, and dozens of imitations during the intervening years.

REFERENCES: Burns Mantle, 1920–1921; Nathan Irvin Huggins, *Harlem Renaissance,* 1971; NYTTR, 1972; EMT, 1976; Al Rose, *Eubie Blake,* 1979; BB, 1980. (BK)

SHUFFLE ALONG IN 1930 (musical comedy), 1930. The vogue for black song and dance shows was past when Flournoy Miller* and Aubrey Lyles*

attempted to resurrect *Shuffle Along* with a new score. J. P. Johnson* and Fats Waller* supplied the songs, including at least two that had a brief popularity: "Willow Tree" and "Go Harlem."
REFERENCE: Burns Mantle, 1930–1931. (BK)

SHUFFLE ALONG OF 1933 (musical comedy), 1932. Like most sequels and subsequent editions, this third version of *Shuffle Along* was a pale imitation of the 1921 original. Noble Sissle* and Flournoy Miller* wrote the book, Eubie Blake* wrote the music, and Mantan Moreland* starred as a replacement partner for Aubrey Lyles,* who had died a few months before the opening. The music and dancing were generally better than the plot about some city slickers trying to fleece Jimtown citizens over a molasses factory. The show ran briefly, beginning 26 December 1932.
REFERENCE: NYTTR, 1972. (BK)

SILENT PROTEST PARADE, 28 July 1917. In protest against lynchings in Waco, Texas, and Memphis, Tennessee, and, particularly, a devastating riot* in East St. Louis, Illinois, four weeks earlier, 10,000 to 15,000 black American citizens marched down Fifth Avenue in absolute silence, save the roll of muffled drums, led by children dressed in white, followed by women in white and then men in black. Even the white onlookers watched silently. Some marchers carried banners with messages such as "Mother, Do Lynchers Go to Heaven?" and "Mr. President, Why Not Make America Safe for Democracy?" Boy scouts distributed a leaflet, later reprinted in both black and white newspapers:

We march because the growing consciousness and solidarity of race, coupled with sorrow and discrimination, have made us one, a union that may never be dissolved in spite of the shallow-brained agitators, scheming pundits, and political tricksters who receive a fleeting popularity and the uncertain financial support of a people who ought to consider themselves as one. We march because we want our children to live in a better land and enjoy fairer conditions than have been our lot.

W.E.B. Du Bois,* James Weldon Johnson,* John Nail,* and the Reverend Frederick Asbury Cullen* organized this first silent protest against racial inequities in the United States, taken seriously enough to move the mayor of New York to close down traffic on Fifth Avenue well in advance and until—still silently—the parade concluded.
REFERENCES: *New York American*, 29 July 1917; New York *Age*, 17 Aug. 1917; JWJ. (BK)

SILVERA, EDWARD [S.] (poet), 1906–1937. Born in Florida, Edward Silvera was reared in New Jersey and attended Lincoln University, where his poems were published in *Four Lincoln University Poets** in 1930. In addition, Silvera was active in athletics there. His lyrics published in 1930 were delicate, but

three years earlier, in Countee Cullen's* *Caroling Dusk*,* Silvera was represented by two strong poems with marked racial themes, "South Street," a grim reminder of ghetto life, and "Jungle Taste," which observed in other words that "black was beautiful," even in 1927. Other poems appeared in magazines and anthologies before Silvera's early death.
REFERENCES: Countee Cullen, ed., *Caroling Dusk*, 1927; Langston Hughes and Arna Bontemps, eds., *The Poetry of the Negro*, 1949. (BK)

SIMS, JOE (comedian), c. 1890–? Joe Sims was born in Mississippi but migrated north to Chicago at an early age. He first worked in a beer garden on State Street and then joined the Pekin Theatre Stock Company. In 1923 he replaced Aubrey Lyles* in *Shuffle Along** in New York, and in 1927 he produced *Sons of Rest*, one of the Harlem shows that failed to make a transition to Broadway.
REFERENCE: BB, 1980. (BK)

SINGIN' THE BLUES (musical play), 1931. During a crap game raid in a Chicago pool room, Jim Williams shoots a policeman and escapes to New York; there he falls in love with Susan Blake, a Harlem nightclub singer, who hides him in her dressing room—all in the first act. In the second act, he makes a long escape through a series of cabarets and clubs, amply populated by "dusky wenches and singing waiters with hot feet," according to Brooks Atkinson in the *New York Times* (17 Sept. 1931, p. 21). "As a musical carnival it has its moment of jubilance, billowing ostrich feathers and kinkless hair," Atkinson continued. "As a melodrama of night life in Harlem it has the raciness of a sharply colored lithograph." Joined into a single entertainment, however, the parts had their "embarrassed moments." Frank Wilson* played the hero, and Mantan Moreland* bugged his eyes as Knuckles Lincoln, a sidekick. As "the jaunty prima donna," Isabell Washington* gave her songs "the exultation of the spirituals," and there was some "wicked stepping by the brown gals . . . and torrid hoofing by the four gleaming youths," all to a book by John McGowan and a score by Jimmie McHugh* and Dorothy Fields,* played by Eubie Blake's* "thumping, squealing band."
REFERENCES: Burns Mantle, 1931–1932; NYTTR, 1972. (BK)

SISSLE, NOBLE (lyricist, actor), 10 July 1889–17 December 1975. Early in life Noble Sissle studied for the ministry at Butler University in his native Indiana, in emulation of his ordained father. Later, after touring with the Thomas Hann Jubilee Singers from 1911 to 1913 and with Joe Porter's Serenaders until 1915, he became the protégé of James Reese Europe,* serving as his drum major in the 369th Regiment during and just after World War I. Sissle teamed up with Eubie Blake*—his only collaborator—about 1915 to tour as the Dixie Duo, and about five years later they produced their first show, the legendary *Shuffle Along*,* produced on Broadway in 1921. *Elsie* followed in 1923, *Chocolate Dandies**

in 1924, *Keep Shufflin'** in 1928, and a new edition of *Shuffle Along** in 1933. Sissle did all of the contracts and paper work for these shows, duties he seemed to welcome, according to his partner's memories as quoted in Al Rose's biography. Blake also recalled, however, that Sissle was "a real square. A goody-goody. He never wanted to do nothin'. He didn't drink, he didn't smoke, he didn't cuss, he didn't gamble. Of course, he was a handsome fellow and he could have had all the girls he wanted, but I always thought all he needed was that audience out there" (*Eubie Blake*, p. 56). In 1923 Sissle and Blake made a short film with sound, using the phonofilm system of Lee De Forest, a pioneer radio inventor. It was called *Snappy Songs* and featured "Those Colored Vaude-villians." That same year they supplied Gertrude Lawrence and Noel Coward, the young English musical performers, with "You Were Meant for Me" in *London Calling*, one of several numbers they wrote for the white theater. In 1926 Sissle and Blake played in London and made extensive tours of the continent afterward as "American Ambassadors of Syncopation." They had their only argument during that period—Blake wanted to return to America; Sissle loved England and wanted to stay there—and broke up their partnership, although only temporarily.

Noble Sissle is credited with having founded the Negro Actor's Guild, and, in a solo act, he was known during the thirties as "The Colored Rudy Vallee," the nasal white crooner who had become America's vocal heart throb during the late twenties. Sissle is better remembered, however, for infectious lyrics like "I'm Just Wild about Harry."

REFERENCES: Daniel Leab, *From Sambo to Superspade*, 1975; EMT, 1976; NA, 1976; Al Rose, *Eubie Blake*, 1979; BB, 1980. (BK)

SMALL'S PARADISE (cabaret), October 1925–? Ed Small's cabaret was called "Harlem's Home of Mirth and Music," a larger place than most of the others in the area, at 2294 Seventh Avenue. It was patronized largely by blacks, although it endured white slummers occasionally. The improvised music, during nightly jam sessions, was called "gut-bucket," and the floor shows featured dancing waiters, in addition to the singers of double entendre blues* and "a real beauty ensemble of winsome maids" in a "Snappy All-Star Revue," according to Ed Small's advertisements. As the "Black Venus," Small's Paradise is described in detail—both its steamy atmosphere and its varied clientele—in the Prologue to Carl Van Vechten's* *Nigger Heaven*.* The place opened in October 1925, and from the beginning its Sundays were considered best, followed by Monday morning breakfast dances that soon became traditional. Small's may have been unique in Harlem in offering both Chinese and American food.

REFERENCES: Carl Van Vechten, *Nigger Heaven*, 1926; *Official Theatrical World of Colored Artists*, 1928; Roi Ottley and William J. Weatherby, eds., *The Negro in New York*, 1967; Jervis Anderson, *This Was Harlem*, 1982. (BK)

SMITH, ADA "BRICKTOP" (singer, nightclub hostess), 14 August 1894–31 January 1984. Ada Beatrice Queen Victoria Louisa Virginia Smith, from

West Virginia, began her nightclub career at the age of seventeen, singing at Jack Johnson's* Chicago Club Du Champ. She was small, freckle-faced, and far from conventionally pretty. With her bright red hair she quickly acquired the nickname "Bricktop." She teamed up with Florence Mills* and Cora Green* to form the Panama Trio,* which toured the vaudeville circuits for several years, and worked TOBA* tours with the Tennessee Ten. But she was a café singer rather than a vaudevillian or stage performer—she seems to have appeared in only one stage show in New York: *The Frolics* (1923)—and by the early twenties she was singing regularly at Barron Wilkins's Club and Connie's Inn* in New York. In 1924 she was summoned hastily to Paris; Florence Embry, the temperamental star of the nighclub Le Grand Duc, had quit in a huff, and they needed an immediate replacement. Bricktop was hardly the glamorous star the management was hoping for. Langston Hughes,* who was washing dishes at the club at the time, described her as having "a cute little voice, with nice, wistful notes. She danced a few cute little steps, tossed her head and smiled, and went around to all the tables and was pleasant to everybody" (*The Big Sea*, p. 179.) But it didn't take her long to build up her own clientele; Cole Porter discovered her at the club and asked her to teach the Charleston to the guests at his parties, and his guests—the International Smart Set—began to go to the club. Within a year Bricktop took over the management of Le Grand Duc and some time later opened her own place, the first of a series of Bricktop's, on the Rue Pigalle. Over the years they became the favorite haunts of royalty, society, and leaders in the arts. During World War II she had a club in Mexico City, and after the war she opened a new series of Bricktop's in Italy.

REFERENCES: Langston Hughes, *The Big Sea*, 1940; *Ebony*, October 1948; *Show Magazine*, May 1973; BB, 1980. (DA)

SMITH, ALBERT (painter), 17 September 1896–1940. Albert Smith was born in New York City and studied at the Ethical School on a scholarship in 1916 and at the National Academy of Design from 1917 until 1920. He won the Henry O. Tanner Gold Medal and Chaloner Prize in 1919, and his work was exhibited in Paris in 1921. Smith won the Harmon Foundation* Bronze Medal in 1929, and his work, both landscape and figure paintings, was exhibited at the Ethical Culture School in 1928.

REFERENCES: WWCA, 1933; Cedric Dover, *American Negro Art*, 1969. (BK)

SMITH, BESSIE (singer), 15 April 1894–26 September 1937. Bessie Smith was one of seven children of a part-time Baptist preacher in Chattanooga, Tennessee. She joined Moses Stokes's travelling show in 1912, appearing with Will Rainey and Ma Rainey,* and worked briefly in an Irvin C. Miller* show but was kicked out of the chorus as being too dark—the theme of Miller's shows was "Glorifying the Brownskin Girl." She teamed with Buzzin' Barton in Park's Big Revue in Atlanta in 1914, toured with Ma Rainey again in Fat Chappelle's Rabbit Foot Minstrel Show in 1915, and worked with Pete Werley's Florida

Cotton Blossom Minstrel Show, the Silas Green Minstrel Show, and other tent shows. She worked in a team with Hazel Green in 1918 and then starred in her own *Liberty Belles* in 1918–1919. By 1920 she was an established blues* star in the South.

Curiously, she was at first ignored by the burgeoning blues recording industry. The Black Swan Phonograph Corporation* rejected her in 1921 in favor of Ethel Waters,* and OKeh also rejected her in early 1923. But Frank Walker, director of race records at Columbia, signed her a few weeks later—at the rate of $125 a side—and her first recording, "Down Hearted Blues"/"Gulf Coast Blues," was a sensational hit, selling 780,000 copies in six months. Billed as "Empress of the Blues," she quickly became Columbia's best-selling artist, and remained with the company until 1931; but she never had a royalty agreement and received a total of only $28,575 from Columbia for all of her dozens of recordings.

On tour she commanded top salaries of up to $2,000 a week, and her popularity continued to grow, particularly in the South. Although she travelled only with black shows and played only in black theaters, she sometimes gave special performances for whites only. She worked the TOBA* circuit regularly but preferred to run her own shows, travelling in her own railroad car, with accommodations for her entire troupe, as well as storage space for a show tent and all of the necessary stage equipment. Her troupes worked hard and played hard. Bessie Smith was stingy about salaries, but she could be spontaneously generous to her fellow artists. She was a 200-pound, rough, tough woman, foul mouthed and with an ugly temper. "Nobody messed with Bessie, black or white, it didn't make no difference," said Ruby Walker, her niece by marriage, who worked with her for many years (Albertson, *Bessie*, p. 66). Once she single-handedly faced down and routed a group of Ku Klux Klansmen who were bent on tearing down her show tent; another time she played her show despite having been stabbed in the side the night before in a party brawl. She was a heavy drinker, and she had strong sexual appetites for both men and women. Her first husband, Earl Love, died about 1920, and in 1923 she married Jack Gee, a security guard. The marriage was stormy, and she later took up with Richard Morgan, a prosperous bootlegger from Chicago.

Generally, Bessie Smith got along well with other performers, at least those who did not encroach on her blues repertoire, but her phenomenal popularity in the twenties was based largely on her recordings. She did not appear often in the New York area. Two early revues, *How Come* and *Tunes and Topics*, both in 1923, opened in Philadelphia; others—*Yellow Girl Revue* (1927), *Mississippi Days* (1928), *Late Hour Tap Dancers* (1929), and *The Jazzbo Regiment* (1929), for example—originated at the Lafayette* or Lincoln* theaters in New York before going on tour. Many of her shows were assembled in New York for tours only, and she appeared in only one Broadway musical comedy, the ill-starred *Pansy*,* in 1929, which lasted only three performances. Bessie Smith made only one film, a two-reel RCA Photophone short, *St. Louis Blues*,* in 1929, with Jimmy Mordecai, Isabell Washington,* a forty-two-voice choir conducted by J.

Rosamund Johnson,* and an orchestra of Fletcher Henderson's* bandsmen conducted by James P. Johnson.*

Her career suffered a sharp decline in the early thirties as record sales dropped and touring became unprofitable. She did attempt to broaden her repertoire and develop a more sophisticated style and began a successful comeback in 1936, when she replaced Billie Holiday in *Stars Over Broadway* at Connie's Inn.* But on tour with *Broadway Rastus*, the car in which she was travelling hit a truck; her right arm was nearly severed and she suffered massive chest injuries. She died at the Afro-American Hospital in Clarksdale, Mississippi, 26 September 1937.

Bessie Smith left an enormous legacy of recordings, of which five albums have been reissued by Columbia. They range from a raucous "Gimme a Pigfoot and a Bottle of Beer" to a banal "Alexander's Ragtime Band," but the blues predominate. Many commentators have remarked on the religious character of Bessie Smith's blues singing. Guitarist Danny Barker said of her: "If you had any church background, like people who came from the South as I did, you would recognize a similarity between what she was doing and what those preachers and evangelists from there did, and how they moved people. She could bring about mass hypnotism. When she was performing you could hear a pin drop" (Shapiro and Hentoff, *Hear Me Talkin' to Ya*, p. 243).

REFERENCES: Nat Shapiro and Nat Hentoff, eds., *Hear Me Talkin' to Ya*, 1955; Robert M. W. Dixon and John Godrich, *Recording the Blues*, 1970; Chris Albertson, *Bessie*, 1972; Giles Oakley, *The Devil's Music*, 1978; BWW, 1979. (DA)

SMITH, CHRIS (composer), 1879–10 September 1939. Chris Smith wrote the perennially popular "Ballin' the Jack" in 1913 and many other songs during the following years. He had appeared in vaudeville in his native South Carolina, and he continued to perform in various cafés as well as with the first stock company at the Lincoln Theatre* in Harlem. In 1927 he supplied some of the songs for the Clarence Williams*–Eva Taylor* musical fiasco *Bottomland.*

REFERENCES: NYT, 28 June 1927; BB, 1980. (BK)

SMITH, CLARA (singer), c. 1894–2 February 1935. Nothing is known of Clara Smith's childhood, but she is believed to have been born in Spartanburg, South Carolina, about 1894. She worked in southern vaudeville from about 1910 and was a TOBA* headliner by 1918. She toured with Al Wells Smart Set tent show in 1920, played the Dream Theatre in Columbus, Georgia in 1921, and settled in New York City in 1923, where she sang in the Harlem clubs, cabarets, and speakeasies. From about 1924 she ran her own Clara Smith Theatrical Club in New York City and appeared in a number of musical revues: *Black Bottom Revue* (1927); *Clara Smith Revue* (1928); and *Ophelia Snow From Baltimo'* (1928–1929), all at the Lincoln Theatre*; *Swanee Club Revue* (1928), at the Lafayette Theatre*; and *Dream Girls and Candied Sweets* (1929), *Hello 1930*

(1929–1930), *Here We Are* (1930), *Dusty Lane* (1930), and *January Jubilee* (1930), all at the Alhambra Theatre.* In 1930 she appeared with Charlie Johnson's Paradise Band at the Harlem Opera House and starred in *Sweet Chariot** at the Ambassador Theatre. In 1931 she starred (with Jackie "Moms" Mabley*) in an all-Negro Western Show, *Trouble on the Ranch*, at the Standard Theatre in Philadelphia, and in 1933 she appeared in *Harlem Madness* at the Harlem Fifth Avenue Theatre.

She made her first recordings for Columbia in 1923, the same year that Bessie Smith* began her recording career with that company, and although there was some professional rivalry between them they were on friendly terms, at least in the beginning. They sometimes pretended to be sisters, although they were not related. Bessie apparently thought that Clara was not a serious threat; she had a more powerful voice than Clara, and Columbia paid her more and promoted her as its top recording star. They even made recordings together, "Far Away Blues" and "I'm Going Back to My Used to Be" (1923) and "My Man Blues" (1925), the latter a humorous duet in which they agree to share the same man "on the cooperation plan." But the two stars got into a fist fight at a drunken party at the end of 1925 and never spoke to each other again.

Clara Smith recorded steadily for Columbia until 1932 and was second only to Bessie Smith as a best-selling blues* artist. One of her most unusual recordings is the overtly sexual "Whip It to a Jelly (if You Like Good Jelly Roll)," for which she wrote the words and melody; the song is most frequently played fast, with strong rhythm; Clara Smith sings it as a slow-drag blues, implying that the imagery is only a sad fantasy. Her voice on her earliest recordings was somewhat light and thin, but it darkened as time went on. Carl Van Vechten,* comparing her to Bessie Smith, wrote that she employed

more nuances of expression, a greater range of vocal color, than the Empress. Her voice flutters agonizingly between tones. Music critics would say that she sings off the key; rather, she is singing quarter tones, and singing them for the full effect of a mystic kind of grief. Thus she is justifiably billed, by the Columbia Recording Company, as the World's Greatest Moaner. She appears to be more of an artist than Bessie, but I suspect that this apparent artistry is spontaneous and uncalculated ("*Keep A-Inchin' Along*," p. 173).

Clara Smith died of a heart attack in Detroit in 1935.

REFERENCES: Robert M. W. Dixon and John Godrich, *Recording the Blues*, 1970; Chris Albertson, *Bessie*, 1972; Giles Oakley, *The Devil's Music*, 1978; BWW, 1979; Carl Van Vechten, "*Keep A-Inchin' Along*," 1979. (DA)

SMITH, MAMIE (singer), 26 May 1883?–16 September? 1946. Mamie Smith was born in Cincinnati, Ohio, and although her birthdate is uncertain it could not have been much later than 1883, since by about 1893 she was touring as a dancer with the Four Dancing Mitchells (a white act). By 1912 she was working, still as a dancer, in the touring Salem Tutt Whitney* Smart Set Company, but from 1913 she appeared as a singer in clubs, cabarets and cafés in New York City and the surrounding area. She headlined in Perry Bradford's* *Maid in Harlem* in 1918, and it was through Bradford's efforts that she received her first recording contract.

Bradford was interested in promoting his own songs and also in persuading record companies to record black artists. Victor rejected a test record, but OKeh agreed to record Bradford's songs, "That Thing Called Love" and "You Can't Keep a Good Man Down," with Mamie Smith backed by an all-white orchestra. (OKeh had wanted Sophie Tucker, but she was under contract to another company.) The record, made on 14 February 1920, was surprisingly successful, and on 20 August 1920 Mamie Smith was called back to record, with a black orchestra, Bradford's "Crazy Blues" and "It's Right Here For You (If You Don't Get It . . . 'Tain't No Fault of Mine)." These were the first solo recordings by a black artist. "Crazy Blues" had originally been titled "Harlem Blues," and she had sung it in *Maid in Harlem*, but the OKeh recording manager Fred Hager was afraid that the word *Harlem* in the title might frighten off prospective buyers. Mamie Smith was not really a blues* singer—she had a light, clear voice more suited to popular songs—but her first blues record was an astonishing hit, selling 75,000 copies in the first month at the high price of one dollar, and all of the recording companies were quick to realize the extent of the market for "race" records. She made twenty-three more records for OKeh in 1921–1922 and toured widely with her own group, Mamie Smith's Jazz Hounds. In 1923 she toured the West Coast in her own revue, *Struttin' Along*, and in New York she appeared in a number of musical revues: *Follow Me* (1923), *Syncopationland Revue* (1924), *Sugar Cane Revue* (1928), *Black Diamond Express* (1928), *Fireworks of 1930* (with Fats Waller* and Jimmie Johnson's Syncopators), and *Rhumba Land Revue* (1931), all at the Lafayette Theatre*; and *Frolicking Along* (1926), *A Riot of Fun* (1928), and *Sun-Tan Frolics* (1929), all at the Lincoln Theatre.* She recorded for Ajax in 1924, for Victor in 1926, and for OKeh again in 1929 and 1931. She toured with Fats Pichon's orchestra in the revue *Yelping Hounds* (1932–1934) and made a European tour about 1936. Mamie Smith made her first film in 1929, the short *Jail House Blues*, and later appeared in a number of Hollywood films: *Paradise in Harlem* (1939), *Mystery in Swing* (1940), *Murder on Lenox Avenue* (1941), *Sunday Sinners* (1941), and *Because I Love You* (1943).

She married three times, first to William "Smitty" Smith, a singer, about 1912; then to Sam Gardner, a comedian, some time in the 1920s; and finally, to a man named Goldberg about 1929. She died in Harlem Hospital after a long illness in 1946, but the exact date is uncertain. Her promotional title "Queen of the Blues," may have been a misnomer, but Mamie Smith was a talented, versatile artist. She was an extremely beautiful woman, and a much-loved personality.

REFERENCES: Robert M. W. Dixon and John Godrich, *Recording the Blues*, 1970; Chris Albertson, *Bessie*, 1972; Giles Oakley, *The Devil's Music*, 1978; BWW, 1979. (DA)

SMITH, N. CLARK (composer, musician), 31 July 1877–8 October 1933. N. Clark Smith's musical training covered many years. He attended Western University in his native Kansas City, Kansas, the Guild Hall in London, the Chicago Music College, the University of Kansas, and Chicago Normal School, all around the turn of the century. Then he joined Ernest Hogan for a world tour that included Europe, Africa, Asia, and South America. In 1911 he served as director of the band, orchestra, and glee club at Tuskegee Institute, and in the early twenties he was director of the Pullman Porter Orchestra and Glee Club. Cab Calloway,* Earl "Fatha" Hines, and Benny Moton all studied under Smith in the high schools in which he taught. He wrote a "Negro choral symphony," *Negro Folksong Suite*, a large choral work based on James Weldon Johnson's* "Crucifixion," as well as many arrangements of spirituals.* In 1928 he completed work for a master of arts degree in music at the Sherwood School in Chicago. His influence on many black composers was considerable.
REFERENCES: WWCA, 1933; BDAM, 1982. (BK)

SMITH, TRIXIE "TESSIE AMES" "BESSIE LEE" (singer), c. 1895–21 September 1943. Trixie Smith was born in Atlanta, Georgia, and attended Salem University, Selma, Alabama. From about 1915 she worked at Edmond's Novelty Cafe in Brooklyn and at the Lincoln Theatre* in New York and toured on the TOBA* circuit, billed as the "Southern Nightingale." In 1922 she won a blues* singing contest at the Manhattan Casino* in New York and was signed by the Black Swan* recording company. Her first release was her own composition, "Trixie's Blues". She later recorded with Fletcher Henderson's* Down Home Syncopators on the Paramount label (1923–1924) and appeared in *New York Revue*, *Highlights of Harlem*, and *Next Door Neighbors* (1928) at the Lincoln Theatre; in *Lily White* (1930) at the Majestic Theatre in Brooklyn and on tour; in *Sunshine* (1930) at the Alhambra Theatre*; in *Brass Ankle* (1931) at the Masque Theatre; in *The Constant Sinner* (1931) with Mae West; in the film *The Black King* (1932); and in the Theatre Guild production of *Louisiana* (1933). She toured through the thirties and in 1938–1939 made more recordings for Decca and Bluebird. Decca's house pianist Sam Price said of her: "Trixie had real depth, real warmth, and appeal. What was she like? She was just another woman called Smith—but she could sing like hell!" (Shapiro and Hentoff, *Hear Me Talkin' to Ya*, pp. 248–49).
REFERENCES: Nat Shapiro and Nat Hentoff, eds., *Hear Me Talkin' to Ya*, 1955; Robert M. W. Dixon and John Godrich, *Recording the Blues*, 1970; BWW, 1979. (DA)

SMITH, WILLIE-THE-LION [WILLIAM BERTHOLOFF] (pianist, composer), 25 November 1897–18 April 1973. William Henry Joseph Bonaparte Bertholoff was of Jewish-Negro parentage; his father died in 1901, and he later took his step-father's name of Smith. He was born in Goshen, New York, but was brought up in New York City, where he learned to play the organ as a child. By the age of seventeen he was playing piano professionally in Newark, New Jersey, Atlantic City, and New York, in clubs and at rent parties. He joined the United States Army in 1916, serving first as a bass drummer with Lieutenant Tim Brymm's* Regimental Band and later with the 350th Field Artillery. During one period of action he stayed at the front for thirty-three consecutive days, and his bravery earned him the nickname of "Willie-the-Lion." After the war he played at Leroy's, Small's Paradise,* the Garden of Joy, and other New York clubs; was featured in the revue *Hollywood to Dixie* (1922); and toured the theater circuits. He appeared in the Broadway play *The Four Walls* (1927) and in the late twenties and early thirties was the featured pianist at the Apollo Theatre* and at New York clubs such as Pod's and Jerry's,* the Onyx, and Adrian's Tap Room. From the forties through the sixties he toured Europe, the United States, and Canada, sometimes with his own band but usually as a single. He was a busy recording artist, an influential pianist and teacher, and an innovative composer. His piano style was a combination of power and delicacy; music historian Rudi Blesh wrote in 1950, "The Lion has never seriously invaded society entertainment or show business. The house shout parties remain, and he remains with them." But Blesh also described Smith's piano pieces "Echoes of Spring," "Zig Zag," "Contrary Motion," and "Here Comes the Band" as "not shouts but atmospheric pieces featuring unusual rhythms and harmonies" (Blesh and Janis, *They All Played Ragtime*, p. 195). Duke Ellington* recognized him as a unique performer and personality and dedicated his "Portrait of the Lion" to him; Willie-the-Lion in return composed a "Portrait of the Duke." His autobiography *Music on My Mind*, written with George Hoefer, was published in 1965.
REFERENCES: Rudi Blesh and Harriet Janis, *They All Played Ragtime*, 1951; EJ, 1955; MBA, 1971; WWJ, 1978; ASCAP, 1980. (DA)

SNOW, VALAIDA (singer), 2 June 1900 or 1903–30 May 1956. Bobby Short, in *Black and White Baby*, recalled the "fabled Valaida Snow, who traveled in an orchid-colored Mercedes-Benz, dressed in an orchid suit, her pet monkey rigged out in an orchid jacket and cap, with the chauffeur in orchid as well" (p. 84). Snow's long career as an entertainer took her around the world many times and included at least one misadventure. Winding up a several-years' tour of all of Europe (during which she also appeared in the French film *Alibi*), she was arrested and deported from Sweden and reportedly spent nearly two years in a Nazi concentration camp.
   The daughter of a music teacher, with three sisters who were also singers, Snow was an accomplished instrumentalist as well, known particularly for her

proficiency on the trumpet. She began playing at clubs on the East Coast around 1920; toured with Will Mastin's Revue as a singer, dancer, and trumpeter; and appeared in three New York shows in 1923 and in *Chocolate Dandies** in 1924. She took her act to Shanghai in 1926 with Jack Carter's Band and after engagements in Chicago toured Russia, the Middle East, and Europe in 1929. She appeared in *Shuffle Along in 1930** and was the costar, with Ethel Waters,* of *Rhapsody in Black** in 1931. Snow sang the title song in that show, as well as "Till the Real Thing Comes Along," "Harlem Rhumbola," and "St. James Infirmary," and conducted a vocal arrangement of Gershwin's "Rhapsody in Blue," wielding the baton, according to the *New York Times* reviewer, "with a frenzy that would abash a roomful of Toscaninis" (5 May 1933, p. 33). She was featured in Lew Leslie's* *Blackbirds [*] of 1934*, which played in New York and London. She appeared in two films, *Take It from Me* and *Irresistible You*, while she and her husband, dancer Ananias Berry, were working as a double act in California, following which she made a repeat tour of the Far East and returned to New York to play the Apollo Theatre.* In 1936 she began her long tour of Europe. Upon her return to America after her release she resumed an active schedule of engagements at the Apollo Theatre and at clubs and theaters throughout the country, moving to California in 1945. She recorded regularly and continued to appear in concerts and shows until shortly before her death.
REFERENCES: Bobby Short, *Black and White Baby*, 1971; WWJ, 1972; DBPA, 1978; BB, 1980. (PO)

SNOWDEN, ELMER (musician), 9 October 1900–14 May 1973. At the age of fifteen, Elmer Snowden was playing his banjo and guitar with Eubie Blake.* Subsequently, he played with Duke Ellington's* trio and by 1920 had his own band, doubling on saxophone. He moved to New York in 1923 and two years later had five bands playing in and around the city under his name. Elmer Snowden's music was familiar in a number of Harlem nightclubs, beginning with Barron Wilkins's place in 1923 and, toward the end of the twenties, at the Bamville Club,* Small's Paradise,* and the Nest.* During the thirties he maintained a small combo in Philadelphia and occasionally in New York, and in later years he taught music at Berkeley, California.
REFERENCES: WW, 1972; NYT, 15 May 1973. (BK)

SPAULDING, CHARLES C[LINTON] (businessman), 1 August 1874–1 August 1952. Perhaps the most successful black businessman of the first quarter of the century was born into poverty on a North Carolina farm. Charles Spaulding worked the land through his teens and then became a dishwasher and bellboy in Durham until, at twenty-three, he completed his eighth-grade education—as far as blacks were allowed to matriculate at the time. A black doctor and a black barber then employed Spaulding to manage their fledgling insurance company. He took in less than a thousand dollars his first year; twenty years later his field agents were taking in an annual million dollars in premiums. As first the secretary-treasurer of the North Carolina Mutual Insurance Company and later as its president, Spaulding was instrumental in founding the National Negro Insurance Association in 1921. Five years later he became president of the National Negro Business League* and received the Harmon Foundation* Gold Medal for Distinguished Achievement. Furthermore, he was cashier and then president of the Mechanics and Farmers Bank and active in many civic and other business ventures.

REFERENCES: WWCA, 1927; Langston Hughes, *Famous American Negroes*, 1954; DANB, 1982. (BK)

SPENCE, EULALIE (playwright), 11 June 1894–? Eulalie Spence was another West Indian-born black who was a literary figure in the Harlem Renaissance. Born in Nevis, British West Indies, in 1894, Spence wrote a number of one-act plays in the late 1920s, including *Fool's Errand* (1927), *Foreign Mail* (1927), *Her* (1927), *The Hunch* (1927), *The Starter* (1927), *Episode* (1928), *Help Wanted* (1929), and *Undertow* (1929). She won a second prize in the Krigwa Players* Contest, sponsored by *The Crisis** in 1926, and directed the Dunbar Garden Players* in *Before Breakfast* and *Joint Owners of Spain* in 1929. She also wrote *The Whipping*, a screenplay, for Paramount in 1933. Later, she completed her education—a B.S. at New York University in 1937 and an M.A. in speech at Columbia University in 1939—and served as a teacher and dramatic society coach at the Eastern District High School in Brooklyn.

REFERENCE: DBPA, 1978. (DS)

SPENCER, ANNE (poet), 6 February 1882–1976. Anne Spencer's delicate lyrics first appeared in *The New Negro** in 1925 and two years later in Countee Cullen's* *Caroling Dusk.** In her note for the latter she described herself as "lonely child, happy wife, perplexed mother—and, so far, a twice resentful grandmother" (p. 47). She wrote about things she loved, she confessed, having no "civilized articulation" for things she hated. Born in West Virginia and educated at the Virginia Seminary and College, Anne Spencer was librarian at the Dunbar High School in Lynchburg from 1920 until 1943. She wrote in traditional forms, rarely directly about black subjects, but observed: "*We* are the PROBLEM—the great national game of TABOO."

REFERENCE: Countee Cullen, *Caroling Dusk*, 1927. (BK)

SPILLER, ISABELLE TALIFERRO (music teacher), 19 March 1888–14 May 1974. Isabelle Spiller was the director of the Spiller Music School, which she established with her husband, William Newmeyer Spiller, in New York in 1926. She began playing piano in her father's church in Virginia as a child, and after attending public schools in Philadelphia, she studied at the New England Conservatory of Music in Boston, at Columbia University Teachers College, and the New School for Social Research in New York. From 1912 to 1926 she was assistant manager of the Six Musical Spillers, a vaudeville act organized by her husband, which toured the United States and Europe. She taught in the

New York public schools from 1929 to 1954 and for the last twelve years of her tenure was orchestral supervisor at the Wadleigh High School. Her other activities included supervising the music education program for the New York World's Fair of 1939 and a music therapy program at Bellevue Hospital.
REFERENCE: BDAM, 1982. (PO)

SPINGARN, ARTHUR (lawyer), 1878–1 December 1971. Like his older brother Joel Spingarn,* Arthur Spingarn devoted his entire life to racial equality. Born of Austrian Jewish parents in New York, he graduated from the Columbia Law School in 1899 and became a member of the bar two years later. From its beginnings he was active in the National Association for the Advancement of Colored People* and was its lawyer from 1909, its vice-president from 1911, and its president from 1940 until his retirement in 1966, as well as its unpaid legal counsel until his death in 1971. Spingarn's first of several legal successes for the race came in 1927, when the Supreme Court upheld his challenge to the all-white Democratic primary election in Texas, but as early as 1914 he was touring with his brother, at their own expense, to picket in Memphis, Tennessee, against Jim Crow practices. At the beginning of his career Arthur Spingarn's law practice suffered because of his racial sympathies, but he believed, in later years, that they actually increased it. Privately, Spingarn was a collector of rare books and of paintings; in 1948 he donated his entire collection of materials relating to the Afro-American to Howard University.
REFERENCES: NYT, 2 Dec. 1971; B. Joyce Ross, *J. E. Spingarn and the Rise of the NAACP*, 1972. (BK)

SPINGARN, JOEL ELIAS (writer, humanitarian, editor), 17 May 1875–1 June 1939. The leading twentieth-century abolitionist, Joel Elias Spingarn devoted his adult life to the National Association for the Advancement of Colored People* and its interests. This white humanitarian was born in New York of Austrian Jewish parents, attended the City College of New York, Columbia University, and Harvard University, and in 1899 the twenty-four-year-old Ph.D. became a professor of comparative literature at Columbia. Despite his formidable reputation as a scholar—he was an authority on Benedetto Croce, the Italian philosopher and art critic—and teacher, Spingarn's academic career lasted barely a decade. A colleague had been dismissed because of a breach-of-promise suit against him; when Spingarn rose in defense of academics being allowed their private lives, he was fired too, although president Nicholas Murray Butler claimed the two issues were unconnected. Spingarn seems not to have mourned long, for twenty-five years later he celebrated the anniversary with a cocktail party for his friends, many of them, perhaps most, Afro-Americans.

Long before he left Columbia Spingarn and his younger brother Arthur Spingarn* had been deeply involved in the new abolitionist movement, motivated by the indifference of the white race, the despair of the black race, and the driving need for integration. Already, he had dismissed politics, failing in a bid for a congressional seat in 1908 and resigning from the Republican party in 1912, because it had no black delegates. By that time, from his family home, Troutbeck, one hundred miles north of New York City, he was editing his suffragist paper *The Amenia Times* and was deeply committed to the NAACP, which he had helped to incorporate. Spingarn served as its chairman of the board (1913–1919), its treasurer (1919–1930), and then as its president until his death. His wife, Amy, completed his final term of office. His long tenure was not entirely smooth. Black newspapers like the New York *Age** regularly complained because of too many whites in influential positions in the NAACP, and W.E.B. Du Bois,* who strongly respected Spingarn's judgment, was nevertheless disturbed by his apparent inability to relinquish any authority. Conversely, no one questioned Spingarn's commitment: from 1914 he toured the country at his own expense, sometimes with his brother, sometimes alone, to protest Jim Crow practices; in 1915 he attempted to stop showings of D. W. Griffith's film *The Birth of a Nation*; in 1916 he organized the first Amenia Conference, with many influential blacks in attendance, to formulate policy combatting racial inequities; in 1917 he drafted the first federal antilynching legislation; in 1918, as a major in the army, he laid aside his antiseparatist stand long enough to force the establishing of a black officers' training school in Des Moines, Iowa. Independently wealthy from inheritance after 1919, he devoted the majority of his time and energy to the NAACP, in part responsible for its 300 branches by 1921.

Through the twenties Spingarn served also as a founder and then literary advisor to Harcourt Brace Publishing Company; he was director of two productive mills; he was the American authority on the clematis, nurturing more than 250 varieties at Troutbeck, and was widely known in botanical circles; he was a founding member of the American Legion, a lieutenant colonel in the reserves until his death; and he was the author of four volumes of literary criticism as well as a collection of verse. Both Spingarn and his wife regularly contributed funds to the NAACP throughout their lives and solicited money from others for its causes. In 1925, when the literary contests in *The Crisis** and *Opportunity** were at their height, Mrs. Spingarn established financial awards of her own, voted by a committee to Rudolph Fisher* for fiction, Marita Bonner* for drama, and Countee Cullen* for poetry, Frank Horne* and Langston Hughes* placing second and third in the latter category. Spingarn himself had long before established the most prestigious award, the Spingarn Gold Medal,* awarded first in 1915 and continuing to the present time through a trust fund from Spingarn's estate. Ruthlessly and single-mindedly integrationist all of his life, Joel Spingarn believed implicitly in W.E.B. Du Bois's theory of the "Talented Tenth."

REFERENCES: NYT, 27 July 1939; B. Joyce Ross, *J. E. Spingarn and the Rise of the NAACP*, 1972. (BK)

SPINGARN MEDAL. Established by Joel Spingarn* in 1914, the Spingarn Medal is a gold medallion valued at $100, awarded annually for "the highest and noblest achievement of an American Negro during the preceding year or years.'' The June 1914 issue of *The Crisis** carried a drawing of the design on its cover. Spingarn insured the medal's continuance by setting up a $20,000 trust fund in his will. It was awarded first in 1915 to Ernest E. Just, professor of physiology at Howard University, and in 1916 to Lieutenant Colonel Charles Young, United States Army. During subsequent years, through the period of the Harlem Renaissance, it was awarded to Harry T. Burleigh,* 1917; William Stanley Braithwaite,* 1918; Archibald Grimké,* 1919; W.E.B. Du Bois,* 1920; Charles Gilpin,* 1921; Mary Burnett Talbert,* 1922; George Washington Carver,* 1923; James Weldon Johnson,* 1924; Roland Hayes,* 1925; Carter G. Woodson,* 1926; Anthony Overton, president of the Victory Life Insurance Company, 1927; Charles W. Chesnutt,* 1928; Mordecai W. Johnson,* 1929; H. A. Hunt, president, Fort Valley Industrial School, Georgia, 1930; Richard B. Harrison,* 1931; Robert Russa Moton,* 1932; Max Yergan, YMCA director in Africa, 1933; William T. B. Williams, dean of the college, Tuskegee Institute, 1934; and Mary McLeod Bethune,* 1935. Later recipients, also active during the Harlem Renaissance, included Walter White,* 1937; A. Philip Randolph,* 1942; Paul Robeson,* 1945; and Langston Hughes,* 1960.

REFRERENCES: *The Crisis*, June 1914, Nov. 1980. (BK)

SPIRITUALS. Negro spirituals gained their first wide public popularity in the 1870s, when the Fisk Jubilee Singers from Fisk University began touring both this country and Europe. Fifty years later, at the center of the Harlem Renaissance, several studies of these powerful ''sorrow songs'' (as they were called, encapsulating ''the soul of black folk,'' in W.E.B. Du Bois's* memorable phrase) were published. Few explanations of the evolution of the spirituals are likely to improve on James Weldon Johnson's* preface to *The Book of American Negro Spirituals*, which he edited in 1925 with his brother J. Rosamond Johnson*

At the psychic moment there was at hand the precise religion for the condition in which he [the African enslaved in America] found himself thrust. Far from his native land and customs, despised by those among whom he lived, experiencing the pang of the separation of loved ones on the auction block, knowing the hard task master, feeling the lash, the Negro seized Christianity, the religion of compensations in the life to come for the ills suffered in the present existence, the religion which implied the hope that in the next world there would be a reversal of conditions, of rich man and poor man, of proud and meek, of master and slave. The result was a body of songs voicing all the cardinal virtues of Christianity—patience—forbearance—love—faith—and hope—through a necessarily modified form of primitive African music. The Negro took complete refuge in Christianity, and the Spirituals were literally forged of sorrow in the heat of religious fervor. These exhibited, moreover, a reversion to the simple principles of primitive, communal Christianity. (p. 20)

Some months earlier, in an article about the spirituals in *Vanity Fair*,* white music critic Carl Van Vechten* had observed that ''Negro folksongs differ from the folksongs of most other races through the fact that they are sung in harmony''

("*Keep A-Inchin' Along*," p. 37), corroborating the "communal" nature of the spirituals. He further contended that they were the source of jazz and popular music, suggesting that a song like "Get on Board, Little Chillun," if set with secular words could be mistaken for a number by George Gershwin.* He credited H. T. Burleigh,* Roland Hayes,* and Paul Robeson* with having popularized the spirituals during the twenties, although for entirely different reasons. Within the decade the spirituals had become an integral part—sometimes the entire foundation, as in Hall Johnson's* *Run, Little Chillun*—of black entertainment on Broadway.

REFERENCES: James Weldon Johnson and J. Rosamond Johnson, *The Book of American Negro Spirituals*, 1925; Carl Van Vechten, "*Keep A-Inchin' Along*," 1979. (BK)

SPIVEY, VICTORIA (singer), 15 October 1906–3 October 1976. A classic blues* singer who wrote most of her own songs, "Queen Victoria" Spivey also played piano, organ, and ukelele. She began as a pianist at a theater in her native Texas when she was twelve and sang her own composition, "Black Snake Blues," for her first recording in St. Louis in 1926. She toured the vaudeville circuit as a single act during the twenties, appearing at the Lincoln Theatre* in New York in 1927. Two years later she was featured in the film *Hallelujah!** During the twenties and thirties she made many recordings with Louis Armstrong* and others, toured with Armstrong and Jap Allen and directed Lloyd Hunter's Serenaders. She later performed with her second husband, dancer Billy Adams, and with her sisters, singers Addie "Sweet Peas" Spivey and Elton Island "Za Zu" Spivey. In *Blues Who's Who* Sheldon Harris quoted one of Spivey's admirers who said she was "in turn joyous, somber, coy and showy, theatrically mirroring the moods of her composition," and another who described her blues as "grim tales of death, despair, cruelty and agony, underscored by her somber piano and stark Texas blues moans" (p. 482). In the late thirties Spivey toured with Ole Olsen and Chic Johnson's *Hellzapoppin'*. She semiretired from music in the fifties to work as a church administrator but returned in 1962 to sing at Carnegie Hall. The same year she formed her own company, Spivey Record Productions, which recorded the old-timers like Lucille Hegamin as well as young talent, and issued *The Victoria Spivey Legacy* in 1969, a collection of recordings made by her between 1927 and 1937. She performed in nightclubs and on radio and television during the sixties and toured Europe with the American Folk Blues Festival (1963). In 1971 she was featured at the U.S. Blues Festival and on PBS-TV in *Free Time*. She continued to appear at colleges, festivals, museums, and concerts until her death in 1976.

REFERENCES: NYT, 7 Oct. 1976; WWJ, 1978; BWW, 1979. (PO)

THE SPOKESMAN (periodical), 1925–1926. *The Spokesman*, "Fearless and Independent," according to its title page, was published during 1925 and 1926 in New York by Heeman's Herb Garden. Many pages were given over to ad-

vertisements for various herb and health remedies, but it included a few articles on political and sociological subjects. William H. Ferris,* formerly associated with Marcus Garvey's* *Negro World,* served as literary editor, and Zora Neale Hurston* was one of the contributing editors.
REFERENCE: JWJ. (BK)

SPOOKS (play), 1925. Dixie Loftin and Cy Plunkett played the black servants who were responsible for a series of shenanigins in a haunted house in which the white heirs to a fortune are obliged to stay. Robert J. Sherman wrote this mildly successful comedy, notable only for having a mixed cast as early as 1 June 1925.
REFERENCES: Burns Mantle, 1924–1925; NYTTR, 1972. (BK)

STAFFORD, MARY (singer), c. 1895–c. 1938. Little is known of Mary Stafford's origins. Her true name may have been Annie Burns, and she is believed to have been born in Missouri. Between 1910 and 1920 she worked occasionally with Eubie Blake* in Baltimore and with Bessie Smith* in Atlantic City; in 1920 she appeared at Barron Wilkins's club in New York and sang in other New York clubs throughout the twenties. She made half a dozen recordings for Columbia in 1921, but her contract was not renewed, and she recorded for Pathé in 1926 for a series of race records on the cut-rate Perfect label. The companies seem to have done little to promote her recordings, although she was regarded as a fine classic blues* singer. She appeared at the Lafayette Theatre* in *Rocking Chair Revue* (1931) and *Dear Old Southland* (1932) and reportedly worked outside the field of music in Atlantic City thereafter. Her eventual fate is unknown.
REFERENCES: Robert M. W. Dixon and John Godrich, *Recording the Blues,* 1970; BWW, 1979. (DA)

STEVEDORE (play), 1934. The Theatre Union produced *Stevedore,* a poweful play by Paul Peters and George Sklar about mob violence. It opened in April 1934 and was sufficiently successful to reopen six months later, as the *New York Times* observed, deserving "a distinguished run" (19 Apr. 1934, p. 33). When a black is falsely accused of beating up a white girl his fellow dock workers rebel against white-trash oppressors and barricade an alley to fight them off. "Acted with gusto," the play had the "ring of authenticity" and was "remarkable for the lithographic color of its scenes and the broadness and keenness of its characterizations," according to the *Times,* but it was notable, too, for its mixed black and white cast and its mixed audience—black and white sitting both in the orchestra and in the balcony, perhaps for the first time. Canada Lee,* Abbie Mitchell,* Georgette Harvey,* Jack Carter, Edna Thomas, * Leigh Whipper,* and Rex Ingram* were prominent in the large cast.
REFERENCES: Burns Mantle, 1933–1934 and 1934–1935; NYTTR, 1972. (BK)

STILL, WILLIAM GRANT (composer), 11 May 1895–3 December 1978. Still was born in Woodville, Mississippi, but his father died when he was an infant, and his mother moved to Little Rock, Arkansas, where she became a teacher in a local high school. Still received musical instruction as a boy and showed talent; he continued his musical studies and activities at Wilberforce University and at Oberlin—with time out for service as a mess attendant in the navy in World War I. While a student he had played in dance bands and for vaudeville acts and worked for W. C. Handy* in Memphis, and in 1919 he joined Handy's music publishing firm in New York as an arranger. He also served as musical director for the Black Swan Phonograph Corporation* from 1921 but continued to play in dance orchestras (he played oboe in the pit orchestra of *Shuffle Along**) and found time to pursue serious musical study with the avant-garde French composer Edgard Varèse and with George Chadwick. Early concert works—*Darker America* (1924), *From the Land of Dreams* (1925), and *From the Journal of a Wanderer* (1925)—received praise from the critics, but it was his *Afro-American Symphony* (1931) that brought him full public recognition. The symphony was performed by the Rochester Philharmonic Symphony under Howard Hanson in 1931 and by the New York Philharmonic at Carnegie Hall in 1935, and in the following years it became his most consistently performed work in America and Europe. Other works of this period include *Levee Land* (1926); a jazz piece written for Florence Mills*; *Africa* (1930); *Symphony in G minor* (1937); three ballets: *La Guiablesse* (1927), *Sahdji* (1930), and *Lenox Avenue* (1937); and *Kaintuck* (1935), for piano and orchestra. The New York Philharmonic-Symphony Orchestra presented premieres of his cantata *And They Lynched Him on a Tree* (1940); *Plain Chant for America*, for baritone and orchestra (1941); and *In Memoriam* and the first New York performance of *Old California* (1944).

Still worked as a staff composer for both WCBS and WNBC and produced arrangements for Donald Vorhees, Paul Whiteman, and Artie Shaw, among others. He also orchestrated musical comedies, including *Earl Carroll's Vanities, Runnin' Wild,** and *Americana*, and did arrangements and orchestrations of popular music such as the song "Shadrack," which became a Louis Armstrong* specialty. He composed the film score for *Pennies from Heaven*, served as musical adviser for *Stormy Weather*, and provided orchestrations and background music for many other films and, later, for television programs.

His first opera, *Blue Steel* (1935), employed Negro folk music, spirituals,* and jazz. *Troubled Island* (1938), to a libretto by Langston Hughes,* had its premiere at New York City Opera in 1949, the first opera by a black composer to be produced by a major opera company. *A Bayou Legend* (1941), to a libretto by Still's wife, Verna Arvey, based upon a Mississippi legend of a man who falls in love with a spirit, was first performed by Opera/South in Jackson, Mississippi, in 1974 and was filmed for television and shown on PBS in 1981.

Still was a prolific and eclectic composer: more than a hundred concert works, seven operas, four ballets, instrumental pieces and songs (including popular songs, sometimes written under the pseudonym Willy M. Grant), arrangements of spirituals, and choral works. He won several prizes for composition and received many commissions from leading symphony orchestras during his long career. He was awarded Rosenwald and Guggenheim fellowships, a Harmon Foundation* Award (1927), and honorary degrees from Wilberforce University (1936), Howard University (1941), Oberlin College (1947), and Bates College (1954). "The Dean of Afro-American Music" died at the age of eighty-three in 1978.

REFERENCES: Sigmund Spaeth, *A History of Popular Music in America*, 1948; MBA, 1971; *Opera News*, June 1981. (DA)

STINNETT, [McCLEARY] MAC (jack-of-all-trades), ?–? One of the remarkable personalities of the Harlem Renaissance, and a familiar figure in many circles, Mac Stinnett was usually identified as a dancer. For a time, however, he was A'Lelia Walker's* social secretary, and others knew him best in his role as a bootlegger. More or less openly he ran a package store unofficially, and he gave dance classes officially.

REFERENCES: CVV; Donald Angus; Richard Bruce Nugent. (BK)

STINNETTE, JUANITA (singer), 3 June 1899–4 June 1932. Thomas Chapelle engaged Juanita Stinnette for Salem Whitney* and Homer Tutt's* *Smart Set* in 1912. Then he married her, and they toured together for several years in a number of revues. In New York she appeared in *Deep Harlem** (1929) and *Sugar Hill** (1931), her promising career cut short by death from peritonitis the day following her thirty-third birthday.

REFERENCES: *Inter-State Tattler*, 9 June 1932; BB, 1980. (BK)

STRIVER'S ROW, HARLEM. "Striver's Row" was the nickname given to the fashionable group of brownstones in Harlem on West 138th and 139th streets, which housed many members of the black upper class in the 1920s and 1930s. Designed by the famed architect Stanford White in 1891, the Italianate-styled homes—106 of them—contained from ten to sixteen rooms each, driveways edged with flowers, and a suburban ambience with the tree-lined streets and the houses set back from the streets to ensure privacy. The Equitable Life Assurance Society, which owned the brownstones, had restricted ownership of homes to whites until 1919, when they put them up for sale. Within eight months practically all were sold to wealthy blacks, after a vigorous advertising campaign was conducted by the real estate firm of John Nail* and Henry Parker, among others.

REFERENCES: Gilbert Osofsky, *Harlem,* 1966; David Levering Lewis, *When Harlem Was in Vogue,* 1981. (DS)

STRUT MISS LIZZIE (musical revue), 1922. *Strut Miss Lizzie*, a Chicago show by Harry Creamer* and Turner Layton seems to have evolved on the Minsky circuit, with Hamtree Harrington* and Cora Green.* It opened at the

Wintergarden, purporting to glorify "the creole beauty," but the comedy scenes struck the *New York Times* reviewer as "deadly," and he was even shocked that the chorines were "bare-legged part of the time" (20 June 1922, p. 22).
REFERENCE: NYTTR, 1972. (BK)

STYLUS (periodical), 1916–1941. The literary society at Howard University, organized in 1916 by Alain Locke* and T. Montgomery Gregory,* published the first issue of its magazine *Stylus* in June of that year, with contributions by William Stanley Braithwaite,* Benjamin Brawley,* James Weldon Johnson,* and several students. The war precluded further issues until May 1921, when a second one included Zora Neale Hurston's* first published story. Although the *Stylus* organization continued to meet during the twenties, it did not publish a third issue until 1929, to which Alain Locke contributed "Beauty and the Provinces," an assessment of the preceding decade and the New Negro's place in it. Some further issues appeared, until *Stylus* ceased publication in 1941.
REFERENCE: Abby Ann Arthur Johnson and Ronald M. Johnson, "Forgotten Pages," *Journal of American Studies*, 1974. (BK)

SUGAR CANE CLUB (cabaret). At the edge of Harlem's slum, where few whites and even fewer educated blacks dared go, the Sugar Cane Club at 135th Street and Fifth Avenue catered to petty gamblers, pimps, and prostitutes. Customers entered through a narrow underground passageway to a room about 25 by 125 feet, big enough to accommodate about a hundred people. Twice that many crowded in. The unsophisticated jazz orchestra "weeps and moans and groans," according to Wallace Thurman's* account of the place in his *Negro Life in New York's Harlem*,* while dancing couples "sweat gloriously together, with shoulders hunched, limbs obscenely intertwined and hips wriggling, animal beings urged on by liquor and music and physical contact" (p. 27).
REFERENCE: Wallace Thurman, *Negro Life in New York's Harlem*, 1928. (BK)

SUGAR HILL (musical comedy), 1931. Charles Tazewell, in the *New York Times* named "what courtesy alone could call a musical comedy" after the section of Harlem where its black aristocracy lived. James P. Johnson* wrote the music, Jo Trent supplied the lyrics, and Flournoy Miller* and Aubrey Lyles* used some of their familiar blackface routines to flesh out this story of young love and murder. Etta Moten* played the heroine and Broadway Jones played Gyp Penrose, a numbers racketeer, dividing his time between "hoofing Hot Harlem and menacing the juveniles" (26 Dec. 1931, p. 15). *Sugar Hill* opened on Christmas night and closed after eleven peformances.
REFERENCES: Burns Mantle, 1931–1932; NYTTR, 1972. (BK)

SUGAR HILL, HARLEM. North from the St. James Presbyterian Church to the Polo Grounds, a distance of about ten blocks, marked Sugar Hill, bordered

on one side by Bradford Park and on the other by Washington Heights. Here a line of brick and granite townhouses and apartment buildings, with canopied entrances and uniformed doormen, sheltered Harlem's aristocracy. Like ''Nob Hill'' in San Francisco and ''The Main Line'' outside Philadelphia, the name of the locale was used to suggest money and social position.
REFERENCE: Roi Ottley and William J. Weatherby, eds., *The Negro in New York*, 1967. (BK)

SUL TE WAN, MADAME (actress), 1873–1 February 1959. The daughter of a Kentucky washerwoman began her long career in the theater when the celebrated white actress Fanny Davenport, then playing soubrette roles in Louisville, became her mentor. Madame Sul Te Wan, who apparently took her real name to the grave when she died at eighty-three, began dancing buck-and-wing routines in amateur contests. In Cincinnati, Ohio, she organized the Black Four Hundred Company and the Rair Back Minstrels and toured with them for several years. She entered films in D. W. Griffith's controversial *Birth of a Nation* in 1915, playing several different roles, although white actors in blackface were cast in most of the black parts. She remained a friend of the director and appeared in other films of his. As late as 1937 she was still acting, notably as the black conjurer Tituba in *Maid of Salem*. Madame Sul Te Wan's publicity photographs show her lavishly gowned and dripping with jewels, even in the last year of her life.
REFERENCE: Valerie Shaw, *Black Hollywood*, 1983. (BK)

SURVEY GRAPHIC (periodical), 1921–1948. Inspired by a Civic Club Dinner* honoring young black intellectuals, the *Survey Graphic* editor Paul Kellog devoted the entire March 1925 issue to the work of black artists and writers, subtitled ''Harlem: Mecca for the New Negro.'' Advertisements for the National Urban League* and *The Crisis* followed the bold cover with its blue and black design by Winold Reiss.* Alain Locke's* introductory essay ''The New Negro'' (later the basis of his full-length anthology) compared Harlem to Dublin and Prague as a center for culture, and he encapsulated the whole movement in a phrase: ''the Negro's latest thrust toward democracy'' (p. 7). George E. Haynes* wrote an essay about Harlem's churches and religious movements; W. A. Domingo* wrote about the West Indians; Charles S. Johnson* wrote about urban workers; Elise McDougald,* about women; Kelly Miller,* about prejudice; Melville Herskovits,* about black and white race relations; Walter White,* about miscegenation; W.E.B. Du Bois* contributed a short story; James Weldon Johnson* wrote about the history of Harlem; J. A. Rogers,* about jazz; Arthur Schomburg,* about Negro history; Rudolph Fisher* wrote a short story; and Langston Hughes,* Countee Cullen,* Claude McKay,* and Jean Toomer* contributed poetry. To its predominately white subscribers *Survey Graphic* served as yet another significant step toward recognition of the abilities of that ''Talented Tenth'' of the race that intellectual Afro-America was counting on to improve the estimation of the race in the eyes of an ignorant white public. The title of the magazine itself is somewhat misleading. The *Survey* appeared twice monthly, a "graphic" issue on the first of the month, fully illustrated in a decorative cover, and a "midmonthly" issue on the fifteenth of the month, printed on lighter stock and unbound. (BK)

SWEATMAN, WILBUR C. (clarinetist), 7 February 1882–9 March 1961. Wilbur Sweatman, from Brunswick, Missouri, played violin before switching to clarinet and in his youth toured with circus bands and W. C. Handy's* Mahara Minstrels. He formed his own orchestra in 1902 in Minneapolis and toured the theater circuits and played residencies in Chicago before coming to New York in 1913. He played in theater orchestras and vaudeville, led his own band (in which Duke Ellington* made his first New York appearance), served as executor for Scott Joplin's* estate, played for the opening of Connie's Inn* in 1923, operated a theatrical agency, and was involved in music publishing. He was the first to introduce syncopated clarinet playing and was famous for his sweet tone and facility in the high register. He was also famous for his ability to play three clarinets at the same time; his hit number was a trio arrangement of Ethelbert Nevin's "Rosary."
REFERENCES: MBA, 1971; WWJ, 1978. (DA)

SWEET CHARIOT (musical play), 1930. There were only three performances of Robert Wilder's *drame à clef* about what might have happened to Marcus Garvey.* After selling fake stock in his steamship company, Marius Harvey becomes inspired by his own eloquence and transports a group of black Americans to Africa, a country "for which they feel no great nostalgia," as the *New York Times* reviewer interpreted the performance (24 Oct. 1930, p. 30). Once settled there they begin to long for the pleasures of their Saturday nights back home and subsequently desert Harvey to return to the United States. To a degree *Sweet Chariot* spoke to the ambivalence many Afro-Americans must have felt toward the philosophy behind the Universal Negro Improvement Association.* Frank Wilson* and Fredi Washington* starred in the play, and the celebrated blues* singer Clara Smith* was featured in the cast.
REFERENCES: Burns Mantle, 1930–1931; NYTTR, 1972. (BK)

SWEET MAN (novel), 1930. One of several novels with black subject matter by white writers, *Sweet Man* by Gilmore Millen recounts the good life gone bad of John Henry, who suffers because of white treachery. When he is denied income from his cotton crop, he leaves his wife and goes to New Orleans to become an irresistible stud, pimping for black whores with white customers. When the law cracks down on Beale Street, John Henry moves on to Los Angeles, inadvertently causes the death of his white mistress, whom he serves as a chauffeur, and then commits suicide. *Sweet Man* perpetuates a number of racial stereotypes, but Walter White,* reviewing it in the *Saturday Review of Literature*,

admired its "strong meat" and thought it was "superbly told" (12 July 1930, p. 1189).
REFERENCE: Walter White, "Sweet Man," *Saturday Review of Literature*, 12 July 1930. (BK)

SYLVESTER, HANNAH [GENEVIA SCOTT] (singer), c. 1900–15 October 1973. "Harlem's Mae West" first performed in her native Philadelphia at an early age. In 1924 she was engaged at Happy Rhone's Club* and, later, for several shows at the Lincoln,* Lafayette,* and Alhambra* theaters. A large, affable woman with a routine of sexy innuendoes and bawdy songs, Hannah Sylvester appeared at the Cotton Club,* the Club Harlem, and finally at the Nest,* where she married the manager, Jeff Blunt. A later black actress, known primarily for her work in films, was billed as the "sepia Mae West"; her name was Bee Freeman.
REFERENCES: Donald Bogle, *Toms, Coons, Mulattoes, Mammies, and Bucks*, 1973; BWW, 1979. (BK)

T

TABOO (play), 1922. Mary Hoyt Wiborg's *Taboo*, produced in a series of special matinee performances at the Sam Harris Theatre, deals with African voodoo, "an ambitious, garrulous and quite artless play," according to the *New York Times* reviewer. A white plantation owner seeks to cure her eight-year-old grandson, mute from birth, with a "luck ball" prepared by her black slaves. One of them, played by Paul Robeson* in his initial appearance on the professional stage, has a dream in which he is an African king and his mistress is a voodoo queen who consigns an albino child to death by fire because it is abnormal. The dream is designed to explain the origins of a curse handed down over many generations. When the grandmother encounters the dreamer on her way home from her "luck ball" meeting, the child regains his speech, since she "expiates the curse by dropping conveniently dead from shock in the final moment of the play" (5 Apr. 1922, p. 22). After its brief run in New York *Taboo* played in London and was better received. Robeson remained with the melodrama and played opposite the well-known English actress Mrs. Patrick Campbell in the double role as grandmother and voodoo queen.
REFERENCES: Burns Mantle, 1921–1922; NYTTR, 1972. (MH)

TALBERT, MARY BURNETT (sociologist), 1886–November 1923. Working behind the scenes, Mary Burnett Talbert contributed to the beginning of the Harlem Renaissance in several ways. After receiving her Ph.D. at the University of Buffalo she worked as a Red Cross nurse in France and sold liberty bonds. From 1916 until 1920 she was president of the National Association of Colored Women's Clubs, and afterward vice-president of the NAACP* and chairman of the Dyer Anti-Lynching Bill Committee. She lectured widely on race relations and women's rights.
REFERENCES: WWCR, 1915; Wilhelmenia S. Robinson, *History of Negro Biography*, 1967. (BK)

TANDY, VERTNER W. (architect), 1885–? Vertner Tandy was born in New York City and educated at Tuskegee Institute. Later, he studied architecture at Cornell University and went on to design St. Philip's Episcopal Church* on 134th Street, with its spacious gymnasium for basketball games and elegant parish house for social events. Earlier, he had designed Sarah Breedlove (Madame C. J.) Walker's* elaborate Villa LeWaro at Irvington-on-Hudson.
REFERENCES: Roi Ottley and William J. Weatherby, *The Negro in New York*, 1967; AAD, 1973. (BK)

TANNER, HENRY OSSAWA (painter), 21 June 1859–25 May 1937. Although by age a member of an earlier generation, Henry O. Tanner exerted a considerable influence over young artists of the Harlem Renaissance. He was born in Pennsylvania and educated at the Pennsylvania Academy of Fine Arts, where he studied under Thomas Eakins. He taught briefly at Clark University in Georgia, but his recognition as an artist came in Paris, shortly before the turn of the century, where he had gone to study. After 1891 Tanner returned to the United States only once, but the number of black painters who went to study with him in Paris is legion. He exhibited at the New York Public Library in 1921 and in Washington, D.C., in 1922. His subjects were predominately religious and rarely if ever exclusively black, but his career is significant proof of the power of talent to overcome the obstacles placed by prejudice. Careers like Tanner's motivated the whole theory of the "Talented Tenth," that Afro-Americans of exceptional abilities could eventually abolish the inequities fostered by bigotry.
REFERENCES: WWCA, 1933; Cedric Dover, *American Negro Art*, 1969. (BK)

TAYLOR, EVA [IRENE GIBBONS] (singer), 22 January 1895–31 October 1977. Eva Taylor was the first black soloist to perform on national radio, and for several years thereafter she and her husband, Clarence Williams,* were regular singers over the National Broadcasting Company. She made her Broadway debut in *Shuffle Along** in 1921 and reappeared there in *Bottomland*,* the catastrophe she and her husband staged in 1927. Eva Taylor gave her date of birth as 1908, but in 1904 she had toured Hawaii, Australia and Europe with Josephine Gassman and Her Pickanninies.
REFERENCES: WWCA, 1933; BWW, 1979. (BK)

TAYLOR, PRENTISS (artist), 13 November 1906–   . Born in Washington, D.C., Prentiss Taylor studied at the Art Students League in New York and later held fellowships at Yaddo and the MacDowell Colony. When through Carl Van Vechten* this white artist met Langston Hughes,* they collaborated on two works, both published by the Golden Stair Press and now among the rarest items in the Hughes bibliography: *The Negro Mother and Other Dramatic Recitations** (1931) and *Scottsboro Limited** (1932). During July and August 1934 *The Crisis**

featured a number of Taylor's works. Subsequently, he taught at the American University in Washington, D.C.
REFERENCE: Prentiss Taylor. (BK)

THEATERS. In addition to the more celebrated Lafayette,* Lincoln,* Renaissance Casino,* and Alhambra* theaters, Harlem had several other theaters. Although vaudeville occasionally played there, they were primarily film houses. The Roosevelt, New Douglass, and Savoy theaters ran many of the same movies shown at the Renaissance; their audiences were made up of poor but honest family groups, although lecherous males frequently used the premises for casual pickups. The white-owned Franklin and Gem theaters were most notable for the stench they shared, according to Wallace Thurman,* and drew their audiences from Harlem's slums. Signs urged patrons not to spit or smoke, but the aisles could prove slippery with tobacco juice by the time the houses closed at 11 P.M. Thurman recalled babies crying in time to the music from the electric piano that accompanied the silent films and a good deal of raucous conversation among members of the audience. Later, about 1932, Oscar Hammerstein's Opera House, built at the turn of the century, reopened as a vaudeville theater, and the Apollo Theatre* opened with a musical revue based on the current floor show at Connie's Inn,* continuing thereafter to feature the kinds of entertainments formerly identified with the Lafayette.
REFERENCES: Wallace Thurman, *Negro Life in New York's Harlem*, 1928; *Inter-State Tattler*, 1932. (BK)

THEATRICAL OWNERS AND BOOKERS ASSOCIATION (TOBA) (booking organization for black performers), 1920–? Thirty-two theater owners, none from New York, founded the Theatrical Owners and Bookers Association in Chattanooga, Tennessee, in 1920, its acronym popularly explained as "Tough on Black Actors." The members sold shares of stock at one hundred dollars each, at a three-share minimum. Through the organization eighty theaters booked black acts on a regular basis, largely because the tight contract favored the theater manager. He was allowed to cancel an engagement on less than a week's notice, leaving the performers stranded in Baltimore, Washington, Atlanta, St. Louis, or Chicago, the TOBA strongholds. Playing "Toby Time," as it was called, was often unfair to actors, who had to suffer through bad bookings, unsatisfactory accommodations, and low pay, but TOBA did offer regular avenues for employment at a time when black performers operated largely without agents.
REFERENCES: Tom Fletcher, *100 Years of the Negro in Show Business*, 1954; Loften Mitchell, *Black Drama*, 1967; BB, 1980. (BK)

THERE IS CONFUSION (novel), 1924. In *There Is Confusion* Jessie Fauset* illustrated the distress caused by American race prejudice in the lives of black people. Through its genealogically complex plot the novel portrays Joanna Marshall's desire for success. Born into a wealthy family of New York caterers, she seeks a career, achieves it, and then finds it disappointing. Her lover Peter Bye comes from an old Philadelphia family. He studies to become a surgeon. He renounces Joanna and becomes engaged to her friend Maggie, which shows Joanna the value of relationships as well as a career. The culmination of the story revolves around the reconcilation and marriage between Joanna and Peter, whose maturity enabled them to find love. This novel of manners includes the complex relationships within their respective families and reveals many of the attitudes of the New Negro middle class of the 1920s. (DI)

THEY SHALL NOT DIE (play), 1934. The Theatre Guild produced white writer John Wexley's didactic play based on the *Scottsboro* case* on February 21. Although in his *New York Times* review Brooks Atkinson referred to its "terrifying and courageous bluntness of statement—thoughtfully developed, lucidly explained and played with great resolution" (22 Feb. 1934, p. 24), Carl Van Vechten* confided in his friend James Weldon Johnson* that he "came away completely unmoved," because "no play in which all the dice are loaded can be very convincing" ("*Keep A-Inchin' Along*," pp. 258–59). *They Shall Not Die* never mentions Scottsboro by name, but nobody missed the connection. Wexley avoided nothing to make his point: anti-Semitism, corrupt politics, mob rule, deliberate subversion of justice, and lust for blood-letting, all of which have less to do with guilt and innocence than with prejudice and bigotry. George R. Hayes, Al Stokes, and Frank Wilson,* all familiar black actors from the twenties, were among those playing the nine defendants accused of raping two white prostitutes, and Claude Rains, Ruth Gordon, and Helen Westley were among the well-known white members of the cast.

For those in the audience "with a social conscience," Atkinson thought it was "a tremendously powerful play." His follow-up essay in the Sunday edition of the newspaper further worked to justify the liberties Wexley had taken with the case to build his play, noting that he was "writing for the theatre and not for a newspaper, which helps to explain why his work will be remembered long after the work of journalists has crumpled to dust" (4 Mar. 1934, sec. 9, p. 1). When the play was about to close a week later because of a slow box office, Atkinson observed that "the great public does not want to be harrowed" and went on to push *They Shall Not Die* as a play "of race hatred, intersectional hatred between city and country, and those are the roots of a malignant national evil" (11 Mar. 1934, sec. 10, p. 1). Still, Van Vechten's assessment may explain the play's failure: "I think it will react against the purpose for which it was written. . . . The interpretation of the facts is so obviously inspired by hate that often you are forced to admit to yourself you just don't believe the author" ("*Keep A-Inchin' Along*," p. 259). Nevertheless, Burns Mantle chose it as one of the best plays of the 1933–1934 season.
REFERENCES: NYTTR, 1972; Carl Van Vechten, "*Keep A-Inchin' Along*," 1979. (BK)

THOMAS, EDNA LEWIS (actress), 1886–22 July 1974. Born in Boston, Edna Lewis began her New York stage career in Flournoy Miller's* *Goin' White* in 1922 and played in *Lulu Belle** in 1926 and *Vaudeville at the Palace* in 1927. More serious roles did not begin to come her way until the thirties. In the meantime, she was one of "the circle of handsome women attending A'Lelia Walker,"* according to David Lewis's *When Harlem Was in Vogue* (p. 167). Her friend Elinor J. Marvel remembered that Edna Thomas's Harlem apartment was the setting for "endless discussions" among Afro-American theatrical and literary people, in "that strange *menage à trois* of herself, her husband Lloyd [Thomas], . . . and Olivia Wyndham, emigré to Harlem who remained the girl who had been the brightest of London's bright young things." Edna Thomas appeared in Hall Johnson's* *Run, Little Chillun,** in 1933 and in *Stevedore** in 1934. At the tag end of the Harlem Renaissance she was "incandescent," in Elinor J. Marvel's memory, as Lady Macbeth in Orson Welles's all-black production of *Macbeth*; about the same time she served on the play-reading committee for the Harlem unit of the Federal Theatre Project. Subsequently, Edna Thomas appeared with Helen Hayes in *Harriett*, about the abolitionist novelist Harriett Beecher Stowe, in 1943 and the miscegenation drama *Strange Fruit* in 1945. She appeared in *A Streetcar Named Desire* in 1947, in its subsequent New York revivals, and in its 1951 film version. In later years she served as secretary of the Negro Actors Guild and worked in radio and television. Throughout her professional life Edna Thomas was one of the most popular figures in Harlem society.
REFERENCES: NYT, 17 Dec. 1938, 24 July 1974; Loften Mitchell, *Black Drama*, 1967; BB, 1980; David Levering Lewis, *When Harlem Was in Vogue*, 1981; CVV; Elinor J. Marvel. (PO, BK)

THOMPSON [PATTERSON], LOUISE (educator, labor organizer), 9 September 1901– . One of the most interesting intellectuals of the Harlem Renaissance brought to the movement an awareness of racism in its various disguises that strongly influenced her later life as well as the lives of many of the young black artists and writers with whom she came in contact. Born in Chicago, Louise Thompson travelled west with her mother at an early age and was raised in several states as her rover stepfather moved from job to job. Often theirs was the only black family in a small town, so Thompson's first exposure to racism was an awareness of isolation. At Berkeley, where she completed her education at the University of California in 1924, she encountered racism in the form of indifference. When W.E.B. Du Bois* lectured there, however, she was awakened to her own potential and, indeed, to that of her race.

Thompson accepted a teaching job in Pine Bluffs, Arkansas—where her students were barely able to read, although she was expected to teach them Spanish, among other subjects—only to discover racism in its violent manifestations. In 1926 she went on to the Hampton Institute to teach business administration and there encountered "a refined racism," as she later called it during an interview, behind the mask of white patronage. At the height of the Harlem Renaissance she was denied the right to any social exchange with her students; black and white faculty members were discouraged from any public or private fraternization; and the predominately white administration demanded strict enforcement of social rules from another age. At a time when F. Scott Fitzgerald coeds rouged their knees and their male counterparts carried hip flasks on white campuses, Hampton students were not allowed to date. Thompson recalled that even during weekend movies shown in the college chapel a faculty member was assigned as chaperone to every four students, and the lights were kept up. A resulting passive rebellion at Hampton caused some adverse publicity, particularly following a visit from South African prime minister Jan Christiaan Smuts. He had come to investigate Tuskegee and Hampton as model schools for blacks that might be emulated in his own country, but when a black singer was obliged to entertain him before a segregated audience in the college chapel, singing a subservient spiritual, the student body marched out in silent protest rather than join in the chorus. That action, and Louis Thompson's letter to W.E.B. Du Bois recounting these antiquated attempts to insure gentility (published anonymously in *The Crisis** to protect her job) effected some minor changes at Hampton.

At that juncture Thompson moved to New York to accept a National Urban League* scholarship in sociology and, as a new friend of Aaron Douglas* and his wife, began to come in contact with many young black intellectuals in Harlem. Among them was Wallace Thurman,* editor of the notorious *Fire!!,** spokesman for the movement, and scandalous bon vivant. They married after a brief courtship; shortly thereafter Thompson filed for divorce, but her Reno stay was interrupted by her mother's illness, Thurman refused to finance a divorce by proxy in Mexico, and the alliance was never legally severed. Although a good deal of bitterness preceded Thurman's death in 1934, Thompson ministered to him in the Staten Island welfare home where he died, and she attended his funeral.

During the period following their initial separation in 1928, Thompson came under the influence of the widow of Rufus Osgood Mason, the formidable Charlotte Louise Vandervere Quick Mason,* who insisted that her protégés call her "Godmother." This rich white philanthropist, who disguised her suffocating and degrading hold on young black writers with largesse, only convinced Thompson of yet another form of racism. In this case, it was all too easily destructive to creative artists. Mason engaged her as secretary to Langston Hughes* and Zora Neale Hurston* when they were collaborating on a play, but Thompson broke the ties over Mason's subtle cruelties and convinced Hughes to do the same.

She took a job with the Congregational Education Society in its department of social relations, conducting seminars on a Pullman car that travelled around the South (except for Birmingham, Alabama, where the organization was denied the right to appear). As editor of the society's newsletter, Thompson came to the attention of James W. Ford,* just back from the Soviet Union and soon to be a vice-presidential candidate for the Communist party. He encouraged her to gather a group of young black intellectuals to accept an invitation from the Meschrabpom Film Corporation to make a movie in Moscow about black life in America, to be called *Black and White*.* Thompson's recollections of this 1932 trip appeared in an article in *Freedomways* in 1968, recounting not only the failure of the project but the affectionate reception accorded the Americans and the strange experience of finding their color a badge of honor entitling them to preferential treatment.

On her return to the United States Thompson became involved in the *Scottsboro* case* and with the National Committee for Political Prisoners. In 1933 she began her fifteen-year service to the International Workers Order, and in 1940 she married William Patterson, who had been lawyer for the Scottsboro boys, afterward remaining an avid worker in various fields of civil liberties.
REFERENCES: Louise Thompson Patterson, "With Langston Hughes in the USSR," *Freedomways*, Spring 1968; Dorothy West, "Elephant's Dance," *Black World*, Nov. 1970; David Levering Lewis, *When Harlem Was in Vogue*, 1981; Louise Thompson Patterson. (BK, PO)

THOMPSON, ULYSSES "SLOW KID" (dancer), 1888– . Husband of Florence Mills* and innovator of slow motion dancing, U. S. Thompson was born in Arizona and at an early age began to tour with medicine shows and carnivals. He had his own jazz band until he was drafted in 1917, and after the war he appeared in a number of Broadway shows, notably *Shuffle Along* in 1921, in which he first appeared with his wife. They acted together as well in *Plantation Revue* the following year, went to London together for *Dover to Dixie* and returned in 1924 for its New York incarnation, *Dixie to Broadway*.* Thompson continued to perform after Florence Mills's early death, and he served as treasurer for the Florence Mills Memorial Fund of the Florence Mills Theatrical Association, Inc.,* which flourished briefly. He was still dancing at the age of ninety-two, demonstrating for a younger generation the boneless undulations that marked his unique style.
REFERENCES: BB, 1980; *New York Voice*, 31 Dec. 1982. (BK)

THREE PLAYS FOR A NEGRO THEATRE, 1917. James Weldon Johnson* called 5 April 1917 "the date of the most important single event in the entire history of the Negro in the American Theatre" (*Black Manhattan*, 1930, p. 175). At the Garden Theatre on that occasion the Emilie Hapgood Players presented three one-act plays by white writer Frederic Ridgely Torrence (1875–1950) about blacks with black casts. Torrence was perhaps the first white writer to use black subject matter sympathetically in the drama. Three years earlier the Stage Society had mounted one of these plays with a white cast, *Granny Maumee*, depicting Afro-Americans from their own point of view, in a terse drama about voodoo, miscegenation, and the power of religious faith. The second play, *Simon the Cyrenian*, was based on the idea that Jesus Christ's cross bearer was black. The third, *The Rider of Dreams*, was a folk play evoking John Millington Synge's comedy of Irish rural life, *The Playboy of the Western World*. In all three, race pride burns brightly. The influential dramatic critic George Jean Nathan singled out Inez Clough* and Opal Cooper as two of the ten best actors of the season. The following day, however, brought President Woodrow Wilson's Declaration of War against Germany, and interest in theatrical matters—white as well as black—was diverted. In 1920 Paul Robeson* made his acting debut in the revival of *Simon the Cyrenian* with a little theater group, and all three of the plays were produced under similar circumstances during the ensuing years.

REFERENCES: James Weldon Johnson, *Black Manhattan*, 1930; Carl Van Vechten, *"Keep A-Inchin' Along,"* 1979. (BK)

THURMAN, WALLACE (writer, editor), 16 August 1902–22 December 1934. Born in Salt Lake City, Wallace Thurman was educated at the University of Southern California and found work, together with Arna Bontemps,* in the Los Angeles Central Post Office. Upon publication of his first poem in *The Crisis* Bontemps left for Harlem in August 1924. Thurman soon followed. He hired on as a literary critic for *The Messenger** (1926) and associated with A. Philip Randolph,* Chandler Owen,* and George S. Schuyler.* Soon after, he became circulation manager for *World Tomorrow* (October 1926) and later a senior editor of Macaulay's, the first black to hold such a position with a white publishing house. Thurman was also a ghostwriter for *True Story*, often appearing in Irish or Jewish dialect.

More important, Thurman was a leader of the younger writers and artists. His residence at 267 West 136th Street, dubbed "Niggerati Manor" by himself and Zora Neale Hurston,* was a meeting place for the avant-garde of Harlem and Greenwich Village. During the summer of 1926 Thurman founded, along with Langston Hughes,* Zora Neale Hurston, Aaron Douglas,* J. P. Davis, Richard Bruce Nugent,* and Gwendolyn Bennett,* *Fire!!*,* subtitled "A Quarterly Devoted to the Younger Negro Artists." Much to the relief of men such as Benjamin Brawley* and W.E.B. Du Bois,* *Fire!!* failed and left Thurman deeply in debt. Nevertheless, he made one more publishing effort, but *Harlem** fared no better. All the while, Thurman wrote articles for *New Republic, Bookman*, and the *Independent* as well as scripts for two Hollywood "adult" films.

Thurman's place in the Harlem Renaissance, however, is most clearly defined in two of his novels, *The Blacker the Berry** (1929) and *Infants of the Spring** (1932), and his play *Harlem** (1929). The irony of the first work—the title derives from a folk saying, "the blacker the berry, the sweeter the juice"— details the profound despair of a girl who experiences rejection and humiliation by her family and others because of her dark skin, a circumstance Thurman himself suffered from irrationally. This novel, along with his play *Harlem* and his short story "Cordelia the Crude" in *Fire!!* served notice that Thurman was brutally frank and willing to shock. But these works also reveal that he was writing out of a deeply felt sense of disenchantment with most of those he met and observed. He mistrusted white patronage as he mistrusted conservative, middle-class black patronage, but in Dorothy West's* observation, he surrounded himself "with a queer assortment of the 'lost generation' of Blacks and whites. They clung to him like leeches, and although he saw them clearly, and could evaluate them in a half dozen brutal words, he chose to allow them to waste the valuable hours of his ripening maturity" ("Elephant's Dance," p. 80).

Between the two novels Thurman married Louise Thompson,* an apparently catastrophic alliance, and she sued for divorce almost immediately. The action was never completed, however. Thurman took a job as an understudy in *Porgy** to learn something about dramaturgy and stagecraft before writing *Harlem*, and in 1928 he wrote *Negro Life in New York's Harlem*,* a monograph of fascinating insights from someone on the scene at the time. In his second novel, *Infants of the Spring*, published in 1932 when the Harlem Renaissance had begun to run down, Thurman offers an assessment of the period. Everyone is present in this *roman à clef*: Zora Neale Hurston, Bruce Nugent, Countee Cullen,* Langston Hughes, and Thurman himself. All of the luminaries gather at Niggerati Manor, and discussions touch on most of the issues and enthusiasms—both public and private, social and sexual—of the preceding decade. To Thurman, "Renaissance" seemed a misnomer, more artifice than serious and sustained accomplishment. Two years later he returned to New York from Hollywood, where he had been trying to write for the movies, gathered his old friends around him for a last party, and stayed drunk until he collapsed. Having ignored the advice of more than one doctor to stop drinking, in despair over an unrealized career, and riddled with guilt over his sexual ambivalence, Thurman waited out six months in the incurable ward on Welfare Island until he died on Christmas Eve 1934 at the age of thirty-four, the first "New Negro" child of the century to make a "break in the ranks," as Dorothy West reflected. In a Harlem funeral parlor the others "assembled in solemn silence, older, hardly wiser, and reminded for the first time of their lack of immortality" (p. 85).

Langston Hughes was certainly right in his description of Thurman as a brilliant man tortured by his own inability to achieve what he knew to be great art. But more than personal failure was at stake, for Thurman was equally sensitive to the ambiguities of sexuality and of race and culture in the twenties.

REFERENCES: Dorothy West, "Elephant's Dance," *Black World*, Nov. 1970; Nathan Irvin Huggins, *Harlem Renaissance*, 1971; David Levering Lewis, *When Harlem Was in Vogue*, 1981; Louise Thompson Patterson. (MH, BK)

TILLIE'S CHICKEN SHACK (cabaret). Located on 133rd Street with a number of other Harlem cabarets, Tillie's Chicken Shack served sweet potato pie and fried chicken to both races. The long-standing entertainer there was called "Elmira" and was best known for singing a scatological number called "Stop It, Joe!"

REFERENCE: Jervis Anderson, *This Was Harlem*, 1982. (BK)

TOOMER, [NATHAN] JEAN (writer), 26 December 1894–30 March 1967. Jean Toomer was born in Washington, D.C., in the home of his maternal grandfather, Pickney Benton Stewart Pinchback, a former lieutenant governor of Louisiana and United States senator. After the desertion of his father, Nathan Toomer (1895), and the death of his mother, Nina Pinchback (1909), Jean Toomer grew up under the stern eye of his grandfather and the critical encouragement of his uncle Bismarck, an omnivorous reader. In Washington he attended Dunbar High School, where he began to experience the spiritual and intellectual restlessness that would mark his life and lead to his lifelong quest to achieve a transcendent state of moral and psychic consciousness. Upon graduating in 1914 he enrolled at the University of Wisconsin. This was the beginning of an inconclusive academic career that meandered through five colleges and universities. After a period of wandering, odd jobs, tentative contact with literary figures in New York—a period of intense effort to learn the craft of writing—Toomer journeyed south in 1921 to assume for a brief period the administrative responsibility for a small, black agricultural and industrial academy in Sparta, Georgia. The experience galvanized his imagination, and in the following year Toomer's creative response to the South began to appear in some of the most important literary journals: *Nomad, S4N, Broom, The Crisis,* Double-Dealer, Liberator,* Little Review,* and the *Dial*. Critical response was overwhelmingly favorable, and Toomer was catapulted into New York literary and artistic circles; his closest relationships were with Waldo Frank,* Gorham Munson, and Alfred Stieglitz.

In early September 1922 Toomer and Frank journeyed together to Spartanburg, South Carolina—Toomer to bring to emotional pitch his experiences in Georgia and Frank to bring to fruition a novel that had been germinating since a trip to Mississippi and Alabama in late 1920. In the following year, after thoughtful criticism and encouragement by each other, Toomer's *Cane** (October 1923) and Frank's *Holiday** (August 1923) were published.

Cane was a financial failure but a critical success. Throughout the spectrum of political and artistic opinion—W.E.B. Du Bois* and William Stanley Braithwaite* to Claude McKay* and Wallace Thurman*—black Americans hailed *Cane* as a masterpiece, a benchmark of creative achievement. In addition, in his own personal life Toomer now had direct contact with many of the black intellectuals of the Harlem Renaissance. But Toomer's interests led to other concerns and other relationships. With Hart Crane, Munson, and Frank, Toomer studied the *Tertium Organum*, the spiritual thought of P. D. Ouspensky, and was converted. In 1924 he spent the summer at the Institute for the Harmonious Development of Man established by the Russian mystic Georgi Ivanovitch Gurdjieff at the Château de la Prieuré near Fontainebleau, France. Upon his return to America late in 1924, Toomer dedicated his life to teaching Gurdjieff's mystical doctrines. At first he lectured in Harlem, drawing curious yet steadily dwindling audiences. Later, he established classes in Chicago; lectured in Taos, New Mexico, at the ardent requests of Mabel Dodge Luhan; helped establish a commune in Portage, Wisconsin; and even found his way to Carmel, California. In 1940 he joined

the Society of Friends in Doylestown, Pennsylvania, where he died twenty-seven years later, his life since *Cane* far removed spiritually and intellectually from its "folksongs . . . heard then as spontaneous with gold, tints of eternal purple" (p. 93). After *Cane* Toomer published a few experimental pieces in the *Little Review* and *Dial*, five chapters of his novel *York Beach* in *New American Caravan* (1929), and the long poem "Blue Meridan" (1936). Until recently, it was widely assumed that Toomer had essentially ceased to write. However, he had indeed filled a trunk with unpublished manuscripts. This work (short stories, plays, literary criticism, poetry, psychological studies, and several full-length novels) is presently housed at Fisk University in Nashville, Tennessee.
REFERENCES: Darwin T. Turner, *In a Minor Chord*, 1971; Arthur P. Davis, *From the Dark Tower*, 1974; Jean Toomer, *Cane*, 1975; Brian J. Benson and Mabel Mayle Dillard, *Jean Toomer*, 1980; David Levering Davis, *When Harlem Was in Vogue*, 1981. (MH)

TOPSY AND EVA (musical play), 1924. After a lengthy Chicago run, where it was called "a freak of the season . . . , a terrible thing," according to the *New York Times*, the Duncan Sisters brought this jazz version of *Uncle Tom's Cabin* by Catherine Chisolm Cushing to Broadway (24 Dec. 1924, p. 11). Neither Vivian nor Rosefta Duncan, who supplied their own music and lyrics, was particularly successful in the offering. The chorus was weak, the script was humorless, and by the end of 1924 white audiences had begun to grow uncomfortable with whites stereotyping blacks, even though they continued to require blackface conventions in the black musical revues. In 1927 the Duncan Sisters made a film version even more grotesque. Vivian, as white Eva, prays for Topsy; Rosefta, as a blackface Topsy, swears, eats bugs, steals, bites, and prays that God will turn her white. Noble Johnson* played Uncle Tom, his role reduced to a small part.
REFERENCES: Burns Mantle, 1924–1925; NYTTR, 1972; Tom Shales et al., *The American Film Heritage*, 1972. (BK)

THE TREE (play), 1932. In Richard Maibaum's melodrama *The Tree* a white girl is assaulted and strangled, after which a black boy who admired her is falsely accused and lynched. His ultimate vindication comes through the religious conversion of the murderer. Brooks Atkinson, in his *New York Times* review, found *The Tree* "blunt and sinewy" when it dealt with the lynching but muddled when it dealt with "Christian remorse." Moreover, the "clumsy and faltering" acting weakened Maibaum's script (13 Apr. 1932, p. 23).
REFERENCES: Burns Mantle, 1931–1932; NYTTR, 1972. (BK)

TREE OF HOPE (touchstone). An aging elm took on such mythic significance that Bill "Bojangles" Robinson* is rumored to have paid to have it transplanted rather than uprooted when demolition for a new building project threatened its long life. The Tree of Hope stood in front of the Lafayette Theatre* at Seventh

Avenue and 132nd Street to serve as a "labor exchange," where out-of-work Afro-Americans rubbed its rough bark for good luck. When in 1941 an automobile destroyed it, Robinson rededicated it with a plaque to mark its place in Harlem's history.
REFERENCES: David Levering Lewis, *When Harlem Was in Vogue*, 1981; Alexander Gumby Scrapbooks, Columbia University. (BK)

TRI-ARTS CLUB (little theater group), 1923–   . At the Harlem YWCA on December 20, the Tri-Arts Club staged three plays: *The Lady of the Hairpins*, a Japanese drama; *The Criminal*, by Leroy N. Jorgeson; and *The Wooing of Frazee*, by Frederick Hogan. Arthur Taylor, Marie Santos, Ruppert Marks, Lillian Mattison, and John Wilson appeared in the casts. In his monthly theatrical column in *The Messenger*,* Theophilus Lewis* wished the group might have devoted its efforts to plays of more relevant subject matter and urged black playwrights to submit their work for consideration. Plays like *Come Along, Mandy*, the current offering at the Lafayette Theatre,* he regretted, were more likely to please the public.
REFERENCE: Theophilus Lewis, "Theatre," *The Messenger*, Feb. 1924. (BK)

TROPIC DEATH (short stories), 1926. *Tropic Death* is a collection of ten stories set, for the most part, in Barbados and Panama. Although the quality of the stories is uneven, Eric Walrond's book ranks with Jean Toomer's* *Cane** as one of the truly avant-garde literary experiments of the Harlem Renaissance. "The Yellow One," "The White Snake," and "Tropic Death" are especially brilliant. Cultural disorientation—the loss of the familiar and the ambiguity of the present—as the result of technological change unify thematically and geographically the several stories. (MH)

TROTTER, WILLIAM MONROE (editor), 7 April 1872–7 April 1934. William Monroe Trotter, businessman, editor, and activist, was born at his grandparents' farm near Chillicothe, Ohio. Monroe, as he was called, was the oldest of three children and the only son born to Virginia Isaacs and James Monroe Trotter. His adolescence was spent within the well-ordered family environment of predominately white Hyde Park, a suburb of Boston. James Trotter was employed by the Boston Post Office and later had successful careers in real estate and local politics. Monroe was a happy, contented child, active in the local Baptist Church and popular in school. He won a scholarship in high school and was elected president of his class, matriculating to Harvard College in 1891, where he spent four pleasant and fulfilling years. Trotter was a superior student who showed interest in a variety of subjects and made Phi Beta Kappa in his junior year, the first black student to win the honor at Harvard. He graduated with his class in 1895. For several years Trotter enjoyed the life of an eligible bachelor and the income he earned working for a white real estate firm. He was sufficiently confident of success to open his own office in 1899. That same year he married Geraldine Pindell, the daughter of a prominent Boston family who was employed as a bookkeeper. Already, though, Trotter's interests were turning from business to civil rights. He, like others of his background and education, had become impatient with the strategy of race leader Booker T. Washington and the encroachment of Jim Crow segregation laws in the South and in Boston. By the winter of 1901–1902 Trotter had made the momentous decision to start his own newspaper, the Boston *Guardian*,* to advocate a more militant and openly political line than the so-called Tuskegee Machine, Washington's influential college. For two years, as he watched the *Guardian's* circulation grow to several thousand, Trotter shared editorial duties with George Washington Forbes. Forbes resigned the controversial enterprise in 1904 rather than jeopardize his other position as a city employee. Thereafter, Geraldine Trotter came to play an invaluable role in what would be her husband's lifework.

Trotter quickly emerged as one of the more militant and controversial spokesmen for racial equality his generation would know. His attacks on Washington were relentless. In July 1903 Trotter was jailed for one month for his part in disrupting a speech Washington gave in Boston. This incident brought him into closer association with the other significant opponent of Booker T. Washington, W.E.B. Du Bois.* The two joined together in the Niagara movement in 1905–1906, but by the time of the formation of the NAACP* in 1909, Trotter and Du Bois had drifted apart. For his part Trotter objected to the white leadership and money behind the new organization, and he preferred to work through his own National Equal Rights League. But there was more to the break than that. Trotter had a strong personality, and he exhibited little tolerance of those who did not share his views. This fault isolated him from other black leaders like Du Bois who found it impossible to work with the gifted but irascible editor. A person of uncompromising principle, it was his unbending will that kept Monroe Trotter from developing the national following he desired. In 1912 Trotter supported Woodrow Wilson for president, but within two years they too had parted company after strong words were exchanged in the course of a White House meeting. In 1915 the editor led a highly publicized protest against the opening of *The Birth of a Nation* in Boston movie theaters. In 1919 he travelled to Paris to advocate a racial-equality plank in the Versailles Treaty. But the death of his wife a year earlier did much to complete Monroe Trotter's isolation from a national constituency. His dwindling influence now limited to Boston, Monroe Trotter kept on publishing *The Guardian* into the early thirties. One of the most militant and principled spokesmen for racial equality in the twentieth century, William Monroe Trotter died on his sixty-second birthday. He apparently committed suicide. REFERENCE: Stephen R. Fox. *The Guardian of Boston*, 1970. (DD)

TUCKER, EARL "SNAKEHIPS" (dancer), c. 1905–21 March 1937. Snakehips Tucker probably taught Gilda Gray how to do the shimmy, although she seems to have named the dance herself. (When asked what she was doing, she is reported to have explained that she was "shaking her chemise.") Tucker

developed his languorous acrobatics at Connie's Inn* and in *Hot Chocolates** and several editions of *Blackbirds*.* As was often the case during the twenties, whites simply took over dances that had originated with black performers—the Charleston, the black bottom, the lindy hop, and Tucker's shimmy—and adopted them as their own. At the Cotton Club,* performing between Broadway runs, Tucker was likened to a boa constrictor, contorting his joints with such suppleness that he seemed to have no bones at all. Still photographs are unsuccessful in conveying such movements, but E. Simms Campbell* executed a series of sketches of Snakehips Tucker in action that give a good idea of his routine.
REFERENCES: Nancy Cunard, ed., *Negro*, 1970; Jim Haskins, *The Cotton Club*, 1977; Jervis Anderson, *This Was Harlem*, 1982. (BK)

TUCKER, LORENZO (actor), 27 June 1907– . The "Black Valentino" was born in Philadelphia and attended Temple University there. He began appearing in romantic films in 1926, the year of Valentino's death, many of them made by Oscar Micheaux.* The first was *Wages of Sin; Bewitching Eyes* followed in 1927 and *When Men Betray* in 1928. Tall, dark, and handsome, and therefore suitable for her well-advertised tastes, Tucker was featured by Mae West in her 1927 play *The Constant Sinner*.* Tucker appeared in a few other plays as well, but most of his work was in all-black films: *Daughter of the Congo* (1930), *The Black King** (1931), and *Veiled Aristocrats* (1932), for example. When talking pictures came in, Tucker was billed as the "Colored William Powell."
REFERENCES: Donald Bogle, *Toms, Coons, Mulattoes, Mammies, and Bucks*, 1973; BB, 1980. (BK)

TURNER, JOE (jazz pianist), 3 November 1907–? Joe Turner, one of the original Harlem stride pianists, along with Fats Waller,* James P. Johnson,* and others, was born in Baltimore. He studied piano with his mother and developed his style listening to piano rolls. Settling in New York in the early twenties, he played the piano in Harlem nightclubs and with various groups, including Louis Armstrong.* He toured widely with Adelaide Hall* in the United States and abroad during the thirties. From 1936 on he made his home in Europe, with the exception of the war years, when he joined the U.S. armed forces and played in the army band led by Sy Oliver. Turner's later piano style reflected the influence of jazz pianists such as Earl Hines, Erroll Garner, and Art Tatum. In 1973 he played at the Newport Jazz Festival in the United States and appeared for a long engagement at a New York nightclub in 1976.
REFERENCE: BDAM, 1982. (PO)

TUTT, HOMER [WHITNEY]. See WHITNEY, SALEM TUTT.

U

UNIVERSAL HOLY TEMPLE OF TRANQUILITY, 1930–? Founded by Bishop Amiru Al-Minin Sufi Abdul Hamid* in 1930, the Universal Holy Temple of Tranquility abolished the use of the word *Negro* and offered political support against white Harlem's discrimination. The New York *Age** denounced its leader Sufi as a "black Hitler," guilty of anti-Semitism and of fleecing members of their dues to his temple. He formed the Negro Industrial and Clerical Alliance to boycott against white strongholds. With Father Divine (George Baker*), Sufi staged a rally at the Rockland Palace Casino to end discrimination. It failed when Sufi was indicted for extortion, but it anticipated subsequent boycotts. REFERENCE: David Levering Lewis, *When Harlem Was in Vogue*, 1981. (BK)

UNIVERSAL NEGRO IMPROVEMENT ASSOCIATION (UNIA), 1914– . Marcus Garvey,* a twenty-five-year-old Jamaican, founded the Universal Negro Improvement Association on 1 August 1914 in Kingston, Jamaica, to build a unified black race, to aid in the development and independence of African states, and, generally, "to work for the general uplift of the Negro peoples of the world." For several years Garvey and the UNIA confined most of their activities to Jamaica, particularly in trying to establish educational and industrial colleges for native blacks. On 23 March 1916 Garvey landed in Harlem with hopes of raising funds and setting up a UNIA chapter in the United States. He slowly built up a following during the next three years, and due to the constant attempts by enemies in New York to divide or control the UNIA, he decided to stay in New York rather than return to Jamaica. Since the headquarters of the UNIA in the early years was wherever Garvey resided, New York and Harlem became the new home of the UNIA in the 1920s. In 1919 and 1920 the UNIA enjoyed phenomenal growth, as Garvey set up chapters throughout the United States, the West Indies, and Latin America. The association's newspaper, the *Negro World*,* helped spread the message of race uplift and black pride, which proved so popular after World War I among blacks around the world who were tired of white oppression and rule. The UNIA reached the height of its popularity during August 1920 at its international convention in Harlem. Garvey and the UNIA astounded the world with a well-organized and exciting program of parades, speeches, and colorful events. In addition, the UNIA had organized a shipping company, the Black Star Line,* which was to compete with white companies.

The sale of stock for the Black Star Line brought hundreds of thousands of dollars into the UNIA treasury and raised the hopes of millions of blacks as no other event before or since. The failure of the company in 1922, the subsequent arrest and conviction of Garvey and other UNIA leaders on mail-fraud charges, and the inability of the UNIA to fulfill its plans expressed in 1924 of colonizing Liberia all helped to deflate the incredible bubble of popularity the UNIA had enjoyed in the early 1920s. Still, the movement did not die even when Garvey was imprisoned in 1925–1927 and deported immediately on his release. Certainly, the UNIA's membership had declined markedly, and requests for dues were made more often and more stridently as the years progressed; yet conventions were held throughout the 1930s, and the movement (although splintered badly into competing factions) continued even after Garvey's death in 1940.

REFERENCES: E. David Cronon, *Black Moses*, 1955; John Hendrik Clarke, ed., *Marcus Garvey and the Vision of Africa*, 1974. (DS)

URBAN LEAGUE BULLETIN (periodical), 1921–1922. The *Urban League Bulletin* was the first regular publication of the National Urban League* and the immediate predecessor of *Opportunity*.* The *Bulletin* first appeared in December 1921 and replaced the occasional bulletins that had earlier been published by the league. The *Bulletin*, edited by Charles S. Johnson,* was a bimonthly tabloid. In October 1922 the league decided to produce a monthly magazine that could attract advertisers and subscribers, and *Opportunity* replaced the *Bulletin* on January 1, 1923.

REFERENCE: Nancy J. Weiss, *The National Urban League*, 1974. (DS)

V

VAN DER ZEE, JAMES (photographer), 29 June 1886–15 May 1984. The dean of Harlem photographers began his career at the turn of the century in Massachusetts where he had been born. In 1916 he opened a studio in Harlem at 272 Lenox Avenue and was actively engaged in his profession until ill health retired him in 1969. Van Der Zee had begun to study for a musical career at the Carlton Conservatory in New York, playing violin with the Harlem Orchestra about 1910 for a variety of social occasions and sometimes playing the piano with Fletcher Henderson,* although only for private parties. By that time he had divorced his first wife, with whom he had two children. He named his studio after his second wife, Gaynella Grenley Greenlee, who took in roomers while he began to build his reputation, frequently but not exclusively as a funeral photographer. Van Der Zee's photographs always had a narrative quality, even in the hundreds of pictures he made of people in their coffins. In one, for example, a man holds a newspaper in his hands, looking, according to the photographer, as if he had dozed off while reading about Florence Mills.* In another, a smiling father holds his dead baby in his lap while his wife perches comfortably on the arm of the chair. In still another, a baby is in his crib, one hand holding a milk bottle, the other petting a teddy bear. In a series of Harlem studios, Van Der Zee continued to photograph until the Metropolitan Museum of Art mounted an exhibition in 1969, entitled "Harlem on My Mind," which brought him to prominence. After Gaynella's death in 1976 Van Der Zee married a third time and in his ninth decade enjoyed speaking engagements and photographic shows as one of Harlem's elder statesmen in the arts.
REFERENCES: Reginald McGhee, *The World of James Van Der Zee*, 1973; James Van Der Zee, Owen Dodson, and Camille Billops, *The Harlem Book of the Dead*, 1978. (BK)

VAN DOREN, CARL (teacher and critic), 10 September 1885–18 July 1950. One of America's most distinguished critics, Carl Van Doren taught literature

at Columbia University (1911–1934), edited *Nation** (1919–1922) and *Century Magazine* (1922–1925), and authored numerous books on American literary and historical figures. During the twenties he frequently socialized with the major personalities of the Harlem Renaissance. Invited to speak at the Writers Guild meeting organized by Charles S. Johnson* at the Civic Club* in March 1924 in New York City, Van Doren gave a stirring address, "The Younger Generation of Negro Writers," in which he foresaw a remarkable opportunity and future for black writers. One year later he served as one of the literary judges at the first *Opportunity** banquet, in May, to award prizes for that year's outstanding black literary talent. Two years later, in March 1926, Van Doren offered further evidence and encouragement in *Century Magazine* ("The Negro Renaissance") that black writers and intellectuals were creating a typically American yet uniquely expressive range of critical and imaginative work. He wrote several books, none of them devoted exclusively to black arts and letters.
REFERENCES: WWW, 1963; AAB, 1972; David Levering Lewis, *When Harlem Was in Vogue*, 1981. (MH)

VANITY FAIR (periodical), 1914–1936. During the twenties Frank Crowninshield's* influential publication was a social barometer of tastes and fashions, publishing work by nearly every celebrated writer and photographs of nearly everybody connected with various kinds of entertainment. *Vanity Fair* was a combination of several later kinds of magazines: *Life, Vogue,* the *New Yorker,* and perhaps *Esquire.* It was the first of the large-circulation periodicals to publish black material, initially in a series of articles by Carl Van Vechten* about the spirituals,* the blues,* a "Prescription for the Negro Theatre," and an analysis of the young black writer's reluctance to exploit his racial gifts. It was one of the first magazines to publish poems by Langston Hughes* and Countee Cullen,* and full-page photographs of Paul Robeson* and Florence Mills* appeared in its pages. (BK)

VANN, ROBERT L. (journalist), 27 August 1879–14 October 1940. For nearly thirty years Robert L. Vann was responsible for the most influential black newspaper in the country, the *Pittsburgh Courier,** with a circulation of a quarter million. Born into an Afro-American's customary poverty in America in 1879, in North Carolina, Vann became one of the first blacks to graduate from the University of Pittsburgh. By 1910 he was practicing law in that city and found among his first clients some acquaintances for whom he drew up incorporation papers for a weekly newspaper. Subsequently, Vann became its treasurer and in 1914 its editor. The *Pittsburgh Courier*'s success motivated Vann's starting a monthly news organ for the black upper middle class, called *The Competitor,* in 1920, but its limited appeal to both readers and advertisers resulted in failure after two years. Twenty years later, at the time of Vann's death, his newspaper continued to exert a powerful influence over its readers, however.

REFERENCES: Theodore J. Vincent, ed., *Voices of a Black Nation*, 1973; Andrew Buni, *Robert L. Vann of the Pittsburgh Courier*, 1974. (BK)

VAN VECHTEN, CARL (writer, photographer), 17 June 1880–21 December 1964. Carl Van Vechten was born in Cedar Rapids, Iowa, and yearned to leave. His satirical look back many years later (*The Tattooed Countess*, 1924) provides some insight into his need to escape. He attended the University of Chicago (1899–1903), earned a bachelor of philosophy degree, and, building upon early exposure in Cedar Rapids to the remarkable voice and retinue of Sissieretta Jones,* was greatly taken with the talents of artists such as James "Slaprags" White, Ernest Hogan, Carita Day, Bob Cole, George Walker, and Bert Williams,* who often performed at the Old Pekin Theatre. Upon graduation Van Vechten began the first of several careers (he was assistant music critic for the *New York Times*, 1906–1912, and drama critic for the *New York Press*, 1913–1914) and greatly expanded his critical knowledge of dance, opera, theater, and music. His admiration and respect for black arts and artists also deepened and broadened. In his "Valedictory" to music criticism in 1924, a career that included six volumes of essays on music, theater, and other interests, Van Vechten counseled that "jazz may not be the last hope of American music, nor yet the best hope, but at present, I am convinced, it is its only hope" (*Red*, 1925, p. xv).

The year before he offered his farewell to music Van Vechten read Walter White's* *The Fire in the Flint*.* Soon afterward they met, and through White's good offices, Van Vechten met Langston Hughes,* James Weldon Johnson* (both lifelong friends), and many other celebrated Afro-Americans. Stimulated by these new friendships, Van Vechten wrote eleven articles and five book reviews on black music, literature, and theater in the next two years. Most important in these writings was his continuing insistence, first voiced in "The Negro Theatre" in 1919, that black actors and actresses not be trapped within the imaginative limitations and commercial ambitions of whites. Despite such writing, however, Van Vechten's career had decidedly taken a new turn. By 1924 he had written three novels. He still had four novels and two books of essays to write (*Excavations* in 1926 and *Sacred and Profane Memories* in 1932) before he would plunge into his third creative passion, photography.

Although Van Vechten is largely forgotten as a novelist, his fifth novel, *Nigger Heaven** (1926), remains the subject of strenuous controversy. At the time of its appearance W.E.B. Du Bois* denounced it as "a blow in the face." Others—individuals such as Alain Locke,* James Weldon Johnson, and Charles S. Johnson*—praised his achievement. Contemporary criticism is not less divided as to Van Vechten's intention and success. Likewise, his counsel offered in *The Crisis** questionnaire series "The Negro in Art: How Shall He Be Portrayed?"* continues to draw criticism.

Only slightly less controversial is Van Vechten's extraordinary involvement and friendship with the writers, artists, poets, and singers of the Harlem Renaissance. He was everywhere, and at his lavish parties whites and blacks drank, sang, and conversed far into the night. His soireés became regular features in both the black and white press. More important was Van Vechten's unremitting effort through encouragement, private influence, and public endorsement to assist many black writers to become published and recognized. The following commentary of Langston Hughes could be that of many others: "What Carl Van Vechten did for me was to submit my first book of poems to Alfred A. Knopf,[*] put me in contact with the editors of *Vanity Fair*[*] . . . caused me to meet many editors and writers . . . cheered me on in the writing of my first short stories" (*The Big Sea*, p. 272).

At age fifty-two Van Vechten gave up writing. In his remaining thirty-two years he photographed nearly every celebrated black person in America from W.E.B. Du Bois* to Sammy Davis, Jr., and from Leontyne Price to Ralph Bunche. In addition, he established several important collections that help to insure that the Harlem Renaissance will not be lost, stolen, or strayed: the James Weldon Johnson Memorial Collection of Negro Arts and Letters at Yale University (1941), the George Gershwin* Memorial Collection of Music and Musical Literature at Fisk University (1944), the Rose McClendon* Memorial Collection of Photographs of Celebrated Negroes at Howard University (1946), and the Jerome Bowers Peterson* Collection of Photographs by Carl Van Vechten of Celebrated Negroes at the University of New Mexico (1954). In 1955 Van Vechten received an honorary doctor's degree from Fisk University. To the last year of his life he continued to correspond with those who were left.

REFERENCES: Carl Van Vechten, *Red*, 1925; Langston Hughes, *The Big Sea*, 1940; Edward Lueders, *Carl Van Vechten*, 1965; Bruce Kellner, *Carl Van Vechten and the Irreverent Decades*, 1968; Mark Helbling, "Carl Van Vechten and the Harlem Renaissance," *Negro American Literature Forum*, July 1976; Bruce Kellner, "Carl Van Vechten," *American Writers*, 1981. (MH)

THE VENGEANCE OF THE GODS AND THREE OTHER STORIES OF REAL AMERICAN COLOR LINE LIFE (short stories), 1922. William Pickens's* short stories are premised on the conviction that unless blacks speak for themselves they will forever remain caricatures of another's ignorance and hostility. The title story, similar to the plot line of Mark Twain's *Pudd' nhead Wilson* in which half-brothers of mixed blood, one white and one black, are confused, investigates environment and heredity as the major determinants defining human destiny. The remaining stories satirize white pretensions to racial superiority. (MH)

VILLARD, OSWALD GARRISON (journalist), 13 March 1872–1 October 1949. The grandson of William Lloyd Garrison and one of the leading white spokesmen for civil rights in the early twentieth century, Oswald Garrison Villard was editor (1918–1932) of the *Nation*,* an influential liberal weekly that gave favorable publicity to black causes and vigorously attacked racism, militarism, corporate greed, and attempts to limit civil liberties. In 1897, four years after he graduated from Harvard, Villard went to work for the New York *Evening Post*, which his father, Henry Villard, a foreign correspondent turned railroad and utilities magnate, had purchased in 1881. When his father died in 1900, he took control of the *Evening Post* and the *Nation* (which had been a weekly edition of the paper) and soon transformed the latter into a vehicle for his brand of crusading liberal journalism and (once again, as it had been at its beginnings in 1865) a worthy successor to his grandfather's famous *Liberator*.

An active neoabolitionist, Villard was a founder of the NAACP*; indeed, in 1909 he accepted the invitation to write the call for the conference in February of that year that led to the formation of the NAACP. In later years he gave that fledgling organization editorial support and free use of space in the *Evening Post* building and was elected vice-president in 1931. In 1918 he sold the *Evening Post*, which was languishing financially due to Villard's unpopular antiwar editorial policy, but held onto the *Nation* until 1932 and continued writing for the magazine until 1940, when he parted ways with the prowar editorial staff. Villard was a prolific writer of books and articles—although none of them was directly connected with Afro-American affairs—even after he was slowed by a heart attack in 1944, five years before his death.
REFERENCES: Oswald Garrison Villard, *Fighting Years*, 1939; Dollena Joy Humes, *Oswald Garrison Villard*, 1960. (DS)

VODERY, WILL (composer, arranger), 8 October 1885–18 November 1951. Will Vodery played the organ for his church when he was nine years old, and at the University of Pennsylvania he was the orchestra's pianist. When he was about twenty, he was writing material for Bert Williams* and George Walker and later for Walker's wife, Aida Overton. Before he was thirty Vodery was supplying material for the Ziegfeld Follies. He served with the 807th Black Regiment during the war. Afterward, he returned to composing and arranging for the Plantation Cabaret Orchestra and the scores for *Dixie to Broadway** and *Keep Shufflin'*.* In 1927 he arranged the chorus routines for *Showboat** and was later active in other shows as well.
REFERENCES: PR, 1969; BB, 1980. (BK)

W

WALKER, A'LELIA (hostess), 1885–16 August 1931. The daughter of the first black female millionaire, Sarah Breedlove (Madame C. J.) Walker,* the inventor of a hair-straightening process, A'Lelia Walker was one of the most colorful figures of the Harlem Renaissance. With a fortune of more than $2 million (some estimates were higher) from her mother, she threw hundreds of parties where all shades of people met and mingled during the twenties. She invited artists, writers, musicians, actors, royalty, and racketeers to her lavish affairs at one of her three addresses: the Villa Lewaro, the half-million-dollar mansion her mother had built at Irvington-on-Hudson in 1917, with pipe organ, swimming pool, and white-wigged footmen; her mother's elaborate limestone mansion on 136th Street; or her apartment on Edgecombe Avenue in Harlem's West End. One of her regular guests became a close friend, white writer Carl Van Vechten,* who put her into his Harlem novel *Nigger Heaven*,* none too flatteringly, but later claimed that she was nicer to him afterward. As "Adora Boniface," a rich social arbiter who surrounds herself with sweetmen and other sycophants, she is described as "undeniably warm-hearted, amusing, in her outspoken way, and even beautiful, in a queenly African manner that set her apart from the other beauties of her race whose loveliness was more frequently of a Latin than an Ethiopian character" (p. 21). A'Lelia Walker was six feet tall, a magnificent dresser. "She looked like a queen," Van Vechten recalled long after her death, "and frequently acted like a tyrant" ("*Keep A-Inchin' Along*," p. 154).

A'Lelia Walker had arrived in Harlem around 1914 from Indianapolis, after her divorce from her first husband, to manage the headquarters of her mother's beauty empire, the Walker College of Hair Culture. After her mother's death in 1919 she embarked on the second of her three short-lived marriages and on her career as a salon hostess and conspicuous consumer of jewels, cars, and champagne. When she wasn't giving parties, she was holding poker or bridge sessions with her circle or going out to dinner, the theater, or a round of parties, ending up at a nightclub like Connie's Inn,* her favorite, dancing well into the night. A'Lelia Walker was not the philanthropist her mother had been. Perhaps she thought the two-thirds of the Walker Corporation's annual net profits, which under the terms of her mother's will went to charity, was enough on that score; but she was lavish in her generosity to her friends, lovers, employees, and adopted daughter, whose wedding in 1923 was one of the most spectacular social occasions ever witnessed in Harlem. In 1928 she opened the Dark Tower* at her 136th Street house, a kind of salon for artists and intellectuals, but which turned out to be more formal and expensive than her bohemian friends had expected. Later, when she moved to her Edgecombe apartment, the Dark Tower became a nightclub, with advertisements in the *Inter-State Tattler*,* presided over by Mayme White or some other member of the "handsome women," as David Lewis described them, or "effete men" who surrounded A'Lelia Walker most of the time (*When Harlem Was in Vogue*, p. 167).

She died at the age of forty-six, while visiting friends in New Jersey. Her death coincided with the dissolution of the Harlem Renaissance, the end of the generous twenties and the onset of the mean-spirited thirties. Her funeral, a final symbol of her largesse, was itself very much like a party, according to Langston Hughes, whose poem "To A'Lelia" was read at the rites. The Reverend Adam Clayton Powell* delivered the eulogy, Mary McLeod Bethune* spoke, and the four Bon Bons sang Noel Coward's "I'll See You Again" and "swung it slightly," Hughes noted, "as she might have liked it" (*The Big Sea*, p. 247). Girls from the Walker beauty shops laid flowers on the $5,000 silver and bronze casket, and an airplane dropped a floral wreath in her memory. "You should have known A'Lelia Walker," Van Vechten wrote to a young black novelist, Chester Himes, many years later. "Nothing in this age is quite as good as THAT. . . . What a woman! ("*Keep A-Inchin' Along*," p. 282).

REFERENCES: Carl Van Vechten, *Nigger Heaven*, 1926; NYT, 18 Aug. 1931; Langston Hughes, *The Big Sea*, 1940; Carl Van Vechten, "*Keep A-Inchin' Along*," 1979; David Levering Lewis, *When Harlem Was in Vogue*, 1981; Jervis Anderson, *This Was Harlem*, 1982. (PO, BK)

WALKER, SARAH BREEDLOVE [MADAME C. J.] (entrepreneuse), 23 December 1867–25 May 1919. Sarah Breedlove Walker, better known as Madame C. J. Walker, went from poverty-stricken washerwoman to immensely wealthy businesswoman after she discovered and successfully marketed a process for treating the hair of Afro-Americans. Sarah Breedlove was born of poor parents in Delta, Louisiana, in 1867. She was orphaned at the age of six, married at the age of fourteen to C. J. Walker, and left a widow at twenty with a small daughter to take care of. She moved to St. Louis, where she worked as a laundress. One day (as legend has it), during a break from her job, the weary Walker nodded off and had a dream that showed her how to smooth the hair of blacks. Starting with a capital of $2 she developed a preparation that proved commercially successful, and by 1910 she had set up in Indianapolis the Madam C. J. Walker laboratories to manufacture her products and train her agents and beauticians. At the height of her business she had more than 2,000 agents in the field selling her "Preparations," and she grossed more than $50,000 annually from those sales alone.

In 1913 she moved to New York City and wowed the inhabitants of Harlem when she built a $90,000 limestone mansion on West 136th Street. As her fortune increased, she decided to move to a better residential section but was rebuffed by the white community of Flushing. Undeterred, she determined that if she were going to be unwelcome in a white neighborhood, she might as well pick the most exclusive one she could afford, and in 1917 she built an elaborate mansion at exclusive Irvington-on-the-Hudson: Villa Lewaro. At her death in 1919 she left a $2 million estate, most of it to her daughter, A'Lelia Walker* Robinson, including the Villa Lewaro country estate.

REFERENCES: DAB, 1937; Roi Ottley and William Weatherby, eds., *The Negro in New York*, 1967. (DS)

WALLER, [THOMAS WRIGHT] FATS (composer, pianist, organist), 21 May 1904–15 December 1943. Thomas Waller's father was deacon and later pastor of the Abyssinian Baptist Church on 40th Street in New York; his mother was a singer and pianist and organist. Thomas learned to play piano and organ as a child and at the age of fifteen won a talent contest playing "Carolina Shout." The composer of that piece, James P. Johnson,* was so impressed with his talent that he offered to give him lessons, and Waller quickly mastered the techniques of stride bass and ragtime piano and joined the select group of New York pianists—Johnson, Willie-the-Lion Smith,* C. Luckyeth "Luckey" Roberts*— whose services were much in demand in Harlem clubs and at rent parties.* His first steady job may have been as a theater organist for silent movies in Washington, D.C., and he followed that with engagements at the Lafayette* and Lincoln* theaters as organist in 1923. He toured with a vaudeville act called Liza and Her Shufflin' Six, played piano at Leroy's Cabaret and other New York clubs, and published his first songs, "Bloody Razor Blues" and "Bullet Wound Blues" in 1924 and "Squeeze Me" in 1925. In 1926 he seems to have done the whole score for a Harlem revue called *Tan Town Topics*. About the mid-twenties he began a collaboration with lyricist Andy Razaf,* which over the years resulted in scores of songs. Their first show together was *Keep Shufflin'* (1928) with songs such as "Willow Tree" and "Got Myself Another Jockey Now," and this was followed by *Hot Chocolates* (1929), which introduced the hit song "Ain't Misbehavin'," sung originally by Margaret Simms but quickly taken up by Louis Armstrong.* (Waller later sold his rights to this song together with eighteen others for $500; he was often badly in need of cash for alimony payments and bar and restaurant bills.) *Hot Chocolates* also introduced "Sweet Savannah Sue" and a greatly underrated song that spoke movingly of the black experience in America, "Black and Blue," Waller's melody underlining Razaf's touching lyric. "Honeysuckle Rose" and "I've Got a Feeling I'm Falling" are sometimes listed as part of the original score for *Hot Chocolates*; more often they are not.

Waller went to Europe in 1932 but, denied entry into England, performed only in Paris (the legend that he participated in a midnight organ jam session in Notre-Dame Cathedral with the French organist Marcel Dupré has been discredited) and on his return to America began a series of broadcasts on radio station WLW in Cincinnati. Whatever immigration difficulties had prevented him from visiting England in 1932 seem to have been settled by 1938, when he made a concert tour of England, Denmark, Sweden, and Norway, and this was followed by another British and Scandinavian tour in 1939. On these trips he completed and recorded his *London Suite*, a set of sixteen piano pieces. Through the thirties and forties he fronted his own bands, made guest appearances with other orchestras and on radio, and toured widely. He appeared as a song stylist in some Hollywood films, notably *Stormy Weather* in 1943 with Lena Horne and Bill Robinson,* singing his "Ain't Misbehavin'." He died of pneumonia aboard the Santa Fe Chief while returning to New York from Los Angeles in 1943.

Fats Waller was gargantuan in size (285 pounds) and in tastes, extravagant and spendthrift, generous to a fault, and feckless in both public and private life, according to those who knew him. He published more than 400 songs and instrumental pieces and was a tireless recording artist. He made his first recordings—piano rolls—for the Q.R.S. Company in 1922 and during the next twenty years performed in nearly 500 recordings as pianist, organist, and singer. He was a serious musician and a fine performer of classical music, blues,* and traditional ragtime, but also, as music historian Rudi Blesh put it, "His humor was vast, innocent, but sardonic; he kidded everything, everybody, and himself" (Blesh and Janis, *They All Played Ragtime*, p. 207). Many of his recordings for RCA Victor transformed banal Tin Pan Alley songs into hilarious burlesques, and some of his songs—"Your Feet's Too Big"—and sayings—"One never knows, do one?"—became classics of American humor.

REFERENCES: Rudi Blesh and Harriet Janis, *They All Played Ragtime*, 1951; ETM, 1961; Charles Fox, *Fats Waller*, 1961; WWJ, 1972; BB, 1980. (DA)

THE WALLS OF JERICHO (novel), 1928. Rudolph Fisher's* satiric first novel is a deftly handled yet biting look at Harlem and the fascination it held for whites and blacks in the twenties. The love of Joshua "Shine" Jones, a burly piano mover, for Linda Young, a maid for the white spinster Agatha Cramp, serves to carry the story and to reveal the tensions and pretensions of class distinctions and racial hatred. Through Joshua we see Harlem low life and through Linda we see Harlem high life. In their eventual union they are contrasted and balanced against the extremes of emotion and ambition that others experience and express. Several scarcely veiled characters represent the most prominent figures of the Harlem Renaissance, including the white matriarch Charlotte Mason,* who supported many young black artists with money during the period, and the white novelist Carl Van Vechten,* who supported them with encouragement. *The Walls of Jericho* is also interesting for its depiction of various familiar locales, like the Savoy Ballroom* and the (Rockland Palace) Manhattan Casino.* (MH)

WALROND, ERIC (writer), 1898–1966. Born in Georgetown, Guyana, Eric Walrond grew up in the English- and Spanish-speaking cultures of Barbadoes and Panama. Educated by a series of private tutors, he first worked for the Health Department of the Canal Commission at Cristobal, and between the years 1916 and 1918 he worked as a reporter on the *Panama Star and Herald*. At the age of twenty he left for Harlem, attending City College of New York and Columbia University, where he studied creative writing before resuming his career as a journalist. After two years as editor and co-owner of the *Brooklyn and Long Island Informer* (a black weekly), Walrond joined the staff of Marcus Garvey's* *Negro World** as an associate editor. He soon left, however, and later served as a business manager for *Opportunity** (1925–1927). By that time he was readily and regularly identified with the group of young artists and intellectuals of the period. Walrond's essays on racial, political, and historical subjects appeared in periodicals such as the *New Republic, Current History*, and the *Independent*. However, it is as a writer of fiction that he is best remembered. His work is roughly divided between his expriences (mostly painful) in New York and his earlier life in the Caribbean. The ten stories that comprise his *Tropic Death** (1926) are his *chef d'oeuvre*, in which "The Yellow One," "The White Snake," and the title story are especially notable for their power of destruction and intensity of feeling. In March 1928 publishers Boni and Liveright announced the appearance of Walrond's book on the Panama Canal. If completed, the manuscript has never been seen, and except for a chance meeting with Richard Bruce Nugent* in London the following year, Eric Walrond also disappeared from view.
REFERENCES: Alain Locke, ed., *The New Negro*, 1925; Robert Bone, *Down Home*, 1975; Chidi Ikonné, *From Du Bois to Van Vechten*, 1981; David Levering Lewis, *When Harlem Was in Vogue*, 1981. (MH)

WALTON, LESTER A. (journalist), 20 April 1882–16 October 1965. Lester A. Walton began his long career as a free-lance journalist for the *St. Louis Globe Democrat* in his home town when he was in his teens, apparently without identifying his race, and then for the *St. Louis Star* as a golf reporter, when that latest sports craze swept America in the 1890s. Under Herbert Bayard Swope, later to become editor of the *New York World*, Walton served as drama critic, after which Ernest Hogan employed him to write the lyrics for *Rastus Rastus*, one of the touring shows of the period. In 1908 Walton went to the New York *Age** as drama critic and then as managing editor until he resigned in 1914. At that time he leased the Lafayette Theatre* and brought the Anita Bush* Company from the Lincoln Theatre* to become the Lafayette Players Stock Company.* Until 1923 the company mounted new productions of recent successes on the

white stage and of the classics—including Shakespeare—nearly every week. Walton sold the Lafayette when musical offerings became more popular than serious drama, although mismanagement seems to have required this action as well. From 1922 until 1931 Walton was an influential editorial contributor to the *New World* as well as to the magazines *Outlook* and *Literary Digest*. Concurrently, he served as publicity director for the National Negro Business League* and the Negro Division of the National Democratic Campaign Committee and later as a member of the New York Commission on Human Rights. Finally, Lester A. Walton may claim credit for having insisted that the word *Negro* stop being printed with a small *n*.
REFERENCES: NYT, 17 Oct. 1965; Langston Hughes and Milton Meltzer, *Black Magic*, 1971; Jervis Anderson, *This Was Harlem*, 1982. (BK)

WARD, AIDA (singer), 1900–23 June 1984. Aida Ward, the "mellow voiced . . . successor of . . . Florence Mills"* (Cunard, *Negro*, p. 188), had a principal role in *Blackbirds [*] of 1928*, in which she sang "Dixie" and "I Can't Give You Anything but Love." She had previously appeared at the Cotton Club,* in small parts in *The Frolics* (1923) and *Dixie to Broadway** (1924), and in the London production of *Blackbirds of 1926*. She played in *Brown Buddies** in 1930 and later appeared in revues at the Apollo Theatre.*
REFERENCES: Nancy Cunard, ed., *Negro*, 1970; BB, 1980; Jervis Anderson, *This Was Harlem*, 1982. (PO)

WARING, LAURA WHEELER (painter, educator), 1887–4 February 1948. Laura Wheeler Waring is known for her portraits and for oils, pastels, and watercolors depicting the life of Afro-Americans. Born in Hartford, Connecticut, Waring studied at the Pennsylvania Academy of Fine Arts in Philadelphia and in 1924 won a Cresson Memorial Scholarship to study at the Grand Chaumière in Paris. She received the Harmon Foundation* Gold Award for achievement in fine arts for her portrait of Ann Washington Derrick in 1927. Waring joined the art department of Cheyney State College in Pennsylvania in 1926 and remained on the faculty until her death, serving for a time as chairman of the department. Her work was shown at the Harmon Exhibition in 1929, 1930, and 1931 and at the Smithsonian in 1933 and in Chicago in 1940. She was director of the Negro Art Exhibit at the New York Sesquicentennial Exposition in 1926 and at the Texas Centennial Exposition in 1935. Her work is represented in the permanent collections of the National Archives and the National Portrait Gallery in Washington, D.C.
REFERENCES: NYT, 5 Feb. 1948; AAD, 1973; EBA, 1981. (PO)

WASHINGTON, FORD LEE "BUCK." See BUBBLES, JOHN [JOHN WILLIAM SUBLETT].

WASHINGTON, FREDI (actress), 23 December 1903– . Born in Georgia and educated in Pennsylvania, Fredi Washington was noted for the intelligence and sensitivity of her acting. She played nightclub engagements as a dancer and toured with *Shuffle Along** in the early twenties. In 1926 she was cast in a leading role in *Black Boy** with Paul Robeson,* for which she took the stage name Edith Warren. She toured Europe as a dancer until she could find appropriate stage roles in New York, where she appeared in 1930 in *Sweet Chariot,** in 1931 in *Singin' the Blues,** and in 1933 in *Run, Little Chillun.** Of her performance in *Mamba's Daughters*, Brooks Atkinson wrote in the *New York Times* that she "beautifully plays the part of Hagar's talented granddaughter . . . with intelligence as well as charm" (4 Jan. 1939, p. 24). Meanwhile she had begun a film career with the Duke Ellington* short *Black and Tan Fantasy* (1929) and *The Old Man of the Mountain* and *The Emperor Jones** (1933). Of the film version of Fannie Hurst's novel *Imitation of Life,** the *New York Times* reviewer wrote that Washington, "a beautiful and sensitive stage actress, played the mulatto daughter with great intelligence, and brought sympathy and understanding to the character" (24 Nov. 1934, p. 19). So convincing was she, in fact, in the part of Peola, the daughter of Louise Beavers* who passed for white, that many blacks believed she must have been in reality anti-Negro to do the part so well. Bobby Short remembered in *Black and White Baby*, however, that "Fredi was one of the first in the fight for equal rights and never hid behind her white complexion" (p. 97). In addition to her activity in the theater—she continued to perform into the forties—Washington was a founder of the Negro Actors Guild and its first executive secretary in 1937, and she was theater editor and columnist for *The People's Voice*, a New York weekly published by Adam Clayton Powell, Jr. In later years she was active in civil rights work and appeared on radio and television. Fredi Washington was married to Lawrence Brown, a trombonist with the Duke Ellington Band.
REFERENCES: NYT, 24 Nov. 1934, 19 Aug. 1937, 9 Feb. 1948; Bobby Short, *Black and White Baby*, 1971; NYTTR, 1972; DBPA, 1978; BB, 1980. (PO)

WASHINGTON, ISABELL (singer), ?–? The sister of actress Fredi Washington,* Isabell Washington sang and danced in nightclubs during the twenties and began a promising stage career in Wallace Thurman's* *Harlem,** in which she "radiated the more scarlet aspects of Negro life with an abandon seldom seen before," according to the *New York Times* reviewer (21 Feb. 1929, p. 30). "Always an ebullient performer," she made the musical *Bombolla** "lustrous by her presence," and when she came on to sing the lilting "Rub-a-dub Your Rabbit's Foot," she threatened "to let nothing more on the program take place" (NYT, 27 June 1929, p. 17). Her vivacious stage personality was seen to advantage again in *Singin' the Blues,** in which, "as the jaunty prima donna of the Magnolia Club, she gave the blues the exultation of spirituals"* (NYT, 17 Sept. 1931, p. 21). Furthermore, she appeared in the Bessie Smith* film *St. Louis Blues** in 1929. She gave up her career in 1933 to marry the Reverend

Adam Clayton Powell, Jr. Powell's father disapproved of his marrying a divorced showgirl but after Powell, Jr., threatened to leave the church if his father refused his consent, Adam Clayton Powell, Sr.,* relented and performed the wedding ceremony. Powell, Jr., adopted Washington's son by her previous marriage. They were divorced ten years later.

REFERENCES: NYTTR, 1972; NYT, 5 April, 1972; Jervis Anderson, *This Was Harlem*, 1982. (PO)

WATERS, ETHEL (singer, actress), 31 October 1896–1 September 1977. Born illegitimate—her mother had been raped at the age of twelve—Ethel Waters grew up in the slums of Chester, Pennsylvania, running with street gangs and stealing food to eat. She received only intermittent schooling, hired out as a domestic worker at the age of eight, and was married at thirteen. She made her first stage appearance in 1917 at the Lincoln Theatre, Baltimore, singing "St. Louis Blues," and then toured the South playing vaudeville, carnivals, and tent shows as one of the Hill Sisters, billed as Sweet Mama Stringbean. Her first New York appearance was a one-week engagement at the Lincoln Theatre,* but from there she went to the notorious Edmond's Cellar.* This was usually the last stop on the way down in show business, but Waters proved such an attraction that she drew clientele of a better class and improved the reputation of the place. She played in *Hello 1919!* at the Lafayette Theatre* and on tour, until the company folded in Akron, Ohio, and auditioned for *Shuffle Along** but was turned down.

She made her first recording for Cardinal Records in 1919: "The New York Glide" and "At the New Jump Steady Ball." Black Swan* records hired her in 1921, for the unprecedented sum of one hundred dollars, to record "Down Home Blues" and "Oh, Daddy," which became a best-seller and was followed by "There'll Be Some Changes Made" and "One Man Nan." To help promote the records Waters toured the South with Fletcher Henderson's* Black Swan Troubadors. Back in New York she appeared in *Jump Steady* (1922) at the Lafayette; in the revue *Oh Joy* (1922), which closed in the out-of-town run in Boston; and in *Dumb Luck* (1922), which also folded on the road. Waters went back to touring in vaudeville, first the TOBA* theaters in the South with Pearl Wright as her accompanist and then on the Keith circuit with Earl Dancer, as Waters and Dancer, playing for the first time to white audiences. In 1924 she joined the faltering *Plantation Revue* in Chicago and received her first real critical acclaim: Ashton Stevens of the *Herald Examiner* hailed her as "the greatest artist of her race and generation" (Waters, *His Eye Is on the Sparrow*, p. 181). She replaced Florence Mills* at the Plantation Club in New York, introducing her great song hit "Dinah" but turned down the offer to go to Paris with *Revue Nègre** (thereby giving Josephine Baker* her big break) and appeared in more revues at the Lafayette: *Tan Town Topics* (1925), *Too Bad* (1925), and *Black Bottom Revue* (1926).

Her first Broadway musical was *Africana** (1927), produced by Earl Dancer with music and lyrics by Donald Heywood* and the dances staged by Will Marion Cook's* son-in-law Louis Douglas. She visited Europe in 1930, playing the Palladium and Holborn Empire theaters in London and the Cafe de Paris in Paris, and returned to New York for *Blackbirds [*] of 1930* and *Rhapsody in Black** (1931). Irving Berlin heard her singing "Stormy Weather" at the Cotton Club* in 1933 and wrote four numbers for her in *As Thousands Cheer** (1933), including "Heat Wave" (a parody of a Josephine Baker routine) and the haunting "Suppertime." The show ran two years on Broadway and on tour, where even in the South Ethel Waters received star billing along with the white players. She appeared with Beatrice Lillie in the revue *At Home Abroad* in 1935 and gave a Carnegie Hall recital in 1938. She made her debut as a straight dramatic actress in 1939 as Hagar in Du Bose Heyward* and Dorothy Heyward's* *Mamba's Daughters*; the play ran 501 performances in New York, followed by a long tour. In 1940 she played Petunia in the musical *Cabin in the Sky*, and in 1950 she appeared in her most memorable role, Berenice in Carson McCullers's *Member of the Wedding*. She played the role in stock and revivals until she was in her seventies. In the late fifties she had a religious conversion and performed regularly thereafter with the Billy Graham Crusade.

Waters made 259 recordings on labels such as Black Swan (twenty-six titles), Columbia* (forty-seven titles), Paramount, Vocalion, Brunswick, and Word. Among the many songs she introduced or that were associated with her were "Dinah," "Stormy Weather," "Heat Wave," "I'm Comin' Virginia," "Am I Blue?" "Supper Time," and her signature song "His Eye Is on the Sparrow." Her movies include *On with the Show* (1930), *Cairo* (1941), *Cabin in the Sky* (1942), *Tales of Manhattan* (1942), *Stage Door Canteen* (1943), *Pinky* (1949), and *A Member of the Wedding* (1952). She published two autobiographies: *His Eye Is on the Sparrow* (1951, with Charles Samuels) and, after her religious conversion, the "truth-telling" *To Me It's Wonderful* (1972).
REFERENCES: Ethel Waters, *His Eye Is on the Sparrow*, 1951; WWA, 1959; Langston Hughes and Milton Meltzer, *Black Magic*, 1967; Ethel Waters, *To Me It's Wonderful*, 1972; BWW, 1979. (DA)

THE WAYS OF WHITE FOLKS (short stories) 1934. A collection of short fiction, uneven in both form and content, Langston Hughes's* *The Ways of White Folks* details relations and relationships between the races, sometimes in good humor, sometimes in deadly earnest. The white Carraways, who take up blacks because it is chic; old Mrs. Dora Ellsworth (a genial if malicious portrait of Charlotte Mason*), who supports a black musician as long as she can, as it were, call the tune; and Mr. Lloyd, who gets involved with a Harlem hooker, are all finely etched and amusing but at their own expense. Stories about a black child humiliated by a white Santa Claus and about a man passing for white who snubs his mother when they meet in public are overly sentimental; but "Little Dog," in which a lonely white woman is incapable of responding to the friendly gestures of the black janitor in her apartment building, avoids the danger of sentimentality and is, instead, a superb analysis of emotional paralysis borne of prejudice. "Cora Unashamed" is a strong story about a black servant and "Mother and Child" an excellent example of Hughes's gift for dialog (in this case, church women gossiping). Two potentially successful stories, however, are marred by facile melodrama: in "Home" a talented violinist returns from Europe to visit his mother and encounters racial jealousy, and in "Father and Son" a black boy murders his white father during a powerful and moving love-hate confrontation; both stories end in lynching, lurid but anticlimactic, true to life perhaps but not to art. Still, *The Ways of White Folks* is an admirable introduction to the prose of a greatly gifted poet. (BK)

THE WEARY BLUES (poetry), 1926. Langston Hughes's* first collection of poems, *The Weary Blues*, appeared in 1926, with an introduction by Carl Van Vechten.* The opening section, named after the title, deals with various aspects of contemporary Harlem: dancers, cabarets, blues.* Later poems in the book are based on Hughes's travels abroad and in Mexico, and two other sections, "The Negro Speaks of Rivers" and "Our Land," are more broadly directed toward public racial matters. *The Weary Blues* is remarkable for its technical proficiency as well as the variety in its subjects; even in this first collection Hughes demonstrated the range of prosodies of which he was capable, not only in traditional rhymes and meters but in organic forms too. (BK)

WEBB, ELLIDA (dancer), 1895–1974. In *Runnin' Wild** (1923) Ellida Webb claimed to have "invented" the Charleston, dancing on "the prettiest legs in Harlem." She studied ballet and later taught white tap dancer Ruby Keeler, staged shows at the Apollo* and Lafayette* theaters in Harlem, and choreographed some numbers for the Ziegfeld Follies. Ellida Webb was married to Garfield Dawson (1892–?), also a dancer, who performed primarily in London. REFERENCE: Hatch-Billops. (BK)

WEBB, [WILLIAM] CHICK (jazz drummer), 10 February 1909–16 June 1939. Chick Webb, the first jazz musician to receive an honorary doctorate, was co-composer of numerous hit songs, including "Stompin' at the Savoy," "Don't Be That Way," "A-Tisket, A-Tasket," and "Holiday in Harlem." Born in Baltimore, he began playing drums early and joined a boys' band at the age of eleven, before going on to play with riverboat bands. He moved to New York in 1925, where he formed his own group. His band became one of the leading bands in the city, playing in nightclubs, theaters, and ballrooms and broadcasting nationally on radio. He toured with *Hot Chocolates** in 1930. During the thirties he played at the Savoy Ballroom* in Harlem, where he introduced Ella Fitzgerald in 1935. Webb received an honorary doctorate from Yale University in 1937. Fitzgerald led and recorded with his orchestra after his death. REFERENCE: BDAM, 1982. (PO)

WEINGLASS, DEWEY (dancer), 1900–? In a series of early children's shows, Dewey Weinglass was one of the "Dancin' Demons" with Dave Stratton, Nina Hunter, and Charlotte Settle, touring the South under grim conditions for TOBA.* Later, Weinglass danced in some Harlem shows like *Who's Doin' It* and *The Harlem Rounders** and on Broadway in *Liza** (1922) and *Dixie to Broadway** (1924). He retired early from the stage to be a bar and grill manager in Harlem. REFERENCE: BB, 1980. (BK)

WELCH, ELISABETH (singer) 1908– . Although she appeared in several New York shows during the twenties, such as *Liza** (1922), *Runnin' Wild** (1923), *Chocolate Dandies** and *Velvet Brown Babies* (1924), and *Blackbirds[*] of 1928,* Elisabeth Welch started out to study social work. She was still in high school when she introduced the Charleston to Broadway in *Runnin' Wild.* Subsequently she found that her remarkable voice was better appreciated in Europe. After an engagement at the Moulin Rouge in Paris Welch returned to New York to sing "Love for Sale" in Cole Porter's *The New Yorkers* (1930) but made her home in England thereafter. She was the principal singer in *Dark Doings* in 1933 and made a hit singing "Solomon" in Cole Porter's *Nymph Errant* the same year. From 1935 on she was one of the principal singers on the radio series "Soft Lights and Sweet Music" and continued to appear on the stage. Welch made her first film, *Death at Broadcasting House,* in 1934 and went on to play opposite Paul Robeson* in the British films *Show Boat, Song of Freedom,* and *Big Fella.* She entertained British troops with Sir John Gielgud's company during the war and was the headliner in the Palladium revue *Happy and Glorious,* which ran more than eighteen months at the end of the war. Welch continued her singing career on the stage and in clubs for the next thirty years in England and appeared in New York in the late seventies.
REFERENCES: Brian Rust, *Elisabeth Welch,* 1979; BB, 1980; NYT, 16 May 1980. (PO)

WELLS, JAMES LESESNE (painter), 1902–? A printer and painter and later a member of the Howard University faculty, James Wells won the Harmon Foundation* Gold Medal in 1930. His soft lines and rounded contours mark work not notably racial in content.
REFERENCE: Cedric Dover, *American Negro Art,* 1969. (BK)

WESLEY, CHARLES (historian), 2 December 1891–? Charles Harris Wesley, eminent historian and educator, was born in Louisville, Kentucky in 1891. He received the B.A. at Fisk University (1911), the M.A. at Yale University (1913) and the Ph.D. at Harvard University (1925). He taught history at Howard University from 1917 to 1942, before leaving to be president of Wilberforce University (1942–1947) and Central State University (1942–1965). Along with Carter Woodson* and John Hope Franklin, he ranks as one of the most prolific and effective black historians of his generation. He has written twenty books and

many articles and essays, primarily on the history of blacks in the United States. He also was editor of the ten-volume *International Library on Negro Life and History* (revised, 1976) and for many years was executive director of the Association for Study of Afro-American Life and History. He sat on the board of countless educational organizations and by 1978 had received honorary degrees from fourteen schools. Other relevant works are *Negro Labor in the United States* (1927) and *The Negro in the Americas* (1940).
REFERENCES: WWCA, 1933; SBAA, 1977; WWA, 1979. (DS)

WEST, DOROTHY (writer), 1908–   . Dorothy West published the first story she ever wrote—"The Typewriter"—in *Opportunity** when she was eighteen years old. Born in Boston and educated in its public schools, she described herself in a biographical note for the magazine as "conventional, . . . a reticent sort" (June 1926, p. 189). She attended Boston University and the Columbia School of Journalism and continued to publish stories, sometimes in the *Saturday Evening Quill,** the literary magazine of Boston's black intelligentsia. In 1931 she joined a group of young black intellectuals who went to Russia, ostensibly to make a film about Afro-Americans in Alabama called *Black and White.** The project never was realized, but the experience heightened West's social awareness, as did her job as a relief investigator in Harlem. Her major contribution to the Harlem Renaissance is her editorship of *Challenge,** later titled *New Challenge*, which during the early thirties attempted to keep the work of young black writers in print. Robert A. Bone, in *The Negro Novel in America*, called Dorothy West's 1948 novel *The Living is Easy* "a diamond in the rough," but "bitingly ironic" and of "a primarily Renaissance consciousness" (pp. 187, 190).
REFERENCES: *Opportunity*, June 1926; Robert A. Bone, *The Negro Novel in America*, 1958. (BK)

WHIP **(CHICAGO)** (newspaper), 1919–1933. A racially militant sheet, the Chicago *Whip* was a strident competitor to the Chicago *Defender** from its inception in 1919 until its death in the Depression. In its early years, under the editorial direction of Joseph D. Bibb,* it preached economic radicalism similar in kind to that of *The Messenger.** Indeed, Chandler Owen,* a *Messenger* cofounder, worked for the *Whip* in the early 1920s. By the late 1920s, however, the *Whip* had changed ownership, and the paper came out strongly against A. Philip Randolph's* attempt to unionize the railroad porters and maids. The *Whip* was primarily a local sheet, of mediocre character according to one newspaper critic. Yet it was popular because of its editorial-page feature "Town Perspectives" and its weekly editorial comment "Under the Lash of the Whip," which critic Eugene Gordon* found "diverting as an example of the kind of personal abuse the old-fashioned Negro editor once revelled in. Nowhere else in Negro newspaperdom is that ancient practice observed to the extent that the *Whip* observes it'' (*The Annals*, p. 253). Still, the *Whip*'s circulation never exceeded 16,000.

REFERENCES: Eugene Gordon, ''The Negro Press,'' *The Annals*, 1928; Allan Spear, *Black Chicago*, 1967. (DS)

WHIPPER, LEIGH (actor, writer), 1877–26 July 1975. Leigh Whipper was born in South Carolina and attended the Howard Law School, where he received a degree in 1895. He practiced law briefly but began to appear with the Philadelphia Stock Company in 1899 and remained involved in theatrical endeavors afterward. He appeared in the film *Symbol of the Unconquered* in 1920; two years later he founded the Leigh Whipper Film Company to make a feature about the life of Frederic Douglass, and that same year he founded the Renaissance Company to make *Whipper Reel Negro News*, although both ventures failed. With Porter Grainger,* he wrote *De Board Meetin'* in 1925, which played the TOBA* circuit briefly. In 1926 he acted in *In Abraham's Bosom*,* and in 1927 he appeared as the Crabman in *Porgy*.* With J. C. Johnson* Whipper wrote *Runnin' de Town* in 1930 and *Yeah Man** with Billy Mills, in 1932. Among the shows he coauthored, only the latter ran on Broadway. In the early forties Whipper had a marked success in two Hollywood films, *The Ox-Bow Incident* and *Of Mice and Men*.

REFERENCES: BAF, 1974; Daniel J. Leab, *From Sambo to Superspade*, 1975; BBW, 1977. (BK)

WHITE, CLARENCE CAMERON (composer, violinist), 10 August 1880– 30 June 1960. White was born in Clarksville, Tennessee, but spent his childhood in Oberlin, Ohio, and Washington, D.C. He graduated from Howard University and the Oberlin Conservatory of Music and taught violin at the Washington Conservatory of Music for several years before going to England for advanced study of violin with Michael Zakarevich and composition with Samuel Coleridge-Taylor. After 1910 he taught music in Boston and toured periodically as a concert violinist, accompanied by his wife, the pianist Beatrice Warrick. In 1924 he became director of music at West Virginia State College, and in 1928 he and his colleague John Matheus,* a poet and professor of romance languages, went to Haiti to research the folk music and folklore of the island, which led to their collaboration on the opera *Ouanga*,* based upon the life of Dessalines, the liberator of Haiti. With grants from the Julius Rosenwald Fund, White was able to study in Paris with Raoul Lappara while completing the opera, and at that time he also composed a string quartet, based upon Negro themes, which was performed at the École Normale de Musique in Paris.

White served as music director at Hampton Institute from 1931 to 1935 and as organizer of community music programs for the National Recreational Association from 1937 to 1941. His arrangements of spirituals* for violin and piano—*Bandana Sketches, Cabin Memories* and *From the Cotton Fields*—were popular concert pieces in the twenties and thirties. He published two collections

of spirituals, *Forty Negro Spirituals* (1927) and *Traditional Negro Spirituals* (1940); orchestral works, including *Katamba Rhapsody*; a symphony, a ballet, a violin concerto, and vocal, choral, band, and instrumental works. He received the Harmon Foundation* Award (1927), Rosenwald Fellowship awards (1930, 1932), and honorary degrees from Atlanta University and Wilberforce University.
REFERENCES: WWA, 1945; MBA, 1971. (DA)

WHITE, LEE "LASSES" (film actor), 1885–1949. Despite his stereotyped roles Lee White was a popular figure with both black and white audiences and a staple in early western films. As the humorous sidekick of Jimmie Wakley and Tim Holt, White rode the Hollywood range for many years, appearing in *Moon Over Montana, Indian Agent,* and *Song of the Sierra*, none of which was sufficiently memorable even to make television movie guides. In later years Lee White acted in at least two serious white films, *Sergeant York* and *Mark Twain*, both made in the forties.
REFERENCE: WWH, 1976. (BK)

WHITE, PRINCESS (singer), 14 January 1881–21 March 1976. As a five-year-old toe dancer Princess White toured Europe and Australia with Salica Bryan and Her Pickaninnies. Later, she joined Sissieretta Jones* ("Black Patti") and her troupe on tour; James Reese Europe*; Salem Whitney* and Homer Tutt*; and others for shows on the TOBA* circuit. Princess White sang in several Lafayette Theatre* shows and in various cabarets in New York during the twenties.
REFERENCE: BWW, 1979. (BK)

WHITE, WALTER [F.] (civil rights leader, author), 1 July 1893–21 March 1955. Walter White was born and reared in the Jim Crow South, and the experience never left him. He spent a lifetime mobilizing Afro-Americans and supportive whites against racial intolerance through his books, syndicated columns, radio appearances, magazine articles, speeches, investigations of racial incidents, lobbying, travels, and widespread contacts. White's background prepared him well for the public life he chose. An Afro-American with blue eyes, blond hair, and a light complexion, from a family of fair-skinned people, he never could accept the notions of racial exclusivity, whether espoused by the Ku Klux Klan or Marcus Garvey's* black nationalists. White never shied from a public acknowledgment that he was a black man, and his loyalties to the Afro-American community were thorough and sincere. This identity was driven home to him at the age of thirteen, as he explained in his 1948 autobiography *A Man Called White*, when he and his father waited fully armed to retaliate if a white mob should try to assault their home during Atlanta's 1906 race riot. Moreover, his upbringing by hardworking, conscientious parents and other adults in the First Congregational Church and then his education at Atlanta University all stressed duty, service to others, and both personal and collective advancement.

Invited by James Weldon Johnson* of the New York headquarters to join the staff of the NAACP,* White became its assistant executive secretary early in 1918; when Johnson retired in 1930, White assumed the post of executive secretary, where he remained until his death from a heart attack in 1955. Thus for thirty-seven years he was a visible, leading fixture in America's most important civil rights organization. Under Johnson's direction in the twenties and then on his own during the next two decades, White became a noted Washington lobbyist, campaigning for a federal law against lynching. He advocated legislation against the poll tax, joined in the crusade for a Fair Employment Practice Committee, argued strenuously for desegregation in the armed services, and promoted the legal work of his younger NAACP colleague Thurgood Marshall in bringing civil rights cases before the United States Supreme Court. It was White, for the most part, who assembled an effective midcentury civil rights coalition comprised of labor, liberal, civic, ethnic, church, civil libertarian, and women's groups and of academic, literary, and artistic individuals. This laid the foundation for the civil rights program of the late forties and for the continuing efforts thereafter on behalf of a civil rights agenda finally achieved in the sixties. By his relentless initiatives among politicians and government officials, his associations with prominent journalists like H. L. Mencken,* his negotiations with academic and foundation leaders, and his insistence that racial injustices at home marred America's image abroad, Walter White forced the issue of race relations to national attention and stripped racists of their most prized resource, public indifference. When White began his career, Afro-Americans were politically isolated by the prevailing assumptions of black inferiority and the tendency to allow whites locally, in states rights' fashion, to set the conditions of black citizenship. By the time of White's death in 1955 no one but the most ignorant or callous could any longer pretend not to know about the prevalent racial injustice that marred the American Dream or about the raging public debate—that White had helped foment—over the need for and wisdom of federal solutions to such injustices.

Walter White's participation in the Harlem Renaissance was a revealing microcosm of his entire career; three aspects of that involvement especially demand attention. First, there was his own need to become a contributing member of the literary circle. After his unexceptional undergraduate performance, with no promise of artistic talent, followed by a year and a half's work with an Atlanta insurance company, he suddenly found himself a new, junior member of a most impressive NAACP hierarchy. James Weldon Johnson, W.E.B. Du Bois,* Mary White Ovington,* William Pickens,* and Herbert J. Seligmann had all published books before 1920, and Johnson and Du Bois had particularly distinguished records in a number of adjacent fields. For Walter White to function and thrive in such company, he too would have to publish, although the pressures to do so doubtless had more to do with his own ego than with any direct admonition from his NAACP colleagues. A second factor that drew White to the Harlem Renaissance involved his boundless enthusiasm for the arts; his genuine excitement at being part of New York's literary, artistic, and cultural swirl; and the exquisite delight he found in mingling with people of talent and accomplishment.

White reveled in after-theater or cabaret parties, "teas" (a white euphemism for more potent refreshment during Prohibition), buffet suppers, and other social gatherings, especially those that he and his wife, Gladys Powell, hosted at their well-known Harlem apartment at 409 Edgecombe Avenue. In such settings Irita and Carl Van Doren,* Carl Van Vechten* and Fania Marinoff,* Blanche and Alfred Knopf,* Sinclair Lewis, Heywood Broun, and other ranking members of the white literary and artistic establishment all had firsthand contact with many black authors, artists, and performers. White worked tirelessly to promote prominent and aspiring black talent, notably Marian Anderson.* Gifted as a publicist, he extended himself generously to introduce blacks and their culture to previously unresponsive white audiences that helped to break down some of the isolation from which all Afro-Americans had long suffered. The third factor involved Walter White's using his own Harlem Renaissance writings to educate Americans to the plight and desires of their black contemporaries. Of his six books, the first three appeared in this period: *The Fire in the Flint** (1924), *Flight** (1926), and *Rope and Faggot** (1929). The first two were novels, statements of black needs as much as fictional pieces, and the third was a carefully researched and vigorously argued condemnation of mob violence. The three books reflected White's experiences and priorities and exhibited his avid and unashamed commitment to civil rights, social justice, and black initiative.

The Fire in the Flint caused something of a minor sensation, for it was one of the first novels from a major publisher—Alfred A. Knopf—to disclose the horrible idiosyncrasies of southern racism. Carl Van Vechten found the book so captivating that he sought out its author for what became a lifelong friendship and series of collaborative ventures on behalf of black culture. More low key, *Flight* treated a young mulatto woman's search for identity. Migrating to the North, as White and millions of his contemporaries had done and would continue to do, she passes briefly into the white world—something Walter White might easily have tried but never would. *Rope and Faggot*, subtitled "A Biography of Judge Lynch," prepared with the aid of a Guggenheim Fellowship, allowed White to compile what still remains a standard work on the causes of and possible remedies for lynching, burning, and attendant vigilante activities.

In multiple ways Walter White and the Harlem Renaissance nurtured each other. When black academician Alain Locke* edited his famous anthology *The New Negro** in 1925, he assigned portions to nearly all of the principals of the era. It was left for Walter White to provide the chapter "Paradox of Color." Not surprisingly, his was a ringing denunciation of racism and a rallying cry for black unity in the search for equality and justice. Walter White lived what he believed and wrote what he lived.

REFERENCES: Walter White, *A Man Called White*, 1948; Nathan Irvin Huggins, *Harlem Renaissance*, 1971; Charles F. Cooney, "Walter White and the Harlem Renaissance," *Journal of Negro History* 57 (July 1972); Eugene D. Levy, *James Weldon Johnson*, 1973; Edward E. Waldron, *Walter White and the Harlem Renaissance*, 1978; Robert L. Zangrando, *The NAACP Crusade Against Lynching*, 1980; David Levering Lewis, *When Harlem Was in Vogue*, 1981; Jervis Anderson, *This Was Harlem*, 1982. (RZ)

WHITMAN SISTERS REVUE (musical revue), 1923. The *Whitman Sisters Revue* had its genesis in Lawrence, Kansas, before the turn of the century in a family act composed of the mother and elder sister, May or Mabel. Afterward, Mabel served as manager, producer, and director, touring with Alberta in drag and with Alice, who was called successively "Baby Alice," "Essie" or "Elsie." When "Baby Alice" had a baby of her own, he joined the act too, billed as "Pops" or "Little Maxie, Jr." Their amalgamation of songs and dances, drawn from many sources and the routines of other performers, including Bert Williams's* well-known "Nobody," toured widely as the *Whitman Sisters Revue*. It played at the Lafayette Theatre,* after which "The Royalty of Negro Vaudeville," as they billed themselves, continued to tour. Mabel died in the early forties, Alberta in 1964, and Alice in 1970.
REFERENCES: BWW, 1979; BB, 1980. (BK)

WHITNEY, SALEM TUTT (actor, producer), 1869–12 February 1934. With his younger brother, who called himself Homer Tutt,* Salem Whitney toured with the *Smart Set Revue* and with Sissieretta Jones's* *Black Patti's Troubadours* at the turn of the century. Both born in Indiana, the brothers later wrote seventeen shows, including *Oh Joy,* * which ran on Broadway in 1922. Most of their work, however, played in Harlem theaters or toured on the TOBA* circuit. A representative sampling gives a fair idea of their product: *Darkest Africa* (1918), in which Abe and Gabe enter Howard University and are commissioned to find Dean Kelly Miller* on an archeological dig all over the globe; *Bamboula* (1921), in which Jasper Jazz and Raspberry Razz (played by the authors) accompany a professor of music to Africa to prove the continent's contribution to modern music; *Jump Steady* (1922), in which the chorines sang and danced in the theater's aisles, while Whitney and Tutt played swindlers and sang "Ja Da Blues"; *North Ain't South* * (1923), with music by Don Heywood,* in which a southern producer falls in love with a girl in his troupe bound for New York, where they fail and return, but notable for a burlesque version of *Othello* en route; *Come Along, Mandy* * (1924), in which Zack and Sudds fight over a boundary line between their plantations until Al LaBabor, a thief masquerading as a lawyer, steals their deeds, while Lovey Jo and Mandy join up to act as detectives to track him down for a happily ever after ending in Harlem.
REFERENCES: *Official Theatrical World of Colored Artists*, 1928; BB, 1980. (BK)

WHO'S STEALIN'? (play), 1918. Flournoy Miller* and Aubrey Lyles* wrote and acted in a touring show three years before they used it as the basis for *Shuffle Along,* * the successful musical comedy on which they collaborated with Noble

Sissle* and Eubie Blake* in 1921. In *Who's Stealin'?* two rival Iowa department store owners employ the same detective to investigate each other. The detective, who turns out to be a crook in disguise, discovers that both are engaged in theft in order to afford to undersell each other.

REFERENCE: BB, 1980. (BK)

WILLIAMS, [EGBERT AUSTIN] BERT (entertainer), 12 November 1874 or 1875–5 March 1922. After a successful early career with his snappy, cake-walking partner George Walker, in the Williams and Walker Company that had played for Queen Victoria as well as for much of the United States, Bert Williams was the best-loved comedian of his generation. After Walker died he drifted into several editions of the Ziegfeld Follies and was last seen in *Broadway Brevities of 1920*, a show he financed himself, with Eddie Cantor. Bert Williams was an institution long before the time of his death, perpetuating racial stereotypes perhaps, and in the blackface makeup that white audiences demanded, but with such compassion that he did much to encourage them to view blacks as human beings. Still, in top hat and zoot suit in *Darktown Jubilee*, a 1914 two-reel film, he was jeered off the screen; but two years later, for Biograph films, he was successful in *A Natural Born Gambler*.

Williams had little talent for either singing or dancing, although his success as an actor was in part due to his ability to convince audiences that he was adept at both. In outsize, battered shoes, an ill-fitting black suit, a kinky wig, and with his light skin hidden by blackface and his hands hidden by white gloves, Williams was "the funniest man I ever saw," his friend W. C. Fields once said, "and the saddest man I ever knew" (Charters, *Nobody*, p. 11). Ann Charters, who had quoted Fields in her biography of Bert Williams, added Williams's own sanguine observation: "In truth, I have never been able to discover that there was anything disgraceful in being a colored man. But I have often found it inconvenient—in America" (p. 12). Eleanora Duse, the celebrated Italian tragedienne, called him the greatest actor of his country; Carl Van Vechten* said that in Germany or Russia he would have been acclaimed a great actor. At the time of his last Broadway appearance, David Belasco, the white theatrical entrepreneur, offered to star Williams in a serious play. The actor refused, however, well aware of his audience's expectations. "I am what I am," Williams had often declared, "not because of what I am but in spite of it" (p. 16). Theophilus Lewis,* writing in *The Messenger*,* disagreed: Williams had "rendered a disservice to black people" by encouraging Broadway not to "countenance the Negro in serious, dignified, classical drama" (Apr. 1922, p. 394). Lewis's comments appeared in his obituary for the greatly beloved actor. Williams died at the age of forty-seven during an out-of-town tryout for *Under the Bamboo Tree*, playing a resort hotel porter in an otherwise white cast. As usual, he was in blackface.

REFERENCES: Theophilus Lewis, "Theatre," *The Messenger*, Apr. 1922; Ann Charters, *Nobody*, 1970; Carl Van Vechten, *"Keep A-Inchin' Along,"* 1979. (BK)

WILLIAMS, CLARENCE (composer), 6 October 1893–6 November 1965. Clarence Williams is best remembered for having written a number of popular songs, "Baby, Won't You Please Come Home?" (1917), "Sugar Blues" (1919), and "Everybody Loves My Baby" (1924), but he wrote 2,000 other songs, spiritual* arrangements, and instrumental numbers, including "Gulf Coast Blues," "I Wish That I Could Shimmy Like My Sister Kate," and Ethel Waters's* erotic "Organ Grinder." Williams was born in Louisiana, where he wrote his first song at the age of six, peddling it and other early compositions from door to door. He was a professional entertainer from the age of twelve. For a time he worked in music stores in Chicago and New York, playing the piano to advertise sheet music; then with his wife, Eva Taylor,* and Clarence Todd he organized a swing trio for radio in 1923. The Clarence Williams Orchestra recorded for Victor, Columbia,* and OKeh during the twenties when Williams and Taylor became popular radio performers. Presumably in response to requests from their fans, they wrote and starred in *Bottomland*￼* in 1927, an unsuccessful musical play. Eva Taylor knocked thirteen years off her age for professional reasons; Clarence Williams only knocked eleven off his own.
REFERENCES: WWCA, 1933; Roi Ottley and William J. Weatherby, eds., *The Negro in New York*, 1967; ASCAP, 1966; BB, 1980. (BK)

WILLIAMS, SPENCER (musician), 14 July 1893–13 December 1969. Spencer Williams was born in Louisiana and attended St. Charles University there, but he quit to go to New York where he first worked as a call boy for Oscar Hammerstein. In 1921 Williams wrote both the music and lyrics for *Chocolate Brown*, a Harlem show about black northern society snubbing southern immigrants. The following year he contributed some of the songs to *Put and Take*.* Williams appeared in several black films, notably *Melancholy Dame* (1929) and *Georgia Rose* (1930), and went on to another career as a sound technician in Hollywood. In the forties he wrote, directed, and acted in two white-backed films about black religious traditions, *The Blood of Jesus* and *Go Down, Earth!* Williams is best remembered for his songs, however: "Basin Street Blues"; "Everybody Loves My Baby"; "I Ain't Got Nobody"; "Squeeze Me but Please Don't Tease Me," which he wrote with Fats Waller; and the ubiquitous "She'll Be Comin' Round the Mountain When She Comes." In later years Spencer Williams appeared on television as Andy in *Amos and Andy*.
REFERENCES: Donald Bogle, *Toms, Coons, Mulattoes, Mammies, and Bucks*, 1973; BAF, 1974. (BK)

WILSON [ARTHUR] DOOLEY (actor), 1894–1953. Best remembered as the café entertainer in the 1942 film *Casablanca*, singing "As Time Goes By," Dooley Wilson began his career in minstrel shows. He was born in Texas and toured widely until joining Anita Bush's* acting troupe when he was twenty years old. He appeared in her first production at the Lincoln Theatre* in 1914, *The Girl at the Fort*, with Charles Gilpin.* When the Lafayette Theatre* bought the Bush company, renaming it the Lafayette Players Stock Company,* Wilson appeared in several of its productions during the years that it offered a wide variety of plays to Harlem audiences. Wilson seems to have dropped out of sight, from Harlem's black stages in any case, and he did not appear on the Broadway stage until 1936, in a dramatization of Rudolph Fisher's* novel *The Conjure Man Dies*,* followed in 1940 by *Cabin in the Sky*.

REFERENCES: *The Messenger*, Mar., Nov. 1917; Allen Woll, *Dictionary of Black Theatre*, 1983. (BK)

WILSON, EDITH (singer), 2 September 1906–31 March 1981. Edith Wilson's singing career spanned the period from vaudeville of the twenties to folk festivals of the seventies. She began singing as a child in her native Louisville and sang there and in Chicago before forming a trio with her husband, Danny Wilson, and his sister Lena Wilson*. She made the first of her forty-some recordings in New York in 1921 and that same year appeared at Connie's Inn* and toured the vaudeville circuit as a single. She had small parts in *Town Top-Piks* in 1920 and *Put and Take** in 1921, but her first major role in a musical was with Florence Mills* in *Plantation Revue** in 1922, which followed its Broadway success with a run in London, renamed *From Dover to Dixie*, the next year. She was much in demand for club and concert dates from then on. In 1925 she toured Europe, Russia, and South America with *Chocolate Kiddies* and toured Europe again with Florence Mills in *Blackbirds [*] of 1926* after appearing in its Harlem run. In 1927 she appeared with Duke Ellington* in *Jazzmania* at the Lafayette Theatre* and returned to Europe with *The Black Revue* the following year, remaining for solo appearances in Berlin and Paris. Fats Waller* wrote "Black and Blue" for Wilson as one of her numbers in *Hot Chocolates** in 1929, in which she, Waller, and Louis Armstrong* were billed as "1000 Pounds of Harmony." She starred in her own show at the Alhambra Theatre* in 1930 and during the next decade made frequent tours of the United States with well-known bands, returned to Europe several times to perform, sang on radio, and appeared on Broadway in *Hot Rhythm,* Shuffle Along of 1933,* Hummin' Sam,* and *Blackbirds of 1933* with Bill Robinson,* to name a few. She appeared with Robinson again in *Memphis Bound* in 1945.

Wilson moved to the West Coast around 1940 and appeared in nonsinging roles in two films, *I'm Still Alive* (1940) and *To Have and Have Not* (1944). During World War II she toured frequently with Eubie Blake* and others with USO shows. She appeared in a continuing role in radio in *Amos 'n Andy* during the forties and as "Aunt Jemima" did commercials and radio and television shows for the Quaker Oats Company. She also appeared frequently as Aunt Jemima in schools, hospitals, and social clubs to benefit charitable and youth organizations. In 1966 she retired from music to become executive secretary of the Negro Actors Guild, of which she was elected vice-president in 1970, and to help talented children in association with St. James Church in Chicago, but during the seventies she recorded again with Eubie Blake and others, appeared

on television in England and France, and made frequent appearances at folk festivals as late as 1977.
REFERENCES: BWW, 1979; BB, 1980. (PO)

WILSON, ELLIS (painter), 1899–6 January 1977. Ellis Wilson was born in Mayfield, Kentucky. He studied at the state agricultural school for two years and then went to the Chicago Art Institute in 1918, where he knew Aaron Douglas* and Richmond Barthé.* He moved to Harlem in 1928 and first exhibited at the Harmon Foundation* in 1931. Working in large blocks of color, Wilson was strongly influenced by Haitian art. Harmon Foundation grants and a Guggenheim fellowship allowed him to continue painting until he had established his reputation.
REFERENCES: Cedric Dover, *American Negro Art*, 1969; NYT, 7 Jan. 1977; Hatch-Billops. (BK)

WILSON, FRANK H. (actor), 4 May 1886–16 February 1956. Frank Wilson did not sing or dance, so stage opportunites for this gifted, handsome actor were rare during the Harlem Renaissance. He attended the American Academy of Dramatic Art, supporting himself as a postman, not only then but between engagements in plays and sometimes during them as well. Wilson first appeared in a number of plays with the Lafayette Players Stock Company,* all revivals of white imports, but in 1924 he acted with Paul Robeson* in *All God's Chillun Got Wings*,* taking different roles in its two productions that year. His first substantial success came in *In Abraham's Bosom** in 1926, Paul Green's* Pulitzer prize drama. He had been playing a small part in the first act, but six weeks after the opening Jules Bledsoe* failed to appear for a performance, and after a thirty-minute delay Wilson went on in the leading role. According to Brooks Atkinson in the *New York Times*, he was "almost letter perfect, . . . swift, direct and extraordinarily moving," and he replaced Bledsoe permanently (20 Feb. 1926, sec. 7, p. 1). In 1927 Wilson seemed destined to follow Charles Gilpin* and Robeson as one of the outstanding black actors of the period when he played the title role in *Porgy** by Du Bose Heyward.* Even in a catastrophe like *Sweet Chariot** in 1930, playing a thinly disguised Marcus Garvey,* Frank Wilson had a notable personal success. He received strong notices in *We the People* (1931), *Singin' the Blues** (1931), *Bloodstream** (1932), and *They Shall Not Die** (1934) as well. Wilson tried his hand at writing plays on occasion, but his *Meek Mose** (1928) was a failure on Broadway, and his other dramas—*Pa Williams' Gal** (1922) is an interesting case in point—played only in Harlem and even then only in little theater groups, where they drew small attention. During the thirties Wilson made several all-black films and was particularly effective as Moses in *The Green Pastures* (1937), leaving at least one permanent record of his abilities as an actor. His one-act play *Sugar Cane* won the *Opportunity** prize in 1925 and was printed in the magazine; but neither Alain

Locke* in his *Plays of Negro Life* (1927) nor James V. Hatch in his *Black Theater, U.S.A.* (1974) chose to represent Wilson's work.
REFERENCES: Nancy Cunard, ed., *Negro*, 1970; NYTTR, 1972; DBPA, 1974; BB, 1980. (BK)

WILSON, LENA (singer), 1898–c.1939. A sister-in-law of singer Edith Wilson,* Lena Wilson played the vaudeville circuit throughout the South from about 1918 to 1920 with her brother Danny Wilson and subsequently worked as a trio with her brother and his wife in Washington and Baltimore. She came to New York in 1921 and had an active career as a singer for the next decade. From 1922 to 1924 she recorded with various bands and performed in clubs and revues. She went to London for Lew Leslie's* *Blackbirds,* with Florence Mills,* in 1926 and toured Europe with the show. She sang with Edith Wilson in *Jazzmania* in 1927 and with the Duke Ellington* Band in *Dance Mania* at the Lafayette Theatre* the same year. She sang at the Lafayette the following year in *Creole Revels* and *The Nifties of 1928.* From 1929 to 1931 she appeared frequently at the Lenox Club and made several recordings. In the midthirties Wilson worked nightclub dates in upstate New York with her husband, Shrimp Jones, a violinist. She is reported to have died of pneumonia in New York City in the late thirties.
REFERENCES: BWW, 1979; BB, 1980. (PO)

WISE, RABBI STEPHEN SAMUEL (civil rights leader), 17 March 1874–19 April 1949. Stephen Samuel Wise, one of the most influential Jewish social reformers of the century and an unstinting spokesman for the rights of blacks, the poor, and the oppressed, held several rabbinates in New York City and Portland, Oregon, before founding his famous Free Synagogue in New York City in 1906. Although he was most famous for his leadership in the Zionist movement, the interfaith movement, and his crusades against corruption, sweatshops, and poverty, Rabbi Wise was also a leading spokesman for civil rights. He was one of the founders of the NAACP,* he fought for the censorship of *The Birth of a Nation* in 1915, and he urged his many friends in the labor movement to stop the "menacing" tendency of barring "the Negro toiler from the ranks of organized labor" (Wise, *Challenging Years*, p. 118).
REFERENCE: Stephen Wise, *Challenging Years,* 1949. (DS)

WOOD, L[EVI] HOLLINGSWORTH (attorney), 1874–22 July 1956. L. Hollingsworth Wood, a white New York City estates lawyer who worked his whole life for interracial causes, pacifism, and higher education for blacks, found ample time to work in a wide variety of causes, particularly in two areas traditionally stressed by the Society of Friends: peace and interracial cooperation. He was a founder of the American Friends Service Committee and active in Quaker religious matters in the city. Most important, however, was his extensive work with the black community. He was president of the National Urban League* from 1915 until 1941, served forty years on the Fisk University Board of Trustees

(and was vice-president of that body at the time of his death in 1956), was president of Howard Orphanage and Industrial School, and was on the board of the Riverdale Colored Orphanage and many other organizations. Wood apparently was free of racial bias and, as one black journal claimed, "though a white man, was most sympathetic with the Negro's claim for equal opportunity and has an unusual understanding of the Negro's point of view in his efforts to attain the higher things of life" (Chicago *Broad Ax*, 24 Mar. 1923).
REFERENCES: *Broad Ax* (Chicago), 24 Mar. 1923; NYT, 23 July 1956; Nancy Weiss, *The National Urban League*, 1974. (DS)

WOODRUFF, HALE (painter), 1900–? Best known for his "Amistad" murals at Talladega College in Alabama, Hale Woodruff was born in Illinois and studied at the John Herron Art Institute in Indianapolis. In 1926 he won a Harmon Foundation* Bronze Medal, and the following year he went to Paris to study with Henry O. Tanner,* dean of an earlier generation of black American artists. Woodruff's abstract and impressionist landscapes, and his portraits of various celebrated black Americans, all rendered in a style reminiscent of the white American painter Thomas Hart Benton, are in many private and public collections.
REFERENCES: Cedric Dover, *American Negro Art*, 1969; NA, 1976. (BK)

WOODSON, CARTER G. (historian), 19 December 1875–3 April 1950. The "Father of Negro History," as Carter Woodson was often called, was born in Virginia, worked as a coal miner to put himself through high school, and then studied at Berea College. After teaching for four years in the Philippines he completed work for the B.A. and M.A. degrees at the University of Chicago and, in 1912, the Ph.D. at Harvard University. He was dean of liberal arts at Howard University and dean of West Virginia State College before beginning his systematic efforts to record black history. In 1915 he organized and became editor of the *Journal of Negro History*,* and that same year he founded and became research director of the Association for the Study of Negro Life and History.* In 1921 he organized an association of publishers to make black textbooks available that white publishers had refused to print, and he established the *Negro History Bulletin* for high school students. In 1926 he established Negro History Week (in February, to coincide with the birthdates of Frederick Douglass and Abraham Lincoln). These pioneering endeavors and a list of distinguished publications earned Woodson not only his popular appellation but the Spingarn Medal* in 1926. His several books are all of some interest to the period: *Education of the Negro Prior to 1861* (1915), *A Century of Negro Migration* (1918), *The Negro in Our History* (1922), *The Mind of the Negro as Reflected in Letters Written During the Crisis, 1800–1861* (1926), and *Negro Makers of History* (1928).
REFERENCES: WWCA, 1933; Charlemae Hill Rollins, *They Showed the Way*, 1964. (BK)

WORK, JOHN WESLEY, JR. (composer, educator), 15 June 1901–18 May 1967. John Wesley Work, Jr., born in Tullahoma, Tennessee, graduated from Fisk University and received the M.A. from Columbia University and the M.B. from Yale University. He attended the Juilliard Institute of Musical Art for two years on a Rosenwald Fellowship and then became head of the music department at Fisk. His compositions include piano and instrumental pieces; *Yenvalou*, for string orchestra; *Isaac Watts Contemplates the Cross*, a choral cycle; *Golgotha Is a Mountain*, to a poem by Arna Bontemps*; *The Singers*, a prizewinning cantata; *American Negro Songs and Spirituals* (1940); and many songs, including the popular "Go Tell It on the Mountain" and "My Lord, What a Morning!" REFERENCES: MBA, 1971; ASCAP, 1980. (DA)

WORK, JOHN WESLEY, SR. (composer, educator), 1873–1925. John Wesley Work, Sr., a native of Tennessee, graduated from Fisk University and studied at Harvard University, returning to teach Latin at Fisk. With his wife, Agnes Haynes, he conducted field research collecting Negro folk songs, which he arranged for the Fisk Jubilee Singers. From about 1900 to 1916 he took small groups of Fisk Singers on concert tours, and later he directed the Fisk Mozart Society and large student choirs in annual concerts. His published works include a number of songs; the collection of spirituals* *New Jubilee Songs* (1901, with his brother Frederick); the second collection *Folk Song of the American Negro* (1907); and the treatise *The Folk Songs of the American Negro* (1915). REFERENCES: *The Crisis*, May 1926; MBA, 1971. (DA)

WORK, MONROE NATHAN (sociologist), 15 August 1866–2 May 1945. Monroe Nathan Work, editor of the *Negro Year Book*, spent much of his life developing a body of information about blacks in Africa and the Americas. Raised in the Midwest by his ex-slave parents, Work spent his first twenty-two years on frontier farms in Illinois and Kansas. He graduated from high school in Arkansas City, Kansas, in 1892, and after working at odd jobs for three years he attended the Chicago Theological Seminary and graduated in 1898. He realized, however, that the ministry was not for him, and he attended the University of Chicago from 1898 to 1902 and received a bachelor of philosophy degree. In 1903 he earned the M.A. degree in divinity in the Department of Sociology, the first black to do so. He taught at Georgia State College from 1903 to 1907, until Booker T. Washington convinced him to come to Tuskegee to compile information on blacks in America and Tuskegee graduates in particular. From 1908 until his death in 1945 Work turned the Department of Records and Research at Tuskegee (which he headed until his retirement in 1938) into a leading research center on black life. He compiled nine editions of the *Negro Year Book* (1912, 1913, 1914–1915, 1916–1917, 1918–1919, 1921–1922, 1925–1926, 1931–1932, 1937–1938), which brought together for the first time in a condensed form an enormous body of facts regarding blacks past and present. It became a standard reference book. His greatest work, however, was a *Bibliography of the Negro* *in Africa and America* (1928), which was the final product of years of research and compilation. Work, a very quiet and studious man, is also noteworthy for being the first black to publish an article in the *American Journal of Sociology* and for his work in compiling extensive data on lynchings in the United States during the twentieth century.

REFERENCES: WWCA, 1933; Jessie P. Guzman, "Monroe Nathan Work and His Contributions," *Journal of Negro History*, Oct. 1949. (DS)

Y

YEAH MAN! (musical revue), 1932. There were four performances of this "shrill and tuneless farrago, light on its feet and lugubrious in its humor," in the view of the *New York Times* (27 May 1932, p. 27). Eddie Rector* and Mantan Moreland* were featured in the cast, and Al Wilson, Charles Weinberg, Leigh Whipper,* Billy Mills, and Ken Macomber wrote the music and lyrics. By 1932 Broadway had begun to grow impatient with obvious imitations. REFERENCES: Burns Mantle, 1931–1932; NYTTR, 1972. (BK)

APPENDIXES

APPENDIX   A

A Chronology of Significant Events, 1917–1935

1917

Three Plays for a Negro Theatre* by Ridgely Torrence staged at the Garden Theatre, April 5.
East St. Louis, Illinois, Riot, June.
Silent Protest Parade* in New York, July 27.
369th Black Regiment embarked for France, November.
Afro-American Liberty League founded.
Claude McKay* published his poems in *Seven Arts*,* the first work by a black writer in a white publication during the century.

1918

The French awarded the Croix de Guerre to the 369th Regiment and named it "Hell Fighters,"* April.
Walter White* joined the National Association for the Advancement of Colored People (NAACP)* staff.
Marcus Garvey* incorporated the Universal Negro Improvement Association (UNIA)* and began publishing *Negro World.**
The Messenger* editors arrested for violation of the Espionage Act.
North Harlem Community Council* founded.
Harlem Conservatory of Fine Arts founded.

1919

369th Regiment marched up Fifth Avenue to Harlem, February 17.
First Pan African Congress,* February.
Red Summer of 1919, with riots* in Washington, D.C., Chicago, Charleston, Knoxville, Omaha, and elsewhere, June through September.
Race Relations Commission founded in Chicago, September.
Brotherhood Workers of America founded, September.

Marcus Garvey founded the Black Star Shipping Line.*
Dr. Louis Wright, first black staff member appointed to the Harlem General Hospital.*
National Association of Negro Musicians* founded.
Associated Negro Press* founded.

1920

UNIA Convention by the Negro People of the World held at Madison Square Garden, August.
Charles Gilpin* starred in *The Emperor Jones*,* November.
James Weldon Johnson,* first black officer (secretary) of NAACP appointed.
Friends of Negro Freedom* founded.
Harlem Stock Exchange founded.
Theatrical Owners and Bookers Association (TOBA)* founded.
National Negro Theatre Corporation founded.

1921

Shuffle Along,* first all-black show on Broadway, opened, May 22.
Marcus Garvey founded African Orthodox Church,* September.
Second Pan African Congress, September.
Black Swan Phonograph Corporation* founded.
Colored Players Guild of New York founded.

1922

Bert Williams* died, March 15.
First Anti-Lynching legislation approved by House of Representatives.

1923

National Ethiopian Art Players (Theatre)* staged *The Chip Woman's Fortune** by Willis Richardson,* first serious play by a black writer on Broadway, May.
Claude McKay spoke at the Fourth Congress of the Third International in Moscow, June.
The Cotton Club* opened, fall.
Marcus Garvey arrested for mail fraud and sentenced to five years in prison.
Lafayette Players Stock Company* ceased production after seven years of serious drama in Harlem.
Third Pan African Congress.

1924

Civic Club Dinner,* bringing black writers and white publishers together, March 21.
*The Crisis** and *Opportunity** announced literary prizes for 1924, May.
Paul Robeson* starred in *All God's Chillun Got Wings*,* May 15.

Countee Cullen* won first prize in the Witter Bynner Poetry Competition.
Immigration Act excluded immigrants of African descent from the United States.
Negro Art Institute* (formerly American Negro Academy) founded.

1925

*Survey Graphic** issue, "Harlem: Mecca of the New Negro," devoted entirely to black
 arts and letters, March.
American Negro Labor Congress* held in Chicago, October.
Brotherhood of Sleeping Car Porters* founded.

1926

Negro History Week founded by Carter G. Woodson,* February.
Savoy Ballroom* opened in Harlem, March.
Krigwa Players* founded by *The Crisis*, July.
Florence Mills* died, November 1.
Wallace Thurman's* *Fire!!** published, November.
Carnegie Corporation purchased Arthur Schomburg's* collection of Afro-Americana for
 the New York Public Library for $10,000.

1927

*In Abraham's Bosom** by Paul Green,* with an all-black cast, won the Pulitzer Prize,
 May.
Ethel Waters* first appeared on Broadway, July.
Marcus Garvey deported.
Walter White* awarded a Guggenheim Foundation grant.
Louis Armstrong* in Chicago and Duke Ellington* in New York began their careers with
 bands of renown.
Opportunity suspended literary contests because of weak material.
Floyd Calvin's* News Service founded.
Harlem Globetrotters* established.
Harlem Businessmen's Club founded.
Chicago Urban League boycotted white stores for discrimination.
Fifth Pan African Congress, in New York, failed.

1928

Countee Cullen married daughter of W.E.B. Du Bois,* April 9.
Wallace Thurman's *Harlem: A Forum of Negro Life** published, November.
The Dark Tower* in A'Lelia Walker's* townhouse opened.
Oscar De Priest* elected as first black congressman.
White vogue for Harlem slumming at its height.

1929

Negro Experimental Theatre* founded, February.
Negro Art Theatre* founded, June.
National Colored Players* founded, September.
Black Thursday, October 29.

1930

The Green Pastures,* with an all-black cast, opened on Broadway, February 26.
Colored Merchant's Association founded.
Universal Holy Temple of Tranquility* founded.
Black Muslims opened Islam Temple in Detroit.

1931

*Scottsboro*ated* trial, April through July.
A'Lelia Walker died, August 16.
Houseowner's League founded.

1932

Twenty young black intellectuals embarked for Russia to make a movie, *Black and White*, June.
James Ford* ran for national office as vice-presidential candidate for the Communist party, November.
Mass defection from the Republican party began.
Alhambra Theatre* closed.
Lincoln Theatre* closed to reopen as Mount Moriah Baptist Church.

1933

National Negro Business League* ceased operations after 33 years.

1934

Rudolph Fisher* and Wallace Thurman died within four days of each other, December 22 and 26.
W.E.B. Du Bois resigned from *The Crisis* and NAACP.
Lafayette Theatre closed.
Apollo Theatre* opened.
Harlem Economic Association founded.

1935

Harlem Race Riot, March 19.

Porgy and Bess,* with an all-black cast, opened on Broadway, October 10.

Mulatto* by Langston Hughes,* first full-length play by a black writer, opened on Broadway, October 25.

50 percent of Harlem's families unemployed.

APPENDIX B

A Harlem Renaissance Library

In addition to the works of writers usually associated with the Harlem Renaissance, many others of significance were printed between 1917 and 1935. The following chronology makes no attempt to account for every work by every black writer or every work by white writers dealing with black subject matter, but it is a reasonably accurate accounting of the contributions of the period. Many of these books went out of print almost immediately; it is encouraging to report that many of them have been recently reprinted, thanks to the efforts of AMS Press, Arno Press, Books for Libraries, and Greenwood Press to make them widely available to a new generation of readers.

1917

Harrison, Hubert H. *The Negro and the Nation*. New York: Cosmo Advocates.
Johnson, James Weldon. *Fifty Years and Other Poems*. Boston: Cornhill.
Micheaux, Oscar. *The Homesteader*. Iowa (?): Western Book and Supply.
Rogers, Joel A. *From Superman to Man*. New York: Lenox Publishing; reprinted, 1924.
Work, Monroe Nathan, ed. *Negro Year Book: An Annual Encyclopedia of the Negro*. Tuskegee, Ala.: Negro Year Book Publishing (preceded by annual or biennial volumes, 1912, 1913, 1914-1915, 1916-1917, and followed by 1918-1919, 1921-1922, 1925-1926, 1931-1932, 1937-1938).

1918

Cotter, Joseph Seamon, Jr. *The Band of Gideon and Other Lyrics*. Boston: Cornhill.
Fleming, Sarah Lee Brown. *Hope's Highway*. New York: Neale Publishing.
Miller, Kelly. *An Appeal to Conscience*. New York: Macmillan.
Woodson, Carter G. *A Century of Negro Migration*. New York: Ames Press.

1919

Brawley, Benjamin. *The Negro in Literature and Art in the United States*. New York: Duffield; reprinted, 1925, 1930.
Jones, Joshua. *The Heart of the World and Other Poems*. Boston: Stratford.

Kerlin, Robert T., ed. *The Voice of the Negro*. New York: Dutton.
Roberts, Walter Adolphe. *Pierrot Wounded and Other Poems*. Trans. from the French of P. Alberty. Chicago: Brothers of the Book.
Scott, Emmett Jay. *Scott's Official History of the American Negro in the World War*. Chicago: privately printed.

1920

Crogman, William, and H. F. Kletzing. *Progress of a Race*. Napierville, Ill.: Nichols.
Curtis [Burlin], Natalie. *Songs and Tales from the Dark Continent*. New York: Schirmer.
Du Bois, W.E.B. *Darkwater*. Washington, D.C.: Jenkins; reprinted, H. B. and Howe, 1930.
Harrison, Hubert H. *When Africa Awakes*. New York: Porro Press.
Hawkins, Walter Everette. *Chords and Discords*. Boston: Badger.
McKay, Claude. *Spring in New Hampshire*. London: Grant Richards.
Moton, Robert Russa. *Finding a Way Out*. Garden City, N.Y.: Doubleday and Page.
Nelson, Alice Dunbar, ed. *The Dunbar Speaker and Entertainer*. Napierville, Ill.: Nichols.
Scott, Emmett Jay. *Negro Migration During the War*. New York: Oxford University Press.

1921

Brawley, Benjamin. *Social History of the American Negro*. New York: Macmillan.
Hill, Leslie Pickney. *The Wings of Oppression*. Boston: Stratford.
Jones, Joshua. *Poems of the Four Seas*. Boston: Cornhill.
Kerlin, Robert T., ed. *Contemporary Poetry of the Negro*. Hampton, Va.: Hampton Normal and Agricultural Institution.
Lovingood, Penman. *Famous Modern Negro Musicians*. New York: Press Forum.

1922

Detweiler, F. G. *The Negro Press in the United States*. Chicago: University of Chicago Press.
Johnson, Charles S., and Graham R. Taylor. *The Negro in Chicago: A Study of Race Relations and a Race Riot*. Chicago: University of Chicago Press.
Johnson, Georgia Douglas. *Bronze*. Boston: Brimmer.
Johnson, James Weldon, ed. *The Book of American Negro Poetry*. New York: Harcourt Brace; revised, 1931.
McKay, Claude. *Harlem Shadows*. New York: Harcourt Brace.
Maran, René. *Batouala*. New York: Seltzer.
Pickens, William. *The Vengeance of the Gods and Three Other Stories*. Philadelphia: A.M.E. Book Concern.
Stribling, Thomas S. *Birthright*. New York: Century.
Wood, Clement. *Nigger*. New York: Dutton.
Woodson, Carter G. *The Negro in Our History*. Washington, D.C.: Associated Publishers.

1923

Frank, Waldo. *Holiday*. New York: Boni and Liveright.
Garvey, Marcus. *Philosophy and Opinions of Marcus Garvey*. 2 vols. New York: Universal Publishing.
Kerlin, Robert T., ed. *Negro Poets and Their Poems*. Washington, D.C.: Associated Publishers; reprinted, 1925.
Pickens, William. *Burst Bonds*. Boston: Jordan and More Press; revision of 1911 ed.
Scarborough, Dorothy. *The Land of Cotton*. New York: Macmillan.
Toomer, Jean. *Cane*. New York: Boni and Liveright.

1924

Du Bois, W.E.B. *The Gift of Black Folk*. Boston: Stratford.
Fauset, Jessie. *There Is Confusion*. New York: Boni and Liveright.
Garvey, Marcus. *Aims and Objects for a Solution of the Negro Problem Outlined*. New York: Universal Negro Improvement Association.
Jones, Joshua. *By Sanction of Law*. Boston: Brimmer.
Maloney, Arnold, and Clarence MacDonald Maloney. *Some Essentials of Race Leadership*. Xenia, Ohio: Aldine House.
Miller, Kelly. *The Everlasting Stain*. Washington, D.C.: Associated Publishers.
Peterkin, Julia. *Green Thursday*. New York: Knopf.
White, Newman Ivey, and Walter Clinton Jackson, eds. *Anthology of Verse by American Negroes*. Durham, N.C.: Trinity College.
White, Walter. *The Fire in the Flint*. New York: Knopf.

1925

Anderson, Sherwood. *Dark Laughter*. New York: Grosset and Dunlap.
Brown, Hallie Quinn. *Our Women: Past, Present, and Future*. Xenia, Ohio: Aldine House.
———. *Tales My Father Taught Me*. Wilberforce, Ohio: Homewood Cottage.
Cullen, Countee. *Color*. New York: Harper and Brothers.
Heyward, Du Bose. *Porgy*. Garden City, N.Y.: Doubleday.
Johnson, James Weldon, and J. Rosamond Johnson, eds. *The Book of American Negro Spirituals*. New York: Viking Press.
Krehbiel, Henry E., ed. *Afro-American Folksongs*. New York: Schirmer; reprint of 1914 ed.
Locke, Alain, ed. *The New Negro*. New York: A. and C. Boni.
McFall, Haldane. *The Wooings of Jezebel Pettyfer*. New York: Knopf; reprint of 1897 ed.
Odum, Howard, and Guy B. Johnson. *The Negro and His Songs*. Chapel Hill: University of North Carolina Press.
Scarborough, Dorothy. *On the Trail of Negro Folksongs*. Cambridge, Mass.: Harvard University Press.
Woodson, Carter G. *Negro Orators and Their Orations*. Washington, D.C.: Associated Press.

1926

Brown, Hallie Quinn. *Homespun Heroines and Women of Distinction*. Xenia, Ohio: Aldine House.

Fisher, William Arms. *Seventy Negro Spirituals*. New York: Oliver Ditson.

Handy, W. C., and Abbe Niles. *Blues: An Anthology*. New York: A. and C. Boni.

Hughes, Langston. *The Weary Blues*. New York: Knopf.

Johnson, James Weldon, and J. Rosamond Johnson. *The Second Book of Spirituals*. New York: Viking Press.

Kennedy, Robert Emmett. *Black Cameos*. New York: A. and C. Boni.

———. *Mellows: A Chronicle of Unknown Singers*. New York: A. and C. Boni.

Nelson, John H. *The Negro Character in American Literature*. Lawrence: University of Kansas Press.

Odum, Howard, and Guy B. Johnson. *Negro Workaday Songs*. Chapel Hill: University of North Carolina Press.

Puckett, Newell Niles. *Folk Beliefs of the Southern Negro*. Chapel Hill: University of North Carolina Press.

Van Vechten, Carl. *Nigger Heaven*. New York: Knopf.

Walrond, Eric. *Tropic Death*. New York: Boni and Liveright.

White, Walter. *Flight*. New York: Knopf.

1927

Covarrubias, Miguel. *Negro Drawings*. New York: Knopf.

Cullen, Countee. *Ballad of the Brown Girl*. New York: Harper and Brothers.

———. *Copper Sun*. New York: Harper and Brothers.

———, ed. *Caroling Dusk*. New York: Harper and Brothers.

Dett, R[obert] Nathaniel. *Religious Folksongs of the Negro*. Hampton, Va.: Hampton Institute.

Fauset, Arthur Huff. *For Freedom: A Biographical Story of the American Negro*. Philadelphia: Franklin Publishing and Supply.

Flanagan, Thomas Jefferson. *The Road to Mount Keithan*. Atlanta: Independent Publishers.

Four Negro Poets. New York: Simon and Schuster.

Hughes, Langston. *Fine Clothes to the Jew*. New York: Knopf.

Johnson, Charles S., ed. *Ebony and Topaz: A Collectanea*. New York: Opportunity.

Johnson, James Weldon. *The Autobiography of an Ex-Coloured Man*. New York: Knopf; reprint of 1912 ed.

———. *God's Trombones*. New York: Viking Press.

Kennedy, Robert Emmett. *Gritny People*. New York: Dodd, Mead.

Locke, Alain, and Montgomery T. Gregory, eds. *Plays of Negro Life*. New York: Harper and Brothers.

Ovington, Mary White. *Portraits in Color*. New York: Viking Press.

Peterkin, Julia. *Black April*. Indianapolis: Bobbs-Merrill.

Wesley, John Charles. *Negro Labor in the United States*. New York: Vanguard.

1928

Du Bois, W.E.B. *The Dark Princess*. New York: Harcourt Brace.

Fisher, Rudolph. *The Walls of Jericho*. New York: Knopf.

Larsen, Nella. *Quicksand*. New York: Knopf.

McKay, Claude. *Home to Harlem*. New York: Harper and Brothers.
Peterkin, Julia. *Scarlet Sister Mary*. Indianapolis: Bobbs-Merrill.
Roberts, Walter Adolphe. *Pan and Peacocks*. Boston: Four Seas.
Thurman, Wallace. *Negro Life in New York's Harlem*. Girard, Kans.: Haldemann-Julius.
White, Newman Ivey. *Negro American Folksongs*. Cambridge, Mass.: Harvard University Press.
Woodson, Carter G. *Negro Makers of History*. Washington, D.C.: Associated Publishers.
Woofter, T. J. *Negro Problems in the Cities*. Garden City, N.Y.: Doubleday Doran.
Work, Monroe Nathan, ed. *Bibliography of the Negro in Africa and America*. New York: Wilson.

1929

Brawley, Benjamin. *The Negro in Literature and Art in the United States*. New York: Dodd, Mead.
Calverton, V. F., ed. *Anthology of American Negro Literature*. New York: Modern Library.
Cullen, Countee. *The Black Christ and Other Poems*. New York: Harper and Brothers.
Fauset, Jessie. *Plum Bun*. New York: Stokes.
Gordon, Taylor. *Born to Be*. New York: Covici-Friede.
Harmon, J. H. *The Negro as a Businessman*. Washington, D.C.: Associated Press.
Kennedy, Robert Emmett. *Red Bean Row*. New York: Dodd, Mead.
Larsen, Nella. *Passing*. New York: Knopf.
McKay, Claude. *Banjo*. New York: Harper and Brothers.
Morand, Paul. *Black Magic*. New York: Viking Press.
————. *New York*. New York: Holt.
Moton, Robert Russa. *What the Negro Thinks*. Garden City, N.Y.: Doubleday Doran; reprint of 1920 London ed.
Thurman, Wallace. *The Blacker the Berry*. New York: Macaulay.
White, Walter. *Rope and Faggot: The Biography of Judge Lynch*. New York: Knopf.

1930

Edmonds, Randolph. *Shades and Shadows*. Boston: Meador.
Four Lincoln Poets. Chester County, Pa.: Lincoln University.
Johnson, Charles S. *The Negro in American Civilization: A Study of Negro Life and Race Relations*. New York: Holt.
Johnson, James Weldon. *Black Manhattan*. New York: Knopf.
Kennedy, Louise Venable. *The Negro Peasant Turns Cityward*. New York: Columbia University Press.
Millen, Gilmore. *Sweet Man*. New York: Viking Press.
Whitke, Carl. *Tambourine and Bones*. Durham, N.C.: Duke University Press.

1931

Bontemps, Arna. *God Sends Sunday*. New York: Harcourt Brace.
Brawley, Benjamin. *A Short History of the American Negro*. New York: Macmillan.
Embree, E. R. *Brown American*. New York: Viking Press.

Fauset, Jessie. *The Chinaberry Tree*. New York: Stokes.

Hughes, Langston. *Dear Lovely Death*. Amenia, N.Y.: Troutbeck.

———. *The Negro Mother*. New York: Golden Stair Press.

———. *Not without Laughter*. New York: Knopf.

———. *Scottsboro Limited*. New York: Golden Stair Press.

Kennedy, Robert Emmett. *More Mellows*. New York: Dodd, Mead.

Loggins, Vernon. *The Negro Author: His Development in America to 1900*. New York: Columbia University Press.

Schuyler, George S. *Black No More*. New York: Macaulay.

Spero, Sterling Denhard, and Abram L. Harris. *The Black Worker*. New York: Columbia University Press.

Toomer, Jean. *Essentials*. Chicago: Lakeside Press.

1932

Bontemps, Arna, and Langston Hughes. *Popo and Fifina*. New York: Macmillan.

Brown, Sterling. *Southern Road*. New York: Harcourt Brace.

Cullen, Countee. *One Way to Heaven*. New York: Harper and Brothers.

Fisher, Rudolph. *The Conjure Man Dies*. New York: Covici-Friede.

Frazier, E. Franklin. *The Negro Family in Chicago*. Chicago: University of Chicago Press; revised 1934.

Hughes, Langston. *The Dream Keeper*. New York: Knopf.

Kelly, Welbourne. *Inchin' Along*. New York: Morrow.

McKay, Claude. *Ginger Town*. New York: Harper and Brothers.

Nearing, Scott. *Freeborn: An Unpublishable Novel*. New York: Urquart Press.

Peterkin, Julia. *Bright Skin*. Indianapolis: Bobbs-Merrill.

Schuyler, George S. *Slaves Today*. New York: Macaulay.

Spivak, John. *Georgia Nigger*. New York: Harcourt Brace.

Thurman, Wallace. *Infants of the Spring*. New York: Macaulay.

———, and Abraham L. Furman. *The Interne*. New York: Macaulay.

1933

Fauset, Jessie. *Comedy, American Style*. New York: Stokes.

Hurst, Fannie. *Imitation of Life*. New York: Collier.

Johnson, James Weldon. *Along This Way*. New York: Viking Press.

McKay, Claude. *Banana Bottom*. New York: Harper and Brothers.

Peterkin, Julia, and Doris Ullman. *Roll, Jordan, Roll*. New York: Ballou.

1934

Bontemps, Arna. *You Can't Pet a Possum*. New York: Morrow.

Cunard, Nancy, ed. *Negro*. London: Wisart.

Edmonds, Randolph. *Six Plays for the Negro Theatre*. Boston: Baker.

Hughes, Langston. *The Ways of White Folks*. New York: Knopf.

Hurston, Zora Neale. *Jonah's Gourd Vine*. Philadelphia: Lippincott.

Johnson, Charles S. *The Shadow of the Plantation*. Chicago: University of Chicago Press.
Johnson, James Weldon. *Negro Americans: What Now?* New York: Viking Press.
Lee, George. *Beale Street Where the Blues Began*. New York: Ballou.

1935

Cullen, Countee. *The Medea and Other Poems*. New York: Harper and Brothers.
Hurston, Zora Neale. *Mules and Men*. Philadelphia: Lippincott.
Johnson, James Weldon. *St. Peter Relates an Incident*. New York: Viking Press.
Richardson, Willis, and May Miller Sullivan. *Negro History in Thirteen Plays*. Washington, D.C.: Associated Publishers.

1937

McKay, Claude. *A Long Way From Home*. New York: Lee, Furman.

1940

Hughes, Langston. *The Big Sea*. New York: Knopf.
McKay, Claude. *Harlem: Negro Metropolis*. New York: Dutton.

Note: Some few writers of the period published subsequent books, notably Zora Neale Hurston's novels *Their Eyes Were Watching God* (1937) and *Moses: Man of the Mountain* (1939) and Langston Hughes's long list of later publications. The three works that conclude this Harlem Renaissance Library appeared in print after 1935, but they are directly relevant to the movement in offering contemporary assessments of it.

APPENDIX C

Plays by, about, or Featuring Afro-Americans, 1917–1935

In addition to the plays and musical comedies that ran on Broadway during the Harlem Renaissance, dozens of revues and vaudeville entertainments played briefly at the Lafayette,* Lincoln,* and Alhambra* theaters, each usually about an hour long. Some few serious plays by black writers tried out there also, but most dramas were consigned, as well as confined, to little theater groups like the Krigwa Players,* National Ethiopian Art Theatre,* Tri-Arts Club,* and Sekondi Players. Some of the musical offerings went on the road as tab shows; some began as nightclub acts; some few moved downtown to enjoy white patronage; but most of them simply closed after brief runs, and little is documented of their content. About *Gay Harlem*,* for example, some tantalizing squibs say only that it was notable for its nudity. The *Pepper Pot Revue* featured a singer who billed herself as the black Galli-Curci, just as Sissieretta Jones,* in an earlier generation, had called herself Black Patti, after soprano Adelina Patti. Amy Garvey's *Hey Hey* was "low enough to have attracted the Dutch Cleanser squad of Gomorrah," according to Theophilus Lewis* in *The Messenger*,* one of the few writers to pay any attention in print to the Harlem shows (Oct. 1926, p. 362). *Raisin' Cane* was so vulgar, according to Lewis, that it "just managed to get a decision over a blue evening" (Sept. 1923, p. 821). But Frank Wilson's* *Pa Williams' Gal** and Flournoy Miller* and Aubrey Lyles's* *The Flat Above*, both early if crude attempts by black playwrights at serious drama, played at the Lafayette Theatre as well. At least one of the Harlem shows—Lew Leslie's* *Blackbirds*,* in 1926—made a great success in England and served as the basis for a Broadway sequel two years later. Some of Billy King's* Chicago shows are included in this appendix because they sometimes served as a foundation for later versions in New York; furthermore, some of his performers went on to successful careers in New York and Europe. Some plays by white writers were strongly identified with black subject matter and are therefore accounted for. Probably no list could claim absolute accuracy or completeness. This compilation is as full as extant records allow. Shows that played in white theaters on and off Broadway are in all capital letters, with their authors and dates of opening; Harlem shows are in capital and small letters, with their authors and dates when available. Sometimes these Harlem entertainments were anonymous variety bills, in which case only the star is listed. Shows with asterisks have entries in the body of the dictionary, with information about plots, casts, critical receptions, and lengths of their runs.

Aces and Queens, Porter Grainger and Freddie Johnson, 1925

Adam and Eve in Harlem, Leonard Harper, Nov. 1929

AFRICANA* (musical revue), Donald Heywood, 3 Sept. 1927

AFRICANA* (operetta), Donald Heywood, 27 Nov. 1934

African Prince, 1920

AFTERMATH, Mary Burrill, 8 May 1928

Alabama Bound, Irvin C. Miller, 1920

Alabama Fantasies, Sam Wooding, Mar. 1925

All Girl Revue, Irvin C. Miller, c. 1928

ALL GOD'S CHILLUN GOT WINGS,* Eugene O'Neill, 15 May 1924

ALL GOD'S CHILLUN GOT WINGS (revival), 18 Aug. 1924

And How!, 1928

Annie Oakley, Quintard Miller, 1924

APPEARANCES,* Garland Anderson, 13 Oct. 1925

APPEARANCES (revival), 30 Mar. 1929

Are We Happy?, 1928

Arrival of the Negro, J. Berni Barbour, 1920

AS THOUSANDS CHEER,* Irving Berlin and Moss Hart, 30 Sept. 1933

Baby Blues, Alex Rogers and C. Luckyeth Roberts, 1919

Backbiters, Flournoy Miller and Aubrey Lyles, 1925

BAMBOOLA* (also *BAMBOLLA* and *BOMBOLLA*), D. Frank Marcus, 26 June 1929

Bamboula, Salem Whitney and Homer Tutt, 1921

Bandanna Land, 1928

Banjo Land Revue, 1924

Bare Facts, Quintard Miller, 1927

BEYOND EVIL, David Thorne, 7 June 1926

Black and White Revue, 1921

BLACKBERRIES OF 1932,* Lee Posner, Eddie Green, Donald Heywood, and Tom
  Peluso, 4 Apr. 1932

Blackbirds* (Lew Leslie's, of 1926), Dorothy Fields and Jimmie McHugh, 26 Sept. 1926

BLACKBIRDS OF 1928, Dorothy Fields and Jimmie McHugh, 9 May 1928

BLACKBIRDS OF 1930, Eubie Blake and Andy Razaf, 22 Oct. 1930

BLACKBIRDS OF 1933, 2 Dec. 1933

Blackbirds of 1934, 1934

Blackbirds of 1936, 1936

BLACKBIRDS OF 1939, 1939

Black Bottom Revue, 1926

BLACK BOY,* Jim Tully and Frank Dazey, 6 Oct. 1926

Black Diamond Express, 1928

Blackouts of 1929, Billy Higgins, Mar. 1929

BLACK SCANDALS,* George Smithfield, 27 Oct. 1928

BLACK SOULS,* Annie Nathan Meyer, 30 Mar. 1932

BLACK VELVET,* Willard Robertson, 27 Sept. 1928

BLOODSTREAM,* Frederick Schlick, 30 Mar. 1932

Blue Baby, Irvin C. Miller, c. 1928

Board of Education, The, Billy King and J. Berni Barbour, 1918

Bon Bon Buddy, Jr., Irvin C. Miller and Maceo Pinkard, 1922

BOTTOMLAND,* Clarence Williams, Spencer Williams, Chris Smith, Donald Heywood, and Eva Taylor, 27 June 1927
BOTTOM OF THE CUP,* John Tucker Battle and William Perlman, 31 Jan. 1927
BRAINSWEAT,* John Charles Bronelle, 4 Nov. 1934
BRASS ANKLE,* Du Bose Heyward, 23 Apr. 1931
BROADWAY BREVITIES, Blair Treynor and George Gershwin, 29 Sept. 1920
Broadway Gossips, Quintard Miller, 1920
Broadway Rastus (revival from 1915), Irvin C. Miller and Maceo Pinkard, 1920
BROWN BUDDIES,* Carl Rickman, Porter Grainger, Leigh Whipper, J. Rosamond Johnson, Millard Thomas, Joe Jordan, and Shelton Brooks, 7 Oct. 1930
Brownskin Models of 1926 (the first of several annual revues that toured), Irvin C. Miller, 1926
BUBBLE ALONG,* 2 June 1930

Canary Cottage, Oliver Moreseo and Shelton Brooks, 1920
Cape Smoke, 1925
Catching the Burglar, Billy King, 1918
CHANGE YOUR LUCK,* Garland Howard and James C. Johnson, 6 June 1930
Charleston Fricassee, Quintard Miller, 1926
Chinatown: The Darktown Follies, Billy King, 1920
CHIP WOMAN'S FORTUNE, THE,* Willis Richardson, 15 May 1923
Chocolate Blondes, Eddie Rector, Jan. 1929
Chocolate Brown, Spencer Williams, 1921
CHOCOLATE DANDIES,* Noble Sissle, Eubie Blake, and Lew Payton, 1 Sept. 1924
Circus Showman, The, Irvin C. Miller, Apr. 1929
Club Alabam, 1924
Cocktails of 1932, 1932
Come Along, Mandy,* Jean Starr, Salem Whitney and Homer Tutt, Dec. 1923
COME SEVEN,* Octavus Roy Cohen, 19 July 1920
Con Man, The, Billy King, 1918
CONSTANT SINNER, THE,* Mae West, 14 Sept. 1931
Crazy Quilt Revue, Jack Johnson, Oct. 1929
Creole Follies, 1923
Creole Revels, 1928

Dance Mania, 1927
DANCE WITH YOUR GODS,* Kenneth Perkins, 7 Oct. 1934
Darkest Africa, Salem Whitney and Homer Tutt, 1918
Darktown Scandals, Eddie Hunter, 1921
Darktown Strutters, 1925
Dear Old Southland, 1932
De Board Meeting, Leigh Whipper and Porter Grainger, 1925
DEEP HARLEM, Salem Whitney, Homer Tutt, Harry Creamer, and Joe Jordan, 7 Jan. 1929
Demi-Virgin, The, 1926
DE PROMIS' LAN',* Jeroline Hernsley and Russell Woodrig, 27 May 1930
Derby Day in Dixie, 1921
Desires of 1927, Irvin C. Miller, 1927

Desires of 1928, Irvin C. Miller, 1928

Devil, The, Quintard Miller, 1922

Devil's Frolics, The, Addison Carey, Nov. 1929

*Dinah,** Irvin C. Miller and Tim Brymm, Dec. 1923

Dixie Brevities of 1926, Quintard Miller, 1926

Dixie Brevities of 1927, Quintard Miller, 1927

Dixie Brevities of 1928, Quintard Miller, 1928

*DIXIE TO BROADWAY,** Lew Leslie, Walter DeLeon, George W. Meyer, Tom Howard, Arthur Johnston, Grant Clarke, Roy Turk, and others, 29 Oct. 1924

Dixie to Harlem, George Green, Oct. 1929

Downtown Affairs, Garland Howard, c. 1920.

Dream Girls and Candied Sweets, Clara Smith, Sept. 1929

Dumb Luck, 1922

Dusty Lane, 1930

*EARTH,** Em Jo Basshe, 9 Mar. 1927

Ebony Scandals, 1932

Ebony Showboat, Earl Dancer and Cora Green, Jan. 1929

Eddie Hunter Company, The, Eddie Hunter, 1922

Elsie, Noble Sissle and Eubie Blake, 1923

*EMPEROR JONES, THE,** Eugene O'Neill, 1 Nov. 1920

EMPEROR JONES, THE (revival), 10 Nov. 1926

*EMPEROR JONES, THE** (opera), Louis Gruenberg, 7 Jan. 1933

Exploits in Africa, Billy King and J. Berni Barbour, 1919

Famous Georgia Smart Set Minstrels, Apr. 1925

Fan Waves, 1934

*FAST AND FURIOUS,** J. Rosamond Johnson, Porter Grainger, and Zora Neale Hurston, 15 Sept. 1931

FIELD GOD, THE, Paul Green, 22 Apr. 1927

Fireworks of 1930, Fats Waller, 1930

Five Star Final, 1930

Flat Below, The, Flournoy Miller and Aubrey Lyles, May 1922

*FOLIES BERGERE REVUE,** Eubie Blake and Will Morrissey, 15 Apr. 1930

Follow Me, Dec. 1923

*FOLLY TOWN,** William K. Wells and Jesse Greer, 17 May 1920

4–11–44, Eddie Hunter, Nina Hunter, and Grace Rector, 4 Sept. 1926

Frolicing Along, 1926

Frolics, The, 1923

From Dover to Dixie (London), Noble Sissle and Eubie Blake, George W. Meyer, Arthur Johnston, Grant Clark, and Roy Turk, 1923

*Gay Harlem,** Irvin C. Miller, May 1927

*GEORGE WHITE'S SCANDALS,** Arthur Baer and George White, 11 July 1921

Get Lucky, Quintard Miller, 1923

Get Set, Donald Heywood and Porter Grainger, 1923

*GINGERSNAPS,** Homer Tutt, Salem Whitney, Donald Heywood, and George Morris, 31 Dec. 1929

GOAT ALLEY,* Ernest Howard Culbertson, 19 June 1921
GOAT ALLEY (revival), 19 Apr. 1927
GO GO, Alex Rogers and C. Luckyeth Roberts, 1923
Going Straight, Flournoy Miller and Aubrey Lyles, 1922
Going to the Races, Eddie Hunter, c. 1920
Going to Town, 1932
Going White, Flournoy Miller and Aubrey Lyles, Apr. 1924
GOIN' HOME,* Ransom Rideout, 23 Aug. 1928
Gold Dust, 1923
Goldfront Stores, Inc., The,* Caesar G. Washington, 1924
GREAT DAY,* Vincent Youmans and William Cary Duncan, 17 Oct. 1929
GREEN PASTURES, THE,* Marc Connelly, 26 Feb. 1931

Ham's Daughter,* Dennis Donoghue, 1932
HARLEM,* Wallace Thurman and William Jordan Rapp, 20 Feb. 1929
HARLEM (revival), 21 Oct. 1929
Harlem Butterflies, Quintard Miller, 1926
Harlem Frolics, Bessie Smith, Apr. 1929
Harlem Madness, 1923
Harlem Rounders,* J. Rosamond Johnson, 1925
Harlem Scandals, 1932
Hawaiian Moon, 1934
Hawaiian Nights, July 1929
Heart Breakers, Billy King, 1918
Hello, Dixieland! Billy King, 1920
Here We Are, 1930
Hey! Hey!, Amy Garvey, 1926
Highlights of Harlem, 1928
His Honor, the Mayor, 1918
Hit and Run, 1924
HOBOKEN BLUES,* Michael Gold, 17 Feb. 1928
Holiday in Dixie, Will Mastin, 1921
Hollywood to Dixie, 1922
Honey, Flournoy Miller and Aubrey Lyles, 1925
HOT CHOCOLATES,* Andy Razaf, Fats Waller, and Harry Brooke, 20 June 1929
Hot Feet, c. 1928
Hot from Harlem, 1931
HOT RHYTHM,* Will Morrissey, Ballard MacDonald, Edward Lanley, Donald Hey-
     wood, and Porter Grainger, 21 Aug. 1930
HOW COME?,* Eddie Hunter, 16 Apr. 1923
How Come? (revival), 1925
HUMMIN' SAM,* Eileen Nutter and Alexander Hill, 8 Apr. 1933

IN ABRAHAM'S BOSOM,* Paul Green, 30 Dec. 1926
IN ABRAHAM'S BOSOM (revival), 19 Feb. 1927

Jangle Land, 1931
January Jubilee, Jan. 1930

Jazzbo Regiment, 1929
Jazzmania, 1927
Jazzola, Shelton Brooks and John Mason, May 1929
Joy Boat, 1930
Jump Steady, Salem Whitney and Homer Tutt, 1922
Jungle Drums, 1934
Junior Blackbirds of Harlem, Mar. 1929

Keep It Up, 1922
KEEP SHUFFLIN',* Andy Razaf, Fats Waller, James P. Johnson, Con Conrad, Clarence
   Todd, Harry Creamer, Flournoy Miller, and Aubrey Lyles, 27 Feb., 1928
K of P, 1923
Krazy Kats, Cliff Jackson, 1927

Late Hour Tap Dancers, Bessie Smith, Aug. 1929
Lily White, 1930
Lincoln Frolics, 1926
Little Theatre Tournament (national competition), 2–11 May 1927
   THE DREAMY KID, Eugene O'Neill
   THE FOOL'S ERRAND, Eulalie Spence
   'LIJAH, Edgar Valentin Smith
   THE NO 'COUNT BOY, Paul Green
   OFF COL'UH, Amy L. Weber
LIZA,* Irvin C. Miller and Maceo Pinkard, 27 Nov. 1922
Look Who's Here, 1927
LOUISIANA,* J. Augustus Smith, 27 Feb. 1923
LUCKY SAMBO,* Porter Grainger and Freddie Johnson, 8 June 1925
LUCKY SAMBO (revival), 26 May 1926
LULU BELLE,* Edward Sheldon and Charles McArthur, 9 Feb. 1926

MAKE ME KNOW IT,* D. Frank Marcus, Roland Irving, and Earl B. Westfield, 4 Nov.
   1929
MALINDA,* Dennis Donoghue, Roland Irving, and Earl Westfield, 3 Dec. 1929
Mandy Green from New Orleans, Quintard Miller and Marcus Slayter, 1928
Man from Bam, Joe Jordan, 1920
Masquerade, Archie Jones, May 1929
Mayor of Jimtown, The, Quintard Miller, 1923
MEEK MOSE,* Frank Wilson, 6 Feb. 1928
MESSIN' AROUND,* Perry Bradford and Jimmy Johnson, 22 Apr. 1929
Messin' Round, Sam Wooding and His Chocolate Kiddies, Jan. 1932
Midnight Steppers, 1929
Miss Bandanna, Clarence Muse, 1927
Miss Calico, Earl Dancer and Donald Heywood, 1926
Miss Dinah of 1926, Quintard Miller, 1926
Mississippi Days, 1928
Miss Nobody from Starland, Shelton Brooks, 1920
Mister George, Noble Sissle and Maceo Pinkard, Apr. 1929
Moonshine, Billy King, 1922

Move Along, Louis Armstrong, June 1929
*MULATTO,** Langston Hughes, 25 Oct. 1935
Musical Aces, 1926
*MY MAGNOLIA,** Alex Rogers and C. Luckyeth Roberts, 12 July 1926
My People, C. Luckyeth Roberts, 1917

Negro Nuances, Will Marion Cook and Abbie Mitchell, 1924
*NEVER NO MORE,** James Knox Millen, 7 Jan. 1932
New American, The, Billy King, 1921
New Year's Revels, 1930
New York Revue, 1928
Next Door Neighbors, 1928
Nifties of 1928, Shelton Brooks, 1928
Nobody's Girl, 1926
*North Ain't South,** Salem Whitney and Homer Tutt, Oct. 1923

*OCTOROON, THE** (revival), Dion Boucicault, 12 Mar. 1929
*Oh Joy,** Salem Whitney and Homer Tutt, 1922
Oil Well Scandal, An, Freddie Johnson, 1924
*OL' MAN SATAN,** Donald Heywood, 3 Oct. 1932
Ophelia Snow from Baltimo', 1928
Over the Top, Billy King and J. Berni Barbour, 1918

*PANSY,** Alex Belledna and Maceo Pinkard, 14 May 1929
Paul Laurence Dunbar's Dream, J. Berni Barbour, 1927
*Pa Williams' Gal,** Frank Wilson, Sept. 1923
PEARLY GATES, THE, Marc Connelly, 1 Sept. 1931
Pepper Pot Revue, 1927
Plantation Days, 1927
*PLANTATION REVUE,** Lew Leslie and Will Vodery, 17 July 1922
*PORGY,** Du Bose and Dorothy Heyward, 10 Oct. 1927
PORGY (revival), 13 Sept. 1929
*PORGY AND BESS,** George Gershwin, Ira Gershwin, and Du Bose Heyward, 10 Oct.
    1935
Pudden Jones, 1925
*PUT AND TAKE,** Irvin C. Miller, Perry Bradford, Spencer Williams, and J. Tim Brymm,
    23 Aug. 1921

Queen at Home, The, 1930

Rainbow Chasers, The, 1926
*Raisin' Cane,** Frank Montgomery, Sept. 1923
*RANG TANG,** Kaj Gynt, Jo Trent, and Ford Dabney, 12 July 1927
*Revue Nègre** (Paris), Sept. 1925
*RHAPSODY IN BLACK,** W. C. Handy, Alberta Nichols, Cecil Mack, Dorothy Fields
    and Jimmie McHugh, Mann Hollinger, George Gershwin, J. Rosamond Johnson, and
    Ken Macomber, 4 May 1931
Rhumbaland, Mamie Smith, Aug. 1931

Rocking Chair Revue, 1931
Riot of Fun, A, 1928
ROLL, SWEET CHARIOT,* Paul Green, 2 Oct. 1934
Rolling On, 1928
ROSEANNE,* Nan Bagby Stephens, 30 Dec. 1923
Roseanne (revival), 8 Mar. 1924
RUN, LITTLE CHILLUN,* Hall Johnson, 1 Mar. 1933
Runnin' De Town, James C. Johnson, 1930
RUNNIN' WILD,* Flournoy Miller, Aubrey Lyles, James P. Johnson, and Cecil Mack,
    29 Oct. 1923

SAVAGE RHYTHM,* Harry Hamilton, Norman Foster, James P. Johnson, and Cecil
    Mack, 31 Dec. 1931
SECOND COMIN', THE,* George Bryant, 8 Dec. 1931
SENTINELS, Lulu Volmer, 25 Dec. 1931
Sepia Music Box, The, Feb. 1932
September Morn, Shelton Brooks, 1920
Seven-Eleven, Garland Howard, Jan. 1923
Shades of Hades, Dave Payton and Tim Owsley, 1923
SHARLEE, C. Luckyeth Roberts
Sheik of Harlem, The,* Donald Heywood and Irvin C. Miller, Sept. 1923
SHOWBOAT,* Jerome Kern and Oscar Hammerstein II, 27 Dec. 1927
SHOWBOAT (revival), 29 May 1932
SHUFFLE ALONG,* Flournoy Miller, Aubrey Lyles, Eubie Blake, and Noble Sissle,
    22 May 1921
SHUFFLE ALONG IN 1930,* Flournoy Miller, Aubrey Lyles, Fats Waller, and James
    P. Johnson, 1930
SHUFFLE ALONG OF 1933,* Flournoy Miller, Noble Sissle, and Eubie Blake, 26 Dec.
    1932
Shufflin' Feet, 1927
Sidewalks of Harlem, 1930
SINGIN' THE BLUES,* John McGowan, Dorothy Fields, and Jimmie McHugh, 16 Sept.
    1931
Solid South, 1930
Some Baby, Quintard Miller, 1921
Sons of Rest, Sidney Easton and Robert Warfield, 1927
Southland Nights, June 1929
Spirit of 1929, 1929
SPOOKS,* Robert J. Sherman, 1 June 1925
Steamboat Days, Bessie Smith, Jan. 1929
Step Along, Quintard Miller and Marcus Slayter, 1924
Stepchildren, 1923
Step on It, Flournoy Miller and Aubrey Lyles, 1922
Steppin' High, 1924
Steppin' Out, Billy Higgins, 1924
Steppin' Time, C. Luckyeth Roberts, 1924
STEVEDORE,* Paul Peters and George Sklar, 18 Apr. 1934
Striver's Row, Earl Dancer and Fletcher Henderson, July 1929

STRUT MISS LIZZIE,* Harry Creamer and Turner Layton, 19 June 1922
Struttin' Along, 1923
Struttin' Hannah from Savannah, Will Mastin and Eddie Hunter, 1927
Struttin' Sam from Alabam, Charles Alpin, 1927
Struttin' Time, Flournoy Miller and Aubrey Lyles, 1924
Strut Your Stuff, Dave Payton and Babe Townsend, 1920
Sugar Cane Revue, 1928
SUGAR HILL,* Jo Trent, Charles Tazewell, James P. Johnson, Flournoy Miller, and
    Aubrey Lyles, 25 Dec. 1931
Sultan Sam, 1920
Sunshine, 1930
Sunshine for All, Eddie Rector, Nov. 1929
Suntan Frolics, Mamie Smith, Aug. 1929
SWEET CHARIOT,* Robert Wilder, 23 Oct. 1930
Swing Along, Will Vodery and Will Marion Cook, Apr. 1929
Syncopation, Danny Small, Mar. 1929
Syncopation Land Revue, 1924

TABOO,* Mary Hoyt Wiborg, 4 Apr. 1922
Take It Easy, Quintard Miller, 1924
Tan Town Tamales, 1930
Tan Town Topics, Fats Waller, 1925
Temple of Jazz, The, Ralph Cooper, Apr. 1929
That Gets It, 1922
They're Off, Billy King and J. Berni Barbour, 1919
THEY SHALL NOT DIE,* John Wexley, 21 Feb. 1934
This and That, Alex Rogers and C. Luckyeth Roberts, 1919
This Way Out, Quintard Miller, 1922
THREE PLAYS FOR THE NEGRO THEATRE,* Ridgely Torrence, 5 Apr. 1917
Tokio, Irvin C. Miller, c. 1928
Too Bad, 1925
TOPSY AND EVA,* Catherine Chisolm Cushing and the Duncan Sisters, 23 Dec. 1924
Town Topiks (sic), 1920
TREE, THE,* Richard Maibaum, 12 Apr. 1932
Trip Round the World, A, 1921
Tunes and Topics, Quintard Miller, 1923

UNCLE TOM'S CABIN (revival), George Aiken, 30 May 1933

Vaudeville at the Palace, 1927
Velvet Brown Babies, 1924
Vendetta, Harry Lawrence Freeman, 1923
VOODOO, Harry Lawrence Freeman, 1926

Watermelon, Garland Howard and Speedy Smith, 1926
We'se Risin', Porter Grainger and Leigh Whipper, 1927
Whitman Sisters Revue,* Mabel Whitman, 1923
Who's Stealin'?* Flournoy Miller and Aubrey Lyles, 1918

Wicked House of David, The, William A. Grew, Feb. 1925
Wift Waft Warblers, Amon Davis and Eddie Stafford, 1921

YEAH, MAN!* Leigh Whipper, Billy Mills, Al Wilson, Charles Weinberg, and Ken Macomber, 26 May 1932
Yellow Girl Revue, Bessie Smith, 1927

REFERENCES: *The Crisis*, 1917–1934; *The Messenger*, 1917–1928; *Opportunity*, 1923–1934; *Inter-State Tattler*, 1925–1932; *Abbott's Weekly*, 1930–1933; ETM, 1961; NYTTR, 1972; EMT, 1976; BB, 1980; CVV; JWJ.

APPENDIX   D

Serial Publications from the Harlem Renaissance

More than 300 newspapers and more than 30 magazines were in print during the period 1917–1935. Some, like the New York *Age** and *Pittsburgh Courier,** were established long before the movement began and continued long after its demise; others, like Wallace Thurman's *Fire!!** ran for a single issue. Several in the following (inevitably partial) compilation are listed neither in the Library of Congress Union Serial Catalogs nor with OCLC, Inc., so their inclusive dates are difficult to determine. Newspapers designed for mass distribution show the cities of their publication in parentheses. This list includes only strongly influential serials.

*Abbott's Monthly,** 1930–1933
Afro-American (Baltimore),* 1892–
Age (New York), 1881–1960
American Musician, 1926–1927
Amsterdam News (New York),* 1909–
Bee (Washington), 1882–1921
Black Man, 1924–1933 (intermittent), 1933–1935
*Black Opals,** 1927–1928
Black Worker, 1929–1930
Broad Ax (Chicago; initially, Salt Lake City), 1895–1927
*Brownie's Book,** 1921–1922
*Challenge,** 1916–1919
*Challenge** (later, *New Challenge*), 1934–1937
Competitor, 1920–1921
*Crisis, The,** 1910–
Cruader, c. 1919–1922; *Crusader Bulletin,* 1923
Defender (Chicago),* 1905–
Dispatch (New York), 1920–1921
Eagle (Washington), 1921
Emancipator (New York),* 1919
Encore, 1926–1933
Fire!! 1926
Guardian (Boston),* 1901–1960

*Gumby Book Studio Quarterly,** 1930–1931
Half-Century Magazine, 1916–1925
Harlem: A Forum of Negro Life, 1928
Harlem Liberator, 1928–1934 (intermittent)
Heebie Jeebies, 1925–1926
Inter-State Tattler (New York),* 1925–1932
Journal of Negro Education, 1931–
*Journal of Negro History,** 1916–
Master Musician (alternately, *American Musician and Sportsman*), 1919–1922
Menu, The, 1931–1933
*Messenger, The,** 1917–1928
Music and Poetry, 1921
Negro Churchman, 1923–1931
Negro Times, 1923–
Negro Voice, 1917–
Negro Worker, 1928–1929, 1931–1933
*Negro World,** 1918–1933
New Negro, 1919
*Opportunity,** 1923–1949
*Pittsburgh Courier,** 1910–
*Saturday Evening Quill,** 1928–1930
Southern Workman, 1872–
*Spokesman, The,** 1925–1926
*Stylus,** 1916–1941 (intermittent)
Tribune (Philadelphia), 1884–
*Urban League Bulletin,** 1921–1922
Voice: A Journal of Catholic Negro Opinion, 1934
Whip (Chicago),* 1919–1933

REFERENCES: Ronald E. Wolseley, *The Black Press, U.S.A.*, 1971; Theodore G. Vincent, ed., *Voices of a Black Nation*, 1973; JWJ.

A Glossary of Harlem Slang

To credit sources for each of the following words and phrases would only result in redundancy, since many of them occur in several circumstances: not only in the conversations of characters in novels about the Harlem Renaissance and on many vintage phonograph records, but in casual essays as well as scholarly studies of black vocabulary. Guy B. Johnson, for example, accounts for the same obscenity in the *Journal of Abnormal and Social Psychology* that Bessie Smith* employs in "Empty Bed Blues," but cabaret or theater audiences required no explanation from Johnson to understand exactly what Smith was singing about. Carl Van Vechten's* sanitized list at the conclusion of his novel *Nigger Heaven** is accurate but far from complete. *Dan Burley's Original Handbook of Harlem Jive*, compiled nearly a decade after the Harlem Renaissance, contains terms that came into popularity during the swing era of the late thirties. Zora Neale Hurston,* however, may be the best source of information on the subject. In her "Characteristics of Negro Expression," published in Nancy Cunard's* *Negro* in 1934, Hurston accounts for the foundation of most of the materials in this glossary. The Afro-American contributions to the language fall into four clear categories, she contends, by offering ample examples for each to illustrate her "will to adorn" speech. The first of these categories is the *metaphor and simile*, as in "sobbing hearted," "mule blood" (meaning "black molasses"), "one at a time, like lawyers going to heaven." The second category is what she terms *double description*, as in "lady-people," "sitting-chairs," "low-down," "kill-dead." Hurston's third and fourth categories are instances of *conversion*, to which others may be added from her own examples: nouns used verbally, as in "funeralize," "I wouldn't friend with her," "She features somebody I know"; verbs used as nouns, as in "She won't take a listen," "That is such a compelment," "Won't stand a broke"; adjectives used verbally, as in "uglying away," "bookooing around" (from *beaucoup*, meaning "to show off"), or "jooking" (playing the piano) in a "jook house" (meaning "whore house"), an adjective later transformed to "juke" as in "juke box" (pp. 24–25).

The mortality rate among slang words and phrases is notoriously high. Either the expressions die early or enter into the language so thoroughly that they are no longer considered slang. The ubiquitous, colorless, contemporary "Wow" approximates the meanings of expressions of former generations: "Hubba hubba" from the forties and "Goodnight, Irene" from the turn of the century; "wow" also will likely fade away in time. Several expressions in the following glossary are long out of date and forgotten; others, however, continue to influence and inform contemporary English as it is spoken in America by many races. Doubtless there are omissions; the absence of "hip" and "hep," so strongly identified with black music, is deliberate, however. "Hip," apparently white in origin, appears as early as 1914 through Sinclair Lewis and into the twenties through F. Scott Fitzgerald but was not used by blacks; "hep" seems to have first appeared in print in *Cab Calloway's[*] Cat-alogue: A Hepster's Dictionary* in 1938.

Ah-ah. A fool, masculine only.

Ain't got'em. Has no virtues, is of no value.

Air out. To leave, to take a stroll.

Arnchy. One who puts on airs or acts superior.

Astorperious. Haughty or uppity (after the wealthy Astor family).

August ham. Watermelon.

Aunt Hagar's chillun. Aunt Hagar is the black race; her children are black Americans.

Bad hair. Afro-American hair.

Balling. Having a good time, having fun of many kinds; also, having sexual intercourse, as in "balling a girl."

Bam, down in bam. South, down South, as in Alabama.

Bardacious. Wonderful, marvelous; apparently, a misappropriation of *bodacious*, meaning "daring."

Battle-hammed. Badly formed about the hips.

Be-be-itching. Bewitching.

Becassin. Because.

Belly rub. A sexy dance.

Belonging-to-us. Personal, used as an adjective.

Beluthahatchie. An invented name for a terrible town, in Hurston's phrase, "next station beyond Hell."

Berries. An expression of approval, as in "She's the berries," usually feminine.

Big boy. A compliment in the North, an insult in the South.

Big sugar. A term of endearment. *See* Sugar.

Biggy. Sarcastic form of *Big boy* in the North.

Black. As an adjective, an insult when employed by blacks to describe blacks.

Black moon. A face.

Block. A suitcase.

Blowing your top. Getting angry beyond control, although sometimes used to indicate something going well.

Blue. A very black Afro-American; alphabetically, the first of a great many expressions to indicate color variations among members of the black race.

Blue vein. As in "blue-blood," the upper crust in black society, organized after the Civil War by mulattoes into the Blue-Vein Circle.

Bolito. A lottery. *See* Numbers.

Boody. A bawdy person; also, the genitals.

Boogie-woogie. A kind of dancing; in the South, a minor case of syphilis.

Boogy. A black person (from Booker T. Washington).

Bookooing. Showing off (from *beaucoup*).

Bottle it, bottle et. Shut up.

Boy. Friend, buddy; derogatory when used by whites.

Bread. Vagina.

Brick-presser. An idler.

Bring mud. To disappoint; to bring "a homely sheba to a dickty shout brings mud," in Rudolph Fisher's succinct example.

Brother-in-black. One Afro-American referred to by another.

Browned. Damned, as a mild ephithet.

Buckra. A white person.

Bull. As a verb, to obscure the facts.

Bull-skating. Bragging.

Bulldiker, bulldycker. A lesbian.

Bum-bole. The buttocks; also used as an ephithet (from *bung-hole*).

Bump, bumpfy-bump, bump the bump. A slow one-step dance, evolved as an aphrodisiac.

Butt-sprung. Clothing that has grown out of shape across the buttocks.

CPT. Colored people's time; that is, tardy, slow, or late.

Cabbage. Vagina.

Carpet-bagger. An apple polisher.

Catch the air. To leave under pressure.

Celt. A white woman.

Charcoal. A color variation among members of the black race.

Chip. To steal.

Choke. To defeat or to cool off, to quiet someone down.

Chorat. A chorus boy.

Cloakers. Deceivers, liars.

Cloud. A black person; derogatory when used by a white person.

Coal-skuttle blonde. A dark-skinned black girl.

Cocoa-brown. A color variation among members of the black race.

Cold. A term of approbation, as in "He knows that neighborhood cold."

Collar a hot. To eat a meal.

Collar a nod. To sleep.

Conk buster. Cheap liquor; also, derogatorily, a black intellectual.

Cookie. Vagina.

Coon. A black person; derogatory when used by a white person.

Cow. An aging prostitute.

Cracker. A poor white, usually southern.

Crap out. To lose, to give up, to be unable to keep up.

Crap yeller. A negative adjective.

Creeper. A man who invades another man's marital or sexual rights; also, a pimp.

Crow. A black person; derogatory when used by a white person.

Cruising. Parading, sauntering; also, looking for a pick-up.

Curb-hopping. Soliciting.

Cut. To do something well.

Daddy. A lover, husband; also, sugar daddy. *See* Sugar.

Dap. A white person.

Dark black. A color variation among members of the black race.

Darkey. A black person; derogatory when used by a white person.

Dat thing. Genitals of either sex.

Dat's your mammy. "So's your old man," a negative reply.

Deal in coal. To have sexual intercourse with a person of very black skin; also, to associate with Afro-Americans.

Diddy-wah-diddy. A far-distant place, a measure of distance.

Dickty, dicty. Swell, grand, high-toned.

Dig. To understand, as in "Do you dig?" perhaps from the Senegambian *dega*, to understand.

Dinge. A black person; derogatory when used by a white person.

Dinky. A black person; derogatory when used by a white person.

Dog. Used as a complimentary noun, as in "Ain't this a dog?"

Dog it. To show off, to strut, as in "to put on the dog"; also, an expression of encouragement, as in "Come on and dog it now!"

Dog mah cats! An expression of astonishment, as in "Shet mah mouf!"

Dogging. Dancing.

Dogs. Feet.

Doing the dozens. In verbal agreement, to insult another person's parents (usually the mother). *See* Playing the dozens; Slip, slip in the dozens.

Down the way. A place familiar to two people talking.

Down to the bricks. To the limit.

Draped down. Fashionably dressed.

Drunk down. Drunk to the point of being helpless.

Dumb to the fact. Ignorant, as in "You don't know what you're talking about."

Dusty butt. A cheap prostitute.

Eastman. A pimp.

Easy rider. An adept lover who devotes himself to satisfying his partner's sexual needs.

Ebony baby. A black person; derogatory when used by a white person.

Eight-rock. An extremely black person, a color variation among members of the race.

Eightball. A black person; derogatory when used by a white person.

Evermore. Extremely, as in "I'm evermore pleased to meet you."

Every postman on his beat. Kinky hair, an excellent example of Hurston's "will to adorn" through metaphor.

Faggoty. Perverted; not necessarily homosexual.

Fagingy-fagade. A white man (in word play for *fay* or *ofay*).

Fay. A white person. *See* Ofay.

First thing smoking. A train, as in "I'm leaving town on the first thing smoking."

Fooping. Fooling around.

40. Okay. *See* 38 and 2.

Frail eel. A pretty girl.

Freeby, freebie. Something for nothing.

Fungshun. A crowded dance, with too many people smelling of sweat, a play on *function*. *See* Funk.

Funk. Body odor, especially in a crowded and poorly ventilated place.

Funky. Smelly; also, sexy.

Gate, gates. Fellow, fellows; probably a portmanteau word from two musical terms, an *engagement* or a *date*, to play a gig.

Gator-faced. A long, black face with a big mouth (from *alligator*).

Get you to go. To get someone to act or perform.

Getting on some stiff time. Doing very well in business or racket.

Ginny Gall. An invented name for a terrible place, another suburb of Hell.

Git up off of me. Stop talking about me; leave me alone.

Give him air. To dismiss someone, to give him the gate.

Go when the wagon comes. A variation on "You're riding for a fall."

Good hair. Caucasian hair.

Granny Grunt. A mythical Afro-American sybil who has all of the answers; also, in derision, "Go tell it to Granny Grunt."

Gravy. Something free; also, semen.

Ground rations. Sex. *See* Rations.

Gum beater. A braggart or idle talker.

Gut bucket. A sleazy cabaret; also, raucous, vulgar music.

Gut-foot. Fallen arches.

Handkerchief-head. An Uncle Tom, a sycophant.

Happy dust. Cocaine.

Haul bottom, haul hiney, haul it. Get moving, get busy, get going; "it" carries sexual connotations, meaning "get to work" or "start working your genitals for my pleasure."

Hauling. Running away on foot.

High. Slightly drunk, feeling good.

High brown. A color variation among members of the black race.

High yaller. A color variation among members of the black race.

Hincty. Snooty.

Honey stick. Penis, a term of endearment. *See* Sugar cane.

Hoof. To dance.

Hot. Wonderful, marvelous.

Hot choo. A term of astonishment, as in "Oh no, now!"

Hootchie pap. A bawdy person: also, sexual intercourse.

Hunky hunk. A term of endearment for a black male.

Hush mah mouf! An expression of astonishment; also, "Shut mah mouf!"

I shot him lightly and he died politely. A typical rhyme play, meaning "I entirely overwhelmed or overcame him," physically or intellectually.

I'll be a cage of apes to you. A warning: Don't push your luck.

I'm cracking but I'm facking. A typical rhyme play, meaning "I may be wise-cracking, but I'm telling you the truth" (from *fact-ing*).

Ink. A black person; derogatory when used by a white person.

Inky dink. A color variation among members of the black race.

Jagging jig. A black person dancing.

Jap. A black person, probably a color variation among members of the race (from *Japanese*).

Jar head. A black male whose hair has not been straightened.

Jasper. A black male, named for a comic character in standard blackface routines, usually an imperceptive fellow.

Jazz. Black music; also, as a verb, to copulate; also, as a noun, semen. *See* Jive.

Jelly. Sex; also, semen.

Jelly roll. Sexual intercourse; also, penis.

Jig, jigaboo. A black person, usually male; derogatory when used by a white person; a corruption of *zigaboo*.

Jig chaser. A white person who enjoys the company of blacks; also, a white person who goes slumming in Harlem; originally, a southern white policeman.

Jig walker. A black person, rare.

Jive. To pursue, to capture, to deceive, to sleep with, depending on the context; also, slang talk, black music; no wide use until the thirties.

John-Brown. A mild adjective meaning "dog-gone" or "very."

Jook. A disreputable house of prostitution (pronounced to rhyme with *took*, although it is the foundation for *juke-box*) where music was supplied by "boxes," a southern name for *guitars*.

Jooking. Playing piano or guitar in the style of jook house music; also, dancing in this style. *See* Scronching.

Juice. Liquor.

July jam. Very hot.

Jump salty. To get angry.

K[itchen] M[echanic]. A domestic servant.

Kack, kackty. Sarcastically or negatively snobbish. *See* Dickty.

Kink out. To straighten the hair.

Knock yourself out. To have a good time.

Kopasetee. A term of approval (from *copasetic*).

Lemon colored. A color variation among members of the black race.

Light yellow. A color variation among members of the black race.

Lightly, slightly, and politely. A typical rhyme play, meaning "perfectly."

Lily-livered. Cowardly.

Little sister. A measure of degree, as in "Hot as little sister!"

Little tee-ninchy. Tiny.

Liver lips. Pronouncedly thick lips, pendulous, distinctively African; derogatory when used by either race.

Made hair. Hair that has been straightened.

Mama. A potential or actual sweetheart, a lover.

Mammy. An insult; derogatory when used by either race.

Martin. A humorous personification for death (from a Bert Williams* monologue that included the line, "Wait till Martin comes").

Miss Anne. A white female.

Mister Charlie, Mister Eddie. A white male.

Monkey back. A fancy dresser, a dude.

Monkey chaser. A West Indian.

Mose. A black person; derogatory when used by a white person.

Mug man. A small-time thug or criminal.

Mule. The fourth waiter in a dining car on a train.

Mule blood. Black molasses.

Mustard seed. A color variation among members of the black race.

My people! My people! An expression simultaneously sad and satirical: sad as a commentary by a black person on the backwardness of some members of his race; satirical as an identification with them.

Naps. Kinky hair.

Nearer my God to thee. Good hair, ostensibly like Caucasian hair, which in a white-controlled society is preferable and, therefore, closer to a good life; the expression is a good example of Hurston's "will to adorn" through metaphor.

Negrotarian. A white do-gooder, coined by Zora Neale Hurston.

Nigger. A black person; derogatory when used by a white person under any circumstances;

it may be used freely among blacks as a term of opprobrium or as a term of endearment.

Niggerati. The black literary circle, a term popularized by Zora Neale Hurston* and Wallace Thurman.*

Nothing to the bear but his curly hair. An identification of false bravado, as in "Don't be afraid of him, because he won't fight."

Now you cookin' with gas. Correct, on the right track.

Numbers. A lottery based on bank exchanges, using three predetermined digits; *Bolito*, a variation of the lottery, uses only two digits; an illegal but widely practiced Harlem pastime.

Ofay. A white person (from Pig-Latin for *foe*), used derogatorily or casually, depending on the context. *See* Fay.

Old cuffee. An African word meaning black person.

On down to the bricks. As good as possible.

Oscar. A stupid person.

P-I. A pimp.

Palmer house. Walking flat-footed from fallen arches.

Pancake. A humble black person.

Pansy. A homosexual. *See* Queer.

Papa. A lover or husband. *See* Daddy.

Paper-brown. A color variation among members of the black race.

Pappy. Father.

Park ape. An ugly, underprivileged black person.

Pass, passing. Used independent of further explanation, as in "She's passing," meaning "to pass for white" or "passing as a member of the white race."

Peckawood, peckerwood. Indigent southern white class, also called "white trash."

Peeping through my likkers. Getting along though drunk.

Peppercorn. Kinks in black hair.

Pe-ola. An extremely light-skinned black girl.

Piano. Spare ribs.

Pick. As a verb, to rob or to gyp.

Pig meat. A young girl.

Pilch. A residence, either house or apartment.

Pink. A member of the white race.

Pink chaser. A black person who curries the favor of whites.

Pink toes. A light-skinned black girl.

Playing the dozens. Insulting the ancestors of an opponent. *See* Slip.

Pole out. To be distinguished or to excel.

Previous. Premature, as in "Don't get too previous."

Punkin seed. A color variation among members of the black race.

Put it on. To injure, as in "I'm going to put it on him."

Put some in. To report on an enemy, as in "I'm going to put some in for him."

Put the locks on. To be handcuffed.

Queer. A homosexual; also, to be homosexual; no derogatory implication in the term during the Harlem Renaissance.

Race man. A black man.

Rat. A person of low tastes; the opposite of *Dickty, dicty.*

Rations. As in ground rations, elementary sexual rights for basic sustenance.

Red neck. A poor southern white man, usually strongly prejudiced.

Reefer. A marijuana cigarette.

Righteous. Correct.

Righteous grass, righteous mass. Good hair.

Righteous rags. Elegant and stylish clothing. *See* Zoot suit.

Rug-cutter. A person too cheap to frequent dance halls who goes to house-rent parties and proceeds to cut up the rugs of the host with his hot feet; also, a good dancer.

Russian. A southern black who has moved North hurriedly (from having rushed there, hence a Russian).

Salty dog. Stronger than dog, as in "put on the dog," meaning "to show off."

Sam. Like Jasper, a name for a black male derived from blackface routines, probably a diminutive of Sambo; also, an Uncle Tom.

Scarf, scarve. To eat.

Scrap iron. Cheap liquor.

Scrimpy. Scarce.

Scronch. To dance, usually with sexual innuendo.

Scronching. A kind of dancing performed by a scroncher; *see* Jooking.

See you go. To give aid or assistance, or to treat, as in "Will you see me go for breakfast?" that is, "Will you have breakfast with me?"

Sell out. To run away in fear.

Sender. A compliment for a capable person, as in "He's a solid sender."

Shaving steel. A razor, described facetiously.

Shim sham shimmy. An erotic dance. *See* Shimmy.

Shimmy. Chemise; also, a dance popularized by white performer Gilda Gray in which she said she was "shaking her chemise," but of black origin.

Shin dig. An extremely crowded party, often identified with house-rent parties, where one's shins got gouged during the dancing; southern in origin.

Shine. A black person; derogatory when used by a white person.

Shortnin' bread. Vagina; an expression that gave rise to a popular song remarkable for its metaphoric obscenity. *See* Bread.

Shout. A ball or prom; also, a one-step dance.

Skirt man. A pimp.

Slip, slip in the dozens. To joke with or to kid either one person or a whole group; also, to insult another's forbears. *See* Playing the dozens.

Smoke. A black person; derogatory when used by a white person.

Smoking over. Looking over critically.

Snow. Cocaine.

Sobbing hearted. Broken hearted.

Solid. Perfect.

Sooner. Cheap or shabby, used to describe people as well as objects.

Spade. A black person; derogatory when used by a white person.

Spagingy-spagade. A black person (in word play for *spade*). *See* Fagingy-fagade.

Spercherly. Especially.

Stanch, stanch out. To begin; also, to step out.

Stomp. A raucous dancing party.

Storm buzzard. A shiftless, homeless person.

Stroll. To do something well, as in "He's really strolling."

   Struggle buggy. A Ford car.

Suede. A black person; derogatory when used by a white person.

Sugar. Love making; also, semen.

Sugar cane. Penis. *See* Sweet loving; Sweet man, sweetman.

Swab. To physically beat someone.

Swab train. Someone preparing to fight, as in "The swab train will run tonight."

Swap spit. To kiss.

Sweet loving. Good sex.

Sweet man, sweetman. A good lover; also, a pimp.

Syndicating. Gossiping.

The bear. A confession of poverty, always with the definite article.

The big apple. New York City, always with the definite article.

The man. The law, the boss, whoever is in charge, always with the definite article.

Thing. Penis.

38 and 2. That's fine. *See* 40.

Thousand on a plate. Beans.

Tight. Tough or hard.

Tight head. A person with kinky hair.

Too bad! Bad! Wonderful, marvelous.

Trucking. Strolling; also, a dance step resembling a stroll.

Unsheik. To get a divorce.

V and X. A five-and-ten-cent store.

Wang. An extraordinary person, used positively or negatively depending on the context.

West Hell. A place worse than hell.

What's on the rail for the lizard? A dense metaphor: rail may mean "fence," therefore out in the open; *lizard*, attached to other words, suggests indulgence, as in "a chow-lizard who eats a lot" or "a couch-lizard who makes love a lot"; a man looking for sex may use this expression to his friends, meaning "who's available for me?" or "Whom can this lounge-lizard pick up?"

Whip it to the red. Beat your head until it is bloody; also used as a threat, as in "I'm going to whip you to the red."

Wobble. A dance; also, to dance.

Woofing. Gossip, casual or aimless talk, as a dog may bark without any reason.

Work under cork. To appear onstage in blackface makeup.

Young suit. Clothing too small or poorly fitting.

Your likker told you. Bad behavior, blamed on drink.

You're breaking me down. You're wearing me out; you're too much.

Zigaboo. A black person; derogatory when used by a white person. *See* Jig, jigaboo.

Zoot suit. A Harlem-style outfit, not widely known until the forties but already worn during the early thirties, with padded shoulders, trousers wide at the knee and narrow at the ankle, high waists, broad lapels; Hurston described Jelly Roll Morton* in "his zoot suit with the reet pleats" in 1942, but she included it in her glossary of Harlem Renaissance slang.

REFERENCES: W. C. Handy and Abbe Niles, *Blues*, 1926; Carl Van Vechten, *Nigger Heaven*, 1926; Claude McKay, *Home to Harlem*, 1928; Rudolph Fisher, *The Walls of Jericho*, 1929; Guy B. Johnson, "Double Meanings in Popular Negro Blues," *Journal of Abnormal and Social Psychology*, 22 (1927–1928); Zora Neale Hurston, "Characteristics of Negro Expression," *Negro*, 1934; *Dan Burley's Original Handbook of Harlem*

Jive, 1944; *Dictionary of American Slang*, 1960; Earl Conrad, "Philology of Negro Dialect," *Journal of Negro Education*, 13 (1944); Alan Dundes, ed., *Mother Wit from the Laughing Barrel*, 1981; J. L. Dillard, *Lexicon of Black English*, 1977; Donald Angus; Nora Holt; Langston Hughes; Richard Bruce Nugent; Prentiss Taylor; Carl Van Vechten.

Bibliography

Aaron, Daniel. *Writers on the Left: Episodes in American Literary Communism*. New York: Harcourt, Brace and World, 1961; Oxford University Press, 1977.

Abbott's Monthly, 1930–1933.

Abdul, Raoul. *Blacks in Classical Music*. New York: Dodd, Mead, 1977.

Adams, William, ed. *Afro-American Authors*. Boston: Houghton Mifflin, 1972.

———. *Afro-American Literature*. 4 vols. Boston: Houghton Mifflin, 1970.

Adoff, Arnold, ed. *The Poetry of Black America: An Anthology of the 20th Century*. New York: Harper and Row, 1973.

Albertson, Chris. *Bessie*. New York: Stein and Day, 1972.

Allen, James S. *The Negro Question in the United States*. New York: International, 1936.

Allen, Walter C. *Hendersonia*. Highland Park, N.J.: Jazz Monographs, 1973.

Amory, Cleveland, and Frederick Bradlee, eds. *Vanity Fair: Selections from America's Most Memorable Magazine*. New York: Viking Press, 1960.

Anderson, Jervis. *A. Philip Randolph: A Biographical Portrait*. New York: Harcourt Brace Jovanovich, 1973.

———. *This Was Harlem*. New York: Farrar, Straus and Giroux, 1982.

Anderson, Lindsey, ed. *International Library of Negro Life and History*. New York: Publishers Company, 1969.

Apatheker, Herbert, ed. *The Correspondence of W.E.B. Du Bois*. Amherst: University of Massachusetts Press, 1973.

———. *A Documentary History of the Negro People in the United States: 1910–1932*. Secaucus, N.J.: Citadel Press, 1973.

Arata, Esther S. *Black American Playwrights: 1800 to Present*. Metuchen, N.J.: Scarecrow Press, 1976.

Archer, Leonard Courtney. *Black Images in the American Theatre: NAACP Protest Campaigns, Stage, Screen, Radio, and Television*. Brooklyn: Pageant-Poseidon, 1973.

Armstrong, Louis. *Swing That Music*. New York: Longman Green, 1936.

ASCAP Biographical Dictionary of Composers, Authors, and Publishers. Edited by Lynn Farnol Group, Inc. New York: R. R. Bowker, 1966, 1980.

Bailey, Ronald W. *Black Business Enterprises: Historical and Contemporary Perspectives*. New York: Basic Books, 1971.

Baker, Josephine, and Jo Boullion. *Josephine*. New York: Harper and Row, 1977.

Ballard, Allen B. *The Education of Black Folk: The Afro-American Struggle for Knowledge in White America*. New York: Harper and Row, 1973.

Barbeau, Arthur E. *The Unknown Soldiers: Black American Troops in World War I*. Philadelphia: Temple University Press, 1974.

Bardolph, Richard. *The Negro Vanguard*. New York: Rinehart, 1959.

Barksdale, Richard, and Keneth Kinnamon. *Black Writers of America*. New York: Macmillan, 1972.

Barton, Rebecca C. *Black Voices in American Fiction: 1900–1930*. Oakdale, N.Y.: Dowling College Press, 1976.

Baskin, Wade. *Dictionary of Black Culture*. New York: Philosophical Library, 1973.

Bearden, Romare. "A Final Farewell to Douglas." *Amsterdam News*, 24 February 1979.

Benchley, Robert. "Hearts in Dixie." *Opportunity* 7 (April 1929): 122–23.

Benét, William Rose, ed. *The Reader's Encyclopedia*. New York: Crowell, 1948.

Benson, Brian J., and Mabel Mayle Dillard. *Jean Toomer*. New York: Twayne, 1980.

Bentley, Gladys. "I Am a Woman Again." *Ebony*, August 1952, pp. 92-98.

Berry, Faith. *Langston Hughes*. Westport, Conn.: Lawrence Hill, 1983.

"Biggest Northern Business." *Ebony*, August 1946, pp. 43–46.

"Birth of a Nation." *The Crisis* 14 (May 1917): 25–26.

Bittner, William. *The Novels of Waldo Frank*. Philadelphia: University of Pennsylvania Press, 1958.

"Black Academy of Arts and Letters." *New York Amsterdam News Special Supplement*, 18 September 1971.

Black Perspectives in Music, Fall 1973, Fall 1981.

Black World. Harlem Renaissance Issue, November 1970.

Blackwell, Jason E., and Morris Janowitz, eds. *Black Sociologists*. Chicago: University of Chicago Press, 1974.

Blesh, Rudi. *Combo USA*. New York: Chilton, 1971.

———, and Harriet Janis. *They All Played Ragtime*. New York: Knopf, 1951.

Bode, Carl. *Mencken*. Carbondale, Ill.: Southern Illinois University Press, 1969.

Bogle, Donald. *Brown Sugar*. New York: Harmony Books, 1980.

———. *Toms, Coons, Mulattoes, Mammies, and Bucks: An Interpretative History of Blacks in American Films*. New York: Viking Press, 1973.

Bond, Horace Mann. *Education for Freedom: The History of Lincoln University*. Oxford, Pa.: Lincoln University Press, 1976.

———. *The Education of the Negro in the American Social Order*. Englewood Cliffs, N.J.: Prentice-Hall, 1934.

Bone, Robert A. *Down Home*. New York: Putnam's, 1975.

———. *The Negro Novel in America*. New Haven, Conn.: Yale University Press, 1958, 1970.

Bontemps, Arna. "The Black Renaissance of the Twenties." *Black World*, November 1970, p. 7.

———, ed. *The Harlem Renaissance Remembered*. New York: Dodd, Mead, 1972.

Bradbury, John M. *Renaissance in the South: A Critical History of Literature, 1920–1960*. Chapel Hill: University of North Carolina Press, 1963.

Bradford, Perry. *Born with the Blues*. New York: Oak Publications, 1965.

Bradley, Henry T. *Out of the Depths*. New York: Avondale Press, 1928.

Brasch, Walter M. *Black English and the Mass Media*. Amherst: University of Massachusetts Press, 1981.

Brawley, Benjamin G. *Negro Builders and Heroes*. Chapel Hill: University of North Carolina Press, 1937.

———. *The Negro Genius*. New York: Dodd, Mead, 1937.

———. *The Negro in Literature and Art in the United States*. 1919. Reprint. New York: Dodd, Mead, 1925, 1929, 1930.

Broad Ax (Chicago), 24 March 1923.

Bronz, Stephen H. *Roots of Negro Racial Consciousness, The 1920's: Three Harlem Renaissance Authors*. New York: Libra, 1964.

Brotz, Howard. *The Black Jews of Harlem: Negro Nationalism and the Dilemmas of Negro Leadership*. New York: Schocken Books, 1970.

Brown, Sterling. *Collected Poems of Sterling Brown*. Introduction by Stuckey Sterling. Selected by Michael Harper. New York: Harper and Row, 1980.

———. *Negro Poetry and Drama*. Washington, D.C.: Association of Negro Folk Education, 1937.

———. *The Negro in American Fiction*. New York: Atheneum, 1969.

Bruner, Richard. *Black Politicians*. New York: McKay, 1971.

Buni, Andrew. *Robert L. Vann of the Pittsburgh Courier: Politics and Black Journalism*. Pittsburgh: University of Pittsburgh Press, 1974.

Burke, W. J., and W. D. Howe, eds. *American Authors and Books*. New York: Crown, 1962, 1972.

Burleigh, H. T. "The Negro and His Song." In *Music on the Air*, edited by Hazel Gertrude Kinscella. Garden City, N.Y.: Garden City, 1934.

Burrill, Bob. *Who's Who in Boxing*. New Rochelle, N.Y.: Arlington House, 1974.

Butcher, Margaret. *The Negro in American Culture, Based on Materials Left by Alain Locke*. New York: Knopf, 1956.

Calloway, Cab. *Of Minnie the Moocher and Me*. New York: Crowell, 1976.

Campbell, Georgettea Merritt. *Extant Collections of Early Black Newspapers*. Troy, N.Y.: Whitson, 1981.

Cantor, Milton. *Max Eastman*. New York: Twayne, 1970.

Carter, Dan T. *Scottsboro: A Tragedy of the American South*. New York: Oxford University Press, 1969.

Carter, Paul J. *Waldo Frank*. New York: Twayne, 1967.

Case, Brian, and Stan Britt. *The Illustrated Encyclopedia of Jazz*. New York: Harmony Books, 1978.

Challenge [1916–1919], October 1919.

Challenge [1934–1937], March–September 1934.

Chapman, Abraham. "The Harlem Renaissance in Literary History." *CLA Journal* 11 (1967): 38–58.

Charters, Ann. *Nobody: The Story of Bert Williams*. New York: Macmillan, 1970.

Charters, Samuel B. *Jazz: A History of the New York Scene*. Garden City, N.Y.: Doubleday, 1962.

Chase, Gilbert. *America's Music*. New York: McGraw-Hill, 1955.

Chederholm, Theresa Dickason. *Afro-American Artists: A Bio-Bibliographical Dictionary*. Boston: Boston Public Library, 1973.

Chilton, John. *Who's Who in Jazz: Storyville to Swing Street*. Philadelphia: Chilton, 1972, 1978.

Chisholm, Ann. *Nancy Cunard: A Biography*. New York: Knopf, 1979.

Christian, Barbara. *Black Women Novelists: The Development of a Tradition, 1892–1976*. Westport, Conn.: Greenwood Press, 1980.

Claerbaut, David. *Black Jargon in White America*. Grand Rapids, Mich.: Eerdmans, 1972.

Clark, Barrett Harper. *Paul Green*. New York: Haskell House, 1974.

Clark, Emily. *Innocence Abroad*. New York: Knopf, 1930.

Clark, John Henry, ed. *Harlem, U.S.A.* New York: Macmilllan, 1971.

Clarke, John Hendrik, ed. *Marcus Garvey and the Vision of Africa*. New York: Vintage Books, 1974.

Coleman, Leon Duncan. "The Contribution of Carl Van Vechten to the Negro Renaissance: 1920–1930." Ph.D. diss., University of Minnesota, 1969.

Connelly, Marc. *Voices Offstage*. New York: Holt, Rinehart and Winston, 1968.

Conrad, Earl. "Philology of Negro Dialect." *Journal of Negro Education* 13 (1944): 150–54.

Contemporary Authors: A Bio-Bibliographical Guide to Current Writers. Detroit: Gale, 1967–1980.

Coombs, Norma. *The Black Experience in America*. New York: Twayne, 1973.

Cooney, Charles F. "Walter White and the Harlem Renaissance." *Journal of Negro History* 57 (July 1972): 231–40.

Cooper, Wayne F., ed. *The Passion of Claude McKay*. New York: Schocken Books, 1973.

Covarrubias, Miguel. *Negro Drawings*. Introduction by Frank Crowninshield and Preface by Ralph Barton. New York: Knopf, 1927.

Craig, E. Quita. *Black Drama of the Federal Theatre Era: Beyond the Formal Horizon*. Amherst: University of Massachusetts Press, 1980.

Cripps, Thomas. *Black Film as Genre*. Bloomington: Indiana University Press, 1978.

The Crisis, 1917–1935.

Cronon, E. David. *Black Moses*. Madison: University of Wisconsin Press, 1955.

Cullen, Countee. *Color*. New York: Harper and Brothers, 1925.

———, ed. *Caroling Dusk*. New York: Harper and Brothers, 1927.

Cunard, Nancy, ed. *Negro: An Anthology*. 1934. Edited and abridged by Hugh Ford. New York: Ungar, 1970.

Cuney-Hare, Maud. Negro Musicians and Their Music. Washington, D.C.: Associated Publishers, 1936; New York: Da Capo Press, 1974.

Current Biography. New York: Wilson, 1940–1955.

Dalby, David. "Americanisms That May Once Have Been Africanisms." *The Times* (London), 19 July 1969, p. 9.

Dance, Stanley. *The World of Duke Ellington*. New York: Scribner's, 1970.

Dannett, Sylvia L. *Profiles of Negro Womanhood*. Yonkers, N.Y.: Educational Heritage, 1964.

Davis, Arthur P. *From the Dark Tower: Afro-American Writers, 1900 to 1960*. Washington, D.C.: Howard University Press, 1974.

———. "Growing Up in the Harlem Renaissance, 1920–1935." *Negro American Literature Forum*, Fall 1968, pp. 53–60.

———, and Michael W. Peplow, eds. *The New Negro Renaissance: An Anthology*. New York: Holt, Rinehart and Winston, 1975.

————, and J. Saunders Redding, eds. *Cavalcade: Negro American Writing from 1760 to the Present*. Boston: Houghton Mifflin, 1971.

————, Sterling Brown, and Ulysses Lee, eds. *The Negro Caravan*. New York: Arno Press, 1969.

Day, Beth. *The Little Professor of Piney Woods*. New York: Messner, 1955.

Dennison, Sam. *Scandalize My Name: Black Imagery in American Popular Music*. New York: Garland, 1982.

Dictionary of American Biography. Edited by The American Council of Learned Societies. New York: Scribner's, 1928–1981.

Dictionary of American Slang. Edited by Howard Wentworth and Stuart Berg Flexner. New York: Crowell, 1960.

Didier, Roger. "(Little Lena) The Mamma Who Can't Behave." *Heebie Jeebies*, 1 August 1925, pp. 5–7, 28–30.

Dillard, J. L. *Lexicon of Black English*. New York: Seabury Press, 1977.

Dixon, Robert M. W., and John Godrich. *Recording the Blues*. New York: Stein and Day, 1970.

"Documents of the War." *The Crisis*, March 1919, pp. 16–17.

Dover, Cedric. *American Negro Art*. New York: New York Graphic Society, 1960, 1969.

Draper, Muriel. *Music at Midnight*. New York: Harper and Brothers, 1929.

Du Bois, Shirley Graham. *His Day Is Marching On: A Memoir of W.E.B. Du Bois*. Philadelphia: Lippincott, 1971.

————. *Paul Robeson, Citizen of the World*. 1946. New York: Messner, 1971.

Du Bois, W.E.B. *The Autobiography of W.E.B. Du Bois*. New York: International, 1968.

————. *Dusk of Dawn*. New York: Harcourt Brace, 1940.

————. "Postscript." *The Crisis*, May 1928, pp. 96–97.

————. Review of "Negro Americans: What Now?" by James Weldon Johnson. *New York Herald Tribune Books*, 18 November 1934.

————. "Returning Soldiers." *The Crisis*, May 1919, pp. 13–14.

Dunbar [Apartments] News, 7 October 1931, 30 November 1932.

Dundes, Alan, ed. *Mother Wit from the Laughing Barrel: Readings in the Interpretation of Afro-American Folklore*. New York: Garland, 1981.

Ebony, 1948–1974.

Ebony Success Library. Nashville: Southwestern, 1973.

Eckley, Wilton. *Thomas S. Stribling*. New York: Twayne, 1975.

Edwards, G. Franklin, ed. *E. Franklin Frazier on Race Relations*. Philadelphia: Temple University Press, 1968.

Eichelberger, Jason Williams. *The Religious Education of the Negro*. Chicago: Herald Press, 1931.

Ellington, Duke. *Music Is My Mistress*. Garden City, N.Y.: Doubleday, 1973.

Emanuel, James A. *Dark Symphony: Negro Literature in America*. New York: Free Press, 1968.

————. *Langston Hughes*. New York: Twayne, 1967.

Emery, Lynne Fauley. *Black Dance in the United States from 1619 to 1970*. Palo Alto, Calif.: National Press Books, 1972, 1980.

Esquire, selected issues, 1934–1938.

Fabre, Michel. "Autour de René Maran," *Présence Africaine* 86 (1973).

Fauset, Arthur Huff. *Black Gods of the Metropolis: Negro Religious Cults of the Urban North*. Philadelphia: University of Pennsylvania Press, 1971.

Fax, Elton C. *Garvey: The Story of a Pioneer Black Nationalist*. New York: Dodd, Mead, 1972.

Feather, Leonard, ed. *The Encyclopedia of Jazz*. New York: Horizon Press, 1960.

Ferguson, Blanche E. *Countee Cullen and the Negro Renaissance*. New York: Dodd, Mead, 1966.

Fernett, Gene. *Swing Out: Great Negro Dance Bands*. Midland, Mich.: Pendell, 1970.

Festeloot, Lilyan. *Les Ecrivains noirs de la langue française: Naissance d'une litterature*. Brussels: Université Libre de Bruxelles, 1965.

Fire!! Metuchen, N.J.: Fire Press, 1982.

Fisher, Rudolph. *"Gingertown." New York Herald Tribune Books*, 27 March 1932, p. 3.

————. *The Walls of Jericho*. New York: Knopf, 1928.

Fleischmann, Wolfgang Bernard. *Encyclopedia of World Literature in the 20th Century*. New York: Ungar, 1967.

Fletcher Henderson: Developing an American Orchestra, 1923–1937 [Record Album Notes]. Washington, D.C.: Smithsonian Institution; New York: CBS, 1977.

Fletcher, Tom. *100 Years of the Negro in Show Business*. New York: Burdge, 1954.

Flynn, Jason L. *Negroes of Achievement in Modern America*. New York: Dodd, Mead, 1971.

Foner, Philip S., ed. *The Voice of Black America: Major Speeches by Negroes in the United States, 1797–1971*. New York: Simon and Schuster, 1972.

Fox, Charles. *Fats Waller*. New York: A. S. Barnes, 1961.

Fox, Stephen R. *The Guardian of Boston: William Monroe Trotter*. New York: Atheneum, 1970.

Franklin, John Hope. *From Slavery to Freedom: A History of Negro Americans*. New York: Knopf, 1948.

Frazier, Edward F. *The Negro Church in America*. New York: Schocken Books, 1963.

Frucht, Richard. *Black Society in the New World*. New York: Random House, 1971.

Garber, Eric. *"Tain't Nobody's Bizness: Homosexuality in Harlem in the 1920's." The Advocate*, 13 May 1982, pp. 39–43, 53.

Garvey, Marcus. *Philosophy and Opinions of Marcus Garvey*. Edited by Amy Garvey. New York: Universal, 1923.

Gayle, Allison, Jr. *The Way of the New World: The Black Novel in America*. Garden City, N.Y.: Anchor Press, 1975.

Gelb, Arthur, and Barbara Gelb. *O'Neill*. New York: Harper and Brothers, 1962.

Gilbert, Peter, ed. *The Selected Writings of John Edward Bruce: Militant Black Journalist*. New York: Arno Press, 1971.

Giles, James R. *Claude McKay*. New York: Twayne, 1976.

Gloster, Hugh. *Negro Voices in American Fiction*. Chapel Hill: University of North Carolina Press, 1948.

Goldstein, Rhoda L., ed. *Black Life and Culture in the United States*. New York: Crowell, 1971.

Gordon, Eugene. *"The Negro Press." The Annals*, November 1928, pp. 248–56.

Gordon, Taylor. *Born to Be, with a New Introduction by Robert Hemenway*. Seattle: University of Washington Press, 1975.

Green, Abel, and Joe Laurie, Jr. *Show Biz: From Vaude to Video*. New York: Holt, 1951.

Green, Stanley, ed. *Encyclopedia of the Musical Theatre*. New York: Dodd, Mead, 1976.

Grove's Dictionary of Music and Musicians; rev. ed. *New Grove Dictionary of Music and Musicians*. New York: St. Martin's Press, 1954, 1980.

Gumby, Alexander. Scrapbooks. Columbia University, New York.

Guzman, Jessie P. "Monroe Nathan Work and His Contributions." *Journal of Negro History*, October 1949, pp. 428–51.

Handy, D. Antoinette. *Black Women in American Bands and Orchestras*. Westport, Conn.: Greenwood Press, 1981.

Handy, W. C., and Abbe Niles. *Blues: An Anthology*. New York: A. and C. Boni, 1926.

Handy, William C. *Negro Authors and Composers of the United States*. New York: Handy Bros. Music Company, 1938.

Haney, Lynn. *Naked at the Feast: A Biography of Josephine Baker*. New York: Dodd, Mead, 1981.

Hare, Maud Cuney. *Negro Musicians and Their Music*. Washington, D.C.: Associated Publishers, 1936; New York: Da Capo Press, 1974.

Harlem: A Forum of Negro Life, 1928.

Harris, Middleton, et al., eds. *The Black Book*. New York: Random House, 1974.

Harris, Sara. *Father Divine*. New York: Collier Books, 1971.

Harris, Sheldon. *Blues Who's Who: A Biographical Dictionary of Blues Singers*. New Rochelle, N.Y.: Arlington House, 1979.

Harrison, Hubert H. *When Africa Awakes*. New York: Porro Press, 1920.

Hart, James D. *The Oxford Companion to American Literature*. New York: Oxford University Press, 1965.

Hart, John E. *Floyd Dell*. New York: Twayne, 1971.

Haskins, James. *Black Theatre in America*. New York: Crowell, 1982.

———. [Jim Haskins.]. *The Cotton Club*. New York: Random House, 1977.

———. *The Psychology of Black Language*. New York: Barnes and Noble, 1973.

Haslam, Gerald. "Wallace Thurman: A Western Renaissance Man." *Western American Literature*, Spring 1971, p. 53–59.

Hatch, James V., ed. *Black Theater, U.S.A.: Forty-Five Plays by Black Americans, 1847–1974*. New York: Free Press, 1974.

Hatch-Billops Collection, Inc. Archives of Black American Cultural History, Taped Oral Interviews, New York.

Hausser, Michel. *Les Deux Batouala de René Maran*. Bordeaux: Collection Études, 1975.

Hayden, Robert. Preface to *The New Negro*, edited by Alain Locke. New York: Atheneum, 1969.

Heermance, J. Noel. *Charles W. Chesnutt: America's First Great Black Novelist*. Hamden, Conn.: Archon Books, 1974.

Heinsheimer, Hans. "Emperor Resurrexit." *Opera News*, 10 February 1979, pp. 15–21.

Helbling, Mark. "African Art: Albert C. Barnes and Alain Locke." *Phylon*, March 1982, pp. 57–67.

———. "Carl Van Vechten and the Harlem Renaissance." *Negro American Literature Forum*, July 1976, pp. 39–47.

———. "Jean Toomer and Waldo Frank: A Creative Friendship." *Phylon*, June 1980, pp. 167–78.

Helm, MacKinley. *Angel Mo and Her Son, Roland Hayes*. Boston: Little, Brown, 1942.

Hemenway, Robert E. *The Black Novelist*. Columbus, Ohio: Merrill, 1970.

———. *Zora Neale Hurston: A Literary Biography*. Urbana: University of Illinois Press, 1977.

Henri, Florette. *Black Migration: Movement North, 1900–1920*. Garden City, N.Y.: Anchor Press, 1975.

Henry, George W., M.D. *Sexual Variants: A Study of Homosexual Patterns*. New York: Holber, 1948.

Hentoff, Nat. *Jazz: New Perspectives on the History of Jazz by Twelve of the World's Foremost Jazz Critics and Scholars*. New York: Rinehart, 1959.

Herbert, Ian, ed. *Who's Who in the Theatre*. Detroit: Gale, 1981.

Herskovits, Melville. *The Myth of the Negro Past*. New York: Harper and Brothers, 1941.

Hill, Errol, ed. *The Theatre of Black Americans*. Englewood Cliffs, N.J.: Prentice-Hall, 1980.

Holmes, Dwight Oliver Wendell. *The Evolution of the Negro College*. New York: Teacher's College, Columbia University, 1934.

Hooker, James R. *Black Revolutionary: George Padmore's Path from Communism to Pan-Africanism*. New York: Praeger, 1967.

Hornsby, Alton. *The Black Almanac*. Woodbury, N.J.: Barron's Educational Series, 1972.

Howard, John Tasker. *Our American Music*. New York: Crowell, 1965.

Howard, Lillie P. *Zora Neale Hurston*. New York: Twayne, 1980.

Howe, Irving. *Sherwood Anderson*. New York: Sloane, 1951.

Huggins, Nathan Irvin. *Harlem Renaissance*. New York: Oxford University Press, 1971.

———, ed. *Voices from the Harlem Renaissance*. New York: Oxford University Press, 1976.

Hughes, Graham Werden, and F. D. Patterson. *Robert Russa Moton of Hampton and Tuskegee*. Chapel Hill: University of North Carolina Press, 1956.

Hughes, Langston. *The Big Sea*. New York: Knopf, 1940.

———. *Famous American Negroes*. New York: Dodd, Mead, 1954.

———. *Famous Negro Music Makers*. New York: Dodd, Mead, 1955.

———. *Fight for Freedom: A History of the NAACP*. New York: Norton, 1962.

———. *I Wonder as I Wander*. New York: Rinehart, 1956.

———. "The Negro Artist and the Racial Mountain." *The Nation*, 23 June 1926, pp. 692–94.

———. "When Harlem Was in Vogue." *Town and Country*, July 1940, pp. 64–66.

———, and Arna Bontemps, eds. *The Poetry of the Negro, 1746–1949*. Garden City, N.Y.: Doubleday, 1949.

———, and Milton Meltzer. *Black Magic: A Pictorial History of the Negro in American Entertainment*. Englewood Cliffs, N.J.: Prentice-Hall, 1967, 1971.

———, Milton Meltzer, and C. Eric Lincoln, eds. *A Pictorial History of Black Americans*. New York: Crown, 1973.

Hull, Gloria T. "Under the Days: The Buried Life and Poetry of Angelina Weld Grimké." *Conditions Five* 2 (Autumn 1979): 17–25.

Humes, Dollena Joy. *Oswald Garrison Villard: Liberal of the 1920's*. Syracuse, N.Y.: Syracuse University Press, 1960.

Hurston, Zora Neale. "Characteristics of Negro Expression." In *Negro: An Anthology*, edited by Nancy Cunard. 1934. New York: Ungar, 1970.

———. *Dust Tracks on a Road: An Autobiography*. Philadelphia: Lippincott, 1942, 1971.

————. *Mules and Men*. 1935. Reprint. New York: Negro University Press, 1975.

Ikonné, Chidi. *From Du Bois to Van Vechten: The Early New Negro Literature, 1903 to 1926*. Westport, Conn.: Greenwood Press, 1981.

Inge, Thomas M. Maurice Duke, and Jackson R. Bryer, eds. *Black American Writers: Bibliographical Essays*. New York: St. Martin's Press, 1978.

Inter-State Tattler, 1925–1933.

Ireland, Norma Olin, ed. *Index to Women of the World*. Westwood, Mass.: Faxon, 1970.

Isaacs, Edith J. *The Negro in the American Theatre*. New York: Theatre Arts, 1947.

Jablonski, Edward, and Lawrence D. Stewart. *The Gershwin Years*. Garden City, N.Y.: Doubleday, 1958.

James, Edward T. and Janet T. James, and Paul S. Boyer, eds. *Notable American Women, 1607–1950: A Biographical Dictionary*. Cambridge, Mass.: Belknap Press, 1971, 1980.

"John E. Nail," *The Crisis*, March 1924, p. 127.

Johnson, Abby Ann Arthur, and Ronald M. Johnson. "Forgotten Pages: Black Literary Magazines in the 20's." *Journal of American Studies*, 8, no. 3 (1974): 363–82.

Johnson, Charles S. *The Negro in American Civilization: A Study of Negro Life and Race Relations*. New York: Holt, 1930.

————, ed. *Ebony and Topaz: A Collecteanea*. 1927. Reprint. Freeport, N.Y.: Books for Libraries, 1971.

Johnson, Charles S., and Graham R. Taylor. *The Negro in Chicago: A Study of Race Relations and a Race Riot in 1919*. 1921. Reprint. New York: Arno Press, 1968.

Johnson, Guy B. "Double Meanings in the Popular Negro Blues." *Journal of Abnormal and Social Psychology* 22 (1927–1928): 12–20.

Johnson, Jack. *Jack Johnson in the Ring and Out*. Chicago: National, 1927.

Johnson, James Weldon. *Along This Way*. New York: Viking Press, 1933.

————. *Black Manhattan*. New York: Knopf, 1930.

————. *The Book of American Negro Poetry*. New York: Harcourt Brace, 1922, 1931.

Johnson, James Weldon, and J. Rosamund Johnson, eds. *The Book of American Negro Spirituals*. New York: Viking Press, 1925.

Johnson, James Weldon, Memorial Collection of Negro Arts and Letters, Beinecke Rare Book and Manuscript Library, Yale University, New Haven.

Jones, Laurence Clifton. *Piney Woods and Its Story*. New York: Fleming Revell, 1922.

Journal of Negro History, 1916–1933.

Jubilee, Vincent. "Philadelphia's Afro-American Literary Circle and the Harlem Renaissance." Ph.D. diss. University of Pennsylvania, 1980.

Kellner, Bruce. "Carl Van Vechten." *American Writers: A Collection of Literary Biographies*, Supplement II. New York: Scribner's, 1981.

————. *Carl Van Vechten and the Irreverent Decades*. Norman: University of Oklahoma Press, 1968.

Kellogg, Charles Flint. *NAACP: A History of the National Association for the Advancement of Colored People*. Baltimore: Johns Hopkins Press, 1967.

Kennington, Donald. *The Literature of Jazz: A Critical Guide*. Chicago: American Library Association, 1971.

Kerlin, Robert, ed. *Contemporary Poetry of the Negro*. 1921. Reprint. Freeport, N.Y.: Books for Libraries, 1971.

Kinscella, Hazel Gertrude. *Music on the Air*. Garden City, N.Y.: Garden City, 1934.

Kirkeby, Ed. *Ain't Misbehavin': The Story of Fats Waller*. New York: Dodd, Mead, 1966.

Kochman, Thomas. *Rappin' and Stylin' Out: Communication in Urban Black America*. Urbana: University of Illinois Press, 1972.

Kornweibel, Theodore, Jr. *No Crystal Stair*. Westport, Conn.: Greenwood Press, 1974.

Krehbiel, Henry Edward. *Afro-American Folksongs*. New York: Schirmer, 1914; Ungar, 1962; Portland, Maine: Longwood Press, 1976.

Kunitz, Stanley J., and Howard Haycraft, eds. *Twentieth Century Authors*. New York: Wilson, 1940, 1955.

Landay, Eileen. *Black Film Stars*. New York: Drake, 1973.

Landess, Thomas H. *Julia Peterkin*. New York: Twayne, 1976.

Leab, Daniel J. *From Sambo to Superspade: The Black Experience in Motion Pictures*. Boston: Houghton Mifflin, 1975.

Levy, Eugene D. *James Weldon Johnson: Black Leader, Black Voice*. Chicago: University of Chicago Press, 1973.

Lewine, Richard, and Alex Simon, eds. *Encyclopedia of Theatre Music*. New York: Bonanza Books, 1961.

Lewis, David Levering. *When Harlem Was in Vogue*. New York: Knopf, 1981.

Lewis, Theophilus. "Theatre." *The Messenger*, 1922–1927.

Lieb, Sandra. *Mother of the Blues: A Study of Ma Rainey*. Amherst: University of Massachusetts Press, 1981.

Little, Arthur. *From Harlem to the Rhine*. New York: Covici-Friede, 1936.

Lockard, Diana N. "The Negro on the Stage of the Nineteen Twenties." M.A. thesis, Columbia University, 1960.

L[ocke], A[lain]. "Harlem." *The Survey Graphic Number*, 1 March 1925, p. 630.

———. *The Negro in Art: A Pictorial Record of the Negro Artist and of the Negro Theme in Art*. 1940. Reprint. New York: Hacker Art Books, 1971.

———, ed. *The New Negro*. New York: A. and C. Boni, 1925. Introduction by Robert Hayden. New York: Atheneum, 1968.

———, and Montgomery T. Gregory, eds. *Plays of Negro Life*. New York: Harper and Brothers, 1927.

Logan, Rayford W., and Michael R. Winston, eds. *Dictionary of American Negro Biography*. New York: Norton, 1982.

———. *W.E.B. Du Bois*. New York: Hill and Wang, 1971.

Loggins, Vernon. *The Negro Author: His Development in America to 1900*. New York: Columbia University Press, 1931.

Longstreet, Stephen. *The Real Jazz, New and Old*. Baton Rouge: University of Louisiana Press, 1956.

———, and A. M. Dauer. *Knaurs Jazz Lexikon*. Munich: Th. Knaur Nachf, Droemersche Verlagsanstalt, 1957.

Lovell, John, Jr. *Black Song: The Forge and the Flame*. New York: Macmillan, 1972.

Lowe, W. Augustus, ed. *Encyclopedia of Black America*. New York: McGraw-Hill, 1981.

Lowie, Robert. "Bibliographical Memoir of Franz Boas." *Biographical Memoirs*. Washington, D.C.: National Academy of Sciences, 1947.

Lueders, Edward. *Carl Van Vechten*. New York: Twayne, 1965.

Lynch, John Roy. *Reminiscences of an Active Life*. Edited by John Hope Franklin. Chicago: University of Chicago Press, 1970.

McCardle, Carl. "The Terrible Tempered Barnes." *Saturday Evening Post*, 21 March 1942, p. 93.

McCarthy, Albert J. *Louis Armstrong*. New York: Barnes, 1961.

McGhee, Reginald. *The World of James Van Der Zee*. Dobbs Ferry, N.Y.: Morgan and Morgan, 1973.

McKay, Claude. *Harlem: Negro Metropolis*. New York: 1940. Reprint. New York: Harcourt Brace, 1968.

————. *Home to Harlem*. New York: Harper and Brothers, 1928.

————. *A Long Way From Home*. 1937. Reprint. New York: Arno Press, 1969.

McPherson, James M. *The Abolitionist Legacy*. Princeton, N.J.: Princeton University Press, 1975.

————. *Blacks in America: Biographical Essays*. Garden City, N.Y.: Doubleday, 1971.

Mainiero, Linda, ed. *American Women Writers*. New York: Unger, 1979.

Major, Clarence. *The Cotton Club*. Detroit: Broadside Press, 1973.

Maloney, Arnold Hamilton. *Amber Gold*. Boston: Meador, 1946.

Mantle, Burns, ed. *The Best Plays of 1919–1920* through *The Best Plays of 1935–36*. New York: Dodd, Mead, 1919–1936.

Mapp, Edward. *Blacks in American Films: Today and Yesterday*. Metuchen, N.J.: Scarecrow Press, 1974.

————. *Dictionary of Blacks in the Performing Arts*. Metuchen, N.J.: Scarecrow Press, 1978.

Martin, Tony. *Race First*. Westport, Conn.: Greenwood Press, 1976.

Mathews, Marcia M. *Henry Ossawa Tanner, American Artist*. Chicago: University of Chicago Press, 1969.

Matthews, Geraldine O. *Black American Writers: 1773–1949*. Boston: Hall, 1975.

Mays, Benjamin Elijah, and Joseph William Nicholson. *The Negro's Church*. New York: Arno Press, 1969.

The Messenger, 1917–1928.

Miller, Kelly. "Looking Backward." In *Voices of a Black Nation*, edited by Theodore G. Vincent. San Francisco: Ramparts Press, 1973.

Mitchell, J. Paul, ed. *Race Riots in Black and White*. Englewood Cliffs, N.J.: Prentice-Hall, 1970.

Mitchell, Loften. *Black Drama: The Story of the American Negro in the Theatre*. New York: Hawthorn Books, 1967.

————, ed. *Voices of the Black Theatre*. Clifton, N.J.: White, 1975.

Moon, Henry. "A Negro Looks at Soviet Russia." *Nation* 28 (February 1934): 244–46.

Moore, Richard B. "The Critics and Opponents of Marcus Garvey." In *Marcus Garvey and the Vision of Africa*, edited by John Henrik Clarke. New York: Vintage Books, 1974.

Mount, Marshall W. *African Art: The Years Since 1920*. Bloomington: Indiana University Press, 1973.

"Movies Turn a Deaf Ear to Colored Plea." *Christian Century*, 47 (24 September 1930): 1140.

Murray, Hugh. "A Movement Begat a Movement." *New York City News*, 23 June 1982, p. 12.

National Cyclopedia of American Biography, 1872–1977. New York: White, 1977.

Negro Artists: An Illustrated Review of Their Achievements...Presented by the Harmon Foundation, 1935. Freeport, N.Y.: Books for Libraries, 1971.

Negro Digest, July 1951.

Negro History Bulletin, April 1970.

Negro World, 4 March 1922.

Nelson, Bernard H. *The Fourteenth Amendment and the Negro Since 1920*. New York: Russell and Russell, 1946.

Nelson, Hart M., Raytha L. Yokley, and Anne K. Nelson, eds. *The Black Church in America*. New York: Basic Books, 1971.

Nelson, John H. *The Negro Character in American Literature*. 1926. Reprint. New York: AMS Press, 1970.

Newsweek, 21 June 1982.

New York Herald Tribune, 16 April 1954.

New York Times, 1915–1983.

New York Times Theatre Reviews. New York: Arno Press, 1972.

New York Voice, 31 December 1982.

Nichols, Charles H., ed. *Langston Hughes–Arna Bontemps Letters, 1925–1967*. New York: Dodd, Mead, 1980.

Nichols, J. L., and William Crogman, eds. *Progress of a Race*. 1920. Reprint. New York: Arno Press, 1969.

Noble, Peter. *The Cinema and the Negro, 1905–1948*. London: S. Robinson, 1948.

———. *The Negro in Films*, London: S. Robinson, 1948.

Nugent, John Peer. *The Black Eagle*. New York: Stein and Day, 1971.

Null, Gary. *Black Hollywood*. New York: Citadel, 1975.

Oakley, Giles. *The Devil's Music: A History of the Blues*. New York: Harcourt Brace Jovanovich, 1978.

Official Theatrical World of Colored Artists: National Directory and Guide. New York: Theatrical World, April 1928.

Oja-Ade, Femi. *René Maran, Ecrivain Negro-Africain*. Washington, D.C.: Three Continents Press, 1977.

Oliver, Paul. *Aspects of the Blues Tradition*. New York: Oak Publications, 1968.

Opera News, 17 October 1964, 30 January 1971, 10 February 1979, June 1981.

Opportunity, 1923–1949.

Osofsky, Gilbert. *Harlem: The Making of a Ghetto, 1890–1930*. New York: Harper and Row, 1966.

Ottley, Roi. *The Lonely Warrior*. Chicago: Regnery, 1955.

———. *"New World a'Coming": Inside Black America*. New York: Literary Classics, 1943.

———, and William J. Weatherby, eds. *The Negro in New York: An Informal Social History, 1626–1940*. New York: Oceana, 1967; Praeger, 1969.

Ovington, Mary White. *Portraits in Color*. 1927. Reprint. New York: Arno Press.

Page, James. *Selected Black American Authors*. Boston: Hall, 1977.

Patterson, Lindsey. *Anthology of the American Negro in the Theatre*. New York: Publisher's Company, 1969.

———. *Black Films and Film Makers*. New York: Dodd, Mead, 1975.

Patterson, Louise Thompson. "With Langston Hughes in the USSR." *Freedomways: A Quarterly Review of the Negro Freedom Movement*, 8, no. 2 (Spring 1968): 152–58.

Peplow, Michael W. *George S. Schuyler*. Boston: Twayne, 1980.

Perrett, Geoffrey. *America in the Twenties*. New York: Simon and Schuster, 1982.

Perry, Margaret. *The Harlem Renaissance: An Annotated Bibliography and Commentary*. New York: Garland, 1982.

Peters, Margaret. *Ebony Book of Black Achievement*. Chicago: Johnson, 1970.

Peterson, Robert. *Only the Ball Is White*. Englewood Cliffs, N.J.: Prentice-Hall, 1970.

Plackskin, Sally, ed. *American Women in Jazz*. New York: Wideview Books, 1982.

Ploski, Harry A., and Warren Marr II, eds. *The Negro Almanac: A Reference Work on the Afro-American*. New York: Bellweather, 1976, 1980.

Portfolio Magazine of the Fine Arts, September–October 1982.

Poston, U. S. "Books." *The Messenger*, April 1926.

"Pot-Pourri." *Opportunity*, June 1925, p. 187.

Powers, Anne, ed. *Blacks in American Movies: A Selected Bibliography*. Metuchen, N.J.: Scarecrow Press, 1974.

Preston, Wheeler. *American Biographies*. New York: Harper and Brothers, 1940.

"Primitive Emotions Aflame in a Negro Film." *Literary Digest*, 103 (5 October 1929): 42–56.

Puttkammer, Charles W., and Ruth Worthy. "William Monroe Trotter, 1872–1934." *Journal of Negro History*, 43 (1958): 298–316.

Ragan, David, ed. *Who's Who in Hollywood, 1900–1976*. New Rochelle, N.Y.: Arlington House, 1976.

Ramsey, Frederic, Jr., and Charles Edward Smith, eds. *Jazzmen*. New York: Harcourt Brace, 1939.

Reed, Addison W. *The Life and Works of Scott Joplin*. Chapel Hill: University of North Carolina Press, 1973.

Rigdon, Walter, ed. *Biographical Encyclopedia and Who's Who of the American Theatre*. New York: Heineman, 1966.

Roach, Hildred. *Black American Music: Past and Present*. Boston: Crescendo, 1973.

Robeson, Paul. *Here I Stand*. New York: Othello Associates, 1958; Boston: Beacon Press, 1971, 1976.

Robinson, Wilhelmenia S. *History of Negro Biography*. New York: Publisher's Company, 1967. Reprint. *International Library of Negro Life and History*. New York: Publisher's Company, 1969.

Rogers, J. A. *World's Great Men of Color*. New York: Macmillan, 1973.

Rollins, Charlemae Hill. *They Showed the Way*. New York: Crowell, 1964.

Rose, Al. *Eubie Blake*. New York: Schirmer, 1979.

Ross, B. Joyce. *J. E. Spingarn and the Rise of the NAACP, 1911–1932*. New York: Atheneum, 1972.

Rublowsky, John. *Black Music in America*. New York: Basic Books, 1971.

Rudwick, Elliott M. *W.E.B. Du Bois, Propagandist of the Negro Protest*. Philadelphia: University of Pennsylvania Press, 1968.

Rush, Theresa Gunnels, Carol Fairbanks Myers, and Esther Spring Arata, eds. *Black American Writers Past and Present*. Metuchen, N.J.: Scarecrow Press, 1975.

Rust, Brian. *Elisabeth Welch*, World Records Album, SH328, 1979.

Sackheim, Eric. *The Blues Line: A Collection of Blues Lyrics*. New York: Grossman, 1969.

Sampson, Henry T. *Blacks in Black and White*. Metuchen, N.J.: Scarecrow Press, 1977.

———. *Blacks in Blackface*. Metuchen, N.J.: Scarecrow Press, 1980.

Schevill, James Edwin. *Sherwood Anderson: His Life and Work*. Denver: University of Denver Press, 1951.

Schiffman, Jack. *Uptown: The Story of Harlem's Apollo Theatre*. New York: Cowles, 1971.

Schoener, Allon. *Harlem on My Mind*. New York: Random House, 1968.

Schuyler, George S. *Black and Conservative: The Autobiography of George S. Schuyler*. New Rochelle, N.Y.: Arlington House, 1966.

———. "Theatre." *The Messenger*, November 1923, November 1924.

Seldes, Gilbert. *The Seven Lively Arts*. New York: Harper and Brothers, 1924.

Seligmann, Herbert. *The Negro Faces America*. New York: Press of Clarence H. Nathan, 1924.

Shales, Tom, et al. *The American Film Heritage*. Washington, D.C.: Acropolis Books, 1972.

Shapiro, Nat, and Nat Hentoff, eds. *Hear Me Talkin' to Ya*. New York: Rinehart, 1955.

Shaw, Valerie. *Black Hollywood: Yesterday*. Los Angeles, D. C. Connection, 1983.

Sherman, Joan R. *Invisible Poets: Afro-Americans of the Nineteenth Century*. Urbana: University of Illinois Press, 1974.

Short, Bobby. *Black and White Baby*. New York: Dodd, Mead, 1971.

Show Magazine, May 1973.

Simpson, George. *Melville Herskovits*. New York: Columbia University Press, 1973.

Singh, Amritjit. *The Novels of the Harlem Renaissance: Twelve Black Writers, 1923–1933*. University Park: Pennsylvania State University Press, 1975.

Sitwell, Osbert. "New York in the Twenties." *Atlantic Monthly*, February 1962, pp. 38–43.

Smyth, Mabel M., ed. *Black American Reference Book*. Englewood Cliffs, N.J.: Prentice-Hall, 1976.

Sochen, June. *The Black Man and the American Dream: Negro Aspirations in America, 1900–1930*. Chicago: Quadrangle Books, 1971.

Southern, Eileen. *Biographical Dictionary of Afro-American and African Musicians*. Westport, Conn.: Greenwood Press, 1982.

———. *The Music of Black Americans: A History*. New York: Norton, 1971.

Spaeth, Sigmund. *A History of Popular Music in America*. New York: Random House, 1948, 1966.

Spear, Allan H. *Black Chicago: The Makings of a Negro Ghetto, 1890–1920*. Chicago: University of Chicago Press, 1967.

Spero, Sterling Denhard, and Abram L. Harris. *The Black Worker: The Negro and the Labor Movement*. New York: Columbia University Press, 1931.

Stearns, Marshall, and Jean Stearns. *Jazz Dance: The Story of American Vernacular Dance*. New York: Macmillan, 1968.

Stetson, Erlene, ed. *Black Sisters: Poetry by Black American Women, 1746–1980*. Bloomington: Indiana University Press, 1981.

Stevenson, Janet. *Spokesman for Freedom*. New York: Crowell-Collier Press, 1969.

Stewart, Rex W. *Jazz Masters of the 30's*. New York: Macmillan, 1972.

Stewart, Virginia. *45 Contemporary Mexican Artists*. Stanford, Calif.: Stanford University Press, 1951.

Stewart-Baxter, Derrick. *Ma Rainey and the Classic Blues Singers*. New York: Stein and Day, 1970.

Survey Graphic Number, 53 (1 March 1925): 11.

Sylvander, Carolyn Wedin. *Jessie Redmon Fauset, Black American Writer*. Troy, N.Y.: Whitson, 1981.

"The Talk of the Town." *New Yorker*, 9 October 1926, pp. 20–21.

Teasdale, May Silva. *Handbook of 20th Century Opera*. New York: Dutton, 1938.

Thomson, Virgil. *Virgil Thomson*. New York: Knopf, 1966.

Thornbrough, Emma L. *T. Thomas Fortune: Militant Journalist*. Chicago: University of Chicago Press, 1972.

Thorpe, Earl E. *Black Historians*. New York: Morrow, 1971.

———. *Negro Historians in the United States*. Baton Rouge, La.: Fraternal Press, 1958.

Thurman, Wallace. *Infants of the Spring*. New York: Macaulay, 1932.

———. *Negro Life in New York's Harlem*. Girard, Kans.: Haldemann-Julius, 1928.

Time, 18 May 1981.

Toomer, Jean. *Cane*. 1923. Reprint. New York: Liveright, 1975.

Toppin, Edgar A. *Biographical History of Blacks in America Since 1528*. New York: McKay, 1971.

Tucker, David M. *Lieutenant Lee of Beale Street*. Nashville: Vanderbilt University Press, 1971.

Turner, Darwin T. *Afro-American Writers*. New York: Appleton-Century-Crofts, 1970.

———. *In a Minor Chord: 3 Afro-American Writers and Their Search for Identity*. Carbondale: Southern Illinois University Press, 1971.

———. ed. *Black American Literature*. Columbus, Ohio: Merrill, 1970.

———. *Black Drama in America: An Anthology*. Greenwich, Conn.: Fawcett, 1971.

Turner, W. B. "Joel Augustus Rogers, An Afro-American Historian." *Negro History Bulletin*, February 1972, pp. 34–38.

Tuttle, William M. *Race Riot: Chicago in the Red Summer of 1919*. New York: Atheneum, 1970.

———. *W.E.B. Du Bois*. Englewood Cliffs, N.J.: Prentice-Hall, 1973.

Ulanov, Barry. *History of Jazz in America*. New York: Viking Press, 1955.

Van Der Zee, James, Owen Dodson, and Camille Billops. *The Harlem Book of the Dead*. Dobbs Ferry, N.Y.: Morgan and Morgan, 1978.

Van Vechten, Carl. "A Few Notes About Four Saints in Three Acts." In *Four Saints in Three Acts*, by Gertrude Stein. New York: Random House, 1934.

———. *Fragments from an Unwritten Autobiography*. New Haven: Yale University Library, 1955.

———. *"Keep A-Inchin' Along": Selected Writings of Carl Van Vechten about Black Arts and Letters*. Edited by Bruce Kellner. Westport, Conn.: Greenwood Press, 1979.

———. "Ma Draper." *Yale University Library Gazette*, April 1963, pp. 125–29.

———. *Nigger Heaven*. New York: Knopf, 1926.

———. *Parties*. New York: Knopf, 1930.

———. Preface to *The Prince of Wales and Other Famous Americans*. New York: Knopf, 1925.

———. *Red*. New York: Alfred A. Knopf, 1925.

———. Typed Inventory, 1941–1964, for the James Weldon Johnson Memorial Collection of Negro Arts and Letters, Yale University, New Haven.

Villard, Oswald Garrison. *Fighting Years*. New York: Harcourt Brace, 1939.

Vincent, Theodore G., ed. *Voices of a Black Nation*. San Francisco: Ramparts Press, 1973.

Wagner, Jean. *Black Poets of the United States from Paul Laurence Dunbar to Langston Hughes*. Urbana: University of Illinois Press, 1973.

Walrond, Edward E. *Walter White and the Harlem Renaissance*. Port Washington, N.Y.: Kennikat Press, 1978.

Walser, Raul, ed. *Paul Green of Chapel Hill*. Chapel Hill: University of North Carolina Press, 1951.

Ward, Alfred Charles. *Longman Companion to 20th Century Literature*. New York: Longman, 1970.

Washington, Mary Helen. "Lost Women, Nella Larsen: Mystery Woman of the Harlem Renaissance." *Ms*, December 1980, pp. 40, 47–48, 50.

Waters, Ethel. *To Me It's Wonderful*. New York: Harper and Row, 1972.

———, with Charles Samuels. *His Eye Is on the Sparrow*. Garden City, N.Y.: Doubleday, 1951.

Watts, Florence. *The Black Man in America: 1905–1932*. New York: Watts, 1974.

Weiss, Irving, and Anne Weiss. *American Authors and Books*. New York: Crown, 1972.

Weiss, Nancy J. *The National Urban League*. New York: Oxford University Press, 1974.

Wentworth, Harold, and Stewart Berg Flexner. *Dictionary of American Slang*. New York: Crowell, 1960.

West, Dorothy. "Elephant's Dance: A Memoir of Wallace Thurman." *Black World*, November 1970.

White, Ray Lewis, ed. *The Achievement of Sherwood Anderson*. Chapel Hill: University of North Carolina Press, 1966.

White, Walter. *A Man Called White*. New York: Viking 1948; Arno, 1969.

———. "A Report on Filmland." *Chicago Defender*, 8 May 1934.

———. "Sweet Man." *Saturday Review of Literature*, 12 July 1930, p. 1189.

Who's Who Among Black Americans. Northbrook, Ill.: Who's Who Among Black Americans, 1976.

Who's Who in America. N.Y.: Marquis, 1930, 1933, 1945, 1950, 1959, 1979.

Who's Who in Colored America. New York: Boris, 1927, 1933.

Who's Who in the Colored Race. Chicago: privately printed, 1915.

Who's Who in the Theatre. John Parker, ed. New York: Pitman, 1939, 1952.

Who Was Who in America. New York: Marquis, 1943, 1947, 1950, 1951, 1963, 1968.

William, Henry. *Black Response to the American Left*. Princeton, N.J.: Princeton University History Department, 1975.

Williams, Kenny J. *They Also Spoke: An Essay on Negro Literature in America, 1787–1930*. Nashville: Townsend Press, 1970.

Williams, Ora. *American Black Women in the Arts and Social Sciences: A Bibliographic Survey*. Metuchen, N.J.: Scarecrow Press, 1973.

Williams, W.H.A. *H. L. Mencken*. G. K. Hall, 1977.

Wise, Stephen. *Challenging Years*. New York: Putnam's, 1949.

Woll, Allen. *Dictionary of the Black Theatre: Broadway, Off-Broadway, and Selected Harlem Theatre*. Westport, Conn.: Greenwood Press, 1983.

Wolseley, Roland E. *The Black Press, U.S.A.* Ames, Iowa: Iowa State University Press, 1971.

Wolters, Raymond. *Negroes and the Great Depression: The Problem of Economic Recovery*. Westport, Conn.: Greenwood Press, 1970.

Woodson, Carter G. *The Negro Professional Man and the Community, with Special Emphasis on the Physician and the Lawyer*. 1934. Reprint. New York: Negro University Press, 1969.

————. "Ten Years of Collecting and Publishing the Records of the Negro." *Journal of Negro History*, October 1925, pp. 598–606.

Work, Monroe Nathan, ed. *Bibliography of the Negro in Africa and America*. New York: Wilson, 1928.

————. *Negro Year Book: An Annual Encyclopedia of the Negro*. Tuskegee, Ala.: Negro Year Book, 1919–1938.

Young, A. S. "Doc." *Negro First in Sports*. Chicago: Johnson, 1963.

Young, James O. *Black Writers of the Thirties*. Baton Rouge: Louisiana State University Press, 1973.

Zangrando, Robert L. *The NAACP Crusade Against Lynching, 1909–1950*. Philadelphia: Temple University Press, 1980.

Zinkoff, Dave, and Edgar Williams. *Around the World with the Harlem Globetrotters*. Philadelphia: Smith, 1953.

Index

Page numbers in *italic* indicate the location of the main entry.

Abbott, Robert S., *3*, 98
Abbott's Monthly, 3–4
Abraham Lincoln, 137
Abrahams, E. Richard, 213
Absent, 251
Abyssinian Baptist Church, 18, 73, 289, 373
Aces and Queens, 214
Addison, Bernard, 150
Africa and Orient Review, 247
Africana (musical revue), *4*, 378
Africana (operetta), *4*
African Blood Brotherhood, 53, 103, 287
African Orthodox Church, *4–5*
Afro-American (Baltimore), *5*, 6, 101, 122, 127, 191, 238
Afro-American Folksongs, 5, 62
Afro-American Ledger, 5
Afro-American Realty Company, 281
Age (New York), *6*, 9, 14, 25, 127, 158, 194, 198, 248, 282, 338, 363
Aldridge Players, *6*
Alexander, Lewis, *6–7*, 37, 67, 122, 278
Alhambra (cabaret), *7*
Alhambra Theatre, *7*, 15, 174, 217, 246, 351, 390
Alix, Mae, *7*, 178
Allen, Cleveland G., *7–8*

Allen, James, 170
All God's Chillun Got Wings, 8, 14, 272, 306, 391
Along This Way, 200
Amber Satyr, 8
Amenia Conference, 338
Amenia Times, 338
American Mercury, 30, 239, 319
American Negro Academy, *8*, 145, 318
American Negro Labor Congress, *8–9*, 126
Amistad murals, 393
Amsterdam News (New York), 6, *9*, 13, 52, 101, 103, 158, 173, 210
Anderson, Eddie, *9–10*, 306
Anderson, Garland, *10*, 14, 247
Anderson, Hallie, *10*
Anderson, Ida, 260
Anderson, Marian, *10–11*, 162, 386
Anderson, Maxwell, 140
Anderson, Mrs. Charles H., 213
Anderson, Mrs. Sherwood, 116
Anderson, Regina M., *11*, 192, 257, 281
Anderson, Sherwood, *11–12*, 86, 95, 129, 263
Andlauer Production Company, *12*, 197, 251
Andrews, Regina, 11, 192, 257, 281